The Crusades, *c.* 1071–*c.* 1291

The aim of this book is to provide for the student and general reader a concise history of the crusades – whose chief goal was the liberation and preservation of the 'holy places' of the Middle East – from the first calls to arms in the late eleventh century to the fall of the last crusader strongholds in Syria and Palestine in 1291.

Professor Richard considers the consequences of the crusades, such as the establishment of the Latin east, and its organisation into a group of feudal states, as well as crusading contacts with the Muslim world, eastern Christians, Byzantines and Mongols. Also considered are the organisation of expeditions, the financing of such expeditionary forces, and the organisation of operations and supply. Jean Richard is the *doyen* of crusader historians and this work, the distillation of over forty years' research and contemplation, is the only one of its kind in English.

JEAN RICHARD is Emeritus Professor at the University of Dijon and a member of the Institut de France. He is the author of many classic books on the period of the crusades, including *Saint Louis* (published under the title *Saint Louis: Crusader King of France*, Cambridge, 1992).

Cambridge Medieval Textbooks

This a series of specially commissioned textbooks for teachers and students, designed to complement the monograph series Cambridge Studies in Medieval Life and Thought by providing introductions to a range of topics in medieval history. This series combines both chronological and thematic approaches, and will deal with British and European topics. All volumes in the series will be published in hard covers and in paperback.

For a list of titles in the series, see end of book.

THE CRUSADES,
c. 1071–*c.* 1291

JEAN RICHARD

TRANSLATED BY JEAN BIRRELL

CAMBRIDGE UNIVERSITY PRESS
Cambridge, New York, Melbourne, Madrid, Cape Town, Singapore, São Paulo

Cambridge University Press
The Edinburgh Building, Cambridge CB2 2RU, UK

Published in the United States of America by Cambridge University Press, New York

www.cambridge.org
Information on this title: www.cambridge.org/9780521623698

Originally published in French as *Histoire des croisades*
by Librairie Arthème Fayard 1996
and © Fayard

First published in English by Cambridge University Press 1999
as *The Crusades c. 1071–c. 1291*
Reprinted 2001
English translation © Cambridge University Press 1999

A catalogue record for this publication is available from the British Library

Library of Congress Cataloguing in Publication data
Richard, Jean, 1921 Feb. 7–
[Histoire des croisades. English]
The Crusades, c. 1071–c. 1291 / Jean Richard; translated by Jean Birrell.
p. cm.
Includes bibliographical references and index.
ISBN 0 521 62369 3 hb. – ISBN 0 521 62566 1 pb
1. Crusades. I. Title.
D157.R52413 1999
909.07–dc21 98–43850 CIP

ISBN-13 978-0-521-62369-8 hardback
ISBN-10 0-521-62369-3 hardback

ISBN-13 978-0-521-62566-1 paperback
ISBN-10 0-521-62566-1 paperback

Transferred to digital printing 2005

CONTENTS

123040

MAPS

GENEALOGICAL TABLES

PREFACE

That the crusades have been and still are studied by so many historians and hold so much interest for the general reader is probably due to the sheer scale of the historical phenomenon they represent. They caused a massive movement of people, at the cost of a scarcely conceivable effort, and their main driving force was the Christian faith. They pose many questions, which have received very different answers; the documentation for them is uneven, but its abundance reveals that contemporaries were aware of the exceptional nature of these enterprises.

At the start of my study of the crusades, I should define the scope of my enquiry. The crusade, in the strict meaning of the term, is an expedition, essentially military, regarded by the papacy as a meritorious work and endowed by it with spiritual privileges granted to the combatants and to those who participated in their enterprise. These privileges were first granted to those who went to the East and in particular to the Holy Places, but they were also granted for other operations launched within Christendom against heretics or enemies of the Church of Rome and on its frontiers against pagans and the infidel. The appearance of a Latin empire of Constantinople was linked to a crusade; crusades were proposed against the Byzantine empire as well as in its support.

I have chosen to confine myself here to the expeditions directed against the Muslim powers of the East with the dual aim of defending the Christians against the Turkish invasion and of securing to Christendom possession of the Holy Land, regarded as unlawfully occupied by the infidel. They did not end in the thirteenth century, though they changed in nature as a result of the renewal of the Turkish threat, but I will remain faithful to the standard terminology, which gives the name 'the age of the crusades' to the period that begins with the councils of 1095 and ends in 1291, with the loss of the last possessions in the Holy Land. We should not, of course, forget that the crusades have their prehistory and that an expedition of the same type as those of the thirteenth century was being prepared as late as the time of Pope John XXII and King Philip VI of France.

The crusades gave birth to a Latin East which survived the fateful date of 1291; the kingdom of Cyprus, the duchy of the Archipelago, Genoese and, above all, Venetian Romania and the Hospitaller presence in Rhodes still appeared on the sixteenth-century map. The history of these states, and in particular of the kingdom of Jerusalem, the principality of Antioch and the counties of Edessa and Tripoli, is closely linked to that of the crusades; it was the dangers faced by these states, and their ordeals or their loss, that caused expeditions to depart. But the life of these political constructions is in itself the subject of studies which are proliferating and which raise questions that go beyond the domain of the crusade proper. I have therefore felt able only to sketch it in broad outline.

Many eastern historians have seen the crusades as part of the history of the East, one of the factors which have influenced the evolution of its societies and states. This approach has led to works of synthesis which come up against the problem that the crusades remained, for the most part, marginal to the life of the easterners, who were only rarely aware of their specific character. Nor did these peoples constitute a unity; Muslim Arabs, Syrians of various Christian confessions, Armenians and Byzantines were all separate communities which had their own existence and which were not deeply marked by the presence of the Franks, even though they were affected by it. Without underrating the interest of the eastern perspective, I have treated the crusades as a phenomenon closely integrated into European history with repercussions for the East.

The history of the crusades is in part that of the confrontation between different civilisations, that of western Christendom and those of the East. We must not, however, consider this confrontation only in the context of the crusades. Jacques Le Goff's little joke that all the Christians seem to have brought back from the crusades is the apricot is well known. Many other elements of a material nature passed from the East to the West, but it was not only the crusaders who introduced them. Pilgrims travelled to Jerusalem and merchants to Constantinople, Antioch and Alexandria before 1095; the latter, though they took advantage of the crusades to expand their trade by establishing themselves in Frankish Syria, continued to seek out precious goods in the Byzantine and Islamic states, before penetrating even deeper.

And with regard to other elements of civilisation, the Franks of the East seem not to have been closed to the world that surrounded them. Admittedly, it was through Spain that most of the translations of ancient works preserved by the Arabs were transmitted, but the example of *The Book of the Secret of Secrets*, which was translated in Tripoli and became the source of a moral and political literature in the West, shows that this effort to penetrate the thought of others was not unknown to the Latin East. The crusaders who settled in the East took an interest in the peoples and the countries they discovered; from Fulcher of Chartres to James of Vitry, we owe to them descriptions that attest to their appetite for discovery. But here too, as in the case of contacts with eastern Christianity or with Islam, others than the crusaders were involved. One cannot encompass the totality of relations between East and West in the history of the crusades, and here again I have not felt it necessary to discuss the issue in detail.

The history of the crusades as I shall approach it here is primarily that of the expeditions from the West which went to the East and, more precisely, to what was called in the Middle Ages 'Syria'. It is the history of an enormous effort accepted by the people of that age, which occupies a unique place in the 'growth of Europe' in that the objective they set themselves was the recovery and preservation of what was in their eyes a Christian patrimony. A *chanson de geste* written at this period, the *Pèlerinage de Charlemagne*, recalled how the West had been concerned about the fate of the Holy Places since the age of the great Carolingians. This concern became more insistent, and it turned men's footsteps in the late eleventh century and for two centuries to come towards the shores of the Levant. What might have been only a chimera became a reality; for two centuries, the Christians of the West lived in contact with the Holy Places they venerated or close enough to hope to return to them.

It was an extraordinary venture. I have chosen, in classic fashion, to trace each expedition from its origin, through its preparation and its progress, in the hope of discovering the feelings that motivated the participants, their anxieties, their ordeals, their victories and their defeats. I will also discuss what made it possible to carry out enterprises that, given the resources of the age, may seem inordinate. It was necessary for the political, institutional, mental and economic structures of the West to be capable of supporting such a prolonged effort. I will emphasise that the crusade was not a fleeting enterprise, something that tended to be forgotten during the commemorations of the ninth centenary of the appeal of Clermont; the crusades continued for two centuries, at a different pace perhaps, but without any real slackening off. It was this permanence that made them a major phenomenon in European history.

To observe the 'men of the crusade' (the phrase is Régine Pernoud's) live is to be made aware of an extraordinary human experience. Men formed in the apparently narrow world of the early medieval West were confronted by societies, political structures and natural conditions very different from those with which they were familiar; they had to conduct military operations and diplomatic negotiations there, conclude alliances, build states and fit their architectural conceptions and religious life into this complex world; they had to do this in a durable way, in a hostile environment; they revealed unexpected skills in coping with what was alien to their customary universe.

The crusades have been assessed, judged and debated, praised and denigrated in ways that reflect the opinions and the sensibilities, even the prejudices, of different epochs, and they will no doubt continue to be so. For me, it is those men who lived a great adventure, to which they brought their courage and their discouragements, their faith, their talents and their failings, who remain the protagonists in this great drama and whom I hope to know better.

The background cannot be neglected. The history of the medieval East, with its complexities, provides the context for the activities of the crusaders and for those of them who settled on Asian soil. This history is not always familiar, and I have thought it necessary to sketch it in broad outline, without going into the detail that is not directly relevant to the crusades.

At this point I should acknowledge my debts. Historical research into the crusades began at an early date, and the humanists collected the texts on which their history is based. The first great synthesis, that of Joseph Michaud, whose *Histoire des Croisades* deservedly remains a classic, did not overlook the Arab sources, which had been quarried by Joseph Reinaud. The end of the nineteenth century was the age of the great scholars: Heinrich Hagenmeyer and Reinhold Röhricht, who established with precision the chronological sequence of the crusades to the Latin East, and Paul Riant, himself an indefatigable editor of texts, who continued the work undertaken by the Académie des Inscriptions et Belles-lettres in the *Recueil des Historiens des Croisades* and founded the Société de l'Orient latin. The *Revue de l'Orient latin* brought together the work of historians. Soon after the First World War, Jean Longnon and Louis Bréhier paved the way for new works, which culminated in the magisterial synthesis of René Grousset, whose *Histoire des croisades et du royaume franc de Jérusalem* (1934–6) can still be regarded as the indispensable starting point for all new research. It benefited from the assistance of many great orientalists – including Paul Pelliot, Gaston Weit and Henri Massé – but it remained the work of one man who took in the totality of this history.

Other works have appeared since which, while distinguishing themselves from that of René Grousset, were in the same tradition, such as those of Sir Steven Runciman and Francesco Cognasso. But the great work of the thirty years following the end of the Second World War was the collection of six volumes, fruit of a collective labour, encompassing the whole domain of the crusades from the eleventh to the fifteenth century, the history of the Frankish, Muslim and Armenian East and that of Byzantium, inaugurated by John L. LaMonte and completed thanks to the perseverance of Kenneth M. Setton. This work is indispensable and I have drawn heavily on it.

Major questions have, however, been taken up again and re-examined in depth. The idea of the crusade, since Carl Erdmann and Etienne Delaruelle, has been the subject of works by Paul Rousset, Paul Alphandéry and Alphonse Dupront. In *The First Crusade and the Idea of Crusading*, Jonathan Riley-Smith has looked at it in a new way and more works have since appeared.

Both the military history of the crusades, an English speciality, and their economic history, have also made great progress. The monographs devoted to the states of the Latin East, beginning with Claude Cahen's *La Syrie du Nord*, those dealing with the lordships and the biographies of the various participants, both Franks and Muslims, have greatly enriched our knowledge, and numerous studies of the documents or of specific topics have thrown new light on many issues. Convenient and well-informed syntheses have appeared for the benefit of a wider audience including students, among which a special place must be reserved for Hans Mayer's *Geschichte der Kreuzzügge*, many times revised and twice translated into English. I should also note the works of Cécile Morrisson, Zoé Oldenbourg, Canon Platelle, Michel Balard and Jonathan Riley-Smith, who each approach this history in their own way, and Régine Pernoud's *Les Hommes de la croisade*, and the recent *Atlas of the crusades* edited by Riley-Smith.

The bibliography is now considerable and proliferating. One can no longer count the articles and contributions to conferences, and I would like to express my gratitude to all those who have sent me extracts and offprints, from which I have benefited greatly. In the face of this rising tide, and to remedy the dispersion of these works, the Society for the Study of the Crusades and the Latin East, distant heir of the Société de l'Orient Latin, has been founded, an initiative in which I myself was involved. This is an opportunity to thank those who have worked and still work within the Society, making it possible to publish an information *Bulletin* and hold many conferences. The large number of participants is in itself evidence of the revitalisation of the history of the crusades.

I hope that I have been able to show the importance of all this new work to our knowledge of the crusades, and that I have not misrepresented the work of all those scholars and researchers, many of whom have become friends, too numerous to name, though I should mention two we have recently lost, Joshua Prawer and Maurice Chehab. I would like also to express my debt to those who, more than fifty years ago, introduced me to the study of the history of the crusades, Claude Cahen, Jean Longnon, Paul Deschamps, Henri Seyrig, Paul Pelliot and, above all, the man I acknowledge as my master, René Grousset, who, in 1947, wrote the preface to my *Royaume latin de Jérusalem*, and hoped that I in my turn would stimulate students to labour in this field of research.

I would also like to thank those who have helped me to complete this book, especially my family; I should make special mention of Agnes Fontaine, without whose insistence I would have hesitated to embark on it; and I am very grateful to Jean Birrell for the great care she has taken over the English translation of this book.

I

THE BEGINNING OF THE CRUSADES

It was on 27 November 1095, at the end of the council he had convened at Clermont in Auvergne, before a large audience of both laity and clergy, that Pope Urban II launched an appeal that was to have far-reaching repercussions. Fortunately, we can be fairly clear about the content of his address, but the response to the pope's appeal is more problematic. It set off shock waves that put tens of thousands of people on the roads to the East and resulted in the birth of a new 'nation' on eastern soil. Its impact was felt for two centuries and more; the initial objective was transformed, though without really changing its nature. It was to continue, in the form of a defence of Europe, even after the Latin possessions in the Holy Land had been abandoned.

THE BIRTH OF THE IDEA OF CRUSADE

The question of the origins of the crusade has long been debated among historians, and the debate will no doubt continue, especially since other perspectives than the strictly historical are involved.

The crusade poses a problem that is still present in the human consciousness, that of the legitimacy of war. It is easy to contrast Urban II's appeal with the image of a primitive Christianity that was fundamentally opposed to all use of force. But the inclusion in the Ten Commandments of a precept forbidding the killing of a human being did not prevent the people of Israel from waging wars which seemed to them wholly justified. And, from the earliest times, the Church included in its ranks soldiers who refused to sacrifice to the gods but did not refuse to fight in accordance with their profession. After it had become Christian, the Roman Empire continued to use war as a means of achieving its political ends and, most of all, for its defence. Theologians laboured to reconcile the demands of divine law and the imperatives of the government of men. Both the Byzantine Church and the Latin Church continued to regard the killing of any man as a reprehensible act. The former required a penance from the soldier who had killed an enemy, but the *Penitential* of Alan of Lille, at the end of the twelfth century, effectively said the same: 'He who has killed a pagan or a Jew', he wrote, in substance, 'ought to submit to a penance of forty days, because the person he killed is one of God's creatures and might have been led to salvation'.

This did not prevent necessities of state from making war inevitable. The Church accepted that the sovereign had the right to resort to it and to summon his subjects to participate, when their defence was at stake; we owe to St Augustine the definition of a just war, namely a war waged for the defence of Christians and the 'homeland of the Christians' against an unjust aggressor.

It was not for the Church to intervene in what was the province of a sovereign power, that of the emperor. At the very most, it might obtain for the clergy and the bishops freedom from the obligation to take up arms, which obliged them to shed blood. But exceptions were made even to this principle. The emperors often devolved some of their obligations to the bishops, and they, performing the role of fathers of their people, were sometimes obliged to organise the defence of their city, for example against the Huns and the Vandals. They more often sought, however, to protect their flock by negotiating with the enemy; during the first Muslim invasions, many prelates were in this way the agents of the submission of their city.

It is generally accepted that when the barbarian monarchies settled in the old Roman Empire, warlike societies replaced a civil society, and this led to an exaltation of war previously unknown to the Christian peoples. I have no wish to dispute this, only to note that many historians see this as the starting point for the concept of a 'holy war', that is, of the recourse to war as a means of extending the reign of Christ by the physical elimination or forced conversion of the infidel. Charlemagne, conducting a war against the Saxons that only ended, in the words of Eginhard, in the destruction of idols and the baptism of pagans, is quoted as an example. We should also note that, according to the same author, the Saxons were highly inconvenient neighbours for the Frankish people, and that the emperor may have been obeying other imperatives than simply the desire to impose the faith.

The image of a 'missionary and warlike' Charlemagne, as Robert Folz has said, owes much to later developments. These provided material for the Charlemagne cycle of *chansons de geste*, which took as their principal theme his battles against the Saracens of Spain and Italy. The *Chanson de Roland* shows the emperor offering the vanquished the choice between death and baptism. But Charlemagne refused to impose this choice on Queen Bramimonda, who converted only 'for love'. The song, a literary genre, hence a work of the imagination, here comes up against the principle firmly proclaimed by the Church. Adhesion to the faith could not be obtained either by force or by threats and only example and persuasion could lead an infidel to it. The 'holy war' as an operation culminating in forced conversion was rejected by all the theologians and canonists. The crusaders, by and large, respected this dictate.

The 'just war', on the other hand, grew in importance after the great emperor's death, because the Christian West was then genuinely in a state of siege. From the north came the murderous and devastating raids of the Scandinavians, who attacked churches and the clergy in particular, because of their wealth and from a hatred of Christianity. From the east, Hungarian cavalry made raids into Germany, Italy and Burgundy. And the Saracens, driven back at the end of the ninth century, after a hundred years of struggle, as far as Llobregat, reappeared in Provence, the Mediterranean and southern Italy, pillaging as far north as St Peter's in Rome.

Western Christendom had not mobilised against the Muslims when they had conquered North Africa and Spain, and only the Visigothic princelings, the dukes of Aquitaine and the kingdom of the Franks had put up a serious resistance. The Carolingians had been satisfied when they had eliminated the march established by the Arabs at Narbonne and covered their frontier by a Spanish march that extended no further than Barcelona. The persecutions endured by the martyrs of Cordova made little impact.

The new Saracen incursions, which began with the conquest of Sicily by the African emirs, transformed the situation. For the papacy, the defence of the 'patrimony of St Peter' was an imperative. It caused the popes, when the iconoclastic emperors left them to their own devices, to appeal to the Franks against the Lombards. In the ninth century, it was to defend itself against the Saracens that the papacy summoned Charles the Bald into Italy. After his death, Pope John VIII asked all Christian warriors to come to the defence of the possessions of the apostles against the Saracens in a bull of 878 in which Etienne Delaruelle saw the first clear grant of an indulgence to these combatants, and the first attempt at a collective organisation of a Christian defence disregarding a faltering imperial protection.

The initiative of 878 was not followed up. German and Byzantine emperors reappeared in Italy; the Saracens were contained in Italy and driven out of Provence. But in the eleventh century, a new danger threatened the 'patrimony', this time from the Normans, who were carving out for themselves in southern Italy dominions that caused great anxiety to their neighbours. In 1053 Pope Leo IX had to make a new appeal for warriors to fight these disruptive elements by promising them spiritual rewards. His army was nevertheless soundly defeated, and the pope was taken prisoner by the Normans, for whom this success was a considerable embarrassment.

Thus, in the name of his responsibility as temporal sovereign, the pope, to assure his defence, in the absence of assistance from the emperors who were in principle responsible for it, had to resort to warriors to whom he presented this defence as a pious work, in the service of the Church, and in particular of the apostles Peter and Paul, a work that deserved to be rewarded. It was not necessarily against the infidel that they fought: Christians who had put themselves beyond the law by their usurpations and their pillage, like the Normans, were also targeted.

Another step was taken with the reform called Gregorian (Leo IX was already a reforming pope). The popes of the second half of the eleventh century increasingly intervened in temporal matters. To combat the 'simoniac heresy', Alexander II encouraged the Milanese to take up arms against those he regarded as their oppressors. He gave his protection to William the Conqueror when he denounced Harold for reneging on his oath to recognise him as Edward the Confessor's heir. Similarly, he and his successors encouraged the Christians of Spain in their *reconquista*.

Above all, faced with the inadequacy of the secular authorities, the Church invested heavily in the 'movement of peace' that characterised the eleventh century, which had the effect of increasing the responsibility assumed by the papacy for the government of Christendom.

WESTERN SOCIETY ON THE EVE OF THE CRUSADE

It was at the end of the Carolingian period that the West and western society took shape in a way that, two centuries later, would enable it to sustain the crusading venture. As we know, the peoples of the East, when they became aware of what differentiated the crusaders from the Byzantine Christians they already knew, called them the 'Franks'. This name expresses a reality, since the majority of the crusaders came from the lands that had been ruled by the kings of the Franks or those incorporated into them.

'King of the Franks' was still, in the eleventh century, part of the title of the sovereigns of the two parts of the old Carolingian empire that were separated by the frontier of the 'four rivers' defined at the time of the treaty of Verdun: western France and eastern France. The sovereigns of the east wore a triple crown, that of the kingdoms of Germany, Burgundy and Italy, but their power in Italy was confined to the old Lombard kingdom, while the Byzantines retained the coastal parts of southern Italy into the eleventh century. The kingdom of the kings of France stretched from Flanders to Catalonia, but their own demesne was confined to the lands lying between Orleans and the valley of the Oise. The rest of the kingdom consisted of principalities whose rulers, usually bearing the title of duke or count, while they remained bound to the sovereign by ties of fealty, enjoyed considerable autonomy. In the Empire, the structure was similar, though the emperors retained under their direct control a number of cities whose bishops, endowed with comital powers, were more closely dependent on them.

In the kingdoms that resulted from the dismemberment of the Carolingian monarchy, what may be called the 'Frankish model', that is, the collection of structures which define feudal society, prevailed. With the end of the Norman and Hungarian invasions, this model spread beyond the boundaries of the old Carolingian domain. Its spread was accompanied by the advance of a Christianisation which reached the Scandinavian, Slav and Hungarian countries. National duchies emerged, and the emperor granted the royal title to their principal rulers, as in Denmark, Poland and Bohemia. Sweden and Norway were unified and became, in their turn, kingdoms; the pope granted a royal crown to the Hungarian and Croatian dynasties. These new kingdoms, in spite of the reservations of the German clergy, who had hoped to keep them dependent on their metropolitans, obtained from the papacy autonomous episcopal hierarchies. In this way, a whole collection of new states enlarged western Christendom, even though a pagan mass persisted, between Germany and Poland, among the Slavs of the region between the Elbe and the Oder.

The Frankish model was also dominant, though in different forms, in the old Visigothic territories which escaped Muslim domination, in the lands captured by the Normans in southern Italy and Sicily from the Byzantines, the Lombards and the Muslims; the conquest of Anglo-Saxon England by other Normans brought that country more fully into Frankish society, whilst the Celtic countries of Scotland and Ireland began to feel its influence.

A new Europe was thus added to that of Carolingian times. Its culture was entirely Latin, and Latin was the common language of all literate persons. The liturgy and the ecclesiastical institutions were its prop. Admittedly, particularisms persisted. Spain, and in particular Castile, still retained a writing, a liturgy and a calendar that were peculiar to it, but which would disappear before the common ecclesiastical culture. The Celts, too, resisted this penetration, as did the Hellenised populations of southern Italy, who alone escaped the domination of Latin civilisation.

Integration into the Frankish model took the form of the adoption of a political and social structure which entrusted government to a warrior nobility. This nobility performed the judicial as well as the military function. It adapted itself to the structures of a vassalic system which gave it cohesion and assured its predominance through technical superiority; it constituted a heavy cavalry, wielding the sword and the lance (the latter no longer employed as a javelin), and protected by the coat of mail and long shield; sweeping into battle in serried ranks, it was supplemented by an infantry which employed missile weapons.

Its leaders belonged to an aristocracy of Frankish origin, or allied to the great Frankish families, who were bound by ties of lineage. They enjoyed a privilege based on blood; the possession of power was legitimised by a dynastic tradition which did not prevent successional disputes, but confined them to those who could claim rights based on membership of a lineage. These dynasties could count on the obedience of their subordinates, in particular of those who were bound to them by the tie of vassalage, which men able to fight on horseback and in a coat of mail rarely escaped. The prime duty of the vassal was to assist his lord to defend his body and his honour; he followed him on his expeditions and, when the lord responded to a summons from the count, duke or king, it was his vassals who made up his contingent. This solidarity was to play a major role in recruitment for the crusades.

Vassalage was accompanied by a feudal system based on the grant to the vassal of a piece of land which supported him, his horse and his equipment. But grants as fiefs went much further; kings and great men enfeoffed their followers with public responsibilities, and the income deriving from them. And lords endeavoured to extend their authority to the owners of estates situated in their neighbourhood by obliging them to become their vassals and by granting them as fiefs lands taken from the latter's own lands. But entry into vassalage was far from complete; the allod, that is, land free of ties of dependence, coexisted with the fief and the allod-holder was able to acknowledge many lords if he received many fiefs. This produced conflicting loyalties, which together with the requirements of family solidarity – which, in particular, obliged the members of a lineage to seek vengeance (the *faide*, or feud) in the case of murder – introduced all sorts of contradictions into feudal society. The vassalic structure, so effective in the military sphere, proved less coherent in other areas; power relations caused conflicts that were something long lasting.

The lords and their vassals, the simple knights dependent on a small fief, sometimes maintained by their master, and the allod-holders of equivalent rank, formed a stratum situated above the peasants who comprised the vast majority of a society that was essentially rural. Slavery had almost disappeared; serfdom, which was the condition most wide-spread apart from a few regions (in particular those adjoining the North Sea), carried the obligation to perform very heavy services for the master, that is, the landlord whose tenant the serf was. But the serf held his land by hereditary title and *mainmorte* was tending to replace serfdom; the peasants were beginning to negotiate a reduction in their services.

This beginning of an evolution in serfdom is linked to a problem that historians have not entirely resolved. The eleventh century seems to have experienced a real demographic growth, except during serious subsistence crises, one of which ravaged Germany shortly before the crusade. *Hospites* settled on lands previously forest or waste; the wave of new town creation which characterised the twelfth century had already begun. Should we conclude that there was a shortage of land to receive an excessive manpower? The fact that so much land was available in the following century on which to establish new villages gives cause for doubt. But it is possible that the structures of the lordship, which required a large area to be set aside for pasture and for the hunt, did not favour the expansion of cultivated areas. Some historians believe that the existence of a mass of landless peasants encouraged the exodus towards new lands.

The income derived by the lords from the rents of their tenants, and from other sources such as the taxes levied for the protection of the merchants who passed through their lands, or on transactions taking place in markets, put them in possession of a certain capital, which meant they could maintain their knights. It is hardly surprising that they were able to finance their expeditions, nor that this financing had its limits.

Seigneurial power was linked to the possession of a castle: a motte and bailey, consisting of an artificial mound on which a tower was erected and which was surrounded by a large fenced and ditched enclosure, like so many built by the Normans in England; or a large, rectangular stone-built donjon, whose main room was the very heart of the lordship. But fortification was developing fast; the art of flanking was still rudimentary, and towers were beginning simply to complete the *enceinte*, on the model of the old walls of Roman forts.

Below these castles there developed *bourgs* which attracted to the protection of the castle walls the marketplace, merchants and craftsmen previously dispersed in the villages. This process had started long ago round the oldest towns, usually surrounded by monasteries and priories. There was a revival of towns in western France, in Germany and in northern Italy, and it was in them that the markets in which agricultural produce and manufactured goods were exchanged were to be found. With the market came the need for credit, which allowed the buyer to defer the moment of payment. This led to a transformation in the activities of the Jews, who specialised in loans against security or at interest; they were attracted into the towns by their lay and ecclesiastical lords both to facilitate their economic development and so that the lords themselves could take advantage of a credit they found useful. The towns of the Rhineland in particular acquired prosperous 'Jewries'. The burgesses also benefited from this revival of trade; they began to stand up to their lords, in Le Mans in 1066 and in Cologne in 1074. In Italy, this trend was more precocious and Milan had already experienced its first urban troubles. This revival of trade, which led to an increase in the circulation of money, is one of the factors which made the crusades possible. Nor should we forget that the churches, and also great men, had long hoarded precious metals in the form of objects of gold and silver, which could, when the time was right, be mobilised.

We should remember, too, the circulation of people. There were many merchants on the roads, as the disputes arising from the imposition of tolls by lords of castles, on the pretext of providing protection, testify. Pilgrims, too, were numerous, and they visited distant sanctuaries, such as Compostella, Rome and even Jerusalem. Society was not immobile. And, like people, news circulated and ideas were spread. The wanderings of itinerant preachers are one proof of this.

This society was faced with a religious ferment that was without doubt one of the major facts of the eleventh century. In the West, admittedly, there was only one faith, that taught by the Church of Rome. Only the Jewish communities escaped this unity of faith, but this exception had long been familiar to theologians, who accepted that the resistance of the Jews to the teaching of Christ would last to the end of time. Heretical tendencies were denounced, here and there, but they were not yet on any appreciable scale, and were, in any case, harshly suppressed.

The religious ferment arose from the aspiration of Christians for a 'reform' which was, to begin with, the desire to liberate the Church from the compromises with the world which it had been obliged to make at the time of the first Carolingians. The reform had at first been aimed at monks and canons, to steer them all to observance of a rule – for the former, that of St Benedict of Aniane, for the latter, that of

Chrodegang. The monastic order was led to conform to a religious life which had as one of its models Cluny, then at the height of its fame under St Hugh (1049–1109). Reform then reached the secular clergy, and first the upper clergy, beginning with the papacy, which was reformed by the Lorrainer popes with the support of the emperor Henry III. Through the intermediary of their legates, the popes attacked simony, that is, the acquisition of ecclesiastical office through the favour of the secular powers. The new emperor Henry IV, deprived of his right to intervene in the choice of popes by Nicholas II's decree of 1059, and reluctant to renounce his authority over bishops exercising governmental functions in their cities in his name, came into conflict with Pope Gregory VII, who was determined to get him to renounce the symbolic investiture of bishops with their bishopric. The conflict worsened to the point where the pope deposed the emperor and the emperor had an anti-pope, Gilbert of Ravenna, elected. The latter was still in possession of Rome when Urban II, elected by the cardinals of the opposing party, went to France. Henry IV had expelled Gregory VII from Rome, and among the emperor's auxiliaries was the duke of Lower Lorraine, Godfrey of Bouillon.

The Church was thus torn between two opposing parties; numerous bishops had been deposed, and many German dukes had rallied to an anti-emperor, while others recognised the authority of the anti-pope. But Gregorian ideas were gaining ground and, with them, the desire for a clearer separation between the spiritual and the temporal. This separation meant that great men and even knights must renounce much property they had received in the form of fiefs: abbatial office, churches and tithes. The cartularies of the period are full of such renunciations, testimony to the crisis of conscience among a noble class that possession of these ecclesiastical properties placed in a state of sin.

The desire to cut oneself off from the temptations of the world went further. Monastic vocations were increasingly frequent in noble society. The monkish life in itself seemed too easy to the most demanding spirits. Abbots left their monasteries to found others that were subject to a more demanding asceticism. Many sought a more absolute solitude and a total absence of possessions. This gave rise to an eremitical movement which culminated in the foundation of new orders, from the Camaldoli to the Cistercians and Carthusians. It was difficult for those who did not enter the cloister to shut their ears to the voice of the preachers calling for moral reform and a more Christian life. The people of the late eleventh century were aware of being sinners and knew that the road to eternal salvation lay in the Christianisation of their life.

This affected the noble world in particular. Since the end of the tenth century, bishops and abbots had been anxious to find a remedy for the exactions and violence perpetrated by those who disposed of force of arms. Quite apart from the greed and brutality often inherent in the condition of these men, society encouraged such violence by failing to provide men with the normal means of maintaining their rights and obtaining justice. The judicial institutions inherited from the Roman and Carolingian past had lost their efficacy by the fact of the absorption of public functions into the feudal order. The vassal might recognise the authority of his lord's court in matters touching his fief, but it was a different matter when his allod was at issue. The two parties might fail to agree on the choice of a judge, and the one that had been condemned might feel justified in rejecting the judgement. There was a resort to private war, which amounted to making one's own justice, by inflicting such losses on an adversary that he was forced to make terms. This led to exactions of every sort: pillage, destruction, abduction of people and cattle, arson.

To remedy this situation, the Church had the idea of proposing limits to the exercise of the right of war, either temporal – the truce of God – or in the nature of the acts of war from which they wished to exclude the clergy, the peasantry and travellers – the peace of God. 'Assemblies of peace', on the pattern of councils, were held, in particular between 1020 and 1030, provoking an enthusiasm comparable to that which was to be ignited by the announcement of the crusade in 1095. Barons and knights swore, on the relics that had been amassed from all around, to respect the peace, and promised to repress infringements of it, the guilty being punished with excommunication. Leagues, the 'institutions of peace', or 'sworn communes of the dioceses', were formed, whose members, at the bishop's summons, would take action against those who broke the peace. The great lords soon took over these operations. The emperor Henry III, Duke Hugh of Burgundy and Duke William of Normandy threw the weight of their might behind them. But it was a long time before private war and its excesses disappeared. And it seemed normal to the men of the eleventh century for responsibility for the establishment of peace, which was the order God wished to reign on earth, to lie with the Church. This vocation of the Church was fundamental to Urban II's appeal.

Thus the pope found a West whose structures already favoured expansion. New forces were ready to be used, the aspiration to salvation encouraged an undeniable fervour, and the Church enjoyed an exceptional authority which extended beyond the strictly spiritual sphere. It was not only the economic structures that were capable of supporting the effort that the pope was to demand of the Franks.

THE EAST IN THE ELEVENTH CENTURY

In the late ninth and early tenth centuries the East was still the theatre of confrontation of two powers which had been facing each other for over two centuries: the caliphate of the Abbasids in Baghdad and the empire of the *basileis* in Constantinople. At this time, the two powers counterbalanced each other. The emperors had driven the Arabs back to the borders of the valley of the Euphrates and the Taurus Mountains, and a chain of fortresses made this situation material. Between the Byzantine fortresses and those of the caliphs lay a glacis exposed to reciprocal raids, whilst the practice of exchanging prisoners in agreed locations had become established.

In 931 a Byzantine general temporarily occupied Melitene. From this point, the balance of power began to swing in favour of the Byzantines, while the caliphs, whose authority was weakening, left the task of containing the Byzantines' advance to the frontier emirs. The emperors of the Macedonian dynasty, aided by a succession of remarkable military leaders drawn from the landed aristocracy of Asia Minor, won new successes. In 965 the town of Tarsus became Byzantine again; in 969 it was the turn of Antioch. Shaizar, in 999, and Edessa, in 1039, became the furthest points of Byzantine conquest. But Nicephorus Phocas and John Tzimisces had pushed even further. In 975 Tzimisces had been as far as Mount Tabor; he had received offers of submission from the towns of Judaea and had declared his intention of advancing as far as Jerusalem. Cilicia, northern Mesopotamia and northern Syria were organised into 'themes' and the Byzantines summoned Christians to repopulate them.

The Abbasid caliphs were in no position to fight Byzantium. Eastern Iran had passed to a local dynasty, that of the Samanids. Other Iranians, the Buyids of Daylam, had taken power in Baghdad itself, exercising it in the name of the caliph. Arabs, the Hamdanid emirs, had formed a principality which had Aleppo as its centre; it was they who had to bear the brunt of the battle against the Byzantines, who at one point penetrated as far as their capital.

Above all, Egypt had been lost to the Abbasids. Rival caliphs, the Fatimids, who proclaimed an extreme Shi'ism (the Buyids were also Shi'is, but accepted the theoretical sovereignty of a Sunni caliph), had seized the country in 969 and made Cairo their capital. They had soon gained a foothold in Palestine; it was their presence that had halted the offensive of John Tzimisces. Damascus obeyed them and their sovereignty was briefly proclaimed in Baghdad. The propaganda of the Ismailite missionaries (the dynasty claimed to descend from the seventh imam, Ismail) gained disciples and had the support of 'houses of knowledge'. It also gave birth to various sects, the Ismailis or Assassins, the Druze and the Nizaris. The caliph al-Hakim (996–1021) even allowed himself to be presented as being of divine essence; it was he who ordered the destruction of the Holy Sepulchre in 1006.

But the pattern of power relations soon changed. The emperor Basil II had directed his efforts towards Armenia, whose principal kingdoms he had annexed. On his death, the military aristocracy, till then dominant, was excluded from power by emperors who were associated with the throne by the empresses Zoe and Theodora, and who endeavoured to maintain peace with the Fatimids, who permitted them to rebuild the Holy Sepulchre. Their attention was directed more towards the Balkans, Italy and Sicily than towards the East.

At this point there was a Turkish invasion. The Ghuzz, the nomadic Turks of the steppe of the Aral Sea, recently converted to Islam, took advantage of the destruction of the Samanid empire by a *condottiere*, also Turkish, Mahmud of Ghazna. Their dominant clan, the Seljuks, settled in 1038 in Khorassan and in Khorezm. Other bands launched raids of pillage as far afield as Armenia. In 1055, on an appeal from the caliph, the Seljuk chief Toghrul entered Baghdad and received the title of sultan. These Turks, practising a strict Sunniism, opposed to the Shi'is an orthodoxy supported by the teaching of the *madrasa* which they established in all their possessions.

Their attention was attracted to Asia Minor by the progress being made there by the Turkoman clans, which, without encumbering themselves with Byzantine fortresses, which they were content to blockade, penetrated deep into Byzantine territory. An emperor put on the throne by the military aristocracy, Romanus Diogenes, attempted to drive them back. The Turks appealed to the new sultan, Alp Arslan, who routed the emperor at Manzikert (1071). In the ensuing anarchy, a Norman soldier of fortune, Roussel of Bailleul, was able to carve out for himself a principality. The new emperor, Michael VII, appealed against him to a cousin of Alp Arslan, Suleiman, who took the opportunity to seize several towns, including Nicaea. Another Turkish chieftain, Tzachas, occupied Smyrna.

Not all of Asia Minor, however, was in Turkish hands. The fortresses of the eastern frontier held firm, under the command of Armenian leaders, one of whom, Philaretus, was generally regarded as duke of Antioch. But the civil wars between the claimants to the throne of Constantinople distracted them from the battle against the invaders, whose aid they sometimes sought, and Antioch fell in 1084. Other towns continued to resist, though some of their leaders came to terms with the Turks, as at Marash, Melitene and Edessa.

In 1081 Alexius Comnenus proclaimed himself *basileus*. He defeated his rivals and seized Constantinople, which his troops conscientiously looted. He resorted to confiscations and the secularisation of Church property in order to restore a treasury that enabled him to assemble an army composed largely of mercenaries. He turned his attention to the enemies of the empire, Normans and Pechenegs, and, having defeated them, could proceed to the reconquest of the lands lost in Anatolia, meanwhile playing the Turkish leaders off one against the other.

His plans were facilitated by the discord reigning among the Turks. Suleiman of Nicaea, who had occupied Antioch, had been almost at once attacked and killed by another Seljuk, Tutush, who had taken Damascus from the Fatimids and who coveted northern Syria. But Tutush's brother, the sultan Malik-Shah, intervened and made himself master of Aleppo and Antioch. After the sultan's death, Tutush set out to seize Baghdad. He died in the attempt, leaving his two sons, Ridwan and Duqaq, respectively *malik* (king) of Aleppo and of Damascus, whilst in other towns governors made themselves practically independent under the nominal authority of the sultan.

The Turkish occupation took a different form in Asia Minor and in Syria. The capitulation of the Byzantine fortresses, usually after a siege, was followed by the installation of Turkish garrisons, who seem sometimes to have treated the Christian population harshly. They, with their bishops, were often obliged to seek refuge in Byzantine territory. The cathedral churches were transformed into mosques. At Ani, the ancient capital of Armenia, Malik-Shah had the cross that surmounted it taken to a mosque where it was built into the doorstep so that believers could tread it underfoot. The rural population had to suffer raids conducted by the *ghazi*, who pillaged their stocks and made off with their slaves; the villagers were subsequently reduced to the status of *dhimmi*, with the burdens inherent to this condition. Among them, the Jacobite Christians, particularly numerous in eastern Anatolia, Mesopotamia and the Antioch region, seem to have found Muslim rule little different to that of the Byzantines.

The situation was different for the Armenians. Deprived of their independence by Basil II and his successors, they had lost their national aristocracy, which had been resettled on Byzantine territory, especially Capadocia and the Taurus region. Those who had been won over to the *Credo* of the council of Chalcedon had received office and commands from the emperors; they sought to remain, even if it meant paying tribute to the new Turkish masters, but at the risk of being evicted by them. They were a group who proved particularly useful to the crusaders.

In Muslim Syria, the Turks left in place the existing administration, consisting largely of Arabs and Iranians with some Christian scribes. They did not persecute the Shi'is, but entrusted office in the mosques and the judiciary to Sunnis. Arab emirs remained in certain fortified towns, recognising the authority of the new masters. It was an Arab leader from the Banu Munqidh clan who took possession of Shaizar, having the gates of the town opened to him by the bishop who was its governor. For the rural population, Muslim or Christian, little changed; at most, they suffered from the passage of troops and from raids made by irregulars. Insurrections might be severely punished, as in the case of Jerusalem where, when the Turk Atsiz reoccupied the town in 1076–7, the rebellious inhabitants who had taken refuge in the al-Aqsa mosque were massacred. Possibly there was also greater insecurity; brigands, Turkish and Bedouin, sometimes severed road links.

The Fatimid caliphate suffered the direct effects of the Turkish conquest. After al-Hakim, the caliphs became hostages to their viziers and lost the support of the Berbers of North Africa who had provided their best troops. The Seljuks deprived them of Damascus after a Turkish adventurer who had previously been in their service, Atsiz, had taken Ramla and Jerusalem in 1071. The governors of the coastal towns made themselves independent; it was an Armenian convert, Badr al-Jamali, who restored the authority of the caliph over Tyre and Sidon, while the qadi of Tripoli, Ibn Ammar, created a small principality around that town. Badr eventually became vizier of the caliph, whose authority he restored; his son considered seeking the assistance of the crusaders against the Turks.

The Byzantine empire might therefore hope to recover the territory it had lost. Alexius Comnenus, having fought off many Turkish attacks on Constantinople, brought relief to the town by reoccupying Cyzicus and Sinope. He took Smyrna from Tzachas. He was probably preparing other operations; the letter he seems to have sent to Robert the Frison, count of Flanders, asking for knights, shows him concerned to reinforce his army to this end. His victories over the Normans and other enemies of the empire had paradoxically added to his troops, in particular by the incorporation of the Pechenegs, auxiliaries who were undisciplined but valuable for their experience in nomad tactics. The bases available for operations in Asia existed, even if there was no longer any contact with the Armenian governors of the eastern towns, and despite the governor of Trebizond behaving as if he were an independent ruler. The Byzantine fleet remained large and assured communications with Cyprus. Admittedly, the devastations had deprived the Byzantines of the solid support for reconquest that would have been provided by a fairly dense Greek population in Anatolia, but the empire still enjoyed many advantages.

Could westerners have remained indifferent to the great drama being played out in the East? It remains difficult to know how well informed they were about it. They could not have been wholly ignorant of it, since relations between the two shores of the Mediterranean were fairly active during the course of the eleventh century.

Trade had long linked these two worlds. For Henri Pirenne the Arab conquest interrupted commercial relations between East and West, but more recent research has considerably modified this view. A famous text of Ibn Khordadbeh describes the activities of the Jews of Babylonia, whose trading network extended from Spain to Mesopotamia by way of the Slav and Frankish countries, and from one end of the Mediterranean to the other; the documents found in the Cairo genizah have revealed the humdrum routine of the journeys and the trade in which the Jews were profitably engaged.

We know little about merchants from the East in the ports of Mediterranean Europe, but William of Malmesbury, in connection with Raymond of Saint-Gilles, mentions men from Ascalon who visited the ports of Languedoc. We are better informed about Italian trade with the East, in particular that of the towns of southern Italy, still under Byzantine control at the beginning of the eleventh century; Bari and Trani, for example, had contacts with Constantinople and with the shores of the eastern Mediterranean; it was sailors from Bari who seized the relics of St Nicholas in Myra when the town was abandoned at the approach of the Turks. Amalfi was a special case; its nationals integrated themselves into Byzantine structures to the point of founding a Latin monastery on Mount Athos and its merchants frequented Constantinople and Alexandria; the Pantaleon family and other Amalfitans founded a Benedictine monastery in Jerusalem, and hospitals there and in Antioch.

The Venetians ran them close. They, too, participated in the life of the Byzantine world, of which they had long been a part. At the end of the eleventh century, they sent their ships to Alexandria and other Fatimid ports, but the *basileus* called them to order and forbade them to transport materials which could be used for war, since the Fatimids were then the enemies of Byzantium. The doge Orseolo complied and in 992 obtained the first of the privileges enjoyed by the Venetians in the empire, in particular in Constantinople. A century later, Venice brought decisive assistance to the Byzantines in their war with the Normans; by the Golden Bull of May 1082 it gained free access to the ports of the various provinces of the empire, and the Amalfitans were obliged to pass under Venetian control. The Venetians also traded in fabrics from Byzantium, in particular the silks that the artists of the Romanesque period portrayed on their statues. Other luxury goods arrived through Egypt.

The West also provided the Byzantine East with much-appreciated assistance in the form of men of war. Amongst these, the Scandinavians held a special place, as they constituted one of the corps of the imperial guard (the *hetairia*), that of the Varangians armed with an axe. But Byzantium also hired Normans; it was the Normans recruited by George Maniakes for the conquest of Sicily who, not having been paid, plotted to subject Byzantine Italy to regular raids. Other Normans, Hervé le Francopoule, Robert Crespin and Roussel of Bailleul, served in the army that disputed Asia Minor with the Turks in the second half of the eleventh century. It was the *Nemitzoi*, the Germans in the service of the empire, who in 1081 opened the gates of Constantinople to Alexius Comnenus. He, to fight the Pechenegs who were attacking the Danube frontier, had recourse to five hundred Flemish knights. He also appealed to Anglo-Saxons, with their prince Edgar Atheling, to Normans and to Aquitainians, one of whom is mentioned in the *Miracles of St Foy*. The warriors who sought fame and fortune in 'Miklagard', in the service of the emperor, found a place in the Scandinavian epic.

But, however numerous the merchants and soldiers who went to the East, it is the pilgrims who most deserve our attention. Since the fourth century, the Holy Places had attracted the Christians of western Europe who went to venerate the tomb of Christ and those of other witnesses of his life. The Arab conquest did not interrupt this stream of veneration, even if it temporarily reduced it. The country's new masters quickly discovered that they could turn it to good account by selling safe-conducts and by imposing on the Christians of the East financial burdens that led them to seek the assistance of their brethren in the West. Every pretext was adopted to demand heavy payments – to allow the repair of churches, to alleviate humiliating obligations, etc. – and the patriarchs of Jerusalem and the religious communities begged for help. It is in this context that Charlemagne and his successors claimed to be protectors of the Church of Jerusalem. The West felt an obligation to those who watched over the Holy Places. Gerbert of Aurillac refers to this in 999 and Raoul Glaber tells us that, after al-Hakim's destruction of the Holy Sepulchre, Duke Robert II of Normandy sent the patriarch a large sum for its restoration. In the West as in the East, the monks who went to seek help for St Sabas or for Sinai or for the Holy Sepulchre were received respectfully, and the first donations of landed property to the latter predated the crusades.

This veneration for the Holy Places was primarily manifested in the flow of pilgrims. They came in large numbers before the ninth century. In 890, the monk Bernard the Wise embarked on a boat transporting Christians from Italy, who had been reduced to slavery, to Jerusalem by way of Alexandria. The conversion of Hungary encouraged pilgrimages by offering the possibility of a journey overland instead of the more dangerous and more expensive sea voyage. By the end of the tenth century, great men were setting out for Jerusalem; they included an abbot of Flavigny, a bishop of Constance, a count of Périgord and Hilduin, count of Arcis, who travelled with Adson of Montiérender. Later, their numbers increased; a viscount of Limoges, a count of Rouergue, a bishop of Périgueux, William Taillefer, Count of Angoulême, and Hugh of Chalon, bishop of Auxerre left between 1000 and 1030. In 1035 Duke Robert the Magnificent of Normandy met Fulk Nerra, count of Anjou, who was making the pilgrimage for the second time and who made it again in 1039. Many prelates, bishops and abbots, and especially many founders of monasteries, also went to Jerusalem; they included abbots Thierry of Saint-Evroul and Raoul of Mont-Saint-Michel, bishops Théoduin of Liège and Liébert of Cambrai, then in 1064 the bishops of Bamberg, Mainz, Ratisbon and Utrecht, who travelled together; the princes included a count of Barcelona, a count of Luxembourg, a count of Flanders, Berenger-Raymond of Barcelona and William IV of Toulouse, the last two of whom died during the course of their pilgrimage, in 1092. There were many others, both rich and poor.

These pilgrimages were sometimes made in large parties. Richard, abbot of St Vannes of Verdun, in 1026–7 joined a group estimated at seven hundred persons. The four German bishops mentioned above were supposedly accompanied in 1064 by seven thousand pilgrims, a figure we should treat, obviously, with some caution. The pilgrimage had become so common a practice that a council of Chalon-sur-Saône, in 813, forbade great lords from using it as a pretext to demand a tax from their subjects. Nevertheless, though certain individuals paraded their wealth, the majority of pilgrims set out as penitents. Many princes decided to go to Jerusalem because their conscience was troubled; this was the case with the count of Arcis in 992, Conrad of Luxembourg around 1060, Count Thierry III of Holland – guilty of having killed an archbishop – before 1039, Fulk Nerra and, possibly, Hugh of Chalon; the pilgrimage to the Holy Places was imposed as penance on those who had broken the truce of God.

I will return to the exceptional nature of the pilgrimage to Jerusalem.

Other journeys, like those to Compostella or to Rome, may have seemed equally meritorious because pilgrims hoped to obtain the support of the Apostles for the pardon of their sins. But the Holy Sepulchre was attractive for other reasons. The conditions in which the pious journey was accomplished were certainly not encouraging. Many pilgrims died en route; for some, death was a blessing, as for Liébald, a knight of Burgundy, who had begged God to remove him from this world at Jerusalem, or for the pilgrim mentioned by Caesar of Heisterbach, who also obtained the blessing of dying there without returning to his native land, where he would once again have found opportunity to sin. Pilgrims could count on enjoying alms and the hospitality offered by hospitals such as that of St Samson of Constantinople. But they had to pay taxes demanded by the Byzantines – Victor IV, in 1055, asked them to exonerate these travellers – and by the Saracens, who required a 'tribute' for entry to the Holy Sepulchre.

They were sometimes forbidden to complete their pilgrimage; St Liébert, bishop of Cambrai, was angered by a prohibition of this type issued by the Byzantine governor of Laodocia on the pretext of the insecurity of the roads. But, arriving in Cyprus, he learned that three hundred pilgrims had been expelled from Jerusalem by the Saracens (1054). The four German bishops of 1064 were attacked by brigands – Bedouins or Turks? – and obliged to seek refuge in a fortress, where they were besieged for three days, until the emir of Ramla came to their rescue. And this was before the Turk Atsiz had seized Palestine from the Fatimids and inaugurated a period of armed struggle. But it did not prevent westerners from embarking on new pilgrimages.

In the years immediately preceding the crusade, many people set out, evidence that the Holy Land was the object of a veneration with deep roots in Christian piety. Within an East that some of them knew because they had been there as mercenaries or as merchants, or even for other reasons (we are told of a Norman who, having been banished in 1077, spent twenty years in Muslim territory before joining the crusaders before Jerusalem), the Holy City and its approaches constituted an ensemble that was more familiar. That the pope's appeal, when he invoked the Holy Sepulchre, should resonate so widely, ought therefore to come as no surprise.

2

THE CRUSADE OF URBAN II
AND PASCHAL II

The expansionist tendency of the Frankish West and the state of unrest prevailing in the East would probably not in themselves have been enough to give rise to the crusading movement – even taking into account the military operations directed during the previous decades against Muslim Spain and against Sicily – but for the intervention of a set of ideas which gave a decisive impetus to the power of the western knights. The analysis of the motives of the two popes of the First Crusade, Urban II and his successor Paschal II, has therefore long preoccupied historians, who have explored very diverse and often conflicting channels to explain both the formation of the concept of the crusade and the success it enjoyed in the countries of western Europe.

Tracing the progress of the crusade may help us to understand the birth and evolution of a 'crusading spirit' which was to retain its principal features. The motives of those who participated in the expedition may also be revealed by their reactions to the events which marked its course, though we should not forget that the First Crusade consisted of a series of 'waves': the premature departure of the first contingents; the third wave, the so-called 'crusade of 1101', launched by Paschal II; and the maritime expeditions of the Italian towns.

THE POPE'S APPEAL

The council convened at Clermont for 24 November 1095 was the successor to one held by Pope Urban II six months earlier at Piacenza in the Po plain. Urban II – Eudes of Lagery – was from Champagne and had been prior of Cluny; he had reasserted the authority of the Gregorian papacy, to the detriment of his rival, Gilbert, who nevertheless remained master of Rome and who enjoyed imperial support. The council of Piacenza, which had been attended by a large number of prelates from Italy and the neighbouring regions, had been intended to restore peace to a Church shaken by the after-effects of Gregorian reform, the reciprocal excommunications and the deposition of prelates. Urban II then crossed the Alps, reaching Valence and then Cluny before arriving at Clermont. There, he assembled perhaps a dozen archbishops, some eighty bishops and about the same number of abbots, mostly French or Spanish, in order to address the same problems. These included the question of the matrimonial situation of the king of France, Philip I, who had been given a reprieve at Piacenza to allow him to separate from Bertrade of Montfort, whom he had married even though she was already married to one of his great vassals. This time, the king was excommunicated, though this did not prevent the crusade from being preached in his lands.

But the council of Clermont was also one of the many councils which, during the course of the eleventh century, were preoccupied with the restoration of 'the peace' in feudal society. The measures intended to make peace a reality had been brought together at the council of Narbonne in 1054. The truce of God and the peace of God were completed by the creation of the leagues called 'institutions of peace', which obliged their members to take action against those who failed to respect the rules laid down by previous assemblies. Private wars continued, nevertheless, to rage, and lords and barons to fight each other.

At the end of the council, and outside the church in which it had been held, the pope addressed a crowd probably composed of those nobles of the region who were recognised as having a certain role in the government of the dioceses by the support they gave to episcopal elections, and their vassals. There seem to have been no great barons present, though a few counts and viscounts were perhaps among the crowd. Urban II vigorously denounced the violence and the injustice that knights could commit. It was then, according to most accounts, that he invited his audience to employ their strength in the defence of their brethren, victims of the ill treatment inflicted on them by the infidel in the East.

Some historians have interpreted this appeal in a simplistic and cynical fashion: the pope and his counsellors were seeking to rid the West of troublesome elements by sending them to the East, in the near certainty that they would never return. The fact that the great lords, responsible for the fate of peoples, were the audience at whom this message was directed suggests we may reject this view. I prefer to think that just as the leagues of peace employed warriors to keep order in the West, so the knights summoned to the crusade would seek to restore peace in the East by teaching the invaders a lesson. Looked at in this way, the crusade resembles an 'institution of peace' which would operate in the East.

The invitation appears in most of the texts of Urban II's speech as it has been handed down by historians. It goes without saying that they, writing after the event, reconstructed this speech in line with the tradition of the 'fictitious discourse' inherited from Antiquity, each bringing to it his own view of the motives for the crusade. We must remember that none of these texts, not even that of Fulcher of Chartres, who was one of those who heard the appeal, faithfully transcribed the pope's words. They are nevertheless sufficiently in agreement overall for us to be able to use them to get an idea of what Urban II said. We may be all the more confident of this in that, in three letters, one addressed to the Flemings, the second to the people of Bologna and the third to the Genoese, the pope used very similar words.

His appeal to bring help to the Christians of the East has been much debated. The pope referred to the defeats suffered by the Christians of the East and to the requests for help he had received from them. There seems no justification for believing that, as frequently claimed, he referred to the restrictions put on pilgrimage or to the persecutions suffered by Christians in the Holy Land. This is the story told by Peter the Hermit, as reported by Albert of Aix and the *Chanson d'Antioche*, which emphasised these very questionable aspects. Claude Cahen has shown that the traditional tolerance Christians enjoyed under Muslim rule had been threatened neither in Palestine nor in Syria, even if westerners were shocked by the humiliations and the extortions of which they were the victims. The destruction of the Holy Sepulchre by al-Hakim was long in the past, even though the emotions it provoked at the time had been strong enough to produce a sympathetic response in the form of financial assistance; the memory lingered on, as is shown by the composition, probably between 1095 and 1100, of an encyclical attributed to Pope Sergius IV, but probably forged to arouse the enthusiasm of potential crusaders. Nevertheless, episodes like those described in the Life of St Lietbert, or the story of the journey of the German bishops of 1065, not to speak of the sufferings inflicted on the inhabitants of Jerusalem by the Turkish conquest, may have played a role.

It seems clear, on the other hand, that the pope, speaking of the Christians of the East, referred to the subjects of the Byzantine empire, Greeks and Armenians, who had suffered directly from the Turkish invasion, which he specifically mentioned. Refugees had been arriving in the West since the time of Gregory VII, and the emperors themselves had told the papacy of the ordeals they faced. But had they sought aid from the West? The reality of Michael VII's appeal to Gregory VII has been questioned, but that Alexius Comnenus asked for help from Urban II seems highly likely. The letter along these lines to the count of Flanders, whose authenticity has been queried, is today accepted as having been written by him. The chronicler Bernold of Constance says that, at the end of the council of Piacenza, Urban II asked the Christians who heard him to take an oath to go to the aid of the empire of Constantinople, which had sent envoys to Piacenza.

Urban II was, in fact, reviving a project which had been conceived twenty years earlier by Gregory VII, at the time of the defeat of Manzikert. The pope had written to several western princes, in particular the emperor Henry IV, to inform them of his intention to accompany the 'faithful of St Peter' on an expedition in aid of the Christians who had suffered from the Turkish invasion, an expedition which was to culminate in a pilgrimage to the Holy Sepulchre. The emperor was to remain in the West to assure its defence. The recurrence of difficulties between empire and papacy, and the deposition of Michael VII, whose side the pope had taken, had helped to abort this project. But it is difficult to imagine that it had not been in Urban II's mind.

The reference to the Holy Sepulchre does not appear in all the versions of the pope's appeal. Fulcher of Chartres, in particular, does not mention it. J. Flori has suggested that the fact that Baldwin of Boulogne, to whom Fulcher was chaplain, left the crusade before it reached Jerusalem may explain an omission that must have been deliberate. Others, including Carl Erdmann, have argued that this reference did not take the form of an appeal for the liberation of the Holy Sepulchre, the grant of the indulgence customarily made for visiting it being interpreted by the crusaders differently from the way the pope had intended. But the course of events taken by the crusade is difficult to explain if this liberation had not been emphasised. And we owe to Alfons Becker a proof that appears decisive, namely that the notion of liberation was familiar to the late eleventh-century mind.

For 'reform' was accompanied by the idea of a 'restoration of the reign of Christ'. This century had seen the Spanish *reconquista* accompanied by the rebuilding of churches, the restoration of the episcopal hierarchy and the disappearance of the marks of humiliation imposed on Christians in the reconquered territories. Urban II had himself restored their archiepiscopal rank to the cities of Toledo and Tarragona. It had been the same in Sicily, reconquered from the Muslims by Count Roger, brother of Robert Guiscard. In both cases, the lands involved had been removed from the rule of Christian sovereigns by conquering Muslims, one in the eighth century, the other in the ninth and tenth centuries. Since the mid-eleventh century, the popes, beginning with Alexander II, had encouraged the Spanish princes and the Normans in their reconquest. The theme of liberation of territories occupied by the infidel with no other justification than the use of force was thus not new.

Does this amount to saying that the pope conceived the expedition announced in 1095 as a war against Islam? This idea, familiar to propagandists today, has been put forward by various historians, in particular Joshua Prawer, for whom the crusade was 'not the defence of the Christians of the East, but a Christian offensive against Islam'. He goes on: 'This is probably how Urban II's objective was formulated and, at any rate, how it was understood in the western world.'

This seems unlikely. The idea of Islam, that is to say of a collection of political and religious beliefs, was alien to western thinking at this period. Some learned clerics might have had a perception of the Muslim faith, especially in Spain, where the Mozarabic Church had had to construct an apologetics to combat Muslim proselytism. The vast majority of westerners, however, saw the 'Saracens' as 'pagans' who, according to contemporary authors, worshipped idols. The legitimacy of the sovereignty of the Muslim princes was not challenged by the papacy, as the correspondence of Gregory VII with those of North Africa testifies. But their rule over the lands that had belonged to the 'kingdom of Christ', where they had abolished the 'reign of Christ', might appear scandalous. One may well wonder where this scandalous situation stopped, since Islam had recovered so many lands from the old Roman Empire. But there could be no doubt that this was the case for the Holy Land, objective of so many pilgrimages, and regarded by Christians brought up in the Biblical tradition as the heritage of Christ and thus of the people of his faith. Latin Christendom eventually regarded it as the 'homeland of the Christians', perhaps only after a certain period of western presence there. At the time of Urban II's sermon, Jerusalem, above all, represented one of the objects of its veneration, and it was the name of the Holy Sepulchre that rallied the crusaders.

Also, to encourage them to join the expedition, the pope offered the crusaders the benefit of an indulgence defined as that which was attached to the visit to the tomb of Christ. This, too, was not entirely new. The pilgrimage to Jerusalem, which might be motivated by the desire to deepen a pilgrim's piety by contact with the places where Christ had lived, and those made familiar by the Bible, also represented a penance. In the course of the development of penitential practice, the Church accepted that a repentant sinner enjoined by his confessor to submit to the often heavy and lengthy obligations attached to absolution (separation from the community, deprivation of the sacraments, the wearing of a special garment, fasts, etc.) might substitute making a pilgrimage. The pilgrim went to seek the prayers of a saint; when his faults were particularly grave, he was required to make the journey to the tomb of Christ, which represented a major ordeal, involving many sacrifices. This pilgrimage assured him of the remission of temporal penalties and of those which might remain to be accomplished in Purgatory. We know that more than one of these pious travellers, having reached the Holy Sepulchre, was overcome by the desire to maintain his state of rediscovered innocence, some praying to God to remove them from their earthly life, others entering a religious order. This had been, for example, on his return from a pilgrimage to the Holy Land, the wish of the Milanese knight Erlembald, whom Urban II canonised in 1095. The visit to the Holy Sepulchre was believed to assure the pilgrim already absolved from his sins plenary remission of their consequences.

The popes had also begun to encourage the performance of pious works, such as the building of churches, by granting their authors the same indulgence as that attached to the veneration of the Holy Sepulchre. Urban II himself had granted it to those who contributed to the restoration of Tarragona, which was regarded as the bastion of the defence of Muslim Christianity, where the Almoravids were posing a new threat. But the grant of the plenary indulgence to those who went to Jerusalem no longer simply as pilgrims but as combatants was new. Gregory VII had intended to accord those who participated in his expedition only the benefit of the prayers of the apostles Peter and Paul. Urban II thought it necessary to specify, in one of the canons of the council that has survived, that the plenary indulgence would only be acquired by those who embarked on the journey motivated neither by the desire for vain glory nor for material gain.

The substance of the pope's appeal, therefore, was for participants to bring the military aid they needed to the Christians of Byzantine lands and to liberate the Holy Sepulchre by restoring it to the reign of Christ, thereby enjoying the plenary indulgence linked to the visit to that same Holy Sepulchre.

WHAT URBAN II DID NOT SAY

Did Urban II, in asking the Franks to set out for the East, have motives that are not apparent in his appeal? Historians have argued about this at length and have offered very different explanations.

Since 1054, the Church of Rome and that of Constantinople, followed, more or less reluctantly, by the eastern patriarchs, had severed ties, as a result of the double anathema hurled by Pope Leo IX's legates against Michael Cerularius and by the patriarch against the Roman Church. The causes of the schism were many, stemming from differences that were both disciplinary (the use of unleavened bread for consecration in the Latin Church, ecclesiastical celibacy) and dogmatic (such as the addition of the *Filioque* to the Creed). But the papacy had never lost hope of reestablishing contact, especially since the Italian policy of the Byzantine emperors suffered as a result of this separation, which had been exploited by the Normans. Negotiations had continued, despite episodes such as the excommunication of Alexius Comnenus by Gregory VII, pronounced after the deposition of Michael VII. Byzantium looked for help from the West, and Alexius Comnenus himself had asked for it. To respond to this appeal would be to demonstrate towards the Byzantine empire intentions that the pope might hope the emperor would acknowledge by persuading his clergy to restore the name of the Roman pontiff to the diptychs.

Might there have been more? Had there been consideration of the possibility of getting Roman primacy recognised by all the eastern Christians thanks to the pressure exerted by a powerful army obedient to the pope? Such a thesis does not bear scrutiny. But the possibility of a reunion of the Greek and Latin Churches may have entered Urban II's considerations; it seems, however, not to have been expressed, and there is no evidence of any discussion of this question during the crusade.

Might papal policy in the West have benefited from the consequences of the pope's appeal? The presence in the crusading army of supporters of the emperor Henry IV alongside those of the pope of Gregorian reform might suggest that the pope had succeeded in imposing his influence even in the area under imperial authority, by getting the emperor to support the enterprise he had launched. But the French crusaders who travelled through Rome in 1096 were insulted by Romans loyal to the anti-pope, unmoved by the appeal of the crusade. Nor was the king of France impressed to the point of separating from Bertrade of Montfort.

It has been suggested that the papacy, already provided by the Donation of Constantine with a vast domain in the West, dreamed of extending its temporal power over territories conquered in the East. This seems unlikely, no thought, apparently, having been given to the future of the lands to be conquered. And none of the Latin states founded as a result of the crusades acknowledged itself to be a vassal of the Holy See, unlike England and Aragon.

Some historians have put forward economic explanations. A bold theory recently advanced starts from the fact of the landed wealth enjoyed by the Church in the eleventh century to argue that the Church as an economic power was anxious to find outlets for its products and to protect itself from the competition of Muslim producers, not forgetting the profits to be made from pilgrimage. This rash hypothesis comes up against the fact that the economy of the Church lands was primarily agricultural and found outlets in western markets without there being any need to search for others beyond Europe.

Around the pope, there may have been those who hoped to use the expedition to introduce western merchants into the eastern world. In fact, they were already there; the Pisans and the Genoese were to take advantage of the crusade to acquire possessions that became trading posts. But, as Claude Cahen has shown, the towns where they settled were not yet great commercial centres. And while the crusade allowed them to go beyond their customary horizon, namely the western Mediterranean, it was to establish commercial relations with Fatimid Egypt, and in particular with Alexandria. In any case, it was Urban II who invited the Genoese to participate in the crusade, not the Genoese who took the initiative.

Here, we are already moving from the motives behind the pope's appeal to those which made westerners respond to it. Some were no doubt material in nature. The conditions laid down by the pope for obtaining the indulgence precluded its being acquired by those who joined the expedition in the hope of material gain. In fact, allowing for the costs the participants incurred, any hoped-for profit risked being illusory. To represent the crusaders as dreaming of the incalculable wealth of the East is mere fancy. Nevertheless, there were in the West younger sons of families not well endowed with property, knights eager to establish themselves. Pope Urban II, like St Bernard after him, lambasted the greed of the knights, which manifested itself on more than one occasion. That it was on such a scale as to have motivated many of them to depart remains to be demonstrated.

Did hopes on the part of landless peasants of finding land on which to settle persuade many to take the road to the East? We know that Norman England, before the Slav lands beyond the Elbe, attracted many settlers. But it is tempting to locate this attraction, in the case of the Holy Land, after the establishment of the crusaders, not before.

We must look, accordingly, beyond the material plane. If we are to believe those who reported the words of Urban II, the pope touched a chord in the minds of the knights by exalting their warlike valour and their courage, even, they say, pandering to the pride of the French by referring to the epic tradition. The *chansons de geste* give us insight into the mentality of noble society. Their heroes were inspired by the quest for achievement, the certainty that in fighting for God they would win the glory of Paradise; they were models of bravery and loyalty. The chroniclers reveal that the barons and the knights did not always behave according to these rules of conduct, but it remains the case that the ideal described by the *chansons* was that offered by the culture of their milieu. Urban II warned them against vain glory, but he proposed an enterprise from which they might win renown. And fighting the infidel was an idea familiar to the audience for the *chansons de geste*, many of whom had experience of feats accomplished in Spain by knights from France.

But, more than this, it was considerations of a religious nature that decided the knights – and many others – to undertake this 'voyage' (*voiage*), whose difficulties and dangers were known in advance. The indulgence promised to the participants, it is clear from their charters and from other evidence, had an extraordinary appeal. The announcement of the grant of a grace so complete had a profound effect on men conscious of being sinners and anxious about their salvation. If the crusaders set out in large numbers, and if Urban II's words gave rise to a collective enthusiasm, it was because these words responded to the aspirations of a society longing for a 'conversion' thanks to which it would escape the rigours of judgement.

Some historians, among them Paul Alphandéry and Alphonse Dupront, have emphasised an idea that is complementary. Jerusalem was traditionally the place where the return of the Lord, his Second Coming, would take place, and it was widely believed that the resurrection of the dead would happen in the valley of Josaphat. It seems that the announcement of this great journey with Jerusalem as its goal led large numbers of people to believe that if they reached it they would actually be present at the Second Coming of Christ. Not everyone, certainly, shared this eschatological perspective (they showed too much concern with planning for their return and for the recovery of the property they had mortgaged), but it had consequences to which we will return.

From the pope's appeal to the most secret motivations of men is a long journey that is difficult for us to retrace, but we need to imagine it if we are to understand the response to that appeal.

THE DEPARTURE OF THE CRUSADERS: 1095–6

At Clermont, Urban II addressed an audience which was probably large, but whose size we should not overestimate. As we have seen, no great baron was present; the count of Toulouse, Raymond of Saint-Gilles, had

probably been informed of the pope's project and his messengers came
to show his support. Those who heard the pope demonstrated their
enthusiasm by shouting 'God wills it' and by wearing on their clothing a
badge, the cloth cross, which had probably previously been that of
pilgrims setting out for Jerusalem. It was to become the badge of those
who were later called the *crucesignati*, those 'marked with a cross'. The
first to make a vow between the hands of the pope to join the expedition
was the bishop of Le Puy, Adhémar of Monteil; the count of Forez may
have been one of these first crusaders.

Urban II made the bishop of Le Puy his legate to the crusade. As we
know, Gregory VII had intended himself to participate in the expedition
he was planning and which he probably intended to lead. Though there
is room for doubt, there seems little justification for the view that Urban
II entrusted Adhémar with the direction of the crusade in his place. In
1100 Paschal II appointed the archbishop of Lyons, Hugh of Die, to be
his legate for his crusade; it was laid down that he was to exercise his
office fully when the expedition was in Asia, that is, once it had left the
Christian countries subject to the authority of a normal hierarchy. And
Urban II, when the contingents of the counts of Blois and Normandy
passed through Rome (where he himself held the Lateran, while
Clement III was recognised on the other side of the Tiber), gave his
legation to the chaplains of the two princes, Arnulf of Choques and
Alexander, which would seem to suggest that the power of these legates
was of a spiritual order; their task was to sustain the participants in their
initial fervour. Urban II probably intended to make the count of
Toulouse the military commander.

Was it because of the success of that first sermon that the pope decided
to go further, or had he already planned to extend his appeal beyond that
first audience? In any case, continuing his journey across southern and
western France, he renewed his appeal in Limoges on 25 December, in
Angers and Le Mans during February 1096, probably in Tours in March
and in Nîmes, where he held a council in July. As we have seen, he had
also written to the Flemings, the Bolognese and the Genoese, this last
letter being dated July 1096. Other letters have not survived; it is possible
that one of them persuaded the king of France and his brother Hugh,
count of Vermandois, to meet in Paris on 11 February, when they
discussed participating in the crusade.

Nevertheless, the pope was anxious to confine the crusade within
certain limits; he wrote to the counts of Roussillon, Besalu, Cerdagne
and Ampurias to dissuade them from joining the expedition, granting
them the benefit of the indulgence on the grounds that their role was to
defend Christendom against the Almoravids. It is likely that the pope did

not wish kings to set out, just as, in 1074, Gregory VII had believed it was the duty of the emperor to keep his people at peace; the first duty of kings was to protect their kingdoms.

The pope's message was spread by preachers. It was a monk, we are told, perhaps the abbot of Saint-Bénigne of Dijon, Jarenton, who made the duke of Normandy, Robert Curthose, decide to depart. The popular preachers, the men Jacques Heers has called 'God's fools', who already attracted large audiences to whom they preached the reform of morals, were associated in the publicising of the pope's message; Robert of Arbrissel is said to have been given a mandate to this effect. The most famous of these preachers was Peter the Hermit, whose surname evokes the eremetical movement of the late eleventh century, of which he was presumably a part. This monk (the Byzantines called him Peter of the Cowl), originally from near Amiens, has become the hero of a legend which portrays him as the instigator of the crusade, having received while on a pilgrimage the complaints of the patriarch of Jerusalem, confirmed by a vision. We know that he preached with great success in northern France and probably in the neighbouring regions. German preachers, Folkmar and Gottschalk, are also mentioned; they were to lead bands of crusaders of all social conditions.

A recent study by J. Flori has once again emphasised the original features of the crusade as it was preached by these men, who went beyond the lines mapped out by Urban II in his speech at Clermont, in particular by introducing into their sermons an anti-semitic note; this was to result in the exactions of which the Jews of the Rhineland and the Danube valley were the principal victims. We know too little about the conditions in which the troops who followed these preachers were recruited to be sure of this. It is only likely that their sermons added to the proclamation of the indulgence and the effusion of graces promised to participants in the expedition the exhortations borrowed from their usual themes aimed at moral reform. A century and a half later, at the time of the Pastoureaux, a note of social protest was to be incorporated into a spontaneous crusading movement. Was this the case in 1096?

It is by no means certain. The crusade that left before the date fixed by the pope was not only a People's Crusade, though this is the name usually given to it. Jonathan Riley-Smith has given us a very detailed analysis of those who set out at this time. Those from northern France included knights and lords of a certain rank, such as the viscount of Melun, William the Carpenter, and many others. The name of Walter Sans-Avoir has given the impression that its owner was a poor knight; in fact, this was the hereditary surname of the lords of Boissy-sans-Avoir, near Mantes. German barons, such as Walter of Teck and the count palatine of Swabia, Hugh of Tübingen, also set out with Peter the Hermit. Other bands included numerous counts from Swabia and the Rhineland. One was led by a layman, the count of Leiningen. One may even wonder whether the proportion of non-combatants or simple people on foot among these first troops was very much higher than in later years.

The revivalist character seems to have been more marked in these bands than in those that followed, and one is reminded of the crowds of penitents that accompanied Robert of Arbrissel on his preaching tours. These sermons urged Christians to a conversion, that is, to a reform of their life that encouraged them to leave their homes. Here, they were given a goal, Jerusalem, and also a prospect, that of the total remission of sins. This joined that of the Second Coming, which, for many, would come to pass at the end of the journey. These men and women are described, carrying their belongings and accompanied by children who asked, every time they saw a town, if it was Jerusalem. They would turn out to be incapable of fighting.

But Urban II had been clear that his appeal was aimed essentially at warriors and had tried to prevent women from setting out. He was only partially heeded, as many crusaders took women along. However, the armies that set out on the day fixed, 15 August 1096, were more highly organised. The date of their departure even took account of the harvest, which guaranteed better possibilities of finding food than were experienced by the first bands. They had left in spring, the earliest contingents reaching the Hungarian border in the month of May; the question of supplies quickly became crucial.

For those who composed what we call the armies of the crusade those of the barons of France, Normandy, the Loire valley, Languedoc and southern Italy, the preparation of the campaign seems to have been more thoughtful. The first concern of the participants was to assure the financing of their expedition. Large numbers of charters show us the future crusaders making donations to churches, which promised them their prayers, adding gifts of cash or horses that were invaluable for the journey ahead. Some great lords amassed large sums of money. Two years later, Raymond of Saint-Gilles was still able to take penniless companions into his pay. Robert of Normandy pawned his duchy to his brother William Rufus for a period of five years in return for a sum of 10,000 marks, which the king of England raised by levying an aid on his kingdom. The bishop of Liège agreed to buy his castle of Bouillon from Godfrey of Bouillon, which meant he had to strip the reliquaries of his cathedral of their jewels. Lords sold and, above all, pawned lands, villages and rights to churches, which struggled to find the necessary sums at the expense of their gold and silver treasures. Before setting out, the crusaders had to make great sacrifices. One can only marvel that the economy of the late eleventh century was able to respond to this sudden increase in the demand for money.

Arrangements of every type had to be made. Within a family, no one could dispose of his property without the agreement of his relatives; their consent had to be obtained. The pope promised those who left to protect their family and their possessions against the greed of others. It was still necessary to have confidence in them. The count of Le Mans, Helias, changed his mind about going when he learned that Normandy would be in the hands of William Rufus, whom he had reason to distrust. William of Poitiers tried to take advantage of the absence of Raymond of Saint-Gilles to assert his rights to the county of Toulouse. There was a lot of negotiating in the months before the expedition left.

Historians have claimed that some of the leaders of the crusade promised, before they left, not to return to their lands, hence to devote themselves to the service of the Lord in the East. Godfrey of Bouillon is supposed to have been one of these, but it has been shown that the duke of Lower Lorraine had stipulated, when he sold Bouillon, that he could repurchase the castle on his return. At the time of leaving, no one could yet tell what form such service might take. I am tempted to think that, if such promises were made, it was during the course of the crusade, when the prospect of a Latin establishment overseas had begun to take shape.

Only two deeds allude to the possibility of not returning, that of Achard of Montmerle, a Burgundian knight, and that of a German knight, Wolfker of Kuffern. But clauses envisaging the possibility of remaining in the East are found even before the crusades in the deeds of pilgrims. We cannot know, therefore, whether the prospect of settling in conquered territory was actually present in the minds of the crusaders. It has been claimed in the case of Bohemond of Taranto, on the grounds that the Normans of southern Italy were already familiar with the idea of settlement in Byzantine territory, and that the prince tried to procure a position in the Byzantine army. This implies that Bohemond, when he took the cross, was less interested in the Holy Sepulchre than in the Byzantine perspectives of the pope's appeal. The example of Bohemond of Taranto is interesting because he was a baron who abandoned an enterprise already under way in order to devote himself wholly to his departure for the crusade. It was while he was besieging Amalfi, which was in revolt, along with his half-brother Roger Borsa, that he learned that the crusade had been preached; he withdrew from the siege, taking several members of his family and many knights with him; Roger had no alternative but to raise the siege. Their nephew Tancred was one of those eager to go; lacking money of his own, he put himself in Bohemond's pay.

Many of those who took the cross did the same. The contingents of the barons included their own vassals, who were not required by their feudal duty to follow the example of their lord, but who were in the habit of accompanying him on his expeditions, alongside less well-off lords who had put themselves in their service on condition they were maintained. The crusading army included both coherent troops, those of the leaders of the feudal principalities, and more or less independent groups, obliged by lack of money to join them. Ordinarily, the command of an army was based on the decision of a leader, duly advised by his vassals; on the crusade, there emerged a council of barons, how large we do not know, whose decisions were not always followed by lords of more independent spirit. Thus Raymond Pilet, a Languedocian lord, in principle responsible to Raymond of Saint-Gilles, frequently behaved in an autonomous fashion. And many crusaders, either because they came to the end of their resources or because they had lost their leader, attached themselves to another who took them into his pay.

Was the time that elapsed before the departure put to good use to compile rules of discipline? Hitherto, pilgrims had been required to behave like penitents, renouncing certain conveniences including the bearing of arms and entertainments, and engaging in devout practices. Those whom the pope sent to the East saw themselves as pilgrims, but they were at the same time potential combatants. Accordingly, the rule of life imposed on pilgrims had to be adapted to their condition; this rule was already well defined by the time of the Second Crusade, but we know little about how it was worked out.

Religious matters came within the competence of the legate Adhémar of Monteil who, as bishop, was a temporal lord, with his own vassals, and took part in the council of barons. He was not the only member of the clergy, since other bishops had joined the expedition; so did many clerics. Some abbots had forbidden their monks to set out for Jerusalem, arguing that the monastic life prefigured that of the heavenly Jerusalem; others went in person. Anna Comnena tells how a monk who had embarked on a ship that was crossing the Adriatic defended himself vigorously against the Byzantines who attacked it, which much shocked her. It has often been argued, on the basis of this incident, that the clergy bore arms like the laity, contrary to the rule accepted in the Latin Church. It is not impossible that some of them took up arms and fought. But their role lay elsewhere; the concern of the pope and of the legates was to provide within the army a normal religious life, with the celebration of offices and the administration of the sacraments. The ordeals experienced by the crusaders were the occasion for collective penances, for absolution given to the combatants before battle, for fasts, penances and processions. The legates even had to assess the authenticity of the visions that occurred during the course of the expedition. We should not forget that marvels accompanied the crusade from the time it was preached to the end of the journey.

We are least well informed about the preparations of a command structure for the crusade. As we have seen, when the leader of a territorial principality, a duke or a count (since crowned kings did not take part), had taken the cross, he was naturally expected to lead the army composed of his vassals, counts, viscounts or barons, themselves followed by their own vassals; added to those were lords bound to them by ties of lineage or neighbourhood. Together they formed one of the large units of the crusading army, which sometimes joined forces to make the journey together, like those of the counts of Flanders and Normandy.

But no overall command seems to have been planned. The great barons and the prelates met in a council and there took decisions of a military character; they appointed one of them as their leader in battle. It is hardly surprising that these decisions had a collective character; in the Middle Ages, leaders always availed themselves of the advice of a council. But the absence of a commander invested with a superior authority weighed heavily on the course taken by events in the First Crusade.

The absence of a single command was compensated for by the quality of the leaders who took part in this council. Most of them already possessed military experience, sometimes of distant expeditions, as was normal for men who ruled great territories and were associated in the power of sovereigns. Bohemond of Taranto had led an army into Macedonia; Godfrey of Bouillon had taken his troops into Italy; Raymond of Saint-Gilles had probably fought in Spain. John France has drawn attention to the experience acquired during the conquest of England. The crusade benefited from the competence of all these barons, whose ability as military leaders was demonstrated. It was they who were required to resolve logistical problems, and in due course to adapt the tactics of the Franks of the West to those of their adversaries. It would be interesting to know whether they made contact before they left, and the extent to which they tried to synchronise their journeys.

LATER DEPARTURES

The armies of 1096 did not consider the possibility of transport by sea; the technical difficulties of shipping horses probably made such an operation impossible at that date. Even Bohemond of Taranto, whose father had transported a large army from the other side of the Adriatic, used the sea route only to reach the Albanian coast, as did the French crusaders.

But Urban II had addressed his appeal also to others. Some knights from England joined Peter the Hermit and, in circumstances which are obscure, an English fleet arrived near Antioch at the end of the winter of 1096–7, which suggests that it may have left at more or less the date fixed by the pope. How many combatants it carried we do not know, but it seems unlikely that its sole purpose was to assure the supply of provisions for the crusaders. The apparently spontaneous nature of their departure is testimony to the depth of our ignorance.

In Genoa, the impact of the pontifical letter was reinforced by the arrival of two prelates, the bishops of Grenoble and Orange, who came to preach the crusade. In 1097 the Genoese nobles joined together in a *compagna* that fitted out a fleet of a dozen galleys, with transports that made it possible to carry to below Antioch some twenty-five knights and six hundred foot soldiers, who rendered great service, in particular in the construction of the siege machines used at Jerusalem. The Pisans seem only to have reacted on news of the fall of Antioch. Their archbishop, lord of the city, then assumed leadership of a huge expedition of 120 vessels. It reached Latakia in September 1099, after having clashed with a Byzantine squadron, and embarked on hostilities with the Byzantines.

It was only later that a fleet left Venice headed for the East. The Venetians took advantage of their voyage along the coasts of Asia Minor to remove some relics of St Nicholas from Myra and clashed with the Pisans who were returning from the Holy Land; it is possible that they had begun to prepare their departure in 1098, but it was not until 1100 that they reached Jaffa. Their expedition coincided more with the crusade of Paschal II than with that of Urban II.

French historians have given the name 'Arrière-Croisade' to the group of armies that set out on news of the crusaders' capture of Jerusalem. In fact, Urban II had been planning to send reinforcements since 1097, in particular by reminding of their duty those who had taken the crusading vow but not followed it up. In the spring of 1099 he had asked the archbishop of Milan to preach the crusade in Lombardy, where he had been enthusiastically received. Paschal II, who succeeded Urban II on 13 August 1099, less than a month after the capture of Jerusalem, faced the problem of whether to use the promised crusade to extend the crusaders' conquests to Egypt, as Urban II had suggested in his letter to the Milanese, or to strengthen their position in Jerusalem. Advised of the precariousness of their situation, he opted for the latter. He also renewed the measures taken by his predecessors, forbidding the Spanish to leave for the Levant, which would have denuded the frontier of Christendom, and reaffirming the grant of the indulgence to the new crusaders.

New regions were invited to provide their recruits. After the Lombards, it was the Burgundians of the duchy and of the county, and of the county of Nevers, who took the cross, with their duke and their counts, at the request of the archbishop of Lyons, Hugh of Die, who was to accompany them in his capacity as papal legate, and of the archbishop of Besançon, who also set out. The Bavarians with their Guelf duke and the archbishop of Salzburg, the Aquitainians with duke William and viscount Arpin of Bourges, provided the principal contingents. But they were joined by many latecomers who had not fulfilled their vow of 1095–6, such as the viscount of Béziers; they had been reminded that defaulting on a vow entailed excommunication.

Some of those who had taken part in the first expedition also went on the second. Among them were the counts of Blois and of Vermandois, who had left the army below Antioch; the former had been fiercely criticised, not least by his wife, Adela of England. Some, who had deserted at the time of the ordeals experienced during the siege of Antioch, had brought shame on their family. They included Guy Trousseau of Montlhéry; his brother and his uncle both took the cross so as to redeem their reputation. There were some, lastly, who had stayed with the crusade right to the end and set off again with this second wave. Their acts of donation, sale or commitment are identical to those of the first crusaders. Particularly well known is the grant made by Arpin of Bourges to the king of France, which became permanent when the viscount became a monk on his return from the expedition; this inaugurated the Capetian penetration of Berry.

The motives of the crusaders of 1101 seem little different from those of their predecessors, on the evidence of the preambles to their charters. At most, one might think that the desire to equal the exploits of the heroes of 1096–9 played a major role; for some, as we have seen, it was the desire to efface a stain caused by an act of cowardice during the first expedition. But most of all we should note the exaltation that was aroused by the conquest of Antioch and, even more, of Jerusalem. Divine favour seemed to have been demonstrated in a manner so striking that the fervour of the new crusaders could only be the greater.

The crusade of 1110 did not enjoy the same success as its predecessor. It was still part of the same movement; but it faced a new situation, and its leaders were less successful than their predecessors in leading it to victory.

3

THE FIRST CRUSADE
CONFRONTS THE EAST

Leaving in three successive waves, with a trickle of departures in between, the First Crusade initiated routes and first confronted problems which, in one way or another, influenced the course of expeditions for two centuries to come. What the participants encountered and experienced seems to have borne little resemblance to what they had imagined before they set off; nor is it likely that Pope Urban II had foreseen all the problems the crusaders would have to face.

Cooperation with Byzantium seems to have been intended, but the way it evolved has led an American historian, August C. Krey, to ask whether the crusade was a success or a failure. The birth of the Latin states in the East, a consequence of the crusade, had certainly not figured in the plans of the pope or the fathers of the Council of Clermont. The experiences of the pilgrims, merchants and mercenaries of the eleventh century had not made it possible to predict the form that the encounter between East and West, sometimes conflictual, sometimes friendly, would take. The rapidity with which so many westerners adapted to a world so different from their own is remarkable.

THE ROAD TO CONSTANTINOPLE

The crusaders who set out in 1096, though taking different routes, all terminated their journey across Europe in the same place, Constantinople. The Byzantine emperor had to attempt to dissuade them from passing through the town itself by offering them other ways of crossing the Bosphorus. But Constantinople was too established a staging point for the westerners not to have seen it as the goal to be reached before crossing into Asia. They seem not to have agreed in advance to meet there; the Byzantines were faced with the problem of preventing them from massing below the walls of the town.

For the crusaders arrived in large numbers. It is impossible to estimate the size of each band, and the figures given by contemporary historians are unusable, except for those concerning the final stages of the expedition. The number of combatants of every rank, both knights and footsoldiers, has been put at over 30,000 and even as high as 70,000 at the point of crossing into Asia. The non-combatants were probably less numerous, perhaps around 30,000. But every estimate remains debatable, allowing for logistical imperatives that are difficult for us to appreciate. In any case, the numbers must have fallen later, as a result of the losses suffered and also of desertions.

The large proportion of non-combatants is explained by the fact that many westerners joined the crusade regarding it as a pilgrimage. This had its effect on the conduct of operations and on their logistical require-ments. The problem of food supplies, in particular, was a major concern from the very beginning. It would be interesting to know whether, before leaving, the leaders of the various contingents had made contact with the sovereigns of the countries through which they were to travel, to prepare for the passage of their troops, to negotiate the conditions of the opening of markets, to fix the rate of exchange and to reduce the possibilities of friction with the local populations. Here, sadly, the sources are silent.

The itinerary was determined by the network of routes used pre-viously by pilgrims and merchants. Those from Lotharingia, Flanders and Picardy usually followed the banks of the Rhine, then the valley of the Neckar, joined the Danube near Ratisbon and descended the river as far as the frontier of the kingdom of Hungary, entered Byzantine territory between Belgrade and Nish, and crossed Bulgaria, also under Byzantine rule. Those from central France took the traditional pilgrim route to Rome to reach the Adriatic and, on the other side, Durazzo, the starting point of the Roman via Egnatia, which they followed all the way to Constantinople. This last stage of the itinerary was also that followed by the Normans of southern Italy. The Provençals chose a less-frequented route, which, starting from Lombardy and Friuli, took them across Croatia until they could join the via Egnatia. The regions through which they travelled had to provide for the needs of these masses of people and sometimes to endure their excesses.

While it would be unjust to assume that the crusaders were necessarily all great sinners needing to expiate grave faults, as has sometimes been claimed, it is the case that many of them, professional soldiers or peasants

required on occasion to bear arms in military operations, were susceptible to the temptation to violence. The morals of the age were crude.
The religious education of many crusaders no doubt remained rudimentary and their leaders had to impose a respect for discipline, which
necessitated recourse to harsh measures; looters were sometimes hanged.
The clergy present on the crusades might also, by their exhortations,
exercise a restraining influence, or urge repentance. But not all of them
were supervised with such rigour.

The inadequacy of supervision and the absence of preparations with
regard to food supplies probably explain many of the incidents that
occurred during the course of the crusaders' march through Christian
Europe. But other factors played a part, especially during the clashes with
the Jews. These first occurred, apparently sporadically, at the time of the
departure of those who joined Peter the Hermit's crusade in northern
France, during the month of December 1095, when serious incidents are
recorded in Rouen and Champagne. We know little about what
happened, but they probably explain the dispatch of a letter by the Jews
of France to their co-religionists in Germany, warning them that they
would have to submit to the financial demands of the crusaders and
facilitate their progress.

The journey of the first bands of crusaders through the Rhineland was
accompanied by abuse of and exactions on the Jewish communities.
They were probably asked to make financial contributions to the
followers both of Peter the Hermit and of Godfrey of Bouillon. We
should remember that such demands were regarded as bound up with
the special status of the Jews, who were allowed by lords to practice
loans at interest on their lands, they themselves on occasion taxing and
even extorting money from them in order to meet their own financial
needs.

The Jewish communities suffered much worse from the passage of
other troops, in particular those led by the priest Folkmar and, most of
all, Count Emich of Leiningen, who had made himself leader of a band
composed of German and French lords which also included a popular
element. On 3 May 1096 they launched an attack on the Jews of Speyer,
a dozen of whom were killed, the bishop managing to protect the rest.
Emich then arrived at Worms, where there was a massacre on a larger
scale; the count of Leiningen's crusaders murdered and pillaged and here,
too, the bishop offered the shelter of his castle to the Jews. But after the
crusaders had left the local people attacked the castle and killed a large
number of Jews, many of whom cut their children's throats or killed
themselves to escape a forced conversion. Similar scenes occurred in
Mainz between 25 and 29 May, but on a larger scale, after which some

groups left Count Emich, who continued his journey towards the Danube, to attack the Jewish communities of Cologne, Metz, Trier and the lower Rhine valley. Forced conversions followed from Ratisbon to Prague, though without the same scenes of carnage; they were the work of the followers either of Peter the Hermit or of Folkmar.

The explosion of violence directed against the Jews which accompanied the crusade had not been part of the project inaugurated by Urban II. Acts of violence were apparently committed against the Jews in Provence, at Monieux, but they seem to have been isolated, whereas in the north the violence was on an unwonted scale. The motives for these outbursts may, of course, be connected to the envy aroused by the wealth of the Jews, and the resentment provoked by their practice of usury. The widespread recourse to credit which began during the course of the eleventh century, and the seemingly brazen prosperity of Jewish moneylenders, no doubt encouraged such explosions, which were not confined to the Christian West; the first great wave of hatred of which the Jews were victims in the eleventh century took place around 1066 in Muslim Spain, at Grenada. An indication of the status enjoyed by these communities is provided by the revival of Jewish proselytism, which resulted in conversions even in noble circles.

But there may have been other factors more directly linked to the crusade. The Church forbade attacks on Jews, and Alexander II had issued reminders of this at the time of the expeditions to Spain. But the Christians who left for the East might believe that the Jews, in the same way as the Muslims, were enemies of Christ. The followers of Emich of Leiningen were characteristically keener to convert Jews to Christianity than to massacre them. Emich himself is presented by the Jewish chronicles as having been blessed by visions and the mark of the stigmata in his flesh, as a sign of his mission. This, according to Paul Alphandéry, is in line with the eschatological perspectives which associated the crusade and the imminent Second Coming of Christ. For Emich and his followers, in accord with the conviction that the conversion of the Jewish people must precede this return, it was necessary to force baptism on the Jews and to punish the obstinacy of those who refused.

This deviation from the idea of crusade, which remained relatively isolated though it reappeared at the time of the Second Crusade, aroused opposition among the clergy and especially the bishops and archbishops of the Rhineland. Not only did they hold to the Church doctrine forbidding the forced conversion of Jews but, as temporal lords, it was their duty to give them protection. This the prelates did, more successfully in Speyer and Cologne than in Mainz and Worms. The emperor, too, disowned the violence of 1096, and in 1097 authorised Jews

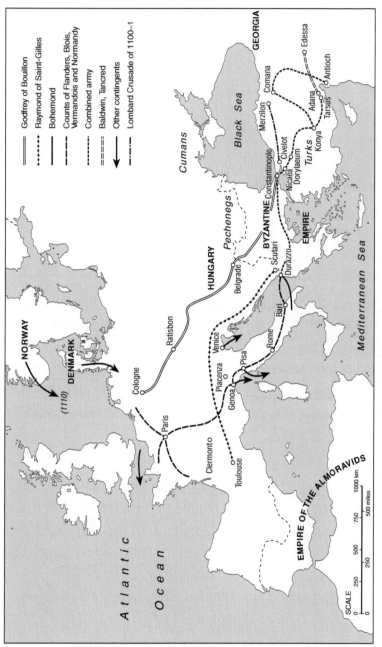

Map 1 The routes of the First Crusade

converted by force to return to their faith, in disregard of the indelible nature of baptism. Henry IV, as soon as he learned of these events, even wrote to Godfrey of Bouillon forbidding him to harm the Jews.

The experiences of the first bands of crusaders after they had left Germany were mixed. The first groups, those of Walter Sans-Avoir, crossed Hungary and the Byzantine provinces to reach Constantinople without notable incident. The followers of Peter the Hermit, more numerous and less disciplined, seem to have been responsible for some depredations in Hungary; such behaviour was probably inevitable, given that it was the beginning of summer, before the harvest, when the resources of the countryside were at their lowest level, in spite of King Coloman's efforts to ensure that they were fed. Before the last Hungarian town, Semlin (now Zemun), a riot erupted that degenerated into an attack on the town, a large number of whose inhabitants were massacred. Duke Nicetas, who guarded the Byzantine frontier, decided to evacuate Belgrade and withdrew to Nish. When the depredations continued, his troops attacked the crusaders and inflicted losses on them, at which point Peter the Hermit promised to control his troops better by forbidding prolonged stays before a town. He then reached Constantinople where he found the first arrivals. The emperor tried to dissuade him from crossing the sea before the arrival of the regular troops, but Peter's companions resumed their looting, and the Byzantines hastily transported them to the Asian shore early in August 1096.

The bands of Folkmar and Gottschalk, arriving in Hungarian territory, engaged in acts of pillage which provoked a furious reaction on the part of the king of Hungary; the former were massacred near Nitra; the latter, surrounded at Pannonhalma, were driven back into Germany. The followers of Emich of Leiningen were forbidden to enter Hungary by King Coloman, who was aware of their violent behaviour. Emich embarked on a siege of the frontier town of Wiesselburg (Moson, on the Leitha); the Hungarian army fell on him, and the crusaders who escaped the rout dispersed; some joined the armies that departed at a later date (around 20 August 1096); Emich himself did not set out again.

It was at just this time that, in accord with the plan devised at Clermont, the armies of the barons departed. Godfrey of Bouillon, duke of Lower Lorraine, accompanied by his brothers Eustace and Baldwin of Boulogne, the counts of Hainault and Toul and many lords from Brabant, Lorraine and Luxembourg, took the route followed by Peter the Hermit, which was likely to make their reception less friendly. But discipline was better observed, and this great lord was able to make terms with the sovereigns of the countries through which they travelled. He kept to the rules laid down by the emperor and refrained from molesting the Jews, though this did not prevent him from accepting the large sums of money offered more or less spontaneously by the communities of Cologne and Mainz. To secure his passage across Hungary, Godfrey had talks with King Coloman, to whom he delivered his brother Baldwin as hostage. After crossing the Danube at Belgrade, he made an agreement with the Byzantine authorities which guaranteed him provisions. The only incident occurred at Selymbria. Around the middle of December, his troops were below Constantinople, where things went less easily.

The brother of the king of France, Hugh of Vermandois, had preceded him. From Rome, he had crossed the Adriatic in October, but the crossing had been difficult and he had suffered serious losses in a shipwreck. The Byzantine governor who rescued him conducted him to the capital, where he was treated honourably (though the Byzantines mocked what they regarded as an infatuation on the part of a 'barbarian' prince), but he was kept under virtual house-arrest.

Bohemond of Taranto and his troops had crossed the Adriatic soon after. Though his army was well disciplined, it had nevertheless clashed with the Byzantines, taking a fortress by storm because its garrison consisted of heretics – probably Paulicians – and finding it necessary to teach the Turkish auxiliaries of the imperial army a lesson. Bohemond had been careful to avoid further clashes and his men reached Constantinople in their turn around 10 April 1097, having crossed Epirus, Macedonia and Thrace in four months. The troops of the duke of Lower Lorraine were already in Asia.

Raymond of Saint-Gilles, at the head of a large army that included the counts of Orange, Béarn and Forez as well as many great men from Limousin, Languedoc and Provence, had crossed Lombardy and entered the mountains of Croatia. The march through the thinly populated forests had been hard; the roads were poorly cleared and the inhabitants ill-disposed and prone to attack stragglers, in spite of the warm welcome provided by King Constantine Bodin. Once arrived in Byzantine territory, the crusaders had also been well received by the governor of Durazzo, who was the future emperor John Comnenus. But the Pecheneg auxiliaries of the Byzantine army, made responsible for ensuring that men did not stray from the road, showed excessive zeal and wounded the legate Adhémar of Monteil, who had to remain at Thessalonika to recover. In his absence, the Provençals, infuriated by the hostility of the inhabitants, sacked Roussa and Rodosto; the Byzantines inflicted a serious defeat on them near the latter, Raymond having left for Constantinople at the request of the emperor. The anger of the count of Toulouse could be appeased, but his army was the one that had experienced the most difficult journey.

The troops led by Robert of Normandy and Stephen of Blois, in contrast, who had passed by way of Rome and Brindisi, also followed the via Egnatia and reached Constantinople in mid-May, when the earlier contingents were already arriving in Nicaea. As we have seen, these various bands, to which should be added that of Count Robert of Flanders, had all crossed south-east Europe without serious difficulty. Only Croatia lacked proper roads. The agreements made by the different leaders with the local sovereigns, perhaps also contacts made earlier with the Byzantine emperor, had made it possible for the troops to be fed. We know little of how this was achieved, but the example of later expeditions suggests that the crusaders would have had access to markets located outside the towns, where merchants supplied them with basic foodstuffs for which they paid a price that had probably been fixed as part of the agreements in question; the merchants would have been given advance notice of the quantities to be provided. It was where the inhabitants refused to take part in the provision of supplies that riots and looting broke out, though we must also remember the activities of the foragers who engaged in irregular requisitioning. The question of horses seems already to have begun to loom large; the emperor Alexius is said to have provided some of the crusaders with fresh mounts.

It is worth noting that tens of thousands of men, many of them on horseback, were able to follow each other along the same roads, at fairly close intervals, without exhausting the resources of the countries through which they passed. This suggests a certain degree of organisation, on the part both of the leaders of these armies and of the sovereigns of the countries in question.

THE BYZANTINE PROBLEM IN 1096–7

The staggered arrival of the various contingents at Constantinople allowed the emperor Alexius I to resolve in his own way the difficult problems posed by the appearance of the crusaders in the Byzantine empire. The influx of these tens of thousands of combatants certainly exceeded by far what the emperor could have expected. It is now difficult to believe, as we have seen, that the crusade had taken him by surprise; the Clermont appeal was in response to another appeal, that from Constantinople. The *basileus* might have expected the arrival of several hundred knights, who would be absorbed into the Byzantine army while retaining their leaders and their individuality, as had happened in the past with those from several countries: soldiers hired for a certain period, paid, and available for use on different battlefields or only in Asia Minor – many possibilities were open. Mercenaries from the

West were already numerous in the imperial army, where they rubbed shoulders with other ethnically defined groups. Byzantium was aware that they were quick to become unruly and were liable to rebel; the example of the Normans of the expeditionary force in Sicily who had founded an Italian state carved out of the empire went back less than a century; leaders of contingents, like Crespin or Roussel of Bailleul, had organised revolts, but the empire was usually able to bring them into line.

This time the groups were much larger and had the appearance of armies commanded by the territorial princes of the lands from which they had been recruited; these men would be difficult to disperse among the imperial armies. From the beginning, the Byzantines saw them as potentially dangerous. These hordes of men flooding into the empire created the impression of an actual invasion. Would the crusaders, when they discovered the wealth of the imperial city, its monuments and its religious treasures (Constantinople had accumulated the most prestigious relics), be tempted to seize whatever they could lay their hands on?

The idea of an attack on Constantinople seems to have been mooted within the imperial entourage. There was good reason to fear such aggression. Was it not Bohemond of Taranto himself who had landed in Epirus with his father and led his troops in the conquest of a territory which Robert Guiscard had destined for him on the eastern shore of the Adriatic? That was fifteen years ago, but the memory lived on, and Anna Comnena, in her *Alexiad*, had revived it.

There were a number of ways in which Alexius could control the crusading armies. First, there was constant surveillance, assured at sea by the Byzantine ships, which did not hesitate to intercept isolated boats, and on land by the knights of the imperial army, recruited in particular from the Turkish peoples who lived adjacent to the northern empire, Pechenegs and Cumans, who, as we have seen, had tried to prevent the Frankish warriors from straying from the route assigned to them. Or the emperor, seemingly committed to ensuring their food supplies, could suspend deliveries; this was how he tried to compel Godfrey of Bouillon to do homage, but Baldwin of Boulogne responded to these measures by looting the suburbs of Constantinople, and the emperor resumed the provision of supplies.

The problem with these policing measures was that they made the soldiers of the emperor appear to be enemies. When one of the ships of Bohemond's fleet was attacked by imperial sailors, the passengers resisted fiercely; it would have been difficult for them to do otherwise. The surveillance by the Pechenegs and the Cumans, which entailed the abduction of stragglers, began to look like simple harassment. And when a town refused to supply the expected provisions, it risked being sacked when the crusaders went on the attack. The precautions taken to limit the possible depredations of the crusaders had the effect of creating a hostile climate.

It is difficult to see how this could have been avoided. The indiscipline of the first bands was hardly likely to inspire confidence in the Byzantines. And the sheer size of the body of combatants that would result if all the crusader armies were to assemble below Constantinople obliged Alexius to accelerate the departure of the early arrivals in order to avoid such a concentration. Some of the leaders of the crusade would have liked to gather in Constantinople before embarking on the roads of Asia, but the emperor would not allow this.

Were some of the crusaders tempted to seize Constantinople? One source claims that Bohemond suggested this possibility to Godfrey, who refused because he did not wish to fight other Christians. Bohemond has been credited with many things, but his attitude at this point in the campaign hardly supports this interpretation.

The emperor's subjects might distrust the Franks, but he was aware that they had set out in order to respond to an appeal, probably loosely interpreted, which corresponded to one strand in his policy, namely to free Constantinople from the danger posed by the Turkish presence only a hundred kilometres from the town and to reoccupy Asia Minor. The crusaders were potential allies, but they were not the army of a sovereign with whom the emperor had negotiated. There had been no alliance between Urban II and Alexius Comnenus. Each army led by a great baron was responsible only to him, and the papal legate did not exercise a higher authority. Alexius Comnenus had to resolve a difficult problem, that of the relations to be established between the leaders of these armies and the imperial power, in such a way as to subordinate the former to him, with a view to joint action. To this end, he had the idea of using an institution familiar to the westerners, of which he seems to have had a good understanding, namely vassalage. By this means, a personal link would be established between the *basileus* and each of the barons, who would then be obliged to act in accordance with the interests of the emperor and to respect his rights.

It seems that Alexius was able to convince the first of the leaders of the crusade he received, Hugh of Vermandois, to agree to do homage. Though deeply imbued with the superiority conferred on him by his membership of the French royal house, the Capetian seems not to have objected to acknowledging himself to be the vassal of the Byzantine emperor.

This was not the case with the duke of Lower Lorraine. When asked to do homage to the emperor, Godfrey refused. Alexius tried to put pressure on him by restricting supplies to the market where his troops obtained their provisions; the troops reacted so robustly that the emperor resumed deliveries. He tried to blockade the Lorrainers in Pera; a series of skirmishes continued throughout the first months of 1097. Finally, a success won by the imperial troops made Godfrey decide to comply with the conditions required by the emperor. He himself and his principal companions knelt before Alexius and took the oath of fealty, promising to hand over the towns they conquered. Alexius declared that he was adopting Godfrey as a son and lavished presents on him; his army was in future treated as part of that of the emperor, receiving wages and provisions (early April 1097).

Bohemond had left his army in order to reach Constantinople more quickly. It seems unlikely that he tried to persuade Godfrey to attack the town, since he proved from the outset ready to accept the emperor's proposals and at once took the oath of fealty. But he would have liked to have gone further; according to Anna Comnena, he asked to be appointed *domestikos* of the East, that is commander of the Byzantine army, which might have made him the leader of the crusade. Whether he also revealed his desire to receive a fief from the emperor in the lands to be conquered, as another source asserts, remains unclear. It is not impossible that Bohemond was already considering making a career in the East, if necessary in the service of the Byzantines, with the prospect of carving out a principality for himself. His nephew Tancred, on the other hand, to avoid becoming a vassal of the emperor, chose not to pass through Constantinople.

Raymond of Saint-Gilles, ill disposed as a result of the humiliations suffered by his troops, refused to become Alexius' vassal on the grounds that he had not left his lands in order to serve the Lord only to become the vassal of an earthly prince. His juridical position was strong. Like Godfrey, he was already the vassal of a sovereign from whom he held his lands as a fief – the western emperor in Godfrey's case, the king of France in Raymond's – and feudal law at this period did not allow for someone to be the vassal of several lords. A compromise was eventually found. Raymond did not become Alexius' vassal, but he swore the oath of fealty by which he was bound not to attack either the body or the honour of his lord. It has been suggested that the count of Toulouse was hoping to further the plans of Urban II, who aimed to create a pontifical dominion in the East, but this thesis does not carry conviction. Raymond of Saint-Gilles seems essentially to have refused what might appear as a personal submission to the Byzantine emperor. Alexius punished this attitude by behaving less generously to him than to the other leaders.

Robert of Flanders, Robert Curthose and Stephen of Blois made no difficulties about doing the homage asked of them. The presents showered on them by the emperor dazzled Stephen, though himself a man of high rank and great wealth, who wrote to his wife expressing his admiration for Alexius and his generosity.

One associated question remained. By undertaking to respect the emperor and his rights, the crusaders were made to realise that they were not going to be conducting their operations in lands without a master. The territories occupied by the Turks were part of the Byzantine empire, and some of them had only recently been lost. Alexius made it clear that the empire intended to repossess them and he made these leaders swear an oath to deliver to him or to his representative any towns they occupied that had previously been Byzantine.

But which were these lands? The tenth-century emperors had revealed that their claims extended to provinces taken from the Roman Empire long ago by the caliphs of earlier ages: Mesopotamia, Palestine, Syria and Phoenicia. Later texts suggest that, in Alexius' eyes, everything from Egypt to the Balkan peninsula belonged to his empire. From this perspective, the question of Jerusalem itself was posed: did freeing the Holy Sepulchre from the control of the infidel mean restoring it to that of the Byzantine emperors? As we will see, imperial policy in this regard remains difficult to interpret.

Nevertheless, when the various contingents crossed the Bosphorus, between the beginning of April and the end of May 1097, the synthesis was achieved; the crusade, which remained an autonomous enterprise, was integrated into a Byzantine policy which aimed to use it for the recovery of the lost lands and the liberation of the Christians enslaved by the Turks.

No document survives that refers at this point to differences or discussions of a confessional nature between Greeks and Latins. If Urban II had seen the crusade as a means of solving the problems that had led to the schism of 1054, this is not revealed by our texts. The problems at issue were purely political, though they had repercussions for religious matters.

THE MARCH ON ANTIOCH

It was in August 1096 that the contingents led by Peter the Hermit, Walter Sans-Avoir and their followers were transported, through the good offices of the Byzantines, to the shores of Asia. They established themselves around the fortress of Cibotos (Civetot), then unoccupied, on the frontier of Seljuk territory. Dissension arose between the French on the one hand and the Germans and Italians on the other. The French launched a raid of pillage into Turkish territory and returned bringing booty; the Germans and Italians pushed as far as Xerigordon, near Nicaea, where they were soon besieged by the Turks, who massacred those who refused to deny their faith. Although Walter advised caution, the crusaders who had remained at Cibotos went to the rescue and were, in their turn, wiped out (21 October). Walter was killed. Peter the Hermit led those who had escaped back to Constantinople, where they awaited the arrival of the barons.

The barons' troops, who had landed in succession in Asia, had gathered near Nicomedia. Godfrey of Bouillon, joined by Peter the Hermit, went on to Nicaea, while Bohemond, with the Byzantines, organised the provisioning of the army and Alexius arranged the construction of siege machines. Arriving a little later, the Provençals intercepted the reinforcements being sent to the garrison by the sultan. A Byzantine fleet, launched on Lake Ascanius, completed the blockade of Nicaea. The Turks, to avoid the town being stormed, negotiated with the emperor and, on the morning of 19 June, the crusaders discovered the emperor's banners on the walls of the city. Some of them demonstrated their chagrin at finding themselves deprived of the booty they had expected, but Alexius, now master of the great fortress, and also of the sultan's wife and children, whom he quickly restored to Kilij Arslan, distributed such generous gifts among the crusaders that their disappointment was soon forgotten.

The crusading army was now complete. Alexius gathered his leaders at Pelecanum to decide on the next stage of the campaign. Tancred himself was present at this meeting and swore loyalty to the emperor; Raymond alone kept his distance. It was agreed that the crusade would continue on its way through Asia Minor. The emperor would provide it with logistical aid; he attached to it a body of light cavalry, the turcopoles, who would frequently in the future accompany the Frankish armies, and put it under the command of one of his best generals, Taticius. The latter, called 'Tatin with the cut-off nose' by the crusaders, alluding to a physical deformity, represented imperial authority. He probably played an important role in the decision to adopt an itinerary which, though difficult, allowed the crusaders to attack Antioch in the best conditions. Alexius was content to complete the occupation of territory; he was to follow the crusaders with his army and join them to take Jerusalem in their company.

It was early summer (late June 1097) when the crusaders embarked on the journey across Asia Minor. Almost at once they encountered a large army which the sultan Kilij Arslan, reinforced by the Danishmend emir of Cappadocia, was leading to the rescue of his capital. As they entered the plain of Dorylaeum (Eskisehir), the vanguard commanded by Bohemond was attacked by the Turks. Bohemond hastily pitched his camp and, with his knights, faced the enemy. First exposed to the fire of the archers, then charged by the Turkish cavalry, the Franks were driven back into their camp, where they stood firm. Alerted by messengers from Bohemond, Godfrey's knights arrived at a gallop; the other contingents, probably on the initiative of the legate Adhémar, attacked the Turkish flank and forced them to flee, abandoning a large quantity of booty. The Battle of Dorylaeum (1 July) freed the road leading into the heart of Anatolia and temporarily wiped out the Turkish forces; the Byzantines took advantage of this to occupy the whole western part of Asia Minor.

This first contact with the Turks had been a rude awakening, and the crusaders quickly realised that they had found worthy adversaries. Their own knights might be practically irresistible when they charged in serried ranks, but the Turkish horsemen, also in armour, constituted a cavalry equally capable of making charges; their mounted archers surpassed the Frankish archers, who fought on foot, thanks to their use of a bow that enabled them to fire rapidly, less powerfully perhaps than did the western bows, but ensuring a formidable harassment. The habitual Turkish tactic of a simulated flight that led the pursuers to break ranks, so rendering them vulnerable when their adversary turned on them, soon became familiar to the westerners, though they were still often surprised by it. A whole new type of warfare had to be learned. The crusaders were quick learners.

The victory at Dorylaeum had opened the road into the interior. Crossing the Phrygian steppe at the height of summer, the army encountered no other problems than those arising from the heat and desert-like character of the countryside, serious though these were. Deprived of water and grass, many horses perished; one of the chroniclers describes knights riding on oxen and loading their baggage on the backs of goats, sheep and dogs. When they reached Iconium (Konya), the crusaders were surprised to find that the town had been evacuated, but a few Christians were able to give them useful advice. A Turkish army was stationed in front of the defiles of the Taurus, at Eregli; it was easily dispersed (10 September).

The army then split up. The main force set out towards the north-east where it occupied Caesarea, then Comana, where there was an Armenian garrison. Taticius took control of the town and appointed as governor on behalf of the *basileus* a Provençal or Norman knight. They next occupied Coxon (Güksün), then Marash, which was in its turn handed over to the Byzantines. From there, the army set off for Antioch, which it reached on 21 October. In many places, the local Christians had risen against their Turkish garrisons.

Two small contingents had, on leaving Eregli, passed through the Cilician Gates to descend into the Cilician plain. Tancred marched on Tarsus, which was occupied by a Turkish garrison. The garrison took flight, and the inhabitants, Greeks and Armenians, hoisted the Norman leader's banner on the walls. But the much larger contingent of Baldwin of Boulogne took over the town, which Tancred had to relinquish to them. The arrival of Guynemer of Boulogne and his ships strengthened Baldwin's hold. Tancred then took Adana and Mamistra from the Armenians, but Baldwin again appeared and the two armies came to blows before reaching an agreement. Finally, Tancred's men remained in what was probably only a light occupation of the towns of Cilicia, while the two leaders rejoined the main army.

There is good reason for the siege of Antioch to have assumed epic proportions in the memory of the Franks. The whole crusading army was involved. The siege was not without its dramatic episodes, since at the very moment when the crusaders were seizing the town, an enormous Turkish army arrived to blockade them. Starting in October 1097, it was June 1098 before the siege ended. The besiegers suffered the worst, to the point where many of them lost heart. The consequence of these dramatic events was to bring cooperation between the Franks and the Byzantines to an end.

The departure of Baldwin of Boulogne, who, at the request of the Armenian leaders, went to occupy the fortresses near the Euphrates, was almost certainly not the result of prior consultation; though he deprived the Frankish army of one of its contingents, if not a very large one, he subsequently proved extremely useful to the besiegers. They occupied many places close to the large town, especially Artesia (Artah), before, on 20 October, seizing the tower that commanded entry to the bridge over the Orontes and, at the same time, a whole convoy of provisions destined for Antioch.

The town itself was defended by natural obstacles. Dominated by the citadel which crowned the escarpments of the Silpius, it was surrounded by an enceinte reinforced by four hundred towers. The Turkish emir who was its commander, Yaghi Siyan, had a large garrison and, to guard against possible treason, he expelled from the town those belonging to the various Christian confessions. The Frankish army, though still large, was unable to enforce a rigorous blockade; right up to the final months of the siege, the townspeople were able to pasture their animals below the walls and receive provisions which were supplied even by the Christian peasantry of the neighbouring countryside.

The crusaders first established themselves to the north of the city, where they built a fortress, christened Malregard, which controlled the Gate of St Paul, and constructed a pontoon bridge to ensure their contacts with the troops who were covering the Bridge Gate. They won themselves a breathing space by repulsing, with heavy losses, an incursion by the garrison of Harenc. The arrival of the ships of Guynemer, who had occupied Latakia, and of those of the Genoese assured them a maritime base accessible to boats bringing provisions from the Byzantine coasts, and in particular from Cyprus. But the road from the port of St Simeon to Antioch was unsafe, and the provisions arrived only in small quantities. By December, famine reigned in the camp, and the leaders of the army decided to send a large expedition into the valley of the Orontes to find food. Under the command of Bohemond and Robert of Flanders, some 20,000 men went up the river as far as the vicinity of Albara, sacking in particular Ma'arrat Misrin, and sending out foragers. Yaghi Siyan tried to take advantage of the weakening of the besieging army, but Raymond of Saint-Gilles repulsed the sortie attempted by the garrison (28 December).

The expedition into the Orontes valley coincided with the arrival of a large enemy army led by the king of Damascus, Duqaq, and the emir of Homs, with one of Yaghi Siyan's sons, which had gathered at Shaizar. The encounter turned to the advantage of the Franks, whose opponents took flight (31 December). Nevertheless, their leaders, reckoning it unwise to prolong their stay in the middle Orontes, returned to Antioch having only partly achieved their aims. The famine grew worse and led to the first defections. Peter the Hermit and William the Carpenter of Melun were surprised trying secretly to reach St Simeon. Bohemond publicly admonished them before the whole army. But others had left, some having even gone to Cyprus in search of provisions.

It was at this point that the leader of the Byzantine contingent, Taticius, who had previously taken an active part in operations, left. One version of his departure attributes it to the intrigues of Bohemond, who had persuaded Taticius that his life was in danger and who wanted to get rid of him so he could achieve his own ambitions for Antioch. Other sources suggest that, in the light of the difficult situation faced by the army, Taticius was given the task of organising supplies. He departed leaving his body of turcopoles at Bohemond's disposition and may even have entrusted him with custody of the places in Cilicia occupied by Tancred. This raises the question of the Norman prince's intentions; he made a pretence of wanting to abandon the siege given the losses suffered by his contingent and obtained from other leaders (Raymond excepted) the agreement that he would be given Antioch once the town was taken. It seems unlikely, however, that, at this date, it was accepted that Bohemond would enjoy permanent possession.

It remains the case that Bohemond played a major role within the army, though its command was assumed in turn by the various leaders of the contingents of which it was composed. It was Bohemond who, to discourage the spies who kept the Turks informed of events among the besiegers, had the idea of having the bodies of some Muslims roasted, letting it be known that they were going to be eaten. This was the starting point for a legend widespread throughout the Arab world concerning the cannibalism of the crusaders; it is referred to in the *chansons*, which attribute it to the *Tafurs*, a picturesque group of ruffians led by a 'king' who had been a Norman knight who had lost, along with his horse, his knightly status.

A new Muslim army gathered, which joined up with the king of Aleppo, Ridwan, hitherto ill disposed towards Yaghi Siyan, the emirs of Shaizar, Homs and Hamah and the Ortoqid Soqman, a commander in the Jazirah. Alerted by the eastern Christians, the Franks went to meet them, leaving their infantry before the besieged town. They were terribly reduced in numbers; there were now only seven hundred knights. But they, after an initial Turkish success, launched a decisive charge and put their enemies to flight. To complete their successes, they seized the fortress of Harenc. This victory of the Lake of Antioch (9 February 1098) ensured them a respite of two or three months before the threatened arrival of a new rescuing army. The crusaders put this time to good use by building two new forts, one to the south and one to the west of the town, and by going in search of reinforcements and materials to St Simeon. As it returned, the convoy was surprised by a sortie from the garrison, but, before it could regain the city, the setback was reversed and the sortie ended in disaster (6 March).

It was, in the end, Bohemond who was responsible for the success of the siege. Time was pressing, because the large army sent by the sultan was approaching. Happily for the crusaders, its leader, Kerbogha, lost three weeks trying to take Edessa, where Baldwin held him at bay. Bohemond, meanwhile, had made contact with a renegade Armenian, possibly called Firouz, who was keeper of the Tower of the Two Sisters. He thus had the means to gain entry to the town, but he was determined to get the other leaders to promise to deliver it to him on condition that he surrendered it to the emperor when he arrived; Raymond remained irrevocably hostile. This was on 29 May, just as Kerbogha raised the siege of Edessa.

On the night of 2–3 June, Firouz delivered the tower to Bohemond and his men, while the Frankish army allayed suspicion by ostentatiously taking the road to the east as if going to meet Kerbogha. The first men to get over the walls opened the gates to the crusader troops, who had by then returned, and Bohemond raised his banner above the highest of the towers close to the citadel. The citadel remained in Turkish hands, but Yaghi Siyan fled and, falling from his horse, was killed by peasants.

The length of the siege had tried the crusaders sorely, despite the arrival, by sea, of some reinforcements. Some, discouraged, had reached the coast or even embarked; others had temporarily left the army, including Robert of Normandy, who had withdrawn to Latakia, and Stephen of Blois, who was then in command, and who, on the eve of the fall of the town, went to St Simeon because he was sick, which was later interpreted as a pretext. To maintain discipline, it had been necessary to take harsh measures, in particular against the prostitutes and those who frequented them. Raymond of Saint-Gilles, anxious for the morale of the knights, who hesitated to risk their horses, which had become so precious, in encounters with the Turks, had taken the initiative of establishing a fund (a 'confraternity') to provide new mounts at common expense. Though victors, the crusaders were much weakened.

On 4 June, the sultan's army arrived below Antioch and, in its turn, seized the Tower of the Iron Bridge; the crusaders had to destroy the fortresses they had built. The *atabeg* of Mosul, Kerbogha, was accompanied by the king of Damascus, the emir of Homs and Soqman, who had already confronted the crusaders, and many chiefs from Iraq. His army was much stronger than that of the Franks, and it could enforce a rigorous blockade of the town. Kerbogha had the advantage of the Turkish presence in the citadel, which he made Yaghi Siyan's son hand over to him and where he installed as governor Ahmad ibn Marwan. He had intended to take advantage of this situation to penetrate Antioch by the citadel, but the Frankish leaders hastily constructed a system of ditches and barricades to isolate the town. There remained, nevertheless, the danger of sorties from his garrison; to guard against it, Bohemond set fire to one of the town's quarters on 12 June in order to force the Franks to leave their lodgings.

The crusaders' situation seemed desperate. According to the *Chanson d'Antioche*, Stephen of Blois became convinced that all was lost when, from the neighbouring heights, to which he had gone in secret, he saw the size of the Turkish camp. Famine was again severe, all the more so since the Franks had found insufficient stocks of grain within the town. The events of 12 June attest to the demoralisation threatening these exhausted men: the legate and Bohemond had to have the gates shut, as the Turks arrived, to prevent a mass flight.

It was at this point that there occurred the episode of the Holy Lance: a Provençal priest, Peter Bartholomew, reported a vision of St Andrew and, overcoming the reservations of the legate and Raymond of Saint-Gilles, carried out an excavation under the pavement of the church of St Peter and found the Lance that had pierced the side of Christ on the cross. This discovery followed other manifestations which helped to create a climate of religious exaltation and restored the crusaders' confidence. They sent an embassy consisting of Peter the Hermit and a knight, Herluin, to Kerbogha to invite him to withdraw. The envoys were greeted with sarcasm; it is possible that the Frankish leaders had been anxious to have all the legal conventions on their side by delivering a formal challenge to their enemy.

Kerbogha, who had meanwhile alienated some of his allies by making his authority felt, demonstrated complete confidence. When, on the morning of 28 June, the crusaders began to leave the town in small batches, he refused to follow the advice of those who urged him to destroy the detachments as they emerged. Bohemond, who had replaced the sick Raymond of Saint-Gilles as supreme commander, leaving the count of Toulouse to contain the garrison in the citadel, divided the army into six divisions which, after crossing the bridge over the Orontes, drove the Turks back into their camp. Kerbogha proposed to attack their flank. Bohemond opposed him with a seventh division entrusted to the count of Toul, which dispersed its adversaries. Finally, the Turks turned tail and the Franks, who had been forbidden to stop to loot their tents, pursued them as far as Harenc. On their return, they proceeded to share out an enormous quantity of plunder, which made it possible for many knights to replace their horses.

The citadel quickly capitulated, on the condition that the governor Ahmad ibn Marwan could withdraw with his family. But, when he was being handed Raymond's banner for it to be raised over the fortress, a Norman warned him that it was not that of Bohemond, and it was Bohemond's that he raised. It has been claimed that he received baptism, while many of his men were killed by peasants as they returned to Aleppo.

Antioch was taken and the Turkish armies had suffered serious defeats. The crusaders now had to decide what to do next.

The six months that elapsed between the fall of Antioch and the departure of Raymond of Saint-Gilles for Jerusalem were decisive for the future of the crusade. With the occupation of Antioch, the status of the Frankish presence in the East had to be defined and, at the same time, the relationship between the Franks and the Byzantine empire, and that between the Franks and the indigenous Christians.

With the capture of Nicaea and the battle of Dorylaeum, the Byzantine emperor, his army then close to the ancient capital of the Seljuk sultan, was in a position to restore imperial sovereignty over the neighbouring territories. This he did, and his troops reoccupied the whole of Bithynia. Under the command of his brother-in-law, John Ducas, a fleet and an army chased the Turks out of Ephesus, the Maeander valley, Caria, Lycia and Adalia.

The crusaders had made possible the restoration of the empire in its provinces adjacent to the Aegean Sea and in part of those bordering the eastern Mediterranean. An English fleet under the command of Edgar Atheling, which had put itself in the service of the empire, recovered possession of Latakia and Latin leaders held in the emperor's name the places reconquered by the crusaders on the confines of the Taurus, including Kayseri (Caesarea in Cappadocia). The road through Anatolia, however, remained at the mercy of bands of Turks thrown into disarray by the passage of the Frankish army but soon reappearing in the steppe. The Danish crusaders, on their way to join the siege, were wiped out not far from Philomelium (Aksehir).

As laid down in the agreement made at Pelecanum, Alexius set out to join the crusader army, then below Antioch, in May 1098. He had reached Philomelium, where he was probably joined by Taticius, when he received Stephen of Blois, who had decided not to return to Antioch on learning of the presence of Kerbogha's army, and, it seems, some others who had escaped from the town before it was completely surrounded. There followed a council of war, which must have been tense. Some leaders of the imperial army, including Bohemond's half-brother, Guy, insisted that the Byzantine troops proceed by forced marches to the rescue of the Christians besieged in Antioch. Others, chief among them Stephen, argued that such a measure would be pointless, given that the crusaders, in their view, must already have perished at the hands of the Turks. Alexius opted for caution and, rather than risk his army in the wastes of the Anatolian desert, ordered a retreat, adding for good measure instructions to evacuate the population of this part of Phrygia to create a void before the Turks.

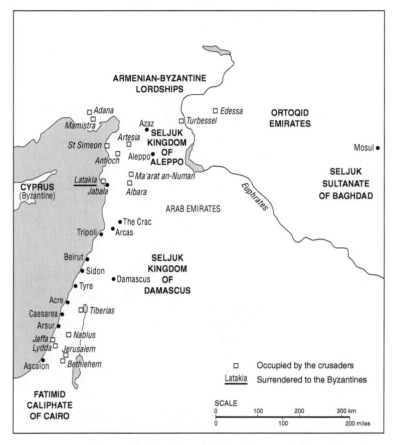

ARMENIAN-BYZANTINE
LORDSHIPS

☐ Adana
☐ Mamistra
☐ Edessa
☐ Turbessel
ORTOQID
EMIRATES

Azaz
☐ Artesia
SELJUK
KINGDOM
OF
ALEPPO

St Simeon ☐
☐ Aleppo
Antioch

Mosul ●

SELJUK
SULTANATE
OF BAGHDAD

☐ Ma'arat an-Numan

Latakia ☐
Jabala
☐ Albara

CYPRUS
(Byzantine)

Euphrates

ARAB EMIRATES

● The Crac
Tripoli ● ● Arcas

Beirut ●
● Sidon
● Damascus
● Tyre

SELJUK
KINGDOM
OF
DAMASCUS

Acre ●
Caesarea ●
Arsur ●
☐ Tiberias

Jaffa ☐
Lydda ☐
☐ Nablus
Jerusalem
☐ Bethlehem

Ascalon ☐

FATIMID
CALIPHATE
OF CAIRO

☐   Occupied by the crusaders

<u>Latakia</u>   Surrendered to the Byzantines

SCALE
0   100   200   300 km
0   100   200 miles

Map 2   The First Crusade in Syria (1097–1100)

Did this retreat come at the right moment to encourage the greed of
Bohemond and of other crusader princes with ambitions to settle on land
that had previously been Byzantine? It is by no means clear that their
ideas had as yet crystallised; in any case, the barons had been quite
specific that, if the emperor came to join them, they would surrender
Antioch to him in accordance with their sworn oaths. This position was
confirmed during a council that met in Antioch at the beginning of July,
and the barons instructed Hugh of Vermandois and Baldwin of Hainault
to convey to the emperor their invitation to come and take possession of
the town and accompany them on the next stage of their journey. One
of the two envoys, Baldwin, was killed on the way, perhaps by

turcopoles of the imperial army, but Hugh delivered his message to Alexius. The emperor did not reply until the spring of 1099, when he asked the crusaders to wait for him until July of that year. By then, however, they were already on their way and, in July, Jerusalem was taken.

Why did Alexius not accept this invitation? It may be that financial difficulties prevented him from embarking on a new campaign so soon after the previous one. His prudence may have warned him against the risk of an expedition whose outcome was, in the last analysis, uncertain. Perhaps also, despite his promises, he had no wish to march on Jerusalem, because he had embarked on negotiations with the Fatimids of Egypt. The vizier al-Afdal was trying to restore their rule over Palestine, that natural glacis of Egypt, and he maintained friendly relations with the empire.

We need to look more closely at the negotiations that took place between the Egyptians and the Franks while Antioch was under siege, between January and March 1098. If we are to believe the letter sent by Raymond of Saint-Gilles to al-Afdal by means of a Turkish convert called Bohemond, after the battle of Ascalon, the caliph's envoys had promised that their master would deliver 'free Jerusalem' to the crusaders, which was interpreted as a promise to hand over the town if the Fatimids reconquered Palestine from their Seljuk enemies, in return for an alliance against them. In fact, during the summer of 1098 the Egyptians conducted a campaign in the course of which they recovered Jerusalem from the Turks. Al-Afdal accused the Christians of perjury because they had attacked the town, and it may be that he had intended only to promise them free access to the Holy Places. The discovery of letters from Alexius in the Fatimid camp after the battle of Ascalon was interpreted as proof of collusion between Byzantium and Egypt, the emperor urging the vizier not to keep the promises he had made to the crusaders. It is possible that Alexius was scaling down his planned cooperation with the crusaders to the recovery of Byzantine Syria, while at the same time agreeing with the Fatimids about the division of the rest of that country.

For the crusaders, the emperor's retreat looked like treachery. Whereas he had promised to assist them and to join them to win Jerusalem in their company, he was now abandoning them in their hour of greatest need. It is only necessary to read the accounts of the crusade or the *chanson* to appreciate the intensity of the emotion and indignation felt by the Franks. This was compounded by the fact that it was not only a matter of the implementation of a treaty of alliance; Alexius had taken the leaders of the crusade as his vassals, which constituted a contract by virtue of which, if the vassal promised to serve his lord, the lord was equally obligated with regard to his vassal, to whom he owed protection. This failure on the part of the emperor meant that the crusaders could regard themselves as released from their oath.

This is what would be argued by Bohemond of Taranto. It is difficult to trace in detail the changing attitudes of the Norman prince, since our sources were put into writing some time after the crusade and provide information which is questionable. At Constantinople, Bohemond had gone a long way in his allegiance to the emperor, putting pressure on the other leaders to do the same. In his entourage it was claimed that the emperor had promised to grant him a large fief, located beyond the ancient Byzantine possessions. He could at least bank on this.

Bohemond seems to have begun to play an anti-Byzantine game during the course of the siege of Antioch; it is difficult to say at precisely what point he tried to get his peers to promise that the town would be handed over to him, perhaps as a proxy of the emperor, especially after the departure of Taticius. It was thanks to his undeniable military talents that the crusaders had won their battles, and to his energy and tenacity that they had taken Antioch. To have worked for a *basileus* who had not made him a firm commitment could hardly have satisfied him. *De facto* master of Antioch, which he would probably have had to relinquish if the emperor had arrived in time, he would not rest until he had transformed this occupation into possession by right and, to this end, kept insisting that the emperor's claims had lost all legitimacy. A whole argument based on imperial perjury and strengthened by denunciation of the state of schism applying to the Byzantines developed from this time.

Furthermore, the absence of any imperial representative made it impossible to assert the emperor's rights over the reoccupied towns. A solution to their lack of status would have to be found. In fact, Bohemond had gone out on a limb. Most of the other leaders still regarded themselves as bound by their promises to the emperor. They included Raymond of Saint-Gilles, whose situation was unusual since he had not done homage to the emperor, which did not prevent him from considering himself bound by the oath regarding the restoration of the towns. We may suspect that a deep hostility to Bohemond influenced his adoption of this position. In any case, Raymond of Saint-Gilles refused to deliver to the Norman lord, as others had done, the towers of the enceinte of Antioch that his men held, and he in future consistently supported the arguments in favour of Alexius.

The question of the Byzantine towns reconquered from the Turks, apart from those handed over to Taticius during the journey, arose even before the capture of Antioch. Baldwin of Boulogne had left the army at

Marash, taking a contingent of about two hundred knights. He had with him an Armenian called Pakrad, who had been a prisoner at Constantinople and who was the brother of Kogh Vasil, master of the castles of Kaisun and Raban. It was probably Pakrad who persuaded Baldwin to expel the small Turkish garrisons holding the fortresses controlling the region between the Taurus and the Euphrates. The whole of this area was in fact held by Armenian lords, often invested with office by the emperor; these, since the fall of Philaretus, had agreed to recognise the sovereignty of the sultan by paying tribute. The arrival of the Franks seemed to offer the chance to get rid of their masters.

This is what happened at Turbessel (Tell Bashir) and Ravendel; as Baldwin approached, the Turkish garrisons fled and the population opened the gates to him (October 1097). Baldwin entrusted the government of both places to Pakrad, then removed him when other Armenians denounced his scheming against the Franks. At the end of January 1098 messengers from the curopalates Thoros, who governed Edessa, arrived to ask Baldwin to come to the rescue of this town, which was threatened by the Turks, promising that he would be associated in its government. Baldwin reached Edessa on 20 February to discover that Thoros had no intention of granting him the town. But the curopalates, because he adhered to the Greek rite, was a target for the hostility of his compatriots. He hoped to rely on Baldwin to escape a plot and adopted the Frankish leader, which did not save him from losing his life in an uprising on 9 March. The Armenians then recognised Baldwin as their lord and he, having lost his wife during the journey to Marash, made a second marriage to the daughter of a great Armenian lord, Arda. As we have seen, he resisted Kerbogha's efforts to take the town and, after the rout of the latter's army, extended his power over Samosata and Saruj, fortresses that their Turkish lords preferred to grant to him, in return for cash, rather than hold against him.

The Franks, who had just seized Antioch, provided Baldwin with recruits who entered his service. Among them was his brother, Godfrey of Bouillon, then without money, to whom he gave the revenues of Turbessel and 50,000 gold bezants. This allowed him to strengthen his control and to substitute Franks for the Armenians he suspected of disloyalty. Many of these crusaders returned to Jerusalem, but Baldwin found among those who remained the men who would settle the future county of Edessa.

At the beginning of July the Franks who had taken Antioch were still massed around that town. On 3 July the barons met to send their message to Alexius Comnenus. They were proposing to prolong their stay in the region in order to recover from the ordeals of the siege and to await the end of the fierce summer heat; they were perhaps also hoping to receive reinforcements, as they were very conscious of the small size of their existing forces, and the desertion by a large number of crusaders had been a heavy blow. But epidemic raged in their ranks and on 1 August removed the legate Adhémar of Monteil. Two ecclesiastics present in the contingents of Stephen of Blois and Robert of Normandy, Alexander and Arnulf of Choques, could take advantage of a legation conferred on them by the pope as they passed through Rome, but they lacked the authority of the bishop of Le Puy, whose death aggravated the differences within the council of barons. The epidemic also encouraged the knights to disperse; it was then that many of them went to Edessa.

When the barons met again on 11 September, they wrote a letter to Urban II that reveals their perplexity. After describing their journey, their ordeals and their victories, they went on:

We beg you to complete your work by coming among us and bringing with you everyone you can bring ... come, then, and help us to end this war which is yours. We have vanquished the Turks and the pagans; we cannot similarly combat the heretics: the Greeks, the Armenians, the Syrians and the Jacobites. We beg you then, most holy father, come among your children. You who are the vicar of Peter, come and sit in his church, come and train our hearts in submission and obedience; come and destroy by your authority every species of heresy. Come and lead us in the path that you have mapped out and open for us the gates of the one and only Jerusalem, come and liberate with us the tomb of Jesus Christ and make the name of Christian prevail over all other names.

The notion of the pope's arrival was probably not alien to Urban II, who announced his intention of leaving for Jerusalem at a council held at Bari on 21 October with the Greek bishops of southern Italy. He did not, however, follow this up. The letter from the crusader princes (it was written in the name of Bohemond, Raymond, Godfrey, his brother Eustace and the two Roberts) reveals their uncertainty with regard not only to the next stage of the expedition but also in the face of their discovery of the realities of the East.

The eastern Christians of the various rites, all separated from Rome either by their refusal to accept the dogmas defined by the ecumenical councils or by differences of ritual, and used to the controversies and vexations inflicted by the Byzantine authorities on the Monophysites and the Armenians, were amazed by the attitude of the Franks who, in the words of the patriarch Michael the Syrian, 'saw as a Christian whoever venerated the Cross'. In occupying Antioch, they had returned the cathedral of St Peter to Christian worship, restored the sacred images and reinstated the Greek patriarch, John the Oxite. They had also allowed the Christians of other rites to recover possessions of their churches. This tolerance was all the more remarkable in that the westerners were strangers to the idea of a coexistence of rites, though the Normans had already practised it in southern Italy; but it did not prevent the leaders of the crusade from experiencing some scruples, and it is understandable that they wanted the presence of the pope to resolve the divisions between Christians.

The discovery of the relationships established with Muslims was another novelty. Putting aside the stories, more or less embroidered, of contacts with the besieged during the siege of Antioch, it is the case that the crusaders negotiated with their adversaries. Ahmed ibn Merwan and many of his men, though authorised to withdraw freely, chose to be baptised and probably reinforced the ranks of the turcopoles; some Muslim women also received baptism after the capture of the town. A Muslim lord, the governor of Azaz, in revolt against the king of Aleppo, appealed to Godfrey for help, giving him his son as hostage. Assisted by Raymond of Saint-Gilles, the duke went to his aid and the Muslim came out of his fortress to make himself the liege man of the Lorrainer. It was on this occasion that the Franks discovered the practice of sending messages by carrier pigeon. It was the first time that a Frank had received the homage of a Saracen.

The crusade, nevertheless, had stalled. The hot season had passed and the barons, whether awaiting the response of the pope or that of the emperor to their appeals, did not decide to resume their journey. As we have seen, they were worried by the problem of numbers; in December they had only about nine hundred knights. The conflict surrounding the occupation of Antioch, where Raymond was refusing to relinquish the palace of Yaghi Siyan and the Tower of the Iron Bridge to Bohemond, dragged on. Gradually, the crusaders began to conduct local operations on their own account. Bohemond seems to have gone into Cilicia to secure the places liberated by Tancred. The need to obtain provisions led the different leaders to extend the occupation.

One region attracted particular attention, the fertile valley of the Ruj, which had already been visited at the end of 1097. Raymond Pilet, a Limousin knight from the contingent of Raymond of Saint-Gilles, led a small body of troops there and seized the small town of Tell Mannas. He was defeated before Ma'arrat an-Numan. In September Raymond himself went to Albara and made himself its master, restoring the town's episcopal see to give it to the clerk Peter of Narbonne. He returned to the same region at the end of November, crossed the Ruj and besieged Ma'arrat. Bohemond went to his assistance, since the town was well fortified and vigorously defended. The besiegers suffered famine, and

Muslim historians tell of cannibalistic practices that horrified them. Finally, William of Montpellier built a rolling tower from the top of which he showered the inhabitants with projectiles. The town fell. Bohemond had promised to spare the lives of the defenders, but his promise was not kept and the inhabitants were killed or reduced to slavery (12 December). After this the two princes quarrelled, Bohemond refusing to surrender a place which he had occupied, whereas Raymond wanted to hand the town over to the bishop of Albara. Bohemond seems to have contemplated using it as a bargaining counter with which to make Raymond relinquish the part of Antioch that he still held.

These quarrels reveal that the leaders of the crusade no longer saw the occupation of the towns as only temporary, while waiting for their restoration to the Byzantine emperor. They were establishing domains on which they began to settle their men. The appointment of the bishop of Albara is characteristic; here was a Latin bishop installed by the count of Toulouse in a fortified town that he regarded as now incorporated into a Frankish lordship. And alongside the Franco-Armenian principality being constructed by Baldwin around Edessa, and the dominion that Bohemond was carving out for himself in Antioch, was the Provençal lordship being built by Raymond in the foothills of Djebel Summaq, at Tell Mannas, Arcekan, Rugia, Albara and Ma'arrat. When he departed for Jerusalem, he left his constable, William Peyre of Conilhac, with seven knights and thirty footsoldiers, to maintain the occupation.

So a 'Latin East' was already emerging during the six long months the crusade spent in Syria. The goal first proposed to the crusaders by Urban II, the freeing of the Christians of the East from the yoke of the infidel, had largely been achieved. But it seemed that, given the failure of the armies of the Byzantine emperor to arrive in these countries remote from Constantinople, it was the Christians from the West who were assuring the permanence of this liberation. The Armenians of the region round Edessa had shown the way; already well established, but no longer in real contact with the empire from which they derived their power, they had been obliged to appeal to the Franks to free them from the Turks; and the crusaders felt that it was incumbent on them to take responsibility for protecting and governing these populations in their place.

The great mass of knights, lesser lords, pilgrims and clergy, however, found it hard to endure the hanging about while the barons disputed towns and castles, and were growing impatient. The march on Ma'arrat had been decided after demonstrations that had led Raymond of Saint-Gilles to accept the task of leading the crusade to Jerusalem. Once

Ma'arrat had been taken, he assembled the other leaders at Rugia, proposing to take Godfrey of Bouillon into his pay for 10,000 sous, Robert of Normandy for the same sum, Robert of Flanders for 6,000, and Tancred for 5,000. Bohemond, invited to join the expedition, refused. Those involved having procrastinated, the mass of pilgrims rebelled and decided to destroy the subject of the latest haggling by demolishing the walls and houses of Ma'arrat, despite threats of excommunication from the bishop of Albara. On 13 January, alone of all the leaders of the crusade, Raymond, in pilgrim's garb and barefoot, set out for Jerusalem.

THE CONQUEST OF JERUSALEM

What remained, in January 1099, of the crowds that had set out some two and a half years earlier? We know that the first bands had suffered very heavy losses, some of them having failed to cross the Hungarian frontier. Those that had followed had been tried by battle, illness, the fatigue of long marches, and famine. Many had gone home, ranging from the French crusaders who turned back at Rome, reckoning that they had done enough by completing the pilgrimage to the tomb of the apostles, to the many deserters who left the army during the siege of Antioch. The latter were so numerous that Raymond of Aguilers and Pons of Balazun set about writing their history of the crusade to refute the rumours they were spreading in the West. A few hundred of the crusaders remained in northern Syria to perpetuate the conquests there. Those who set out for Jerusalem certainly numbered no more than 25,000. They were, however, tried and tested warriors, experienced in the tactics required for war in the East, and they enjoyed a reputation based on all the victories they had won. Their leaders were worried by their small numbers; their enemies were reluctant to confront them. This explains the course taken by their march on Jerusalem.

The march was made over difficult terrain, particularly along the Lebanese coast, where some defiles could have been held against the crusaders. But power here was very fragmented. Along the Orontes valley, the Arab emirs of Shaizar, Hamah and Homs were practically independent; along the coast, a string of fortified towns, some of them subject to the Fatimid caliph, were abandoned to their own devices. These were the human obstacles that might have opposed the army of the crusaders, but none felt strong enough to do so.

Raymond of Saint-Gilles had marched from Kafr Tab in the company of Tancred and Robert Curthose, leaving the fortress of Apamea to the west. The emir of Shaizar tried to persuade him not to pass close to his town; unable to do so, he provided the Franks with guides who led them into a valley where, it appears, the local flocks and herds had been driven for safety; they were seized by the Franks who accumulated so much booty that they had to buy pack animals in Homs. The same good fortune awaited them at the Castle of the Kurds (Crac des Chevaliers), which its defenders evacuated, as the inhabitants of Rafaniya had already done. The army advanced without haste and without problems of supply. The emir of Homs paid tribute to prevent an attack, and the qadi of Tripoli, Ibn Ammar, also offered rich gifts and a large sum of money if they would pass by in peace. It seems that the wealth of Tripoli decided Raymond to try to extort more and, to this end, he laid siege to the town of Arqah (Akkar). Raymond Pilet led a raid on Tortosa, which he took, thus opening a port to the ships bringing supplies to the crusaders. But Arqah resisted; the siege lasted from 14 February to 13 May, punctuated by raids on the suburbs of Tripoli.

Godfrey of Bouillon and Robert of Flanders had also set out for Jerusalem. After leaving Antioch, they had reached Jabala, which they besieged. They then received an appeal from Raymond, who had been told of the imminent arrival of the caliph of Baghdad at the head of an army; this rumour seems to have been started by Ibn Ammar to force Raymond to raise the siege of Arqah. The two barons abandoned the siege of Jabala, though not before obtaining a ransom from the town, and came in haste, only to discover that the report was false. Much discontented, they joined with Tancred, who was also discontented at how little pay he was receiving from Raymond, to force the count of Toulouse to resume the march. The credit of the clergy in Raymond's entourage had suffered as a result of a controversy over the authenticity of the Holy Lance, which Peter Bartholomew had wanted to prove by ordeal by fire, which had got out of hand and led to his death. At this point, the envoys of Alexius Comnenus arrived to complain about Bohemond's intrigues and to ask the crusaders to await the arrival of their master before proceeding to Jerusalem. Raymond pronounced himself in favour, but the other barons refused. In the end, the siege of Arqah had to be raised (13 May).

It was on the advice of the Christians from the mountains that it was decided to take the route that was most dangerous but richest in sources of water, on the strength of predictions reported by them. No one contested the difficult stretches. The masters of Tripoli and Jubail (Gibelet) paid a ransom. On 19 May, the crusaders reached Beirut, which also ransomed itself, as did Sidon, Tyre, Acre and Caesarea. These towns provided without difficulty the supplies that were needed. Some of the knights left at Antioch rejoined the army, which the Christian fleet followed along the coast. All the forces had come together by the time they arrived at Ramla, where they stayed for three days. Discovering the great church of St George at Lydda, which was in ruins, they installed here a new Latin bishop (3–6 June).

At this point there arrived some Christians from Bethlehem, who warned the crusaders that the governor of Jerusalem on behalf of the Fatimids, Iftikhar al-Dawla, was preparing the city to withstand a siege. The crusaders debated what plan of campaign to adopt, some arguing that they should carry the war into Egypt to destroy Fatimid power. During the siege of Arqah, the envoys who had gone to Cairo with the Egyptian ambassadors of the previous winter had returned with al-Afdal's final offers; there was no more talk of returning free Jerusalem to the hands of the Christians, but only of allowing them, in groups of up to two hundred and unarmed, to make their devotions in a Jerusalem that was once again Fatimid. This no longer amounted, clearly, to the liberation of the Holy Sepulchre, and these new offers seemed to be breaking an agreement, though it is difficult to know how seriously it had been taken by the crusaders; the idea of a campaign against Egypt had also been aired in the letter written by Urban II to the Milanese in April 1099, that is, when the pope was ignorant of the negotiations between the crusaders and the Fatimids. But the barons gathered at Ramla agreed that, given the state of their forces, a campaign against Egypt was unrealistic.

The arrival of the Bethlehem Christians decided them to delay no longer before approaching the Holy City. Two detachments were soon dispatched, one to Bethlehem with Tancred, the other to Jerusalem with Gaston de Béarn. Bethlehem was occupied on 7 June, and the local Christians gave the crusaders a warm welcome.

The whole army massed before Jerusalem, which they attacked on the western side of the enceinte where the Tower of David was the strong point. The emotions of the crusaders were strong, but they soon realised the difficulty of their task; Iftikhar had poisoned the wells and expelled the Christians from the city, which was strongly garrisoned. They launched, nevertheless, a vigorous assault, which failed due to a shortage of ladders, on 13 June. The lack of water meant they had to send fatigues as far as the River Jordan.

But they learned that two Genoese galleys had arrived at Jaffa; a detachment commanded by Raymond Pilet went to meet them, dispersing an Egyptian corps near Ramla. The Genoese returned bringing the wood from their ships to construct war machines, and they were lucky enough to find beams, concealed in caves, that had been used in the construction of the Fatimid's siege machines the year before. They also obtained wood from the mountains and from Samaria. The siege was now methodically pursued with wooden towers and catapults.

On 8 July, on the advice of the priest Peter Desiderius, who claimed to have been blessed by a vision of the legate Adhémar, a general fast was called, followed by a procession which marched round the walls; Arnulf of Choques preached a sermon. The warriors now decided to concentrate their main efforts on the eastern section of the enceinte, which was dominated by three wooden towers. The assault began on the evening of 13 July and continued till the 15th. A rolling tower which contained Godfrey and Eustace of Boulogne got close enough to the wall for it to be possible to throw out a footbridge, across which two brothers, natives of Tournai, passed first, while other crusaders scaled the wall with the aid of ladders. Soon, the city was invaded from all sides.

The battle had been particularly fierce. The defenders had the advantage of a larger number of machines than the besiegers and they had very effectively returned the enemy fire. They had inflicted very heavy losses on the crusaders. Their entry into the city, where fighting seems to have continued, was accompanied by a massacre that shocked contemporaries. Many Muslims had taken refuge in the al-Aqsa mosque (the unlikely figure of 70,000 persons has been suggested), where there was a repeat of the scenes that had taken place in the same mosque in 1077. To describe them, historians, in particular Raymond of Aguilers, used an image borrowed from a text in the Apocalypse, which spoke of 'blood rising to the bridles of their horses'. The crusaders massacred those who rushed into the streets to take refuge in the Tower of David. The citadel still resisted and the governor, Iftikhar al-Dawla, eventually surrendered to Raymond of Saint-Gilles, who kept his promise to conduct him and his men to Ascalon. Tancred and Gaston de Béarn had given their banners to those who had taken refuge on the roofs of the al-Aqsa mosque as a sign of their protection, but they were massacred all the same. In the Jewish quarter, a synagogue was burned with all who were inside.

This massacre, whose description has been endlessly repeated, was not, however, systematic. Hebrew letters discovered in the Cairo genizah tell how a party of Jews from Jerusalem was led under escort to Ascalon where their co-religionists of Egypt ransomed them and their books. And it is noted, with surprise, that the Franks respected the women. The Christians had been expelled by the Fatimid governor and the Jacobite bishop had taken refuge in Egypt; the crusaders, in their turn, seem to have emptied the city of its Muslim population; it has been claimed that these refugees began to populate the Damascus suburb of Salihiyé and Saladin tried to discover their descendants, to bring them back. In the short run, the pilgrims, at last arrived at their goal, made haste to venerate the tomb of Christ and give thanks for their victory. It seemed miraculous, so great had been the dangers and obstacles to be surmounted. And the siege of the city could not have been prolonged without exposing the crusaders to a reversal of fortune. It is hardly surprising that a liturgical feast was instituted in the breviary of the Holy Sepulchre to commemorate the capture of Jerusalem. And the whole historical literature born of the crusade, like the epic, ends with this wonderful event.

All was not over, however, with the arrival at the tomb of Christ. The clergy present in the army had to arrange for it to be served in these new circumstances, and the barons had to prepare for an Egyptian counter-attack. These matters were debated in a council which met on 17 June. The bishops and the clergy argued that Jerusalem should belong to the Holy Sepulchre and not to a lay prince, which would not have been aberrant, since towns in western Europe were often ruled by their bishops. They advocated the immediate election of a patriarch who would assume this role. But the great episcopal figures – Adhémar of Monteil and William, Bishop of Orange – were dead; the other bishops were less outstanding, including the Norman bishop of Martirano in southern Italy, who had procured Bethlehem. The barons were able to insist on the appointment of a lay prince who would assume responsi-bility for the defence of Jerusalem.

The debate then turned to the choice of the future king of Jerusalem. The leader of the crusade since the departure from Ma'arrat had been Raymond of Saint-Gilles, who had borne the financial cost of the expedition, taken the other barons into his pay, negotiated with the Muslim leaders and recently occupied the Tower of David. But he had made enemies; he was criticised for having appropriated the indemnities received from the towns and leaders with whom he had negotiated; in fact it was he who managed the army's treasury. Above all, his companions, Provençals, Toulousains and Limousins, showed little enthusiasm for remaining in the East and providing the personnel for the occupation. In the end, Raymond refused the honour offered to him.

Robert of Flanders and Robert of Normandy supported the candida-ture of Godfrey of Bouillon, which was now compelling. The duke eventually accepted, though refusing the royal title; where Christ had worn the crown of thorns, he did not wish to wear a crown of gold. Did he take the title of Advocate of the Holy Sepulchre? The documents and chronicles normally refer to him as 'duke'. The designation 'Advocate' (*advocatus*) would imply that he was regarded as responsible for the protection and the maintenance of order in a city whose true owner was the sanctuary. This would suggest that the debate about the sovereignty of Jerusalem was not finally settled.

The appointment of a patriarch came next. Here, too, one person seemed the obvious choice by reason of the role he had played, namely Arnulf of Choques, chaplain to the duke of Normandy; Arnulf had received the powers of a legate and, since Adhémar's death, had effectively exercised them, exhorting the army and pronouncing on the authenticity of Peter Bartholomew's visions. But Arnulf had made enemies; he was illegitimate and, though he was learned, his morals were open to criticism. He was nevertheless elected, in circumstances which would be disputed.

The fall of Jerusalem entailed the occupation of the neighbouring region, Nablus, from which the city drew its resources. Tancred of Hauteville and Eustace of Boulogne went to receive the submission of the local small towns and tribes, who made no difficulty about recognising their new masters.

The mass of crusaders wanted only to go home. The counts of Flanders and Normandy had already left when news arrived of the approach of the army that the vizier al-Afdal had assembled for the support of Jerusalem on hearing of the crusaders' arrival. He had reached Ascalon on 4 August and denounced what he saw as the unjustified aggression of the Franks, to whom he had offered the chance to make a pilgrimage, unarmed, to the Holy City, accusing them of treachery. But he waited for the arrival of the fleet, whose movements he planned to combine with those of his land army, which seems to have been very large. So the Franks had time to react.

The counts of Flanders and Normandy had already reached Ramla; Raymond of Saint-Gilles, in response to an instruction from Peter Bartholomew, was with his men on the banks of the Jordan. Godfrey got news to them, and the three counts, after taking the time to confirm the Egyptian presence, rejoined the duke's army at Ibelin (Yebna). The whole army now numbered barely 1,200 knights and 9,000 infantry. But, having seized the flocks accompanying the enemy army and interrogated their shepherds (11 August), who provided information about the enemy dispositions, they made a surprise attack on the Egyptians on the morning of 12 August; with their right wing against the sea, they drove them from the field, pushing the fleeing troops back to the shore, where only a few of them could be taken onto their boats, while the vizier and his men took refuge in Ascalon. The captured camp yielded an immense quantity of booty as well as the documents already mentioned. The Egyptian threat was lifted for the time being.

THE AFTERMATH OF THE CONQUEST

Alone among the leaders of the crusade, Raymond of Saint-Gilles had revealed his intention of prolonging his stay in the Holy Land for several months, until Easter 1100. But his plans assumed his continued occupation of the tower he had captured, the Tower of David, which Godfrey refused to accept, demanding that the citadel of Jerusalem should be delivered into his hands; this was done in circumstances that are by no means clear and with which Raymond was clearly unhappy. After the battle of Ascalon, the crusaders marched on the town, which the vizier had just left, and began to besiege it. The inhabitants offered to surrender, but to Raymond, whose conduct towards the Egyptian garrison of Jerusalem was remembered. The count of Toulouse was inclined to accept their submission. But Godfrey intervened and claimed for himself a town that seemed intended to belong to the lordship he was to construct round Jerusalem. Furious, Raymond urged the people of Ascalon to hold out, and he left the army, along with the counts of Flanders and Normandy. As he was passing before Arsur, the inhabitants of the town offered, in their turn, to surrender to him. Godfrey, arriving on the scene, forced him to withdraw. If Raymond had intended to carve out a lordship for himself in Philistia, his plans were frustrated.

He joined the other two counts and took the road north in their company. With them went the majority of the crusaders – 20,000 persons according to Albert of Aix; they included Peter the Hermit, who returned to the West to found the monastery of Bellevaux, near Belfort, then that of Neufmonastier, near Huy. The governors of the towns along the coast offered them the same facilities as during their descent on Jerusalem; they found in passing that Tortosa had been reoccupied by Muslims and arrived at Latakia.

They were surprised to find that the town, which had become Byzantine again after it had been taken from the Muslims by Guynemer of Boulogne, was being besieged by Bohemond's forces, joined by some new arrivals, the crusaders from Pisa. As we have seen, they had left at the beginning of the summer and, after a first clash with a Byzantine squadron, had arrived on the Syrian coast in September. Their leader, archbishop Daimbert, had responded to an approach from Bohemond to attack the Byzantine maritime base. Angered by this war between Christians, the three barons vehemently reproached Daimbert, who claimed that he had been misled. Robert of Normandy and Robert of Flanders, with their followers, embarked on Byzantine boats which carried them to Constantinople, where Alexius received them with honour.

Raymond remained at Latakia with some of his men. Regarding himself as representing the emperor Alexius, he also retained, not far from Latakia, vassals who held on his behalf the settlements in the Orontes valley, round Albara. Holding the town of Latakia for the emperor, he remained afar from negligible political force, well established south of Antioch, at a time when the conflict between Bohemond's Normans and the Byzantines was hotting up; his declared respect for the oath taken to Alexius in 1097 made him an ally of the emperor. Leaving his wife and young son at Latakia, he set off for Constantinople in the late spring of 1100.

It would be interesting to know if Bohemond took advantage of the presence of Daimbert, who enjoyed the powers of a pontifical legate, to strengthen his claims to maritime Cilicia by appointing Latin archbishops to the sees of Tarsus and Mamistra. At all events, and perhaps after a joint demonstration against Jabala, the archbishop and the prince, joined by Baldwin of Boulogne, set out for Jerusalem in order to fulfil their vow of pilgrimage. Despite the presence of the Pisan fleet which sailed down the coast, their march encountered some difficulties; in many places, stragglers were attacked, and provisions ran short. But on 21 December the two Frankish leaders and the archbishop, with the Pisan sailors, reached Jerusalem. For Bohemond and Baldwin, who had abandoned the march of the main army in order to establish themselves in northern Syria, this was the completion, only a little delayed, of their pilgrimage.

For Daimbert, archbishop and legate of Urban II, with a devoted army at his disposal and enjoying much greater prestige than Arnulf of Choques, this was also an opportunity to revive the question of the status of Jerusalem, to which the decisions of the baronial council of the previous July and August had not provided a solution he regarded as satisfactory. He deposed Arnulf, whose election was irregular, and who had to be content with the double title of archdeacon of the Holy Sepulchre and guardian of the relics, which left him with real power. Daimbert had himself proclaimed patriarch of Jerusalem. By this title, after celebrating Christmas at Bethlehem the new patriarch successfully demanded that Godfrey and Bohemond acknowledge themselves to be his vassals and publicly do homage. This was an entirely new situation, because Daimbert was acting not as legate and in the name of the Holy See but by virtue of his patriarchal title, without regard for the fact that the see of Antioch and its dependencies had never been under the jurisdiction of the patriarchate of Jerusalem. The pope had probably never intended to establish a pontifical sovereignty over the conquests of the crusaders; still less had he planned to create such a sovereignty for the benefit of the patriarch of Jerusalem. A few months later, at Easter

(1 April 1100), Daimbert went further; he got Godfrey to recognise his possession of Jerusalem and of Jaffa, whose duke remained its lord only for life. The Holy City thus became what had been decided against in July 1099, an ecclesiastical lordship. And Jaffa, the only port in the kingdom, whose fortifications had been built in January 1100, passed under Pisan control.

Bohemond and Baldwin started back for the north, this time travelling along the Litani and Orontes rivers, through the Beqa'a, and the regions of Homs, Shaizar and the Ruj, without the Muslim princes putting any obstacles in their way. Godfrey and Tancred had taken advantage of the months following the victory of Ascalon to extend their occupation. Godfrey had occupied Hebron; he made several attempts to subjugate Arsur, which resisted vigorously and which, finally, in February to March, agreed to pay tribute to the Franks of Jerusalem. He also imposed his sovereignty on the leaders of the Arab tribes, nomadic and sedentary, confirming their rights to roam freely and their customs.

Tancred, the only leader of the crusade to have chosen to remain with Godfrey, had occupied the region of Nablus soon after the capture of Jerusalem. He seems to have got the territories extending to the north-east of Jerusalem granted to him as a fief by the advocate of the Holy Sepulchre; he took possession of Tiberias, abandoned by its Muslim inhabitants, and fortified Bethsan, the old Scythopolis, which controlled the crossing of the Jordan. From there, in May 1100, he crossed to the east bank of the river to subjugate Sawad, which effectively gave him control of all the shores of Lake Tiberias and of the Jordan valley to the south. But here, he came up against the dependencies of the Seljuk kingdom of Damascus. The emir of Sawad, whom the Franks called *grossus rusticus*, appealed to Duqaq, who asked the Franks to evacuate this area. Tancred, taking a gamble, sent ten knights to Damascus to ask the Muslim sovereign to become a Christian and agree to pay tribute. Duqaq had the envoys beheaded; Tancred appealed to Godfrey and together they made a show of force in the region of Damascus. After this, Sawad continued to pay tribute.

Tancred was even able to add an outlet to the sea, thanks to the arrival of the Venetian crusaders, who represented yet another 'wave' of the First Crusade. Having left after the Pisans, and having defended Byzantine interests against them, the Venetians arrived at Jaffa in June 1100 and offered to assist the Franks in seizing Acre. But having met too fierce a resistance, they marched on Caiphas (now Haifa), which they occupied in August 1100. Godfrey had promised the town to one of his supporters, Galdemar Carpenel; taking advantage of the duke's death (18 July 1100), Tancred attached Haifa to Galilee, which seemed likely to

take its place among the constellation of Latin states when circumstances
changed.

Once Antioch had fallen, the leaders of the crusade suddenly became
aware of the numerical weakness of their army; the desertion of several
hundred, perhaps thousands, of men made it even more apparent. Many
of those who had left, of course, would return; a priest in the entourage
of the count of Toulouse, Elrad, told how, below Arcas, 'when the
Turks were besieging our army in Antioch', he had gone to Tripoli to
procure foodstuffs and there had a revelation through the intermediary
of a Syrian Christian; he had then rejoined the army after the victory.
But many had gone home. The letters sent to the pope and to various
prelates, in particular the archbishops of Reims, all return to the same
theme: that they should compel those who had forgotten their crusading
vow or had abandoned the expedition to join them, and that others
should set out. The circulation of texts, true or false, the *excitatoriae*, did
the same. The crusaders were in dire need of reinforcements.

As we know, these were being prepared, urged on by Urban II and
Paschal II. Duly provided with legates (the archbishop of Lyons, Hugh
of Die, and probably the archbishops of Milan and Salzburg), the
crusaders set out from the end of September 1100. First to leave were the
Lombards, to whom Urban II had appealed in April 1099, who overwintered in Bulgaria and Thrace, having followed the valley of the
Danube. Like the first crusaders, they had the benefit of having
provisions assured by the Byzantines, but the excesses of some of their
number persuaded the emperor to isolate them not far from Constantinople, then to have them transported to Asia, not without provoking a
riot, the Lombards fearing they would be exposed to Turkish attacks
(April 1101). A group of French barons, with the counts of Blois
(Stephen had taken the cross again) and Burgundy, the duke of
Burgundy and the constable of the empire, Conrad, joined them near
Nicomedia. Raymond of Saint-Gilles, then in Constantinople, was
chosen as their leader and Alexius gave him a corps of turcopoles.
Stephen of Blois and Raymond wanted to retrace the route taken by the
First Crusade; the Lombards, learning that Bohemond was a captive of
the Danishmend Turks at Niksar, between Sivas and Trebizond,
demanded that they go to his rescue. They took Ankara in passing,
which was handed over to the emperor in accord with the oath sworn in
1097. But they were defeated before Gangra, entered barren regions and
met an army of the Danishmends combined with the troops of the

Seljuks Kilij Arslan and Ridwan. Their lines broken, the crusaders scattered. Stephen of Blois and the count of Burgundy attempted to contain the enemy; Raymond of Saint-Gilles, abandoned by the turcopoles and surrounded on a height, was extricated by Eudes of Burgundy, but, during the course of the night, seized by panic, he in his turn took flight; the other barons followed him, abandoning their camp, the women and the non-combatants to the Turks (about 5 August). They suffered heavy losses; the number of those killed or taken prisoner has been estimated at between 50,000 and 160,000. Those who escaped were able to regain Constantinople by sea.

This disaster was followed by others. Count William II of Nevers, who had set out with 15,000 men in February 1101, had travelled by way of Brindisi, Avlona and Thessalonika and attempted to join the earlier army. From Ankara he marched to Konya to find the town solidly held; he was forced to press on to Eregli, across a countryside devastated by the Turks. His army was almost totally wiped out nearby at the end of August and he arrived in Antioch with only a handful of knights.

The army of William the Troubadour, count of Poitiers, reinforced by the Bavarian army of Duke Welf IV, was much larger. It crossed Hungary and then, not without incident, Bulgaria, and did battle with the emperor's Pechenegs near Adrianople. Alexius provided it with the means to cross into Asia around the beginning of June 1101. The count of Nevers was trying to join the Lombards while the main army embarked on the route taken by the First Crusade.

The Turks employed scorched-earth tactics, so that the troops were exhausted by the time they reached the neighbourhood of Eregli, where they were spotted and massacred by the combined forces in early September. William and Welf were able to reach Antioch, but Hugh of Vermandois, who had taken the cross again, and Duke Eudes of Burgundy both died at Tarsus.

Historians have judged both the crusaders and their leaders harshly, but it is by no means clear that they were less disciplined or less able fighters than those of 1097–9. The latter became hardened and very quickly accustomed to the Turkish methods of warfare; the waves of mounted archers harassing the Franks with their arrows and the simulated flights had soon become familiar to the soldiers of the First Crusade. But these tactics took the new arrivals by surprise. The Turks employed against them a strategy involving the desertion of villages and the devastation of the countryside. We must also take account of human frailty. The count of Toulouse, to whom Alexius made known his displeasure, had helped to aggravate the wave of panic that seized the army he commanded. The numbers of the Crusade of 1101 were probably comparable to those of the First Crusade; they failed to reinforce those who had been given the task of preserving its conquests. But we should not forget that those who escaped the disaster provided help that was often extremely effective to the Franks in the East; it was they who, having helped Raymond of Saint-Gilles to conquer Tortosa, fought at Ramla under Baldwin I. It was there that Stephen of Blois was killed and Harpin of Bourges taken prisoner, to be ransomed three years later.

The West did not see the failure of the last wave of the First Crusade as decisive. The clergy explained this failure by attributing it to the sins of men; the Muslims failed to take immediate advantage of their victory. It is difficult to say whether Alexius Comnenus would have been able to take advantage of the intervention of the new arrivals to resolve the question of Antioch. Of course, had they been successful, the projects bandied about in May and June 1099, which even included a march on Baghdad, would have changed the course of events, but their utopian character makes this unlikely.

There followed an episode that brought to an end one of the confrontations that had marked the course of the First Crusade, the conflict between Bohemond of Tarento and Raymond of Saint-Gilles. This was a clash between two strong personalities, neither disposed to give way to the other, perhaps because both men – in Bohemond's case certainly, in Raymond's case probably – were hoping to create an establishment in the East. It was also a conflict between two interpretations of a solemn promise, made on the relics of the Passion, the oath sworn to the emperor Alexius obliging the crusaders to return to the empire what had belonged to it. Bohemond regarded himself as released from this oath as soon as the failure of the emperor could be seen to justify this; Raymond observed it strictly, and was observing it still when, returning from Constantinople, he set out to rejoin his family in Latakia.

The ship which carried him, and also Stephen of Blois, Stephen of Burgundy and other leaders of the Lombard army, landed in Cilicia. There, a knight, Bernard the Stranger, arrested and imprisoned Raymond on the pretext that he had betrayed the crusaders the previous June. Tancred, who then ruled the principality of Antioch, took possession of the prisoner; he agreed to release him, at the request of his companions and of the patriarch of Antioch, but on condition that Raymond ceased to contest possession of Antioch with the Normans and prevent them from occupying Latakia. Tancred also fixed a limit north of which the count of Toulouse was to renounce all claims, which meant abandoning the lordship he had created in the valley of the Ruj in 1098 and which was still in the hands of the Provençals, whose numbers had gradually increased while the count was pursuing his adventures. Some of them, probably including the Mazoir who became sires of Margat, seem then to have become vassals of the prince of Antioch (January 1102). Raymond may have promised not to settle between Antioch and Acre, but this is not certain.

In any case, with the men he had left guarding Latakia and the other places he now abandoned, and with the agreement of the crusaders who remained in his company (William of Poitiers, the counts of Blois, Burgundy and Biandrate and Conrad the Constable), and thanks to the aid of Genoese ships, he laid siege to Tortosa, in February 1102, and captured it. His companions were expecting him to accompany them to Jerusalem, but he decided to stay in Tortosa, and was able, despite the small size of his army (300 knights), to put to flight an army sent to recover the town by the emir of Homs, the lord of Tripoli and the king of Damascus. Raymond had finally found his establishment in the East.

The crusaders continued on their way. They reached Jerusalem in time to celebrate Easter, and then expected to return to the West. But adverse winds threw most of them back onto the coast, where they were persuaded to join in the campaign led by Baldwin I against the Egyptians, which ended in the disaster of Ramla. Conrad escaped death (he was freed only in 1107), but Stephen of Burgundy, Stephen of Blois, Hugh of Lusignan and Geoffrey of Vendôme lost their lives.

The only lasting legacy of the Crusade of 1101 was what was to become the county of Tripoli. It was not much in comparison with the hopes aroused by the scale of the effort. The last wave of Urban II's crusade ended in failure. But only two of the historians of this crusade, Ekkehard of Aura, who had taken part in this final expedition, and Albert of Aix, describe this defeat. Other accounts concentrated on the crusade of 1096–9, as if its success overshadowed the failure of its successor. God's design, as it had been defined at the council of Clermont, seemed to be confirmed by events: the Byzantine East had escaped the Turks, the Holy Sepulchre the domination of the infidel. Admittedly, a high price had been paid, the armies having left a trail of dead behind them; no one knows how many of the men and women who had left the West for Jerusalem had been enslaved and sold in the markets of the East. The financial sacrifices had been considerable, and the massive booty described by the chroniclers must have been rapidly dissipated, given the cost of these expeditions.

On the map, the result of the various campaigns of the First Crusade, by the time it ended, was the appearance of the Frankish dominions, seemingly quite unplanned; they had not yet assumed their definitive form, but the first lineaments of the Latin states were already visible. Problems had arisen, those of relations with Byzantium, of political and ecclesiastical structures, and of contacts with the easterners. Others were yet to emerge or to gain definition, especially in the economic sphere. But the First Crusade defined what was in future to be the purpose of the crusades: the survival of a Latin East.

4

THE HOLY LAND: A NEW COUNTRY OVERSEAS

The Latin states of the East were a creation of the First Crusade, not as part of some grand design, but as an unforeseen consequence of the way events unfolded. It was during the siege and capture of Antioch that, round it and Edessa, two states were formed that aimed to bring under their authority the former Byzantine lands recaptured from the Turks. The occupation of Jerusalem presented the council of crusader barons with the problems of how to keep the city in Christian hands. And the county of Tripoli began to take shape when the participants in the crusade of 1101 took Tortosa. In this case, however, a baron revealed his desire to take advantage of this occupation to settle permanently in the East and build himself a lordship there.

Raymond of Saint-Gilles was not alone in his wish to stay in the East. More than one pilgrim, having obtained redemption of his sins by completing the pilgrimage, wished not to leave the place where divine grace had manifested itself in his favour, and the vow 'to die in Jerusalem' was already found in the eleventh century. The Cistercian Caesar of Heisterbach, who wrote at the beginning of the thirteenth century, tells how this idea came to Wicher the German, a knight from the diocese of Utrecht whom he identifies with one of the heroes of the crusade; he had every intention of returning home, but seeing, during the course of a battle (Ascalon?), the soul of his squire, killed before his eyes, rise to heaven, he realised that death in defence of the Holy Sepulchre would be the most direct route to eternal bliss, and decided to remain.

Many of his companions must have thought like him, and the conquest of Jerusalem, regarded as quasi-miraculous, may have provided the decisive impulse in making them decide to devote themselves in future to the defence of a liberated Syria.

Was this so in the case of the count of Toulouse? At the time of the siege of Arcas, he was apparently still intending to return to Provence, where Peter Bartholomew was asking him to build a church, near Arles, to house the Holy Lance. After the capture of Jerusalem, he seems to have wanted to settle in Philistia, which Godfrey would not accept; once Tortosa had been taken, he established himself there, leaving his companions in arms to depart for Jerusalem. The case of Godfrey of Bouillon is similar; a sincere crusader who had fulfilled his vow of pilgrimage was true to himself in deciding to devote his remaining years to the service of the Holy Sepulchre.

Such motives were perhaps not unknown to Bohemond of Taranto and Baldwin of Boulogne, who may have felt responsible for the Christians they had liberated from the Turkish yoke. But, unlike Raymond and Godfrey, both rulers of great principalities in the West, they lacked possessions in their native land. Bohemond, as part of his inheritance, before his father's death, had received the lands he had conquered in Albania; he had been reduced to possession of Taranto. Baldwin could not hope to inherit the county of Boulogne or the duchy of Lower Lorraine, and he had at one stage sought his fortune in the possessions of William the Conqueror. For both of them, an establishment in the East was very tempting. The same was true of Tancred, a younger son of the house of Hauteville, and of Baldwin of Bourcq, younger son of that of Rethel.

These founders defined the principalities they were owed by their birth. They even gave them their title in the noble hierarchy. Prince of Taranto, Bohemond remained 'prince' and founded the principality of Antioch. Count of Toulouse, Raymond gave the title of county to his future possessions in Tripoli. Born of a comital family, Baldwin did the same in Edessa, just as Tancred made Galilee a 'principality', the term in use in Norman Italy.

The royal title that Godfrey had refused was nevertheless instituted in Jerusalem. But here the title was traditional. The title 'King of Jerusalem of the Latins' referred back to the previous dynasty of kings of Jerusalem of the people of Israel: David and Solomon. The future St Anselm wrote to Baldwin I to remind him of the eminent dignity of this monarchy and of the moral obligations attaching to it.

THE DYNASTIES

If these creations took root, it was not only as a result of the wishes of their founders; it was also because they were surrounded by a group of men who were mostly by tradition vassals of their family and who had joined the contingent that had accompanied them on the crusade. It was primarily Normans from Italy who followed Bohemond, and Provençals and Languedocians who accompanied Raymond, and it was from among these men that Raymond chose those who settled in his lands around Albara, then around Tripoli. Godfrey's *mesnie*, or household, was composed of men from Brabant, Hainault and Lower Lorraine, with the addition of men who had joined his army; they probably included Wicher, possibly a knight of the abbot of Fulda, and Galdemar Carpenel, who had probably left with the count of Forez and, after his death, led his own contingent under his banner.

Historians used to see Godfrey and his successors as kings elected by those who were to become their vassals. This is not so; Godfrey was elected by his peers and he made his vassals those men who were already for the most part under his command. And the kingdom, like the principality and the counties, was transmitted according to the rules of hereditary succession. Only the descendants or relatives of the founder were regarded as qualified to succeed him. This is not to say that the transmission of power took place without disputes. In the absence of direct heirs, it was necessary to choose between the claims of the possible candidates to the succession, and whether the most legitimate heir would be capable of rapidly assuming the heritage was a factor to be taken into account. And in all these Eastern states, women, when they were widowed, found it hard to accept being forced to give way to their son when it was they who had transmitted the royal or princely title to their deceased husband; this was a cause of intrigues and sometimes of open conflicts.

The kings of Jerusalem

Godfrey died, childless, on 18 July 1100; as he was only Advocate of the Holy Sepulchre, and had promised to leave Jerusalem and Jaffa to the patriarch, the latter proposed to take possession of the inheritance, with Tancred's support. But Godfrey's *mesnie*, led by Count Garnier of Grez, refused to deliver the Tower of David to the prelate and appealed to Godfrey's brother, Baldwin of Boulogne. Learning of this, Daimbert tried to get Bohemond to intervene, but his envoy was intercepted by the Byzantines; Bohemond, in any case, was then a prisoner of the Turks. Baldwin arrived with all speed, having crossed swords with the Damascenes, who had laid an ambush for him, on the way. Garnier of Grez had died, but his companions delivered the citadel to Baldwin and Daimbert had to give way and even crown Baldwin king, at Bethlehem, on Christmas Day.

On 2 April 1118 Baldwin died, returning from a raid into Egypt. His barons were divided, some appealing to his brother Eustace, Count of Boulogne, others to his cousin Baldwin of Bourcq, who had succeeded him as count of Edessa. It was the latter, led by Joscelin of Courtenay, who won the day; Eustace had got no further than Italy, but Baldwin II bore a grudge against those who had supported him. Then, when he was captured by the Turks (1123–4), some of the barons wanted to bring in a relative of Baldwin I, Charles the Good, Count of Flanders. Baldwin II therefore took care to arrange his succession during his lifetime by marrying the eldest of his four daughters, Melisende, to a powerful and recently widowed baron in the West, Fulk V, Count of Anjou, to whom he explicitly promised the kingdom. Pope Honorius II expressed his admiration for a prince ready to relinquish the government of a great fief for a more arduous task.

On the death of Baldwin II (1131) Fulk succeeded, and Melisende was crowned alongside him. But it was Fulk who ruled and he had brought with him Angevins who made up his entourage. This gave rise to discontent and even revolts, like that of the count of Jaffa, Hugh of Le Puiset, the queen's cousin, who was forced into exile. Melisende took her revenge on the death of her husband (10 November 1143), determined to behave as queen and not as regent, with the support of her cousin, Manasses of Hierges. The young Baldwin III had to form his own party, get himself crowned, and share the kingdom with his mother, then resort to arms to force her to withdraw (1152). Once again, old scores were settled, and Manasses was exiled.

Baldwin's younger brother, Amalric, who would probably have been Melisende's choice, had received a splendid apanage, namely the county of Jaffa and Ascalon. On his brother's death (10 February 1163), he succeeded him, but he had first to separate from his wife, Agnes of Courtenay, whom he had married even though she was promised to a baron. He was nevertheless able to transmit the crown to his son by Agnes, Baldwin IV, on 11 July 1174.

Baldwin, a young man of great ability, suffered from leprosy. Despite his energy, he could not prevent intrigues from developing over his succession. His sister Sibylla had married as her second husband a Poitevin nobleman, Guy of Lusignan (1180). Guy having quarrelled with the king, the latter had Sibylla's son by her first marriage to William of Montferrat, then still a child, crowned, putting him under the tutelage of his cousin, Raymond III of Tripoli; Raymond acted as regent after his death (May 1185). But the boy king, Baldwin V, soon died (13 September 1186). Raymond insisted that Sibylla had been disinherited but she, thanks to the Master of the Temple and her uncle Joscelin III of

Map 3   The kingdom of Jerusalem

Courtenay, acted with great speed and had herself crowned with her husband, forcing the count of Tripoli into an opposition which began to look like rebellion.

Though the transmission of the crown had obeyed the rules of heredity, there had been a number of interventions, which had sometimes looked like palace revolutions, though without deteriorating into wars of succession; it is as if cliques formed round each sovereign, and the change of ruler produced tension within the entourage.

The princes of Antioch

Antioch experienced other problems; the principality's situation, close to powerful enemies, rendered it susceptible to serious crises. Bohemond, who had become master of the town during the course of 1098, was captured by the Danishmends during the summer of 1100; Tancred arrived to assume the regency, though he was forced to swear to restore the principality to his cousin. In 1103 Bohemond was freed in return for a large ransom, but he had to go in search of reinforcements to the West, where he died. Tancred, until 1112, then his cousin, Roger of Salerno, acted as regents for the child Bohemond II. But Roger died fighting at the Field of Blood (*Ager Sanguinis*) on 28 June 1119. King Baldwin II had to assume responsibility for the government while awaiting the arrival of Bohemond II, to whom he married his daughter Alice in October 1126. But in February 1130 Bohemond in his turn was killed and his head sent to the caliph of Baghdad. His widow Alice proposed that she should assume power and won the support of the count of Tripoli; King Fulk had to intervene and assume the regency in the name of the young princess Constance, for whom he found a husband, the second son of the count of Poitiers, Raymond (1136). It has been claimed that he resorted to trickery, and that the patriarch led Alice to believe that Raymond was coming to marry her and that she discovered the truth too late.

Raymond in his turn fell on the battlefield (29 June 1149), and Baldwin III arrived to act as regent. But Constance fell in love with a knight of good family but no fortune, Reynald of Châtillon-sur-Loing, whom she married in 1153. Reynald was captured in 1161, and Constance intrigued with the Byzantines to remain in power, negotiating the marriage of her daughter Maria to Manuel Comnenus. The barons of Antioch forced her to grant her son Bohemond III the land of Latakia, then the title of prince, but it was still necessary for the king of Jerusalem to intervene before oaths were sworn to the young prince. His stepfather, Reynald, was freed only in 1176, and lost all rights to Antioch.

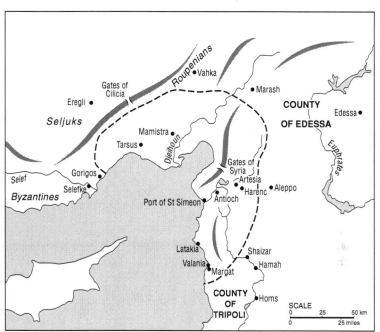

Map 4   The principality of Antioch in the first half of the twelfth century

The counts of Edessa

Both Baldwin of Boulogne and then Baldwin of Bourcq having exchanged the title of count of Edessa for that of king of Jerusalem, it was eventually a family from the Gâtinais, the Courtenay, who took possession of the county. Joscelin I (1119–31) was succeeded by Joscelin II, who was driven out of Edessa in 1144, remained at Turbessel until his capture by the Turks in 1149, and died in the prisons of Aleppo. His wife, Beatrice, had to resign herself to granting what remained of the county to the Byzantines (1150); her children, Agnes and Joscelin III, lived in Jerusalem after Agnes' marriage to Amalric. But, during the first years of the county's existence, the capture of Baldwin II and Joscelin by the Turks had given Tancred, who took charge of its defence, the opportunity to try to keep it for himself.

The counts of Tripoli

Raymond of Saint-Gilles, master of Tortosa by 1102, called himself

Map 5   The county of Edessa

count of Tripoli, but died without having taken the town (1105). His widow left for Toulouse with her young son Alfonso Jordan. His vassals then took as their leader a cousin of his, the count of Cerdagne, William Jordan. But Raymond's eldest son, Bertrand, arrived to `claim the county. King Baldwin I intervened and assembled all the Frankish leaders below Tripoli so they could come to an agreement. Tancred renounced Edessa and the county of Tripoli was divided between the two claimants, William Jordan becoming Tancred's vassal and Bertrand

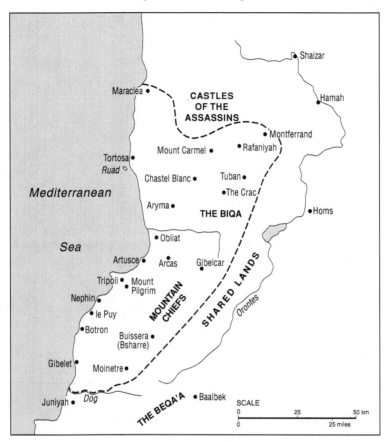

Map 6   The county of Tripoli at its greatest extent

becoming Baldwin's. William Jordan was killed soon after in obscure circumstances and Bertrand occupied Tripoli; Tancred had to abandon the north of the county to Bertrand's son Pons, who became his page and who was to marry his young widow Cecily of France.

When Pons was killed by the Damascenes (1137), Raymond II succeeded him. During the Second Crusade, he had to confront the claims of Alfonso Jordan's son, whom he got rid of by appealing to Nur al-Din. He himself having been murdered by the Assassins (1152), his son Raymond III governed the county till 1187, except for the period 1164–72 when he was a prisoner in Damascus and King Amalric acted as regent. When he died, Raymond left his county (reserving the possibility of a member of his family arriving from Toulouse) to his godson Raymond, son of Bohemond III, who substituted for him his younger son, Bohemond IV. In this case, too, the consequences of war weighed heavily on the county's fortunes; the ransom of Raymond III alone came to 80,000 gold bezants.

A fifth barony might have taken its place on the map of the Latin East, the principality of Galilee. Tancred, after the capture of Jerusalem, had put himself in Godfrey's service. He seems to have occupied Samaria (where the castle of Nablus took the name of 'Tancred's spring'), the land of Tiberias and Bethsan and the lands situated east of the Jordan, perhaps with designs on Damascus, and also Caiphas. By supporting Daimbert, he might have hoped to achieve his independence with regard to whichever prince succeeded Godfrey. He had even founded a Latin convent on Mount Tabor whose abbot claimed the title of metropolitan of all Galilee, a claim briefly recognised by Paschal II. But Baldwin I, responding to the complaints of Galdemar Carpenel, angered by having been deprived of Caiphas, signalled his intention of bringing this over-mighty vassal to heel. Tancred was summoned to Antioch and surrendered his principality to Baldwin, who made haste to divide it up; but, at the Tripoli meeting, the king recognised Tancred's rights to Galilee.

He was never, however, able to exercise them, and the lordship of Tiberias remained a fief of the kingdom of Jerusalem. At most, Count Raymond III of Tripoli, husband of the lady of Tiberias, defied Guy of Lusignan, then king, in 1186–7, but without claiming to repudiate this feudal dependence. It may be remarked that Tancred had with him only eighty knights, perhaps too small a force to found a lasting state.

Regional differences were significant to begin with, but the accidents of succession lessened them. At Antioch, the Poitiers succeeded the Hauteville; at Jerusalem the house of Boulogne was replaced by that of Rethel, and the latter by that of Anjou. Matrimonial ties were soon formed. Baldwin I and Baldwin II both married Armenians when they were rulers of Edessa, and the former, having sent his wife back, obtained the hand of the mother of Roger II of Sicily, from whom he was obliged to separate, since his first wife was still alive; but one daughter of Baldwin II married Bohemond of Antioch, another Raymond II of Tripoli.

Other marriages connected them to the Comnenus family: Baldwin III married Theodora, the emperor's niece. Manuel Comnenus himself married Maria of Antioch, after having allowed the hand of Melisende of

Tripoli to be requested on his behalf, a change of mind which enraged Raymond III, who took his revenge by a raid of pillage into Byzantine territory.

These dynasties of the Latin East raised themselves to the level of the reigning families of the West, even if Amalric, writing to Louis VII, intimated that he had not forgotten that his relatives were the subjects of the king of France. Bohemond and Tancred married Capetians; Tancred's widow married Pons of Tripoli. Above all, the marriage of Melisende of Jerusalem made the kings of Jerusalem a cadet branch of the house of Anjou which was soon to conquer the throne of England. Baldwin III and Amalric were the half-brothers of Geoffrey Plantagenet, and Henry II of England took a keen interest in the fate of his cousins across the seas; in January 1185, when the succession to Baldwin IV was being debated, the patriarch of Jerusalem even went to offer him the keys to Jerusalem and, it has been claimed, the crown for his son John; this seems unlikely, however, since the infant Baldwin V had already been placed on the throne.

FEUDALISM OR FEUDALISMS?

Created at the turn of the eleventh and twelfth centuries, the Frankish states of Outremer were inevitably constructed according to the feudal model then prevailing in the West. But western feudalism was changing, in the direction of a strengthening of ties of dependence, in particular as a result of the introduction of liege homage and the obligations attached to it. There were also significant differences between regions. Feudalism had not developed in the same way in the lands of the Normans, in Capetian France, in the Mediterranean Midi and in the countries of the Empire, and the institutions they each exported to the East were not identical.

There was no link between the four political formations deriving from their origins; the four territories took shape, as a product of circumstances and in the light of possibilities, independently of each other. Nor were they attached to foreign powers outside the Latin East; they were threatened only by the rights claimed by the Byzantine empire.

The patriarch Daimbert had, admittedly, succeeded in obtaining the homage of Godfrey of Bouillon and also that of Bohemond, which might have formed the basis for a patriarchal claim of rights of suzerainty over all the Latin states. But the patriarchate in question was that of Jerusalem and it would have been difficult to assert its preeminence in the face of a patriarchate of Antioch revived in favour of a Latin patriarch. It has been argued that Daimbert, papal legate as well as patriarch, was acting as representative of the Holy See, and that the homage in question made the two Frankish leaders vassals of the pope. But there is no evidence that the papacy ever claimed a suzerainty of this type. In 1128 Honorius II certainly confirmed to Baldwin II the 'dignity' that Baldwin I had received from Honorius' predecessor Paschal II, but this dignity was not the crown of Jerusalem; it was the prerogative of restoring bishoprics within his kingdom, and a prerogative that Urban II had already conferred on Roger of Sicily. The king of Jerusalem was no more the vassal of the Holy See than were the prince of Antioch or the counts of Edessa or Tripoli.

The four states were created independently of each other; none of them had grounds for claiming a feudal preeminence over the others. The case of Edessa, nevertheless, presents a problem: Baldwin I, when accepting the crown of Jerusalem, left the county to Baldwin II, and he to Joscelin of Courtenay; it is possible that Baldwin II and Joscelin on this occasion did homage to the new king. But above all, when, in 1104, Baldwin of Bourcq and Joscelin were captured by the Turks, the Edessenes asked Tancred to assure their defence. When, in 1108, Baldwin was freed, the Norman prince agreed to pay his ransom and re-equip him, but he meant to restore Edessa to him only if he did homage. The county of Edessa would thus have become a feudal dependence of Antioch, which was in line with the attempts of the princes of that town to revive to their advantage, territorially speaking, the old Byzantine duchy of Antioch. Baldwin refused and resorted to arms; in the end, it was Baldwin I who, in 1109, having summoned the Frankish leaders to Tripoli to resolve their differences, persuaded Tancred to renounce his claims, at the same time agreeing to stop supporting those of William Jordan to Tripoli.

In the case of Tripoli, Bertrand of Saint-Gilles did homage to the king, and William to Tancred. Did this entail feudal dependence on the part of the former as regards Jerusalem, and of the latter as regards Antioch? It does not seem, however, that the county was held as a fief from the king; the count was his vassal by personal title. In the case of Antioch, Count Pons behaved like a vassal, in particular when he supported Princess Alice against the king. He probably held the castles of Arzghan and Chastel Rouge of the prince, which Tancred had given to his wife Cecily, later remarried to Pons, on their marriage; but it is not clear whether the same was true of the Crac, which Tancred left him. The feudal situation of the county of Tripoli remains obscure.

In the case of Antioch, the reverses suffered by the princes led the kings of Jerusalem to intervene, beginning with Baldwin II after the Field of Blood (1119); they exercised a hegemony which enabled them to control the princely succession, while conferring on them the obligation to go to the principality's aid in times of danger. It is quite possible that a homage sanctioned this position of preeminence, the prince holding a piece of land or a rent as a fief of the king.

In fact, the Frankish states constituted four lands practically independent of each other, but the king of Jerusalem was able to secure a preeminent authority which enabled him to frustrate the aspirations of the princesses of Antioch to rule their land themselves, and to crush the rebellion of Pons of Tripoli in 1122. The king was also obliged to assume responsibility for the defence of the principality and the counties when they were in danger, without prospect of gain for himself or for his own barons, who sometimes made their discontent at this plain.

We see this independence in the fact that each of these lands had its own law. The *Assises de Jérusalem*, that is, the corpus of customs and legislative provisions governing the kingdom, were not the same as the *Assises de Tripoli*, known to us only by name, or the *Assises de Antioche*, which have survived in an Armenian adaptation. But we are very far from understanding the profound differences between the law of each state. It is possible that the custom of Tripoli recognised the existence of noble lands not held in fief, that is, allods, as was often the case in southern France; Norman features can be detected in the institutions of Antioch. Overall, however, the feudalism of the four states was governed by very similar rules.

The county of Edessa was in one respect unique. Here, the Franks had been appealed to by the Armenians, who hoped to make use of them to drive back the Turks. But the Armenian leaders had to let the Franks take pride of place, often giving them their daughters in marriage. Masters of the chief fortresses and playing a dominant role in the county as a whole, the Franks had initially left places like Kaisun, Raban, Khoros, Bira and Samosata to Armenian lords. But the first defeats had led them to doubt their loyalty, and they had been gradually dispossessed in favour of Franks, though the practice of mixed marriages had created bonds between them thanks to which the Armenians continued to occupy a position of some importance in the county.

Elsewhere, non-Frankish elements were less prominent. They were found in the domestic entourage of the princes; the king of Jerusalem had a chamberlain who was a Turkish convert by the name of Baldwin. A few knights seem to have been Greeks or Armenians, and there were lords of villages with Arab names. But they remained exceptions; the ruling aristocracy was composed of Franks. They are found close to the kings, the princes, the counts and the barons, where they performed the duties of the great officers who reproduced the model customary in the West: a seneschal, the king's lieutenant; a constable who commanded the army; a marshal whose role was both military and administrative, since he was responsible for both the stable and the provision of mounts for the knights, it being usual to replace their horses if they had been lost in the king's service (the *restor*).

There were non-Franks in the central government, however, in the offices which managed the finances and which stored the grants of the *diwan* (the latter held the cadastre, or land register). This service was given the name of *Secrète*, inherited from the Byzantines; it kept a record of grants and changes of fiefs.

The *Fonde* and the *Chaine*, which collected the taxes on merchants and gave judgement in their lawsuits, also had their 'Saracen scribes'. The drawing up of deeds, often written in Arabic, also required the use of scribes versed in this language. The administration of the royal, princely or comital demesne employed eastern Christians, perhaps even Muslims.

It was this demesne which provided the king and the rulers of the other states with the means to feed and support their entourage and, on occasion, to hire *soudoyers* (paid soldiers) to reinforce their army. The private resources of the sovereign allowed him to grant 'fiefs in bezants', that is cash rents, to knights who owed him the same services as those who had been granted landed fiefs. The demesne comprised towns, fortresses, guarded by a castellan paid by the sovereign, and villages and fiscal rights. Thus the king of Jerusalem was lord of Jerusalem, Tyre and Acre; at the beginning of the twelfth century, he was also lord of Jaffa and Nablus, which he later enfeoffed to vassals. Jaffa became the seat of a county granted to Hugh of Le Puiset, from whom it was confiscated in 1132, then to the brother of Baldwin III, Amalric, and lastly to the husband of Sibylla of Jerusalem, Guy of Lusignan. Nablus was returned to the royal demesne when the king gave in exchange for it to Philip of Milly the various territories which constituted the important lordship of Montreal and Oultrejourdain. Amalric was able to restore Beirut to his demesne by exchanging it for the small lordship of Blanchegarde.

The feudal map of the Frankish states was thus not fixed. Vassals might hold their fiefs by hereditary title, but the powers of the sovereigns allowed them to exploit the rules of feudal law to their own advantage, recovering possession of the lands of an insubordinate vassal, or exerting pressure by a variety of means; in order to acquire Beirut, it is claimed, Amalric prevented its lord, a prisoner of the Muslims, from raising the sum necessary for his ransom.

But the fiefs played an essential role in the survival of the Frankish states, and it was not in the interests of the leaders of these states to weaken their vassals. The occupation of the land was based on a system of fortifications whose surviving remains are vivid witness to the fact that they assured the permanence of the Frankish regime. The crusaders, who were accustomed in the West to base their authority on the possession of castles, found in the East fortresses of Byzantine or Arab origin which they renovated, completed and strengthened, and they built an impressive number of new castles, some large, others quite small. Fortresses like Margat and the Crac des Chevaliers, which still stand today, attest to the progress of their skill in fortification. We know less of the human and financial means that enabled such constructions to be built; with regard to the fortification of Kaisun, Michael the Syrian wrote that Baldwin of Marash 'made the yoke weigh heavily on the Christians, to the point of turning them into slaves', suggesting that the population was subjected to forced labour.

The system of fortifications of the kingdom of Jerusalem began to fill out in 1099–1100, with the building of the walls of Jaffa, which were to frustrate Egyptian offensives from Ascalon. To keep the garrison of Ascalon at bay, Chastel Hernault was built at great speed, and later Ibelin, Blanchegarde and Bethgibelin. Baldwin I built Montreal to control the Wadi al-Araba, the great valley which extends the Dead Sea in the direction of the Gulf of Aqaba. Kerak (the Crac of Moab) was the centre of the system of fortifications that covered the land of Oultrejourdain and which included, in particular, the castle of Ahamant, the modern Amman. Belvoir and Bethsan were built along the Jordan; access to Galilee was defended by Saphet and La Fève; Beaufort dominated the valley of the Litani and the first passes of the Lebanon, Chastel Neuf and Subeibe the upper valley of the Jordan. Other fortresses had only an ephemeral existence, such as Qasr Bardawil ('Baldwin's castle'), razed to the ground by the atabeg Tughtekin almost as soon as it was built, and the chastellet of Jacob's Ford, destroyed by Saladin after he had slaughtered its garrison.

To the north, the Tripolitanian castles of Moinetre and Gibelcar defended the passes of the Lebanon, the Crat – later the Crac des Chevaliers – and Montferrand commanded the approaches to the valley of the Nahr el-Kebir; Safitha (Chastel Blanc), Tortosa and Maraclea were closer to the coast. In the principality of Antioch, after the fall of the fortresses of the region of Apamea, it was on Margat (Marqab) and Saone (Sahyun) that the defence of the region of Latakia was based. The interior, too, was dotted with fortresses of lesser importance. Some had been built to blockade towns whose conquest was awaited, such as Mont Pèlerin, from which Raymond of Saint-Gilles conducted the siege of Tripoli, and Toron, which overlooked Tyre.

Each castle was the centre of a territory which supplied it with foodstuffs and which provided the lord with the rents from which he drew his financial resources, enabling him to maintain a garrison of knights. In the West, these knights mostly lived in the surrounding countryside, where they had their houses alongside those of their dependent tenants, and took it in turns to guard the castle. In the Latin East, though a few fortified manor houses where such lesser lords may have lived have been discovered, the vast majority lived permanently in the seigneurial castle, while collecting the rents from the village where they had their fief. Defensive necessities were seemingly more constricting here than in the West.

The masters of the great fortresses often had several castles to defend, and the monarchy sometimes found it useful to constitute these into large commands. King Amalric granted to Philip of Milly the lordships of Oultrejourdain (Kerak), Montreal and Hebron (St Abraham) to form a single block covering the whole south-east of the kingdom. It was to prove dangerous in the time of Reynald of Châtillon.

The lords of these great fiefs were able to stand up to their suzerains, even to impose their views on them. There were rebellions: that of Roman of Le Puy, lord of Oultrejourdain, against Baldwin II; that of Hugh of Le Puiset, count of Jaffa, allied to the former and perhaps mouthpiece for the opposition of certain barons to King Fulk, against whom he appealed to the Muslims. We may also quote, though with few known details, that of Gerard of Sidon which has been related to acts of piracy committed by him and which culminated in collusion with Nur al-Din; but this was seen by the jurists of the thirteenth century as originating in a conflict between Gerard and one of his vassals who had appealed to the king. Guy of Lusignan, deprived by Baldwin IV of hopes of his succession, took up arms against the king, and Raymond III of Tripoli, summoned by Guy to account for his conduct as regent of the kingdom, refused to obey the summons and made contact with Saladin. At Antioch, Bohemond III clashed with some of his barons who had sided with the patriarch he had molested (1181). Such revolts on the part of powerful barons who did not hesitate to seek the aid of Muslim princes endangered the Frankish states. The other lords and the rebels' vassals, conscious of this danger, seem to have acted to limit the consequences.

Baldwin II had taken drastic measures against such rebellions, providing for the possibility of the king confiscating without further ado the fiefs of the barons who rebelled or who failed to respect the rights of the crown. This *Establissement de Baudoin de Borc* has been much debated, but its existence seems hardly open to doubt. Amalric, after the rebellion of the sire of Sidon, promulgated an *Assise sur la ligece* which was designed to assure the king the loyalty of his rear-vassals and of the burgesses of the fortified town in the case of a revolt by their lord; he recognised the right of vassals to 'conspire' if their lord claimed to deprive them of their fief without a judgement. But this right was also recognised for the vassals of the king and might lessen the impact of Baldwin II's ordinance. It remains the case that by demanding from each member of the feudal hierarchy a homage attaching him directly to the person of the king, Amalric strengthened royal power.

So the monarchy was strong, and the king could make the rules of feudal law work to his advantage. But pressure by the vassals enabled them to lessen some of their rigour; initially, the king could marry the daughter of one of his deceased vassals to a person of his choice; the liege men obtained an agreement that the heiress should be offered a choice between three candidates of the same social rank as her own. Seigneurial arbitrary power was further limited by the marriages which united the members of the great families, allowing the concentration of inheritances and favouring the cohesion of 'lineages'. A family of relatively obscure origins, the Ibelin, was able gradually to rise to the first rank: Balian II of Ibelin even married Queen Maria Comnena, widow of Baldwin III.

The Frankish nobility of the East proved little different from that of the West. Though it was sometimes necessary to reinforce its ranks by conferring knighthood on the sons of burgesses or sergeants, it remained attached to the notion of noble blood transmitted hereditarily. The higher category, that of the lords of castles, was recruited from families of equivalent rank in the West. It even seems that certain families, especially in Tripoli, formed the habit of dispatching a member of their family to the East when one of their relatives there died without heirs. But we should not forget that this nobility suffered from terrible bloodlettings. This was the case in 1119 for the principality of Antioch, in 1104 for the county of Edessa, and in 1132 for that of Tripoli. The kingdom of Jerusalem had the good fortune to avoid such losses until 1187.

The feudal system on the Western model seemed very different to the easterners from anything they knew. That a warrior aristocracy should concentrate all powers in its own hands, in accord with the form of decentralisation of government accepted in the West since Carolingian times, greatly astonished the emir Usama ibn Munqidh, himself from a good Arab family; he remarked that, whereas in the East all that was demanded of a knight was that he know how to manage his horse and his weapons, the Frankish knights were expected even to administer justice. He had seen how things were done at the royal court when visiting it to present grievances to King Fulk. The king summoned a group of knights, instructed them to investigate the complaint and prepare a judgement, and gave orders for its execution. For the Muslim, it was for men of the law to pass judgement.

The Latin East was a true province of feudal Europe. The division of the land into fiefs, each of which remunerated the service of a vassal who came to the aid of his lord both to administer justice and to defend his lordship; the creation of territorial units round fortresses each of which housed one of the groups of warriors which together comprised the royal army; the granting of all the powers of government to the masters of these castles; the tie of personal loyalty that bound each of these men to the sovereign: all were characteristic features of this structure. It had its weaknesses; the lord could only be sure of the cooperation of his vassals if he kept his commitments to them, and rebellions were possible. But it also had the undeniable advantage of great flexibility, especially when it came to the defence of territory. In the twelfth century, thanks to a sufficient landed base, the feudal regime was able to do what was necessary to maintain Frankish domination.

A COLONIAL SOCIETY

We who were Occidentals have now become Orientals. He who was a Roman or a Frank is here a Galilean or a Palestinian. He who was once a Rémois or Chartrain has now become a citizen of Tyre or of Antioch. We have already forgotten the places where we were born; for many of us, they are unknown, or we have never even heard tell of them. Some of us possess houses and servants as by natural and hereditary right; another has taken as his wife not a compatriot but a Syrian or an Armenian, or even a Saracen who has received the grace of baptism. Yet another has by him a father-in-law, a mother-in-law, a son-in-law, a stepson or a stepfather; another has a nephew or a great-nephew; some own vines, others fields. Everyone uses different languages in turn, and a foreign language that has become common is known to every nation, faith uniting those who are ignorant of their race ... He who was a stranger here is now a native ... Our dependants and our relatives daily follow us, leaving all their possessions behind and losing all interest in them. Those who were poor there, God has made rich here. He who had a few pennies possesses bezants without number; he who held not even a village now by God's grace enjoys a town. Why should anyone return to the West who has found an Orient so desirable?

This famous passage from Fulcher of Chartres testifies to the development overseas of a whole society originating in the West and now settled in the East, where it had forged family ties and where its members had prospered. Admittedly, the author here mixes nobles and non-nobles, and he emphasises the interpenetration of the Franks and the eastern Christians. But his text suggests the formation in the Frankish states of a Frankish society comprising all the levels it had comprised in its country of origin.

It was the crusade that had produced this colonial population. Among those who had followed the barons, the knights constituted only a minority. Medieval armies included a considerable proportion of sergeants, on foot or mounted, who assisted the knights in battle and served them between battles. There were servants and valets who performed the mundane duties about the camps, taking up arms on occasion to repel looters without being, properly speaking, combatants; and there were pilgrims following the expedition without belonging to it; many westerners had reached Antioch or Jerusalem or some other destination in the footsteps of the warriors. And many of them were to remain where they were, for lack of means to return home, or because they continued to serve those they had followed, or even because to prolong their stay close to the Holy Sepulchre satisfied their religious aspirations. Others followed in their footsteps. Fulcher of Chartres warns us not to underestimate the appeal exercised by an East where there were places to be taken, land to be exploited and wealth to be acquired close at hand for those who wanted to improve their lot.

Very soon, we find the word 'bourgeois', and this even responds to a military necessity; the defence of the occupied towns could not be left to the knights alone, and the indigenous Christians who often accounted for the majority of the population, at least in the regions previously Byzantine, did not appear to the Franks to be endowed with the warlike qualities required by this defensive duty. But the needs of the knights and of the other Franks belonging to the military or religious personnel of the new states necessitated the presence of merchants and artisans, among whom the westerners found a place similar to the one that they had occupied in their native country.

This settlement did not happen all at once. The occupation of Jerusalem, in particular, took many years. The city, emptied by the Egyptians of its Christian inhabitants, who took time to return, and by the crusaders of its Jewish and Muslim inhabitants, is described as almost deserted, the new arrivals occupying scarcely more than one street and insecurity reigning in the still uninhabited spaces. But twenty years after the crusade, the situation had changed. Bourgeois of Jerusalem engaged in commercial activities and trades similar to those of the 'Syrians'; prominent among them were goldsmiths, money changers and minters. John of Wurzburg, around 1165, refers to Frenchmen, Lorrainers, Normans, Provençals, Auvergnats, Italians, Spaniards and Burgundians, while regretting that the Germans had not formed themselves into a group; we know also of Hungarians. And the town seems by then to have had a large Frankish population, which provided a contingent of sergeants for the royal army; these bourgeois enjoyed rights that can be compared to franchises; their juries sat in the royal court presided over by the viscount of Jerusalem, and their tenures, known as 'burgess tenures', were normally burdened with a money rent paid to the lord responsible for each quarter.

Similar Frankish colonies were found in all the towns conquered by the crusaders; the Frankish bourgeois had their own law, administered by a court composed of juries chosen from among them; they were required to come to the defence of the town and to provide sergeants for the royal, princely or comital army; as we have seen, Amalric demanded an oath of loyalty to the king from them to forestall rebellions.

But it was not only a question of installing a population 'of the law of Rome' (that is, Catholic) in Antioch, Tripoli, Latakia, Edessa, Turbessel, Jaffa, Nablus, etc. The influx of settlers was on such a scale as to produce in the Latin East a phenomenon well known in the West at that time, that is, the birth of 'new towns'. A whole group of villages was established on the lands of the Holy Sepulchre, near Jerusalem, the most important of which took the name of Mahumeria, probably after an ancient mosque.

As in the West, these new foundations received grants of franchises. Thus the Hospitallers, to attract inhabitants to Bethgibelin, where they had built a castle, granted a true charter of liberties. A 'promoter' took on the job of setting a population at Casal Imbert, offering new arrivals favourable terms of settlement. It is even possible to detect relationships between these charters, that of one of these localities serving as a model for others.

This wave of colonisation, which seems to have found favourable ground in the East thanks to the low density of population, is an aspect of the expansion experienced by the West in the twelfth and thirteenth centuries and which scattered Flemish, Frisian and German colonies from England to the Baltic, as well as producing many settlements in Spain, France and Germany. But it had a particular character in the East, as is shown by the preference of the settlers for the kingdom of Jerusalem; religious motives played a part, and those who settled in these new villages – and archaeological surveys are currently adding to their number – must often have originally been pilgrims.

This colonial society was not purely agricultural and there were commercial as well as religious motives. One of the peculiar features of the Frankish states was the presence of the colonies of the mercantile towns, in particular those of Genoa, Pisa and Venice. Other merchants came from other maritime cities, from Saint-Gilles and Narbonne and from the towns of the kingdom of Sicily, but their settlement was of a different type. This is explained by the circumstances in which the nationals of these three towns joined the crusades. As we have seen, these were maritime enterprises which required the fitting out of fleets and the involvement of urban authorities – of the prelates, of the 'captains' and of the merchants who invested in the building and equipping of the ships. It was the 'commune' that negotiated with the Eastern Franks, as it negotiated with the Byzantines or with Muslim princes, wherever it sought to obtain commercial privileges.

By the month of July 1098, the Genoese who had participated in the siege of Antioch had obtained from Bohemond, as a result of their 'prowess', the grant of a church, dedicated to St John, a *fondaco* (what in the East was called a *khan*, that is, a collection of shops surrounding a central court, put at the disposal of the merchants), a well and thirteen houses. It was a modest quarter, but it was the first collective property of a community represented by the cathedral of St Laurence (just as the donations to Pisa and to Venice were made in the name of St Peter and of St Mark) and intended for the use of merchants. And, in proportion to the services rendered by the Genoese to the princes of Antioch, these privileges increased; Genoa owned quarters and collected rents in Latakia, St Simeon and Mamistra, and enjoyed tax exemptions.

In the kingdom of Jerusalem, the Genoese took part in the capture of the Holy City and, for a long time, an inscription in letters of gold recalled this at the Holy Sepulchre. But others arrived and obtained concessions, which usually consisted of a third of the cities conquered with their assistance and the grant of a *fondaco*, a church and its dependencies elsewhere. This was the case with the Pisans, who had arrived with Daimbert, and with the Venetians. The share-out by which they acquired this third applied also to booty: at Caesarea, in 1104, the Genoese were very conscious of this, and it was then that they appropriated the precious vase which, believed to be the Holy Grail, was carried back to Genoa. For these sailors, such conquests resembled raids of pillage, but the communal authorities were anxious to secure permanent establishments. To acquire Tripoli, Bertrand negotiated with the Genoese, promising them a third of the city, a neighbouring castle, and the extension of what his father had given them at Gibelet.

The most important of these concessions was made at Tyre; here, the Venetians had obtained from the patriarch Gormond and the barons the promise of a third of the town, which they were to hold in full sovereignty, and of its dependencies. Freed from captivity, Baldwin II reduced the scale of this concession; Venice retained the third of the lordship, but on condition that it was held in homage to the king (1124–5).

The reality was more limited; the maritime towns which had acquired these embryonic autonomous trading posts, with rights of justice, tax exemptions and all the equipment of a quarter, including bath, mill, well and oven, exempt from the *banalités* owed to the lord, even, as in the case of the Venetians at Tyre, the use of Venetian rather than local measures, had to come to terms with the Frankish powers; the whole history of these trading posts in the twelfth century is one of claims, lawsuits and falsifications of documents which cast doubt on the scope of the first privileges.

Above all, the communes were unable to enjoy everything they had been granted. The trade generated by the Frankish towns failed to live up to expectations. The principal purpose of the maritime traffic with the Latin East was then the transport of pilgrims and probably also already of basic foodstuffs from Italy (dried fruits and corn). But the precious fabrics, spices and other oriental products were found essentially at Alexandria and Constantinople, and the trade routes which made Antioch, Tripoli, Tyre and Acre into markets capable of attracting trade in valuable merchandise were only gradually established. The ships that carried the pilgrims then set sail for Cyprus and, from there, for the Egyptian and Byzantine ports; it was scarcely possible to make use of all the *fondachi* originally provided for.

These Italian quarters were therefore urban territories in which only colonies of very limited size lived all year round, with much larger groups arriving for the period between the 'spring passage' and the 'autumn passage'. The communal authorities were represented by judicial officers, sometimes called 'consul and viscount', who administered justice in the internal affairs of their community, and who ensured that their fiscal privileges were respected, in particular that exemption from right of wreck which was supposed to prevent the lords from appropriating goods thrown overboard when a vessel was lost; the emir Usama reveals that, on occasion, a shipwreck was caused so as to benefit from these profits, he himself claiming to have been a victim of one on the part of King Amalric.

But this administration was expensive and Genoa decided in 1154 to grant its possessions in Latakia, Gibelet, Antioch and Acre on a twenty-nine-year lease to members of the Embriaco family. The Embriaco of Gibelet – probably already established in the town – eventually failed to pay their rent to the commune and behaved as vassals of the count of Tripoli. At Tyre, the rural possessions of the commune, which represented in principle a third of the lordship, were in the hands of the Contarini, who were also vassals, of the king.

The extra-territorial nature of the quarters of the 'communes' had its implications for housing; at Acre, non-Franks were forbidden to live in the streets between the market and the port, so that transactions would not escape payment of the taxes from which the inhabitants of the Genoese, Pisan and Venetian streets were exempt. This did not, however, prevent the natives of these maritime towns, and of other towns which had obtained privileges, though less far-reaching, from being integrated into the life of Frankish society. And by stimulating the mercantile economy, they contributed to its prosperity, and to that of the people of other origins who inhabited the Frankish towns; it was thanks to them that many foodstuffs such as sugar, soap and various fabrics found markets in the West.

No picture of the Frankish society of the Latin East would be complete that did not include that other equally temporary element, the pilgrims, who probably numbered several thousand each year. We know very little about some of them, those who travelled overland, and who probably included the poorest, who could not afford the cost of the sea passage. They are rarely mentioned, except when they accompanied a crusade that itself followed the route of the First Crusade, but we know that a hospital was reserved for them in Constantinople and that they were still to be found on the roads of Seljuk Turkey in the thirteenth century. The majority of pilgrims seem to have travelled by sea, leaving from the ports of Italy or Languedoc; we know that Genoa claimed to limit the transport of pilgrims by the ships of Narbonne to one vessel a year. Large fleets might be involved; storms caused the loss of many ships, for example in 1102, off Jaffa, watched by the English pilgrim Saewulf. The timing of the voyages depended on the conditions of navigation in the Mediterranean; ships left southern Italy, especially Bari, or Venice or the Tyrrhenian ports in the spring, and returned in the autumn, which meant a stay of several months in the East. This influx of pilgrims, to which we will return, had its consequences for the Frankish states. The ports had to be equipped to receive them, by sheltering them from pirates, which necessitated several galleys to be in a position to intervene if need be. The pilgrims had to be provided with lodgings, fed and cared for; special bodies were created, organised along the same lines as ecclesiastical institutions.

Not all these pilgrims were poor. The story of the pilgrimage of the duke of Saxony, Henry the Lion, in 1171, is instructive; a great lord, he enriched with his donations the sanctuaries he visited, and he was received by the great men of the kingdom. The duke of Hungary,

preparing to set out on a pilgrimage with his wife, around 1168, sent a
sum of 10,000 bezants to the Hospitallers to be used to buy land and
casals near Jerusalem, the revenues from which would support them
during their stay, and which they would then leave in the ownership of
the Hospital. But, in the absence of well-situated villages and lands, they
had to be content with estates close to the castle of Emmaus, or at Acre,
with the 'palace' bought by the Hospitallers from Gerald of Conilz with
four houses, an orchard and a *casal* close to the town. This noble pilgrim
clearly intended to maintain his lordly lifestyle during his stay. The
religious establishments would also benefit from his journey.

The king of Jerusalem himself did not hesitate to levy a tax on
pilgrims; the texts relating to the rights of the Venetians at Tyre refer to a
tax of a third on the price of the passage for the ships carrying them. The
pilgrims provided a livelihood for the local traders. Opposite the Holy
Sepulchre was the rue des Paumiers which was where they could buy
the palms that were the sign that they had completed their pilgrimage
and which earned them the name of 'palmers'. We are reminded of the
souvenir sellers who haunt places of pilgrimage today.

And the pilgrims could be very useful to the Franks; it was wise to
await the arrival of the 'passage' before embarking on military operations,
as pilgrims could use the time remaining to them after visiting the Holy
Places to enter the service of the princes and share in the defence of the
kingdom, receiving a wage that was very welcome; a list of the services
due from the royal vassals stipulated for one of them to provide the
service of a 'pilgrim knight'.

The pilgrims were not, therefore, a foreign body within the Frankish
states; they participated in their life and their presence gave a peculiar
character to the colonial society they temporarily reinforced.

EASTERNERS WITHIN THE FRANKISH STATES

The Frankish society established overseas was, as we have seen, made up
of very diverse groups, nobles and non-nobles, peoples of different
languages and origins, permanent and temporary residents. But these
different elements had fused into a coherent synthesis. The Franks might
form the backbone of these new states ruled by them, but this rule
extended to a whole mosaic of communities that can together be
described as eastern, without attempting to disguise the fact that the term
in reality encompasses very heterogeneous elements. Personal statuses,
national identities, customs and benefits differed; and the letter written in
September 1098 by the leaders of the crusade shows that they had soon
realised this.

Nor should we forget the regional variations; in the north, in the mountains of the Taurus, the crusaders found Armenian lordships that had only recently passed under Turkish rule; the mountain tribes of the Lebanon represented another type of occupation; on the edge of the desert, the routes followed by the Bedouin tribes overlapped with Frankish territory. The Islamisation of the Syrian peoples had not progressed uniformly; nor had it entailed a profound transformation of agrarian structures. The towns had been more affected by the successive occupations.

Generally speaking, the basic structure was that of the village, which, in the Byzantine system, constituted a fiscal unit, which continued under Islam. The Franks introduced the feudal system, with the transfer of state rights to the lord to whom the land was enfeoffed. But the village, which the Franks called the *casal*, retained its characteristics. It was surrounded by *gastina*, which might be landed reserves at the disposal of the village, or hamlets. Responsibility for the village lay with a group of notables, chief of whom were the *ra'is*, who performed the role of leaders of the community. Alongside them, but in the same social group, were men who served as intermediaries between the lord and the inhabitants, regarded by the former as seigneurial officials, who enjoyed concessions analogous to the 'fiefs in sergeanty'; they included the indispensable dragoman, who acted as interpreter, the scribe and the official who supervised the allocation of water and looked after the irrigation channels. In fact, the village administered itself, the *ra'is*, responsible for the collection of taxes under the previous system, assuming rural police functions with the aid of the village assembly. It was the *Cour du Ra'is* which judged village disputes according to local custom, which derived essentially from Romano-Byzantine law. The Franks were careful not to interfere with this traditional organisation, which was integrated into the feudal lordship. In the vast majority of cases, the *casal* as a whole was granted as a fief, the enfeoffed knight receiving the totality of the revenues. The manorial system, where the lord lived off his estate, cultivating his own land by the labour services he demanded from his tenants, who themselves had their gardens, orchards and fields, was practically unknown in the Syrian East, with the exception of the sugar-cane plantations, found especially near Tripoli, or other cultures of this type, where the labour force was often servile.

The villager was primarily obliged to hand over part of his crop according to a system, the Arab *kharaj*, itself inherited from the Roman and Byzantine land tax; the part seems usually to have been one third. It might be replaced by a fixed rent, paid in money. Fruit trees, especially olive trees, were also liable to a levy of a proportion of their crop. A series of taxes, such as the right of *tuage* demanded of anyone who killed a pig, completed the rents. They appeared modest to a Muslim traveller, Ibn Jubayr, compared with those found in the other Mediterranean countries.

The condition of these peasants can be compared to that of the serfs in the West – men who were free but subject to seigneurial constraints, in particular the prohibition on leaving the lordship. Muslims had to pay a head-tax. This has been seen as a measure of reprisal for the levy of a poll tax on the *dhimmi* in Muslim lands, but it was also in force in Byzantine lands, and corresponded to the chevage characteristic of western serfdom. It is unclear whether the Franks also demanded it of their Christian subjects. *Mainmorte* seems not to have been practised in the East, although it is possible that lords seized escheated property. The term *vilain*, which was used for the villagers in the East, was perhaps not exactly synonymous with serf. Nevertheless – and here again we find situations similar to those in the West – the Franks were careful to ensure that their estates were exploited to a degree that provided for their towns and castles and allowed them to trade in agricultural surpluses. They organised, therefore, the recolonisation of abandoned lands, as, for example, when the construction of the castle of Gaza restored security to southern Philistia. To ensure the provisioning of Jerusalem, Baldwin II not only exempted from taxes at the town gates the Christian and Muslim villagers who supplied the city's market, but he appealed to the Christian inhabitants of the lands of Oultrejourdain which remained under Muslim rule by offering them liberties if they would settle in Judaea.

The Muslim princes did not demand armed service from their Christian subjects. Nor, probably, did the Franks of their Muslim subjects, even though, at the end of the thirteenth century, the princes of Antioch were accused of having employed Saracens in their armed conflicts with a prelate of the county of Tripoli. On the other hand, the use of 'Syrians' in the Frankish armies is well attested, especially in those of the county of Tripoli, in addition to the Christian archers from the mountains of Gibelet – Maronites – employed by the lord of that town. We observe here the extension to the Latin East of that right to resort to the armed service of the people of their land, in particular for *chevauchées* which were local wars, enjoyed by lords in the West.

There were easterners serving in the Frankish armies, namely the 'turcopoles', probably introduced into the service of the Franks when Taticius left his soldiers to the leaders of the crusade. They were Turks recruited essentially from the prisoners who had converted to Christianity, often bearing Latin names (those of their godfathers, who were

Frankish knights). Wearing light armour and armed in the Turkish fashion (with lighter lances), they constituted a body of light cavalry that harassed the enemy. They received tenures very similar to fiefs and formed a sort of domestic guard of warriors; they were found in the service of the military orders, of convents and of lords. They completed the defensive system of the Frankish states and were the counterparts of the Frankish renegades such as the Provençals who defended one of the towers of Sidon when it was besieged by the Franks in 1108.

The situation in the towns was in many ways very different. Here, the 'Syrians' and the Saracens were in contact with the Franks. For the former, this contact soon became familiarity. The picture we are given of Jerusalem shows Franks and Syrians as in principle each established in their own quarter. The 'Syrian Exchange' was separate from the 'Latin Exchange'; Latin drapers did not sell in the same street as Syrian drapers, less in order to separate the 'nations' than to facilitate the application of different fiscal and juridical systems. In the streets, adjacent houses belonged to owners with Frankish and Greek or Arab names. Fulcher of Chartres refers to the mixed marriages which might give a Frankish settler Syrian in-laws, and to the way they each used the other's languages. The wealth of some bourgeois Syrians, such as the Saïs of Tripoli who lent Guy of Lusignan the money he needed to acquire the lordship of Cyprus, might be greater than that of their Frankish homologues.

But complete integration was precluded by the fact that Frankish Syria lived under a system of laws according to person – as did the kingdom of Sicily until Frederick II. The Frankish bourgeois came under the court of the viscount, served by juries chosen from among their number; the Melchite or Jacobite bourgeois came under either the *Cour du Ra'is*, purely eastern in its composition, or under a mixed jurisdiction (because competent in commercial matters), the *Cour de la Fonde*, which had four Syrian and two Frankish jurors. The law that was applied was not the same. The law of the Muslims was different again; they came under other jurisdictions.

As a general rule, the urban Syrians were regarded as being of free status (and they took advantage of this when they settled in Cyprus). At Antioch, the influence of the Melchites was particularly strong and the princes were very attentive to them. As we have seen, in 1193 Greeks and Latins there made common cause against the threat of an Armenian take-over. In contrast, in the principality of Edessa, it was the Armenians who were in a majority.

The definition of these different communities was based on con-fessional adherence. Here, the Franks were careful to avoid wounding the sensibilities of the various groups. On occasion, they seized property belonging to the religious establishments of one or other rite. This was the case with those of the Jacobite bishopric of Jerusalem, whose holder had left for Egypt at the crusaders' approach; the Franks appropriated the villages of his estate, which made a knight's fief. The prelate returned, whereas the knight disappeared, which made it easier to restore the villages to the Jacobite community. But the knight eventually reappeared after a long captivity and Queen Melisende had to seek a compromise that would reconcile the rights of each party; in the end, the Jacobites remained in possession of their property. A scandal erupted at Edessa when Joscelin II, to punish the monks of St Barsauma for their alleged collusion with the Turks, seized the monastery's property. He was careful to have recourse to a priest before taking possession of the sacred objects, but the Jacobites saw the defeat which deprived him of his liberty as a just punishment for this sacrilege. The easterners readily accused the Franks of greed, and the latter were indeed quick to resort to confiscations at their expense. But we should remember that this was hardly a new phenomenon in the East.

Respect for the sanctuaries of the other confessions was, however, one of the dominant characteristics of Frankish behaviour. They felt a spontaneous reverence for the saints honoured by the easterners and for their sanctuaries, invoking them and showering gifts on them. We know that a Frankish knight of Antioch, after a miraculous cure obtained through the intercession of St Barsauma, who was the object of particular veneration on the part of the Jacobites, built a church in Antioch in his honour, which was consecrated by the patriarch of the Syrians. Eastern monasteries remained numerous; the Greek traveller John Phocas noted those that were built in the twelfth century; the great monastic ensembles of the Black Mountain, near Antioch, and those which surrounded Jerusalem, like St Sabas or the Holy Cross of the Georgians, and, most of all, Sinai, enjoyed exceptional prosperity. The pontifical bull granted by the pope in 1216 to St Theodosius, 'Cenobiarch of Berrie' (the desert of Judaea), shows that this convent owned temporalities comparable to those of the richest Latin monasteries. The situation was similar for the Armenians and the Syrians.

In the case of the Muslims, we need to distinguish between the time of conquest and their later situation within the Frankish states. During the conquest, they suffered badly. The capture of the fortified towns entailed violence and massacres, some of which have been described in lavish detail, for Jerusalem, Ma'arrat, Caiphas or Beirut among others. When a town was stormed, such excesses were sadly only too common. It was also sometimes the case that capitulations negotiated by those under siege, assuring them of safety in more or less generous conditions (the right to leave the town freely, for example, or to remain on condition of accepting Frankish rule), were not respected, the Frankish leaders being disobeyed by their troops. Where the conquest was peaceful, the Franks left the existing population alone, as at Nablus.

The capture of a town, or the taking of prisoners on the battlefield, was for the Muslims who fell into Frankish hands likely to mean being held to ransom or reduced to slavery; King Amalric gave the knights of St Lazarus one slave in ten of those comprising his share of the booty 'on condition he was not a knight', prisoners of knightly rank normally being ransomed. Slavery, which had fallen out of use in the West, was rediscovered by the Franks in the East, and they put a high value on a servile labour force. King Amalric, with the conquest of Egypt in mind, reminded the Hospitallers that it was forbidden to deprive a Christian of his liberty. Slavery could therefore apply only to Muslims. This raised the question of what was to be done with those slaves who converted to the Christian faith. The Church recommended that they should be freed and this was, it seems, initially the attitude of the crusaders; a bond persisted, nevertheless, between the freed slave, the *batié* (baptised one), and his former master, similar to that which had existed in Antiquity and also in the Islamic world. Arrangements were made for this in the *Assises de Jérusalem*. But there were soon complaints about the attitude of masters reluctant to lose their labour force as a consequence of conversions. The popes intervened to urge that no obstacles be put in the way of such conversions; it has, however, to be accepted that baptism did not automatically entail enfranchisement.

Only those who had been taken fighting, whether on the battlefield or in a fortress that had not opened its gates, all the inhabitants of both sexes being in this case considered as having taken part in the defence, could be reduced to slavery. Of the women captured in Caesarea, conquered in 1104, the historian tells us that 'beautiful or ugly, they had to turn the grindstone of the mills', that is, they became domestic slaves. Unlike Christian women taken captive, they usually escaped concubinage, which was forbidden by the councils, in particular by that of Nablus in 1120.

But the vast majority of Muslims agreed to submit to the new rulers, in particular the rural population, largely Muslim in many areas. The Franks had every incentive to keep them where they were, since they assured the cultivation of the conquered territories. In Samaria, in particular, the traditional population remained as it had been before the conquest, which had the inconvenience that the peasants from this region, when the Muslims gained the upper hand (in 1113 and in 1187), fell on the Frankish establishments to pillage them; and, according to Ibn Jubayr, the Muslim villagers of the hinterland of Tyre helped captives of their religion to escape. Nevertheless, the Franks respected local customs and status, except perhaps for the introduction of the poll tax, if indeed it was imposed systematically on the Muslim subjects of their estates.

In the towns, the Muslims were usually in a minority. They nevertheless constituted a bourgeoisie. At Tyre, for example, there was a '*ra'is* of the Saracens', who was called Sadi, in 1181. At about the same date, a merchant by the name of Abu Ali obtained from King Baldwin IV a safe-conduct to take a ship to Egypt. Ibn Jubayr visited the Muslims of this town, who seem to have been living in peace.

Freedom of worship for Muslims was the rule, but many mosques were converted into churches; many of them had, of course, originally been churches converted into mosques. Here and there, for example in Tyre and Acre, mosques or oratories are mentioned. Public summonses to prayer were probably forbidden, since they constituted affirmations of the sovereignty of Islam. There are references, however, in the Nablus region, to gatherings of peasants for public prayer. In this region, too, we see a Hanbali group, between 1156 and 1173, decide to leave for Damascus to escape Christian rule. But religious identity was recognised; before the courts, Muslims were allowed to testify by an oath on the Koran. In the twelfth century, we see little attempt made to convert Saracens. The emir Usama, who travelled in the kingdom of Jerusalem in his capacity as ambassador, was even allowed to pray in the al-Aqsa mosque, although it had been turned into a church, at the invitation of the Templars.

The nomadic Bedouins were a special case; they continued to roam with their flocks over their territory along their traditional routes, retaining their tribal organisation. Regarded as serfs, they were in principle attached to a lordship whose lord gave them his protection in return for payment of rent; their tents, with the families they sheltered, might be the subject of grants and exchanges. Their way of life led them, however, to drive their flocks across frontier zones, at the risk of being targeted by razzias. We even see the turcopoles of Bethgibelin, in the service of the Hospitallers, make raids on the Bedouins of the Templars. But these same Bedouins did not hesitate to make themselves the accomplices of the Franks to assist them in raids of pillage or in operations directed against their co-religionists.

The situation of the Jews was not exceptional. Expelled from Jerusalem in 1099, they sometimes returned there, and Benjamin of Tudela, who visited the town in the second half of the twelfth century, found several Jewish craftsmen there. They were found in other towns, for example in Latakia, where a deed shows them alongside Latins, Greeks and Armenians whose tenures – and the tenants – were the subject of a grant at the same time as theirs.

Easterners might mix even with Franks of the ruling class. A seigneurial family which owned many *casals* in Philistia, the Arrabiti, could trace its lineage back to a Musa who was regarded as a knight and who had been forced to sell his *casals*, with the agreement of the lord of his fief, to pay a ransom. His descendants seem to merge with the Frankish nobility. Similarly, in the kingdom of Jerusalem, an Armenian is called a knight, as are some Greeks. In the county of Edessa, many Armenians had seigneurial status. And a story, sadly unverifiable, has it that a king of Jerusalem entertained a project designed to attract to his kingdom Armenian warriors to whom tenures would be granted, though we cannot know whether these would have been true fiefs. The scheme failed because the Latin clergy wished to make them pay tithes, which, in practice, applied to all lordships, whatever the confessional adherence of their holders.

The subjection of the easterners to Frankish rule left the Franks with the power and their non-Frankish subjects with their own customs and law, and some areas remained outside Frankish power. The mountainous regions of the kingdom of Jerusalem, the county of Tripoli and the lands of Antioch and Edessa lent themselves to the preservation of such autonomy. Mountain clans made the kingdom insecure until after 1120, and Baldwin I was wounded in the course of pacification operations conducted in the mountains of Judaea. On the borders of Galilee, the valley of the Bouquiau served as a hideout for raiders who often cut the roads. By means of a military operation they were driven back into the territory of Damascus, before 1180; in the end, King Baldwin IV captured them during one of their raids. In the mountainous hinterland of Tyre, Sidon and Beirut, an Arab clan held the fortified cave, the Cave de Tyron (Tirun Niha), recognising both the Franks and the Turks of Damascus, until around 1130. The Bohtor emirs of the Gharb and Maan of the Schuf came under the principality of Damascus, but made agreements with the Franks, who regarded their principal haunts as coming under their sovereignty; it was around 1160 that the Franks of Beirut seized many of these, by means of an ambush, from the Bohtor. In the Lebanese mountains, the Melchite or Maronite *ra'is* held their villages or groups of villages under the authority of the counts of Tripoli or the lords of Gibelet, but with a very high degree of autonomy; it was probably one of them who was supposed to have betrayed Count Pons in 1136–7, and his fortified cave was given by Raymond II to the lord of the Crac in exchange for his fortress.

Further to the north, it was the Ismailis, the Assassins of our texts, those Shi'i who practised the murder of princes to retain their independence, who formed, largely at the expense of the Franks, what amounted to a principality around the castles of Masyaf and Qadmus, in the hinterland of Margat and Maraclea. The payment of tribute to the Frankish lords, the Hospitallers and the Templars assured their security, and the Franks occasionally protected them from the greed of their Muslim neighbours.

Further north still were the Armenian barons of the Mountains, holding the impregnable castles of the Taurus chain (Vahka, etc.), who had for a while moved in the orbit of Antioch; the Byzantines had subjugated them in the time of John Comnenus, but they had escaped a forced residence in Constantinople and, not content with recovering their eyries, had taken advantage of the differences between Franks and Byzantines to occupy the plain of Cilicia, which they had made into a Little Armenia, though with close links to the Latins of the East.

A whole fringe of 'Syrian', Arab and Armenian lordships formed a sort of buffer zone between the Muslims of the East and the Franks of the West. The Franks might regard them as coming under their sovereignty, because they paid tributes disguised as rents or did homage; the Latin Church even considered them as potentially liable to the payment of tithe, as forming part of the Latin kingdom. Their autonomy, which enabled them to play one off against the other, remained, nevertheless, real.

This diversity of statuses, which allowed the dependence of the easterners on the Frankish masters of the Latin states to take different forms, was another peculiarity of these states. They might call themselves Latin by reason of another characteristic, namely the establishment of the Latin Church.

THE FRANKISH STATES AND THE LATIN CHURCH

The ethnic and religious diversity of the lands which passed under Frankish rule makes it difficult to measure statistically the predominance of any one element in the Frankish states as a whole. At most we may note the features specific to each region: Jacobite Armenians and Syrians were probably most numerous in the county of Edessa and probably also in Cilicia; Melchites of Greek obedience in and around Antioch and in various coastal and mountainous districts, both in the Lebanon and Palestine, and Maronites in a large part of the Lebanese mountains – to note only the Christians. Muslims of various types were found everywhere, but in greatly varying numbers. The Franks were nowhere numerically preponderant within this mosaic, but they were everywhere supreme in the possession of political power. In the ecclesiastical domain, this was expressed in the preeminence of the Church to which they belonged, that which came under the see of Rome. To define 'Frank', legal texts used the expression 'of the law of Rome'. And, as conceived by medieval Christianity, whether eastern or western, it was the Church to which the politically dominant element belonged that should have priority in the structures of the state. Byzantium had set the example, in both its eastern territories, in contact with Syrians and Armenians, and in the West, where the bishops of Southern Italy had been attached to Constantinople.

Is it appropriate to use the expression 'established Church', reminiscent of the status of the Church of England in modern Britain, in relation to the ecclesiastical structure of the Frankish East? It probably is, since the decision taken in 1120 by the Nablus *parlement*, also called a council because prelates took part, gave the Latin Church an essential prerogative, that is, the right to levy tithes throughout the kingdom of Jerusalem. This assembly was held at a time when the Franks were feeling the precariousness of their power and had only recently suffered various calamities. They were anxious, therefore, to avert the wrath of God, to the extent that it was the cause of this difficult situation. Among the measures taken to achieve a moral recovery was the recognition by the king, the barons and the 'terriers' of the kingdom of the right of the Latin bishops to collect tithes. This was not, as in France, by a levy of a percentage on harvests, in practice rarely equivalent to a tenth, which operated at the level of each tenant, but by a levy on the totality of seigneurial revenues. Whatever the personal status of the lord, who might be a Greek monastery, a Latin religious establishment, an Armenian, a Maronite, a Melchite, or even a Muslim, with seigneurial rights over a *casal*, it was he who was required to deliver to the Latin bishop of his diocese a tenth of his income; various accommodations, of course, were possible.

This basic principle gives the impression that the whole territory of the Frankish states was divided between the dioceses of the Latin Church. As we have seen, during the crusade bishops had been appointed by the crusaders to occupy cathedral sees, as at Albara, Artesia and Lydda. These appointments started from the fact that these were churches, apparently of cathedral rank, lacking incumbents, and that after having restored them to the service of God it seemed proper to the crusaders to provide them with bishops. But very quickly, between the summer of 1098 and the end of 1099, the situation was regularised, and an episcopal hierarchy was put in place. One threat had to be lifted, that of the presence of Greek prelates legitimately exercising their authority in the context of these dioceses. Here and there, it had been possible to take advantage of their absence, temporary or permanent; in Jerusalem, for example, the Greek patriarch had left shortly before the arrival of the crusaders, whom he may have joined at the time of the siege of Antioch. Elsewhere, the victorious Turks had probably driven into exile Greek prelates who incarnated the authority of the Byzantine emperor. At Antioch, the crusaders had restored the Greek patriarch to his see, in the cathedral church previously converted into a mosque, and had treated him with great respect. But Bohemond, when he decided to eliminate all trace of imperial authority over Antioch, obliged the patriarch John V to resign and leave for Constantinople, where Alexius Comnenus quickly confirmed him in his patriarchal dignity. As a general rule, however, where bishops of the Greek rite remained in possession of their cathedrals (where these had not been systematically transformed into mosques), the Latins took possession of them by installing bishops of their own rite.

It was still necessary to take account of realities. The episcopal organisation of the Byzantine period was well known, thanks to the *notices*, whose Latin translations survive. The new episcopal hierarchy restored by the crusaders accounted for only some of the preexisting sees. In the county of Tripoli, only three bishoprics were reinstated (Tripoli, Gibelet and Tortosa) where there had been at least seven according to the *Notice* of the metropolitan province of Phoenicia. Towns abandoned or of secondary importance were attached to one of those where the episcopal title had been maintained: thus Botrys, Arcas and Orthosias, for example, episcopal cities reduced to little more than large villages, were merged into the bishopric of Tripoli.

The Franks considered that a bishop should enjoy a situation worthy of his rank. A bishop, therefore, was provided with an endowment comprising, with the cathedral, property in his episcopal town, shops, houses and gardens forming a quarter, villages in his diocese of which he was lord and from which he collected rents, and churches and chapels to which he might appoint the priest (though not make them over, in return for a rent, to eastern Christians). Finally, he had the right to collect tithes throughout the diocese. This was laid down in the bull of 1183 confirming the rights of the bishop of Beirut.

This restoration of churches, which may be seen as an essential element in Urban II's programme, was carried out in the old patriarchate of Antioch on a fairly regular basis. Archbishops took possession of sees previously occupied by other archbishops (Tarsus, Mamistra, Apamea and Edessa), even if these sees were transferred to what were now more important towns (that of Doliche was established at Turbessel); bishops took over those of the episcopal sees which had been revived.

In the kingdom of Jerusalem, the situation was different, for two specific reasons. The first was the incoherence of the *Notice* of the patriarchate of Jerusalem, swollen by the exertions of a patriarch anxious to enhance the importance of his see by inserting after the name of each metropolitan an impressive number of localities, some of which had never had bishops, and many of which, in any case, had disappeared during the long Muslim occupation. The second was a consequence of the crucial role played by pilgrimage in the kingdom. It was because the great church of Lydda, with its associations with St George, had been found intact that, in June 1099, this deserted town had been made the seat of the first bishopric restored in Palestine, even though Jerusalem was still in Muslim hands.

At first, the Franks entrusted the Holy Sepulchre to a patriarch. The election of Arnulf of Choques was undeniably irregular and, using his powers as legate, Daimbert had him deposed without difficulty less than six months later. But, having enjoyed the support of the Normans against King Baldwin, Daimbert was deposed in his turn, to be replaced by Evremar. A new legate deposed Evremar and was then made patriarch. Finally, Arnulf regained possession of the patriarchal see, but in the meantime, with the title of archdeacon, he had in practice ruled the Church of Jerusalem and retained the confidence of King Baldwin. It seems likely that he played an important role in the construction of the episcopal hierarchy in his patriarchate.

The three Palestines of ancient geography, with their metropolitans of Caesarea, Scythopolis and Petra, were not immediately revived. The archiepiscopal see of Caesarea was restored by 1101 and it fell to Evremar when he was deprived of the patriarchate (1108). In Galilee, however, the title of archbishop was at first given to the abbot of Mount Tabor, regarded as the site of the Transfiguration; the appointment in 1109 of a bishop of Nazareth – home of the Holy Family – provoked a conflict that was eventually resolved in favour of the newcomer, who in 1128 had the archiepiscopal see of Scythopolis transferred to Nazareth. Like Nazareth, Bethlehem – scene of the Nativity – had not been the seat of a bishopric before 1099 when it was raised to this rank, though it was not until 1110 that the pope transferred to it the see of Ascalon. It was the places most venerated by the pilgrims that were chosen to receive bishoprics. The kings of Jerusalem and their patriarchs, unlike in Antioch, seem to have wished to build their church with regard essentially to the veneration attaching to the great sites distinguished by events reported in the Gospels, paying little heed to the traditional map of provinces and cities.

This seems not to have caused any problems with the papacy. But things changed when Baldwin I, having seized Beirut and Sidon, and planning the occupation of Tyre (1110–11), meant to appoint there two bishops and an archbishop who would be subordinate to the patriarchate of Jerusalem. This was no longer Palestine but Phoenicia, and this country lay within the traditional sphere of the patriarchate of Antioch. The patriarch of this town protested; the conflict dragged on, all the more so after the restoration of the see of Tyre, in 1124, had further embittered the situation. Antioch argued that the division between the patriarchates had been decided in ancient times and that there was no justification for this drastic reduction in its sphere of authority. Jerusalem argued on the basis of a decision of the council of Clermont to the effect that, when diocesan circumscriptions were lost, each prince should be able to choose the towns in which bishoprics would be placed; this was a decision which, as R. Hiestand has recently shown, did not apply to the countries to be conquered by the crusaders, but repeated a measure passed by Urban II in favour of Roger of Sicily. It was further mentioned that Adhémar of Monteil had fixed the Nahr el-Kebir as the frontier between the two patriarchates, which was obviously pure invention. The pope could not decide who to support. Then, after 1124, the archbishop of Tyre intervened in his turn to request the restoration of his province, since the Tripolitanian bishoprics which traditionally belonged to Tyre had been restored before that town was taken and had been attached to Antioch. The papacy accepted his arguments, but the patriarch of Antioch stood firm.

Jerusalem had succeeded in annexing the bishoprics of the province of Tyre situated to the south of the frontier of the county of Tripoli; Antioch lost Tyre, but retained its authority over the Tripolitanian bishoprics. Then, in 1168, it was decided to revive, in Oultrejourdain, the see of Kerak, which the Franks erroneously identified with Petra (it was called *Petra Deserti*, 'the Stone of the Desert'). Petra was the archbishopric of Palestine III; the patriarchs of Antioch claimed that Kerak formed part of the province of Arabia, whose capital was Bosra, and which belonged to their see. This caused another dispute, which dragged on after the loss of these towns by the Franks.

The year 1168 saw the creation of three new episcopal sees: with Kerak, they were Hebron (the tomb of the Patriarchs) and Sebastia (the tomb of St John the Baptist). Here, too, it was the veneration of the places of pilgrimage that determined the choice of site.

Thus, in the south of Lebanon, the ecclesiastical map was drawn on a different basis from that in the north. Less weight was given to meeting the needs of the religious life of the faithful than to catering for the pilgrims. Each episcopal see was also the residence of a cathedral chapter which served the great church; pilgrims found there an imposing liturgical service, which sometimes preceded the establishment of a bishopric; Sebastia and Hebron were endowed with chapters before receiving bishops.

We know very little about how the parishes were served; it is likely that each castle and each new town with a Latin population had its priest. Outside the towns, the number of parishes seems to have been few. But our documentation is very incomplete.

The life of these dioceses and patriarchates was sometimes stormy. There were conflicts between the patriarchs and the sovereigns. Rome was forced to intervene, in particular when the patriarch Radulph of Domfront quarrelled with Prince Bohemond II, although he had helped to put him on his throne. The papal legate took advantage of this dispute to take action against the claims of Radulph and his predecessor Bernard of Valence, who seem to have wanted to exploit the fact that their cathedral, too, had been the seat of the Throne of St Peter, to demonstrate a degree of independence as regards Rome. Radulph was deposed by the council that met in Antioch in 1140.

The councils that were held in the East on the arrival of papal legates were not intended only to solve problems internal to the Latin clergy. They also considered the situation of the eastern Churches.

The question put to Urban II in September 1098 had never been answered. Rome had given instructions neither to its legates nor to the faithful regarding the attitude to be adopted towards the eastern communities. The princes had quickly understood that the loyalty of their Christian subjects of the eastern Churches was linked to a respect for their customs and their ecclesiastical hierarchies. The Latin prelates had sometimes taken it upon themselves to arbitrate in the disputes that arose within these communities, where personal rivalries were rife, and the princes had sometimes had to moderate their initiatives. But overall, the Latin patriarchs and bishops had accepted the coexistence of Eastern prelates on whom the whole ecclesiastical hierarchy of their respective communities depended. The case of the patriarch of the Jacobites, Michael the Syrian, is particularly noteworthy; he was treated on equal terms by the patriarch of Antioch, Aimery of Limoges, who even received him in his cathedral church. The Jacobite metropolitan of Edessa enjoyed generally friendly relations with the Frankish counts, and it was in the Latin cathedral of Turbessel that the election of the Jacobite patriarch was held, in 1130. The clergy had contacts with each other and, on occasion, debated theological and liturgical questions; the Syrians of Jerusalem asked for the help of the bishop of Amida, Denys bar-Salibi, who wrote for them a treatise on the mass to reply to the arguments of the Franks (1169). Aimery even suggested to Michael the Syrian that he accompany him in 1179 to the Lateran Council; his Jacobite homologue drew up for the benefit of the Latins a treatise against the Manicheans to assist them in their battle against the Cathar heresy.

More difficult to resolve is the question of relations between Rome and the Greek Church, since, despite the schism of 1054, the two Churches regarded themselves as professing the same faith, and therefore bound by the canon of the council of Sardica prohibiting the coexistence of two bishops in the same see. Further, it was at the expense of the Greeks that the Latins took possession of some great churches, and, when the Byzantines reoccupied a town occupied by the Franks, as at Tarsus or Mamistra, they expelled the Latin prelates from the cathedrals. The substitution of Latin patriarchs for Greek patriarchs at Antioch and Jerusalem was also a source of tension, as much political as ecclesiastical in nature; in fact, the emperors were less worried by the presence of a Latin patriarch in the see of Jerusalem than in that of Antioch. The *basileus*, whenever he had the upper hand, forced the prince of Antioch to restore his patriarch in the cathedral of that town.

In practice, compromise solutions were fairly quickly worked out. There could be no question of subordinating the Melchite clergy to a Latin bishop who conferred investitures or ordinations. An indirect method was therefore found; since many episcopal sees were brought together in one diocese entrusted to a Latin bishop, the Greeks gave the title of one of these sees, not occupied by the Latin, to one of them, who became the leader of the Greek clergy for the whole diocese. From the canonical point of view, he was regarded as the vicar for the Greeks of the Latin bishop, to whom he probably swore loyalty without submitting to his authority.

Other solutions were found. In the Holy Sepulchre in Jerusalem, which was served by a chapter of Latin canons, there existed a Greek clergy which served the same sanctuary, and which obeyed an archbishop of Gaza and Eleutheropolis, who had every appearance of being the Greek prelate of the patriarchal diocese. In Edessa, on the eve of the conquest of 1144, there were four archbishops with their cathedrals: that of Saints Mary, Thaddeus and George for the Latins, St Sophia for the Greeks and the Melchites, St Euphemia for the Armenians and St Abraham for the Jacobites. Could co-existence be more complete?

No doubt some reservations were felt. The Latins regarded themselves as bound by the word of Christ urging his disciples to remain united, and they could imagine this union only under the crozier of the successor of Peter. The easterners were anxious to preserve their identity based on a particular Christology. The Greeks hoped for union to follow the negotiations conducted between Rome and Constantinople. In the case of the other confessions, talks proceeded at the local level.

The council held at Jerusalem in 1141 by the papal legate had been an opportunity for him to invite the patriarchs and *catholicos* of the Syrians, the Armenians and probably also the Maronites. They had all sent the legate professions of faith affirming their unity of doctrine and their respect for pontifical primacy. These were no more, perhaps, than pure formalities but, at least for the Armenians and the Maronites, there was progress towards a more real union. In moments of crisis, this showed itself at grass-roots level. On Holy Saturday 1101 the sacred flame failed to ignite in the Holy Sepulchre. The Christians of the various rites united in one procession and in one common prayer to procure the enactment of what was regarded as a miracle, and it was Fulcher of Chartres who delivered the sermon. The pilgrims, finally, visited the sanctuaries without worrying too much about who was responsible for them. There were even Muslim pilgrims, like Ali al-Harawi, who travelled through the kingdom of the Franks visiting the holy places of his faith, including the tomb of Abraham at Hebron, where he heard how the Franks had searched for the exact site of the sepulchre of the Father of the faithful, which served to deepen his veneration.

A RELIGIOUS LIFE AND ITS ORIGINAL FEATURES

The kingdom of Jerusalem had a particular association with pilgrimage because it was at its ports that pilgrims normally landed to visit a group of sanctuaries situated within its frontiers. But the northern states, too, were involved; throughout the twelfth century, the route through Byzantine territory, even when it had become Turkish, and through Antioch, was still used by pilgrims and it was hoped to see it freed of its obstacles. Antioch, Edessa and Tripoli were, as it were, annexes and access roads to the kingdom that constituted more precisely the Holy Land. And these lands were redolent with Christian history; was it not at Antioch that the name of 'Christians' had appeared, and at Edessa that, for the first time, a king had declared himself a Christian?

The religious life of the Frankish states was therefore bound to take account of pilgrimage. The pilgrims, when they arrived in the Holy Land, wanted to share in the liturgy specific to each of the holy places they visited. It was therefore essential for there to be clergy attached to these and, with westerners of the Latin rite arriving in large numbers, it

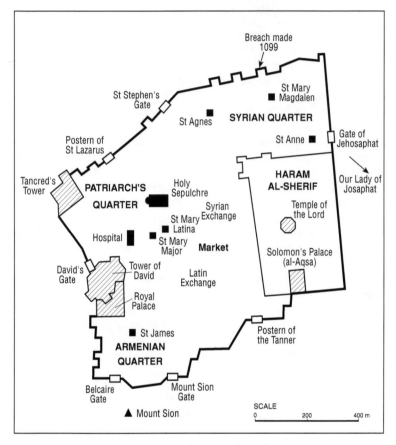

Map 7   Jerusalem at the time of the crusaders (after Fathers Vincent
and Abel)

seemed necessary to provide them with the services they wished to
attend. In the sanctuaries themselves, the Latins often established
themselves by replacing priests of the Greek or Melchite rite, but more
often it was by associating with them. In the Holy Sepulchre, for
example, the Latins held services in the choir, the Greeks at a nearby
altar. The Latins formed a chapter here, which was created very soon
after the occupation of Jerusalem, each canon enjoying a prebend drawn
from the revenues of the Holy Sepulchre. These revenues often derived
from donations made before the crusades, coming as often from the East
(in particular from Georgia) as from the West. The crusade naturally

stimulated new donations and, in the East, Godfrey of Bouillon granted the canons, with the church of St Peter of Jaffa, some twenty villages close to Jerusalem; the count of Toulouse founded a priory of the Holy Sepulchre on Mont Pèlerin with the grant of landed property. The chapter, well endowed, was ruled by dignitaries who were also provided with prebends.

It was within the chapters that the young clergy received their training; as a result, they attracted masters, such as the future cardinal, John of Pisa, first teacher of William of Tyre and, according to Hans Mayer, the scholar in charge of the cathedral school of the Holy Sepulchre. William himself refers to many learned men among the clergy of the Latin East. The chapters also encouraged an intellectual life, attested most notably by the treatise of Rorgo Fretel on the Holy Places and the hagiographical works of Gerard of Nazareth, to be followed by the *Historia transmarina* of the future archbishop of Tyre. But these learned clerics were not only familiar with the Latin language; some of them were in contact with their eastern homologues; the cantor Anceau, who sent a relic of the True Cross to Notre Dame in Paris, acquired it from the Georgians. William of Tyre used the work of an eastern Christian to write his *History of the eastern princes*. And at Tripoli, an important intellectual centre for the eastern Churches, the clerk Philip of Tripoli translated from Arabic a pseudo-Aristotelian text, *The Book of the Secret of Secrets*, which was widely read in the West where it provided the material for the moral treatises known as 'Mirrors of princes'; at Antioch, Stephen of Pisa translated the great medical treatise of al-Majusi. The chapter libraries probably owned other similar works but their almost total disappearance leaves us ignorant on this point.

The secular chapters did not enjoy as much prestige among the faithful as those that adopted the rule of St Augustine, which brought the way of life of the canons closer to that of the monks. William of Tyre, who had no love for the patriarch Arnulf, accused him of having forced the canons of the Holy Sepulchre to adopt this rule so that he could appropriate the estate of Jericho as a dowry for his niece. But transformations of this type were common in the West at this period, and the cathedral chapter of Jerusalem was not the only one to become a chapter of regular canons; the same happened at Bethlehem and at Tripoli. This rule was also that adopted in the sanctuaries that the pilgrims venerated most in Jerusalem, for example the Temple of the Lord, which replaced the mosque of Omar, where Godfrey installed canons, and Mount Sion and the Mount of Olives. The sanctuary of the latter was in 1100 entrusted to a Latin priest, and it was probably he who became head of the chapter instituted soon after. Outside Jerusalem, there were regular canons at Hebron and Sebastia. The Augustinian rule was well suited to the service of these sanctuaries of pilgrimage, assuring the regularity of the liturgy and causing it to be celebrated by religious practising the common life and renouncing personal property, according to the ideal of the time. It may also have been adopted in a sanctuary known only from its ruins and from a seal: the Table of Christ, on Lake Tiberias, where the mission of the apostles Peter and Andrew was commemorated.

The Benedictine monasteries were not necessarily founded on the precise sites with major Gospel and Bible connections. St Mary Latina, an Amalfitan foundation of the eleventh century, was close to the Holy Sepulchre, as was the nunnery of St Mary Major. But Benedictines were also established close to the Tomb of Our Lady (St Mary of Josaphat), and nuns of the same order near the Tomb of St Anne, site of the convent of St Anne, where Baldwin I put his wife Arda when he had to separate from her. Some forty years later, a new abbey for women was founded at Bethany, probably an extension of Fontevrault, by King Fulk; the queen's youngest sister, Joetta, soon became its abbess; this site was associated with the Resurrection of Lazarus. Latin monasteries were less numerous away from Judaea. Mount Tabor had a Benedictine house alongside a Greek monastery. At Antioch, the great monastery of St Paul was also Benedictine; the presence of monastic communities in association with the great lordships should come as no surprise.

What is more surprising is how slow the great congregations of the new monasticism were in deciding to establish themselves in the Latin East. It may be that their leaders hesitated to found abbeys too far away to participate in the life of the order; St Bernard did not want a foundation in Palestine. The Cistercians were only established there in 1157, at Belmont, above Tripoli, and in 1161 at Salvatio, in the kingdom of Jerusalem; the Premonstratensians at St Habakkuk of Ramla and St Samuel of Mountjoy (1161).

In fact, as we know only from the recent discovery of extracts from a hagiographical work by Gerard of Nazareth, the movement which had given birth to these orders was quite widely represented in the East. It was pilgrims from the West, above all, who wanted to end their days in the Promised Land. A wealthy western baron, Radulph, became a hermit in Jerusalem, as did Gerard himself on Mount Tabor; a Hungarian built his cell on the walls of the Holy City so that he could contemplate it; many were attracted by a great centre of eremitical life in the eastern tradition, the Black Mountain, near Antioch. Like the western founders, they were seeking a way of life that conformed to their ideal, spending some time in a community, trying to live according to the rule of St Benedict in all its rigour, in the manner of the Cistercians. A whole world of souls longing for both solitude and regularity in asceticism founded houses, such as Machanath, Jubin, Carraria and Palmarea, without constituting what could be called an organised order. Some eventually joined an obedience: that of Cluny in the case of Palmarea, and, later, that of Cîteaux in the case of Jubin. The first Carmelites have been seen as part of this trend, but they seem not to have appeared before the last years of the twelfth century.

These religious houses seem largely to have drawn their recruits from outside the Frankish states, whose locally born population could hardly have provided the religious for all these communities. Those whose lives were described came mostly from the West, and some returned after a longer or shorter stay in the East. For many of them, the religious life of the Latin states of the East was bound up with pilgrimage and the veneration of the Holy Places.

The Franks encouraged pilgrimage and provided assistance to pilgrims in another way. We know very little of the origin of the first texts drawn up for their use, anonymously, to which their first editors gave the generic name of *Innominatus*. Other texts were written in the mid-twelfth century by pilgrims returning from their long journey, such as Theodoric or John of Wurzburg. But it was a Frank from the Holy Land, Rorgo Fretel of Nazareth, who, around 1148, produced the first of these pilgrim guides to adopt a systematic form, giving information about itineraries, distances, notable sites and the memories attached to them, continuing the tradition of the books devoted by St Jerome to the identification of the Holy Places.

Equipped with a guide, the pilgrims could take to the road. These, when the Franks arrived, were far from safe; we are told of brigands hiding in caves in order to pounce on travellers. And raids were mounted from territory in Muslim hands like those which, from Tyre and Ascalon in 1120, were directed against seven hundred pilgrims, killing three hundred and capturing sixty; nor should we forget those who were taken prisoner when their ships were wrecked on the coast or seized by pirates. These dangers led a group of knights, probably in 1119, to band together to provide an escort for pilgrims. The exact circumstances of this development have been much debated. It appears that some of the knights had come on a pilgrimage and entered for a period the service of the Holy Sepulchre, among them the future King Fulk of Anjou. But those who joined together at the instigation of Hugh of Payns and Geoffrey of St Omer laid the foundations of a new religious order which took the name of the Temple of Solomon (the former mosque al-Aqsa and its dependencies) which was given to them by King Baldwin II as their residence. The early days of the new order are shrouded in obscurity. But Hugh of Payns succeeded in getting it recognised as an institution of the Church and its rule accepted; it is said to have been written by St Bernard at the time of the council of Troyes of 1128.

Soon after, while Hugh was still in the West recruiting knights and building up a landed estate that would provide the wealth necessary to support them, a crisis erupted, some of the knights indicating their preference for the contemplative life. Hugh was obliged to remind them of their vocation and St Bernard wrote his *In praise of the new knighthood* to acclaim the merits of a life devoted to the protection of others and the defence of the Holy Places.

To receive the pilgrims it was necessary to establish a support system, in particular to accommodate the poor and tend the sick. The Hospital of St John, founded some forty years before the crusade and continuing to function throughout it, experienced rapid growth; its autonomy with regard to the chapter of the Holy Sepulchre was maintained, while in Bethlehem and Nazareth congregations of Hospitallers emerged under the patronage of the canons. The numbers of sick cared for in the Hospital at Jerusalem, which also received those wounded in battle, and the volume of the provisions and medicaments it required, attest to the importance of this institution, which occupied a whole block near to the Holy Sepulchre. Donations poured in, in the Latin East and in the West, to finance this establishment, which gradually took over most of the hospitals founded in the Frankish states.

The Temple was military in origin; the Hospital became military in conditions that are obscure, probably between 1130 and 1140. It has been suggested that, like the Templars, the Hospitallers recruited paid knights to protect the pilgrims. What is certain is that, when some of their lands, like Bethgibelin, were fortified so as to be incorporated into the kingdom's defensive system, they were required to ensure their defence. And the men of knightly family who put themselves at the service of the poor were obliged to take up arms to join the royal host. In any case, even before the Second Crusade, Hospitallers and Templars seemed like two military orders. When, in 1142 or 1144, the count of Tripoli granted the whole fortified ensemble of which the Crac was centrepiece to the Hospitallers, before, in 1152, abandoning Tortosa to the Templars, the vocation of the two orders was well established. And as the dangers increased and as the numbers of the military nobility proved insufficient, kings, princes and counts began to regard the knights of the two orders as an indispensable adjunct; one, furthermore, that was self-renewing thanks to the recruitment practised by the two orders in the West, where they had landed estates that enabled them to meet their financial needs in the East. This even encouraged delusions: the master of the Hospital, Gilbert of Assailly, believed he could make his order participate in the conquest of Egypt planned by King Amalric in 1168–9, at the cost of heavy investment; the order was brought to the brink of bankruptcy. But the crisis was overcome, and the Temple, like the Hospital, was able to face the catastrophe of 1187 and survive. The Spanish orders produced by the *reconquista* also attempted to establish themselves in the East, in both the principality of Antioch and the kingdom of Jerusalem, where one of them, that of Mountjoy, came into existence. But this tardy intervention was ephemeral. It reveals, however, how the participation of the military orders in defence had become essential.

It was not only pilgrims who were in need of assistance. The Franks encountered in the East an illness which was not unknown in the West but was here on an unexpected scale, that is, leprosy, which afflicted even King Baldwin IV. The disease exacted a heavy toll. It was found necessary to establish an order devoted to the care of lepers, that of St Lazarus, whose convent was at first situated on the road to Jericho, but which, by the end of the twelfth century, was below the walls of Jerusalem. The originality of this order was that it allowed knights suffering from leprosy to serve in the army, in a special contingent reinforced by knights who were 'healthy'. The crusader barons and princes who, like King Louis VII of France in 1148, learned of this order's existence, gave it dependencies in the West. But it was only in the East that the lepers, led by a master who was himself a leper, combined their segregation with participation in the common military effort. The rule of St Augustine was sufficiently flexible to be adapted to their way of life.

The religious life of the Frankish states developed features that distinguished it from that of the West, while remaining essentially within that tradition. It also found expression in a programme of restoration directed in particular at the monumental patrimony that had suffered from centuries of Muslim occupation. The Franks restored and rebuilt in their own style a large number of buildings dating back to Byzantine times. These included cathedrals and abbeys but also many simple priories, often depending on the chapters and monasteries of Jerusalem, served by a few priests or monks, and visited by pilgrims. The great religious houses had spawned these priories, sometimes endowed with parish rights, close to the chief towns and larger villages, and wherever a venerable site attracted a devotion. The most prestigious of these reconstructions was that of the Holy Sepulchre, in which masons, sculptors and painters, some from the West, others from Byzantium, yet others recruited on the spot, participated. The emperor Manuel Comnenus collaborated by making gifts and sending artists. But the cathedrals of Tyre (now lost), Beirut, Lydda and Sebastia, and the priories like that of Abu-Gosh, were sites in which the techniques of Romanesque and Gothic architecture, the artistic trends imported by sculptors in the western tradition, the decorative elements of which the Syrian ornamentalists had long been masters, and the art of the painters to whom we owe the famous icons of Sinai, were all combined. There were also discoveries of holy bodies such as those of Saints Thaddeus and Abgar, found after a vision by Archbishop Benedict of Edessa; at Hebron, the canons of St Abraham explored the crypt to discover the tombs of the patriarchs, thereby responding to the passion of the men of the twelfth century for the veneration of relics.

'Outremer', to give it a name familiar to writers of that age, was an ensemble of great diversity. As we have seen, the northern territories – Antioch and Edessa – differed in many ways from those of the south, and above all from the kingdom of Jerusalem. The former continued to bear the mark of their Byzantine origins and of the traditions of the patriarchate of Antioch. The latter were much influenced by the preeminence of pilgrimage, which ensured them a renewal of their numbers and substantial financial assistance.

To designate this ensemble, the popes frequently used the term *Ecclesia orientalis*, which, having at the time of the First Crusade indicated all the Christians of the East, came to mean more precisely the Latins of the Frankish states. Other ecclesiastical authors spoke of the Promised Land, or of the Holy Land, though well aware that, in the Biblical sense of the term, this applied only to the lands between Dan and Beersheba, so not even to the whole of the kingdom of Jerusalem. Nevertheless, it, the county of Tripoli, the principality of Antioch and even the county of Edessa formed a whole with a real unity.

Antioch and Tripoli protected the road to the Holy Sepulchre. Our texts tell us almost exclusively about the sea passages of pilgrims, but they and the crusaders also used the land route. And when the emperor Manuel Comnenus announced his intention of bringing to an end the Turkish presence in Asia Minor, Pope Alexander III was delighted that he would also, in so doing, free from obstacles the road to the Holy Sepulchre. The northern states were the antechamber of Jerusalem, and also its military cover against the dangers threatening from the north and the east of the Fertile Crescent.

The unity of this Frankish ensemble was apparent in its ecclesiastical structures. That Our Lady of Josaphat should make a prayer association with St Paul of Antioch was typical of the monastic practice in the Middle Ages. But the way so many priories were attached to the Holy Sepulchre and to the communities of Jerusalem, and the granting for their needs of so many rural estates, shows that these lords, established all over the Frankish East after taking the cross for the liberation of the Sepulchre, remained deeply attached to it. Raymond of Saint-Gilles and his successors made donations both to the churches of their native countries, for example in Arles and in Marseilles, and to those of their new conquests. But, around the castle built on Mont Pèlerin, it was a priory of the Holy Sepulchre, a priory of St Mary Latina, a priory of Bethlehem and a dependence of the Hospital that came to represent the ecclesiastical entourage of the capital of the future county of Tripoli. The same was true elsewhere. The 'Holy Land' formed a true human and political reality. There was even a lack of comprehension between new arrivals from the West and those who had been established for two or three generations. When a knight, indignant at seeing Usamah praying by turning towards Mecca in the church of the Templars, took him by the shoulders to make him turn towards the West, the Templars apologised to the emir; the man was, they explained, a newcomer, ignorant of local customs. For the westerners, the Franks of the East were the *poulains*, a term it has been attempted in vain to explain by reference to a mixing of the races. The *poulains* responded by calling the westerners the 'sons of Hernaud', which is, for us, equally sibylline, but which was hardly intended to be friendly.

'Outremer', 'Holy Land', even *regio peregrinorum* in a passage in Albert of Aix, the Frankish East became a 'nation', with the sense of its own individuality within Christendom. A William of Tyre, son of a bourgeois of Jerusalem, educated in the school of the Holy Sepulchre before receiving his university education in the West, who returned to the kingdom to climb the rungs of the ecclesiastical ladder, was well aware of this.

Nevertheless, this nation knew that it was dependent on the help it received from the West. Pilgrimage, a permanent unifying feature, served to make these links material. The Christian of the West, if he could travel to the Holy Land or at least live there in spirit, hoped thereby to recharge the batteries of his religious life. Homeland of those who had been born there and who devoted themselves to its survival, Outremer was also, in the phrase of Albert of Aix, the 'homeland of Christians'. It is this that explains how the latter could devote so much effort to it and make so many sacrifices in its service.

5

FROM THE FIRST TO THE SECOND CRUSADE

By settling in the East, the Franks altered the character of the initiative launched by Urban II and his successor. Having embarked on an enterprise whose initial objectives seem not to have included an indefinitely prolonged effort, they had entered into a long-term commitment: the maintenance under the 'rule of Christ' of a group of territories which by 1102 stretched from the upper valley of the Euphrates to the Dead Sea; and this brought them face to face on the one hand with the Byzantines and their claims, and on the other with Muslim princes who could only be their enemies.

Chief among the latter were the Fatimid caliphs of Cairo, from whom the Franks had taken Jerusalem; we are told that, after the battle of Ascalon, Raymond of Saint-Gilles tried to resume the contacts tentatively established before the seizure of Jerusalem, but this attempt proved abortive. Still masters of the coastal towns, the most southerly of which, Ascalon, was the key to Egypt, the caliphs were doomed to permanent hostility towards the kingdom of Jerusalem.

A grave danger seemed about to materialise when the Almoravid conqueror Yûsuf ibn Tâshfîn, in 1105 or 1106, mounted an expedition with Jerusalem as its goal, but his seventy ships and the thousands of warriors they carried were lost in a storm.

In the north, the situation was more complex. The two Seljuk kings of Damascus and Aleppo, the brothers Duqaq and Ridwan, were on bad terms; they had little inclination to embark on joint action against the Franks. The emirs who held the towns of lesser importance – those of Homs and Shaizar, who were practically independent, and those of Sawad, Baalbek, Bosra, Apamea and the other towns, who were more or less closely bound to these kings by ties of loyalty – had no wish to see the Seljuks gain a foothold in their tiny principalities.

There was more vigour in the dominions founded by Turkoman chiefs beyond the Euphrates; the Danishmends of Cappadocia and the Ortoqids of Upper Jazirah were to prove formidable adversaries for the Franks. But the chief danger lay in the mighty command entrusted by the sultan of Baghdad to the governor of Mosul, a high dignitary of the sultanate who bore the title of atabeg; in 1098 Kerbogha had led a large army to the assistance of Antioch; his successors frequently appeared in Syria with the intention of destroying the Frankish principalities. It was lucky for the Franks that the Seljuk dynasties and their successors in Damascus, the Burid atabegs, the first of whom, Tughtekin, was a formidable enemy of the Franks, viewed these governors with some distrust, fearing their intentions regarding their states, since they represented the authority of the sultan and might wish to put an end to local autonomies.

It was effectively from Mosul that a unification of Syria began at the time of the atabeg Zengi, who succeeded in reuniting Aleppo and Mosul in 1128, as his predecessor, Bursuqi, had briefly done in 1125. Already, some years earlier, the assumption of power in Aleppo by an Ortoqid, Ilghazi, had proved a real danger to the Franks; now, a great Muslim state adjoined their northern frontier. Zengi's son, Nur al-Din, despite leaving Mosul to his brother, pursued a policy of conquest in Muslim Syria which was to culminate, in 1154, in the reunification of Aleppo and Damascus.

Admittedly, the Syrian theatre was not the only one to attract the attention of the masters of Mosul and the emirs of Upper Jazirah; the crises of the Seljuk sultanate of Iran, and the victorious war waged by the Georgians against their Muslim neighbours (and Frankish knights went to the assistance of King David II of Georgia), occasionally distracted them from the Frankish frontier. But, with their establishment on Syrian territory, the situation of the Frankish states changed. The fluctuations of the political map of internal Syria had great influence on their fate, and consequently on the need to appeal for new crusades.

WOULD THERE BE ANOTHER CRUSADE? THE NORTHERN FRANKISH STATES UNTIL 1110

In 1102, when the survivors of the crusade of 1101 returned to Europe, was the crusade regarded as over? It was then that many witnesses to the expedition – a Poitevin priest, a Norman knight, a chaplain from the county of Toulouse – described it, drawing edifying lessons. Others, who had not taken part, like Baudri of Bourgueil and Guibert of Nogent, offered a theological interpretation. For Guibert, in particular,

Map 8   'Bella Antiochena': the frontier between the principality of
Antioch and Aleppo

the crusade was a new route to salvation offered to the knightly world. It
could be said that after the crusade came the definition of a doctrine of
the crusade. Richard the Pilgrim composed an epic song (it has come
down to us in a later version, the work of Graindor of Douai), the
Chanson d'Antioche, continued by a *Chanson de Jérusalem*, which can be
regarded as a popular history of the expedition, telling of the mighty
deeds of the barons, of moments of exaltation and despair, and of the
courage of the prisoners who had been put to death for their faith; here,
the 'Tafurs' make their appearance, those ruffians who respected neither
the conventions of war nor the commandments of God, but whose

earthiness added spice to the story. The 'matter of the crusades' entered both scholarly and popular literature, while the pilgrims took advantage of the opening of the road to the Holy Sepulchre. No text suggests that, in Rome or in the capitals of the great principalities, a new expedition was contemplated.

In the East, attention was focused on northern Syria. Here, nothing was settled. When the main army left for the south, Bohemond returned to Antioch, from which he expelled the men of Raymond of Saint-Gilles, and, in the final months of 1099, he embarked on a siege of Latakia which was held by the Byzantines; as we have seen, Raymond forced him to raise this siege. At this point, the prince of Antioch left for Jerusalem. When he returned, it was to attempt an assault on Apamea, then to repulse the troops of Aleppo (5 July 1100). A series of minor operations seemed to indicate an impending siege of Aleppo. But Bohemond also had his eyes on the Armenian-Byzantine lands to the north and was harassing Marash, when the master of Melitene, the Armenian Gabriel, called for his assistance against the Danishmend Turks who were besieging his town. Bohemond responded to this appeal, but fell into an ambush and was captured by the emir Malik Ghazi (August 1100). He was able to warn Baldwin of Boulogne of his situation, and Baldwin arrived post haste before Melitene; he was in time to save the town, but too late to free Bohemond, who had been taken to Cappadocia.

Tancred, summoned to Antioch, found that the townships close to Aleppo had fallen once again into Turkish hands. He had to confront a Byzantine offensive which had occupied Cilicia. He recovered Mamistra, Tarsus and Adana from the Byzantines and besieged Latakia, which capitulated after a siege lasting a year and a half (1102). But he had also provided his neighbour, the new count of Edessa, Baldwin of Bourcq, with the reinforcements that enabled him to save Saruj (Sororgia) from an Ortoqid attack, at the beginning of 1101.

At this point, Bohemond managed to procure his freedom; when Alexius Comnenus was offering a large sum to the Danishmend to buy the Norman prince's freedom, the latter was able to exploit rivalries between the Muslim leaders to pay a ransom of only half this size (130,000 instead of 260,000 dinars), also obtaining an alliance with Malik Ghazi against the Seljuks and the Byzantines. He resumed his projects against Aleppo; Ridwan redeemed himself by paying tribute.

Baldwin of Le Bourg then conceived a bold scheme which needed the support not only of his cousin and vassal, Joscelin of Courtenay, but also of Bohemond and Tancred, namely the conquest of Harran, one of the principal fortresses of the Jazirah. The town was on the point of capitulating. But the Frankish leaders had failed to reach agreement about the manner of its occupation, when an army led by the atabeg of Mosul, Jekermish, and an Ortoqid emir arrived. Battle was engaged, and a simulated flight by the Turkish cavalry led to the destruction of the Edessenian contingent, the Normans managing to beat a retreat (7 May 1104).

The battle of Harran marked a turning-point; the momentum of Frankish expansion, previously unchallenged, was checked. Tancred saved Edessa, and took on its defence while Baldwin and Joscelin were prisoners; but we are told that he was in no hurry to take advantage of the atabeg's offer to free them, and they remained in captivity until 1108. Aleppo recovered the whole line of fortresses conquered by the Franks, from Albara and Ma'arrat to Artesia, most of them being spontaneously evacuated by their garrisons. The Byzantines, remaining masters of the ports of Corycus and Silifke, recovered the towns of Tarsus, Mamistra and Adana, and even the lower town of Latakia. The Armenian mountain chiefs, both those holding the fortresses controlling the passes of the Taurus to the north of the Cilician plain, of the Roupenian family, and those who had previously recognised the supremacy of the count of Edessa, recovered their independence, and even resumed contacts with the Turks, to whom many of the villages transferred their allegiance. This crumbling of Frankish domination seemed to return the position of the Franks in the north to where it had been in 1098.

Bohemond soon realised this. He assembled his knights and addressed them along the following lines: 'We are few and daily becoming fewer. We need help from overseas, and we will only find it by calling for assistance from the people of France.' He entrusted the defence of Antioch to Tancred and that of Edessa to Roger of Salerno and set off for southern Italy, which he reached early in 1105, before proceeding to the kingdom of France. He had made contact with the pontifical court, obtaining the support of some of the cardinals, and Paschal II had agreed to entrust him with the mission of recruiting new crusaders.

For this was, indeed, a resumption of the crusade. The pope had appointed a legate, the cardinal Bruno of Segni, to preach it. Bohemond himself called the enterprise the *Iter Hierosolymitanum* – precisely the term used in the Latin texts to refer to the crusade; Orderic Vitalis regarded this expedition as 'the third departure of the Christians for Jerusalem'. On 26 May 1106 a council was held at Poitiers, where Bruno of Segni confirmed the summons to the crusade: the 'vow of the Sepulchre'. King Philip I demonstrated his esteem for Bohemond, whose reputation was at its peak (and he knew how to maintain it by skilful propaganda); he gave him his daughter Constance in marriage and at the same time married another daughter, Cecily, born outside marriage, to Tancred, whom she was to join in the East.

We are told that Bohemond had assembled a huge army, 'not only from France, but even from the whole of the West'. We should note, however, that none of the great barons who had led their contingents on the previous expeditions had responded to his appeal; the captains who are mentioned, Hugh of Le Puiset, Rainier Brus and Robert of Vieux-Pont, belonged to the seigneurial world, but not to the highest aristocracy.

What seems to have prejudiced Bohemond's expedition was his scarcely veiled intention of leading it against the Turks, but bringing the Byzantines to their senses on the way. This caused some unease. Bohemond explained himself in the letter he wrote to the pope in September 1106, calling himself 'the servant of the Christian army'. In it, he deplored the delay affecting the expedition and asked the pope and the cardinals, at the council that was about to meet, to hurry its departure. He recalled that Urban II, at the council of Bari, had expressed the intention of setting out himself, and urged Paschal II to do the same, in order (and here we find the very words used in the baronial letter of September 1098) to eliminate heresy. He then launched into a catalogue of the grievances of the Latins against the Greeks, with regard to the procession of the Holy Spirit, the rite of baptism, the Eucharist and married priests. Above all, he listed his own complaints against the emperor Alexius, recalling that the Byzantine owed his throne to a usurpation, and that he had put every obstacle in the way of the crusaders and the pilgrims; he demanded justice against him, at the same time begging the pope, so as to destroy the ferment of heresy among the Greeks, to send with the army a theologian, John Burgundio. But he attacked those in the papal entourage who accused him of having taken up arms against a Christian emperor, denouncing them as having been bought by Alexius. In fact, we know that the emperor had sent representatives to Europe and in particular to Monte Cassino; behind Bohemond's complaints, we may detect the activities of a pro-Byzantine party. Paschal II could not disown the enterprise, especially since one of Bohemond's complaints, the obstacles put by the emperor in the way of the pilgrims travelling to the Holy Land, seemed well founded. But one suspects that he was somewhat embarrassed; he took no action with regard to Bohemond's proposals in the theological sphere.

Bohemond's army assembled at Bari, supported by a large number of transports thanks to which it was able to land at Avlona on 9 October 1107. It then proceeded to the great port of Dyrrachium (Durazzo) which it began to besiege, after devastating part of Epirus.

Alexius had prepared his defence, not only by contacting the Italian towns, but by strengthening the town's defences; he himself was at Thessalonika, where he had assembled a large army (it has been estimated at 60,000 men), in particular by recruiting Turkish mercenaries, thanks to the cooperation of the Seljuk sultan of Anatolia. While Bohemond was blockading the great city, the imperial troops occupied the passes which dominated it, and the Venetian ships intercepted communications between the besieging army and the Italian ports. In spite of successes in a few skirmishes, the crusaders were suffering from famine, and Bohemond was forced to negotiate with the emperor, in September 1108, at Devol.

This treaty has been called a 'diktat' by René Grousset, but the careful analysis of Ralph Lilie suggests we should qualify this judgement. The discussions were long, and each party abandoned some of its claims. First, the conventions of 1097 were abolished (though Alexius was still referring to them in 1104). Bohemond relinquished Cilicia; he kept Antioch, his port of St Simeon and the Black Mountain; he ceded to the empire Latakia and the ports situated to the south, which were, in any case, in the hands of the counts of Tripoli, like Tortosa. In compensation, the emperor gave him Aleppo and its territory (which he would have to conquer), and Edessa, as a fief which would be held of him, and the borders of Cilicia, with Til Hamdun. For all this, Bohemond became the emperor's vassal, or, more precisely, his liege man, with all the obligations this implied, as customary in the West: he was obliged to bring military assistance to the emperor, except in wars in which he was involved, and to serve him against all his enemies, in Europe and in Asia (we should remember that Bohemond was prince of Taranto and of Bari, which might involve him in Italian matters). If he occupied a town which had belonged to the empire, he was to consider himself, until more fully informed, as invested with it by the emperor – and if the latter demanded its restitution, he could not compel his vassals to accept. An oath would be required of those of Antioch, and also from the crusaders who had accompanied him in Epirus, if they wanted authorisation to travel through Byzantine territory.

Was Bohemond the victor or the vanquished? Admittedly, he retained Antioch as a vassal of the emperor, and the latter intended him to have everything that lay to the east. The rules of feudal law to which he had to submit were in no way humiliating. He could regard himself as the military leader of the Syrian borders of the empire, which was not very different from the office of *domesticos* (Grand Domestic) that he had sought in 1097. But he was obliged to renounce the lands occupied by the Normans in Cilicia and on the coast of Latakia and, above all, to persuade Tancred to agree to this renunciation. Finally, the restoration of the Greek patriarch in Antioch, stipulated in the treaty, marked the acceptance of submission to the empire. It posed canonical questions which were difficult to resolve. For the emperor, the principle of imperial sovereignty was recognised, not only over Antioch but over Edessa; and the emperor's new vassal might, in the short term, bring Aleppo into the Byzantine sphere of influence. The price was recognition of the usurpation for which he had criticised Bohemond since 1098, and also the annual payment of the huge sum of 200 *livres* of gold. And William of Tyre stresses that the Franks could once again pass freely through the Byzantine empire.

In accepting the treaty, which committed him to certain obligations that it was difficult to get his men to accept, was the prince of Antioch thinking simply of finding a means of escape from the difficult situation he was in, or did he believe he had found a reasonably satisfactory compromise to the 'question of Antioch'? We do not know. For, while the treaty refers to those crusaders he was proposing to lead to Antioch through Byzantine territory, in practice he left for Apulia, where he died on 6 March 1112, leaving an infant son, Bohemond II. It has been suggested that, broken by defeat, he had abandoned all idea of returning to Syria. William of Tyre claims the opposite, saying that he was preparing a large fleet when he fell ill. He had already been sick during the course of 1106; perhaps his inactivity between the end of 1108 and 1111 was due at least in part to his declining health.

Bohemond's return to Italy did not mark the end of the crusade he had led. A whole section of the army set out for Jerusalem, probably by sea rather than by land. A significant number of the crusaders were to settle overseas, going some way to bringing the reinforcements Bohemond had hoped for. At least, we find many of its leaders among the Frankish baronage of the ensuing years: Rainier Brus became lord of Banyas; Robert of Vieux-Pont distinguished himself during the campaign which culminated in the battle of the Field of Blood; Hugh of Le Puiset, who had left his young son Hugh (the future rebel of 1132) in Apulia, seems to have received the county of Jaffa from Baldwin I. Bohemond's crusade thus takes its place, if a modest one, among those of the twelfth century.

THE NORTHERN FRANKISH STATES BETWEEN BYZANTIUM AND THE SELJUKS

If the figure of Bohemond dominates the history of Frankish Syria between 1098 and 1108 it is that of Tancred which is the focus of

attention during the years that followed, when it seemed as if the fate of
the Frankish states was being decided in the area lying between Antioch
and Edessa. It was the attitude of the regent of the principality towards
the Treaty of Devol that delayed resolution of the question of Antioch,
and his claim to build around that town a hegemony extending to all the
Frankish possessions north of the Nahr el-Kebir finally resulted in this
hegemony passing to the king of Jerusalem. But Antiochene power
experienced a further disaster, perhaps more serious even than that of
Harran, though it still managed to survive.

While Bohemond was making his preparations for a crusade, Tancred
had resumed the offensive against the Turks of Aleppo. Before Artesia,
he met Ridwan's army, which he put to flight on the plain of Tizin on
20 April 1105, which enabled him to reoccupy not only Artesia but also
Zerdana and Sermin. The fortified town of Apamea then fell into his
hands, after the murder of its lord by the Ismailis, the extreme Shi'i who
were then attempting to seize power in Muslim Syria, at first with the
help of the princes, then in spite of them (11 September 1106). The
Byzantines took advantage of the fact that Tancred was occupied before
Apamea to seize the citadel of Latakia which was still resisting them;
Tancred marched on the town, which agreed to open its gates to him,
and he also seized Mamistra and Tarsus from the men of Alexius
Comnenus (1108–9). The desperate situation that had made Bohemond
decide to leave for the West had thus already been reversed.

Alexius had sent an ambassador to the Norman leader to ask him to
observe the treaty of Devol. Tancred refused; the emperor then set
about constructing a network of alliances directed against him. He even
sent an ambassador to Baghdad to ask the sultan Muhammad to attack
the Franks, probably early in 1111. He had obtained from Raymond of
Saint-Gilles' son Bertrand, who was coming to the East to revive his
father's designs on Tripoli, the promise to respect Byzantine territory.
Consequently, when Tancred proposed that Bertrand attack Mamistra
with him, he refused, which led to a rupture between the two men;
Alexius then counted on the support of the new count of Tripoli which
his ambassador, Manuel Boutoumites, went to seek in 1111, placing his
treasure on deposit in Tripoli. Boutoumites tried also to convince
Baldwin I, without success; and Bertrand's death deprived him of the
ally he was expecting. Alexius had also negotiated with Pisa, which, in
October 1111, obtained important privileges in the empire, of which it
had previously been the enemy, in return for a commitment to assist
the emperor against anyone who wished to seize his lands and the
promise of loyalty. The emperor could also count on Venice and he
negotiated with the pope. But this grand design came to nothing, and

Tancred died early in 1112 without having had to face a Byzantine attack.

Alexius Comnenus had counted on the support of the other Frankish princes for the success of his schemes against Tancred, who had not behaved tactfully towards his Frankish neighbours. The motives underlying this aggressive policy may be discerned in the declaration he made in 1110 to the king of Jerusalem; in his eyes, Edessa and its region should be dependent on Antioch, since it had belonged in Greek and Muslim times to the district that had Antioch as its centre. The same claim might be made with regard to the northern part of the county of Tripoli (with Tortosa), and to Cilicia. As we have seen, in the Treaty of Devol it was precisely these regions and towns that Alexius I demanded that Bohemond restore.

Further, Tancred and, after him, and under his authority, his cousin Roger of Salerno, had governed Edessa during Baldwin of Bourcq's captivity (1104–8). The return of these rich lands to their previous holder was hardly an attractive prospect. But what Tancred wanted most of all was for Baldwin to acknowledge himself as his vassal, and hold Edessa and his county from him as a fief. But Baldwin had already done homage for his Edessenian possessions to Baldwin I when he became king of Jerusalem and left them to him; Tancred's demand came up against the precedence of this homage, as well as seeming to lack a legal basis.

The situation deteriorated; Baldwin, finding himself denied access to his town, took refuge in Turbessel, with his cousin Joscelin. At the end of 1108, the two rivals confronted each other, without result. Baldwin went in search of allies. The first was the Muslim leader who had freed him and who admired the valour of his former prisoners, the atabeg of Mosul, Jawali; the second was the Armenian lord of Kaisun and Raban, Kogh Vasil. This led to a rapprochement between Tancred and Ridwan of Aleppo, who had been attacked by the atabeg's troops. Despite the intervention of the patriarch of Antioch, hostilities commenced. Tancred broke through Baldwin's lines, obliging him to take refuge in Duluk, where Tancred made as if to besiege him. But the Armenians of Edessa, determined not to fall once again into the power of the prince of Antioch, appear to have wanted to secure the citadel. Only the unexpected arrival of Joscelin and Baldwin frustrated what seems to have been a conspiracy, which was ruthlessly put down (October 1108).

The following year, a new quarrel broke out, this time over Tripoli. Bertrand of Saint-Gilles was demanding his father's inheritance from William Jordan, who appealed for Tancred's help and declared himself his vassal. Learning of this, Bertrand appealed to King Baldwin I, who reacted forcefully, reprimanding William, Tancred, Baldwin of Bourcq and Joscelin 'in the name of the whole Church of Jerusalem' (April 1109). We should probably see in this not so much the memory of the homage once done by Bohemond to the patriarch Daimbert as the assertion – as Baldwin was to spell out to Tancred in 1110 – that the Franks 'had made a king for him to serve them as leader, protector and guide in the preservation and expansion of the conquest'. However that may be, Baldwin I gave his decision: he left Tortosa and the countries to the north of the Nahr el-Kebir to William, under Tancred's suzerainty, while Tripoli, which opened its gates on 12 July, was to fall to Bertrand. The king asked the regent of Antioch to renounce his claims to Edessa, returning to him his rights over the principality of Galilee. The first part of the agreement was soon obsolete, as a result of William's death. Tancred contented himself, it appears, with seizing, as he returned to Antioch, the coastal town of Jabala and, a little later, the future Crac des Chevaliers, which he was forced to relinquish to count Pons of Tripoli. The feudal dependence of Tortosa on Antioch remained hypothetical, but the territories situated between Latakia and the Tripolitanian frontier were in future firmly assured to Antioch. The last Muslim enclave on the coast, Margat, was taken in 1114.

A new phase was about to begin, that of the 'counter-crusades'. This term, used by René Grousset, has been challenged. But it expresses a reality: for the first time since the intervention of Kerbogha below Antioch, the sultan's authority was manifested in Syria by the dispatch of an army specifically intended to eliminate the Frankish presence. It was the qadi of Tripoli, Ibn Ammar, who had asked for this intervention, in 1108, when he had gone to Baghdad to draw the attention of the sultan and the caliph to the situation of his town, besieged for four years by the Franks. The sultan had promised to send an army to assist him, which he entrusted to Mawdud, appointed atabeg of Mosul in Jawali's place. In fact, the Seljuk sultan was hoping to kill two birds with one stone; to restore his authority over the lands of Syria, where the heritage of Tutush remained divided between princes who had made themselves practically independent, and to eliminate the states established by the Franks. To entrust this double task to the governors of Mosul was to introduce into Syria an essentially Turkish military force, able to draw on a reservoir of men far larger than that at the disposal of the Syrian princes.

When news of the capture of Tripoli became known, the sultan urged Mawdud to go into action; reinforced by the troops of the Ortoqid emirs of Khilat and Mardin, Mawdud marched on Edessa, which he besieged in April–May 1110. Baldwin of Le Bourg had sent Joscelin to

Jerusalem to ask for the king's help; Tancred stayed where he was. The royal army, swollen by the troops of the count of Tripoli and the Armenian lords, arrived when the situation of Edessa was desperate; Mawdud withdrew to Harran. Baldwin I summoned Tancred, who came with five hundred knights, and persuaded the prince of Antioch and the count of Edessa to bury their grievances; the former remained, however, reluctant.

The two Baldwins then resolved to adopt a new and essentially defensive strategy, that is, to put the fortified towns in a position to resist sieges, and to clear the open countryside of its inhabitants. The whole Christian population from the lands situated to the east of the Euphrates was to be transported to the other side of the river. But the Turks arrived when the Frankish army had crossed the Euphrates, and massacred or reduced to slavery the unarmed crowd. Edessa was now surrounded by a ruined countryside. This disaster seems to have opened Tancred's eyes to the danger threatening Frankish rule.

It was then that Ridwan of Aleppo, deciding the time was ripe to break the truce he had made with Antioch, began to ravage Antiochene territory. Tancred attacked the lands of Aleppo, seizing Cerep (Athareb) and Zerdana, the two fortresses that controlled the passes leading from the territory held by the Franks beyond the Orontes to Aleppo. To get the truce renewed, Ridwan had to accept all the Frankish leader's demands, including the liberation of his Armenian captives. The emirs of Shaizar and Hamah made haste to pay tribute (1111). This time, it was pious circles in Aleppo who took action, sending a delegation to Baghdad whose cause was taken up in legal and clerical circles; faced with a riot, the sultan and the caliph decided to mobilise all their forces against the Franks, and Mawdud regrouped his army, with the addition of the contingents of the emirs of the Iranian borders (Hamadhan, Maragha and Arbil). Before this enormous force, Ridwan took fright; even though he had appealed to Mawdud, he took refuge in the fact that he had given his word to justify refusing to break his truce with Antioch and kept the population of Aleppo at bay. The atabeg of Damascus, Tughtekin, had joined Mawdud before Ma'arrat, but remained uneasy about the latter's intentions. The Franks had held Edessa and Turbessel, abandoned by the atabeg; they assembled all their forces in the region of Apamea, content to keep the enemy army at bay, and it soon broke up.

Mawdud reappeared two years later, in 1113, this time in the vicinity of the kingdom of Jerusalem. Baldwin I let himself be drawn into attacking him and suffered a major defeat, but the arrival of troops from Antioch and Tripoli saved the day. Then Mawdud, who had decided to spend the winter in Damascus, was assassinated in the great mosque.

Tughtekin was suspected of having fomented this murder, which helped to reinforce suspicions within the Muslim coalition. This became apparent in 1115, when the new atabeg of Mosul, Bursuq, found united against him the Franks of Antioch, Jerusalem and Tripoli and the Turks of Aleppo, Damascus and Mardin, Aleppo having refused to open its gates to him. He succeeded in causing the enemy forces to break up by making them think he had left, then launched an attack on the fortress of Kafr Tab. But Roger of Antioch and Baldwin of Edessa, surprising his army in full marching order, inflicted on him the serious defeat of Tell Danith (18 September 1115).

The campaigns of the atabegs of Mosul had thus encountered a resistance in which the Muslim princes of Syria had gradually made common cause with the Franks. A curious atmosphere had developed between the two, as is shown by the anecdotes recounted by Usama ibn-Munqidh concerning the visits of the Franks to Shaizar and the mutual admiration felt for each other by the combatants. But, though they had fought off the forces assembled at the instigation of the sultan of Baghdad, thanks to the unease that the designs of the sultan and his representatives aroused among their neighbours, the Franks of Antioch and Edessa were to suffer some hard knocks at the latter's hands.

Roger of Antioch had practically reduced Aleppo to the condition of a protectorate. The town had been without a prince since the death of Ridwan's son in 1114, and it was governed by a regent who had to agree not only to pay tribute but to allow the prince of Antioch to control the passage of pilgrims on their way to Mecca. All the fortresses covering the approaches to the town, those of the Djebel Summaq which separated it from the lands across the Orontes and that of Hasart (Azaz) to the north of Aleppo, were in Frankish hands. But the people of Aleppo appealed to the Ortoqid of Mardin, Ilghazi, who took possession of the city and, with strong Turkoman and Arab contingents, descended into the valley of the Orontes. Roger, instead of waiting for the arrival of the other Frankish princes, gave battle; his army, surrounded, was destroyed and he himself was killed at the Ager Sanguinis (Field of Blood), on 28 June 1119; only a hundred and fifty men escaped, and, next day, all the prisoners were massacred.

This disaster put the principality at the mercy of Ilghazi, but he was unable to press his advantage. The patriarch of Antioch, Bernard of Valence, armed all the Franks, clergy and laity, warded off the indigenous Christians who would have offered their submission to the Turks, and put the town in a defensive state, while awaiting the arrival of Baldwin II and Pons of Tripoli. They, having taken urgent measures to rebuild the infrastructure of the principality by comforting the survivors and promising to respect the rights of the widows and children to the fiefs of dead knights, returned up the valley of the Orontes and, at Tell Danith, met Ilghazi's troops, reinforced by the Damascenes, who were defeated on 14 August.

It took five successive campaigns (1119, 1120, 1121, 1122 and 1123), and as many stays in Antioch on the part of King Baldwin, before the line of fortifications that defended the lands beyond the Orontes was restored. The principality of Antioch, throughout the alternating successes and reverses, had managed to retain its territorial integrity and hold Aleppo at bay, though without having tried to seize the town itself; the situation of the county of Edessa, however, directly exposed to attacks from Mosul or the Jazirah, gave cause for concern. The loyalty of the county's Armenian subjects had faltered; during the attacks by Mawdud, especially in 1112, some of them had delivered towers of the enceinte of Edessa to the enemy, and, in 1113, Baldwin of Bourcq had expelled a part of the population. In 1114 the atabeg Bursuq had obtained the submission of the adopted son of Kogh Vasil, Vasil Dgha. The count of Edessa punished him by confiscating his castles, in particular Kaisun, then deprived the other Armenian leaders of their lordships, that is, those of Bira, Corice and Gargar, who were replaced by Franks. The heavy financial costs entailed by a constant state of war meant, for the county's subjects, fiscal demands that they found intolerable. Joscelin of Courtenay, who succeeded Baldwin II in 1118, seems to have been more popular among his Armenian subjects.

Joscelin was captured in September 1122 by an Ortoqid emir, Balak. Baldwin II assured the regency of the county before he, too, fell into Balak's hands, on 18 April 1123. Both men were taken to the fortress of Kharpurt, and Balak, flushed with success, seized power in Aleppo before embarking on a campaign against Antioch. He had taken Albara when he learned that a party of Armenians had occupied Kharpurt and freed its prisoners. Baldwin, hoping to be able to hold the town, sent Joscelin in search of assistance. He rushed to Jerusalem, but, when he returned, Balak had retaken Kharpurt and put his captives to death, except for Baldwin; he was freed only in June 1124 in return for a huge ransom, for which he had to give hostages, among them his little daughter Joetta. Joscelin had to take responsibility for the defence of the whole of northern Syria until the king was freed; he had the good fortune to profit from Balak's difficulties, by giving assistance to the Muslims of Menbij, who had risen against him; Balak was killed besieging the town.

Since the crusade of 1107 had been cut short, the northern Frankish states had been left to their own devices. Without the assistance of the king of Jerusalem, now recognised as the leader of all the Frankish states, they would have been unable to withstand the formidable waves of attack launched against them, between 1110 and 1115, from Iraq. This new cohesion had frustrated the plans of Alexius Comnenus to exploit the rivalry between the Franks to isolate Antioch, and at the same time take advantage of an alliance with the sultan against them (the rioters in Baghdad in 1111 accused the sultan of being less zealous for the Holy War than the Byzantine emperor). Rather it was the crusaders established in the East who had been able to take advantage of the divisions within the Muslim world; they had been able to form friendships, even develop camaraderie, with those who were on occasion their enemies. But the disappearance of the Seljuk dynasty of Aleppo heralded a new situation, the principality of Aleppo now being incorporated into a more powerful grouping that was foreign to the Syrian world.

In the short run, the material losses accumulated during a decade of fighting, the terrible bloodshed of the Ager Sanguinis and the losses suffered by the Frankish knights had dangerously weakened the Frankish forces. Their leaders saw only one solution: a new appeal for a crusade, which was a consequence of the catastrophe of 1119.

THE LABORIOUS CONSTRUCTION OF THE KINGDOM OF JERUSALEM AND THE CRUSADE OF CALIXTUS II

Unlike the county of Edessa and the principality of Antioch, the kingdom of Jerusalem – and the history of the county of Tripoli was in some respects similar – was not founded in its complete state. Godfrey of Bouillon had been left with a very small number of men, and the occupation which had followed the capture of Jerusalem was limited to the town itself, its surroundings area, Samaria and the part of Galilee close to Lake Tiberias. With the exception of Jaffa, Frankish rule did not extend to the coast, and in the mountainous regions it remained precarious. To build a coherent construction extending through the whole of Palestine and the southern parts of Phoenicia was to take time, even though Raymond of Saint-Gilles' intervention provided assistance to this long-term project.

On the other hand, Jerusalem was less exposed to expeditions launched from Iraq, and the frontier with Egypt was only a few dozen kilometres long and in any case largely desert. Above all, the fact that the Holy Sepulchre was the goal of the pilgrimage which brought pilgrims flooding in from the West was to make this country the principal theatre of the operations that can be regarded as part of the crusades.

Christopher Tyerman has recently asked whether one can speak of 'crusades' in the twelfth century, and particularly during the first half of the century, before 1147. He concludes that one can, assuming a precise juridical definition is given to the term, that of an enterprise for which indulgences were granted by the papacy. In fact, the pilgrimage, since it was the fulfilment of a vow, did not change its nature if a person who set out to venerate the Holy Sepulchre agreed to fight in its service. A typical example is that of the English pilgrims who refused to take part in a military operation on their arrival but who, once their pilgrimage had been completed, offered their services to the king (1106). Jerusalem could take advantage of such occasional back-up assistance for operations with limited objectives.

As long as the vizier al-Afdal lived (he was murdered in 1121), the government of Cairo was not resigned to the loss of Palestine, especially since the Franks had moved quickly to conquer the coastal towns that still belonged to the Fatimids. In May 1101 an army arrived and camped at Ascalon and, in September, began to march in the direction of Ramla; after a fierce battle, whose victims included Galdemar Carpenel, it was put to flight (7–8 September). In 1102 a new army marched on Ramla; it clashed with Baldwin I, who was reinforced by the survivors of the crusade of 1101 but had not waited for the rest of his troops. The king was almost alone in managing to escape, while his companions, besieged in Ramla, were massacred (19 May). A fleet of two hundred ships arrived at the same time as the troops from Galilee; the battle of Jaffa (27 May) erased the consequences of the defeat of Ramla. In 1105 there was a new offensive, in which the Egyptian army and fleet were joined by a contingent from Damascus. Baldwin defeated them once again on the plain of Ramla (27 August). In 1106 detachments from Ascalon, Tyre, Sidon and Beirut massacred a crowd of pilgrims near Jaffa then attacked the fortress of Chastel Hernault – built specifically to guard the road to Jerusalem – and destroyed it after killing its defenders. In 1107 the Egyptians raided Hebron; in 1110 they appeared before Jerusalem. But in 1111 the governor of Ascalon, who was in revolt, put himself under Frankish protection; Baldwin gave him a garrison of 300 men, who were killed by the inhabitants. There was another Egyptian sally as far as the walls of Jerusalem in 1113, and another attack on Jaffa in 1115. Tired of being the target of all these attacks, Baldwin risked crossing the desert with 216 knights and 400 footsoldiers, having negotiated with the Bedouins, and occupied the Egyptian town of Farama (22 March 1118) without meeting any resistance. It was as he was returning from this expedition that he died at el-Arish, by the side of the lake that bears his name.

The capture of Baldwin II by the Ortoqids offered the Fatimids a

chance that they did not let slip; in May 1123 an army and a fleet laid siege
to Jaffa, but the constable Eustace Grenier gave battle before Ibelin and
routed them decisively. All the attempts made from Ascalon had ended in
failure. The Fatimid presence in that town nevertheless constituted a
permanent threat, especially for the roads, rendered perilous by the raids
conducted by its garrison; when the Franks besieged Tyre, Egyptian
runners dared to attack Magna Mahumeria (al-Bira), to the north of
Jerusalem, where only those inhabitants who had taken refuge in a tower
escaped death. The building, then rebuilding, of Chastel Hernault helped
to reduce the danger run by pilgrims between Jerusalem and Jaffa. From
1135, however, the Latins embarked on a programme of fortification
to reduce the area accessible to the Ascalon garrison. First to be fortified
was Bethgibelin, which was then entrusted to the Hospitallers, followed,
in 1141, by Ibelin, which was enfeoffed to the constable of Jaffa, Balian,
and then, in 1142, Blanchegarde, which remained in the king's hands.
The fortification of Daron and Gaza, to the south of Ascalon, marked a
new phase, which was to culminate in the fall of Ascalon. Many castles
of lesser importance completed this defensive system.

To neutralise Ascalon was also to make possible an occupation of the
coastal towns. This was desirable because of the danger presented by
these dens of pirates and bandits who, on land and sea, conducted raids
from which travellers, pilgrims and villagers all suffered. The occupation
of Jaffa, followed by that of Caiphas, had given the kingdom two
openings to the sea; to enlarge this outlet to the Mediterranean was
another imperative. But the presence of a large and active Egyptian fleet,
able to make use of all its bases, rendered any operation against these
towns difficult; the Franks could only act when they had at their disposal
larger naval forces than the handful of galleys and other ships customarily
stationed in their ports. Baldwin I discovered this in 1103, when he tried
to besiege Acre without naval support; Tyre, Sidon and Tripoli soon
sent reinforcements which obliged him to retreat.

It was therefore necessary to take advantage of the arrival of fleets
carrying pilgrims, and use the ships to assure the sea blockade by keeping
off the Fatimid squadrons, while the passengers, their pilgrimage completed, were available to reinforce the army of the king and his barons. It
was with the assistance of some Genoese who had arrived at Caiphas in
March 1101 and who had gone to Jerusalem for Easter that Baldwin,
having come to an agreement with them, marched on Arsur, which soon
opened its gates, thereby escaping the fate soon suffered by Caesarea;
here, it was necessary to conduct a full-scale siege, terminated by the
storming of the town; the sack was total and the majority of the
inhabitants were massacred (17 May 1101).

In March 1104 a new Genoese fleet sailed along the coast; it helped Raymond of Saint-Gilles to take Gibelet, then Baldwin I to attack Acre, which capitulated after a siege of twenty days. The conditions agreed by the king (the right of the inhabitants to leave with their belongings or to remain) were not wholly respected, the Genoese sailors attacking those who left. Two attempts on Sidon, in 1106 and 1108, coincided with the arrival, first of a large number of pilgrims from England, and then of sailors from various Italian towns, but this time the intervention of an Egyptian squadron caused the operation to fail.

In 1109 Bertrand of Saint-Gilles succeeded in obtaining the capitulation of Tripoli, which, thanks to the assistance it received by sea, had been able to hold out for many years, though the castle built by the count of Toulouse at Mont Pèlerin had subjected it to a strict land blockade. The same Genoese fleet then put itself at the disposal of the king, who was able to take Beirut, whose governor had fled, abandoning its population (May 1110).

At this point a large fleet arrived that had left Norway with the king's brother, who, after the pilgrimage, agreed to help Baldwin to take Sidon. The Norwegians much impressed the Egyptians, who were unwilling to tackle them, and the town capitulated on 4 December 1110. There remained only Tyre, which had been blockaded since 1105, when the lord of Tiberias, Hugh of St Omer, had built the castle of Toron, which severed relations between the town and the interior. Another castle, Scandelion, built in 1116, blocked access to the town from the south. However, its governor had made an agreement with the atabeg of Damascus, who sent him a troop of soldiers and who frustrated the Frankish efforts by making diversionary attacks. Baldwin I had been obliged to raise the siege in 1111–12. Egypt was also sending provisions and men; in 1123 advantage was taken of this to remove the Damascene commander of the garrison. But before the Frankish threat, the Fatimid caliph decided to cede Tyre to the atabeg of Damascus.

Baldwin II was then a prisoner. But a large Venetian fleet, commanded by the doge himself, arrived in Syria in May 1123. The leaders of the kingdom, the patriarch Gormond and the constable William of Bures, after lengthy debate (the barons of Judaea wanted to attack Ascalon), made a treaty with the doge aimed at the capture of Tyre. The Venetians set a trap for the Egyptian fleet, into which it fell, assuring them mastery of the sea. The siege lasted from 15 February to 7 July 1124; the diversions attempted by the Egyptians of Ascalon and the Turks of Damascus were abortive, and Tyre finally capitulated. The leaders of the army had strictly forbidden any looting; Tughtekin himself came to receive the refugees. There followed strange scenes of fraternisation, the combatants of the two parties visiting the enemy camps, besiegers and besieged expressing their admiration for each other's valour.

The Fatimids had lost their last base in Phoenicia. They were still able to send their squadrons to raid the Frankish coast, which they frequently did during the next forty years. The fate of the raid launched in 1125 shows that such enterprises were now risky; the Egyptians ships were effectively able to conduct their operations all along the coast, but they needed at some point to put in for fresh water and the Franks of Beirut fell on them and inflicted such heavy losses that their leaders chose to retreat to Cyprus before regaining Egypt. The safety of Frankish navigation, and that of the districts close to the coast, had been greatly increased.

At the time of its creation, the kingdom of Jerusalem seems not to have been defined at all precisely. The title 'king of Babylon or of Asia', occasionally found, suggests that it might have expanded either in the direction of Egypt or in that of Damascus; in fact, negotiating with the Genoese in 1104, Baldwin I promised them a third of the city of Cairo, if he were to conquer it with their assistance.

In practice, such illusions were soon dispelled. Godfrey was left with scarcely more than three hundred knights and about two thousand other combatants. Baldwin I tried to strengthen their ranks, instructing his vassals to double the number of their squires, but there were not enough war-horses for this measure to be really effective (1101). New arrivals joined them, but only gradually. It was with very much reduced numbers, even reinforced by recruits from the Syrian population, that they had to hold a territory that already, in the first months of Frankish conquest, extended from the shores of Lake Tiberias to the Dead Sea. The policy of the first two Baldwins was primarily aimed at the consolidation of this occupation by absorbing pockets of defiance and by securing the frontiers, but without losing sight of the possibility of controlling, beyond them, the fertile lands and the routes that would be sources of wealth for a prince who was often short of cash.

Thus in 1108 King Baldwin himself, with some sixty knights, having been informed of the unobtrusive passing of a caravan from Egypt headed for Damascus, Tyre and Beirut, surprised it as it crossed the Jordan; in the ensuing battle, prisoners were taken and the whole caravan – eleven camels loaded with sugar, four with pepper and spices, seventeen with oil and honey – was seized. Albert of Aix, who describes this incident, adds that 'the country of the crusaders was enriched'. This suggests that the scale of the operations conducted by the king might be very limited. But it is likely that this operation was designed to impose on merchants the obligation to pay tolls before crossing the Frankish occupied zone, which this caravan had attempted to avoid.

The appeal of booty and the desire to impose a political order were probably combined in other operations which were effectively razzias with the nomadic tribes as their victims. Albert of Aix describes several of them, during which the king seized flocks and men. It was during one of these expeditions that Baldwin showed towards the heavily pregnant wife of an Arab chief a humanity which won him her husband's gratitude – and it was his warning that enabled Baldwin to escape capture on the occasion of the defeat of Ramla. When Joscelin of Courtenay tried to capture another tribe, in 1119, things went badly wrong and he lost many of his knights. The Arabs made haste to prevent reprisals by offering to pay blood money and by accepting the requirement to pay a tax to be allowed to lead their nomadic existence in peace.

The desire to control these routes was one of the reasons for Baldwin I's interest in Transjordan and Arabia, where, in 1115, he built the castle of Montreal, which assured him domination over the Wadi Musa ('Le Vaux Moyse'). In 1116, he reached the Red Sea, where the new castle of Aila, modern Eilat, was constructed.

Here he clashed with the government of Damascus, under Duqaq and above all under the atabeg Tughtekin, though the two states confronted each other all along the eastern frontier. The operations often took the form of raids of pillage, which sometimes ended in disaster; two of the sires of Tiberias, Hugh of St Omer and Gervase of Basoches, lost their lives in this way. A system evolved by which the harvests in the contested districts were shared: the king of Jerusalem or his vassals took one third of the revenues from the Terre de Sueth (Sawad) and from the regions of Jerash and Jaulan (the Golan), the Damascenes took another third, leaving the final third to the peasants. The counts of Tripoli did the same in the Beqa'a and also, further north, in the valley of the Orontes, where they dealt with the emirs of Homs and Hamah. But there was a strong temptation to secure the whole of these revenues; Baldwin I built, to the east of Lake Tiberias, the castle of Al, which Tughtekin destroyed in 1105; in 1119 Baldwin II built, close by, that of Habis Jaldak (the 'Cave de Sueth').

To consolidate their hold over the lands left to the rule of the atabeg of Damascus, the Franks tried to control the Lebanese mountain passes. The counts of Tripoli had deprived Damascus of the castles of Moinetre and Gibelcar, which Toghtekin had granted them in 1109 and from which they conducted razzias into the Beqa'a; further north, they secured Rafaniyah in 1116, which they lost in 1126, but later recovered, and Tuban, which gave them access to the plain of Homs. Here,

Tughtekin riposted by summoning warlike tribes that he and his son installed in the mountains, opposite Beirut and Sidon, and which took their place in the system of coexistence peculiar to this part of the Lebanon. He tried to do the same south of the Dead Sea, but Baldwin was able to frighten off the Turkomans by employing the services of a Melchite priest, and they withdrew (1107).

Periods of hostilities alternated with truces, observed more or less strictly by one side or the other, and Franco-Damascene relations testify to the balance of power. They were also affected by the general situation; in 1113 Tughtekin and Mawdud took up a position opposite the Franks to the south of Lake Tiberias, and Baldwin I's rash behaviour cost him the defeat of Sinn al-Nabra. The Muslims were then able to ravage Samaria and pillage Nablus, with the support of the local peasantry, until the arrival of troops from Antioch and Tripoli put a stop to the campaign. The murder of Mawdud drove the atabeg of Damascus into an alliance with the Franks (1115). But with the death of Baldwin I, when his successor offered to renew their agreement, the atabeg demanded that he relinquish his share of the crops, attacked Tiberias and pillaged the town, which led to reprisals; Baldwin II ravaged the region of Deraa and fortified the Cave de Sueth. Overall, however, the frontier remained stable.

Within the kingdom, insecurity remained a problem. Brigands occupied hideouts from which they made forays against travellers and pilgrims, even against villages. It was during the course of an attack on one of these dens, near Athlit, that, in 1103, Baldwin I was seriously wounded. And in 1125 Baldwin II had to build the castle of Mont Glavien in the hinterland of Beirut to force the villages of the area to pay taxes. The Frankish occupation remained fairly tenuous and at the mercy of any defeat on the battlefield.

This gave cause for concern. A letter survives, written, probably in 1120, by the patriarch Gormond of Picquigny to the archbishop of Compostella which contains echoes of the preamble to the acts of the 'council of Nablus', where barons and prelates discussed how to obtain divine mercy. After deploring a series of poor harvests, aggravated by a plague of grasshoppers, Gormond wrote:

What am I to say about the enemy attacks? We are besieged on all sides by the Saracens: Babylon [?Baghdad] to the east, Ascalon to the west, Tyre on the coast, Damascus to the north. Every day, we are invaded, killed, captured, beheaded, thrown to the wild beast and the birds. What next? For the name of Jesus, before abandoning the holy city of Jerusalem, the cross of Our Lord and the most holy tomb of Christ, we are ready to die. That is why, in such distress ... come to our aid ... let the incomparable labours of our knights, alas few in number, touch the bottom of your heart; what shall I say of the sufferings of the footsoldiers? They are shut up in the towers and walls of Jerusalem, in caves in the ground ... No one dares to go more than a mile, if that, beyond the walls of Jerusalem or of the other towns without an armed escort ... Strive to come and join the army of Christ and bring us speedy aid, or, if you cannot come, send whoever you can.

The patriarch's letter contains echoes of another, that of King Baldwin II, the prelates and the barons of the Frankish states who, after the disaster of the Field of Blood, had appealed to the pope. Baldwin referred not only to the danger from Aleppo, but to that from Egypt and Damascus. We know that his letters and those of the two patriarchs were conveyed to Calixtus II and to the doge of Venice. It is quite possible that others in the West received the same appeal.

The pope's reply was favourable; for the patriarch Gormond, there existed a 'host of Jerusalem' for which he sought many recruits. And the doge recalled to Venice the ships then in Romania for the month of April 1121. The date of the bull of crusade promulgated by Calixtus II is unknown; he refers to it in a letter in which he extended to those who went to the aid of the Christians of Spain 'the same remission of sins that we have granted to the defenders of the Church in the East'. This grant of an indulgence for the crusade in the East was confirmed at the first Lateran council (27 March 1123), with an injunction to those who had not yet departed to do so before Easter 1124.

The only response known to us came from Venice, which prepared a large fleet which set out in the summer of 1122, but delayed en route at Corfu, where it laid siege to the island's capital, as a result of difficulties between the republic and the Byzantine emperor. It arrived in the spring of 1123 to embark on the siege of Tyre. If other crusaders set out, their arrival is unrecorded, and the crusade of 1123–4 remains for historians 'the Venetian Crusade'. It may have been in response to the pope's appeal that Fulk of Anjou arrived with a hundred knights to spend a year in the Holy Land in 1120–1. And perhaps the Genoese expedition of 1104, during which the town of Caesarea was taken, deserves to be called a 'Genoese Crusade'. The citizens of Genoa participated in large numbers and if the Genoese made sure they benefited from their cooperation with the Franks to obtain substantial advantages in the conquered towns, this was exactly what the Venetians did in 1123. There had been no need of a specific grant of indulgences by the pope to encourage them. The letters of Urban II were sufficient for the participants to feel confident that they would enjoy the remission of sins granted by the pope. And the same was probably true for the great Norwegian expedition of 1110; it carried pilgrims, but their collective 'passage' was the result of operations conducted country-wide and the northerners entered the service of the Holy Sepulchre, surely regarding themselves as beneficiaries of Urban II's indulgence. Perhaps the same was true of the groups of English pilgrims leaving in their ships, who sometimes allowed themselves be recruited in passing by Spanish or Portuguese leaders.

Pilgrims did not always leave in organised fleets. Here and there, we hear of the departure of groups of knights who travelled together to Jerusalem. On the borders of Forez and the Brionnais, for example, a celebrated baron, Hugh Damas, ancestor of the great family of that name, brother of the lord of Semur and lord of many important castles, left for an *iter Hierosolymitanum* in 1118; many minor lords from the region, so as to leave in his company, abandoned some of their possessions to the prior of Marcigny who gave them in return money and horses; on their arrival in the Holy Land, when their pilgrimage had been completed, they entered the service of the Franks of Jerusalem.

In fact, it is difficult to separate crusade and pilgrimage; the Franks of Outremer received limited but important assistance from their brethren in western Europe, some of whom were able to remain in the East. But it was Jerusalem that attracted the pilgrims, and it was the king of Jerusalem who, in the crucial years that included the crusade of Calixtus II, was responsible for the Frankish states as a whole. The real danger lay, it seems, on the borders of Edessa and Antioch. But it was difficult for a Venetian fleet to be of use there, and it was for the benefit of the kingdom of Jerusalem that the Venetian crusaders fought.

FRANKISH SYRIA BETWEEN JOHN COMNENUS AND ZENGI: THE FALL OF EDESSA

Following the capture of Tyre, the freeing of Baldwin II marked a brief apogee for the Latin states in the East. The king persuaded the patriarch of Antioch to free him from the commitments he had made to the Ortoqid emir whose prisoner he had been, on the grounds that, holding the principality in the name of Bohemond's son, he could not dispose of this heritage. Further, he reached an accord with an Arab emir, Dubais, who coveted Aleppo, and laid siege to that town with his Muslim allies. The citizens of Aleppo, abandoned by the Ortoqid, entrusted themselves to the atabeg of Mosul, Bursuqi, who drove off the besiegers. But Baldwin, at the head of an army comprising all the available Frankish forces, inflicted a crushing defeat on him at Hasart and reoccupied the line of towns closest to Aleppo, including Cerep and Zerdana (1125). Returning to Jerusalem, he attacked Tughtekin and conducted a raid into the heartlands of Damascus, dispersing the enemy soldiers (1126).

The arrival of Bohemond II at Antioch (October 1125) freed him from the obligation to assure the principality's defence. He could now devote himself to his kingdom, whilst Bohemond recovered Kafr Tab and tried to take advantage of Bursuqi's assassination to seize Aleppo.

The king had conceived the project of conquering Damascus and, to this end, sent messengers to the princes of the West to ask for their support; chief among them was Hugh of Payns, who used his journey to recruit knights of the Temple. A considerable number of crusaders seem to have responded to this appeal; Baldwin was able to lead a large army as far as the approaches to Damascus, but a serious reverse on the plain of Marj al-Suffar obliged him to beat a retreat before he could embark on the siege (5 December 1129). Nevertheless, the king had been able to take advantage of the troubles that followed the death of Tughtekin; the population of Damascus having massacred the Ismailis in whom the aged atabeg had placed his confidence, their leader surrendered to him the castle of Banyas, at the foot of Mount Hermon. It does not seem that the Franks had colluded with the Ismailis to get their hands on the town, as later historians have claimed. The acquisition of Banyas opened the road to Damascus.

The situation was changing for the worse, however, in northern Syria. Bohemond II had had his difficulties with Joscelin of Courtenay, and the king had been forced to intervene to end them. Then the prince of Antioch was killed in a battle with the Danishmends, in Cilicia (February 1130). The king had to return to Antioch, where he found that his daughter Alice, whom he had married to Bohemond, had appealed to the new atabeg of Mosul, Zengi, to maintain her in power.

This intrigue, which Bohemond was able to frustrate in time, was all the more dangerous in that the arrival of Zengi saw the first moves in pursuit of a project for which the ambitious atabeg had won the sultan's agreement, namely the constitution of the whole of Syria as one great command which would be entrusted to him. He took possession of Aleppo without difficulty in 1128 and embarked on hostilities, initially limited, against the Franks, at the same time imposing his authority in Hamah, at the expense of the principality of Damascus, where Buri had succeeded his father Tughtekin. In future, Damascus distrusted the atabeg and his proposals of an alliance against the Franks.

Franco-Damascene relations alternated between entente and conflict. In 1132 Buri took Banyas from King Fulk, and, at the beginning of 1133, the fortified cave of the Cave de Tyron, on the hills west of the Jordan, from an Arab sheik friendly to the Franks. But when Zengi's ambitions became more formidable and threatened Damascus directly, the new atabeg Muin al-Din Unur sought an alliance with the Franks and, in return for the assistance he received from Fulk, he helped him to recover the Cave de Tyron and Banyas. It needed cooperation between the troops of the king and the atabeg to capture that town from the troops stationed there by Zengi, who were threatening Damascus (1139). The Franco-Damascene accord reached on this occasion was to hold Zengi in check for many years.

The Damascenes were nevertheless responsible for a serious weakening of the county of Tripoli. The emir Bazwaj, who exercised power in the name of the son of the atabeg Buri, led a raid across the Lebanese mountains as far as the approaches to Tripoli. Count Pons, who had hastily assembled his knights and the burgesses of the town, was defeated and his army destroyed (the bishop of Tripoli, whom the Muslims had failed to recognise, was freed in return for a ransom). Pons took refuge in the mountains, but was handed over to Bazwaj by Syrian Christians, who were also accused of having guided the enemy before the battle (March and April 1137). The young Count Raymond II took reprisals against the culprits, who were taken to Tripoli to be executed. But the count had lost many men and his richest plain had been devastated.

Two years earlier Zengi had led a campaign against Antioch during which he had recaptured from the Antiochenes the fortresses which surrounded Aleppo: Cerep, Zerdana, Ma'arrat and Kafr Tab (1135); he had forced the emirs of Shaizar to recognise his authority, though he had been unable to subject Homs; but, through Hamah, he had become a neighbour of the county of Tripoli. He took advantage of the county's weakened state to attack the fortress of Montferrand, built a few years earlier to cover Rafaniyah from the direction of the Orontes valley. The count appealed for assistance from King Fulk, but both were surprised as they marched on Montferrand. Raymond II was captured, the larger part of the army destroyed, and the king could only take refuge in the besieged castle with his barons. Hearing of this, the northern princes rushed to his aid, while the patriarch of Jerusalem raised a large army. Faced with these forces, Zengi, who also feared the arrival of the Byzantine emperor, preferred to negotiate, freeing the prisoners and allowing the king and his men to leave Montferrand, which he then occupied, along with Rafaniyah (summer of 1137). The emir Bazwaj had taken advantage of these events to pillage Nablus. But the loss of the two castles dominating the Orontes valley between Homs and Hamah was definitive.

The county, weakened by the loss of so many of its knights, was now incapable of assuring the defence of all its frontiers, and the treachery that had delivered Count Pons to the enemy gave cause to fear that the loyalty of its Christian subjects was exhausted. So Raymond II resolved, in 1142 or 1144, to abandon to the Hospitallers the castles which commanded the pass of Homs and the valley of the Nahr el-Kebir: Lacum (Tell Kalakh), Felicium and the Crat, which then became the Crac des Chevaliers, as well as his rights to Rafaniyah and the neighbouring lands. The lord of the Crat, in compensation, was enfeoffed with a fortified cave which may have been the headquarters of the lordship held by a perfidious *ra'is*, the Cave of David the Syrian, probably close to Bsharré (Buissera).

The reordering of the county's defensive system in response to the new situation seems primarily to have been inspired by the desire for retrenchment. In the kingdom of Jerusalem, on the other hand, the building of new castles, Beaufort, which dominated the valley of the Litani in the hinterland of Sidon (1139) and the Crac of Moab (Kerak), to the east of the Dead Sea (1142), marked the tightening of the Frankish hold over the rich valley of Marj Ayun on the one hand and over the Transjordan, long subject to the system of crop sharing, on the other.

This reorganisation coincided with the emergence of a new factor, the creation of a dominion of the Assassins, like a wedge driven between the county of Tripoli and the principality of Antioch. The sectarians had previously failed in their attempts to take power in Damascus and in Aleppo, and they had been unable to remain in Banyas. But, thanks to the weakness of the principality of Antioch following the death of Bohemond II, and perhaps with the implicit consent of the Franks, who did not react, they acquired the fortress of Qadmus and neighbouring castles from a Muslim lord, captured Khariba from the Franks and then Masyaf from the Munqidhites of Shaizar, in the years after 1130. Agreements reached with the Franks – payment of annual tribute, payments corresponding to rents for certain villages, etc. – insured them against any future action from that quarter. The terror they inspired in the Muslim princes threatened with assassination guaranteed them against the latter (Count Raymond II himself was to fall to their attack as he was leaving a church). This new domination neutralised a whole sector of the Franco-Muslim frontier.

In the short term, the most important development was the revival of Byzantine power in northern Syria, where a new prince, Raymond of Poitiers, had established himself in Antioch by marrying Constance, the daughter of Bohemond II; this was despite the efforts of the king of Sicily, Roger II, who claimed the principality, and the schemes of Bohemond's widow, Alice (1136). In Edessa, meanwhile, Joscelin II had succeeded his father Joscelin I. The quarrels between Raymond and Joscelin added to the difficulties then being caused by the Armenian barony of the Roupenians, who, from their fortresses in the Taurus, had

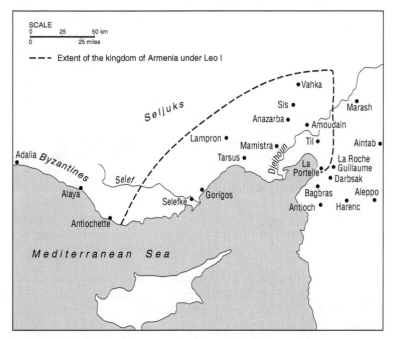

Map 9   The northern frontier of the principality of Antioch

taken possession of a large part of Cilicia, with Sis and Anazarbus, in spite
of Antiochene claims; Raymond of Poitiers had even imprisoned the
Armenian leader Leo I, while the Danishmends invaded his lands. These
conflicts favoured the schemes of the emperor John Comnenus, who
was determined to restore the authority of the empire over its Syrian
borders, reviving the projects of his father Alexius; Raymond, Joscelin
and Leo barely had time to settle their differences before the arrival of
the Byzantine, but were incapable of resisting him.

Alexius Comnenus had conducted negotiations with Roger of
Antioch aimed at finding a solution to the unresolved question of the
implementation of the treaty of Devol. His envoy, Ravendinos, had
been present at the battle of the Field of Blood. And Princess Alice,
when widowed, had considered a marriage with a son of John Comnenus, which may help to explain the campaign conducted against her
and her ally, Count Pons, around 1132, by Fulk.

But in 1137 the emperor assembled an army with which, beginning
with Silifke, he occupied the part of Cilicia belonging to the principality,

Tarsus, Adana and Mamistra, replacing the Latin bishops with Greek bishops to signal the reintegration of these towns into the empire. He then occupied part of the lands of Leo of Armenia and, in August of the same year, arrived at Antioch, which he proceeded to bombard with his siege machines. Raymond of Poitiers entered into talks and negotiated on bases which were no longer quite those of the treaty of Devol. John Comnenus received his liege homage and left him Antioch as a hereditary fief, but only while waiting for him to create an equivalent fief, through the conquest of Aleppo, Shaizar, Hamah and Homs. Raymond promised free access to his town to the emperor and his troops, which corresponded to what feudal law called a fief *jurable et rendable*, the liege vassal being obliged to surrender his castle to his lord when the latter had need of it for his wars. It seems that the counts of Edessa and Tripoli also acknowledged themselves to be vassals of the emperor.

Joscelin and Raymond accompanied the emperor the following spring, when, after a show of force before Aleppo and the reoccupation of Cereb and Kafr Tab, he began to lay siege to Shaizar. But the town held out. William of Tyre tells us that the two Frankish princes failed to help the emperor, which is not confirmed by the Greek sources. Finally, John raised the siege in return for the payment of a tribute by the emir and returned to Antioch. There, he asked Raymond to implement the clause relating to the surrender of the town, with a view to later operations. Joscelin of Edessa pointed to the need to obtain the agreement of the prince's vassals, which gave him time to raise the inhabitants of Antioch, who were extremely hostile to the prospect of passing under Byzantine rule, which seemed to them the inevitable consequence. The emperor, recalled to Constantinople, to which he took Leo of Armenia as a prisoner, had to leave Antioch.

John Comnenus repeated his operation in 1142, but this time he began by marching on Turbessel to force Joscelin to surrender hostages. On 15 September, having reached Baghras, he asked Raymond to surrender the citadel and fortifications of Antioch. The barons of the principality objected that its true heir was the princess Constance and that her husband could not deprive her of her rights. The emperor also asked King Fulk to authorise him to make a pilgrimage to Jerusalem with his army. Fulk agreed, but, to spare the kingdom's resources, asked him to limit the army's size to 10,000 men, which John refused to do.

At this point, the emperor died following a fall from his horse, and his army withdrew. His aim had probably been to restore Antioch to his lands, to make it, with Cilicia, Cyprus and Adalia, an apanage for his youngest son, Manuel. But when the death of his two elder sons made Manuel his heir, this project, which would have resulted in the creation of a Byzantine bastion surrounded by Latin fiefs, lost impetus. The question of Antioch remained unresolved, but Cilicia was now lost to the Franks. And the expulsion of the archbishops of Tarsus and Mamistra had shifted the emphasis to a confessional opposition; it was probably this which led Pope Innocent II, in a letter of 28 March 1138, to protest against this aggression on the part of a schismatic 'king of the Greeks' and to threaten to release his Latin mercenaries from their loyalty towards him.

The atabeg Zengi had refrained from interfering during this campaign, which had in part cancelled out the territorial gains he had made in 1135. He had engaged in talks with the emperor and reoccupied the towns he had taken. But his main aim throughout this period had been to gain possession of Damascus. While he was content to maintain an observation post opposite the Byzantines and the Franks who were besieging Shaizar, he got the Damascenes to relinquish Homs (1138). In 1139 he tried to surprise Damascus and seized Baalbek, whose garrison he massacred, which helped to alienate the population of Damascus and throw Unur into the arms of the Franks. The emir Usama ibn Munqidh, who had already had occasion to negotiate with the Franks, went to Jerusalem to conclude a formal treaty, at the beginning of 1140, obtaining from the king the liberation of his Muslim captives and a military intervention; on 4 May, the Frankish army broke the blockade of Damascus. The relations between the two states sometimes took a friendly turn; Unur himself made a visit to Fulk, who showed him round several of the kingdom's towns. This did not prevent occasional border incidents, but they were resolved by peaceful means; when a nomadic tribe fell victim to a raid of pillage led by the lord of Banyas, Rainier Brus, Usama complained to the king, who had the matter judged by his court and ordered Rainier to compensate his victims.

Obliged to loosen his hold on Damascus, Zengi returned to the north, where his ambitions brought him into conflict with both the Ortoqids of the Jazirah and the Seljuks of Anatolia, who had reappeared on the frontier of the Euphrates. But the Franks got on with each other no better. Raymond of Poitiers had quarrelled once again with Joscelin II, after the death of John Comnenus had removed a common danger, and he had tried in vain to regain a foothold in Cilicia. Joscelin, who is described in unfavourable terms by Syrian historians because of his disputes with the monks of the monastery of Mar Barsauma, led expeditions of pillage into the Jazirah and allied with the Ortoqids against the atabeg. King Fulk had died, also in a hunting accident, on 8 April 1143, and his widow Melisende was in no position to intervene effectively in the northern states.

It was then that Zengi conducted a lightning campaign, first seizing places which, to the east of Edessa, stretched in a crescent towards the valley of the Khabur. On 28 November 1144 he laid siege to Edessa; as Joscelin was at Turbessel, it was the Latin archbishop, Hugh, who took charge of its defence; he was accused of not having paid the soldiers, which suggests that money was short. The atabeg did not want to allow the other Franks time to intervene and hastened operations: the construction of wooden towers, bombardment, the digging of mines, to which the besieged responded with counter-mines. The Franks refused to capitulate; then, when a stretch of wall that had been heavily undermined collapsed on 24 December 1144, the assailants invaded the town, massacring large numbers of people. The inhabitants rushed to the citadel, to find the gates closed; Archbishop Hugh, who had given the order, was among those who perished. The citadel surrendered on 26 December. The number of dead has been estimated at 15,000; the town was sacked and the churches of the Latin rite destroyed. Zengi had given orders to respect the other Christian churches, but we are told that many monasteries were also destroyed. The Franks were systematically massacred. Saruj was evacuated by its defenders early in January 1145.

In the face of this disaster, Raymond of Poitiers realised that he needed to obtain the aid of the Byzantines, whom he had alienated by attacking Cilicia. Manuel Comnenus would only pardon the Frankish prince for this act of hostility when he had made honourable amends at the tomb of John Comnenus.

But at this point Zengi, who had begun to push on with his campaign, was recalled to Mosul. We should not forget that his Syrian policy clashed with the imperatives of his situation in the Seljuk sultanate, where his conquests, which put him in a position to form an independent state, aroused the disquiet of both the sovereign and his peers; his campaigns against the Franks, even against the Damascenes, were frequently interrupted by his need to resume contact with his base in Mosul. The danger brought about by the capture of Edessa was once again averted in the short term. Further, the assassination of the atabeg, on 14 September 1146 when he was besieging an Ortoqid fortress, seemed likely, for a while, to create a power vacuum in Mosul. The Damascenes restored their authority over Baalbek.

Joscelin II attempted to take advantage of the death of his great adversary, thanks to the welcome he knew he would find among the Armenians of Edessa; they had already, in May 1146, considered a plot which Zengi had thwarted, at the same time attracting a large number of Jewish families to the town. On 27 October they opened their gates to Joscelin, who was accompanied by Baldwin of Marash. But the assailants spent time pillaging the town instead of immediately attacking the citadel. Zengi's son, Nur al-Din, was soon on the spot and his arrival caused panic. Fearing they would be unable to defend the city, the inhabitants evacuated it in haste. Joscelin and Baldwin tried to organise their escort. But the Turks overcame the Frankish defence and massacred the fugitives before returning to the slaughter inside the town, where they destroyed and sacked the churches. Joscelin managed to escape, but Baldwin of Marash was killed; the number of dead has been estimated at 30,000 and the number enslaved at 16,000; among them was the Armenian archbishop (9 November 1146). The Jacobite archbishop was spared and assured Nur al-Din of the submission of his flock, who had also suffered badly. After this, the new prince of Aleppo proceeded to attack several fortresses in the vicinity of his capital.

The fall of Edessa, which had been one of the bastions of Frankish occupation since 1098, and which had withstood many attacks by the atabegs of Mosul, is probably explicable in terms of its remote location, separated by the Euphrates from the main Frankish possessions. The speed of Zengi's attack had forestalled the arrival of the help being brought by the constable of Jerusalem; the improvised character of the reoccupation of 1146 had not allowed a proper preparation of the town's defence. And the Byzantine intervention of 1142, which had seen Joscelin's submission to the emperor, had brought additional protection neither to Edessa nor to its county.

Until this point, the years since 1124 had seen no episodes as dramatic as those of the previous decades. The Frankish expansion had made little progress. The minor war for primacy around Aleppo had ended in success for that town, rid of the Frankish forts closest to it. The county of Tripoli had been more seriously affected by the loss of its most easterly march. The reappearance of the Byzantines, come as allies against the Muslim danger, had proved to be a threat to Frankish domination. The greatest danger came from the union of Aleppo and Mosul, which had enabled Zengi finally to conquer Edessa; but, until the fall of that town, the Franks had succeeded in containing it.

Had the crusade, in the form it had taken until 1124, been in abeyance? As we have seen, Baldwin II had made an appeal to the West for his campaign of 1129 against Damascus. It had had little effect. We may note the arrival, in particular with Fulk of Anjou, of reinforcements consisting of the vassals of those who had assumed eastern thrones; to establish themselves, they had had to sideline some of the barons who had served their predecessors, but very few had, like Hugh of Le Puiset, returned to the West.

An incident recorded by William of Tyre reveals that the flow of pilgrims prepared to provide assistance to the Franks in the East continued. In the summer of 1139 the count of Flanders, Thierry of Alsace, went on a pilgrimage with a fairly large group of knights. Fulk of Anjou, who was his brother-in-law, and the barons of the kingdom proposed to take advantage of this to conduct with their assistance an expedition east of the Jordan, into the 'land of Gilead' (the valley of the Yarmuk), where the occupants of a fortress had been conducting raids of pillage into Frankish territory. Having learned that the defence of Judaea was depleted, a band of Turkomans went to pillage Thecua, a small township situated between Bethlehem and the Dead Sea, whose inhabitants had had time to flee. The knights remaining in Jerusalem attempted a rescue operation and fell into an ambush. The king and Count Thierry continued with their expedition as planned. Had it not been for the failure of the counter-attack which claimed several victims, we would have been told nothing of Count Thierry's 'crusade'.

The fall of Edessa led to a revival of the crusade, on a quite different scale from that of these occasional 'passages', which nevertheless help us to understand the way the Second Crusade ended.

As this was being prepared, the situation in Syria changed. Nur al-Din, who had left Mosul to his brother, now lord of Aleppo, wanted to mend fences with Unur, whose daughter had married in March 1147. In June of the same year the two men joined forces to repel the Franks of Jerusalem who, while attempting to keep to the letter of the truces concluded with Damascus, had agreed to reinstate in his fortresses the governor of Bosra, Altuntash, who had rebelled against Unur. This expedition, which was notable for the maintenance of a strict discipline thanks to which the Franks could avoid being distracted by the men of Aleppo and Damascus, who were harrying them, was a failure, and the Hauran continued to escape the Franks. Unur seems to have tried to come to terms with them, but the Franco-Damascene alliance had had its day. This, too, was to influence the fate of the crusade.

THE CRUSADE OF EUGENIUS III

Was the shock caused in the West by the fall of Edessa as great as historians have claimed? Admittedly, the educated clergy knew that King Abgar had been the first sovereign to embrace the Christian faith, and that the town was famous for the memory of its saints (even if Christ's letter to Abgar, its most famous relic, had been transferred to Constantinople). But the name of 'Rohais' did not resonate like that of Jerusalem. And the taking of the cross in 1147 was not done spontaneously. In any case, the example of the crusade of Calixtus II shows that enthusiasm for an expedition, even one endowed with a plenary indulgence, was far from automatic.

There had to be a convergence of factors. The Roman Curia probably learned of the fall of Edessa by various routes. Otto of Freising emphasises the visit of a bishop from the Nivernais, Hugh of Jabala, who came to seek justice against his patriarch. He brought news of all sorts, in particular of the victory won on the borders of the Khorassan over the sultan Sanjar by a Christian king of the Indies, the famous priest-king, Prester John (who was in reality the khan of the Kara Khitai, a Turco-Mongol people driven out of China, who had effectively vanquished this Seljuk in 1141). Hugh claimed that he was coming to the aid of the Christians, but that he had been unable to cross the river that would have given him access to the Near East. Rome set little store by the prospect of assistance from this source, and registered only the news of the fall of Edessa. Other news was brought by Armenian ecclesiastics. But it is likely that Eugenius III had other sources of information. In any case, the pope decided to proclaim, on 1 December 1145, by the bull *Quantum predecessores*, the grant of the crusading indulgence to those who went to the aid of the Eastern Church.

At the same time, the king of France, Louis VII, who had probably received news from the envoys of the Frankish princes, convoked at Bourges, for Christmas, the festive 'crown-wearing' at which he informed the French barons and prelates of his firm intention of going on a crusade. He had probably already been in touch with the pope, but the bull had almost certainly not yet reached him. The personal motives of the king have been variously interpreted: the desire to expiate by the appropriate penance the burning of the church of Vitry; the fulfilment of a vow made by his dead brother Philip; scruples associated with the excommunication proclaimed against him on account of his actions in ecclesiastical matters. But his audience remained wary, and the abbot of Clairvaux, asked by the king to preach the crusade, waited until he was given a papal mandate.

Eugenius III was persuaded to amend the bull. In his new version (1 March 1146), he recalled the crusade of Urban II and the generous response to the French and the Italians:

But now, because of our sins and those of the people of God, something has happened that we announce with sadness and lamentation. The city of Edessa, that we call Rohais, the city which, it is said, was alone in submitting to the law of Christ when the whole of the East was pagan, has been taken by the enemies of Christ's Cross who have also seized many castles from the Christians. The archbishop of the city, his clergy and many other Christians have been killed, the saints' relics dispersed and trodden underfoot by the infidel . . . we enjoin you in the name of the Lord and for the remission of your sins ... that the faithful of God, and above all the most powerful and the nobles act vigorously to oppose the multitude of the infidel ... and strive to liberate from their hands the many thousands of our brethren who are captives ... we accord them that same remission of sins that our predecessor Pope Urban instituted.

The pope listed the measures which show that lessons had been learned from experience: the protection of the Church for the women, children and property of the crusaders; suspension of lawsuits under way concerning ownership of property until the crusaders' return or until their death was known with certainty; prohibition of extravagant clothing and weapons and the use of beasts for hunting; moratorium on the interest on debts already contracted; freedom to mortgage fiefs with churches or other persons if lords could not or would not accept them. Eugenius III had been a monk under St Bernard and it was to him that he entrusted the task of disseminating his appeal. The abbot of Clairvaux composed a circular intended for the princes and prelates to explain the pope's intentions; rather than dwelling on the fall of Edessa and the other ordeals of the Christians of Outremer, he emphasised the name of penitence and the exceptional grace offered to the faithful who responded to this appeal. 'See, the time is right'; the crusade was a chance of salvation not to be missed.

Bernard agreed to preach the crusade before the king and his barons, assembled at Vézeley on 31 March 1146. His words were enthusiastically received and a large number of people took the cross. The abbot of Clairvaux probably thought he had completed his task by launching the movement that others would soon relay, in England and France.

But at least one of those preachers who spontaneously took up the baton gave to his words a slant that was soon causing concern to St Bernard, who had been careful in his circular to say that the conversion of souls was a matter for God and that he alone would decide when the Jews would embrace the faith of Christ. For, as at the time of the First Crusade, a movement emerged that was in direct contradiction to this; a Cistercian by the name of Rudolf, who preached the crusade, invited his audience to revenge Christ on his enemies. Collective murders are recorded at Ham, Sully and Carentan; the names of these places have been the subject of controversy among historians, and it is difficult to relate them to Rudolf's activities. The monk intervened in the Low Countries, perhaps, but primarily in the Rhine Valley, at Cologne, Mainz and Worms, in August and September 1146, and probably at Würzburg in February 1147. The archbishop of Cologne had left his castle at Wolkenburg to the Jews where they found refuge, and their skilful distribution of gifts – which sometimes amounted to ransoms –

acquired them protectors. The archbishop of Mainz had warned St
Bernard, who immediately asked him to stop this anti-Jewish preaching,
and who himself set off for Flanders, the Low Countries and the
Rhineland to counteract the consequences of Rudolf's incitements and,
at the same time, to confirm the appeal to the crusade. In October 1146
Bernard arrived in the Rhineland and he sent Rudolf back to Clairvaux.

The arrival of the abbot of Clairvaux in Germany had unforeseen
consequences. Finding the ground already prepared by Rudolf's
preaching, Bernard extended his own sphere of activity to the Germanic
countries. He went to the Diet of Frankfurt, in November, to try to
convince King Conrad III to leave on crusade. Conrad resisted, and
Bernard had to be content with going to preach in the lands of the duke
of Zähringen (modern Switzerland). Many German princes were already
planning to join the expedition, among them Duke Welf VI, who had
been Conrad's principal opponent. During the Christmas festivities,
Bernard returned to the attack; at Speyer, he preached in a manner so
pressing that Conrad took the cross, followed by his principal vassals.

There remained one uncertainty; the barons from the eastern part of
Germany pointed out that their departure for the East would empty the
frontier between their country and that of the Wends, who remained
pagans, especially in Lusatia, and they might take advantage of this to
attack Christian lands. At the Diet of Frankfurt (March 1147), Bernard
gave his consent for these barons to do their duty as crusaders by fighting
the pagan Slavs, which was in accord with the pontifical doctrine
concerning the non-participation of the Spanish in the crusades in the
East.

The 'Wendish Crusade' proposed to force baptism on the pagan
peoples living to the east of the Elbe. The Obotrites of the north,
governed by Prince Niklot, raided Lübeck, at which the barons besieged
their capital, Dobin. Niklot then promised to forbid the worship of idols
and to pay tribute to the count of Holstein, which remained in practice a
dead letter. In the case of the Liutizians, the main army, led by the Duke
of Saxony, the margrave Albert the Bear and the legate, Bishop Anselm
of Havelberg, also vainly laid siege to Demmin, then moved to Szczecin
(Stettin), where they were surprised to find the inhabitants parading
crosses. The crusade ended in the autumn, without having achieved its
objectives. These had, in any case, probably been defined with an eye to
the ambitions of the frontier margraves; the missionary perspectives laid
out before St Bernard were illusory.

Conrad III's decision was itself probably not free from political
calculation. The German king had only recently triumphed over the
opposition provoked by the accession of the Hohenstaufen to the

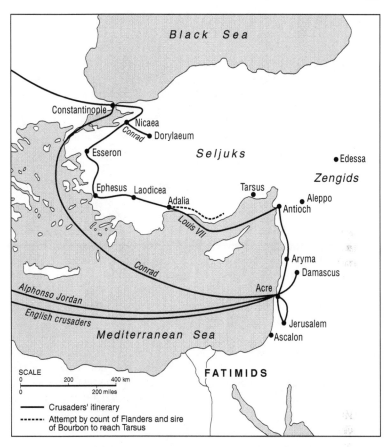

Map 10   The Second Crusade in the East

throne. In taking the cross, he obliged his opponents to rally to him; even Duke Welf VI, who had planned to join the army of Louis VII, joined him. The majority of the great men of the kingdom of Germany, beginning with his nephew Frederick, Duke of Swabia, the future Emperor Frederick Barbarossa, also took part in the crusade under his leadership. This unanimity matched that which had emerged in the kingdom of France.

The crusade launched by Eugenius III, as a result of Louis VII's decision and Conrad III's support, was very different from that of 1096. It was better organised, the pope turning his attention to questions such

as the financing of the expedition, which remained the responsibility of
the crusader; there survive large numbers of acts of donation or of sale
drawn up for lords who took the cross and who appealed, as well as for
the prayers of the monks or canons, for gifts to help them to make their
journey; mortgages of property which were to be returned to the
crusader on repayment of the sum which had been advanced to him are
even more numerous, though we have none of those which were
reimbursed. Eugenius III had specifically made provision for such cases.

Though they bore the cost of their own equipment, the crusaders
were nevertheless taken on by their sovereigns. King Louis VII levied an
aid on his kingdom, to ask his subjects to share in the costs of the
expedition; the barons probably did the same. The two kings each led an
army which was very similar to the army of the kingdom, even if the
combatants were volunteers bound by their personal vow.

The spiritual climate of the departure on the crusade is primarily
known to us through the correspondence of St Bernard. But he referred,
when he had to explain the crusaders' failure, to the fact that his
preaching had seemed to him to be confirmed by the miraculous
manifestations which had accompanied it.

Eugenius III may have been outflanked by his auxiliary. He himself
was in conflict with King Roger II of Sicily and above all with the
Romans, who had risen against his authority, and he was counting on
Conrad's assistance. His involvement in the crusade thus ran counter to
his plans. He nevertheless confirmed the privileges granted in his name
to the Germans by St Bernard and crossed the Alps to visit France where
he personally handed the oriflamme to Louis VII, at St Denis, a
ceremony which shows that it really was the army of the kingdom that
the king meant to lead to the East (8 June 1147).

The crusade attracted the usual train of pilgrims, as anxious to benefit
from the indulgence as to enjoy the aid and protection of the knights.
Odo of Deuil, who told the story of the expedition, deplored the fact
that these unarmed men had not seen fit to equip themselves with the
bows and swords that would have been so useful in battle.

Odo also described the king's hesitation over the route to adopt. This
had been discussed at the assembly of Etampes on 16 February 1147.
Louis had had talks with Roger II of Sicily, who had offered him ships
and supplies, as well as his own and his son's participation in the crusade.
Manuel Comnenus, also consulted, strongly urged Louis VII to pass
through his lands, where he would open up the markets to him and his
followers. He did not conceal the fact that he had made peace with the
Turks, but let it be known that if they were to break this peace, he
would be pleased (August 1146). The same conditions – free passage and

provisions – had been obtained in Germany and in Hungary. The assembly opted for the route already taken by the First Crusade. Some, however, still went by sea, including the count of Toulouse and a large number of the English crusaders, though others of them, with William of Warenne, accompanied Louis VII. Like others before them, the English crusaders, joined by ships from Flanders and the Rhineland, were drawn into operations being conducted against the Muslims of Spain. They had set sail from Dartmouth in May 1147; when they put in at Porto, its bishop asked them to join the siege of Lisbon recently embarked on by the king of Portugal, Alfonso Henriques (16 June). The crusaders were divided, some wishing to accept, others arguing that their vow had been to go to Jerusalem; a split was avoided by emphasising the need for the crusade to remain united (a debate that was to be heard again during the Fourth Crusade). Finally, the English took part in the siege, in particular by constructing the machines that battered the walls. And when the town capitulated, in accord with the promise given them by the king, they sacked it systematically (24 October). The season being far advanced, they overwintered in Lisbon and, leaving some of their number behind (among them the new bishop of Lisbon), they set sail once again for the East on 1 February 1148.

Having entrusted the regency of the kingdom to Suger, Louis VII went to Metz, to which he had summoned his army. The pope had appointed legates – the cardinal Theodwin for the German army, the cardinal Guido for the French – but certain bishops, such as Godfrey of Langres and Arnulf of Lisieux, assumed a *de facto* authority. They waited at Ratisbon for the Byzantine emperor's representative and, by means of the ships that had been prepared, they descended the Danube as far as Branichevo, through which Conrad III had passed some weeks earlier.

The German army, when it crossed the Danube, numbered some 900,000 men if we are to believe the Byzantines. This figure is clearly too high; a total of 70,000 combatants has been suggested, itself a figure to be treated with caution. The German army had only been able to cross Hungary after difficult negotiations with King Geza II, who had been one of Conrad's opponents the year before. And before authorising its passage through the empire, the representatives of the Emperor Manuel asked the leaders of the crusade to swear not in any way to infringe the rights of Byzantium. A troop of Byzantine soldiers followed the Germans to prevent any straying by laggards. Not all incidents could be prevented, but they remained few.

On 10 September Conrad III arrived before Constantinople. The French who followed him complained about the vexations they suffered at the hands of the Germans, and the depredations the latter had committed; they seem not to have jeopardised the provisioning of Louis VII's army. But the two sovereigns could not agree; Conrad crossed the Bosphorus just as Louis arrived in Constantinople (4 October), saying that he had set out to deliver Edessa and that he would not cease until this had been done.

The diplomatic situation was confused. Manuel Comnenus had warned the pope that he would ask the crusaders to make the same promises as in 1096–7. The king of France only learned of this at Ratisbon and contented himself then with making a commitment not to injure the emperor; this oath has been compared with that sworn by the count of Toulouse in 1097. But the promise to restore to the empire the places that had belonged to it prior to the Turkish invasion, which Manuel listed, aroused the strong opposition of the French barons, whose spokesman was Godfrey of Langres. The emperor could only obtain this promise when the army had crossed into Asia, where it was dependent on him for supplies. Conrad III seems not to have been presented with the same request; we should not forget that Manuel and he were brothers-in-law, that the empress Irene (Bertha of Sulzbach) promoted relations between them, and that the two sovereigns had common interests in Italy.

Louis VII found himself faced with a new situation. Roger II, whose offers he had refused in favour of those of Manuel, had attacked Corfu and launched a raid of pillage in Greece. Manuel proved to have no intention of breaking the truce he had made with the Seljuk sultan of Anatolia at the end of the campaign of 1146, when he had penetrated as far as Konya; he also needed to be in a position to repel the Normans. This pact with the Turks enraged the barons. Many of them, following the bishop of Langres, urged the king to attack Constantinople, denouncing the duplicity of this emperor whose ill will towards the Latins had been demonstrated by the expulsion of the Latin bishops of Cilicia.

On the Byzantine side, there was unease at the prospect of collusion between Roger II and the French. King Louis did his best to dispel these fears; he agreed to transport his army over to the Asian shore, which would protect Constantinople from the possibility of attack.

It was at Nicomedia that agreement was finally reached; the king of France promised to return to the emperor the places he conquered, saving his right to pillage them if they refused to hand over supplies; the emperor would provide him with guides of noble rank who would indicate the route to be followed and organise the markets – they even agreed a suitable rate of exchange. The last contingent expected, that of the count of Maurienne, the marquis of Montferrat and the count of

Auvergne, which had travelled through Italy, had arrived. Louis VII's army could set off; they were unaware that the army of Conrad III had suffered a disaster.

THE FAILURES OF THE SECOND CRUSADE

We should probably not believe Odo of Deuil when he accuses the Greeks of having misled the king of France by falsely reporting that Conrad III had taken Konya. On the other hand, Conrad had under-estimated the provisions needed for his march across Asia Minor; he had equipped himself with supplies for only eight days on leaving Nicaea, and his army was soon going hungry. A detachment of some fifteen thousand men, led by his brother, Otto of Freising, separated from the main army to take the coastal route, but the pilgrims remained with the majority. Having reached Dorylaeum (Eskisehir), they encountered the Turks who, by resorting to a simulated flight, threw them into disorder and inflicted heavy losses. Conrad ordered a retreat, which turned into a rout. The rearguard, under the count of Plötzkau, was destroyed, and the remains of the army reached Nicaea at the beginning of November; many crusaders then left it. Otto of Freising's contingent was ambushed in its turn as it approached Laodicea in Phrygia; Count Bernard of Carinthia was killed with most of his companions, Otto managing to escape (December 1147).

Louis VII received and re-equipped Conrad's troops, and the two sovereigns set off for Ephesus, where the German king, who was sick, halted; at Manuel's invitation he returned to Constantinople with his men; he left it by the sea route in spring, heading directly for Jerusalem.

The French continued on their way, ascending the valley of the Maeander, where they frustrated a Turkish attack, on 1 January 1148; the fugitives took refuge in a nearby Byzantine township, and the French then discovered the realities of the situation they faced, which Odo of Deuil defined by saying that where the Greeks held the fortresses, the revenues from the land were shared between them and the Turks. The treaty concluded between Manuel and the Seljuks prevented the imperial troops from protecting the crusaders; the Greeks of the townships were in daily contact with their Muslim neighbours and, while they provided supplies to the Franks – sparingly, it seems, and at high prices – they assisted the Turks by keeping them informed of the crusaders' move-ments, even joining them in their looting. The passage through lands that were theoretically Byzantine was tantamount to a march through enemy territory.

Having left Laodicea, they reached the spot where the bishop of

Freising's troops had been wiped out, then Mount Cadmus (the Baba-Dagh), where an act of disobedience on the part of the commander of the vanguard put the king in great danger; having pushed on beyond the defile, Geoffrey of Rancon effectively left the convoy which included Louis VII at the mercy of a Turkish attack. The king, separated from his men, defended himself on a rock until William of Warenne and a few others came to his rescue. Famine devastated men and horses, and it was the master of the Temple, Everard of Barres, who enabled them to extricate themselves. It was even necessary to burn the baggage that was abandoned to prevent it from falling into the hands of the Turks.

The army at last reached Adalia, on 19 January. There, they found provisions for the men, but the horses perished and it was impossible to buy more. It was this that decided Louis VII to accept the offers of the emperor Manuel's representatives, who had opportunely arrived and who proposed to provide them with ships to reach the port of Antioch. But the number of ships that could be obtained was too small for the whole army, and Louis negotiated – at an exorbitant price – to transport the knights constituting his field forces. The Byzantines promised to lead the healthy men who remained to Tarsus, under escort, in return for 500 silver marks, and to tend the sick until they could leave. Archimbald of Bourbon and the count of Flanders were left at Adalia to see the agreement was kept. But after the king had left, the Turks launched new attacks right up to the walls of the city, and it was necessary to take into it the crusaders camped outside. The two barons were able to embark with some of these men. But the ships were too few for all of them and seven thousand men set out for Tarsus. They were stopped at the crossing of a river swollen by the winter rains. The lot of the pilgrims left in Adalia, a prey to famine and epidemic, was hard; some chose to enlist as mercenaries with the Turks. How the others reached Syria is far from clear.

Although severely tried by this journey across Asia Minor which had provided many reasons for rancour against the emperor and his subjects, Louis VII's army was still a formidable force when it gathered at Antioch in March 1148. Prince Raymond welcomed and fêted the crusaders, amongst whom was his niece, Queen Eleanor of Aquitaine. He had long ago sent messengers to the king of France and his barons urging them to come. He was counting on them to restore the situation in northern Syria in the face of Nur al-Din.

One of the crusading songs written to encourage the French to depart, *Chevaliers, mout estes guaris*, presented the crusade as 'a tournament arranged between Hell and Paradise', the date of which was fixed 'at Rohais'. The objective proposed by Eugenius III was less specific, namely to bring aid to the Christians in the East; but the *trouvère* had repeated the pope's words in recalling the capture of Edessa and the destruction of its churches. Raymond had therefore good reason to believe that the crusade would attack the formidable master of Aleppo, responsible for the fall of that town. And, according to Conrad III's reply to Louis VII, when he was setting out on his journey across Asia, it was to Edessa that the German king was going.

But at the outset, and without having been asked to do otherwise, Louis VII had announced his intention first to accomplish his pilgrimage to Jerusalem. This was, as we have seen, quite normal for knights who went to the Holy Land and who, while ready to fight alongside the Franks, first made their visit to the Holy Places. But the situation in this case was different; the army that had landed at St Simeon was well placed to attack Aleppo or Shaizar, and it was doubtful whether it would return to the north after it had reached Jerusalem. Nor had the crusade been launched as an ordinary pilgrimage. But Louis VII's personal vow was probably that of pilgrimage, and the king stuck firmly to his decision. Raymond of Poitiers tried to make him change his mind, and wanted to involve Queen Eleanor in his plans. It was later even said that she had been too susceptible to her uncle's charms. What is certain is that the king took his wife's intervention badly and that Raymond urged her to separate from her husband. In the end, Louis used force to make her accompany him to Tripoli.

There, he met the patriarch of Jerusalem, Fulcher, who had been sent by Queen Melisende and her barons to persuade him to come to the Holy City. Some of the Germans were already there; Otto of Freising had arrived on 4 April and Conrad a few days later. Fulcher was instructed to dissuade the king from turning against Aleppo and to draw his attention to the situation in Jerusalem. If Conrad still intended to go to Edessa (which we do not know), the desire to act jointly led him to follow Louis, who now had the more powerful army.

A third contingent was expected, that of Alfonso Jordan with crusaders from Toulouse. Alfonso reached Acre at the end of April, but died at Caesarea on his way to Jerusalem, poisoned, according to William of Tyre, though no one knew at whose instigation. Suspicion later fell on Queen Melisende, who might have wished to rid her brother-in-law, Raymond II of Tripoli, of a potential rival, Alfonso having been born at Mont Pèlerin of the second marriage of Raymond of Saint-Gilles.

It was on 24 June, at Acre, that there met a great *parlement* attended by Louis VII, his barons and his prelates, Conrad III with Welf VI, the dukes of Bavaria and Swabia, the marquis of Montferrat, the margrave of Verona and the count of Biandrate, Queen Melisende, her son Baldwin, and the prelates and barons of the kingdom, but no representative of the three other Frankish states. The decisions regarding the use of the military forces of the crusade were therefore taken in the light of the needs of the kingdom of Jerusalem alone. Some of the crusaders, in any case, regarded themselves as quit of their vow because they had completed the pilgrimage, among them Bishop Arnulf of Lisieux, the count of Flanders and perhaps also King Conrad. We do not know if an attack on Aleppo was mooted, but the year was already well advanced and this idea had been rejected at Antioch. The majority of those present pronounced themselves in favour of a military operation that would render the crusaders of 1148 worthy of their ancestors.

The debate turned to the choice of objective. Contrary to what has long been said, the frontiers of the kingdom were no longer protected by the truce made with Damascus; the rapprochement of Unur and Nur al-Din had revived the possibility of danger from that quarter. The barons of the south of the kingdom proposed, as in 1123, to concentrate their efforts on Ascalon, but the council resolved to attack Damascus.

Some of the crusaders left the army, including Welf VI who went to Sicily. The others made their way to Tiberias, where a rendezvous had been fixed for the middle of July. Having reached Banyas, the leaders of the army decided to concentrate their efforts on the west flank of the enceinte of Damascus, probably the best protected but also where the gardens of the oasis would provide food and water for the besiegers.

The conduct of the siege has been much debated. It is clear that, on learning of the Franks' decision, the atabeg Unur appealed to the two sons of Zengi, Saif al-Din and Nur al-Din, who brought troops from Mosul and Aleppo towards Homs, and that he put the town in a defensive state, in particular by summoning archers from the Beqa'a. On 24 July the crusaders and their allies arrived at the entry of the Ghuta; next day, they encountered a large force which Conrad destroyed, and they were able to transfer their camp to the hippodrome, nearer to the ramparts. But progress through the gardens was extremely difficult, as the many hedges and channels made it possible for the defenders to harass the attackers. On 27 July the crusaders changed the site of their camp. It has been suggested that this was to move to the east of the town, where the walls were weaker and that this was on the pernicious advice of the Syrian Franks, in order to lead the crusaders into a waterless plain, but more recent research seems to contradict this. What is certain is that, two days later (29 July), the Franks raised the siege.

The siege of Damascus was surprisingly short, and rumours of every sort abounded. William of Tyre, who gathered his information twenty years later, confessed his uncertainty. Conrad III blamed King Baldwin, the patriarch Fulcher and the master of the Hospital for betraying the crusaders by giving them bad advice; others accused the Franks of having allowed themselves to be bought by the Damascenes; yet others pointed to the choice of Thierry of Flanders as lord of the town after it had been conquered, which had alienated the Franks from the project by dashing their hopes of expanding their kingdom. That the army had grown discouraged after a short week of siege is unlikely. All these explanations testify, however, to the enormous disillusionment felt by the participants.

The most likely reason for the raising of the siege is the approach of the troops of Mosul and Aleppo, even though they never got within reach of the city. Muin al-Din Unur, who had appealed to them, could scarcely have wanted to let into his town, as they requested, the sons of the Zengi who had tried so hard to make himself its master. And his contacts with the Franks allowed him to draw their attention to the risk they ran by driving him to the necessity of opening Damascus to the Zengids. The fortress had, in any case, proved too powerful for it to be taken by brute force; a long siege would have been necessary. The bishop of Langres and several French barons argued for pressing ahead. Conrad, Thierry of Flanders and the eastern Franks won the day, and the army withdrew.

A further council was held and it was decided to attack Ascalon. But Conrad III waited in vain for the arrival of the other leaders and, after a delay of eight days, decided to re-embark. On 8 September he left Acre for Thessalonika, from which he journeyed to Constantinople where he was fêted by Manuel. The alliance between the Hohenstaufen and Byzantium, united by their common hostility towards Roger II of Sicily, emerged strengthened.

Louis VII remained in the Holy Land, where he celebrated Easter, and manifested his desire to bring some assistance to the Christians of the East, to whom he also gave generously. The ships carrying him home were intercepted by a Byzantine squadron; Queen Eleanor and some of the royal household were captured. Louis VII himself landed in Calabria on 28 July 1149. From then on, he gave his full support to Roger II, and recognised the royal title contested by the pope by placing the crown on his head. He showed little enthusiasm, however, for the alliance proposed by Roger against Byzantium.

The biographers of St Bernard have commented at length on the treatise *De consideratione* which the abbot of Clairvaux addressed to Eugenius III and in which he drew lessons from the failure of the crusade, which he imputed to the sins of Christians, in accord with the theological interpretation of the age. But he expressed himself more vigorously elsewhere on the subject of the barons, whom he regarded as having conducted the crusade incompetently. And he remained persuaded that in preaching it he had been the interpreter of God's will. He listened favourably, therefore, to Suger, when the abbot of St Denis conceived the project of resuming the expedition.

This time, it was the clergy who agitated in favour of the crusade. Suger, St Bernard, Cardinal Theodwin and Peter the Venerable tried to convince Conrad III. In their eyes, it was Manuel Comnenus who was responsible for the misfortunes of the crusade, and they echoed Roger of Sicily in saying that the new expedition should be directed against Byzantium. Eugenius III, on 25 April 1150, disowned these initiatives. Suger resumed his project, reducing it to a new enterprise intended to bring succour to the Christians of the East; the pope confined himself to confirming the privileges granted to those who participated. But the assemblies of Laon and Chartres (7 May 1150) showed how unenthusiastic were the French bishops; the barons, so harshly criticised, declared that they would leave the conduct of the campaign to the clergy. The council of Chartres made St Bernard of Clairvaux himself its leader. But the council, which was to convene at Compiègne on 15 July 1150 to put the finishing touches to the project, never met.

The main difference between the Second Crusade and the First is probably that the latter had enjoyed Byzantine support, which was almost entirely lacking to the former. Apparently as large, as well led, and with a comparable fervour, the Franco-German crusade wore itself out crossing Asia Minor, where the crusaders of 1097 had been able to benefit from the experience of Taticius, an old soldier with long experience of Byzantine wars. Odo of Deuil's complaints about the greed of the Byzantine merchants were probably not without some truth, but it seems that the provisioning of Adalia was not adequately carried out by the imperial authorities. Manuel Comnenus, who had wanted the crusade to travel through his lands to deflect it from a cooperation with the king of Sicily that might have been dangerous for the empire, left Louis VII without real support.

Whatever the strategic and tactical faults of the leaders of the crusade, they lacked the assistance that Alexius I had provided to their predecessors, and the emperor Manuel deprived himself, by making long-term truces with the Seljuks of Anatolia, of the possibility of using the forces of the crusade for the benefit of the empire. The Damascus campaign, decided on unexpectedly though the barons of Jerusalem had earlier considered it, was conducted with no more preparation. The atabeg Unur was certainly capable of extricating himself from a difficult situation.

The crusade, however, had been decided on just when Frankish power had received a first shock which was followed by the collapse of a whole section of its defences. It was an opportunity that was not seized. Did it discourage the westerners on a long-term basis, or jeopardise the hopes that might be placed in Byzantine support? Though the efforts of Suger and St Bernard to resume the crusade were abortive, zeal for the Holy Land remained real and was to continue to be expressed, if not on the same scale.

6

BETWEEN BYZANTIUM AND SALADIN:
THE PERILS OF THE LATIN EAST

Not all the crusaders had yet arrived back in the West when the first cracks appeared in the edifice constructed by the First Crusade. The anxiety of the leaders of the Latin East is now directly accessible to us; though the crusade of 1148 had achieved so little, they pinned their hopes on a new effort on the part of Christendom, and their appeals were increasingly pressing. A whole section of the defence of the Holy Land collapsed in the space of a few years, and there emerged at their gates a Muslim power, which the Franks had long feared, with the clear aim of putting an end to their presence.

The Franks did not give up; they fought bravely against the danger. They were forced, nevertheless, at enormous cost, to accept what amounted to a Byzantine protectorate, which did not keep all its promises and which did not survive the death of the emperor Manuel Comnenus, for whom the entente with the Franks was an element in a policy directed at Italy, winning him the sympathy of the pope. The Franks tried to find a solution to their Syrian problems in Egypt; they failed to prevent the formation of Saladin's empire. In the end, helped by the inconsistency of the Frankish powers, Saladin dealt what seemed to be a fatal blow to the existence of the Latin states at the battle of Hattin.

But the Franks had been careful to keep the West informed of their difficulties and to involve it in an increasingly sustained support. It was this that paved the way for the rapid revival that followed the defeat of 1187, which should not be seen as unexpected.

THE COLLAPSE OF NORTHERN SYRIA AND THE CRUSADE
OF THIERRY OF FLANDERS

In a curious turn of events, the alliance between the regent of Damascus and the atabeg of Aleppo, which was maintained for just over a year after the crusaders' departure (Unur died in August 1149), resulted, in September 1148, in a joint operation against a crusader, but on behalf of one of the Frankish princes. Alfonso Jordan's son, Bertrand, had made himself master of the castle of Araima, between Tortosa and Tripoli. He may have been hoping to assert, thanks to the crusade, the rights that were his through his grandfather, Raymond of Saint-Gilles, to the county of Tripoli. Raymond II appealed to the two Muslim princes, who did him the service of seizing the castle. Bertrand was taken as a prisoner to Aleppo and his sister became one of Nur al-Din's concubines. Nur al-Din then led a raid of reprisal in the direction of Antioch, but he made contact with Joscelin II of Edessa, who was once again at odds with his neighbour, Raymond of Poitiers, and concluded a truce with him.

A Damascene contingent also supported the campaign which Nur al-Din led in May 1149 against the Antiochene castles of Harenc and Inab. The prince of Antioch went to Inab's rescue. Despite the warnings of an Ismaili chief who had joined him, he let himself be led into a trap; his army was wiped out; he himself and the son of Baldwin of Marash were killed. The defeat of Fons Murez (between Apamea and Rugia), on 29 June 1149, echoed that of the Field of Blood, but this time Nur al-Din followed it up. He appeared before Antioch, which the patriarch Aimery of Limoges succeeded in putting in a defensive state, while the young king Baldwin III approached by forced marches. The atabeg preferred to capture the fortresses of the Djebel Summaq which covered the Orontes valley, including Albara and Apamea, and those which commanded the approaches to Antioch on the Aleppo side, that is, Artesia and Harenc. He also took the Tripolitanian castle of Tortosa, which he contented himself with dismantling; in 1152 Raymond III granted it to the Templars, who restored it.

It was now the turn of the county of Edessa to be put to the test. Count Joscelin (who had pillaged the monastery of Mar Barsauma in 1148, the monks being suspected of collusion with their Turkoman neighbours), though covered on the Aleppo side by his alliance with Nur al-Din, was exposed to the attacks of the Ortoqids and Seljuks of Anatolia. The sultan of Konya, Masud, had taken advantage of the death of the count of Marash at Fons Murez to seize that town, granting free exit to the inhabitants, though they were massacred nevertheless. He then pushed as far as Turbessel, and Joscelin had to acknowledge himself to be his vassal and pay tribute. Baldwin III's constable, Humphrey of Toron, had come to his rescue. But some Turkoman prowlers surprised the count of Edessa and handed him over to Nur al-Din (1150); he was to die in the prisons of Aleppo in 1159. His Muslim neighbours hastened to exploit this stroke of luck. The Ortoqid Qara Arslan seized Gargar, the Seljuk Kaisun and places nearby, and Nur al-Din Hasart (Azaz).

The countess Beatrice no longer felt able to defend the county, which still constituted a large territorial mass. The Byzantines offered to buy her fortresses in return for a rent to be paid to her and her children. She accepted, after getting the agreement of Baldwin III, who had come to assume the defence of the lands deprived of their lords; in fact, with the loss of Artesia, Harenc and Hasart, the county was practically cut off from the other Frankish states, and John Comnenus had obliged it to acknowledge his suzerainty. The inhabitants, Franks, Armenians and Syrians, unwilling to pass under Byzantine rule, evacuated the towns that were ceded; Baldwin III was able to organise the defence of this convoy which reached Frankish territory without losses. The castle of Ranculat (Hromgla), given to the Armenian *catholicos* by the Countess and where he resided, remained in his possession.

The loss of the county of Edessa was definitive, all the more so since the Byzantines proved incapable of assuring the defence of the places they had acquired. Within a year, the Muslims, primarily the Seljuks, had captured them. Nur al-Din occupied Turbessel.

Baldwin III had wanted to take advantage of his presence in Antioch to find a husband for Constance, the widow of Raymond of Poitiers. But she refused the candidates he put forward. She turned to Manuel Comnenus, who offered to marry her to his brother-in-law, the Caesar John Roger, who was of Norman origin, but the princess seems to have found him too old. Then, suddenly, she fell for a new arrival, Reynald of Châtillon, who obtained the king's approval and married her early in 1153.

The emergence of Reynald of Châtillon is worthy of note; he provides an example which is not unique, that of those westerners who were attracted to the East by pilgrimage or the thirst for adventure and who found a wife there; another was Calon of Avallon, who married Agnes of Beirut, and whose descendants made their careers in the kingdom of Jerusalem. Among the candidates rejected by Constance in 1150 were the count of Soissons, Yves of Nesle, who had come to northern Syria with Baldwin III's army. Reynald, sire of Châtillon-sur-Loing, belonged to a great family, that of Donzy, and his father was sire of Gien. He was a *chevalier soudoyer* of King Baldwin, as were other 'pilgrim knights'. He may have experienced some reversals of fortune; he asked Louis VII to restore his patrimony, which he had been deprived of by his enemies. His undeniable bravery hardly compensated for his lack of wealth, and he might appear inferior in nobility of birth to his wife. Above all, he could bring to the defence of Antioch only his own person. He lost no time in appealing to the king of France.

His letter shows that the memory of the crusade of 1148 had conferred on Louis VII a prestige undimmed by the paucity of the expedition's achievements:

> You have often heard tell, most excellent lord, and you will more often hear tell, if God does not spare us, of the unhappiness and the poverty of this land ... The ears of all Christians are daily open and turned towards you, from whom they expect their deliverance ... We know that your heart impels you often to this deliverance, and we pray that you will come to visit it and free it from the hands of the impious.

Reynald, reminding him that he was one of his 'natural' subjects, begged him to find husbands for Raymond of Poitiers' two daughters. But what he really wanted was another visit by the king of France. A decade later, his son-in-law Bohemond III was to repeat to Louis VII: 'Everyone is asking: when will he come?'

There was, however, no question of a crusade. Louis VII had other concerns, at a time when Eleanor of Aquitaine was bestowing her hand and her duchy on Henry Plantagenet. And the Franks of the Holy Land continued to be left to their own devices.

Happily for them, the coalition between Aleppo and Damascus had not survived. Nur al-Din, who had tried to get his hands on Mosul on the death of his brother, had got his nephew to grant him Homs instead; he was clearly reviving the schemes of his father, Zengi, concerning Damascus. The atabeg Abaq, heir of the Burid dynasty, had resumed friendly relations with the Franks of Jerusalem by 1149. When Nur al-Din arrived with his army in the south of the Hauran, asking him to join the campaign he was planning to lead against the Franks, Abaq refused to break the treaty he had made with them. The atabeg of Aleppo returned in June 1151, this time to lay siege to Damascus; the Franks, summoned to the rescue by Abaq, arrived in time to relieve the town, then to march on Bosra, where the Zengid had installed a governor. When the army of Aleppo returned to Damascus, the Franks forced it to retreat (July 1151). Abaq, meanwhile, tried to dissuade an Ortoqid younger son who wanted to attack Jerusalem from carrying out his project, which failed lamentably (1152). In 1153, he agreed to join with Nur al-Din to create a diversion in order to compel the Franks to raise the siege of Ascalon, but the mutual distrust of the two princes prevented this from materialising. In return for their protection, Abaq paid tribute to the Franks and even authorised them to come to Damascus to free the Christian slaves they found there.

But the internal conflicts of the principality of Damascus weakened Abaq's position, and he was abandoned by the urban militias on whom the Burids had relied. In April 1154 the atabeg was deposed and Nur al-Din at last took possession of Damascus; the following year he drove the last Burid from Baalbek. And thanks to the earthquake of 1157, in which the entire family of the Munqidhite emirs of Shaizar perished, he also gained possession of that town. Thus his lands adjoined the Frankish states for the full length of their border.

The Franks had every reason to fear Nur al-Din's intentions. A deeply pious prince, whose piety was even stronger after the serious illness that threatened his life in 1157, he demonstrated a Sunni zeal which boded ill for his Shi'i subjects. The prescriptions of the Koran were applied in all their rigour, in particular as regards the use of wine. He had strengthened the most warlike elements in his army by summoning to Syria large numbers of Turkomans, and by recruiting from among the Kurds; this was how the father and uncle of Saladin, Ayyub and Shirkûh, entered his service. Lastly, he posed as a protagonist of the *jihad*, the holy war against Christians, aimed in particular at the Frankish states. This stance was not new and the Burids of Damascus had also proclaimed themselves 'fighters in the holy war', but with Nur al-Din the intention was more explicitly expressed; he had a preaching chair made which was destined to be placed in the mosque of Al-Aqsa when it was restored to the Muslims. Faced with the Zengid state, the kingdom of Jerusalem had maintained its frontiers; the county of Tripoli had retrenched. In the north, the retrenchment was substantial. Not only had the county of Edessa been erased from the map, but the principality of Antioch, one of whose richest regions had been the Orontes valley, saw its border reduced to west of the river; the ecclesiastical metropolis, Apamea, was lost; and it was for possession of Harenc, which covered Antioch, and not for that of the fortresses of the mountainous barrier separating Aleppo from the Frankish lands, that the Franks and the Muslims were in future to fight.

There was one compensation for this collapse; the Fatimid frontier, so long a threat to the security of the Holy City itself, had ceased to be so. In 1150, using stone from the ancient city, the Franks had rebuilt Gaza, in future a fortress severing the road which linked Ascalon to Egypt.

An internal crisis in the kingdom of Jerusalem gave Egypt a respite. In 1152 the young king Baldwin III, confined by his mother to possession of the north of the kingdom, got himself crowned, without associating the queen in his coronation, and demanded the surrender of Judaea and Samaria, which Queen Melisende had retained. They resorted to force; the constable Manasses of Hierges, the queen's confidante, besieged in Mirabel, had to capitulate and Melisende, besieged in her turn in Jerusalem, relinquished power to her son. He was then able to resume his campaign.

The Franks were camped before Ascalon by the end of January 1153. The king requisitioned, as they arrived, the ships carrying the pilgrims and the pilgrims themselves, offering them good wages. They were unable to prevent the Egyptian fleet from provisioning the town, but an attempt to destroy the siege machines resulted in the collapse of a whole section of the walls. The master of the Temple, who wanted to reserve the best of the booty for his own knights, prevented the other besiegers from exploiting this breach, and the Templars were driven back. The Franks did not lose heart; the diversion requested by the Egyptians from the atabegs of Damascus and Aleppo failed to materialise. On 19 August the town capitulated, yielding great wealth to the victors. The evacuation was conducted in an orderly fashion, the besieged being allowed to take their movable possessions with them.

We should note here the role played by Franks from Europe. By reinforcing the royal army, the pilgrims of 1153, who stayed in the Holy Land no longer than was usual, had assured the success of the siege. There had been no need, seemingly, to resort to a special crusade; the normal influx of pilgrims and their mobilisation constituted an essential element in the success of the Frankish army. Also, in opening up to the Franks the road to Egypt, the capture of Ascalon helped to prolong the life of the Frankish states.

In 1158–9, the West was to make a more substantial effort. This seems not to have resulted from a papal initiative; referring to the count of Flanders' arrival, Adrian IV described it as an 'unexpected aid', in a letter of 13 November 1158 in which he asked the archbishop of Reims to help the Templars to replace the knights and the weapons they had lost; the pope would certainly have claimed that this aid was due to his intervention if this had been the case. It is likely that it was a personal decision on the part of a great lord, taking with him his vassals and his neighbours. Nevertheless, it seems that he was not alone; an Arab source tells us that it was the arrival of a 'large troop come by sea' that encouraged King Baldwin to attack the flocks that the Turkomans had put out to pasture near Banyas, relying on the agreements they had made (February 1157); Thierry of Flanders set sail only in July.

This attack brought a huge booty, much appreciated by a heavily indebted royal treasury, but the rupture of the truces concluded three months earlier with Nur al-Din (as a good jurist, William of Tyre criticised this violation of rights) allowed him to resume the war. Fearing he would be unable to hold Banyas, the king granted it to the Hospitallers, but they fell into an ambush and relinquished it. Humphrey of Toron, besieged there, offered to capitulate; Nur al-Din did not respond, which suggested the garrison faced massacre. The king was able to get the blockade lifted, but fell in his turn into an ambush, at Jacob's Ford. His men sacrificed themselves so that he could take refuge in Saphet; eighty-seven Templars and three hundred other knights were killed or captured (June 1157). But Banyas was saved thanks to the arrival of troops from Antioch and Tripoli.

It was then that Thierry of Flanders, making his third journey to the Holy Land, arrived in Beirut with a large contingent of knights; he joined his nephew Baldwin III to lift the blockade of the Crac des Chevaliers, threatened by Nur al-Din, and reached Antioch. There followed the earthquake of August 1157 during which the family of the lords of Shaizar was wiped out. It is not clear whether it was the men of Nur al-Din or the Ismailis who took advantage of this to establish themselves in the town, but the Franks decided to seize it. They occupied the low town without difficulty, but a dispute ensued when it was proposed to give the town to Count Thierry. The prince of Antioch, Reynald of Châtillon, claimed the town as belonging to his principality and demanded that Thierry do homage. Lord of one of the great principalities of France, Thierry refused. Faced with this impasse, the Franks chose to abandon the partly conquered Shaizar (October 1157).

Thierry and Reynald nevertheless continued the campaign. They took Harenc, in February 1158; the count of Flanders then joined the king for a short campaign against Daraiya, near Damascus. Nur al-Din prepared a riposte and embarked on the siege of the Cave de Sueth, east of the Jordan, Baldwin, still accompanied by Thierry and also by Reynald of Saint-Valery, defeated the Damascenes to win the victory of Butaiha, south of Lake Tiberias. The Flemish knights, in particular, distinguished themselves.

It seems that the count of Flanders had not come on a simple pilgrimage. It has been suggested that he intended to settle in the Holy Land to end his days there in the service of Christ; the offer that was made to him to take possession of Shaizar would seem to support this (though the capture of this town could not have been envisaged before August 1157); it is difficult to say if the tradition to the effect that he was offered Damascus during the Second Crusade is authentic; but the fact that he was making his third visit, and that the countess Sibylla of Anjou, who had accompanied him, retired to the convent of Bethany instead of leaving for the West would seem to suggest that the count of Flanders felt a very deep devotion to the Holy Land. His voyage of 1157–8 was different from the simple pilgrimages made by others during which they might agree to hire themselves out as mercenaries, even to settle in the East. His aim was very clearly to bring his assistance to the defence of the Holy Land. His ties of kinship with King Baldwin, his wife's nephew, may have been an added attraction. But his voyage should be seen as a true crusade, even if limited in its recruitment to Flanders.

THE RETURN OF BYZANTIUM AND MANUEL COMNENUS' APPEAL FOR A CRUSADE

After the Second Crusade, Manuel Comnenus could congratulate himself on having escaped the danger of collusion between the crusaders and Roger II of Sicily and on having maintained peaceful relations with his Turkish neighbours. Nor had he lost ground in northern Syria; Bohemond II's widow and Joscelin II's wife had both turned to him, one to ask for a husband, the other to grant him her county – two acts which fell within the obligations of vassals to their lord. The results had been less happy: Constance had married Reynald of Châtillon and the Turks had conquered the county of Edessa. The emperor could never-theless consider that he had maintained his hegemony over the Frankish lands of the old duchy of Antioch.

It had not been the same in Cilicia; the Armenian prince of Vahka, Thoros, who had been placed under house arrest in Constantinople, had escaped and reoccupied his fortresses and also some Byzantine towns. Manuel had hoped that the Seljuks would make him see reason; Thoros soundly defeated them (1154). The emperor turned to Reynald of Châtillon, who attacked Armenian Cilicia on Byzantium's behalf, but whom Manuel failed to pay. Reynald and Thoros were reconciled, and the former decided to pay himself by going to pillage Cyprus (1156); in so doing, he made himself a rebellious vassal.

In contrast, King Baldwin III seems to have been convinced at an early stage that Byzantine help had become a vital necessity for the Frankish states. He had given his agreement in 1150 to the cession of the county of Edessa to the emperor. And in 1158 he sent his constable, Humphrey of Toron, and other ambassadors to ask for the hand of an imperial princess. Manuel gave him as his wife his niece Theodora, with a generous dowry, and promised to assist the Franks against Nur al-Din.

When, therefore, Manuel set out to bring Reynald and Thoros to heel, if the king of Jerusalem, with his knights, also took the road for

Antioch, it was less to bring assistance to its prince than to be on the spot to offer his mediation. Thoros barely had time to take refuge in the mountains when the Byzantines reoccupied the Cilician plain. Manuel established his winter quarters at Mamistra, and it was there that Reynald came to make honourable amends. The bishop of Latakia, Gerald of Nazareth, had made the prince understand that the emperor was seeking a sop to his pride and that by accepting a humiliation, the rebellious vassal would be pardoned. Reynald took an oath of loyalty, promising to return the citadel and walls of Antioch on request and to provide a contingent. There was no longer any question of restoring Antioch to the Byzantines, and it seems that Manuel did not ask for the Greek patriarch to be reinstated in his see, to which Reynald, then on very bad terms with the Latin patriarch, might well have agreed. The accord of 1159 went further, therefore, than its predecessors.

Baldwin III then arrived in Mamistra, where he was warmly received; Manuel, much taken with the chivalric customs of the West, admired this handsome knight who had become his nephew. Thoros, through his intermediary, obtained his pardon in his turn and the right to retain his mountain fortresses. Then Manuel set out for Antioch where he made a solemn entry, Reynald serving as his squire and Baldwin riding behind him.

Without waiting for a show of military force, Nur al-Din sued the emperor for peace. He agreed to free several thousand Frankish prisoners, notably Bertrand of Saint-Gilles and many German knights captured during the Second Crusade, and he promised Manuel his help against the Seljuks (May 1159). The following year, Manuel led a campaign against the Seljuk sultan Kilij Arslan, who acknowledged himself his vassal; Frankish contingents had participated.

But two years later, during a raid he had led into Muslim territory to seize flocks which were pasturing in the region of Marash, Reynald fell into the hands of Nur al-Din (23 November 1161). He was to spend fifteen years as a prisoner in Aleppo, and Manuel seems not to have intervened in his favour as he did for other captives. Once again, the princess Constance found herself the governor of the principality, with no intention of recognising the princely title to her son Bohemond III; but Baldwin III went to Antioch nevertheless and was made regent. The princess made contact with the emperor, and it was then that he broke off the talks which were under way regarding his marriage to Melisende of Tripoli.

In fact, Manuel, on being widowed, had asked Baldwin III to give him a Frankish princess as a wife and the king had offered the Byzantine ambassadors the sister of Raymond III of Tripoli, an offer which they had accepted in their master's name, in the summer of 1161. But, during the summer of 1162, Manuel announced that he had decided in favour of Maria, the sister of Bohemond III. Furious at the insult to his sister, Raymond used the galleys which he had fitted out to carry her to Constantinople to ravage the coasts of Cyprus. But Baldwin had to accept the emperor's decision. This was probably a consequence of the capture of Reynald of Châtillon; Manuel would in this way make the Antiochene marriage which he had already considered some decades earlier. And the princess Constance of Poitiers might hope for his support to maintain herself in power. The barons of Antioch were probably less favourable to a strengthening of Byzantine control. They supported the young Bohemond III, whose mother had wanted to restrict him to possession of Latakia and Jabala. He was able to get himself recognised as prince of Antioch in March 1164.

The unease of the Antiochenes is apparent in the letters sent to the king of France in 1162 and 1163. Bohemond and the new king, Amalric, urged him to come, emphasising the difficult situation of the principality, impoverished, devastated by recent earthquakes and in danger of falling into the hands of the Greeks or the Turks. It was being said that the emperor was gathering troops with the intention of taking it over, and Amalric went so far as to beg Louis VII to come to the East 'before the arrival of the emperor'. These were probably only rumours; Manuel was to provide military assistance to the Franks in 1163 and 1164. But at this date the Franks visibly lacked confidence in his intentions.

Nur al-Din, however, had resumed his harrying of the Frankish states. In 1163 he had attacked the Crac des Chevaliers, but a group of French lords, including Hugh VIII of Lusignan and Geoffrey Martel of Angoulême, returning from a pilgrimage to Jerusalem, joined the forces of the county of Tripoli and the principality of Antioch, reinforced by a Byzantine detachment under the command of the duke of Cilicia, Constantine Coloman. The atabeg, surprised on the plain of the Biqa, had only just time to flee to Homs. He took his revenge the following year; having summoned the Ortoqid emirs of Mardin and Hisn Kaifa and the atabeg of Mosul, he laid siege to Harenc and, before that town, routed the Frankish army – six hundred knights and twelve thousand footsoldiers strong – on 11 August 1164. Only the Armenians of Thoros escaped the defeat. The Franks and their allies were almost all killed or captured; out of sixty Templars, only seven rejoined the Frankish lines. Bohemond III, Raymond III, Constantine Coloman, Joscelin III of Courtenay and Hugh of Lusignan were all taken to Aleppo as prisoners; Harenc fell into Muslim hands.

According to the historian Ibn al-Athir, Nur al-Din's allies urged him to march on Antioch. The atabeg refused, explaining that he did not wish to provoke the intervention of the imperial forces. He soon freed the duke of Cilicia, and also Bohemond III (Hugh of Lusignan died in captivity). Byzantine protection was not without its value.

Bohemond had to pay the heavy ransom of 100,000 pieces of gold, for which he had given hostages. He went to Constantinople, where Manuel agreed to provide him with this sum. But he asked in return for the restoration to the see of Antioch of the Greek patriarch, who was then living in Constantinople. Driven out of his cathedral, the Latin patriarch, Aimery of Limoges, left the town after placing it under an interdict, and retired to the nearby castle of Cursat (Qusair) which belonged to the patriarchal estate; there he continued to exercise his functions and even received the Syrian patriarch Michael. The Greek patriarch Athanasius III, who was in Constantinople in 1166, seems to have had no authority over the Latin clergy. During the earthquake that shook the region in July–August 1170, the cathedrals of Tripoli and Antioch collapsed, claiming many victims; Athanasius was buried under the rubble. Seeing this as a sign from Heaven, the prince went to Cursat to beg Aimery's pardon and restored him to the patriarchal see.

Nur al-Din had left Antioch without attacking it, but he had not spared the other Frankish states. Taking advantage of the king's absence in Egypt, he attacked Banyas, which capitulated so rapidly, on 17 October 1174, that the defenders were suspected of treason. Count Thierry of Flanders, who was making his fourth journey to the Holy Land, had no time to intervene. The county of Tripoli, deprived of its count, Raymond III, who was freed only in 1174, lost the castles which threatened the Beqa'a: Moinetre (1165 or 1166) and Gibelcar; in 1167 it was the turn of Chastel Blanc (Safitha) and Aryma; and the atabeg laid siege to Arcas. These castles had to be reconquered (Gibelcar in 1169); some of them had simply been dismantled. It is clear that, south of Antioch, Nur al-Din was uninhibited by Byzantine protection.

The agent of this protection was the duke of Cilicia. After Constantine Coloman, this was Alexius Axuch (the son of a Turk who had been captured at Nicaea in 1097), then a cousin of the emperor, Andronicus Comnenus, invested with wide powers, but of whom Manuel quickly became suspicious. Fearing arrest, he fled to Antioch, then to Jerusalem, where Amalric gave him the fief of Beirut. The Byzantine prince (who had taken with him the money collected in taxes in Cyprus) abducted Baldwin III's widow, Theodora Comnena, and fled with her to Nur al-Din. Constantine Coloman returned, only to see the Armenian principality of the Cilician mountains fall into the hands of a brother of Thoros, Mleh, who seized Tarsus, captured the duke and joined Nur al-Din. He intercepted a well-born pilgrim, the count of Sancerre (1171), and King Amalric was obliged to lead an expedition against him in 1173. Amalric, who in 1163–4 was still expressing his fears of Byzantine intervention, had changed his attitude. In 1165 he sent Archbishop Erneis of Caesarea and Odo the Butler of Saint-Amand to Constantinople to ask in his turn for the hand of an imperial princess. It was not until 1167 that the ambassadors returned with a niece of the emperor who was soon married to the king. We are told that he renewed the oath of loyalty that Baldwin III had sworn to Manuel; however that may be, it appears that the defeat of Harenc and the realisation of the precariousness of the situation of the Frankish states, which was the subject of letters to Louis VII, had led him to revive the policies of his brother.

Manuel and Amalric had probably considered, during these matrimonial negotiations, the idea of an expedition to Egypt, to which we will return; but it was only in 1169 that a joint expedition was attempted, which was unsuccessful. It was soon after this campaign that Amalric, having explained to his barons the necessity of seeking the aid of the Christian princes of the West and also of the emperor who, by his proximity and his wealth, was best placed to intervene effectively on their behalf, took them by surprise by announcing that he himself intended to visit Manuel. By March 1171 he had arrived and had been given a sumptuous reception by Manuel; he acknowledged himself to be the servant of the emperor; he had previously agreed to his participation in the work of rebuilding the basilicas of Bethlehem and Jerusalem where Manuel's name appeared in the inscriptions. Byzantine hegemony was thus recognised.

Manuel Comnenus was soon planning a new operation for which the support of the Franks of the East and the West would be useful. The Seljuk sultanate, brought to heel in 1159, had recovered its power and annexed the lands of the Danishmends, who had taken refuge in Constantinople. In 1175, Manuel embarked on the restoration of his authority over the central part of Asia Minor; he rebuilt the fortress of Dorylaeum and placed a garrison there. The next stage was to be the reconquest of Konya.

The emperor then wrote to Pope Alexander III to explain his plans, noting that he had entrusted the protection of Dorylaeum to Greeks and Latins; he declared his intention of reopening the road which took pilgrims to the Holy Sepulchre and asked for the pope's assistance. The situation was strangely reminiscent of that of 1095. Alexander III answered as Urban II had done; he appealed to the kings of France and England and to all the princes, counts, barons and other faithful of their

kingdoms, to go and fight against the Turks; the legate Peter of Saint-
Chrysogonus was asked to preach the crusade in France (29 January
1176).

Without waiting for the help requested, the imperial army set out to
march on Konya. Manuel refused to accept the sultan's offers of peace.
But he allowed himself to be surprised by the Turks in the upper valley
of the Maeander, at Myriokephalon, in circumstances that recall those
experienced by Louis VII at Mount Cadmus. The Turks destroyed the
rearguard, then the convoy which included the emperor. He, seized by
panic, joined the vanguard almost alone and, with it, beat a retreat (21
September 1176). He was forced to accept the conditions of peace
offered by Kilij Arslan, which were, in fact, generous, and to dismantle
Dorylaeum.

When the kings of France and England declared themselves ready to
depart, Manuel could therefore only offer them free passage through his
lands, in return for the usual promise to restore the conquered towns to
the empire; he asked that a papal legate accompany the two kings. He
also added a promise to work for a union of the Churches (March 1180).

Things had almost reverted to the situation of the Second Crusade.
The emperor, who had been the one to ask for the crusade associating
the Franks and the Byzantines, was no longer in a position to pursue his
projects. The slowness with which the crusade had been prepared must
be allowed for, but the haste with which Manuel had embarked on his
campaign had rendered this cooperation impossible. Once protector of
the Frankish states, Manuel was now in need of the Franks; the
reoccupation of the Anatolian lands was abandoned. He continued to see
the Latins as the saviours of his empire. In February 1180 he married his
daughter to Rainier of Montferrat and, in March, his son to Louis VII's
daughter. On 24 September, he died.

The regency of the empress Maria of Antioch ended in the terrible
riots of the spring of 1182, during which Genoese and Pisans were
massacred, the papal legate decapitated and his head tied to a dog's tail,
and the Latin churches sacked. Andronicus, now emperor and having
got rid of Rainier, Maria and Alexius II, adopted a policy of friendly
relations with Saladin, which seems to have gone as far as the conclusion
of a treaty providing for the division with the atabeg of the Frankish
lands. The abandonment of close relations between the empire and the
Franks came just as Bohemond III sent back the niece of Manuel whom
he had only recently married (1180), which signalled the end of
Antioch's dependence on the empire. The empire was beginning to split
up and was increasingly incapable of making its influence felt in Syria.

EGYPT AND THE CRUSADES OF ALEXANDER III

The evolving situation within the Byzantine sphere of influence and on the borders of the Aleppo–Damascus state is inseparable from that in a third zone, the battle for control of Egypt, which was the main business of the reign of King Amalric.

The establishment of the crusaders had been helped by the schism between the lands of the Fatimid caliph of Cairo and those which recognised, in principle, the sovereign authority of the Abbasid caliph, represented by a sultan gradually being driven out of the Baghdad region and increasingly confined to his Iranian territories. It hardly mattered, as we have seen, that the Egyptian frontier was calm; the Fatimids had alarmed the kingdom of Jerusalem, and sometimes made alliances with the rulers of Damascus. But for them, Palestine, though a natural complement to their kingdom, remained an annexe of Egypt, and its possession by the Franks did not damage Egypt's vital interests; at most, the occasional interception of caravans heading for Syria was a hindrance to Egyptian commerce. On the other hand, the growth of shipping between the West and the East contributed to its prosperity, and it is hardly surprising that the Italian towns which, like Pisa, provided ships to the Frankish princes, tried to obtain privileges to trade with Alexandria. The caliphs exercised power in name only; it was their viziers who governed the country, with the backing of an army recruited from amongst Sudanese slaves and Armenian mercenaries; a caste of military leaders provided with hereditary tenures and Muslim, Coptic and Jewish secretaries staffed the government. The rivalries and conflicts within the entourage of the caliph determined the accession to power or the fall of the viziers.

It was thanks to these internal quarrels that the Franks came to penetrate Egypt. But it was in the reign of Baldwin III that the advance of the kingdom at the expense of the Egyptians became obvious; the construction of the fortresses of Gaza and Darun and the capture of Ascalon had eliminated the march which covered the Nile valley on the Holy Land side. Also, to assure the peace of this frontier, the vizier Ibn Ruzzik had agreed to pay a tribute which provoked Amalric's first intervention in Egypt, in September 1163; he probably felt he need not fear a diversionary attack on the part of Nur al-Din, who had just suffered the defeat of the Biqa. The Frankish army reached the fortress of Bilbais and began to besiege it, but the Egyptians cut the Nile dykes, and the flood forced the Franks to retreat.

The letter that Amalric wrote to the king of France to describe this expedition survives. He explains it not by the refusal of tribute but by his

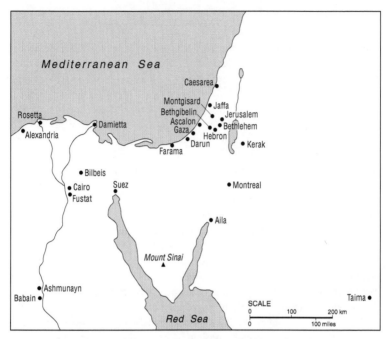

Map 11   The Egyptian campaign of King Amalric and operations in
Oultrejourdain

conviction that Egypt was threatened by Nur al-Din, whom he wanted
to prevent from occupying it.

His fears of a possible intervention in the Nile valley by the atabeg of
Aleppo and Damascus were not illusory; the king seems to have been
well informed about the internal situation of Fatimid Egypt. But he went
on: 'If, as usual, your magnificent force wishes to help us, and if God
wills it, Egypt could easily receive the mark of the Holy Cross.' The
conquest of Egypt seems already to have been in his mind.

The office of vizier was then in dispute between two contenders:
Dhirgham, who had had to confront the Frankish incursion, and Shawar,
who had asked for help from Nur al-Din, who gave him one of his
emirs, the Kurd Shirkûh, previously governor of Baalbek. Shirkûh
ensured that Shawar became vizier, but asked as the price of his services
Bilbais and its province. The new vizier could see only one way out of
his problem, an appeal to the Franks.

Amalric received Shawar's envoys, who promised to implement the conventions agreed the previous year with Dhirgham. Leaving the government of the kingdom to Bohemond III, the king set off for Bilbais, which he besieged in August–September 1164. But while this was happening, Nur al-Din destroyed Bohemond's army at Harenc and had the heads of the dead and their banners taken to Bilbais to be exposed on the walls. Amalric, in a hurry to return, granted free exit to Shirkûh, and the two armies left Egypt. Nur al-Din had meanwhile taken Banyas.

Following these disasters, on 10 July 1165 Alexander III promulgated a bull with the same title as that of Eugenius III, *Quantum predecessores*. He evoked the capture of Bohemond III and the ravages of the Saracens reaching the very gates of Antioch in asking the princes, counts, barons and faithful of the kingdom of France to go to the aid of the Holy Land. Amalric himself approached Louis VII. But these appeals seem to have made little impact, except for the imposition in England by Henry II of a tax, the proceeds of which were sent overseas in 1167. It was then that Amalric turned to Byzantium with a view to negotiating the marriage that would make him a member of the imperial family. Egypt was probably now a less pressing concern; he had been obliged to assume responsibility for the defence of the county of Tripoli.

It was in 1167 that the Egyptian question re-emerged. Once again, the initiative came from Damascus; Shirkûh had revived the projects he had been forced to abandon three years earlier and prepared an expedition for which he was assembling money and men. These preparations became known to Amalric, who convinced his barons and prelates of the mortal danger to the Holy Land represented by the creation in Egypt of a power closely linked to that Nur al-Din had created by uniting Damascus and Aleppo. He was able to persuade the *parlement* assembled at Nablus to agree to impose a tax corresponding to a tenth of movable goods to finance his operations. An attempt to intercept Shirkûh's forces in the desert having failed, Amalric assembled his troops at Ascalon and, on 30 January 1167, set out for Egypt. Shawar was greatly surprised by the unexpected arrival of the Franks, but learned almost at once of that of the Damascenes. Shirkûh tried to persuade him to join with him against Amalric; but Shawar chose to trust the king of Jerusalem rather than the Kurdish emir and made a treaty with Amalric on the basis of the payment of an indemnity of 400,000 dinars to the Franks, they, for their part, promising not to leave Egypt before they had driven Shirkûh out of the country. For greater security, the treaty was ratified by the caliph himself; William of Tyre tells how the Frankish envoy, Hugh of Caesarea, insisted on the caliph putting his ungloved hand in his, which represented an almost unheard-of affront to protocol.

Shirkûh had crossed the Nile and positioned himself at Giza; at the approach of the Franks, he moved south. The two armies met at Babain, on 18 March, when Amalric suffered a defeat, though not a very costly one; it nevertheless allowed Shirkûh to enter Alexandria, to which the Franks began to lay siege. Leaving his nephew Salah al-Din – our Saladin – inside the town, the Kurdish emir again moved to upper Egypt, pursued by the Franks. Saladin still held Alexandria, but sensing that the operation had failed, Shirkûh negotiated with the Franks on the basis of a mutual evacuation of Egypt (September 1167).

Amalric had succeeded in saving Egyptian independence. He had also won payment of an annual tribute, guaranteed by the presence in Egypt of a Frankish representative with a small garrison. But the idea of the conquest of Egypt, mentioned to Louis VII four years earlier, remained in his thoughts, and was the subject of negotiations with Byzantium. William of Tyre, who was involved, assumed that the king had revealed his intentions to the emperor during the talks preceding his marriage. But it was two envoys from Manuel, Alexander of Gravina and Michael of Otranto, who arrived early in 1168 bringing a message which William of Tyre summarises as follows:

The kingdom of Egypt, till now powerful and rich, has fallen into the hands of men who are weak and effeminate. The neighbouring peoples have realised this. So, since it seems things cannot go on as they are, and that we must fear that power will pass to foreign nations, the emperor thinks that with the aid of the lord king, it will be easy for him to unite it to his empire.

Probably warned by Amalric of the risk involved in allowing the government of Egypt to pass to the Syrians, Manuel had conceived the idea of conquering the country, leaving part of his conquests to the king of Jerusalem. These proposals called for a response, and William, then archdeacon of Tyre, was instructed to convey this to Manuel. Agreement having been reached, William returned to the Holy Land, where he was surprised to find that the army was already on the move.

He himself pondered the reasons for the abandonment of a project so far advanced, and historians continue to try to explain it. It seems that King Amalric decided only under pressure from his barons; he said himself, in excuse, that it was the Franks from overseas who had persuaded him. William referred to the talks taking place between Shawar and Nur al-Din, which are known from other sources. But he primarily blamed the master of the Hospital, Gilbert of Assaily, who dreamed of a conquest of which his order would be the chief beneficiary; whereas the master of the Temple argued that they should honour their sworn word to Shawar.

However that may be, in the summer of 1168 the decision was made. On 13 August the king promised Pagan of Caiphas a fief of a hundred knights in Cairo, when the town had been taken; on 20 August he gave Bilbais and its province, that is an income of 150,000 bezants a year, to the Hospitallers; on 17 September the Pisans obtained privileges and quarters in Cairo and at Rosetta, Damietta and Tinnis, the three ports of the Delta. The Hospitallers staked everything on the project; their master procured the necessary money by mortgaging their possessions.

The conquest was clearly intended, therefore, to enlarge the kingdom, and the king disposed of it in advance. It was probably on this point that the project of the emperor Manuel – which a politician as wise as King Amalric, primarily concerned for the future of the Latin East, had been inclined to accept – had offended his council; for Egypt would have been added to the empire, the Franks being granted only a part of the conquered territory 'on certain conditions'.

Did the Franks have the means to occupy Egypt? Their numbers were much reduced; they had to rely on the effect of surprise, speed of operations, and the lack of Egyptian combativeness. The Franks from Europe to whom Amalric referred seem not to have been numerous; we know of the arrival of Count William IV of Nevers – who died on 24 October, before the campaign began – 'with an goodly band of knights'; his intention was to 'serve Christendom against the enemies of the faith, at his own cost'; this was hardly a major reinforcement.

As before, the Franks took the road to Cairo, barred only by the fortress of Bilbais, passing through the desert. Shawar's messengers tried to deflect them from their purpose, offering money and reminding them of the treaty that had been agreed. But on 1 November Amalric reached Bilbais. On 4 November, after the failure of a first attempt, the town was stormed. Many of the inhabitants were killed, the rest reduced to slavery, though Amalric freed those who fell to him. Nevertheless, the fate of Bilbais exerted a great influence on the rest of the campaign by encouraging the Egyptians to resist. Shawar's son was among the captives.

The march on Cairo was slow. The Franks arrived before the town on 13 November, to discover that Shawar had given orders to burn old Cairo (Fustat). Some of them wanted to attack, but the king and his seneschal, Miles of Plancy, opposed this, to avoid pillage. The Egyptian ships prevented the Franks from crossing the Nile; their fleet, however, had penetrated the Delta and pillaged Tinnis. At this point, they learned of the arrival of Shirkûh; the Fatimid caliph had summoned him to the rescue, and Amalric was too late when he tried to intercept him before he entered Egypt. When Shirkûh crossed the Nile, Amalric, afraid of being caught between him and other Turks, decided to retreat (2 January 1169).

Not only had the expedition failed, but, on 18 January, Shawar was murdered and Shirkûh took his place as vizier. He died soon after, to be succeeded by his nephew Saladin, who was vizier for two years under the Fatimid caliphate which he eventually abolished at the instigation of Nur al-Din; but he had already, in August, massacred the black and Armenian soldiers of the caliph's guard.

The failure of the campaign came close to causing the collapse of the order of the Hospitallers, and it was probably this that prevented them from retaining the castles of Arcas and Gibelcar, which had been given them by Amalric in 1171 on condition they restored them. The master, Gilbert of Assaily, was forced to resign, causing a crisis in the government of the order. The finances of the kingdom, too, were severely depleted. But, worse, the conjunction between Egypt and Damascus that Amalric would have liked to prevent – and it was in this that the operation of 1168 had a desperate character – had come about. With it, a mortal danger threatened the Latin kingdom, all the more so in that the Egyptian expeditions had shown the limitations of its forces. Every time that Amalric had led his knights into Egypt, Nur al-Din had attacked the borders of the Frankish states; the retreat of these in the years 1163–9 was due to the inability of the Franks to fight on two fronts.

Their only option was a new appeal for a crusade. This time, it took a dramatic form. Amalric sent the bishop of Banyas, bearing a letter for Louis VII in which he described his defeat. A new mission, with the archbishop of Tyre, the master of the Hospital and other prelates joined him, entrusted with urgent messages for Frederick Barbarossa, Louis VII of France, Henry II of England, William II of Sicily, for various princes and, of course, for Alexander III.

Louis VII's reception of the king's envoys, in September 1169, was memorable. They presented him with a key to Jerusalem, a symbol which has been seen, though this seems unlikely, as an offer to the king of France of suzerainty over the Latin kingdom. In fact, this symbol was used on other occasions, notably when the patriarch of Jerusalem sought aid from Charlemagne, and it is possible that it was used in the case of other sovereigns. Louis VII was much moved, but could not abandon his duties to his own kingdom. Of all the kings approached, only one was to respond positively, and tardily, the king of Sicily. Count Stephen of Sancerre, who made the journey to the Holy Land in 1171, went as a pilgrim not as a crusader; the same was true of the duke of Saxony, Henry the Lion (1172), and probably of Duke Hugh III of Burgundy (1171).

The pope, therefore, in spite of the difficulties he was experiencing as a result of his conflict with Frederick Barbarossa and the anti-pope Victor IV, devised a new form of crusade. The bull *Inter omnia* of 29 July 1169 refers not to the matter of Egypt but to the 'need experienced by the eastern Church and the faithful Christians'. It refers to the diminished population of the Holy Land, 'reduced by repeated ordeals', and to the duty of assistance imposed by 'brotherly charity'. The pope renewed the privileges granted to the crusaders by his predecessors, on condition that those who were ready to go to the Holy Land to share in its defence would remain there for two years, agreeing to fight under the orders of the king and great men of the kingdom; this was addressed to all nobles, knights and faithful of Christ. This remission of sins would be additional to the indulgence granted to those who visited Christ's tomb. The pope was trying to make the service of Christ and of Christians more attractive than the simple pilgrimage. In the short run, not much was to be expected of this papal appeal.

On the other hand, the agreements made by the king of the Franks with the emperor Manuel were implemented, as if Amalric's campaign had been only a minor episode, which would seem to confirm that the plan to conquer Egypt had been conceived, on the Byzantine side, from the perspective of an extension of imperial sovereignty and not as a way of assisting the Franks. The Grand Duke Andronicus Contostephanus, who commanded the Byzantine fleet, took 150 galleys, 60 *huissiers* (the ships intended for the transport of horses) and a dozen dromons loaded with provisions and siege machines to Acre at the beginning of October 1169. Amalric had great difficulty in assembling his army, especially since he had to leave enough men behind to contain Nur al-Din. The Franco-Byzantine army reached Farama on 25 October and, two days later, Damietta. Preparations were made without haste for the siege of the town; Saladin had time to send it food and reinforcements; the Nile remained open and the besiegers, especially the Byzantines, ran short of food before the besieged. Contostephanus tried to break the deadlock by storming the town, while Amalric negotiated with the Egyptians, who bought the departure of the besieging army (December 1169).

The retreat of the Byzantine fleet, which was largely destroyed by a storm, did not sound the death knell of cooperation between Franks and Byzantines. Cooperation was contemplated once again in the spring of 1171, when Amalric went to Constantinople, the two sovereigns considering that the circumstances were propitious for a joint enterprise in Egypt.

In fact, the conquests of Egypt by Shirkûh and Saladin, though it had been achieved thanks to the assistance of Nur al-Din, was based on an ambiguity. For Nur al-Din, Egypt was united to his lands and he intended to be obeyed there and to collect its revenues. Saladin was content to be the vizier of a Fatimid caliph; he was quite ready to assist his former sovereign by attacking the fortresses of the kingdom of Jerusalem which intercepted relations between Damascus and Egypt (Darun and Gaza, in December 1170, and Aila, on the Red Sea, later the same month). He submitted to him and, not without hesitation, agreed to depose the caliph and to have public prayers said in the name of the caliph of Baghdad, to comply with a particularly pressing injunction.

But the growing dissension between Nur al-Din and Saladin, which saved Montreal when it was besieged by the latter in the autumn of 1171 and, in 1173, Kerak, which the two princes had agreed to attack, seemed to offer a respite to the Christians. Amalric even intrigued with Fatimid supporters; he probably also made contact with the Norman king of Sicily, who sent a fleet and an army to Alexandria in July–August 1174. But King Amalric died a few days before they landed (11 July 1174) and the Franks of Jerusalem took no part in this operation, which should probably be seen as a late response to the crusading appeal of 1169, which had been renewed in 1170.

A Byzantine fleet appeared once again in the ports of the Frankish kingdom, at the end of 1177; its purpose was to proceed to Egypt in liaison with the army of Baldwin III. The king and the barons struggled to persuade Count Philip of Flanders, who had arrived on a pilgrimage with many knights, to join the expedition. Philip tried every means of escape; in spite of the good will of the Byzantines, who offered to wait a few more months, and thanks also to the intrigues of the prince of Antioch and the count of Tripoli, who wanted to use his contingent in the interests of their respective principalities and not in that of the kingdom, he ended by causing the project to fail.

With the departure of the Byzantine ships, the prospect of an entry into Egypt by an alliance of Christian states, chimera though it had been, evaporated. The count of Flanders, who took the palm to show that he considered his pilgrimage had been completed and to persuade the Franks of Jerusalem to agree to his wishes, had only partly conformed to the image of the crusader in the service of the Christian princes of the East conjured up by Alexander III; he bore some responsibility for the failure of the project of Amalric I and Manuel Comnenus.

THE HOLY WAR AND THE RISE OF SALADIN

In Muslim historiography, Saladin (Salah al-Dîn Yusuf) appears as the supreme protagonist of the *jihad*, the holy war against the Franks which he had the distinction of carrying through to its conclusion, the recovery of Jerusalem.

The ideology of the holy war had never been forgotten during the previous centuries, but it had become blunted as a result of the preoccupations of those who shared the heritage of the great Abbasid caliphs. It had experienced a resurgence, for a long time visible primarily in pious circles, during the twelfth century. The settlement of the Franks in the Near East had encouraged this; the qadis of Tripoli and Aleppo had frequently resorted to this theme. But it was the Sunni revival, linked to the emerging power of the Seljuks, that led to the revival of the holy war as a means to salvation. A particular aspect of the propaganda on its behalf was the emphasis on Palestine as an element in the Muslim patrimony. Jerusalem acquired a much greater significance as a holy city of Islam; accounts of pilgrimages made at the time of Frankish domination, like that of Ali al-Harawi, reveal that many minor sanctuaries were then claimed for a Muslim veneration that even benefited from the efforts of the Franks to revive certain places of worship, such as the tomb of Abraham at Hebron.

The ideology of the holy war found its champion in Nur al-Din. The atabeg was sincerely attached to the battle against the Franks and their expulsion from the Holy Land, now, in his eyes, the Holy Land of Islam. This did not stop him from using the argument of the holy war in furtherance of his political aims with regard to other Muslim powers, without hesitating to make truces with the Franks to achieve his other ends. Thus, in 1171, when he annexed Mosul, which he had long coveted, and when he contested the sovereignty of the Seljuk sultan, now relegated to his Iranian lands, his justification was that he alone was repelling 'the Franks, the bravest people on earth'; this enabled him to obtain from the caliph a diploma of investiture applying to Mosul, Aleppo, Damascus and Egypt, thereby giving legitimacy to the sovereignty of the Zengid dynasty.

Saladin, in succeeding Shirkûh, was in a difficult situation; Nur al-Din had given the latter troops from his own army who remained loyal to him; further, he had been installed as vizier by a caliph whose deposition was being demanded by Nur al-Din at the urging of the Abbasid caliph. In 1171 Saladin acceded to this demand and participated in the operations conducted at the instigation of the master of Damascus. But Nur al-Din also had financial needs which he intended to see were met by the man he saw as his lieutenant in Egypt, taking no account of the needs of that country's government, where the reorganisation of the army and navy and the rebuilding of the fortress were costing dear.

Nur al-Din also aimed to take advantage of the power he had acquired

through his lieutenants in Egypt to destroy one of the salients of the
Frankish kingdom most inconvenient for the new Syrio-Egyptian unity,
that constituted by Transjordan and Arabia Petraea. In the autumn of
1171 Saladin besieged Montreal, and Nur al-Din Kerak; but the former
beat a retreat, much to the latter's annoyance. A new attempt was made
against these two fortresses in 1173, led initially by Saladin to bring the
Bedouins, who were acting as auxiliaries to the Franks, to heel. Nur
al-Din wanted to join him to besiege the Frankish castles, but Saladin
withdrew before his arrival. His military operations were then directed
against Cyrenaica, the Yemen and Nubia, to consolidate Egyptian
power, while the Franks of King Amalric continued to encourage the
intrigues of the supporters of the Fatimids. Nur al-Din, exasperated by
his lieutenant's procrastinations, was preparing an expedition to Egypt
when he died (15 May 1174). He left a young son, al-Salih Ismail, as his
heir. The people of Aleppo demanded and obtained that he return to
their town.

The people of Mosul recovered their independence, and King
Amalric tried to recapture Banyas; he agreed to raise the siege and
concluded a truce with the regent, in return for the freeing of the
knightly prisoners. Then, taking advantage of Amalric's death and of
quarrels between Aleppo and Damascus, Saladin responded to an appeal
from the Damascenes and entered their town on 27 November 1174.
Baalbek, Homs and Hamah rallied to him, and he marched on Aleppo,
which closed its gates against him and appealed to the Franks.

Count Raymond III of Tripoli then reverted to the traditional policy
of the Latin states, that is, to impede the unification of the territories
adjoining their frontiers. He marched on Homs, where the garrison of
the citadel still supported the Zengid prince, which obliged Saladin to
abandon Aleppo to relieve Homs. Casting off the mask behind which his
aims were concealed, Saladin declared his independence of Zengid
sovereignty, while seeking to obtain from Aleppo the promise to support
him against the Franks. This did not prevent him, late in 1175, as he
received an emissary from Frederick Barbarossa, from concluding a truce
with the latter and returning their captives. The people of Aleppo,
threatened by a new campaign, also made a gesture in favour of the
Christians, freeing Joscelin III and Reynald of Châtillon, prisoners since
1164. Fighting continued, and the net tightened round Aleppo. The
Franks then operated a diversion by making a raid in the Beqa'a during
which Saladin's brother, Turanshah, was beaten at Ain Anjarr; the new
sovereign had to return to Damascus, then to Egypt, threatened by the
arrival of the Byzantine fleet which was preparing to conduct joint
operations with the Franks.

These operations, as we know, were cut short. They gave way to enterprises involving Philip of Flanders, whose arrival had at first appeared likely to favour the proposed Egyptian campaign. But Philip rejected this on various grounds, and by objecting to Reynald of Châtillon as commander of the expeditionary force. And it was in the company of Bohemond III and Raymond III that he set out for the north with his troops, reinforced by a large contingent from Jerusalem. Philip of Flanders' campaign was aimed first at satisfying the ambitions of the count of Tripoli, by attacking Hamah, which was besieged in September 1177, but without success. The allies next marched on Antioch, then decided to attack Harenc, whose governor had rebelled against the king of Aleppo. The siege lasted four months (from the end of November 1177 to March 1178), during which al-Salih Ismail tried to persuade the besiegers that they were playing into Saladin's hands and that it was not in their interests to weaken the principality of Aleppo. The Franks eventually raised the siege.

Saladin, however, had tried to take advantage of the fact that the king was without part of his army, by making a surprise attack. At the head of a large army, he crossed the desert to El-Arish, which he made his operational base, and arrived before Ascalon, which King Baldwin IV had only just had time to reach with what knights he could muster – fewer than three hundred. Contenting himself with blockading Ascalon, Saladin was able to pick off all the contingents which responded to the king's summons and which arrived one after the other; he then returned across the Philistian plain, devastating it as he went, with the intention of reaching a Jerusalem denuded of troops. But the king, advised by Reynald of Châtillon, Reynald of Sidon, Joscelin III and Baldwin of Rames, joined the master of the Temple and the eighty knights he held in Gaza, marched up the coast to beyond Lydda, and surprised Saladin by arriving from the north. The Franks launched into the middle of the enemy army, which numbered 26,000 warriors, and put it to flight. Saladin himself fled to Egypt, while his Mamluks let themselves be killed to protect him. The Franks collected an enormous amount of booty and many captives, their numbers swollen by those who, finding themselves doomed to cross the desert, preferred to surrender. The victory of Montgisard (25 November 1177) had been dearly bought (1,000 dead and 750 wounded), but it relieved the south of the kingdom.

Saladin soon rebuilt his army, but had to wait until 1179 to renew his offensive; he was in any case made uneasy by Kilij Arslan's claim to certain places in northern Syria and by family rivalries. The Franks, who had granted him a truce, took the opportunity to fortify two sites on the upper Jordan, Le Chastellez by Jacob's Ford and Châteauneuf; the

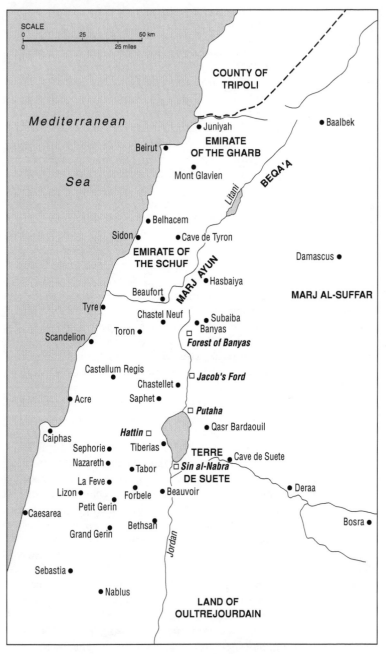

Map 12   The frontier with Damascus: Galilee, Samaria and Terre de
Suethe in the twelfth century

former was built by the Templars, the latter entrusted to Humphrey of Toron; and Baldwin IV had been able to destroy a pillaging tribe which, driven out of its hideout in the Bouquiau, had established itself near Damascus from which it made raids into Frankish territory (November 1178).

War resumed in 1179. The Franks suffered two serious defeats, one in the forest of Banyas, in which Humphrey of Toron was killed, the other at Marj Ayun (10 June 1179), which allowed Saladin to destroy Le Chastellet where he took many prisoners. At the same time, he launched his fleet against the Frankish coast; it spent two days in the roads of Acre, in October. The arrival of many French barons, with Count Henry of Champagne and Peter of Courtenay, who came soon after the defeat of Marj Ayun, relieved the pressure on the kingdom from Saladin's army. It moved to the county of Tripoli which was devastated at the beginning of 1180.

Saladin was then in a position to get the king and the count to agree to new truces to last two years. Thanks to these, he was able to intervene in the quarrels between the Seljuks of Anatolia and the Ortoqids, and above all to impose his hegemony in northern Syria, pointing out that he would need the assistance of the princes of the Jazirah to fight against the Franks; the caliph renewed the investiture he had obtained in 1175.

In 1182 the beaching of a pilgrim ship near Damietta gave Saladin the opportunity to break the truces and to make several devastating raids at the expense of the kingdom of Jerusalem, in the region of Montreal, the Terre de Sueth and at the foot of Mount Tabor, where he seized the small Frankish town of Buria; he then marched on the castle of Belvoir, but the Frankish barons defeated him at Forbelet, in spite of being greatly outnumbered. Saladin then tried to take Beirut by a combined operation of his army and fleet. The arrival of Baldwin IV obliged him to raise the siege (August 1182).

Once again, Saladin turned in the direction of Mosul; the Zengids had redistributed their possessions between them, and many emirs were favourable to the Ayyubid, who believed he could take advantage of this. He tested the defences of Mosul, which stood firm, thus provoking a coalition of the local princes, who feared his ambition. He then denounced to the caliph the prince of Mosul's dealings with the Franks, claiming that he had promised them an annual tribute for eleven years, and the restoration of Banyas, the Cave de Tyron and the Cave de Sueth in return for intervention against Damascus. Baldwin IV had, indeed, conducted razzias deep into Damascene territory, in the Hauran, and recovered the Cave de Sueth, causing concern even in Damascus. But Saladin refused to be deflected from his operations against Mosul.

It looked as if the Franks had returned to the policy that had served them well in the past when they had prevented first Zengi, then Nur al-Din, from taking Damascus. But Saladin, by his persistence, managed to overcome the resistance of the Ortoqids; on 21 May 1183, he laid siege to Aleppo, which its lord, Zengi II, surrendered on 11 June. The capture of Aleppo worried Bohemond III, who went to Jerusalem to seek help from the king and sought a reconciliation with the Armenian prince of Cilicia. But Saladin ignored Antioch.

Reynald of Châtillon, now, by his marriage, prince of Oultrejourdain, had in 1181 revealed his intention of cutting contacts between Egypt, Syria and Arabia; he had seized a large caravan at Taima, in spite of the truces. In February 1183 he fitted out a small squadron which he launched on the Red Sea, where it captured many ships and attempted a landing not far from Mecca. The Ayyubid reacted vigorously; the Frankish ships were sunk and the prisoners ruthlessly massacred.

This raid, regarded as sacrilege, and without doubt primarily motivated by the appeal of rich plunder, was probably not part of the policy intended to deflect Saladin from annexing the Zengid principalities. Nor, probably, was it responsible for his decision to launch his most important campaign yet against the Frankish states; the seizure of Aleppo obliged Saladin to give substance to his claims to the effect that his sole aim was to unite the Muslim forces against the Franks.

On his return to Damascus in August 1183, the Ayyubid assembled his army and marched with it to Bethsan, the fortress which controlled the crossing of the Jordan some twenty kilometres to the south of Lake Tiberias. Finding the fortress evacuated, he burned it, and also the neighbouring small towns of Petit Gerin and Forbelet. The *bailli* of the kingdom, acting for Baldwin IV, whose illness now prevented him from commanding the army, had assembled the kingdom's forces at a point where a large spring, Sephorie, made it possible to water men and beasts, a little to the north of Nazareth. Once again, crusaders from the West had reinforced the Frankish army, this time the duke of Brabant, Godfrey III, and Ralph of Mauléon. Saladin advanced to another watering place, the spring of Tubania; the Franks made a move and took up a position nearby, then occupied Tubania which Saladin had evacuated and fortified their camp by surrounding it with a ditch. In spite of the harassment of the Muslim archers, and of the starvation which was beginning to threaten and which led to outbursts of impatience on the part of the footsoldiers, many of whom were hoping to leave in the 'October passage', and of the raids made by Ayyubid detachments which threatened Mount Tabor and Nazareth, the Frankish barons refused to be drawn out of their entrenchment, where they stayed for nearly a week (2–7 October 1183). Saladin eventually withdrew and returned to Damascus. The Frankish tactic had on this occasion triumphed, though not before the countryside had suffered badly.

But Saladin did not relax his efforts. This time he directed them once again against the crucial sector of Frankish Transjordan, where the presence of Reynald of Châtillon, whose enterprises in Arabia and the Red Sea had made him a particularly detested enemy, appeared provocative. On 22 November, having summoned the Egyptian troops commanded by his brother al-Adil, Saladin laid siege to Kerak, where the wedding of the heir, Humphrey of Toron, to the youngest sister of Baldwin IV, Isabella, had just been celebrated, filling the town with many guests. Baldwin, though almost incapacitated, led his army into Transjordan; Saladin raised the siege (4 December), but he reappeared the following year with a larger number of siege machines and an army strengthened by Ortoqid contingents (August 1184). Once again, the Frankish army, commanded by Raymond III of Tripoli, forced him to raise the siege, early in September; Saladin was nevertheless able to sack Nablus, Sebastia and Grand Gerin before returning to Damascus.

This war, which had lasted two years, had not enabled the sultan – this is the name given him by his Muslim historians, because it was borne by the Egyptian viziers, though it had not been conferred on him by the caliph of Baghdad – to undermine the kingdom's defences. The forts he had destroyed were not the great fortresses on which the defensive system of the Frankish possessions was based. The human and material losses, on the other hand, had been heavy; the reinforcements brought by the 'passages' and in particular those led by the great pilgrim lords had probably made a major contribution to the resistance fielded by the kingdom to the Ayyubid attacks.

The question of subsistence became acute; a succession of bad harvests marked the decade 1177–87, that of 1185, in particular, threatened to be very poor. Raymond III, regent for the new king Baldwin V, assembled the barons and, with their assent, proposed to Saladin that they make truces to last for four years. The sultan accepted, all the more willingly in that Egypt was experiencing a serious economic crisis, and provisions were pouring into the kingdom from Muslim lands (the spring of 1185).

Saladin, in any case, once again had other worries. The Zengid king of Mosul, Izz al-Din, had attacked one of his Ortoqid allies with the aid of the atabeg of Azerbaijan; Saladin made two attacks on Mosul, in June and November 1185; in March 1186, Izz al-Din agreed to provide him with military assistance against the Franks. In this way, Saladin built up a system of vassalage which put him at the head of all the armed forces of the Jazirah and Syria; the various princes of the region were bound to

him either by pacts or by recognition of his sovereignty, which made
material the investiture granted him by the caliph. Nevertheless, this
edifice remained fragile, the autonomy of each having to be respected,
unlike the situation in Egypt.

But the rise of Saladin had provoked serious reservations on the part of
the Muslim sovereigns. The caliph himself remained suspicious with
regard to this Kurdish adventurer who had constructed a formidable
power at the very gates of the tiny state which the Abbasids had begun to
restore around Baghdad, and Saladin's letters, always full of protestations
of respect and obedience, were coldly received. The Seljuks of Iran, who
had as direct vassals the powerful atabegs of Azerbaijan, did not look
favourably on the Ayyubid advances in the direction of Khilat and Irbil.
The Seljuks of Anatolia and the Almohads of North Africa felt directly
threatened by this enterprising neighbour, and his appeals for the union
of the Muslim forces against the Franks seemed to them primarily a
screen for his territorial appetites at their expense.

The question arises as to what Saladin's true aims were. He is one of
those builders of empire who, in Muslim countries, were carried along
by a religious movement. He adopted the role of leader of the Sunnis,
earlier held by Nur al-Din, and it has been assumed that he wanted to
restore the unity of the Muslim world to his own advantage. The
achievement of his projects to the detriment of his co-religionists often
took precedence over the holy war, and convenient truces with the
Franks allowed him to relegate this to the second rank of his preoccupations.

The commercial privileges granted to the Genoese or the Pisans have
been seen as intended to divert international trade to the Egyptian ports
in order to weaken the economy of the Frankish states; they might
simply have been, for a prince always in financial difficulties, a way of
increasing the volume of a trade from which he benefited.

Saladin's ultimate aim of eliminating the Franks was loudly proclaimed. A German chronicler, Magnus of Reichersberg, whose statements are corroborated by Arab authors, has preserved for us the
substance of a Golden Bull of the emperor Isaac Angelus, which has been
dated to the beginning of his reign (1185–6), and which refers to an
earlier letter from Andronicus I; Isaac, who had spent some time at
Saladin's court, and whose brother Alexius had been arrested by the
Franks after being denounced by 'certain noble Saracens whose relatives
had been strangled on Saladin's orders', professed himself anxious to
preserve an alliance with Saladin and proposed, when he had conquered
Jerusalem 'with [his] aid and counsel', a partition leaving Antioch and its
territory to Byzantium and the rest of Syria to Saladin, with the

exception of the town of Jerusalem and the coast (except Ascalon), which would revert to the emperor. There was also the question of the eventual conquest of the lands of the sultan of Konya; the emperor asked to receive the territory extending as far as Antioch and the land of the Armenians. It is clear that the conquest of Frankish lands was taken by the Byzantine emperor to be Saladin's objective, his only desire being to secure for himself in the division what was directly of interest to the empire.

The Ayyubid sultan's attitude was well known to the westerners and to the Franks, as is shown by their repeated appeals for a crusade, and by the response in the form of the arrival of noble pilgrims ready to participate in the defence of the Frankish lands. But the prospect of a crusade, during the years when Saladin was building up his power, was linked to other problems of a political and dynastic nature.

CRUSADE AND ROYAL SUCCESSION: A DIFFICULT DECADE

During the years in which Saladin was alternating between threats and periods of truce, the kingdom of Jerusalem saw the arrival of many pilgrims, but the great crusade so devoutly hoped and prayed for by the Franks of the East failed to materialise. The circumstances, it is true, were not propitious; though Frederick Barbarossa had resigned himself to signing the peace of Venice (1177) with Pope Alexander III, the dispute between Louis VII, then his son and Henry II of England was still unresolved. And on top of this came the complications arising in the Latin East itself.

The accession of Baldwin IV, who was crowned on 15 July 1174, when he was not yet thirteen years old, had placed on the throne a very gifted child – as we are assured by his tutor, William of Tyre – in whom the first signs of leprosy were already apparent. His reign, of less than twelve years, was to be, in the words of René Grousset, 'a long agony, but an agony on horseback, steeled by the consciousness of royal dignity, Christian duty and the responsibilities of the crown, in that tragic period when the drama of the king was echoed by the drama of the kingdom'. From the beginning, rivalries were rife around him. The seneschal Miles of Plancy, confidante of King Amalric, wanted to hold on to power; the young king's uncle, Raymond III of Tripoli, liberated from a Muslim prison in 1172, claimed the regency. The murder of Miles of Plancy, at the end of 1174, left the way clear for Raymond.

Raymond had been freed in return for a huge ransom (80,000 bezants) which he had only been able to pay by contracting a heavy debt to the order of the Hospital. He was obliged, therefore, to grant it important concessions. In 1180 he surrendered to them the fortress of Tuban, furthest outpost of the county of Tripoli in the direction of Hamah, and the whole eastern side of the Lebanon from the lake of Homs to the southern hills giving access to the Beqa'a, traditional terrain of Tripolitanian razzias. On the other hand, Raymond had married the widow of Walter of St Omer, sire of Tiberias, and he exercised the powers of *bailli* of the principality of Galilee in the name of his stepsons, which made him one of the principal lords of the kingdom. He had entrusted the chancery to the archdeacon William, soon archbishop of Tyre, who was one of his strongest supporters.

Raymond ceased to be *bailli* in 1176. But, from this point, the king's health deteriorated, and he was in danger of being unable to exercise the responsibilities of government. In November 1176 he married the eldest of his sisters, Sibylla, like him the child of Agnes of Courtenay, to the son of the marquis of Montferrat, William Longsword, who died three months later, leaving a son, the future Baldwin V.

Before a remarriage for Sibylla could be arranged, there arrived on the scene a great baron of the kingdom of France, the son of the Thierry of Flanders who had demonstrated so much zeal for the Latin east, who had come on a pilgrimage in 1177 with a large number of knights. Philip of Flanders, through his mother, Sibylla of Anjou, was cousin to King Baldwin, who offered him the regency. He refused, just as he refused to lead the projected expedition to Egypt. But he proposed to marry Sibylla and her younger sister, Isabella, daughter of Maria Comnena, to the two sons of the advocate of Béthune; he had hopes of the lordship of Béthune being acquired for the county of Flanders. The barons of the kingdom rejected this proposal.

With Philip's arrival, oppositions emerged. Philip rejected the candidature of Reynald of Châtillon, freed in 1176 from the prisons of Aleppo in return for a ransom of 120,000 bezants, whom Baldwin IV had in mind as regent and as commander of the Egyptian army; he supported the prince of Antioch and the count of Tripoli, who involved him in their expedition against Hamah and Harenc. Reynald, however, had married Stephanie of Milly, widow of the constable Humphrey of Toron and lady of the land of Oultrejourdain, and had become one of the principal barons of the kingdom.

The historian Ernoul, whose statements should sometimes be treated with caution, says that the king and his counsellors then considered providing Sibylla with a new husband in the person of Baldwin of Rames, a member of the family of Ibelin – and that Baldwin even got rid of his wife to make himself available. But he was captured at the battle of Marj Ayun, and Saladin, knowing of the proposed marriage, would only free him in return for a ransom of 200,000 bezants, an enormous sum which Sibylla refused to pay; Baldwin rushed to Constantinople where Manuel Comnenus agreed to provide him with this sum, but when he returned, he found that Sibylla had remarried.

The version given by William of Tyre is different. He confirms that Baldwin had to seek the assistance of the *basileus* to pay his ransom, but he says that the king of Jerusalem had approached another great baron, Duke Hugh III of Burgundy, about accepting the regency, and Sibylla's hand, in 1179, and that the duke had announced his arrival for 1180.

But Sibylla had meanwhile fallen in love with a Poitevin knight whose brother, Aimery, was constable of the kingdom and, so it was said, very close to the queen mother. Guy of Lusignan lacked neither family nor experience; he belonged to the powerful family of Lusignan and had taken an active part in the rebellion of the lords of Poitou against Henry II. But he was only a younger son; Baldwin IV nevertheless consented to the marriage, and made Guy count of Jaffa and Ascalon. By this marriage, Guy became the future king's closest male relative; he was the obvious candidate for the regency, which Baldwin gave him. Thanks to the support of Agnes of Courtenay, he became the leader of a party that included his brother Aimery, Reynald of Châtillon and, above all, the queen's brother, Joscelin III of Courtenay, who had been freed from the prisons of Aleppo at the same time as Reynald, and who had been granted several lordships situated between Acre and Tyre, round Château-du-Roi, which had put him in possession of a vast territory that was called the 'Seigneurie de Joscelin'.

Opposing them were the Ibelin, whose leader, Balian, had married Amalric's widow, who held Nablus; they had close ties with Raymond III of Tripoli. Raymond and Bohemond III of Antioch were Baldwin IV's uncles and, as such, in a position to challenge Guy's rights to the regency. When they wanted to enter the kingdom, where Raymond held, by right of his wife, the principality of Galilee, Baldwin was persuaded that they were coming to seize power and forbad them access.

Guy, however, lacked the authority to make the barons obey him. When Reynald of Châtillon returned from his raid in Arabia, where he had pillaged Taima, Saladin demanded reparations for the damage inflicted; Reynald refused to surrender his booty, though requested to do so in the king's name, so causing the truces to be broken (1182).

While the kingdom was given over to intrigues and Baldwin IV was increasingly handicapped by his disease, the principality of Antioch was experiencing other problems. Bohemond III put away his wife, Theodora Comnena, for love of a Sibylla whom he married in spite of the patriarch; he seized the latter's temporalities and alienated his barons, which provoked a civil war. The compromise which ended it (1182) did not prevent Bohemond from expelling some of his great vassals.

The political climate of the Latin East had deteriorated, and this at a particularly unfortunate time. In 1177 the kingdom had barely escaped an invasion; in 1179 the war in the upper Jordan had inflicted heavy losses on the Frankish baronage. And, as we have seen, Saladin's ambitions were sufficiently transparent to cause the Franks continuing unease.

They had not failed to appeal to the westerners. Alexander III's appeal, in 1169, had been conveyed to the kings of France and England who, at their meeting at Montmirail, discussed a project crusade, to the annoyance of the supporters of Thomas Becket, who remembered the failure of the Second Crusade. But Henry II used this project to try to settle to his own advantage his disputes with the archbishop of Canterbury and promised to depart at Easter 1171. The archbishop's murder threw this into question, while obliging Henry to clarify his intentions. In 1172 he swore to serve for three years overseas and to provide the Temple with a sum of money sufficient to maintain two hundred knights for one year, but he used this promise to obtain the pope's support against his enemies. Alexander III begged Louis VII of France to make peace with Henry on account of the dangers threatening the Holy Land; he agitated with the archbishop of Reims 'so that the king of England may fulfil his vow to depart for Jerusalem', and the patriarch of Jerusalem implored the king and his sons to be reconciled so that they could come to the aid of the Holy Land (1173).

Henry II was due to leave in 1176–7 but he let Philip of Flanders set out alone, though providing him with one of his advisors, William de Mandeville. The king did not forget his links with the royal house of Jerusalem, to which he referred when making his commitments in 1170, and he probably intended to play a role in the choice of a husband for his cousin Sibylla.

In 1177, at their meeting at Ivry, the two kings, this time swayed by Alexander III's letter describing the projects of Manuel Comnenus, promised once again to depart. As we have seen, in 1180 Louis VII approached Byzantium to obtain free passage through Byzantine territory, but he died before putting his plans into practice. Then, in the bull *Cor nostrum* (16 January 1181), Alexander III informed all Christians of the 'sinister rumours reaching us from the region of Jerusalem ... devastated by the incursions of the infidel and deprived of the strength of men of valour and of the counsel of men of experience', referring to the serious illness of King Baldwin and renewing the indulgences granted to those who 'believe they ought to visit our Lord's sepulchre in

the present necessity' and to those who entered the service of the
Frankish princes for a period of one or two years. At once, the young
King Philip of France and Henry II renewed their commitments; it is
said that the former expressed some scepticism, so frequently had Henry
made such promises. In 1182, however, Henry bequeathed 20,000 silver
marks to be divided between the Temple, the Hospital, a common fund
for the assistance of the kingdom and the religious houses of the Holy
Land.

The two kings stayed put, but the count of Flanders, in 1177–8, and
the count of Champagne and Peter of Courtenay, in 1179, went to bring
their support to the Franks of the East, and the presence of pilgrims from
the West at Tubania in 1183 shows that the westerners had not remained
deaf to these appeals.

This last campaign had provoked great hostility in Jerusalem towards
Guy of Lusignan, whose tactics, though prudent, had failed to protect
the kingdom from devastation. Bohemond III and Raymond III, fearing
Saladin's attacks on Antioch, had made acts of submission to Baldwin IV
and thus returned to favour. Guy of Lusignan, on the other hand, had
displeased the king, made increasingly irritable by his illness, by refusing
to exchange Tyre, where Baldwin wanted to live, for Jerusalem;
Baldwin removed him from the regency of the kingdom and, in his own
lifetime, had the son of Sibylla and William of Montferrat, the young
Baldwin V, crowned (20 November 1183). Guy, summoned to appear at
the royal court, refused; he shut the gates of Ascalon against the king and
Baldwin deprived him of Jaffa. The prelates who tried to reconcile them
were sent packing. Guy attacked the king's Bedouins. Baldwin then
decided to give the regency to Raymond, while Joscelin III became
guardian of Baldwin V. Finally, the king put into question his sister's
right to the succession; if Baldwin V died before the age of ten,
Raymond III was to remain regent, and the pope, the emperor and the
kings of France and England were to be asked to decide if the crown
should go to Sibylla or to Isabella, who married Reynald of Châtillon's
stepson, Humphrey IV of Toron. Baldwin IV was dead by 16 May 1185.

It was during the course of 1184 that the king had decided to send to
the West a particularly solemn embassy to ask once again for the
departure of a crusade, but also with a view to the settlement of his
succession. The patriarch Heraclius and the masters of the Temple and
the Hospital went to the West, to Henry II, to whom pope Lucius III
had specially commended the kingdom of Jerusalem. It seems that, either
because of the many promises he had made, or because of his family ties
with the Jerusalem dynasty, Henry was regarded as particularly likely to
provide his protection for the Holy Land.

Heraclius, who may have tried similar approaches elsewhere, arrived in London with the pope's letters and with the keys to the Holy Sepulchre and the Tower of David and the banner of the Holy Cross, which he offered to the king, perhaps more as a symbol of the Holy City than as marks of sovereignty. This was at Reading on 29 January 1185; Baldwin IV was still alive and there could be no question of deposing him. But, in the absence of the hand of one of the two royal princesses, the patriarch probably proposed that Henry or one of his sons should assume the government of the kingdom in the name of the young Baldwin V, or until the Western sovereigns appointed the legitimate heir to the kingdom. Henry's youngest son, John, seems to have been tempted by this role, but the king would not allow him to accept and he himself was forbidden by his barons and prelates from leaving the kingdom.

The patriarch, though regarded by some as one of the pillars of the Church, displeased others by the opulence of his robes and the perfumes he used. His mission failed. Several English barons left the following year, but they arrived to find the kingdom of Jerusalem and the Ayyubids enjoying a truce, and only a few of them remained in the East until 1187. The famous William Marshal obtained financial help from the king to go to the Holy Land; it seems that he represented Henry, the king's eldest son, who had taken the cross in 1183, but who had been discouraged by his father and who had died prematurely.

Nevertheless, though he had failed to persuade the king or a significant contingent to depart, Heraclius had achieved some of his ends. Pope Lucius III, in November 1184 had stipulated, for those who failed to go on a crusade, payment of a financial aid which would procure them a reduction in their penances; the poor could benefit from this by saying prayers. The kingdom was in urgent need of money; in February 1183, a general tax had been instituted on the income of Baldwin IV's subjects, at the rate of two per cent, including that from fiefs. Henry II and Philip Augustus agreed, in either 1184 or 1185, to levy a 'tithe' on the laity and the clergy of their countries, not excepting even those who took the cross, for a period of ten years. The two kings had also arranged for the bishops to preach the taking of the cross, but they seem then to have decided to confine their assistance to the dispatch of these sums of money. It has been estimated that in England this tax raised nearly £20,000, which was probably conveyed to the Holy Land in 1186. Though he never carried out his proclaimed intention of going overseas in person, the king of England was recognised in the Holy Land as having been particularly generous to it. He had deposited a treasury there, entrusted to the care of the Templars and Hospitallers, to meet the needs of his crusade. It was to be called upon during the dramatic events of 1187.

Soon after the envoys' return, on 13 September 1186, the child-king Baldwin V died. Joscelin III advised the regent, Raymond III, to withdraw to his lands of Tiberias for the period of the funeral ceremonies. He took advantage of this to seize Acre and Beirut, urging Sibylla and Guy to proceed without delay to Jerusalem. Raymond wanted to assemble the barons in a *parlement* at Nablus; during this period, Reynald of Châtillon and the patriarch rallied to Sibylla, who enjoyed the support of the new master of the Templars, Gerard of Ridfort, who had never forgiven Raymond for preventing him from making an advantageous marriage. It was in vain that messengers from the barons in Nablus reminded them of the oath sworn to Baldwin IV to submit the question of the succession to the western sovereigns; Sibylla succeeded in getting the crown given to her, possibly after a mock divorce; the patriarch crowned her and she made Guy king (September–October 1186). Humphrey IV, husband of Isabella, supported the new king, and the majority of the barons resigned themselves to recognising him by doing homage. Raymond III had been duped by Joscelin; it is difficult to know whether he wanted the crown for himself, because it was to Isabella that the crown would revert if Sibylla and her husband were excluded, or whether he wanted to remain *bailli* of the kingdom for a further period. As we have seen, this position had been offered to a number of great persons from the West and none of them had accepted what was only a temporary position; it was no doubt more tempting for a Frankish prince of the East like Raymond.

However that may be, the count of Tripoli's opposition hardened, especially when Guy summoned him to account for the administration of the kingdom, while he had been deprived of Beirut, whose revenues had been assigned to him to defray the costs of the regency. Not content with refusing homage to the king, Raymond III approached Saladin and asked for his protection, not without reason, since Guy had assembled his army to march on Tiberias. Balian of Ibelin managed to dissuade him (March 1187). But as negotiations got under way, war broke out with Saladin.

HATTIN AND THE COLLAPSE OF THE FRANKISH KINGDOM

In giving his protection to Raymond III of Tripoli in his principality of Galilee, Saladin was no doubt intending to exploit the internal disputes of the kingdom of Jerusalem in order to split the customarily united front of the Frankish princes. In any case, a series of truces with Antioch,

Tripoli and Jerusalem left his hands free for his other objectives. These truces were due to last until 1189, but an initiative by Reynald of Châtillon brought them to an abrupt end.

Reynald, either at the very end of 1186 or early in 1187, intercepted a large caravan on its way from Cairo to Damascus under strong escort. It is arguable whether the presence of this escort could be seen as justifying the attack, since free passage was generally accorded to unarmed caravans, or whether Reynald simply succumbed to the appeal of the rich plunder that would be his if he captured it. Saladin asked for the prisoners to be freed and the booty returned; Reynald refused. The sultan then appealed to Guy of Lusignan, who was rebuffed in his turn by the lord of Oultrejourdain, who told him he was master of his own lands just as Guy was master of his. Saladin now regarded himself as released from the obligation to observe the truce, and vowed to do Reynald to death at the earliest opportunity.

He summoned to Damascus his Syrian troops and the contingents of the vassal princes of upper Mesopotamia. On 18 March 1187 he marched in the direction of Oultrejourdain, devastating the environs of Kerak and Montreal. After this he turned north, and asked Raymond III for free passage for a large detachment which was on its way to pillage lower Galilee. The count, deeply embarrassed, authorised the passage, stipulating that it should not attack the fortified towns and that the raid should last for only one day, and he then warned the people of the threatened region so that they could retreat into the fortresses.

By chance, on that very day (30 April 1187) a delegation sent by Guy of Lusignan to negotiate his reconciliation with Raymond arrived in the area; it was to consist of the archbishop of Tyre, Josias, Balian of Ibelin, Reynald of Sidon and the masters of the Temple and the Hospital, the three first named not yet having joined it. The master of the Hospital, Roger of Moulins, wanted them to withdraw into a fortress as Raymond III had asked, but the master of the Temple, Gerard of Ridfort, brushing these objections aside, assembled the Templars of the garrison of Caco and the knights of Nazareth and made a sally from the castle of La Fève to go to the rescue. The Muslim raid was ending; the two forces met near Sephorie and the Franks were defeated and taken prisoner. As was his custom, Saladin had all the captured Templars beheaded; Roger of Moulins had been killed; Gerard of Ridfort escaped. Further, the Frankish inhabitants of Nazareth had joined in the counter-raid; they, too, were captured, and Raymond III watched the victors pass before Tiberias with the prisoners and the heads of the dead. He at once made his peace with the king and returned to Saladin the small garrison that he had symbolically positioned in Tiberias.

The danger for the kingdom was obvious, and enormous effort was put into assembling a huge army; Gerard of Ridfort, who held half of Henry II's treasure on deposit, used it to hire a large troop of knights and footsoldiers. Raymond III and the elder son of Bohemond III, Raymond, joined them; Bohemond himself and Baldwin of Rames, who had gone into exile on Guy's accession, also arrived. The army assembled at Sephorie numbered between 1,200 and 2,000 knights and 20,000 other combatants.

Saladin, however, attacked Tiberias, taking the lower town, while the Countess Eschiva, Raymond III's wife, retreated into the citadel (2 July). On hearing of this, the Frankish army had to decide whether to adopt a stalling strategy – remaining encamped round a spring, surrounding themselves with entrenchments, until the forces of the sultan dispersed – or whether to march on Tiberias. Raymond III argued for the former, though Tiberias was his fief and it was his wife who was in danger; Gerard of Ridfort managed to convince King Guy by suggesting that Raymond was trying to make him take responsibility for an unpopular decision, and the army set out on the morning of 2 July.

Saladin, abandoning the siege of Tiberias, managed to prevent the Franks from reaching the springs near the hills of Hattin. A surprise attack might perhaps have enabled them to rush the slopes leading to Lake Tiberias; Raymond advised instead occupying the strong position of the Horns of Hattin, a basalt peak dominating the plain. But the fate of the Frankish army was bound up with the question of water; heat, fanned by brush fires, and thirst overcame their resistance, whilst Saladin had organised a camel transport of goatskins from the lake, which provided his troops with drinking water. Many of the infantry laid down their arms; the knights attempted two charges in which they showed great bravery, but they were overwhelmed. Only a strong detachment led by Raymond III, with Raymond of Antioch, Joscelin III, Reynald of Sidon and Balian of Ibelin, charging through the Muslim ranks, reached the lake and, from there, Tyre. King Guy, Reynald of Châtillon, the marquis William III of Montferrat, who had arrived in 1185, Humphrey IV of Toron, Aimery of Lusignan and many other barons were prisoners; and the True Cross, which accompanied the army, fell into Saladin's hands.

Saladin treated the barons and the king courteously, but upbraided Reynald, reproaching him for his perfidy. Reynald was unapologetic and the sultan beheaded him with his own hand. The turcopoles suffered the same fate, Saladin regarding them as having reneged on Islam; so did all the captured Templars and Hospitallers, as during earlier campaigns, since they were seen as sworn enemies of Islam. In their case, the task of executing them was given to those who had volunteered for the holy war. The fate of the other prisoners depended on their rank; those who might be ransomed were set apart, the rest reduced to slavery; the price of slaves plummeted in Damascus, falling as low as three dinars.

The destruction of this Frankish army deprived the kingdom of almost the whole of its army. Its fortresses had been denuded of their garrisons, except in the case of the great frontier castles where this had clearly been out of the question. Kerak held out till November 1188, Saphet till December, Belvoir till January 1189, Montreal till April of that year. The defenders of Montreal, to obtain provisions, sold their wives and children to the Bedouins; the sultan ordered that they be redeemed. Reynald of Sidon managed to hold out in Beaufort, on the pretext that he had his family in Tyre and that he needed to procure the means to arrange their escape. One of his servants denounced this manoeuvre to Saladin, whom Reynald, who spoke Arabic well, regularly visited. The sultan had him arrested (August 1189) and tortured below the walls, without breaking the garrison's will, and it capitulated only on 22 April 1190, nearly three years after Hattin. Beaufort had played its part to the end, because by delaying Saladin under its walls it diverted his attention from the march of the Franks on Acre.

The sultan had decided it was not worth spending time on these great fortresses, whose capacity for resistance he had already experienced. It seemed more important to eliminate the Frankish presence from the coastal regions and reap the fruits of his victory. He went first to Tiberias, which capitulated on 5 July, the population and the garrison being given the right to withdraw to Tripoli. He then marched on Acre, which the barons who had escaped from Hattin had failed to put in a defensive state; Joscelin III withdrew, and the burgesses offered Saladin the keys of the town (9 July).

Here, the sultan seems to have suffered a setback; he wished to preserve the bases of the town's prosperity, its merchant colonies and sugar factory, but the inhabitants refused to accept his offer to remain where they were and pay a head tax, and preferred to leave the town, which the Muslims plundered with great thoroughness. In future, the conditions laid down by Saladin for accepting the surrender of towns included the right of free exit only for the Franks and their belongings; it seems that they were accompanied by many Christian Syrians, who eventually settled in Cyprus.

From Acre, Saladin had ordered his brother al-Adil to proceed to Palestine with the Egyptian army and to send the Egyptian fleet up the Frankish coast. He himself led his troops southwards, seizing Nazareth, Sephorie, Caiphas and Caesarea in passing, reducing the population to slavery; the castle of La Fève put up a semblance of opposition and obtained a capitulation. The Muslim peasants of Samaria pillaged Nablus. Saladin arrived before Jaffa, which refused to open its gates; the town was stormed and the inhabitants massacred or reduced to slavery.

Instead of marching on Jerusalem as had been expected, the sultan then turned north. He had left his nephew Taqi al-Dîn to reduce Tyre and the neighbouring townships. Taqi appeared before Tyre, which was probably defended by the preceptor of the Temple, Thierry, the other barons having for the most part left. Negotiations began; they were, it seems, sufficiently far advanced for the Ayyubid banners to have been hoisted above some of the towers. But the arrival at that very moment of the son of Marquis William III, Conrad of Montferrat, gave new heart to the inhabitants, who recognised him as their leader; the Ayyubid banners were thrown into the moat and Taqi al-Din informed his uncle (14 July). It was this that made Saladin decide not to go straight to Jerusalem. On 26 July Toron surrendered to him; he then proceeded to Sidon, which capitulated on 29 July; Beirut did the same only after a week of fighting, on 6 August. The two chief towns of the county of Tripoli, Gibelet and Botron, also opened their gates in exchange for the liberation of their lords, taken prisoner at Hattin, and on the usual conditions.

Al-Adil was making little headway at Ascalon, which defended itself fiercely. Saladin joined him, and tried to get the town to surrender in return for the liberation of Guy of Lusignan. He, led out in front of the town, was careful not to ask for its surrender, but asked the inhabitants, if the worst came to the worst, to make the restoration of his liberty one of the conditions of their capitulation. They surrendered only on 5 September, when their walls, weakened by mine works, threatened collapse; they obtained a respite to withdraw to Alexandria with their belongings; the sultan's representatives had to use threats to compel the Italian ships to take them on board. Gerard of Ridfort ordered Gaza, held by the Templars, to surrender in return for his own freedom. The smaller places nearby were also evacuated.

With the coast – except Tyre – now in his hands, Saladin could turn his attention to Jerusalem. The town had already been made uneasy by Muslim runners; it seems that talks had taken place between some elements of the population, either Syrian or Latin, and the sultan; *The History of the Patriarchs of Alexandria* accuses a Melchite, Joseph Batit, who enjoyed Saladin's favour, of trying to get the town to surrender. But the patriarch Heraclius remained in Jerusalem, and Balian of Ibelin, after Hattin, had gone there in search of his wife; the patriarch released him from the oath he had sworn to Saladin not to remain in the town; he took command of the defenders and got them to do homage to him. He knighted the sons of knights and the young burgesses, and minted coins. An Ayyubid detachment which approached was defeated.

Saladin was probably unwilling to grant to Jerusalem the conditions he had conceded elsewhere. He says this in a letter to the caliph in which he tells how, a breach having been opened, the Frankish leaders had asked him for the *aman*;

We refused point blank, wishing only to shed the blood of the men and to reduce the women and the children to slavery. But they threatened to kill the prisoners, and to ruin and destroy crops and buildings. We granted them the *aman*, in return for a ransom equal to their value if they had been made prisoner and reduced to slavery. Those who did not pay the ransom became slaves.

Between the Ayyubid sultan and the Frankish barons, nevertheless, relations were more courteous, as they generally were between the members of the two military aristocracies, for whom religious opposition did not preclude mutual appreciation; a knight of some rank (and the Franks gave this title to Muslim combatants of high rank) was not doomed to slavery, but liable to be ransomed. Saladin had authorised Queen Sibylla to leave the town to rejoin her husband in Nablus, and the wife and children of Balian to reach the coast. Some Franks wanted to attempt a sortie to try to break through the enemy ranks; the patriarch Heraclius pointed out that, if they failed, the refugees, the women and the children would be delivered to the Ayyubid soldiery. In the absence of provisions, the flow of refugees into the town ruled out a lengthy siege.

Here, however, Saladin did not intend simply to allow the Franks to leave, as he had done elsewhere, so they had to haggle. The Muslim prisoners, who numbered some five thousand, were freed. The ransom of the Franks was fixed at 10 bezants for a man, 5 for a woman, 1 for a child. Because there were so many poor, the sultan agreed in principle to a package: 7,000 of them were redeemed for 30,000 bezants. Al-Adil bought 1,000, whom he freed. Some 16,000 others were left. Saladin was selective; as they left the town, the young men and the young women, doomed to slavery, were separated out, and those who lacked market value were let go. The sultan thus gained a reputation for generosity, which he enhanced by restoring to the young women and wives their captive fathers and husbands. What remained of the king of England's treasure in the hands of the Hospitallers had been exhausted and people struggled to turn their possessions into money, with extreme difficulty. The exiles set out for Tripoli, in three strongly escorted convoys; smaller groups fell victim to Muslim attacks, and Tripolitanian knights, among them the sire of Niphin, did not scruple to plunder the refugees.

No Latin was allowed to remain in Jerusalem, except perhaps for an old man who had arrived with the crusade of 1099 and another who had been born in the city that year. 'As for the rest of the people who remained in the town, consisting of Armenians, Byzantines and Syrians, each man had to give ten dinars and each woman five; they could then leave and go where they wished', wrote one Syrian author. The Christian inhabitants of the eastern rite were made to pay the same ransom as the Franks, but they could remain if they paid the head tax and accepted the status of *dhimmi*.

It has often been said that the eastern Christians were not altogether sorry to see the end of Frankish rule. The Syrian Jacobite quoted above, an eyewitness, does not give this impression. 'Words', he says,

cannot describe the crimes we saw committed in the town; nor could any books contain them; how the sacred vessels were sold in the town's markets to men of various races; how the churches and the altars became stables for the horses and cattle and places of debauchery, drinking and singing. Added to which was the shame and derision of the monks, of noblewomen, of pure nuns who were delivered to impurity with all sorts of people, of the boys and girls who became Turkish slaves and were dispersed to the four corners of the earth.

A Nestorian poet from Iraq has left us a similar lament.

Indeed, it was before the eyes of the Christians that the victors triumphed and destroyed the religious signs they held dear. The great cross of the Temple of Our Lord was pulled down and the building became once again the mosque of Omar. 'The churches were stripped of wood, iron and doors; even the marble which covered the walls and floors was taken and carried to other countries.' The Holy Sepulchre was spared; but the basilica was provisionally closed and only opened after the institution of a fee of 10 bezants payable by every visitor. After the expulsion of the Latin canons, who took with them the Holy Sepulchre's treasure, the basilica was served only by Greek clergy; Isaac Angelus, in his letters to Saladin, while congratulating him on his victories, asked him to reserve to them exclusive rights to serve churches in Syria. But the Greeks obtained little benefit from being assigned the Latin churches. As Saladin wrote soon after taking Acre, 'the churches have become mosques ... the altars transformed into *minbar* for our preachers'. Many churches were closed, sometimes to become Muslim oratories, sometimes *madrasa* or Sufi convents.

To replace the Frankish population and those Syrians who had opted for liberty in Christian territory, Saladin seems to have imitated Nur al-Din, who, at Edessa and elsewhere, had recalled the descendants of the former Muslim inhabitants and also appealed to the Jews. But the reality of a proclamation issued to the latter immediately after the capture of Jerusalem is disputed; it is recorded by Jewish writers of the thirteenth century; all that is certain is that Saladin authorised the settlement of Jews in Jerusalem, contrary to the practice of the Franks. But the true Zionist movement which emerged in Jewish communities both in the West and in the Maghreb had other causes. Jewish pilgrimages had become more frequent in the twelfth century (Moses Maimonides made his in 1165), and the movement for a return to the Holy Land was becoming more important in the thirteenth century. The Muslim victory certainly played a part in encouraging it, but was not its cause.

Saladin's attitude to the conquered territories was now clear; he aimed to eliminate the Frankish presence, including that of the clergy and the religious, reserving for the future the possibility of pilgrims coming to pray, in return for cash, and this not only to Jerusalem but throughout the Latin states. If he spared Frankish lives, it was to discourage them from a desperate defence of their fortresses; to drive them back towards one or two places on the coast – Tyre or Tripoli – was effectively to provide them with the possibility of leaving before these towns, in their turn, fell.

Tyre did not, however, fall. The sultan went there in person; he tried the method that had succeeded elsewhere, offering Conrad of Montferrat his father's freedom – he had been captured at Hattin – in return for the surrender of the town. Conrad, who was strengthening his power over it, refused on grounds which also show that a page in the existence of the Latin kingdom had been turned: 'I am the lieutenant of the kings overseas.' One of Saladin's lieutenants, Dildîrim, took Châteauneuf on 26 December, but he had to be content with leaving a body of observers before Tyre, to which Conrad, by new concessions, had attracted Italians, in particular Pisans, and other representatives of the western Maritime towns. On 30 December Conrad seized five Egyptian galleys which were blockading the port and destroyed the rest of the enemy fleet.

In fact, Saladin's army had begun to disperse, the various contingents, exhausted by such a long campaign, wishing to return home with their booty. The sultan resumed his operations, to suffer a defeat at the hands of the Hospitallers of Belvoir in March 1188, and assembled his troops at Damascus in May. But a Sicilian fleet, under the command of Margarit, had arrived off the Syrian coast; after reinforcing Tyre by landing a body of troops sent by King William II, it proceeded to Tripoli and helped to force Saladin to abandon his attempt to take the town; when he marched north, after testing without insistence the defences of the Crac des Chevaliers, the sultan was able to occupy the lower town of Tortosa, where the keep resisted; Guy of Lusignan and Gerard of Ridfort, both freed from captivity, contributing to its defence; then, avoiding Margat, where he would have faced a Sicilian landing party, he easily occupied Jabala and Latakia, thanks to the intermediary of the qadi of Jabala, Mansûr ibn Nabîl, who had previously served the prince of Antioch (21 July). On 24 July he attacked Saone and seized several neighbouring castles; here, he was unimpeded by the inconvenient presence of Margarit's ships. Lastly, the sultan took the two fortresses which controlled access to Antioch from the north: Baghras and Darbsak (26 September). After this, he agreed to grant a truce to Bohemond III stipulating the freeing of all the Muslim captives and the surrender of Antioch if it was not rescued in eight months.

Dazzling though it had been, the campaign of 1188 had left many places where the Franks continued to hang on. Saladin had restored their mountain retreats to the emirs dispossessed by the Franks, where they made inconvenient neighbours, but the region between Margat and the south of Tripoli, including the lands of the Templars and Hospitallers, had hardly been touched. The successes had been more spectacular in the principality of Antioch; the Sicilian intervention, which had caused the Egyptian fleet to stay close to its bases, had probably been the main cause of this relative failure. It remains the case that, in less than two years, the Frankish system of fortifications had been largely destroyed, the places in the interior that still held out being doomed, sooner or later, to fall.

More serious still, the social and religious structures of Frankish settlement had been destroyed. The nation which had developed overseas, with its specific religious life and culture, had been systematically eradicated; the small towns and the villages with Frankish populations no longer existed; many towns had been emptied of their populations of westerners. The Franks, in settling in the East, had not proceeded to such a radical elimination. The sultan's tolerance, celebrated even by his enemies, was demonstrated by numerous humane, even compassionate, gestures, but it did not extend to admitting the coexistence of a Frankish element or the Latin Church with the structures of the restored Muslim state.

But, by giving free rein to the humiliation of the Christians through the symbols of their religion, Saladin encouraged a radicalisation of the battle between them and the Muslims and a revival on a scale he could not have anticipated. The destruction of Frankish Christianity having been incomplete, it was the Latins of the East themselves who embarked on a restoration which would be made possible by a crusade.

The crusade had never ceased to be present in western minds. The expedition of 1148 had been the last great enterprise achieved with the

participation of sovereigns before the catastrophe of 1187. In the meantime, the popes had launched appeals to go to the aid of the East – in
1165, 1169, 1176, 1181 and 1184. In so doing, they were relaying the
approaches of the Franks of the East, who, for their part, addressed their
messages to the kings and to certain prelates, such as Archbishop Henry
of Reims, urging them to send assistance. The mission of the patriarch
Heraclius had been particularly important.

The response had been varied. It is not always possible to relate
directly the departure for the East of a particular great baron accompanied by his knights with one of these appeals; the individual character
of the decisions taken by these men means we cannot always know what
their motives were. But it is rare for an appeal signalling the gravity of a
given situation not soon to be followed by an important departure.

No less remarkable is the role of financial contributions. From the
beginning of the century, the churches in the Holy Land had usually
benefited from western generosity; but, when Adrian IV appealed to
Christians on behalf of the Templars, hard hit by a defeat (1157), it was
in response to an urgent request for financial assistance. Kings Louis VII,
Philip Augustus and Henry II imposed taxes on their subjects to provide
for the needs of the Latin East. In general, the West made a significant
contribution, in money and in men, to its defence.

It is undeniable that the appeals from the Latin East encountered some
resistance. Alexander III had to seek new incentives to persuade the
pilgrims to enter, for a period, the service of their brethren, and how
successful he was is not known. A Gerhoh of Reichersberg might argue
that the Second Crusade had been inspired by the anti-Christ, but
criticism of the crusade remained limited; the attitude of the Franks of
the West towards those of the East remained, nevertheless, mixed.
Henry II told Gerald of Wales that 'if the patriarch comes here, it is in
his interests and not in ours'. The westerners had frequent experience of
the opposition between their own intentions – to earn their remission by
fighting in God's service – and those of the Franks of the East, who did
not hesitate to make truces with the Muslims and refused to break them
so as to give their allies an opportunity to fight, thereby rendering vain
the sacrifices they had made. James of Vitry was to say this in the 1220s,
but others had experienced it before.

The *poulains'* flowing robes and taste for jewellery and perfumes
irritated the westerners; the English clergy were shocked by Heraclius.
They were accused of preferring baths to battle and of enclosing their
women like Orientals. Caesar of Heisterbach attributes to a Muslim emir
the claim that the Franks deserved their fate by their vices – ready even
to prostitute their wives and daughters to the pilgrims. They were

primarily reproached for a pragmatism which, in their relations with the Muslims, went as far as collusion. While the Franks of the East mocked the naivety of the freshly landed 'sons of Hernaud', the latter feared they were being manipulated by special interests. For the Franks of the East, the 'wars of Our Lord' were often frontier disputes; the Franks of the West saw them rather as a global confrontation with the infidel. And zeal was sometimes tempered; more than one great lord, like the Duke of Saxony, Henry the Lion, returned home without having drawn his sword against the 'pagans', and showing no sign of regretting it.

Such considerations may have weakened the response of pilgrims to the appeals in aid of the Franks of the East. But they were counter-balanced by the valour that the latter displayed and which many witnessed. The bravery of Baldwin IV at Montgisard, and the panache of Reynald of Châtillon, about whom Peter of Blois wrote a *Passio Reginaldi*, aroused great enthusiasm, and Guyot of Provins included 'King Amauri of Outremer' in his pantheon of the great men of past times.

It is possible that the feeling of 'brotherly charity' invoked by the popes in their appeals may have been a little dulled, but veneration for the Holy Places remained intact. Without the permanent influx of pilgrims, without their willingness to agree to fight in their defence, which made it possible to recruit from among them the *soudoyers* who were particularly numerous in July 1187, and without the frequent arrival of great lords with 'a goodly company of knights', the Frankish colonies would have disappeared. But the crisis of 1187 revealed that such occasional volunteers were not enough; recourse to kings was inevitable. And, if Alexander III and his successors redoubled their efforts to reconcile the kings of France and England, as their letters make plain, because of the danger threatening the Holy Land, it is because they recognised this necessity.

7

CRUSADES OF RECONQUEST (1188–1205)

With the fall of Jerusalem, this history of the crusades changes course. Throughout the twelfth century, the life of the Frankish states and the support they enjoyed in the West revolved round pilgrimage. The states assured the defence of the Holy Places and the religious establishments that served them and protected the routes followed by pilgrims. The West provided help, sometimes on a considerable scale, in particular when the popes urged westerners to join in the defence of the Frankish lands in the East. Though major ventures might be proposed, their objective could not be clearly defined, since there seems never to have been any serious intention to extend the conquests of the western Christians, except in the case of Egypt. The only large-scale crusade, that of 1147–8, had been a great disappointment.

After Saladin's conquests, the situation changed. The infidel had occupied Jerusalem, destroyed the Christian defences and committed repeated acts of profanation, thereby reawakening the conscience of the West. The need for access to the Holy Places was only one of the imperatives that spurred Christians into action; the notion of their duty to restore the Holy City and Holy Land to the kingdom of Christ was no less pressing; nor was the thought of the violations of divine commandments that had led to the fall of Jerusalem.

As a result, the West expended considerable effort on the reoccupation of the Holy City and Holy Land, mobilising all its resources. This effort was sufficient to keep Saladin's forces in check and, after three years of war, to oblige the sultan to abandon his ambitions to eliminate for ever the Frankish presence in the Levant. The combatants drew breath. But a new effort was soon made, thanks to an initiative of the emperor Henry

VI, which in a way revived the schemes of William II of Sicily, whose successor he claimed to be. When this expedition was cut short, Innocent III organised a new one, which deviated strangely from its route to culminate in the occupation of Constantinople. The project was not resumed until 1213, when it took another form. But from 1188 to 1213, it was the loss of Jerusalem and the duty of reconquest that primarily dictated crusading activity.

THE THIRD CRUSADE ON ITS WAY TO THE EAST

News of the disaster suffered by the Franks and of the threat hanging over the Holy City reached the West very quickly by various routes. The Grand Preceptor of the Temple, Thierry, wrote to Pope Urban III, to his brethren in the order, to the count of Flanders and to all Christians to tell them of the crushing defeat inflicted on the Frankish army and of Saladin's siege of Tyre, while the Hospitallers informed the master of their order in Italy of these same events. Archbishop Josias of Tyre himself set off to visit the pope and the kings of France, England and Sicily.

Urban III died soon after receiving the news. His successor, Gregory VIII, was elected after Cardinal Henry of Albano, who had first been approached, had refused the tiara in order to devote himself to preaching the crusade. Even before his consecration, Gregory announced it, in a letter to the bishops of Germany whom he asked to intervene with the emperor Frederick on behalf of the 'liberation of the Holy Land' (27 October 1187). Two days later, by the bull *Audita tremendi*, he informed the whole of Christendom of the scale of the disaster, emphasising the capture of the Holy Cross by the infidel and the intolerable nature of their profanations. He recalled that, after the capture of Edessa, the generosity of the Christian people had persuaded God to spare the Holy Land and he launched an appeal for penitence, for the restoration of peace between princes and for departures in aid of the recovery of that Land so precious to Christians.

Gregory VIII's appeal, repeated by Celestine III, who succeeded him three months later, placed three imperatives at the forefront of Christian preoccupations: penitence, peace and the taking of the cross. Henry of Albano, Peter of Blois and others devoted themselves to preaching the crusade. It is the tour made by Archbishop Baldwin of Canterbury that we know best, thanks to Gerald of Wales, who was an eyewitness; the archbishop preached throughout Wales, arousing great enthusiasm; miracles were performed, and nearly three thousand people, among them some formidable Welsh archers, took the cross. Such individual commitments were probably very common; a man taken prisoner by the Muslims told how his mother and he owned only a house, and that they had sold it so that he could equip himself and leave on crusade. The preachers ordered fasts and public penances. To avert the wrath of God, provoked by the sins of men, of all men, since the pope refused to lay the responsibility solely on the Christians of the East, was the highest priority. And such acts of penance were a necessary preliminary to the taking of the cross.

Both to remedy a state of sin and from a concern for efficiency, the pope also instructed his envoys to restore harmony between princes, kings and cities. He succeeded in reconciling the Genoese and the Pisans, and the Venetians and the king of Hungary, and in restoring peace between William II of Sicily, who had led a vigorous offensive against the Byzantines, and the emperor Isaac Angelus. The kings of France and England met at Gisors on 21 January 1188, with the count of Flanders. Archbishop Josias persuaded them to take the cross, and it was then that the three princes agreed on the distinctive mark that was to be worn by their troops, a red cross for the French, a white cross for the English and a green cross for the Flemings.

But already, without seeking the advice of his father, Richard of England had taken the cross at Tours, with his Poitevin barons, in November 1187. Frederick Barbarossa, who had met the king of France at Ivois in December 1187, had summoned a diet at Mainz, known as the *Curia Jesu Christ*, during which he was reconciled with those of his barons who had opposed him and together they took the cross (27 March 1188). Philip Augustus and Henry II had also assembled their barons, the latter at the end of January, the former on 27 March.

In practice, however, the quarrels between the Capetian and the two Plantagenets had not been settled; Richard was afraid that his father would take advantage of his absence to increase his brother John's share in the inheritance. Henry died on 6 July before these difficulties could be resolved.

The first sovereign to have responded to the appeal to crusade had been William of Sicily, whose state of health prevented him from departing (he died on 18 November 1189), but who sent a fleet and a small expeditionary force to the East which, as we have seen, greatly impeded Saladin's operations in 1188. He had offered his assistance to Henry II by proposing to equip a fleet of two hundred ships, with provisions for two years, to transport his troops.

They first had to decide whether to depart by sea or by land. The land route had initially been intended, and that was the route the Byzantines were expecting the three sovereigns to take, as the kings of France and

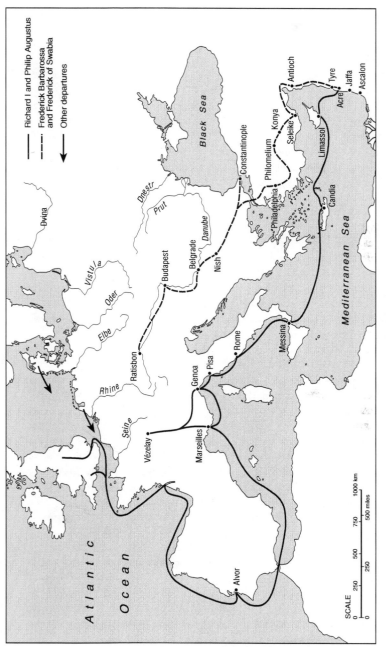

Map 13 The Third Crusade

England had made contact with them. There was dithering even at the Diet of Mainz. Many German princes favoured a sea journey; the emperor eventually opted for the land route and even asked the Mediterranean powers not to respond to the approaches of those of his subjects who disagreed; the Frisons and the Danes, nevertheless, who left in their own ships, took the sea route.

The French and the English had agreed to form a common army; they finally opted for the sea route. But, contrary to what had been intended by Henry II, Richard decided to use his own ships, which had to be built in England. Philip negotiated with the Genoese, dispatching Duke Hugh III of Burgundy to Genoa to negotiate for the transport of 650 knights, 1,300 squires and 1,300 horses, for the sum of 5,850 silver marks, with provisions for eight months and wine for four, plus fodder for the horses (February 1190). The English army left in a hundred ships, but King Richard had to charter in Marseilles the ships that were needed to transport those who had accompanied him across France.

All these operations were inevitably expensive; the imposition of a tax, the 'Saladin tithe', calculated on the basis of a tenth of income and movable goods, in both France and England made it possible to raise the necessary sums. While Richard seems to have enjoyed ample resources, Philip was less well provided, and money problems played a major role during the expedition. The simple crusaders could expect to receive wages.

The two kings promulgated a very strict disciplinary code; the sailors of the English fleet had committed many depredations during their voyage along the Iberian coast, and the ordinances of Messina were probably necessary to maintain order on board.

It was the army of Frederick I that left first, after the emperor had sent his messengers to Byzantium, Hungary and even Konya, where the sultan Alp Arslan welcomed the emperor's request for passage, and to Serbia. It was agreed to rendezvous at Ratisbon on 23 April 1189. The size of the imperial army has been estimated at 15,000 men, including 3,000 knights. However that may be, it left Ratisbon on 11 May, made rapid progress across Hungary and reached the Byzantine frontier on 28 June.

Frederick had obtained from the emperor Isaac right of passage through the empire, with the promise to provide him with guides and to open markets to him. But he found himself prey to attacks by brigands and he had to use force to gain access to the pass of Trajan, which had been fortified and which was held against him. Learning that his envoys had been detained in Constantinople, he made contact with the Serbian prince, Stephen Nemanya, and with the Vlachs and the Bulgars, who had rebelled against the Byzantine empire, and arrived at Philippopoli on 26 August.

There, he received messages from Isaac accusing him of wishing to seize Constantinople. His envoys, finally freed, told him of the situation in the capital, where the patriarch was preaching against the Latins and where it was known that the emperor had negotiated with Saladin, asking him for the return of the Holy Cross and for the churches of the Holy Land to be assigned to the Greeks, and telling him of the crusaders' intentions. The German emperor then considered himself to be at war with Isaac; he defeated the Byzantine forces at Dhidhimotikon and reached Adrianople (22 November), after taking the principal fortresses of Thrace and Macedonia and burning Philippopoli. He established his winter quarters at Adrianople. Isaac, fearing an attack on Constantinople, eventually negotiated with him by returning to the conventions agreed with Frederick in September 1188; the German army, supplied with provisions, was then able to cross the Dardanelles between 21 and 30 March 1190, Isaac meanwhile making his excuses to Saladin. This incoherent policy was severely criticised by the historian Nicetas Choniates, governor of Philippopoli, who had been one of the principal negotiators between the two emperors; it had delayed the German army and weakened an empire already undermined by rebellions.

There were further misadventures in Asia Minor. The Byzantines of Philadelphia failed to provide the expected food supplies; the town escaped reprisals thanks to negotiations with its governor, but some of its inhabitants attacked the German rearguard. The sultan of Konya had promised the Germans a favourable reception, but his sons, between whom he had divided his estates (the eldest had even imprisoned his father), harassed the crusaders, who had to fight a pitched battle near Philomelium and who were wracked by hunger and thirst. They succeeded, nevertheless, in seizing the lower town of Konya, and the sultan, who had taken refuge in the citadel, offered them the chance to recuperate by opening a market where they would be able to obtain up to six thousand horses. Thus, tired but intact, the army reached the territory of Armenian Cilicia. It was then that, having attempted to swim across the River Göksu which barred their way, Frederick was drowned on 10 June 1190.

His son, Frederick of Swabia, was unable to maintain the cohesion of his forces. When he regrouped them at Antioch, it was to face an epidemic which claimed two bishops, many counts including the count of Holland, and the margrave of Baden. Others set sail to return to Europe, for example the count of Holstein, whose lands were under attack from Henry the Lion. Sickness dogged the army, which followed the coast and which was attacked between Antioch and Tripoli. The places on the Antiochene frontier occupied by Saladin in 1188, however, offered no resistance, and Frederick arrived before Acre, where, on 20 January 1191, he died. The trials of the German crusade and its disintegration were a great relief to Saladin who had much feared it; his camp was exultant when news of the emperor's death arrived.

Nothing so dramatically illustrates the shock felt in the West at the fall of Jerusalem as the steady stream of contingents which successively arrived by the sea route. The first were the Pisans, led by their archbishop, Ubaldo, whom the pope had made his legate (6 April 1189). The Genoese and the Venetians followed soon after. On 1 September 1189, there came a great fleet of fifty cogs, carrying, we are told, 12,000 Frisians and Danes, only a hundred of whom would survive the crusade, and who, in passing, had conquered Alvor on behalf of the Portuguese. The following night saw the arrival of a great baron of Hainault, James of Avesnes, with some Flemings; a famous warrior, he became the leader of the crusaders. Some Bretons, and after them many French barons, with Henry of Bar, Erard of Brienne, the count of Dreux and the bishop of Beauvais, arrived in the middle of the month. On 24 September it was the turn of the archbishop of Ravenna and the landgrave of Thuringia, who succeeded James of Avesnes as the leader of the crusaders. In October, there followed some lords of Burgundy and Champagne, those of Montréal, Noyers, Toucy and Joinville. Soon after, lastly, came the Danes, with the king of Denmark's nephew, and princes and barons from other regions.

Winter caused a lull in these arrivals, which resumed in the spring of 1190; Count Henry of Champagne, with a large contingent, which represented a significant part of the army of Philip Augustus, arrived on 27 July and soon took command. The contingent from Franche-Comté, with the archbishop of Besançon and the sires of Champlitte and Salins (he chartered a ship at Genoa on 6 August), arrived next, as did some Normans; they included Yves of Vieux-Pont, who distinguished himself by his maritime exploits during the interception of a Muslim ship loaded with reinforcements and provisions for Acre, on 6 June 1191.

It was this steady flow of men, ships and resources of every type, including parts of siege machines, which was largely responsible for the crusade's success. The English and the French, it has been claimed, had grown weary of waiting for their kings to depart; this is true primarily of the French and of the crusaders from the fringes of the empire. Thanks to all these elements, and even before the arrival of Frederick of Swabia on 7 October, the siege of Acre was well under way. Nevertheless, the arrival of the two kings was decisive. The misfortunes of Frederick

Barbarossa's army had comforted the sultan, who could hope that the crusaders would be incapable of sustaining their efforts for long, given the heavy losses they had suffered. But, a few months later, the reinforcements in the form of the two armies of Philip Augustus and Richard I altered the balance of power.

The English army was larger than that of the Capetian. This was partly because many French barons had left before their sovereign, and partly because Philip had been unable to raise as much money as Richard. Henry II had rigorously enforced the levy of the tithe and demanded contributions from those who had renounced their vow. Philip had encountered much greater opposition to the collection of this tax. Richard could behave generously towards the French barons and towards the king himself.

The English fleet left first; it was to meet up at Marseilles with the troops that King Richard was to lead across the kingdom of France. Philip and Richard met at Vézelay on 4 July 1190; they travelled by way of Lyons, where the bridge collapsed under the crusaders' weight. Philip reached Genoa, but Richard failed to find his ships at Marseilles and he had to hire from the Marseillais the ships which carried the contingent led by the archbishop of Canterbury and the bishop of Salisbury to the Holy Land, and his own contingent to Sicily. Finally, the English fleet reached Messina on 14 September, Philip on the 16th and Richard on the 22nd. They had no alternative but to winter in Sicily.

Richard put the time to good use by setting the succession to the dead king William II, whose widow was his sister and who had bequeathed a large sum to his father Henry II. The throne of Sicily had been occupied by Tancred of Lecce, and Richard had soon clashed with him. He established himself in a wooden castle built before Messina, seized the town and looted it; Tancred made terms, especially since Philip Augustus refused to come to his aid. Richard obtained a generous financial settlement, which enabled Philip to appeal to the clause in their agreement stipulating an equal division of all the conquests made during their joint expedition; the king of England surrendered some of the money in question. In spring, the two kings set sail, Philip on 31 March 1191, Richard, in splendid array, on 10 April.

On 20 April Philip Augustus and his barons, the two chief of whom, Hugh III of Burgundy and Philip of Flanders, already knew the Holy Land, reached Acre. Richard arrived only on 7 June, having, in the meantime, conquered a kingdom.

Was the king of England's conquest of Cyprus, as is often claimed, a consequence of ambitions he harboured concerning Byzantine territory, or even the whole Mediterranean world? It seems to have been essentially a product of chance circumstances, in which the passionate and brutal temperament of the Plantagenet was given free play. His fleet had been scattered by a storm; many vessels were thrown onto the coast of Cyprus, near Limassol. The despot Isaac Comnenus, who had rebelled against Andronicus I and assumed the imperial title in the island, with the aid of the king of Sicily, wanted to exercise right of wreck by capturing the survivors; when he asked Richard's sister and his fiancée to disembark, they refused. The royal fleet arrived at this point; the king demanded the liberation of the prisoners and the return of the goods that had been seized. When Isaac refused, he landed and put his army to flight (6–7 May). Reinforced by Guy of Lusignan and other barons of the Latin East, Richard received Isaac, who sued for peace, in return for homage and the provision of a Cypriot contingent to the crusade. But, changing his mind, Isaac took refuge in his castles. Richard proceeded to occupy the island, capturing the emperor's daughter, then the emperor himself. After this, he resumed his journey to the Holy Land, leaving a small occupying force on the island, whose principal notables, who had suffered much from Isaac's rule, had submitted, after promising to grant the king half of their lands (5 June 1191).

Cyprus had been the granary of the Holy Land and its capture was a valuable haul, in which Philip Augustus quickly demanded his share; no doubt this wealth had played a large part in the king of England's decision. Richard had paid little heed to Isaac's family ties with western princes, including the duke of Austria, or to the rights of the Byzantine empire. Nor had he really organised his conquest, which he soon, after a first revolt by the island's Greek population, granted to the order of the Temple which, after a second rebellion, handed it back. The satisfaction of a rich conquest, and the capture of an emperor whom he put in chains of gold because he had promised not to clap him in irons, probably so flattered the king of England's pride that he hardly bothered to reflect on the consequences.

The unexpected result of this episode, which seems to have been fortuitous, was to attach the island of Cyprus to the Frankish states and to protect it, until 1571, from the Muslim powers.

THE ACHIEVEMENT OF THE THIRD CRUSADE: THE SIEGE OF ACRE

That the various elements of the crusade assembled round Acre, and that the siege of that town was the main event of the expedition, was a consequence of the divisions and rivalries that had marked the last years of the kingdom of Jerusalem.

The party grouped round Guy of Lusignan, with Humphrey of Toron and the constable, Aimery, had been particularly hard hit by the defeat. Those who had supported Raymond III had lost their leader, but they found in Balian of Ibelin, husband of Queen Maria Comnena, who had defended Jerusalem against Saladin, a new charismatic figure. The accounts of the circumstances of the loss of the kingdom bear the mark of the rivalries that were rife. The patriarch Heraclius is denounced for his lax morals, Raymond of Tripoli is accused of treason and Guy of Lusignan is presented as a young man lacking substance, according to whoever is the author of the account, and it is only recently that historians have tried to go beyond these stereotypes.

The conflicts had not been resolved. The arrival of Conrad of Montferrat, who had almost fallen into Muslim hands at Acre but who had managed to escape and land at Tyre, had complicated the situation. Conrad seems to have been determined to remain master of the town that he had successfully defended against Saladin; only a few of the great barons of the kingdom, like Pagan of Caiphas, had joined him. When Guy of Lusignan was freed by Saladin in May 1188, Conrad refused to receive him in Tyre and the king went to take part in the defence of Tortosa. It was then that, in the presence of Saladin's envoys, he went to the island of Ruad, to get round the promise he had made to the sultan to take to the sea. The marquis of Montferrat, whose father had also been given his freedom, refused access to Tyre to Guy's eldest brother, Geoffrey of Lusignan, who had to join his brother in Antioch; he also expelled Reynald of Sidon, who withdrew to Tripoli.

Guy then began to assemble the knights who had escaped the defeat and Saladin's conquest of the fortresses, most of whom had taken refuge in Tripoli. At the head of some six hundred of them, including Sicilians left without employment by the truces agreed between the sultan and Tripoli, he marched south. Conrad of Montferrat once again refused him entry to Tyre, on the grounds that he recognised the sovereignty not of Guy but of 'the kings overseas', who would decide the fate of Tyre. Without insisting, on the advice of his brother Geoffrey, Guy continued his march to Acre, while Saladin, occupied with the siege of Beaufort, assumed that this was a diversion intended to make him raise the siege. When he reached the outskirts of Acre, Guy had already taken up a position on a hill close to the town which he had hastily fortified (29 April 1189). The king had obtained the naval support of the Pisans, and had been joined by many of the defenders of Tyre.

Guy's small army was encamped before the walls of Acre, without the power to invest it completely, and Saladin's army, established on the Tell al-Kharruba, kept it in its sights. From September, successive crusader arrivals made it possible to extend the siege front; on 16 September Saladin gave battle to break it and moved his camp closer to the town. On 4 October the crusaders attacked him; they first broke through the enemy army, then were driven back, and only the vigorous defence of Geoffrey of Lusignan prevented them from being trapped between the sultan's forces and the garrison of Acre, which risked a sortie. The Templars covered the retreat; Gerard of Ridfort fell into Saladin's hands and was put to death; but the sultan returned to his earlier positions and the crusaders resumed the siege of the town. Acre retained its sea contacts, but they were severed in March 1190, thanks to the arrival of an increasing number of Frankish ships; the first cogs, those of James of Avesnes, provided the timber for entrenchments and siege machines. In future, the provisioning of the town was dependent on the skill of those who ran the blockade. In April, the crusaders were able to build wooden towers, which their adversaries attempted to burn. There were frequent skirmishes, which were the occasions for many feats of arms.

In July the sergeants of the Frankish army, exasperated by the slow progress, attempted a surprise attack on the Muslim camp; they were massacred and the knights intervened in time to rescue the survivors. Henry of Champagne, then Frederick of Swabia, tried to inject more energy into the operations, but the forces were evenly balanced. For Saladin, this was at the cost of immense efforts to obtain the assistance of his vassals or to retain them. He tried to persuade the Almohad caliph of North Africa, though he had fought against him in recent years, to intervene on the grounds that the Muslim West ought to provide for the Muslim East assistance comparable to that provided by the Franks of the West to their co-religionists; he was flatly refused (January 1191). His letters to various Muslim princes reiterate this theme:

Look at the Franks, what point they have reached, what concentration they have realised, what aim they seek, what help they have provided, what goods they have lost and dissipated, what resources they have accumulated and then distributed and divided between them! In their nations and their islands, there remain not a king nor a single one of their great men or nobles who has not vied with his neighbour in the sphere of assistance, emulating his peers in efforts and devotion. To preserve their faith, they have reckoned a small thing the gift of their souls and of their lives; they have aided their impure races with all sorts of arms and of warriors skilled in battle. They have only acted and given out of religious fervour and enthusiasm for their faith.

To this the sultan contrasted the neglect, idleness and lack of zeal of the Muslims (October 1189).

Things were hardly as harmonious in the Frankish camp as the sultan described. Conrad of Montferrat had joined the besieging forces, and

Guy had even saved his life in battle, but he stuck to his guns. The death of Queen Sibylla and her two daughters by Guy, in October 1190, once again put the question of the succession at the forefront of the preoccupations of the leaders, as Guy owed the crown to his marriage; in losing his wife, he also lost his right to reign. Conrad then joined forces with Amalric's widow, Maria Comnena, mother of Sibylla's half-sister Isabella; the legate, Archbishop Ubaldo of Pisa, the bishop of Beauvais, Philip of Dreux and the duke of Swabia joined with them to pronounce the annulment of Isabella's marriage to Humphrey of Toron and to remarry her to Conrad. He was connected by family ties both to the Capetians and to the Hohenstaufen and therefore enjoyed the support of the French and German contingents, and of the Pisans. Isabella resisted and found a supporter in the archbishop of Canterbury, Baldwin, who judged this decision contrary to canon law and who represented the interests of the English royal house, which regarded the branch of the family of Anjou established in Jerusalem as its close relatives. But Baldwin died. Maria Comnena swore that her daughter had been married to Humphrey without her consent. Humphrey was challenged to do battle in the lists, but he slipped away. In spite of her protests, Isabella was married to Conrad, on 24 November 1190, though Guy refused to relinquish his right to reign. Conrad withdrew to Tyre, and the disputed king made haste to join Richard of England when he landed in Cyprus, to make sure of his support; Bohemond III of Antioch accompanied him, thus declaring in his favour.

The siege of Acre continued, periods of activity alternating with periods of weariness. The besiegers were victualled by sea, though food sometimes ran short. The financial resources of the crusaders were running out; the arrival of the kings of France and England was therefore very welcome, as they could offer to take the warriors into their pay. Nevertheless, on 13 February 1191, when the Egyptian fleet ran the blockade in order to bring in troops to relieve and provision the town's garrison, the crusaders were able to thwart the operation and the relief was only partly achieved.

With the arrival of Philip Augustus, activity was stepped up, but the resistance of the besieged town never faltered. The fighting reached a peak when the English army in its turn disembarked. Philip undertook to batter the walls, while Richard tackled the Ayyubid army. The Franks made a breach in the enceinte but were unable to enter the town; Saladin tried to relieve the garrison by launching a vigorous attack on the English army; he was repulsed (1–3 July). The citizens had tried to negotiate a capitulation with the king of France on the basis of their free exit; they had to agree to surrender to the two kings, after an intervention by Conrad of Montferrat, Saladin promising to restore the True Cross to the Franks and pay a ransom, completed by the exchange of the men of the garrison for a certain number of Christian prisoners (11 or 12 July 1191). On the day fixed for the exchange, Saladin failed to appear; thinking he had been duped, Richard had all his prisoners, who numbered about three thousand, beheaded.

The question of the throne of Jerusalem was posed once again; Philip Augustus having taken Conrad's side, Richard declared for Guy of Lusignan. On 27 and 28 July, an assembly of barons confirmed Guy in possession of the crown, making Conrad his heir, and leaving him the lordship of Tyre, with the expectation of the fiefs of Beirut and Sidon, whilst the county of Jaffa and Ascalon would revert to Geoffrey of Lusignan. It was also necessary to solve the problems relating to the restoration to their former owners of the houses of Acre which the crusaders claimed by right of conquest; the king of France got their right of ownership recognised, on condition they provided the crusaders with lodgings.

At this point, Philip Augustus decided to return to France, on the grounds of his state of health, but probably primarily because Philip of Flanders had been killed before Acre, and he wanted to lay his hands on part of his heritage, the Vermandois. He embarked early in August, entrusting command of the ten thousand or so men he left in the East to Duke Hugh III of Burgundy.

King Richard remained at the head of the crusader army. Saladin, fearing that he might march from Acre on Egypt, ordered the dismantling of Ascalon, at the beginning of September, having already done the same in the case of Caesarea and Jaffa. So when the king of England set out southwards, he could find nowhere to shelter, while the Muslims harried his army. On 7 September the crusaders arrived at Arsur, where they were surrounded and showered with arrows, but a massive charge put the larger part of the enemy to flight. Saladin managed to check the stampede and mount a counterattack, during which James of Avesnes was killed, but a new charge forced the sultan to retreat.

Richard could then have marched on Ascalon, where the walls had only just begun to be dismantled, or on Jerusalem; he preferred to embark on the rebuilding of Jaffa, which would provide him with an operational base, and waited till the end of October before marching on Jerusalem. But Saladin had improved the fortifications of the Holy City and, after spending a fortnight at Bait Nuba, before entering the defiles which led to Jerusalem, Richard ordered the retreat (13 January 1192). Some said it was the duke of Burgundy who withdrew his contingent in order to deprive the king of England of the glory of the reconquest;

others said it was the Franks of the Holy Land who advised Richard against an enterprise which might easily have turned out badly, especially since a new army was on its way from Egypt. Richard, who had got as far as Montjoie, two leagues from Jerusalem, and who had said his prayers there, returned to Jaffa; it is likely that he was reluctant to chance a siege in unfavourable conditions.

The king of England abandoned Jerusalem, but began to plan a campaign aimed at Egypt; at the end of January he began to rebuild the walls of Ascalon. This done, in May he marched on Darun, which capitulated. Learning of this, Saladin evacuated Tinnis, the most easterly of the Delta ports. But the kings marched once again towards Jerusalem, having assembled all the elements of the crusader army, on 7 June 1192, and enthusiasm was reignited within its ranks. Henry of Champagne had gone in search of reinforcements; Richard waited for them at Bait Nuba for several weeks, which allowed Saladin to implement defensive measures. Duke Hugh III urged the king to march on the town; Richard refused, referring to the difficulties of a siege and the advice of the Syrian Franks. The French threatened to begin the siege without him, but resigned themselves; a fortunate raid on a large caravan, whose approach had been signalled by the Bedouins and which was surprised near the well of the Round Cistern by Richard and Hugh III themselves on 23 June, raised the army's morale. A further show of force was made before Jerusalem, where panic had swept through Saladin's entourage, but the army finally withdrew on 4 July.

Richard's reluctance to risk an operation against Jerusalem, which might have dragged on and immobilised his army far from its bases and surrounded by Muslim forces, is easily explained; the Franks of the East drew on their experience of the country. It is nevertheless possible that, as in 1099, the enterprise might have succeeded. His withdrawal sounded the death knell for combined operations.

Saladin tried to take advantage of the Franks' retreat to Acre to surprise and seize Jaffa; the town and its citadel were almost in his hands when Richard arrived and, with a small body of men, recovered the city (31 July). On 5 August, having received no reinforcements, at the head of two thousand men he inflicted a total defeat on the Muslims, who had tried to take him by surprise. This exploit ended the campaign on a victorious note.

In fact, for almost a year negotiations had been under way; some operations can be seen as designed to apply pressure to speed them up. However, Saladin was able to exploit the discord among the Franks. On 5 September 1191 Richard had met Saladin's brother, al-Adil, and had let it be understood that, if the kingdom was restored to its former boundaries, peace might be achieved. He resumed these negotiations in October–November, pointing out that the two sides were exhausting themselves in a disastrous war, whereas the restoration to the Franks of the part of the kingdom situated west of the Jordan and of the True Cross would not diminish the sultan's power. Saladin replied by saying that he had no intention of renouncing Ascalon or of dismantling Kerak, and by emphasising the sacred character of Jerusalem for the Muslims. Richard then suggested that the kingdom might be governed by al-Adil, who would marry the king of England's sister Joanna, the Holy Sepulchre being returned to the Christians; but Joanna objected.

At the same time, Saladin received the visit of Reynald of Sidon and Balian of Ibelin who, in the name of Conrad of Montferrat, made him a different proposition, namely that he grant Beirut, Sidon and half the kingdom to the marquis, who would hold them as a fief of the sultan. The Montferrat–Lusignan quarrel was unresolved, and in February 1192 the Genoese made an attack on Acre to deliver the town to Conrad. Finally, Richard summoned a meeting at Ascalon in April to settle the issue. It was unanimously agreed that the kingdom should be left to Conrad. Richard invited the marquis to Acre to be crowned. At this point, in a dramatic turn of events, on 28 April the master of the Assassins, to whom Conrad had refused to return a merchant ship he had seized, had him murdered by two accomplices. The Franks and the crusaders then asked that Henry of Champagne, nephew of both Richard and Philip Augustus, be made king and be married to Queen Isabella, who was then pregnant with Conrad's daughter. Henry accepted, not without hesitation, and thus became 'lord of the kingdom of Jerusalem' (he refused the royal title) on 5 May 1192.

Guy of Lusignan, now deprived of the throne, had found compensation in offering to buy the island of Cyprus, relinquished by the Templars, from the king of England. His chancellor managed to borrow 40,000 bezants from the bourgeois of Tripoli as a down payment, and Richard invested him with Cyprus. Guy was to confirm his possession of the island by attracting to it a large number of knights, burgesses and turcopoles who formed the feudal cadres of what became, in 1197, the kingdom of Cyprus, when his brother, Aimery, obtained the crown from the emperor Henry VI.

Richard was now freer to negotiate with Saladin, but he was anxious to return to Europe, on account of the intrigues between his brother John and Philip Augustus. He made an agreement with Saladin, who presented it as an act of submission by crusaders impressed by his victory at Jaffa; it consisted of a truce to last three years and eight months, and the surrender to the Muslims of Ascalon, Gaza, Darun and the neighbouring fortresses (Richard refused to renounce Jaffa); the Franks were allowed to make pilgrimages to the Holy Sepulchre, which they made haste to do, including the French of the Capetian army whom Richard would have liked to have excluded; Saladin authorised two Latin priests and two deacons to reside at the Holy Sepulchre, and the same at Bethlehem and Nazareth. Oddly, the True Cross seems to have been forgotten. Perhaps James of Vitry was right and neither Christians nor Muslims any longer knew what had happened to it.

The truce was to extend to the territory of Antioch and Tripoli. Saladin agreed to restore to Bohemond II the plain of Amq, east of Antioch, as far as the castle of Arzghan. He also granted as a fief to Balian of Ibelin the small lordship of Caymont, and to Reynald of Sidon the southern half of the lordship of Sidon.

So the Third Crusade, if it failed to reconquer the kingdom of Jerusalem and the other lands lost in 1187–8, culminated in the recognition of the Frankish presence in Syria. Saladin not only accepted the existence of one fairly large coastal enclave round Acre, Tyre and Jaffa, and another round Antioch, not to speak of a reduced county of Tripoli and the lordships of the Hospitallers (Margat, the Crac des Chevaliers) and the Templars (Tortosa and Chastel Blanc), but he integrated them into his empire. His project to eliminate the Franks had failed.

This long and painful crusade, during which both disease and battle had exacted a heavy toll, was notable for a climate of religious exaltation reminiscent of the First Crusade. Even the Muslim historians were struck by this. For the Franks, the events of the Third Crusade provided the material for new epics, whose heroes were King Richard, Andrew of Chauvigny and William of Preaux, his loyal supporters, Hugh of Tiberias, James of Avesnes transformed into John of Avesnes, and Saladin himself. What clearer illustration could there be of the place it was to occupy in the imagination of future centuries?

THE CRUSADE OF THE EMPEROR HENRY VI

Richard I left the Holy Land six months before Easter 1193, the date he had fixed as the end of his crusade, under the pressure of the news he had received of negotiations between Philip Augustus and his brother John. He decided to return to his kingdom as quickly as possible. While his army was re-embarking for the West, he himself went on ahead. But his ship having been tossed by a storm onto the Dalmatian coast, he tried to cross, in disguise, the lands of Leopold, duke of Austria, whom he had deeply insulted in Syria. He was recognised, arrested and thrown into prison in the castle of Dürnstein. Leopold's grievances arose primarily from the conquest of Cyprus; Isaac Comnenus was related to the duke of Austria, who refused to accept his dispossession by the king of England. The emperor Henry VI made Leopold hand over his captive, and kept him in prison in spite of an intervention by Pope Celestine III, who was being urged by Eleanor of Aquitaine to excommunicate the emperor for having arrested a crusader. Richard eventually recovered his freedom in return for a large ransom, support for imperial policies and renunciation of his suzerainty over Cyprus, which was transferred to the emperor (Isaac, meanwhile, having died).

Henry VI thus gained a foothold in the East. An envoy of the new lord of Cyprus, Rainier of Gibelet, went to the imperial court at Worms in December 1195, to do homage to Henry VI, who in return sent a royal crown to Aimery of Lusignan. He had earlier, on 29 May 1194, received in Milan the envoys of the Armenian prince Leo, who asked for the grant of a royal crown and declared himself ready to recognise imperial authority. It was probably at this point that the emperor began to consider the possibility of a crusade, when he had already taken possession of the kingdom of Sicily, to which his wife Constance, sister of King William II, was the legitimate heir. On 25 December 1194, he was crowned at Palermo.

When he took the cross at Bari on Good Friday 1195, he was responding neither to an appeal from the Franks of the East nor to one from Pope Celestine III. In a bull of 11 January 1193, the pope had drawn the lessons of the Third Crusade. He regretted that the crusaders had put greater trust in their own forces than in God and reminded the faithful that the people of Israel had waited a long time before they could enter the Holy Land. The duty of Christians was thus above all to persist in penitence. They should hold onto 'that tiny piece of the land of Our Lord which still remains in the possession of the Christians so that it does not fall into the hands of the impious', while waiting until, by an immense effort, they could liberate the Holy Land and the Holy Sepulchre. The only immediate measure he envisaged on the material plane was to forbid tournaments – those who wanted to practise war could do so overseas – and wars between Christians. Celestine III clearly felt no pressing need to organise a new crusade, especially since Christendom was then more threatened by the Almohads, who were about to defeat the king of Castile at the battle of Alarcos.

The Franks of the East had no intention of abandoning the reconquest of their lands or of Jerusalem. But the expiry of the three years' truce had ceased to worry them; Saladin was dead, his heirs were quarrelling and al-Adil, who ruled Damascus, though he had allowed a raid into Christian territory, seems to have renewed the truce.

The announcement that the emperor of Germany had taken the cross was accompanied by activity in Rome. Celestine III, whose attitude to Henry VI was guarded, was probably persuaded by his cardinals to give the imperial decision the guarantee of his bulls, and he granted the customary indulgences.

Henry VI's motives were probably primarily a matter of his own conscience. The son of Frederick Barbarossa, who had died on crusade, like his brother Frederick of Swabia, he may have wished to perform in his turn what was regarded as a princely duty. Other motives, of a political nature, have been attributed to him, arising from the aspirations of the Hohenstaufen to a universal domination, and the resumption of the Normano-Sicilian monarchy's schemes for the Mediterranean. We have to accept that we cannot know the deep motives for Henry VI's decision; the papacy endorsed it by organising the preaching of the crusade, but it was the act of the emperor that dominated the planning of the project and its execution. No other sovereign was associated with it, or seems to have been asked to take part.

Nevertheless, Henry VI seems to have integrated the announcement of the crusade into a grand design that was aimed to make permanent the reunion of the kingdom of Sicily and the empire – which was unlikely to be looked on favourably by the papacy – and to assure the transmission of this double crown to his recently born son, Frederick Roger, the future Frederick II. He needed to get the German princes to accept this project, and at the diets at which he urged them to take the cross he also attempted to get them to recognise the young Frederick as the future king of the Romans, on the grounds that the absence of his father made a premature appointment necessary. In the end, faced with the opposition of some of the princes, Henry abandoned the theme of the hereditary nature of the imperial crown, retaining only that of the crusade.

Contacts were made with the Byzantine empire. The situation was very different from what it had been in 1188–90. Isaac II had moved closer to the westerners and the strongly anti-Latin patriarch Dositheus had been replaced by the much more moderate John Xiphilinus. The historian Nicetas, who held the office of Great Logothete, even suggests that the papacy was looking to Byzantium as a counterweight to Hohenstaufen power. The question of the union of the Churches was once again on the agenda. Isaac had married his daughter to Philip, Henry VI's brother, and relations between the two emperors were relatively cordial. The overthrow of Isaac by his brother Alexius III failed to cool this atmosphere, Alexius putting even greater emphasis on his interest in a union of the Churches.

But when envoys from the German emperor arrived in Constantinople, where Alexius tried to dazzle them with his splendour, they
brought what amounted to an ultimatum: Henry was counting on the
basileus to put his roads and ports in a condition to receive his troops and
his ships, supply them with provisions and send a contingent of his own
soldiers with the crusaders. As a contribution to Henry's efforts, Alexius
was to pay him 5,000 pounds of gold a year. If not, Henry would come
to Constantinople to force him to do so.

The abrupt nature of this instruction is perhaps here a little exaggerated, but it remains the case that Alexius was very pressingly invited to
participate in the crusade and make a financial contribution which,
thanks to a new Byzantine envoy, Eumathius Philokales, was reduced to
1,000 pounds. This was a large sum for an empire that was in reality
impoverished, and Alexius was obliged to levy a tax, called the
Alamanikon, which had the appearance of a tribute to be paid to the
Germans. Some historians have suggested that Alexius saw this contribution as a way of claiming a place in the victorious camp.

After the emperor, many of the princes of the empire and the great
prelates took the cross. By early March 1196 they included the duke of
Brabant and the landgrave of Thuringia; others followed at the diet of
Würzburg at the end of the month. Henry the Lion preferred to leave
the empire, but a number of great Guelph lords committed themselves.
The archbishop of Mainz, Conrad of Wittelsbach, had been made legate,
and it was he who led the crusaders from the Rhineland and Franconia
across the Alps to reach the ports of Apulia, from which they sailed at the
beginning of April 1197. Conrad put in at Cyprus and reached Acre in
May.

The north Germans had left in their own ships – forty-four cogs –
with the archbishop of Bremen, the count palatine of the Rhine and the
duke of Brabant. In passing, they attacked Silves, in Portugal, before
arriving at Messina. The main contingent from Germany, with the dukes
of Austria and Bavaria, the count of Holstein and the bishops of Passau
and Ratisbon, had reached Bari, where, on 1 May, it set sail for the
rendezvous which had been fixed at Messina.

The emperor had made sure that only combatants were involved.
Their number has been estimated at 4,000 knights and at least 12,000
other men, the emperor providing at his own cost 1,500 knights and as
many esquires. Some 250 ships were needed to carry them. They set sail
on 1 September and the armada arrived in Syria at the beginning of
autumn.

The first arrivals had demonstrated their insolence by attacking the
Muslims without warning the 'lord of the kingdom'; the Franks of the

Holy Land feared their brutality; Hugh of Tiberias put the women and children into the care of the Templars and Hospitallers and urged the crusaders to camp on the 'beach' rather than in the town.

But the Ayyubid princes had already assembled their troops; those of Damascus and those of Egypt, reinforced by contingents from Syria and Mesopotamia, gathered at Ain Jalut, nor far from Nazareth, from which they threatened Acre. A provocation by Waleran of Limbourg opened hostilities at a moment when Henry of Champagne had gone to meet his aunt, Queen Margaret of Hungary, who was leading 'a goodly company of knights'. Hugh of Tiberias was forced hastily to raise the royal army, which halted the Muslim offensive. But al-Adil launched an attack on Jaffa, which was defended by Reynald Barlais, who was later accused of negligence, and the town very quickly fell (beginning of September 1197); Henry of Champagne was sending reinforcements when he was killed in an accident, falling from a window (10 September).

The new king – who was to be the new husband of the already thrice-married Queen Isabella – was the preferred choice of Archbishop Conrad. Some would have preferred Ralph of Tiberias, but the decision went to Aimery of Lusignan, the new king of Cyprus, widower of Eschiva of Ibelin, seen by the Germans as a vassal of the emperor, but highly regarded by the local barons.

Aimery accompanied the German army, now under the command of the duke of Brabant, on a march northwards, where an emir by the name of Usama had turned Beirut into a nest of pirates. Al-Adil had ordered the dismantling of all fortifications, but Usama had destroyed only the town walls, leaving the castle intact. He was unwise enough, with other local leaders, to go out as if to face the enemy, and lost heart when he saw their number. But when he wanted to return to his castle, he found it in the hands of a Christian carpenter who had freed the emir's prisoners on seeing the square sails – sign of Nordic origin – of the Frankish fleet. He was eager to deliver the fortress into Aimery's hands (24 October).

Bohemond III of Antioch, who had joined the crusaders, took advantage of his return to Antioch to reoccupy Latakia and Jabala but, as they had been dismantled, he was unable to hold them. The lady of Gibelet, on the other hand, had succeeded in recovering her fortress by bribing the emir entrusted with its defence. With Botron, reoccupied in circumstances of which we are ignorant, the continuity of the Frankish occupation of the coast was almost restored, from north of Tripoli to south of Acre.

The German crusaders seem to have learned, before leaving Beirut, whose walls were hastily rebuilt, of the death of the emperor Henry, on

28 September. The army was thrown into confusion, but its leaders managed to restore calm by making their men swear oaths to Frederick, whom the dead emperor had appointed his heir. The duke of Brabant announced to the archbishop of Cologne that he intended to march on Jerusalem and that he proposed to rebuild the defences of the kingdom, by distributing fiefs or tenures to the crusaders. On 28 November they arrived below Toron, one of the sites which commanded access to the Jordan valley. The siege was actively pursued; the Saxon miners had already made great progress when the inhabitants offered to surrender the town. The leaders of the army were divided, some wanting to take it by force. In the end, nothing was agreed; a breach was opened up, but without success. News then arrived of the approach of the Egyptian army.

The consequences of Henry VI's death worried the crusaders, who feared for their fiefs. When the chancellor, Bishop Conrad of Hildesheim, and many of the other leaders secretly left the siege to return to Tyre, the army broke up. Henry's death had effectively divested the imperial chancellor of his powers, and there was no longer a recognised leader. The situation was aggravated by news that the transmission of the royal title of king of the Romans to the young Frederick had been contested; Otto of Brunswick and Philip of Swabia both had their supporters and, even in Sicily, a reaction set in against Henry VI's rule. The injunctions of the new pope, Innocent III, who asked the crusaders not to abandon their enterprise, were ignored; everyone was preoccupied with the fate of his lands and his lordships and was in a hurry to return to them. In March, the crusaders re-embarked, with a few exceptions, such as the count of Oldenburg, and the Minnesänger Otto of Henneberg who was shortly to marry the heiress of Joscelin III.

It was left to Aimery of Lusignan to make peace with the Muslims. He negotiated with al-Adil on the basis of the renewal for five years and eight months of the treaty concluded with Saladin in 1192, noting the loss of Jaffa and the reoccupation of Beirut, and stipulating freedom of access to the Holy Places for pilgrims. But a new clause was added to the treaty which made the continuation of the truce dependent on no powerful sovereign arriving in the East ('nisi aliquis rex christianorum potens in parte illas veniret'). This was implicitly to recognise that, during a crusade, the sovereignty of the king of Jerusalem must now bow before persons more powerful than he. The days when the pope instructed the crusaders to enter the service of the Latin king of the Holy Land were over.

The crusade of Henry VI, unlike its predecessors and although Richard I had vaguely aspired to behave as the heir of Fulk of Anjou and maintain a suzerainty over an eastern land, marked the entry into the equation of European politics. Imperial suzerainty over Cyprus and Armenia and the type of protectorate imposed on the Byzantines represented new factors in the crusading context. The crusade of 1197 was truly the emperor's crusade.

There was a further innovation. During the Third Crusade, German crusaders had founded a hospital which had initially been intended for the sick and wounded from the German contingent. Frederick of Swabia had sponsored it. With the end of the siege of Acre, this 'German hospital' was moved into the town. This caused friction with the order of the Hospitallers, which claimed a quasi-monopoly of this type of foundation, and which, in the twelfth century, had had a priory in Jerusalem intended primarily for the Germans. The chancellor Conrad assumed responsibility for the fortunes of the new hospital and gave it a military character which it had previously lacked. The hospitaller and military order of St Mary of the Germans may thus be seen as a creation of the crusade of 1197, on the basis of the foundation of 1191. It introduced into the Holy Land a presence indissolubly linked to the Hohenstaufen empire.

The Teutonic Order also acquired what remained of the 'Seigneurie de Joscelin', which the latter's daughter and her husband, Otto of Henneberg, granted it in 1208, thus providing it with an estate close to Acre, starting point for all their territorial possessions. The order was then in a position to compete with the orders of the Temple and the Hospital, and, like them, to participate in the politics of the Latin kingdom.

THE REVIVAL OF THE FRANKISH STATES

It had looked, at one stage, as if the crusade would make a clean break with the past of the Frankish states, and above all the kingdom of Jerusalem. It was probably the marriage of Conrad of Montferrat and Isabella of Jerusalem that made it possible to re-establish continuity between the old kingdom and the one which emerged from its ruins.

In 1192 the territory occupied by the Franks was reduced to a principality of Antioch consisting only of the town's immediate surroundings, including the Amq; a county of Tripoli which had briefly lost Botron and Gibelet, which had been recovered in 1197; the two estates of the Hospitallers of the Crac and the Templars of Tortosa; and the coastal strip extending from the Tripolitanian frontier to Le Destroit south of Acre, with an interruption corresponding to the dismantled town of Sidon; to which should be added the island of Cyprus, which became a kingdom in 1197.

The principality of Antioch had escaped the disruption suffered by the kingdom of Jerusalem. Bohemond III, however, had clashed with his neighbour and vassal, the Armenian prince Leo, who entrapped him by inviting him to a meeting, and demanded the cession of Antioch. But the population, Franks and Greeks together, drove the Armenians out. Leo had to release his prisoner after an intervention by Henry of Champagne (1193). He nevertheless succeeded in freeing himself from the suzerainty of the prince of Antioch and, by making an agreement with the pope and seeking a crown from the emperor Henry VI, he managed to have his 'barony' elevated into a kingdom of Armenia which took its place among the Frankish states (1197–9).

Leo had married his daughter to Bohemond III's eldest son, Raymond. The child born of this marriage, Raymond Roupen, would become, on the death of his father, heir to both Antioch and Armenia, which revived the fears of the people of Antioch. On Bohemond's death, they appealed to his younger son, Bohemond IV, who disputed the principality with King Leo and Raymond Roupen for many years (1201–18). A new marriage sealed the reconciliation between Bohemond and Leo, but this time the Armenian barons got rid of the son of the prince who had married their queen, and the two states remained on bad terms for a long time. The Seljuks of Konya took advantage of these battles to make the Armenian kingdom a vassal state.

In Tripoli, Raymond III had died by the end of 1187; he had left his county to his godson Raymond, elder son of Bohemond III, but Bohemond substituted his younger son, Bohemond IV. The barons of Tripoli proved amenable, and it was in that county that Bohemond found the resources to secure Antioch.

On the advice of Saladin, if we are to believe the Frankish chroniclers, Guy of Lusignan attracted many Latin settlers to Cyprus and thus substituted a Frankish aristocracy and feudalism for the dominant Byzantine class, without changing the status of the villagers. His brother Aimery reorganised Guy's excessively generous distribution of fiefs and, with the agreement of Celestine III, established a Latin Church on the model that had been developed in Jerusalem to regulate relations between the Greek and Latin clergy. Aimery's marriage to Eschiva of Ibelin, daughter of Baldwin of Rames, gave, though only after Aimery's death, a dominant role in the island to members of the Ibelin family, at the expense of the companions of Guy of Lusignan, most of whom were 'Poitevins', causing a rivalry that proved dangerous.

The position of Cyprus with regard to Jerusalem had been left in suspense by Richard of England, who had transferred to Henry of Champagne the debt of 60,000 bezants he was still owed by Guy of Lusignan. After a plot involving the Pisans and in which Aimery, then constable of Jerusalem and count of Jaffa, was compromised, the latter was banished. But the two men were reconciled and the debt written off; Aimery, once king of Jerusalem, was careful to separate the finances of the island and those of his new kingdom, foreseeing the time when his two possessions would go their separate ways, since Jerusalem would fall to Maria, daughter of Conrad of Montferrat and Isabella, whilst Cyprus would pass to his son by his first marriage.

While Henry of Champagne seems to have devoted his main efforts to reconciling the princes (he negotiated the agreements between Leo and Bohemond III) and the barons, Aimery seems to have been preoccupied with the restoration of royal authority. The barons of the new kingdom of Jerusalem were much less wealthy than their ancestors; the powerful fortresses and landed lordships of the twelfth century were no longer in their possession; they continued themselves with preserving their memory, so as to be able to claim them if they returned to Christian hands. But they retained their prerogatives and their feudal law, and the military strength of the kingdom continued to be based on the service they owed to the sovereign. They attempted to exploit this to put pressure on the monarchy, but without much success. Thanks to the 'liege men', the king of Jerusalem disposed of a power which was far from negligible.

To this power was added that provided by the military orders, of which there were now three, thanks to the appearance of the Teutonic knights. Practically independent in their estates of the county of Tripoli, the principality of Antioch and Armenia, they remained at the disposal of the king for his campaigns.

The territorial basis of the new kingdom was no longer comparable to that of the twelfth century. Nevertheless, the coastal districts – the plain of Acre, that of Tyre, the land around Tripoli, the district of Antioch and the Biqa round the Crac des Chevaliers – still represented considerable stretches of agricultural land, with tropical crops such as sugar cane, and olive groves which provided their owners with a handsome income. The royal demesne, of which Tyre and Acre were the two principal centres (it was at Tyre that the king was crowned), remained substantial. The resources derived from the exploitation of the land had been much reduced since Hattin, but their losses were to some extent compensated for by the growth of urban activity, which benefited from the expansion of trade. The king, the prince and the count drew increased revenues from this, which enabled them to grant vassals 'fiefs in bezants' in place of 'landed fiefs'. They were thus able to perform their functions and obtain the obedience of their subjects; they could even keep in check the powerful merchant 'communes' of Italy, which attempted to expand their privileged position. Royal authority remained, in general, respected, if not without some frictions.

There had been serious difficulties with regard to the transmission of the crown. The rejection of Guy of Lusignan had established the rule by which this crown passed from the king, if he had no male heir, to his daughter and to her husband, who was crowned king but who lost his rights if his wife died. As royal authority could only be exercised once the barons did homage to their sovereign, the barons wielded a power comparable to that of election. Isabella of Jerusalem, forcibly separated from her first husband, then married in succession to Conrad, Henry and Aimery, legitimated the choice of these three sovereigns. And it was her eldest daughter, Maria of Montferrat, who, on Aimery's death on 1 April 1205, became heiress to the kingdom. She had been engaged to Aimery's eldest son, Guy, who had died before his father.

After spending several years under the regency of her uncle, John of Ibelin, sire of Beirut, Maria married, in 1210, a French baron, John of Brienne, who had been chosen by Philip Augustus at the request of the barons of the kingdom; he was a brave knight and a poet, but poor.

Henry and Aimery had been able to maintain the king's preeminence over the northern princes; the former had taken Antioch under his protection at the time of Leo of Armenia's attempt on the principality (1194); the latter had constituted a fief (a rent of 4,000 bezants on the *Chaine* of Acre, that is, on the revenues of the port) for the count of Tripoli, who did homage for it (1198). They had also kept the Church dependent on the crown, trying to control the election of the patriarchs and the bishops. But papal activities in this sphere were becoming more numerous, making this prerogative increasingly illusory.

The recovery of the Frankish states is in part explained by the situation in the Muslim East. Saladin had died at Damascus, on 3 March 1193, but his emirs had not waited till then to demonstrate their opposition, and those of Syria made no objections to swearing oaths to his eldest son al-Afdal, while those of Egypt refused. In the end, the sultan's inheritance was divided between his sons; al-Zahir took Aleppo and al-Aziz Cairo, al-Afdal retaining Damascus. Saladin's brother, al-Adil, who had governed Aleppo, then Egypt, in his name, and whom the sultan had begun to mistrust when he lost his most faithful lieutenant, his nephew Taqi al-Din, had received as his share the Jazirah, where he held the Zengids of Mosul at bay, while his son al-Muazzam had taken possession of Kerak. If we add the emirates of Homs and Hamah, not forgetting the

Yemen, also part of the Ayyubid heritage, it becomes clear that Saladin's empire had been replaced by a confederation linked by family ties which barely survived him. Twice, in 1194 and 1195, al-Aziz tried to take Damascus from his brother al-Afdal. On both occasions, al-Adil, acting as the most senior member of the family, intervened. But in 1196, having removed al-Afdal, he established himself in Damascus as lieutenant of al-Aziz.

On the death of al-Aziz in 1198, two clans opposed each other: the emirs recruited in the past by Shirkûh from among his Mamluks and those who had been recruited by Saladin, the Asadiyya and the Salahiyya. The latter declared for al-Adil, who escaped his nephews, who had combined against him, defeated al-Afdal and took possession of Cairo in February 1200. Al-Adil then proclaimed himself sultan and entrusted the government of Damascus and the Jazirah to two of his sons, al-Muazzam and al-Kamil. The surviving sons of Saladin tried in vain to recover Damascus; they had to be content with Aleppo, in the case of al-Zahir, and Samosata in the case of al-Afdal. Confirmed in his title by the caliph, al-Adil redistributed his possessions between his sons: al-Kamil was to succeed him in Egypt, al-Ashraf received the Jazirah and al-Awhad the Diyarbakir. Al-Awhad died and his possessions reverted to al-Ashraf.

Saladin's inheritance thus constituted four groupings, three of which were in the hands of his brother and his nephews, Aleppo alone remaining to his descendants. It is understandable that their covetousness with regard to each other took precedence over their relations with the Franks. Al-Zahir was ready to establish friendly relations with Bohemond IV of Antioch-Tripoli, whom he supported against the king of Armenia. The Seljuk sultan of Konya did the same.

The Seljuks had been reduced to impotence during the last years of Kilij Arslan II, who died at the age of seventy-seven in 1192, having seen his authority challenged by his numerous sons; the sultanate passed to his son Kai-Kushraw I. He was at one stage expelled by his brother Suleiman and obliged to take refuge with the Byzantines (1196), but then returned to power and restored the unity of Seljuk rule. In 1207 he annexed Adalia, which gave Turkey an outlet on the Mediterranean. His son Kai-Kawus (1211–20) further expanded the empire, but it was under Kai-Qobad, who conquered Alaya, Sinope and Erzincan, and definitively drove the Byzantines back to the west of Phrygia, that the sultanate of Konya became a dominant power. By allying with the prince of Antioch against the Armenians, the Seljuks obliged the latter to become their tributaries. They clashed with the Ayyubids against whom they had to wage many wars. They felt no hostility towards the Franks; after the Fourth Crusade, they readily allied with them against the Greeks of Nicaea and employed many Frankish mercenaries in their army.

Nor did the Franks have to fear the hostility of the Abbasid caliph. Al-Nasir, who ruled in Baghdad from 1180 to 1225, was primarily preoccupied with making the caliphate the supreme authority in the Muslim world, thanks to the *futuwa*, an institution by which the princes contracted personal ties with the caliph. At the same time, he tried to rid himself of the last vestiges of the influences of the Seljuk sultans of Iran; by allying with the shah of Khorezm, in 1194, he provoked the fall of the last sultan, Toghrul III, who died on the battlefield. The holy war against the Franks seems to have meant little to him; at most he provided symbolic assistance to Saladin during the siege of Jerusalem, but the latter's many missives failed to persuade him to give his backing to an aggressive policy which he distrusted.

Even the Assassins, established on the confines of the principality of Antioch, the county of Tripoli and Aleppo, came to terms with the Frankish presence; Henry of Champagne, returning from Antioch to Tripoli, was invited by their master to stay in his castle of al-Kahf, where he treated him to a demonstration of his power by ordering his followers to throw themselves off the ramparts. Nevertheless, the redoubtable Assassins posed a threat both to the Frankish princes and to the Muslims; Conrad of Montferrat died at their hands, as did one of Bohemond IV's sons, Raymond, stabbed as he said his prayers in the church of Tortossa. And Bohemond had to abandon the idea of granting Maraclea to the Hospital as he had intended, as a result of the threats he received from the Ismailis, who had no wish to find themselves in closer contact with the Hospitallers, to whom they already paid tribute.

The Muslim princes encouraged the economic activity of the Frankish merchants. Al-Adil granted privileges, in 1207–8, to the Venetians and the Pisans and, in 1212, when the Frankish merchants in Alexandria were arrested, they were said to number three thousand.

The dangers posed to the Frankish presence gradually diminished, though the Franks took time to realise this. In the short run, the continued Ayyubid domination over Jerusalem and the larger part of the Holy Land was not contested.

THE FOURTH CRUSADE

When Innocent III became pope, the death of Henry VI had left his crusade rudderless and doomed to disintegration, and it seemed that the Franks of the East might have to face the whole might of the Ayyubids alone; it was not until 1 July 1198 that the truces were renewed. The crusade was to be the main concern of the new pope, who adopted the scriptural passage: 'If I forget you, Jerusalem ...' He did not hesitate to use the weapon of the crusade elsewhere than in the Holy Land, in the kingdom of Sicily against Markward of Anweiler, in the Albigeois against the Cathar heretics and, above all, against the Saracens in Spain.

Innocent III wrote to the leaders of the German crusade to try to persuade them to carry on with their enterprise. But he quickly realised the necessity of taking it over himself. He announced the imminent departure of a new expedition to the patriarch of Jerusalem and wrote to the emperor Alexius III reminding him of the Christian duty to liberate the land of Christ's birth from the stain of the 'pagans' and asking him to lend his support to this liberation; he extended to him the benefit of the indulgence. On 1 August 1198, an encyclical was addressed to all the archbishops to announce the imminent crusade and to seek commitments. Two cardinals, Sofredo and Peter Capuano, were appointed legates to organise the preaching. They were also to work for peace in the West, by reconciling Philip Augustus and Richard I, though they failed to persuade the two kings – John having meanwhile succeeded his brother – to depart themselves. Peter won from the French bishops assembled at Dijon the promise of a contribution estimated at a thirtieth of their incomes. The great religious orders agreed to do the same, and so, in 1201, did the Cistercian general chapter; a large number of Cistercian abbeys eventually participated in the expedition.

A famous preacher, Fulk, curé of Neuilly-sur-Marne, who had hitherto devoted himself to the battle against immorality, was made responsible by Peter Cantor, to whom Innocent III had entrusted this mission, for inviting the faithful to join the crusade. He gathered colleagues such as the Breton monk Herluin, Robert of Courçon, Stephen Langton and Peter of Roussy, and tried in vain to obtain the assistance of the Cistercians in 1198; his success here came later. It seems, however, not to have been Fulk who obtained the crusading vows of the group of nobles who had gathered at Ecry (the modern Asfeld, in the Ardennes) for a tournament, in November 1199; it may have been Peter Capuano who instilled shame into the knights for indulging in games forbidden by the Church (because very dangerous) when Christ was in need of their aid. In fact, the circumstances of this collective taking of the cross by, among others, Count Thibaut of Champagne, his cousin Louis of Blois and Count Baldwin of Flanders and Hainault, are obscure. The movement gathered support in the valleys of the Loire and the Saône, in Forez, and in Germany, from which came Count Berthold of Katzenelnbogen.

The French barons met at Compiègne in the summer of 1200, and appointed six of their number, representing the counts of Champagne, Blois and Flanders, to prepare their voyage. They included Geoffrey of Villehardouin, marshal of Champagne, and Conan of Béthune. They arrived in Venice at the beginning of 1201, possibly after having made abortive contacts with Genoa and Pisa. Doge Enrico Dandolo agreed to transport 4,500 knights with their horses, 9,000 squires and 20,000 footsoldiers, to provide foodstuffs for nine months and an escort of 50 galleys, at the rate of 5 silver marks per horse and 2 per man, that is, a total of 85,000 marks. It was further agreed that, if conquests were made, they would be shared equally between them. Venice asked for a year to complete the enormous building programme required. Dandolo got the treaty accepted by the councils and by the people. Innocent III confirmed it in May 1201, but also prohibited the allies from attacking Christians, except if they impeded the crusade, the pontifical legate to be the judge of any such cases. The pope probably felt some unease as to the ulterior motives that might be harboured by the Venetians. He also accepted the excuses presented by King Emeric of Hungary, who had taken a vow of crusade, that the attacks by his neighbours, supported by the pagan Comans, prevented him from leaving his kingdom, on condition that he joined the crusade later.

On his return, Villehardouin found that the count of Champagne was sick. His death, on 24 May 1201, deprived the crusade of its chosen leader and probably of the support of many knights from Champagne. The duke of Burgundy and the count of Bar-le-Duc, invited to replace him, refused. Eventually, Villehardouin proposed the marquis of Montferrat, Boniface, who was also recommended by Philip Augustus, to whom he was related. In August 1201, at Soissons, Boniface announced his acceptance and was recognised as the expedition's leader. After this, he went to Hagenau to discuss matters with his suzerain, Philip of Swabia, brother of the emperor Henry VI and a candidate for the imperial crown.

These conversations took a particular turn, unknown, it seems, to the crusaders. After the palace revolution in Constantinople which had cost Isaac II his throne, his son, Alexius Angelus, whose sister Irene was married to Philip of Swabia, had been put under house arrest. Alexius, escaping the surveillance of his uncle, Alexius III, went to the West to seek help, where he was favourably received by Philip. Boniface, whose brothers had played an important role in Constantinople between 1180 and 1187, was also won over to the young prince's schemes. Alexius had tried to convince the pope of his rights to the throne and of the need to drive out the usurper. But Innocent III distrusted Philip of Swabia and preferred to continue to seek an alliance with Alexius III; he nevertheless used, particularly in a letter of 16 November 1202, the threat represented by the ambitions of the young Alexius and his Hohenstaufen supporters to try to persuade the Byzantine emperor to take a more decisive step in favour of the union of the Churches; Innocent III, who was anxious to end the Greek schism, hoped that the patriarch of Constantinople would make an act of obedience towards the see of Rome. The young Alexius had dangled before the pope his intention of achieving this union, but Innocent III remained wary.

Although Alexius had met many of the crusader leaders as they passed through Verona, they seem not to have listened to his proposals. They had other worries. The fleet promised by the Venetians for 24 June 1202 was ready, but the 35,000 crusaders had failed to materialise, not, according to Villehardouin, because they had reneged on their vows, but because many of them had opted for other routes, regardless of the commitments entered into. The bishop of Autun, Walter, with the count of Forez and the Burgundian crusaders, who had not taken part in the meeting at Soissons, had embarked at Marseilles for Syria; the castellan of Bruges, John of Nesle, was to have led a Flemish fleet to Venice but made directly for Syria. The count of Brienne, Walter, asked by the pope to deal with one of the German adventurers who were trying to establish themselves in southern Italy, Diebold of Vohburg, had promised to join Villehardouin at Venice; but, his job done, he had gone straight to Acre.

The six barons had been grossly over-optimistic in estimating the number of crusaders. There were apparently only about 15,000 pilgrims assembled at Venice, inconveniently camped on the island of San Niccolo. And, by calling on all their resources, including the precious objects the barons had brought with them, the most they could come up with was 51,000 silver marks. Fulk of Neuilly had collected large sums, but they had been entrusted to the legate Sofredo, who dispatched them to the East where they made possible the rebuilding of the fortifications destroyed by the earthquake of 1202; they were not available to the crusaders.

Doge Dandolo suggested a solution. Let the Venetians join the crusade and allow the crusaders to delay payment of the remaining 34,000 marks, in return for the assistance they would provide to the Republic in recovering the Dalmatian town of Zara (Zadar), which had freed itself, in 1186, from Venetian rule. But it had put itself under the protection of the king of Hungary, himself a crusader, and Innocent III had prohibited attacks on his possessions. Peter Capuano wanted to intervene; Dandolo informed him that Venice accepted him in his capacity as preacher, but refused to recognise his powers as legate.

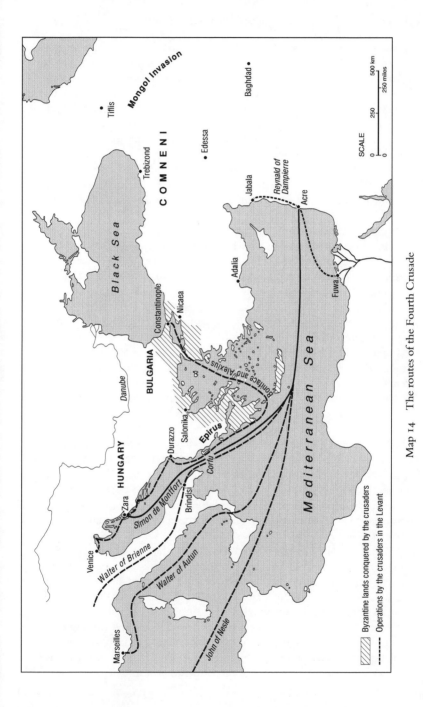

Map 14 The routes of the Fourth Crusade

An agreement was reached on 22 July; it laid down that, after the seizure of Zara, they would overwinter in the town before proceeding to Egypt, given that the crusade, reviving a project mooted in the time of Richard of England, had opted for a landing in Egypt, intending to compel the sultan to evacuate the Holy Land. This agreement met with strong opposition. The barons and the knights were, of course, accustomed to the wars in the West in which they fought against other Christians to obey their lords or to uphold their alliances. But the vow of crusade obliged them to devote themselves to the battle against the infidel and to make the pilgrimage. Many of them abandoned the army and proceeded to Syria; others asked the legate to release them from their vow. Peter Capuano found himself in a dilemma; was he to authorise the campaign against the king of Hungary, despite the pope's orders, basing himself on the clause concerning those who put obstacles in the way of the crusade, or was he to disband it? He asked the crusaders not to leave the army, then went to Rome to explain matters to Innocent III.

But the army, reinforced by German crusaders, though fewer than expected, left Venice at the beginning of October and landed before Zara on 10 November. There was dissension; some of the crusaders, including Simon de Montfort, made their scruples known to those under siege and dissociated themselves from their companions. At this point, a letter arrived from the pope, forbidding an attack on Zara; but the crusaders ignored it and the town capitulated on 24 November and was sacked.

The barons then sent their representatives to Rome, where two of them, Abbot Martin of Pairis and Robert of Boves, left their colleagues to go to the Holy Land. Innocent III agreed to pardon the crusaders their disobedience, recognising that they had been blackmailed; he left the Venetians under the sentence of excommunication they had incurred by attacking a crusader.

But how was the crusade to proceed without the cooperation of those in possession of the ships? Boniface of Montferrat, who had joined the army, held on to the letter intended for the Venetians. Peter of Capuano, to avoid contact with the excommunicates, left for the Holy Land, which deprived the crusaders of the authorised voice of the pope's representative. It was during the course of the winter, on 1 January 1203, that a decisive event occurred. Envoys from the young Alexius arrived to present proposals on his behalf: if the crusaders gave him their assistance in recovering the throne that was his by right, he would pay them 200,000 silver marks, supply them with provisions for their expedition and a contingent of 10,000 men, and he would

maintain in the Holy Land a body of 500 knights; he also promised to
ensure the submission of the Greek Church to that of Rome. These
proposals were favourably received by the leaders of the crusade, the
counts of Blois, Flanders and St Pol and, above all, Boniface of
Montferrat.

Historians have debated the question of Venetian involvement in the
decision to divert the crusade to Constantinople. In the nineteenth
century, Louis de Mas-Latrie repeated an accusation emanating from the
Franks of Syria to the effect that the sultan had bought the Venetians,
who had important commercial interests in Egypt, to divert the attack
which threatened him. Others have repeated this thesis, emphasising the
conflicts which, since 1171, had opposed Venetians and Byzantines
concerning the rights claimed by the former in Constantinople. It has
been suggested that the rapprochement between Byzantium and Genoa,
taking place after the resolution of these conflicts in 1198, worried
Venice, which therefore welcomed a military intervention which would
settle the disputes with the Byzantines in its favour and assure it a
privileged position in the commerce of the capital. The hatred of
Dandolo for the Byzantines who had blinded him also remains pure
supposition. On the other hand, the support of the Venetians for
Alexius' proposals was probably decisive, without there being any need
to suppose that Dandolo had conceived, from his first contacts with the
crusaders, a Machiavellian plan assuming that they would find it
impossible to fulfil their financial obligations and would then be obliged
to promote Venetian interests in both Zara and Constantinople.

Voices were raised in the council against accepting Alexius' proposals;
Abbot Guy of Les-Vaux-de-Cernay was the spokesman for the opposition. But others pointed out that the detour by Constantinople, assuring
the crusaders the support of the Byzantine emperor, would be the best
way of achieving the projected expedition to Egypt and, as a result, the
liberation of the Holy Sepulchre. The pope's letters condemning the
agreement with Alexius and ordering Boniface to publish the sentence of
excommunication against the Venetians were slow to arrive, probably
because Innocent III could not decide how best to avoid the collapse of
the crusade. But already many great persons were leaving the army for
the Holy Land, among them Simon de Montfort, Reynald of Mont-
mirail-au-Perche, Werner of Bollanden and the abbot of Les-Vaux-de-
Cernay; others tried to cross Croatia, but had to turn back. The army left
Zara for Corfu on 20 April 1203. Alexius joined it there after having got
himself recognised as emperor at Durazzo. On his arrival, the agreement
reached at Zara was published; feelings ran high, and the leaders of the
army, with Boniface at their head, had to beg their companions, in tears,

not to leave them. It was agreed to depart for Syria at Michaelmas at the latest (29 September 1203).

Alexius III had made his fears known to the pope, who had assured him of his good intentions, telling him that he had forbidden a landing on Byzantine soil. On 23 June, nevertheless, the Venetian fleet dropped anchor off Scutari, and the crusaders landed on the Asian shore of the Bosphorus. A Byzantine detachment made as if to intervene and was put to flight. Alexius III sent a messenger to express his astonishment and to offer his assistance to the Franks. Conan of Béthune conveyed to him in return an ultimatum, enjoining him to surrender the throne to its legitimate heir, the young Alexius – whose legitimacy Alexius, of course, denied. A Venetian ship presented the pretender to the population by sailing round the walls of the city; it had been hoped there would be a rising in his favour but none materialised. It was necessary to resort to arms.

Some of the crusaders landed at Galata, which they occupied, and a Venetian ship forced the chain which barred the Golden Horn; some Byzantine ships anchored in the bay were seized. A simultaneous sea and land assault was then launched; the crusaders were held in check; the Venetians seized several towers (17 July). During the following night, Alexius III lost heart and fled; some officials took Isaac II from his prison and restored him to the throne. The crusaders sent an ambassador to ask him to confirm the promises of his son, which he did, not without expressing some doubts as to the possibility of carrying them out. On 1 August Alexius IV was proclaimed co-emperor.

Innocent III, informed of this new situation, insisted on achieving the union of the Churches; he had just sanctioned the proclamation of the union of Rome with the Armenian Church, and the tsar of the Bulgars and the Vlachs, who had regained their independence, had himself proclaimed the submission of his Church to Rome in November 1202. The pope demanded that the patriarch of Constantinople come to request the grant of the pallium, sign of his office. Alexius was well aware of the impossibility of his compelling, even asking, the prelate to do this.

Alexius also had to face the exhaustion of the imperial treasury and the difficulty of collecting taxes given the independence acquired by various 'despots'. He was able to find 100,000 marks, most of which went to the Venetians. He made a tour of the provinces in the company of some Frankish barons, but without much success. Fearing that the army's departure, fixed for 29 September, would leave his position on the throne insecure, he asked the crusaders to prolong their stay by one year, which provoked further unrest within the army.

This prolongation was to prove fatal. There were incidents. Some of the crusaders attacked the mosque of Constantinople and some of the citizens confronted them. A fire was started which ravaged a whole section of the town. The Latin inhabitants, feeling themselves threatened, took refuge in the crusaders' camp. Alexius IV tried to destroy the Venetian fleet by launching fireships against it, which the Venetians managed to deflect (1 January 1204). A month later, a riot broke out. Alexius IV was killed, his father was put aside and one of his distant cousins, Alexius Ducas Murzuphlus, became Alexius V.

The situation of the crusaders became impossible. Appeals for their aid were arriving from Syria. The murder of the emperor who had convinced them of his legitimacy offended their feelings of loyalty. Alexius V did not regard himself as bound by his predecessor's promises. The crusaders were without food or money, far from the theatre of operations they wanted to reach. The Venetians were no better placed; they too had counted on the subsidies promised by Alexius IV. The situation was in a sense summarised by two phrases in our chroniclers: 'Know that by Babylon (Egypt) or by Greece will the Holy Land be delivered, if it is ever delivered', and 'What will we do in Babylon or Alexandria if we have no food?' The assistance of the Byzantine empire had seemed to be the crusade's only chance of success; the very survival of the expedition was now at risk.

It was in these circumstances that, after two months of raids of pillage and acts of reprisal, crusaders and Venetians agreed to embark on the conquest of Constantinople and the empire. Dandolo, Boniface and the three counts made meticulous arrangements for the division of the booty which was to be assembled in one place, and of which three quarters was to go to the Venetians, up to the total of the crusaders' debt; beyond this sum, the division was to be half and half; the foodstuffs were to be divided into two equal shares. The Venetians would retain their rights and property, which would be excluded from the share-out, in the town and its dependencies. An emperor was to be elected, who would receive, with the two imperial palaces, a quarter of the empire; the remaining three quarters would be divided equally between the crusaders and the Venetians. The party from which the emperor had not been chosen would choose the canons of St Sophia, who elected the patriarch. The property of the Church, except for whatever was necessary for the support of the clergy, would be secularised. They also reached agreement about the conditions for the granting of fiefs and the service due to the emperor. What was envisaged, clearly, was the replacement of the Greek empire by a Latin one.

It was also stipulated that the capture of the city should take place in a manner appropriate to the occupation of a Christian city; no woman was to be molested, no church or monastery to suffer depredations; everyone was to swear to observe these conditions.

On 9 April 1204 the fleet began the attack and was repelled. On Sunday 11 April all the participants were asked to attend sermons; around noon the following day two towers were seized and a group of combatants made a breach in the walls. Alexius V put up a valiant resistance, but eventually gave up. Confused fighting followed and fire broke out; many nobles and citizens fled the town in haste; an attempt was made to elect a new emperor, but, on the morning of 13 April, the two Lascaris brothers, one of whom had been chosen, took refuge in Asia, while the patriarch sought asylum in Thrace.

The attackers, without regard for their oaths, indulged in pillage on a massive scale, sparing neither churches, whose gold and silver ornaments excited their greed, nor the monuments and works of art inherited from Antiquity; the population, without there being a true massacre, suffered badly; it seems to have been primarily the Frankish residents who revenged themselves for the atrocities suffered by their families in 1182. The sack of Constantinople remains a famous event; the admiration of Robert of Clari for the riches which fell to the victors finds its counterpart in the feelings of shame expressed by Hugh of Berzé when he remembered those fateful days. In his eyes, the crusaders who had respected divine law as long as they had been in poverty 'forgot God' when they were victorious and indulged in every temptation. More brutally, Ernoul wrote that the Franks had entered Constantinople wearing God's colours, and that once inside they had adopted those of the devil. When he learned what had happened, Innocent III, who had initially congratulated the Franks on a victory which seemed to him to be an unexpected demonstration of divine will, expressed strong indignation.

The sack of Constantinople also, as is well known, provided material for an anti-Latin polemic which has led more than one historian to believe that the schism separating the Greek and Latin Churches only really took effect in 1204; this remains to be proved, the crimes committed by the Latins at this time only adding one more argument to an already well-supplied arsenal, to harden a position already firmly established.

Questions remain. Was the seizure and the sack of the town, as has so often been claimed, the realisation of an aspiration long inscribed in 'the collective subconscious of the Latin world'? Had the town's material and spiritual wealth, with the incomparable collection of relics which formed the most precious part of the conquerors' booty, encouraged a greed that had long been looking for ways of satisfying itself? Had the desire to return the Byzantine Church to the bosom of the Church of Rome exacerbated the resentment of the Latin clergy, so that they were ready to use force to achieve it? As Christopher Daly has remarked, every time the crusaders had passed under Constantinople, there had been those who had called for an attack on the town; every time, they had been silenced. The Byzantines had often demonstrated their hostility towards the crusaders; but they had still often helped them in their enterprises, if without ever wholeheartedly embracing these inconvenient allies; and right to the end, the papacy had, in general, had confidence in them.

The affair of 1203–4 has to be seen in the context of Byzantine dynastic instability. Alexius IV was not the first pretender who engaged foreign mercenaries to seize the imperial title and those of Alexius I had already systematically pillaged the town, if admittedly not quite on the scale of 1204. The sequence of events that led the crusaders of 1202 to enter his service, then to conquer the empire he had lost, raises the question of premeditation, though its reality remains debatable. The mistaken estimates of Villehardouin and his peers, the pope's loss of control of an expedition he had wanted to make his own, and the intrusion of Venetian interests into the goals of the crusade are all factors that must be taken into account. The theory of chance and that of premeditation will no doubt each have their proponents for a long time to come.

In practice, the intrigues of some and the problems of others wove a complex web which it is impossible now to disentangle. The crusaders found themselves at the mercy of forces which wished to use them in pursuance of their own goals, in the absence of a leader able to impose a unified direction, which allowed departures to be fragmented; they suffered also from the assignment to the Holy Land of the money raised from ecclesiastical sources which was not available to finance the crusade itself, leaving it to whatever means the participants alone could muster.

THE CONSEQUENCES OF THE FOURTH CRUSADE

The first consequence of the fall of Constantinople was the creation of a Latin empire which aspired to continue that of the Comneni and the Angeloi, and in particular to restore imperial authority in the regions which had broken free; the various states that had been constituted in the provinces since the death of Manuel Comnenus were to be brought to heel. Although Innocent III had just recognised the royal title of Kaloyan, Tsar of the Bulgars and the Vlachs, recalling that his ancestor Boris-Michael had received the royal crown from Nicholas I, and received the submission of the primate of Bulgaria, the new emperor aimed to restore them to the empire and it was the Bulgars and their allies who inflicted their first defeats on the Franks, so allowing the Byzantine dynasties to recover.

The election of Baldwin of Flanders as emperor by a group of twelve electors, six appointed by the Venetians and six by the crusaders, on 9 May, allowed the count of Flanders to don the purple boots of the Byzantine emperors whose ceremonial he adopted. But he organised the structures of the empire on a purely feudal base, granting to his companions in arms the fiefs provided for in the agreement of March 1204. Boniface, who had himself sought election, received Asia as his share; he exchanged it for Thessalonika and the provinces of continental Greece. Venice kept for itself in full ownership the whole western side of the Byzantine empire, and also Crete (which Boniface ceded to it), Euboea and part of Thrace. The new feudalism was not installed without some problems: a Venetian, Marco Sanudo, created a duchy of the Archipelago which was dependent on the empire and not on Venice, and a nephew of the chronicler, Geoffrey of Villehardouin, made the Peloponnese, conquered by William of Champlitte, a principality of Morea, without regard for Venetian claims; it needed a war to make the kingdom of Thessalonika recognise the emperor's rights of suzerainty.

But many Byzantine dynasties, sometimes already established in the provinces of the empire, escaped Baldwin's authority. The Comneni of Trebizond may have recognised him on occasion, but the Angeloi Comneni of Epirus and the Lascarids at Nicaea behaved as heirs of the twelfth-century *basileis*. The former seized Thessalonika in 1224; in 1225 the latter inflicted on the emperor Robert a defeat which cost the Latins almost all their possessions in Asia. And in 1261 Michael Palaeologus, who had ousted the Lascarids, was to seize Constantinople and some lands which still belonged to the imperial estate. But the duchies of Thebes, Athens and the Archipelago, the principality of Morea, the lordships of Negroponte and Venetian Romania were destined to have a longer life.

How far does the history of these Latin rulers belong to the history of the crusades? Many historians have concluded that once the crusaders began to anticipate their establishments in Romania, they forgot Jerusalem. This is rather what is implied by Innocent III in a letter to the legate Peter Capuano: 'Your mission was not to take Constantinople, but to protect the remains of the kingdom of Jerusalem and to recover what has been lost.' But the crusaders had not forgotten the perspectives which had made them agree, in Corfu, to divert the crusade and this meant that the Byzantine empire served the cause of the Holy Land.

Crusaders and pilgrims hoped for the reopening of the land route leading to Jerusalem, on which Manuel Comnenus had based his appeal to the pope in 1176. A few pilgrims followed this route; Simon of St Quentin refers to a German pilgrim who passed through Konya around 1240. And when Baldwin I distributed his fiefs, he made Louis of Blois duke of Nicaea, Stephen of Perche duke of Philadelphia and Peter of Bracieux master of a territory adjoining Konya; a Graeco-Italian adventurer, Aldobrandin, briefly took possession of Adalia. As we know, the Lascarids on the one hand and the Seljuks on the other eventually occupied these territories lining the route in question. It remains the case that the Latin emperor had hoped to restore it.

The Templars, the Hospitallers and the canons of the Holy Sepulchre and the Temple of the Lord received generous donations in the Latin empire. The knights of the Holy Land were also granted fiefs, but this was in the hope of making them come to the defence of the empire. By the end of 1203 some crusaders had left Syria to join the army before Constantinople. In 1204 there was a veritable exodus of prelates, knights and turcopoles, among them Ralph of Tiberias, who hoped to find in Romania the establishment he had lost in the Holy Land. Innocent III was alarmed: 'We can no longer, through lack of men', he wrote, 'defend the maritime regions which are still held by the Christians against the Saracen attacks, and scarcely hold on to the kingdom of Cyprus.'

Even the legate Peter Capuano and the abbot of Pairis went to Constantinople, where the latter found relics, while the former, who had just, in the name of the pope, handed mitres and croziers to the *catholicos* of Armenia and to fourteen of his bishops, embarked on discussions with the Greek clergy of Constantinople.

Was the empire in a position to provide assistance to the Holy Land? The Muslim princes seem at first to have feared this. In fact, it rather diverted western efforts to its own defensive needs. Those westerners who settled there might otherwise have settled in Syria. The popes, who found themselves responsible for an establishment they had not wanted, tried to introduce into Romania a monastic reform and ecclesiastical structures which conformed to the needs of the western Church, while trying to find common ground with the Greeks. And they had to watch over the survival of these lands entrusted to their care and threatened by the greed of their neighbours.

In 1224 Thessalonika was on the point of falling into the hands of the despot of Epirus. William of Montferrat begged for the assistance of Honorius III, who granted the crusading indulgence to those who went to the rescue of the young Demetrius, son of Boniface of Montferrat.

But the crusade was preached only in the lands neighbouring the marquisate and Thessalonika fell before an expedition could set out. In 1235 the emperor John of Brienne sent his ward, Baldwin II of Courtenay, to seek aid in the West because of the danger posed to the empire by the alliance of the tsar of the Bulgars, John Asen, and the emperor of Nicaea. Gregory IX decided in his turn on a crusade, which clashed with the one he wanted to send to the Holy Land and suggested that those who had already committed themselves should change their goal by taking their assistance to the Latins of Constantinople (1238). This proposal met with little enthusiasm and only a few great French barons, like Humbert of Beaujeu, responded to it. The anxieties of the Latins were linked to the fears provoked by the power of the tsar of the Bulgars, John Asen. But his shifts of attitude, posing sometimes as protector and sometimes as adversary of the Latin empire, left the purpose of the crusade uncertain. Gregory IX had asked for the aid of the king of Hungary, Bela IV, but he chose not to turn against his Bulgarian neighbour. And the latter authorised the crusaders, of whom there were not many (2,000 men), to pass through his lands. Though they briefly reinforced the defences of the empire, these crusaders were not called on to fight. The contingent which was to have embarked at Venice never set sail.

Since 1204 the papacy had been keen to maintain the Latin empire, which Innocent III had initially seen as likely to favour the reunion of the Greek and Latin Churches. But the popes quickly realised that the presence of a Latin emperor on the throne of the *basileus* and that of a patriarch of the same rite at St Sophia were not enough to convert the Greeks to the Church of Rome; the Greek patriarch proclaimed at Nicaea after some hesitation became an intermediary, as did the Greek emperor. Negotiations were soon under way. The emperor John Vatatzes urged the patriarch Germanos II to participate from 1232. The dialogue quickly relapsed into a Graeco-Latin polemic; but in 1234 the emperor revealed his proposals: Constantinople would be returned to the Greeks in exchange for the restoration of the pope's name to the diptychs. Gregory IX was indignant, but Innocent IV took up the idea, which fitted into his new vision of relations between Greeks and Latins, which undermined the claims of the Latin clergy of the East to their supremacy over the other rites.

In the pope's eyes, the union of the churches, made material by an identical profession of faith and by the recognition of the primacy of the See of Peter, was more important than the rights claimed by the Latin patriarchs and archbishops. He told Vatatzes that, if the Church of Constantinople accepted union, the papacy was prepared to see the imperial town revert to the emperors of Nicaea. The throne of the emperor Baldwin II was thus hardly secure. After the reoccupation of Constantinople, which took place without premeditation, Michael VIII Palaeologus was to adopt the policies of John Vatatzes and try to close the interlude of the Latin empire of Romania by achieving a union of the Churches.

The creation of this empire had neither brought help to Frankish Syria nor permanently diverted the attention of the West towards Constantinople. But it still signalled a break in the attempt at reconquest inaugurated soon after Hattin and tirelessly pursued ever since. This became plain with the arrival of the first contingents of the Fourth Crusade in the ports of the Holy Land. First came John of Nesle and his Flemings, at the end of 1202, then Bishop Walter of Autun and the count of Forez, in 1203, neither party having passed through Venice. They were followed by the dissidents who had left the army at Zara or Corfu, such as Stephen of Perche, Rotrou of Montfort, Reynald of Dampierre and Reynald of Montmirail. In all, there were hardly more than three hundred knights.

When Reynald of Dampierre urged King Aimery to break the truces made with the sultan in order to allow the crusaders to demonstrate *apertise d'armes*, the king refused in view of this small number, and replied that he was awaiting the arrival of the 'big men'. Reynald then decided to enter the service of Bohemond IV of Antioch, not to fight the Muslims but to take part in a warlike enterprise alien to the purpose of the crusade, that is, to join his war against Raymond Roupen and King Leo of Armenia. John of Nesle, too, went north, but in his case it was to assist Raymond Roupen against Bohemond IV. Reynald took the coastal route. At Jabala, the local emir welcomed him warmly, but advised him not to venture further without having obtained permission from the sultan of Aleppo to cross his states, explaining that, because of the truces agreed with the Christians, he wanted to protect him from unfortunate incidents. Reynald, reckoning that his eighty knights represented a sufficient force, ignored him and fell into an ambush in which many of his companions perished; he himself spent long years as a prisoner and Giles of Trazeignies was almost alone in escaping captivity.

When the truces were broken, in 1204, it was as a result of acts of piracy committed by a Muslim emir from the coast near Sidon, which remained a Franco-Ayyubid 'condominion'. There followed reprisals against a convoy of Egyptian ships, a raid of pillage in the Delta during which Fuwa was sacked (20 May 1204), the mustering of the Ayyubid army near Acre and shows of military force, without there ever being a real battle. In September, Aimery and al-Adil agreed to renew the truces for six years, and the sultan relinquished Jaffa to the Franks, renounced his share of the revenues from the lands of Sidon, Ramla and Lydda, and authorised the return of the Latins to Nazareth. It is possible that the success of the crusaders in Constantinople persuaded him to accept terms so favourable to the Franks. But the death of King Aimery in 1205 and the departure of the crusade and many of the kingdom's warriors for Romania precluded new operations.

When these happened, it was on the frontier of the county of Tripoli. They were initiated by the Hospitallers of the Crac des Chevaliers who wanted to reoccupy the castle of Montferrand (1206–7). Al-Adil had to intervene in person to persuade the count to renew the truces after having destroyed two small fortresses (July 1207).

The other military order, that of the Templars, was hoping for a resumption of hostilities; in September 1210, when the sultan offered to renew the truce of 1204, the master of the Temple objected. Al-Adil's son, al-Muazzam, then went to Acre and ravaged the surrounding area. The Franks responded with a new raid of pillage in the Nile Delta, to which Walter of Montbéliard led an expedition in July 1211. But no crusade had been sent to the defence of the kingdom; the fortification by al-Adil of Mount Tabor, a convenient base of operations against Acre, made the Franks uneasy. In 1211 the new king, John of Brienne, renewed the truces for six years.

The immense effort made by Latin Christendom between 1188 and 1205 had borne fruit. Saladin had been forced to abandon his attempt to eliminate the Frankish presence entirely, and had to take it into account in defining his future policies. His successors, still united by a tie of kinship, though one showing signs of dissolving, were resigned to the fact that every significant enterprise against the Franks was likely to lead to the arrival of numerous crusaders, well trained and provided with substantial financial resources and a firm resolve. Every arrival of new crusaders meant they had to assemble an army, well equipped and numerous, whose upkeep was expensive, and whose quasi-feudal contingents usually balked at prolonged campaigns. Consequently, they agreed to minor concessions, which increased the extent of the lands controlled by the Franks, now masters of almost the entire coastal region.

That the Franks had run out of steam was, nevertheless, undeniable. Whereas, for the Third Crusade, wave after wave of new arrivals had maintained the strength of the crusader army, the death of Henry VI had been enough to bring about the collapse of the German Crusade.

For the Fourth Crusade, even without its unplanned deviation, it had only been possible to assemble numbers well below the perhaps over-optimistic estimates. Innocent III, after this discouraging experience, had to rethink his plans, all the more since the Albigensian Crusade and the crusade he wanted to mobilise against the Almohads in Spain seemed more urgent than that in the East.

There were lessons to be learned from the experience of fifteen years of war against the infidel. The West had suffered heavy losses, and the large number of captives had led the pope to encourage the foundation of an order devoted to redeeming them and to making contact with the eastern Churches to ensure them religious support. When a new crusade set out for the East, it was organised according to clearer rules. The Lateran Council of 1215 can thus be seen as an extension of the crusades of 1188–1204.

8

THE CRUSADE AS AN INSTITUTION

More and more expeditions were mounted in order to save as much as possible of the lands conquered by the crusaders and to recover, with the Holy Places, the whole of the Holy Land as they had rebuilt it as a political unit. The practice established in the twelfth century of a pilgrimage accompanied by a limited period of time spent in the service of the Christians of the East was replaced by an institution which was tending to become permanent: the crusade. And, though the terminology was not yet fixed, the *crucesignatus* (crusader) and the *croiserie* (a word used in 1231 by Balian of Ibelin) acquired a more precise meaning. The essential elements were already in place in the twelfth, even the eleventh, century. It was still the indulgence granted by Urban II and the protection accorded to the crusader by the Church that defined the spiritual and juridical status of the individual who went on a crusade. It was in the time of Eugenius III and Louis VII that the elements of a financial system complementing the material sacrifices accepted by the crusaders began to emerge. It was also then that a discipline was developed and imposed on them.

It was the repercussions of the expeditions, and the experiences of the crusaders between 1188 and 1204, that taught new lessons, revealed pitfalls to be avoided and created an awareness of the compromises that were inevitable. In 1204, soon after the Fourth Crusade, there was still great uncertainty as to its consequences. In order to identify the features which would in future characterise the crusade, it is convenient to begin in 1215, the year in which Pope Innocent III, at the Lateran Council, promulgated the bull *Ad liberandum* (December 1215); as Maureen Purcell has shown, this was repeated unchanged but for minor details in the bull *Afflicti corde* adopted in 1245 by the First Council of Lyons. And the bull *Zelo fidei*, promulgated in 1274 by the Second Council of Lyons, was still profoundly influenced by that of Innocent III, even though it was differently arranged.

Innocent III tried to lay down a complete programme. The bull *Ad liberandum* announced the departure of the crusade and fixed the date (in 1215 a delay of eighteen months was allowed). It specified what the prelates, the clergy and the laity were expected to do to prepare themselves spiritually. It indicated the privileges the participants would enjoy. It prescribed the organisation of the army and the nature of the contingents to be provided; it was concerned with logistics, in particular the conditions of sea transport, and addressed financial matters, both with regard to the participation demanded of the clergy and the procedures governing the loans contracted by the combatants. It attempted to remove the obstacles in the way of the smooth running of the crusade, aiming in particular at the pirates and those who gave military assistance to the Saracens and promulgating an embargo on trade with them. Lastly, it extended the benefits of the indulgence to those who, without going themselves, sent combatants to serve at their expense, or provided them with financial assistance.

THE JURIDICAL THEORY OF THE CRUSADE AND THE CRUSADER'S VOW

Between 1097 and 1187, large numbers of western Christians had set out for the Holy Land and had there done battle with the infidel. They had mostly departed when the pope proclaimed a crusade, but they had also left on their own initiative or in response to an appeal from the East. The process was still very similar to that of the pilgrimage, with which it was inextricably associated; the crusading indulgence, at least until Alexander III tried to give it a more specific content, was linked to the visit to the Holy Sepulchre.

The definition of the crusade itself remained fluid; the essential element was the fact of taking the cross. But theologians and canonists, at least since St Bernard laid down the first elements of a theology of the crusade, had attempted to make it more specific. It gained greater substance in the thirteenth century.

An expedition could be endowed with the plenary indulgence without it having been initiated by the pope. The emperors Henry VI and Frederick II and King Louis IX of France seem to have taken the cross on their own authority. But it was necessary for the pope to confirm the intentions of the sovereigns and endow the expedition with the character of a crusade. A king might undertake a 'just war' in the interests of his subjects, but he could not authorise the participants to adopt the sign of the cross. Only the pope could do this. The canonists debated the motives that could justify the launching of a crusade. For some, the legitimacy of the ownership of the soil – which belonged to God – by the infidel might be challenged. This view was attacked by the majority of jurists; Pope Innocent IV, himself a canonist, specified that one could not wage a war against the infidel to convert him to the faith, but only to prevent him from invading or retaining the lands of Christians.

A crusade could be undertaken against Christians if they were endangering the faith (as was the case in Albigeois), broke the peace or attacked the Church or its rights. But the crusade par excellence, the one which served as reference when the pope decided to grant the indulgence specific to those who fought at his request, remained that which had the Holy Land as its objective.

Only the pope, then, was able to give the character of a crusade to an expedition. In the thirteenth century the crusade was the subject of a particular type of pontifical bull, noting the reasons which necessitated it and the date fixed for the departure, its essential measure consisting of the grant to the crusaders of the material and spiritual privileges they would enjoy.

The indulgence was granted to the crusader, still in the form fixed by Urban II, but now without any reference to a visit to Christ's tomb:

Trusting therefore in the mercy of the Omnipotent God, and the authority of the blessed apostles Peter and Paul, by virtue of the power which has been given us by God, notwithstanding our unworthiness, to bind and to loose, we grant to all those who, in person and at their own expense, accept this duty, full remission of their sins which they have truly confessed, and of which they have repented in their heart, and we promise them an increase of the eternal salvation granted as a reward to the just.

The theologians and canonists of the thirteenth century defined the doctrine of the indulgence with increasing precision, emphasising, in the words of Alexander of Hales, that 'the greatest penance consists of exposing oneself voluntarily to death from faith in Christ or to fight the enemies of that faith'. Such definitions always allowed for the possibility of obtaining the indulgence for other battles than those with the recovery of the Holy Land as their objective. The link between the crusading vow and the pilgrimage to the Holy Sepulchre nevertheless persisted in the minds of the great majority of crusaders, and they took advantage of the opportunities they were offered (for example, when a truce ended military operations) to visit the Holy Places.

The temporal privileges remained, first, in line with Urban II's promise, the protection accorded by the Church to the crusader's family and property, to shield them from the abuses or extortion to which they might fall victim; to this was added extra protection regarding the debts with which the crusader might be burdened or might burden himself in connection with the expedition. The moratorium on interest on loans contracted, in particular with the Jews, had appeared by 1145. In the thirteenth century this was extended to render the crusader and his property exempt from taxes and dues. The clergy enjoyed another privilege; they could continue to collect the revenues from their benefices during their absence.

To enforce these measures, the Church disposed of an arsenal of ecclesiastical censures such as excommunication and the interdict; in the case of the Jews, who were not affected by these sanctions, it was necessary to resort to the relevant secular authority. The effectiveness of these measures was uneven, especially when temporal princes were involved. Philip Augustus attacked the lands of Richard of England when he was on crusade; Richard himself was thrown into prison by the duke of Austria and freed after paying a ransom, and Celestine III, despite the entreaties of Eleanor of Aquitaine, dared not excommunicate the emperor, who might attack the Patrimony of St Peter. But when Thibaut of Champagne was threatened with the confiscation of his fiefs by the king of France in 1236, the Church intervened in his favour because he had taken the cross.

This privilege could be used by those who feared a challenge to their rights. King Haakon V of Norway, whose rights to the crown were far from sure, and who took the cross in 1237, probably did so to enjoy papal protection; he showed little enthusiasm for leaving for the East and his vow was eventually commuted to an expedition against the pagans in the Baltic. Some, like him, were slow to keep their promise, which caused difficulties with the lay justices, who saw crusaders escaping their courts by claiming ecclesiastical justice. The pope eventually decided that the privilege of the cross took effect only on departure for the crusade (1286). It was still sometimes necessary to threaten with canonical censures those who dragged their feet, but, in general, the papacy freely granted delays; Raymond VII of Toulouse, who had taken the cross in 1229, promising to serve for five years in the Holy Land, died in 1249, just as he was about to depart.

The vow was, in principle, irrevocable, except where there were prior commitments, respect for which was stipulated in the time of Urban II; this subordinated its fulfilment to the approval of the wife, the lord, or the bishop or abbot. Over time, the practice of commutation developed.

When, in 1237, Gregory IX received the appeal for help from the Latins of Constantinople, he emphasised its urgency to ask the barons who were preparing to leave for the Holy Land to go to Romania instead. Commutation could take other forms; St Elizabeth of Hungary, who had taken the cross, was persuaded by her confessor to devote the money she would have spent on the crusade to the foundation of a hospital where she herself tended the sick. Nevertheless, these commutations of vows were usually made in favour of a crusade, not necessarily in the Holy Land.

The vow was always made material by the affixing of a cross of cloth onto the clothing of the crusader, who was then 'marked with the cross' (*cruce signatus*). Other rites were borrowed from the ritual of pilgrimage; Joinville went to the abbey of Cheminon to be given by the abbot the staff and pouch of a pilgrim, and a special blessing was provided.

The vow might be taken by a dying person, which put the responsibility of performing it on his executor. Duke Eudes III of Burgundy, on the point of death at Lyons in 1218, in this way obliged his wife to send fifty knights at his expense to the Holy Land. Raymond VII of Toulouse did the same in 1249, and many other examples could be quoted. The heirs were then required to provide the contingents that the testators had stipulated to the army in the case of barons, or pay a pecuniary compensation.

Was the vow always voluntary? It could be imposed as a punishment, or rather as a reduction of a penalty. A knight from the diocese of Rouen who had wronged a monastery was sentenced to pay a fine of 60 *sous* and leave for the Holy Land. St Louis frequently used this punishment in the case of rebellious barons. Peter Mauclerc, count of Brittany, promised in 1234 to go to the Holy Land as soon as his son was old enough to govern his county; some knights of Narbonne who had manhandled inquisitors were ordered in 1237 to serve overseas; Enguerrand of Coucy, condemned for having unjustly hanged three young men, had to promise to spend three years in the Holy Land (1259).

To what extent were vows made in such circumstances comparable to those taken freely? The ecclesiastical authorities seem to have had no objection to accepting them. Some, like James of Vitry and Burchard of Mont-Sion, complained that they were used to get rid of undesirables who came to the East to swell the number of shady elements rather than to recover the grace of God. One such, banned from England for his faults, went to Acre, where he lost his *chevance* gambling; ruined, he took to the road, passing through Muslim territory where he was eventually recruited by the Mongols and captured below Vienna, where he was serving in their army. But the practice of dispatching the guilty to the

Holy Land and reducing their penalty resembled that of the 'judicial pilgrimages' that were common in the Low Countries until the end of the Middle Ages; they represented both an expiation and a means of avoiding acts of family vengeance after a murder, without depriving the condemned person of the possibility of enjoying a spiritual rebirth.

The crusading vow might include a time clause. In 1215 Innocent III asked people to commit themselves for three years. During the Fifth Crusade, some crusaders left once the set time had elapsed. Sometimes, the crusade ended as a result of the decision to disband the army. This happened in 1250 for that of St Louis, though the king himself only laid down the cross on his return to St Denis in 1254. After the crusade of Tunis, when the crusaders returned to France, the pope made it known that their vow had not been accomplished, as the crusade had only been suspended.

It was both for practical reasons and from a concern for moral perfection that the pope called for peace to be established within Christendom. 'To achieve this project', he stated in 1215, 'it is essential for the Christian princes and people to keep the peace between them.' Innocent III asked that truces be concluded for at least four years; the prelates were to compel those who refused by recourse to sentences of excommunication or interdict; secular princes might be encouraged to force observance of a peace or a truce on the recalcitrant. He added the prohibition of tournaments, already pronounced by several councils, but which appeared even more necessary at the time of a crusade; these gatherings, military in nature, at which attendance was obligatory, might hinder the mobilisation of an expedition.

Other prohibitions were added. Innocent III, and Innocent IV after him, legislated against Christians who, directly or indirectly, gave aid to the enemies of the crusade. First, they denounced the pirates who attacked ships on their way to the Holy Land; Philip Augustus had destroyed a den of pirates on the coast of Karamania; we have already noted the exploits of those Christian corsairs who attacked the infidel and their co-religionists alike, abducting men and women from the coasts of Cyprus or attacking ships; some of them seem to have put their galleys at the service of the Muslims.

Others hired themselves as mercenaries to eastern princes; the Turks of Anatolia employed large numbers of them from 1147 until the Mongol conquest, and we know of others who served the Ayyubids. Artisans built war machines which might be used against Christians. Not content with excommunicating them, the popes declared that they could be reduced to slavery if they were captured. But the *Livre au Roi*, written for Aimery of Lusignan, also mentions knights who served Muslim princes, and we know that some joined the army of Theodore Lascaris, irrespective of the conflict between him and the Latins of Constantinople. The Christians who ventured to fight alongside the enemies of the crusaders were not a figment of the imagination.

The popes, both so as to be sure of the vessels necessary for transport and to weaken the enemy economically, also proclaimed an embargo on trade with lands subject to the sultans. The provision of ships, arms and materials of a strategic nature was forbidden at all times; when a crusade was proclaimed, all commercial relations were suspended – for four years in 1215, and again in 1245.

THE RECRUITMENT OF THE CRUSADERS

The organisation of a crusade might concern the whole of Christendom (with the exception of the regions bordering non-Christian countries, especially Muslim Spain) or only certain countries. The papal encyclicals were then addressed to the archbishops and bishops of a group of dioceses, with instructions to spread word of the impending expedition to the faithful of those dioceses.

In the case of general crusades, letters were directed 'to all the faithful of the Church of Christ', but it was the prelates who were responsible for spreading this message. Sometimes they did it themselves, but usually the pope entrusted this task to legates appointed specially for the purpose. Letters might also be sent to the princes who had expressed their intention of taking the cross.

The constitutions of 1215 and 1245 instructed prelates to preach the crusade to those within their sphere of authority, and to appeal to kings, princes, dukes, marquises, counts, barons and other great lords, as well as to the populations of the cities, towns and castles, asking them to provide contingents with the sums necessary for their maintenance. For individual engagements, processions were arranged, usually monthly, which culminated in a sermon, after which the vows of those who took the cross – and the offerings of the rest – were collected. The prelates were advised to rekindle the zeal of those who had taken the cross by reminding them of their commitment, threatening them, if necessary, with excommunication or interdict, or to commute the vows which had proved impracticable.

Except in the case of the princes who might regard themselves as being obliged by their position to participate in the crusade or to send participants, the role of preaching was crucial. One of the great preachers of the Fifth Crusade, the master of the cathedral school of Cologne, Oliver of Paderborn, has left us a description of the atmosphere which surrounded his own appeals to the crusade in Frisia, with miraculous occurrences. James of Vitry, another preacher of the same crusade, delivered a sermon in Acre itself to an audience he described as ill prepared to hear him; yet he was received with as much enthusiasm as a revivalist preacher, distributed crosses, collected offerings and went on to preach in the other Frankish towns. In Lombardy, the cardinal-bishop of Ostia, Hugolin of Segni, travelled from town to town, obtaining here the promise of a contingent of twenty knights (Milan), there of ten (Brescia), elsewhere only of four (Lodi); he endeavoured to restore peace between cities and between citizens and he collected money.

For every crusade there were similar tours; those preceding the Third and Fourth crusades have already been described. For the Fifth, the legates turned to famous preachers such as James of Vitry, who had already preached the crusade against the Albigensians, and whose sermons dealt primarily with moral reform and called on people to repent. Entrusted by Cardinal Robert of Courçon with the task of inducing Christians to depart for the Holy Land, he called on yet other preachers, including Hellin of Florette and Gervase of Prémontré. The preaching could therefore reach a wide audience. Later, it was to be primarily the activity of the brethren of the mendicant orders, Franciscans and Dominicans. It was for the benefit of the latter that the master of the order of Friars Preachers, Humbert of Romans, wrote, around 1266, a treatise on the preaching of the Cross which provided model sermons to assist them in their task.

The themes tackled by these preachers, from the time of St Bernard, have been studied by Valmar Cramer, who has shown how the same ideas recur. Henry of Albano, at the time of the Third Crusade, emphasised how the cross of Christ had fallen into the hands of unbelievers. Henry of Strasbourg, at the same date, introduced a novel theme by appealing to the honour of the knight, who could not fail to respond to the request of his lord, that is, Christ.

The content of the pontifical bulls provided a number of ideas that the preachers could take up and develop. On the eve of the Fifth Crusade, Innocent III emphasised that God had not needed men to prevent the Holy Land from being conquered, but that in allowing this conquest he had hoped to revive the faith of Christians by testing it, like gold in a furnace; he compared God to a king who had been driven out of his kingdom and asked which vassals would refuse to fight on his behalf; was it not for the vassal to 'avenge the shame' of his lord? He then referred to the many Christians held captive by the Saracens, who must be freed.

James of Vitry has left us many of the crusade sermons he preached in the West before leaving for the Holy Land. He evokes the distress of this land of promise and takes up the idea of the *tempus acceptabile*, the moment to be seized to benefit from the effusion of graces, an idea which had been used by St Bernard: the pilgrimage as a festival. He dwelt on the theme of the Cross, altar of Christ's sacrifice and emblem of that of the Christian. According to the method of thirteenth-century preachers, he larded his speech with telling anecdotes and examples. Philip of Oxford, his contemporary, included a collection of them in his *On the preaching of the Holy Cross in England*. Eudes of Châteauroux, legate for the Seventh Crusade, also preached before and after it; the main purpose for taking the cross, he reminded his audience, was the love of Christ. These were all themes taken up by Humbert of Romans, with examples, some of which were taken from the history of the crusades.

After the sermon came the collection of the vows. Innocent III had lain down that they should be accepted whatever the condition or sex of those who made them. He was aware that some of these vows would be impossible to fulfil. Women took the cross and experience had taught that it was unwise to encourage them to accompany the expeditions. The sick also committed themselves in a surge of enthusiasm. Others lacked the resources that would enable them to undertake a costly and long-term project. At Châteauroux in 1248, a number of burgesses joined together in a confraternity to provide a warrior for the crusade; the legate granted each of them forty days' indulgence. Innocent III, in 1215, had stipulated the extension of the plenary indulgence to those who provided a replacement and also to those who served at another's expense; the remission of sins being freely granted, mercenaries might be tempted to join the crusaders. This probably explains how St Louis, when loading his army in 1248, discovered that it contained a large number of Italian soldiers, many of whom he had to leave behind.

Finally, Innocent III had extended the grant of the indulgence to those who provided their own ships to transport the crusaders, and to those who had ships built for this purpose.

The organisation of the crusade bore the mark of these measures. The crusader was not only someone who, in the words of the bulls, left for the war against the infidel bearing the cost of his commitment. He could also be someone who accompanied his lord on the expedition for the wages he would be paid. The crusading army, in the thirteenth century as already in the twelfth, was composed of quasi-feudal contingents; those who followed a great lord were from among his vassals or his neighbours who had placed themselves under his command. Jean de Joinville set out with a dozen knight from his lands, intending to transport and maintain them at his own expense; when the stay in

Cyprus dragged on, he came to the end of his resources and was greatly relieved when the king offered to take him and his men into his pay, as they were threatening to leave him. In 1221 Hugolin of Segni enrolled, in addition to the contingents of the towns, the hundred knights of the marquis of Montferrat and bodies of similar size provided by other magnates. These were clearly the men whom these great barons had taken into their pay. The crusader still had to bear part of the material costs of the expedition. Huon of St Quentin, who joined the Fifth Crusade, complained about this in one of his songs, speaking in the name of the 'bachelors' and the poor vavassors 'who have mortgaged their land – and have neither bounty nor aid – nor the comfort of the great lords – when their money is exhausted'.

Songs played their part in the crusading propaganda. But the 'crusade songs' include works with very different objectives. Some were intended to sustain the enthusiasm of the crusaders or instil shame into the pusillanimous who were reluctant to depart. Others – the 'departure songs' – expressed the sentiments of the lover who would be separated from his loved one by the crusade. Yet others reported events; they told of the resentment of the ordinary participants against leaders who had proved incompetent and against the clergy who took advantage of the crusade to satisfy their greed, and they recorded reactions to events, sometimes in a way that verged on satire. Written in French, Provençal and German, these texts are an invaluable guide to the crusaders' state of mind.

We should note here the songs that seem to have been composed and recited to encourage the knights to take the cross, and also those *chansons de geste* that recount the exploits of heroes who fought against the Saracens, of whom they paint a repulsive picture, firing the bellicose sentiments of the audience. Whether the heroes were the companions of Charlemagne or of William of Orange, it was usually the Saracens they fought, and those who listened to these poems being recited were probably tempted to transpose them into expeditions to the Holy Land.

It remains the case that these *chansons* were firmly located in Spain or Italy or southern France, and in an already distant past, that of the eighth, ninth and tenth centuries. The attempts that have been made to relate them directly to the crusade have produced hypotheses that, while interesting, do not always carry conviction.

Let us look rather at the song *Chevalier, mult estes guariz*, which was probably composed around 1147; in it, the poet evokes the fall of Edessa, 'where God was first served and recognised as Lord', where the churches were burned and deserted, and where divine worship had ceased. God, he says, made 'his clamour' against the infidel, 'who did him such dishonour'. The knights, who are proud of their exploits, ought to respond to his appeal. King Louis, richer than any of those listening to the poet, did not hesitate to leave everything to serve 'him who for us was put on the cross', who suffered his Passion, and on whom 'the people of the perfidious Zengi have played many evil tricks'. He employs the vocabulary of his audience from the knightly world:

> God has arranged a tournament between Hell and Heaven.
> He summons all his friends who wish to come to his defence.
> Let them not fail him.

The refrain concludes:

> He who accompanies Louis, need have no fear of Hell,
> Because his soul will go to Paradise with the angels of Our Lord.

It is in very much the same tone that the troubadour Marcabru expressed himself, in Provençal: 'The French are unnatural if they say no to God's work.'

Forty years later, a Master Renaud repeated this appeal, but, criticising the delays of the kings of France and England, he evoked the loss of the Holy Sepulchre, the desertion of the Holy Places and the need to recover these treasures. A little later, Huon of St Quentin attacked the clergy who allowed crusaders to renounce their vow by substituting a gift of money, adding that the reward that awaited the crusader was so great that no one should hesitate. When St Louis took the cross, an anonymous poet began his poem with the words: 'All the world should be joyful.'

In the middle of the thirteenth century we find a professional *trouvère*, one of those who occupied the role held today by journalists, recording events and propaganda. Rutebeuf had been unenthusiastic about the prohibition of tournaments and festivals which had accompanied the announcement of the crusade of the years 1262–3, because it was at such festivities that the minstrels found their audiences. But he put himself at the service of those who preached the cross, perhaps not without being rewarded for it. He sang the praises of those who had left to fight overseas, such as Geoffrey of Sergines and Eudes of Nevers, urging his audience to go to their aid. In 1264–5 he repeated the appeal to the crusade launched by the pope against Manfred; in 1265–6 the *Complainte d'Outre-mer*, repeated a little later in the *Voie de Tunes*, reads almost like a crusading sermon. The *Nouvelle Complainte d'Outre-mer* lambasted young men who ran after girls, tournaments, and prelates who were too greedy to spend money on combatants, and he repeated the themes emphasised by the Council of Lyons of 1274.

In the *Dit du Croisé et du Décroisé*, probably written in 1268 or 1269, Rutebeuf repeated all the arguments advanced by those who did not wish to leave their homes or reduce their children to poverty, who reckoned that 'you can very well reach God in this country without damage' or that it was for prelates to bear the burden of the war since they lived on 'God's rents', and by those who said that the sultan was not coming to attack them and they were not going to go looking for him and, lastly, that God was surely as present in France as elsewhere. To each of these arguments, the crusader responds victoriously, and the *décroisé* eventually gives in and agrees to take the cross.

All this propaganda – and I use the word advisedly – had the same goal, that is, to persuade the knights, in the words of Conan of Béthune that, though the crusade was a *dure départie*, a painful separation, and though the heart of the crusader remained with his loved one, he must go 'sighing to Syria, for I must not fail my Creator ... and great and small know that one must do one's knightly duty, there, where one will win heaven and honour, and prizes, and praise, and the love of one's mistress'.

The *trouvère* does not hesitate to appeal to sentiments that Urban II would have found worldly: the love of glory and the conquest of one's mistress. The poets were not writing sermons but addressing the men of their own social milieu, whose ideas and aspirations they shared.

We should probably also include in this arsenal of propaganda the writings of historians. Those of the First Crusade wrote to encourage departures and to praise mighty deeds; the authors of songs – the *Chanson d'Antioche*, the *Chanson de Jérusalem* and Ambroise's *Estoire de la Guerre Sainte* during the Third Crusade – might help to arouse enthusiasm, but this was not their prime aim.

In fact, the recruitment of crusaders was primarily dependent on preaching. Other means might reinforce it, but could not substitute for it.

Those who responded to the appeal included men of war – knights, esquires and 'sergeants' – but also burgesses accustomed to defending their walls, forming the urban militias sometimes forced to take part in those simulations of war, tournaments, the 'footsoldiers' trained in combat who constituted the bands of mercenaries and, in particular, the crossbowmen. The crusade also attracted the clergy, in particular the prelates, used to providing their contingents for the royal host. There were also peasants, who were also not without experience in the art of war since they were expected to serve in their lords' campaigns, but the problem of finding the necessary resources limited their involvement.

THE FINANCING OF THE CRUSADES

Finance was a constant problem for the crusaders. One sign of this is the stream of complaints about the rising price of foodstuffs and the extortionate exchange rates practised on Byzantine territory that were recorded by historians. Songs such as that of Huon of St Quentin recapture that moment, familiar to Joinville, when the knight came to the end of the money he had brought with him. Throughout his journey, Louis VII wrote to Suger asking him to send more money and, on leaving the Holy Land, he had to borrow a large sum from the Templars. It was financial problems that caused the Fourth Crusade to divert to Zara, then to Constantinople, and decided the crusaders to attack the latter.

It is impossible to estimate the total cost of the crusades, especially since some of the money spent by the crusaders remained in the West, where it paid for the hire of ships, the purchase of horses and pack animals, equipment, foodstuffs, weapons and vehicles, as well as the wages of the workers and sailors who were employed to prepare or transport the expeditions. In the East, the purchase of foodstuffs and of new horses and mules and many other costs had to be settled in the money current in the various countries; what foragers could get their hands on in the countryside could only ever be supplementary. All these expenses must have exceeded by far the usual budget of the princes and the lords. It comes as something of a surprise to find that even a great baron like Raymond of Saint-Gilles might still be relatively well off after two years of campaigning.

The principle reaffirmed in the conciliar decrees goes back to the First Crusade: the person who took a vow of crusade was responsible for the cost of carrying it out. As we have seen, at this date the practice of selling or more often of mortgaging their lands enabled the crusaders to equip themselves and to take a little money with them. Cluny advanced 2,000 *sous* and two mules to Achard of Montmerle, and 50 *sous* and two mules to Stephen of Neublans. The churches were induced to convert part of their treasuries of precious objects into cash to respond to these requests for loans, these being in principle repaid on return, with no interest other than what the lender collected in income from the land.

The financial system was regularised at the time of the Second Crusade. It was still for the crusader to raise the money that was needed for his equipment, a horse, his own keep and that of the men he took with him. But the pope wanted to make it easier to raise money; the vassal wishing to contact a loan by mortgaging his fief must first offer it to his lord; the pope recognised that he might be obliged to offer it to a church and ordered religious establishments to respond to such requests, which required them to make further inroads into their treasuries.

When sovereigns departed for the East, they resorted to taxation. Louis VII hoped to extort huge sums from the French abbeys; he asked St Benoît-sur-Loire for a gift of 1,000 silver marks; the abbot bargained, and they settled on 400 marks. To raise this sum, the monastery had to melt down two large silver chandeliers and a gold censer. Nor did his other subjects escape the taxation levied by the king; whether it was a feudal aid or a tallage demanded of subjects may be debatable, but the general character of this tax is clear. Louis VII levied taxes for the Holy Land calculated according to individual wealth or revenue, though there was no question of him going himself; in 1166, for example, the rate, which was hardly exorbitant, was one penny in the pound (which, in England, Henry II raised to twopence).

During the course of the twelfth century, the practice was introduced of including a lord's imminent departure for Jerusalem among the purposes justifying the levy of an aid on his subjects (an aid which, in some countries amounted to double the annual rents); in 1182 the duke of Burgundy made his eventual departure for the East one of the 'four cases' which became traditional. In 1185 the count of Vendôme asked the abbey of the Trinity for a sum of 3,000 *sous* for his imminent departure for Jerusalem. Songs spoke of lords who took the cross so they could *dixmer* their subjects, that is, ask them for ten per cent of their income.

So the lord who had to finance his own departure demanded a contribution from the population of his lands, including the religious institutions, which were already under the obligation to grant loans with land as security, an obligation which often left them in possession of that land when the crusader died on the expedition or was unable to repay them; in some cases, it was stipulated that the loan only allowed the income to be collected for a fixed period. In any case, the impossibility of repaying the money borrowed led many a lord or knight to grant the mortgaged land either to his suzerain or to a better-off relative or neighbour.

Right to the end, the crusader was obliged to assume responsibility for part of the cost of the expedition, in particular as regards his equipment and his keep, and that of his horses and his men. When some great person took him into his pay, however, his keep was usually provided. The great men, for their part, were able to resort to taxation.

With the exception of the taxes imposed by sovereigns in the last decades of the twelfth century, which were intended to finance the defence of the Holy Land against Saladin, taxation hit ecclesiastical revenues hardest. This situation originated in the decision taken by the French bishops assembled in council at Dijon in 1199. The pope had asked them to send to the crusade a certain number of warriors, or the corresponding sum; the legate Peter Capuano got them to agree to a tax of a thirtieth of their income. Innocent III reduced this to a fortieth, setting at a tenth the levy on the revenues of the apostolic see. Several religious orders tried to take advantage of their exemption, including the Cistercians and Carthusians; they refused to pay the tax but agreed to make a voluntary contribution.

The system was regularised after 1215. The conciliar bull of that year stipulated that all the clergy would be subject to a levy of a twentieth of their ecclesiastical resources for a period of three years 'for the assistance of the Holy Land', with the exception of certain religious, and that the pope and the cardinals would accept a levy of a tenth. This was the origin of the 'tenth', the rate of which was in practice very variable; in 1225 it was a tenth in France and a fifteenth in England, it being understood that this tax was agreed to by the taxpayers; in 1245 it was a twentieth, in 1263 a hundredth; in 1274 it was again a tenth, this time for five years.

This tax entailed the development of a fiscal system. In Denmark in 1245 the tax was levied on the income from ecclesiastical tithes, at the rate of a third; otherwise, the tenth was applied to the whole of the income from ecclesiastical benefices: crops and livestock, rents and foundations, with no deduction for the cost of the upkeep of buildings. Canons were taxed both on the *gros fruits* of their prebend and on the daily distributions (*diées*). At first, the bishops were made responsible for the taxation (the evaluation of the taxable revenue) and its collection; once the tax base had been decided at the diocesan synod, it was the archdeacons and the archpriests who saw to its collection. But from 1218 the legates controlled this fiscal activity; under Innocent IV they were appointed as collectors general, archdeacons and archpriests becoming sub-collectors.

The income from the tenth was large; it has been calculated that St Louis received from this source, for his crusade, the sum of 1,537,570 *livres tournois*. The clergy complained about the tax, but could not escape it; when the French clergy showed themselves recalcitrant in 1267, Clement IV threatened to deprive the culprits of their benefices and status, and hand them over to the secular arm. The princes who were to receive the income from these taxes did not hesitate to resort to force; in 1254 Duke Hugh IV of Burgundy sent his troops to attack the estates of the abbey of Cluny. Joinville had to tell the king of France in 1250 that people were saying that all he had so far spent on his crusade was the Church's money.

Yet other contributions were demanded from the faithful. Fulk of Neuilly made collections which seem to have been very profitable; Innocent III stipulated that when the crusade was preached appeals should be made to the generosity of the audience. Many testators included among their last wishes legacies for the Holy Land, for the crusade, and even for the rebuilding of the fortresses of the Latin East, hoping in this way to benefit from the grant of the partial indulgences attached to these works. To this might be added the allocation to the Holy Land of ill-gotten gains; for example, when, in return for money, a baron authorised Lombard usurers to lend at interest on his lands, the sum he received might be assigned to the crusade.

Innocent III, so as to encourage voluntary payments for the purpose of financing the crusade, recommended his legates to accept vows made by people unable to participate in an expedition, in particular women, and to commute these vows into a payment corresponding to the cost of sending a warrior to the crusade. The conciliar bull of 1215 confirmed this practice. Canonically, a vow could be assigned to another purpose than that initially stipulated, especially since, by defining it separately from the vow of pilgrimage, the vow of the crusade seemed to be made for the good of Christendom, and not as a personal atonement. In 1240 the Mongol invasion of Hungary was felt to represent a danger to the Christians of the West; the pope authorised German crusaders to commute their vow to go to the Holy Land into a participation in the battle against the invaders. Subsequently, Innocent IV and his successors accepted, even encouraged, what appeared to crusaders setting out for the East as a distortion of the crusading ideal: the English, German and Scandinavian crusaders were asked to join the army of the anti-king opposed by the pope to Frederick II, William of Holland, instead of that of St Louis; and Henry III of England asked to commute his vow to go to the Holy Land into participation in the expedition that the king of Castile was proposing to lead into Africa.

The commutation of vows might take the form of a conversion into money of the physical obligation. It thus came to be confused with the redemption of a vow, which itself had originally been the payment of the cost of a replacement by a person who found he was unable to depart. Many crusaders, struck down by illness before they were able to fulfil their vow, bequeathed the sums necessary to provide someone to replace them. But eventually redemption took place without recourse to the recruitment of combatants. Introduced in the time of Celestine III, the redemption of vows was confused by contemporaries with the annulment of the vow and one poet attacked Rome for having 'uncrossed for money those who had crossed themselves for God'. The resentment caused by these alleged withdrawals provoked hostility towards Rome. To Matthew Paris, it was a system designed to replenish the coffers of the Church of Rome, which he found shocking.

In fact, as we have seen, the financial needs were considerable and explain why every avenue was explored in an attempt to lessen the burden on those who went to fight. But how was the money collected by the Church – the tenths, offerings, legacies and redemptions of vows – used? We know that in 1201–2 the sums collected, particularly by Fulk of Neuilly, and assembled by the efforts of the Cistercians, were conveyed to the Holy Land by one of the pontifical legates, and were therefore not used to the benefit of the crusade. Subsequently, the papacy was careful to ensure that the money was at the disposal of the crusaders; during the Fifth Crusade there was a common treasury replenished by the legacies of the crusaders who had died below Damietta. It was the legate Pelagius who received the money sent to him by, for example, Cardinal Hugolin of Segni, who established a depositary at Bologna in which he put the revenue from the twentieth, and some Bolognese merchants sent money to Damietta. Other sums were put at the disposal of the marquis of Montferrat, who was preparing his departure (1221).

This solution was eventually adopted systematically. St Louis could draw on the largest of the tenths levied in France, but part of this sum was assigned to certain great barons who were to lead their contingents. In 1262 Urban IV stipulated that, as well as the king, many great lords should receive sums deducted from the total raised by the hundredth: 30,000 *livres* in the case of Alphonse of Poitiers, 20,000 *livres* in that of the count of Flanders. In addition to the income from the tenths, other sums were assigned to the financing of the crusade; in 1215 Innocent III allocated to it 3,000 silver marks drawn from various alms, and there were also the sums already sent to the patriarch and the masters of the orders 'for the needs of the Holy Land'.

The practice of assigning the resources earmarked for the financing of the crusade to the leaders who took their armies with them, who were beginning to be called *chevetaines* or captains of the crusade, resulted in every crusade, or every component, now having a leader who disposed of a war chest and therefore exercised a much stronger authority than in the past. This system had its disadvantages: the princes, in particular the kings of Denmark, Norway and England, grew accustomed to seeking the grant of tenths for crusades that never materialised; this led to the aberrations of pontifical fiscality.

The handling of the sums destined for the crusade was responsible for major advances in the techniques of conveying cash. In 1096, when Hugh of Vermandois had been shipwrecked, barrels full of coins had sunk with his ship. In 1148, when Louis VII returned to France, he assigned, on his treasury, the reimbursement of the sums that had been advanced to him in the East by the Templars. The latter received deposits which they kept on the ships (as in 1250, off Damietta, when the king's army was on land), without in principle being able to use them, but they accepted transfers from account to account. St Louis' orders on his treasury, to pay the knights he maintained in the Holy Land, went through Italian bankers. The system was sometimes even more complex. For the tenth instituted in 1274, the diocese of Gardar in Greenland paid in walrus teeth and ox skins, which were converted into cloth in Iceland, then into money in Norway, to be forwarded on Italian banks.

The importance assumed by financial questions is evident in the formulation of the powers granted by the pope to those he made responsible for preaching the crusade. On 1 August 1274 Gregory X wrote to his legate in France, Cardinal Simon of Brie, to the effect that the general council had decided on the levy of the tenth of all ecclesiastical revenues for six years from St John's Day next (24 June), and that he was to collect this tenth in the kingdom of France and the diocese of Lyons, and also to preach the crusade. He was authorised to grant the indulgence prescribed for those who would leave in person and to those who, accepting the obligation of confession, paid an appropriate sum; to commute all other vows into a vow of crusade; to release from the vow of crusade those who could not fulfil it and wished to redeem it; to release from excommunication those who had not fulfilled their vow if they wished to send combatants in their place or pay the corresponding sum; to permit the barons and prelates to convert ill-gotten gains into grants for the crusade; and to collect in legacies made for the assistance of the Holy Land. He asked him to deliver to King Philip III the sums raised by the tenth, by legacies and other grants and by redemptions of vows in the kingdom of France and the dioceses of Lièges, Cambrai, Toul, Mainz and Verdun. The Council of Lyons, meanwhile, had asked for chests to be placed in churches to receive offerings for the crusade.

In fact, a complex financial system had been created which added to the personal participation of the crusader the grants of those in whose name he was to fight and the financial contribution demanded of both subjects and ecclesiastics. The criticism made by the chroniclers and songwriters against those who 'uncrossed' themselves was only partly justified, since the redemption of a vow served to recruit other combatants or to enhance the military and material potential of the army.

But this development took time and the fiscal system which had matured by the time of Gregory X was still very rudimentary in the days of Innocent III. The crusades that followed that of 1202–4 enjoyed a much more solid financial base than their predecessors.

THE LOGISTICS OF THE CRUSADES

Expeditions on such a large scale, probably mobilising almost as many people, in the case of the crusades of 1147 and of 1188–92, as in the First Crusade, inevitably made large demands in the spheres of material preparation, transport and maintenance – what in military history goes under the name of logistics.

The initial equipment probably cost less than the subsequent stages; those who set out were men already trained in combat who owned mounts and weapons. But, as we have seen, when a campaign dragged on, it was necessary to renew a significant proportion of the offensive and defensive weapons; the gifts made by St Louis to less well-off knights to enable them to go on crusade are evidence of this. Each knight needed a hauberk, that is, a coat of mail, the lightly armed horsemen needed a short, sleeveless habergeon, the footsoldiers padded jackets. Lances, swords, bows and crossbows all had to be ready for use, not to speak of ordinary clothing.

The need for horses varied according to whether the land or the sea route was chosen, the latter the more common after 1190. As a result, the number of pack animals was smaller; Joinville and his cousin of Sarrebruck had their baggage taken by river to Marseilles, while the great warhorses were led overland. In the eleventh and twelfth centuries, in contrast, the crusaders had to find mules for their baggage.

The English accounts enable us to see how Richard I prepared for his departure. The royal officers bought large quantities of cheeses in Essex, dry vegetables in Kent and Cambridgeshire, and more than 14,000 pigs in Hampshire, Essex and Lincolnshire. Salt pork, peas and beans, and cheese were the basic foodstuffs that could be preserved, to which were added the wheat indispensable for making bread and barrels of wine. St Louis appointed one of his sergeants to assemble provisions in Cyprus to await his troops; Frederick II had authorised him to make large purchases, probably of wheat, in Apulia and Sicily, and Joinville described the hills made by the sacks of wheat whose outer layers had germinated, giving the appearance of grass, and the stacks of barrels which looked like barns that the crusaders found in 1248 near the port of Limassol. There were other purchases; horseshoes were made by the thousand, and bows and arrows in huge quantities.

What had been prepared before the departure was, of course, soon consumed; throughout the crusade, ships from the West brought foodstuffs. Joinville explained how he contrived the provisioning of the men the king had entrusted to him: he made his purchases in the autumn, because prices rose in winter as a result of the difficulties of navigation. It was early in October that he 'filled his pigsties with pigs and his sheepcote with sheep' and bought flour and wine for the winter. The regularity of supply could not be relied on, and the accounts of historians testify to shortages, and to the speculations that drove up food prices. Nevertheless, when St Louis had to evacuate Damietta, he left behind large quantities of foodstuffs, in particular salt pork, which the Mamluks destroyed, contrary to their promises. And when Queen Margaret, during the weeks preceding the town's surrender, bought up all the available foodstuffs to avert a panic, she spent more than 360,000 *livres*. There were clearly large quantities of foodstuffs on the market, which had been brought by the merchants, whose role was crucial.

During the first crusades, it had been necessary to negotiate rates of exchange with the Hungarians and the Byzantines, to allow purchases in the markets opened for the benefit of the crusaders. Even within the army, it had been necessary, during the First Crusade, to settle the equivalences between the different moneys circulating in the East. It is likely that rules had to be established during the following crusades, but it seems that the crusaders, once arrived in the East, used local money, the bezant in use in the Latin states, as a monetary yardstick. This is suggested by, for example, the will of a Bolognese, Barzella Merxadrus, who, in 1220, specified the amount of his legacies in bezants. This will lists this crusader's equipment: a Barbary horse, armour consisting of a long-sleeved coat of mail and a cowl, and his personal weapons. His provisions, at the end of December, consisted of two sacks of biscuit, two bags of flour, two measures of wine and a quarter of a chine of pork; he stipulated six bezants for the purchase of bread and wine. This gives an idea of the daily needs of a fighting man – in this case a knight – and of those for whom the leaders of the crusade were responsible.

The chief distinguishing feature of the crusades was that the theatre of operations was separated from the bases for departure and support by the length of the Mediterranean, from the Italian peninsula to the shores of Syria. From 1191, Cyprus was a valuable staging post, since the island's resources were considerable; even before this date, ships had put in and provisioned there. The Frankish lands of Syria also made a contribution, over and above the reinforcements the crusaders found there. Nor were the Muslim, Byzantine and Armenian lands closed to them; Seljuk Anatolia appeared a possible source of supplies, and, during a truce, St

Louis sent one of his sergeants to Damascus to procure the horn essential for the manufacture of his crossbows.

In 1215 the bull *Ad liberandum* still assumed that not all the crusaders would leave by sea; in 1245 the bull *Afflicti corde* used only the word *transfretare*, 'to cross the sea'. The former assumed the participants would embark at Messina or Brindisi; later crusades left from Aigues-Mortes (in 1248 and 1270) and other ports. The expeditions of the late twelfth and early thirteenth centuries tried various solutions; Richard I built or bought his own ships and hired the sailors to crew them, on the basis of a hundred ships and fourteen large *busses*; Philip Augustus chartered his boats at Genoa, reserving places for the knights, the other combatants and the horses; the barons of the Fourth Crusade had eventually negotiated with Venice for the transport of the whole army, on the basis of a flat rate for each individual and agreeing, as Philip Augustus had done, that the Republic would have the right to a share of any conquests made.

It was perhaps the experience of 1202–4 that put a stop to this type of contract. No future agreements referred to a share of the booty or conquests; the shipowners hired out their ships to or put them at the disposal of the crusaders without reference to an association of this type. Innocent III promised them the benefit of the crusading indulgence, without requiring them to make a vow.

Some princes, like Frederick II in Sicily and his father Henry VI in Germany, had their own fleet because they were able to requisition the ships of their subjects. For the others, another possibility was to hire 'by the place', which was stipulated in the statutes of the maritime towns for the transport of pilgrims, who were offered various grades of comfort: for the knights, rooms, below the bridge; less comfortable places in the two steerages were leased at a lower price. An intermediary was some-times employed: at Marseilles, a certain Garnier of Marigny reserved two hundred places, at 45 *sous* per place, for crusaders from Burgundy and Champagne, and promised to find passengers to fill the available places. In 1268 Venice proposed a tariff of $2\frac{1}{2}$ marks for a knight, 7 *onces* for an esquire, $4\frac{1}{2}$ marks for a horse and its groom, and $\frac{3}{4}$ mark for a footsoldier. The barons preferred, if possible, to hire a whole ship; in 1248 the archbishop of Tours booked, for 1,500 marks, a ship manned by a crew of thirty-three men, with stables for the horses, provided with sufficient water (the horses drank a lot), provisions and all the necessary equip-ment. The contracts also specified what was necessary in the way of sails, cordage, rigging and anchors.

In 1246–8 St Louis wanted to take advantage of the arrival of the Norwegian fleet; when this failed to materialise, he negotiated with

Genoa, which provided him with a dozen large sailing ships (*nefs*) and four other vessels, and with Marseilles, which offered him twenty ships with ten escort galleys. The king also constructed ships on his own account, in particular *huissiers*, ships suitable for the transport of horses and fitted with a gate that allowed them to embark; Joinville even described how these gates were closed after embarkation. For this crusade, others procured ships by hiring them in Marseilles (Alphonse of Poitiers and the counts of Toulouse, Braine and Forez), while the count of St Pol had a large sailing ship built at Inverness to transport the crusaders from Artois, Flanders and the Low Countries; Raymond VII of Toulouse had one built on the Atlantic coast; and Elnard of Seninghem, a baron from Artois who only arrived in 1252, had bought one in Norway. It is clear that the assembly of the tonnage necessary for a crusade required a massive effort.

We know that the transport of pilgrims had assumed major proportions; the Marseillais had even had to limit the number of those that the Hospitallers and Templars carried in their ships, to reduce their competition. It was also necessary to arrange for the transport of the horses and fodder and that of sufficient provisions for a lengthy period, much longer than that of the voyage itself (sometimes for as much as a year). It even seems that there were fears of a shortage of timber for shipbuilding; negotiating with St Louis in 1268, Genoa obtained permission to procure from the royal forests the trees destined for the masts and rudders of its boats. But, at the same date, the king's commissioners noted that both ships of lower tonnage and escort galleys were widely available.

In 1248 the king of France had negotiated with the Genoese on the usual terms, which a Venetian contract of 1219 defined as follows: 'When the ships have arrived in one of the cities listed below [Damietta, Tyre, Acre or Alexandria], the pilgrims will unload the ships as quickly as they can, and the captain and sailors of each will have the power to do what they want with it.' Having landed in Cyprus, the king dismissed the sailors, who took the opportunity to go to Acre on business of their own and settle scores with the Pisans, so that St Louis had no ships at his disposal when he wanted to set off for Egypt. In 1268–70, therefore, he stipulated that the ships must remain available when they put in somewhere, which allowed his army to re-embark at Tunis for Sicily. And though in 1248 he left the command of the fleet to the Genoese admirals, in 1270 he entrusted it to a French admiral, Florent of Varennes.

Having a fleet at their disposal, whether it consisted of chartered vessels or vessels built specially (that of the king of France, in 1270, included a number of ships for which contracts had been agreed specifying details of the construction) allowed the crusaders to direct their efforts wherever they chose. But the late arrivals who joined the army after it had landed might run into difficulties. When they put in at Messina, the passengers on the *St Victor* of Marseilles learned that the king of France had left Egypt; as their agreement was for their carriage to Damietta, the captain wanted to take them back to Marseilles and the judges of Messina had to compel him to carry them to wherever the king of France then was.

The great Mediterranean ports, Genoa, Venice, Pisa, Marseilles and Barcelona, and also those of the kingdom of Sicily, were thus associated with the crusade in their capacity as carriers. But, as we have seen, the maritime republics and communes had ceased, at least in principle, to cooperate institutionally in the war itself.

The crusaders' dependence on the shipping routes was often inconvenient. Navigation in the Mediterranean was subject to the constraints of the prevailing winds; storms were common, especially in winter. The sailors were beginning to use the compass, but had not wholly mastered ocean navigation, and were often driven at random onto the Barbary coast. Ships often ran aground; St Louis' sailing ship hit a sandbank off Limassol and came close to being abandoned. Shipwrecks were frequent; Richard of England took the precaution of loading the barrels of silver constituting his war chest onto several different ships, but that bringing the money collected by Blanche of Castile to St Louis was lost at sea. In 1249 the royal fleet assembled before Damietta was badly hit by a storm; that of Philip III, in 1270, was almost wiped out in the harbour of Trapani. To the Mongol khan Hülegü, nevertheless, St Louis still seemed to be the master of the sea.

The constraints of the sea route also affected the transmission of news; events taking place in the Latin East and the successes and failures of the crusaders only became known after a longer or shorter delay, and the response, already slow owing to the methods of recruitment and financing of the crusades, could not always be made in time. We should note, in this connection, the existence of information networks. Bohemond IV of Antioch kept spies in Muslim territory, who kept him informed, in particular, about the first Mongol invasions in the Near East; the sultan Baybars had his own spies, who told him of the disaster suffered by the French fleet in 1270. The master of the Temple, William of Beaujeu, even had informers in the sultan's entourage.

There probably did not exist what we would call a health service. During the siege of Acre, in 1190–1, the German crusaders, and in particular Duke Frederick of Swabia, founded a campaign hospital to tend their sick and wounded; it was this hospital that took the name St

Mary of the Germans and continued in existence after the town had fallen, then adopting the organisation of the existing hospitals and military orders; like them, it provided care in hospitals located in towns, without creating infirmaries accompanying the armies.

When Joinville described the death of Gaucher of Autrèches, however, he told how 'many of the surgeons and physicians of the host' came to visit him and decided to bleed him. The presence of doctors and surgeons is therefore well attested, though we do not know what status they enjoyed. Were the sick and wounded from the camp before Mansurah evacuated to Damietta to be taken to a place where they could be looked after? We know that the king left his sick men at Damietta to await their recovery, and that the Mamluks put them to death in spite of the agreements they had made; they were probably sheltered in a temporary hospital.

For lodgings, the crusaders established themselves in the houses seized in the towns they occupied, as in Damietta. The capture of Acre gave rise to problems which were settled by the recognition of the rights of the former Christian owners, on condition they lodged the crusaders in their houses. During operations, 'pavilions', that is, tents, sheltered the combatants. Joinville described these tents, their cords, and the way he set up his bed in his own.

THE ARMY'S MORALE

The first article of the conciliar bulls concerned the priests and the other clergy present in the Christian army, beginning with the prelates; it instructed them 'to persist in prayer and preaching, to teach by example as well as by words, having always before their eyes the love and the fear of God', and to avoid excesses in food and clothing. For it was the job of the clergy to foster in the army the sentiments which would make God look kindly on it.

The military and financial arrangements described above should not make us forget that the crusade was meant to be an exercise in penitence and a work in the service of Christ. A few sentences of the legate Eudes of Châteauroux, speaking to Joinville at the end of St Louis' crusade, are worth recalling here. 'Seneschal', he said, 'I am happy; and I give thanks to God, that the king, you and the other pilgrims are escaping the great danger you have experienced in this land; and I have a heavy heart that I have to leave your holy company.'

It was not that the crusaders were saints or that their behaviour was beyond reproach. The sack of Constantinople led some of them to reflect on their conduct, and to admit that they had forgotten God.

Joinville expressed himself in a similar vein with regard to the capture of Damietta in 1249; the occupation of the town, achieved without having had to fight, was clearly, in his eyes, a divine blessing. But after this success, the crusaders 'forgot God, who had saved them', and he listed the faults they had committed: the king himself, by setting apart from the division of the spoils, contrary to custom, the cheese, barley, rice and other foodstuffs; his officers, by charging too much for the stalls offered to the merchants; the barons, by their feasting; and the common people, who frequented women of easy virtue.

The presence of prostitutes in the camp at Damietta was not an isolated occurrence. Ibn al-Athir noted it at the time of the siege of Acre and even marvelled at these women's devotion, which seemed to him an act of piety. St Louis took measures against them, but only on his return from captivity. Acts of dishonesty and in particular the withholding of objects which ought to have been pooled during the division of the spoils seem to have been common.

When the legate spoke of 'your holy company', we must accept that he regarded the crusaders, despite their failings, as aspiring to lead a Christian life. This was the purpose of the sermons and the appeals to confession and penitence, and of the processions which were so many manifestations of collective repentance in the hope of enjoying divine mercy. This entreaty was not confined to the earliest crusades; right to the end, the crusaders were conscious that their armies had set out to perform a pious work, and that their sins were an obstacle to its achievement.

The crusaders were subject to a discipline whose rules were established by the time of the Second Crusade. It was on leaving Messina in 1190 that Philip Augustus and Richard I issued an ordinance stipulating obedience to certain measures during the voyage. It was forbidden to swear or to wear luxurious clothing – furs of vair, ermine or sable, and scarlet fabric. Gambling was also prohibited if the stake was in money, at least to the sergeants, the sailors and the servants, on pain of flogging (keel hauling for the sailors). The knights and the clergy were permitted to gamble as long as their losses did not exceed 20 *sous* in twenty-four hours, on pain of a fine of 100 *sous*. Meals were to be confined to two courses. Brawling would be severely punished, by the loss of a fist for the use of a knife, by triple immersion for a blow with a fist, and by death in case of murder; no women were to be allowed on board.

These rules were relaxed for persons of high rank, many of whom were accompanied by their wife. In 1250 St Louis, learning that his brother Charles was gambling with Walter of Nemours on the boat which was carrying them to Egypt, threw the dice overboard, though

Walter, Joinville tells us, managed to hide the stakes. Charles of Anjou had not broken a rule, but the king thought he might have had the decency to wait a little. When they arrived at Acre, the king's brothers resumed their gambling, and Alphonse of Poitiers even made himself conspicuous by his lavish distribution of his gains and reimbursement of his partners' losses. The austerity remained relative; for his crusade, Richard I bought luxury fabrics of exactly the type he forbade to others.

It remains the case that the crusaders were conscious of having promised to change their life, and that they endeavoured to keep this promise. They are seen settling disputes before battle, and collecting alms for the aid of the poor; this was recorded during the siege of Acre (1189–90), and these acts of charity were regarded as one of the causes of the success of the siege, because they were pleasing to God.

The desire for purification was particularly evident when danger threatened; contemporary sensibility attached great importance to acts of repentance. But the authors of the crusade *chansons*, as we have seen, expressed less the emotions of the combatants as nostalgia for the 'sweet country' left behind, and their regret at having abandoned a mistress. This was the counterpart to their renewed affirmation that they could not shirk their duty to serve their master, Christ who had suffered his passion for their sake, and to liberate the place of his suffering from the occupation of the infidel. Here, too, the sincerity of the sentiment cannot be doubted, but the expression remains stereotyped. Sometimes there emerges the feeling of the 'great honour' represented by the fact of exposing oneself to danger in God's service. Chivalric sentiments combined with the Christian aspiration for eternal salvation.

There are occasional references to the satisfaction that would be experienced in recounting their exploits; the count of Soissons, addressing Joinville in the thick of battle, said they would remember that day when they conversed together in the 'ladies' chambers'. But a song written after the defeat suffered by the count of Bar in 1239 deplored the fact that there were some who wanted to demonstrate their prowess and exposed themselves, and exposed others, rashly: 'You were too proud to demonstrate chivalry.' The excessive pride of the knight was criticised, but it remained one of the characteristics of the spirit of the crusader, who loved to demonstrate his disregard for danger. But some of their leaders, like St Louis, refused to express their admiration for those who were led by this love of glory to disobey the orders that put them under a strict discipline.

Warriors may not have liked to mention their fear, but it was real. They feared the sea, its depth and its treachery: when Oliver of Termes, a valiant knight, was shipwrecked off Cyprus, it was a long time before he would again entrust himself to a boat. They feared Greek fire, that rain of burning projectiles which so cruelly tried the royal army in Egypt. And they had learned from experience to fear the enemy. To go on a crusade was to face dangers about which there could be no illusions.

In a delightful poem (*Chanterai pour mon courage que je veux réconforter*), a *trouvère* who is probably Guiot of Dijon, who died in the thirteenth century, put this anxiety into the mouth of a mistress who feared her lover would not return and imagined the mêlée:

> God, when they cry 'Onward!'
> Lord, help the pilgrim
> For whom I am terrified,
> For the Saracens are *félons*.

The enemy was indeed formidable (the meaning of *félon* here) and the knights and the footsoldiers were required, for long hours, to remain stoical under a hail of arrows until those in front could launch their charge. Nor should we forget the broken ranks, the sudden panic and the massacres.

Joinville described such moments: he had held a bridge with a few companions where they were hit by so many arrows that they were covered with tiny wounds and unable to put back on their coats of mail; he had experienced the rout of the royal army and the laying down of arms on a false rumour; he had seen the throats of the sick cut in the boats and many prisoners put to death; at one point, he himself and some other barons believed they were going to be killed and hastily confessed each other.

Captivity was the lot awaiting many crusaders, and from 1096, when the bands of Walter Sans-Avoir and his followers were defeated by the Turks, when the armies of the Crusade of 1101 were destroyed in their turn, and during the ordeals of the Second Crusade in Asia Minor. The historians described these masses of prisoners transported as far as Khorassan, reduced to slavery. Saladin's conquests were accompanied by an enormous haul of captives; the fate of these prisoners, and of those seized by the Almohads after their victory at Alarcos, was a major preoccupation of Innocent III. During the Fifth Crusade the Ayyubids captured a number of barons and many prisoners of lesser rank, as had also happened at the siege of Acre. In 1239 Walter of Brienne, count of Jaffa, was taken prisoner with many French crusaders, including Philip of Nanteuil, who gave vent to his complaints from his prison in Cairo; Walter was put to death after an incident during his captivity. The whole army of St Louis experienced a similar fate.

Captivity was a terrible ordeal. Prisoners of modest condition risked being reduced to permanent slavery, sold in the markets of the Near East; it is known that the capture of so many Franks by Saladin caused the price of slaves to collapse. Those of higher rank might experience long periods of captivity – Reynald of Dampierre was a prisoner for thirty years – hoping to be freed *par bataille ou pour avoir*. In the thirteenth century, the burden of the ransoms probably weighed more heavily on the leaders of the crusade than on the crusaders themselves, but it was often in the context of negotiations for a truce that an exchange of prisoners was agreed. Some of them lacked the patience to wait.

Innocent III agreed to the foundation of an order, the Trinitarians, which collected alms to allow the repurchase of prisoners; it approached the patriarch of the Syrians and the Melchite patriarch of Alexandria to secure for the prisoners the consolation of religion. The temptation for them to deny their faith was strong. Joinville tells how he and his companions were asked under threat to declare themselves Muslims; he met a crusader from Champagne who had adopted Islam without great conviction and made a successful career for himself in Egypt; all the sailors from his ship had renounced their faith as soon as they were captured, which was not something in which the emir with whom the chronicler was conversing took any great pride. But the constancy of the crusaders in remaining true to their Christian faith gives an idea of how deep this was.

The songs always quote this faith as the counterpart to the regrets of absence. Thibaut of Champagne said he left everything for the one he loved so dearly. Others developed this idea or another: 'One must conquer paradise by accepting suffering'; the most common theme was that a man could not shirk the appeal addressed to him by God 'in his need', because God had deigned to die on the Cross for men. The castellan of Arras put it like this: 'I must go there where I will suffer in that Land where God suffered.' The idea of the Holy Land was always present in association with the memory of the Passion.

'He who remembers Our Lord ought to pursue his vengeance and deliver his land and his country', said the count of Champagne. 'It is very painful to lose the true Sepulchre where God was placed', wrote another; a third spoke of the 'great injury and pain that the pagans cause overseas in the land of Our Lord'. No doubts were expressed as regards the duty to recover the land where Christ had suffered, in gratitude for his sufferings, or as regards the justice of the cause the crusaders served.

One poet exclaimed that one should 'die happy and joyful for Christ'. But when a servant of the captive barons suggested that they should all let themselves be killed to go at once to Heaven, those who heard him did not agree and preferred to endure the sufferings of captivity.

Devotion to God's cause and the desire to serve him stopped short of fanaticism. The crusaders were men of their time, that of the balanced reason of the great medieval thinkers.

Their confidence in God, the Virgin and the intercession of the saints remained unshaken by ordeals and defeats. Many of those who had already experienced one or two expeditions and failures set out yet again for the East with a new crusade. Joinville did not leave again in 1270 with St Louis, but this was because he was harbouring grievances against the officers of the king and of the count of Champagne; it was perhaps also because he believed the king was ill advised in deciding to take the cross again. But he said not one word against the crusade itself.

It has to be acknowledged that if, in the thirteenth century, enthusiasm had been tempered, it was still present. But in the knightly and baronial world it had taken the form of the acceptance of a service, that which was owed to God, which had as its goal the recovery of the Holy Land, and which responded to Christ's sacrifice for men.

NON-INSTITUTIONAL CRUSADES

Though it had recruited from well-defined groups and disciplined the enthusiasm of the combatants, the crusade remained a movement which triggered the forces of collective emotion and exhilaration. It did not, therefore, remain confined within the parameters laid down by the conciliar decrees, and it strayed beyond the boundaries assigned to it by the promoters of regular expeditions. It is hardly surprising that, here and there, not only the Jews but also the clergy and its hierarchy came under attack.

There were anti-Jewish riots in England at the time of the Third Crusade, in March 1190. It seems that, in Stamford, it was the visible prosperity of the Jews that provoked the resentment and greed of the young men who gathered for the crusade, attacked their houses, looted them and committed other acts of violence. The movement had begun further east, in King's Lynn, where the looters fled in a boat with their booty.

The riots were more serious in York, where there were episodes reminiscent of those experienced in the Rhineland in 1096. Taken into the city castle, the Jews took refuge in the keep, pursued by the rioters. To escape the forced baptism they feared, the besieged Jews killed each other and, as in the Rhineland, this aroused the horror of the attackers who massacred those who tried to escape.

Doubts have been cast on the accounts of this event, which may owe something to the description of the capture of Masada by Flavius

Josephus. It remains the case that, after this bloodshed, the mob rushed to the minster, where the titles of the debts of the Jewish moneylenders were stored, and destroyed them; the movement seems to have originated among the small landowners of Yorkshire, and probably also those of Norfolk and Lincolnshire, heavily indebted to the Jews, for whom the moratorium on interest was not a sufficient relief at a time when they were incurring new costs in connection with the crusade; a social element is here combined with a religious element, of which there were other examples in England, where the Jews seem to have been widely unpopular. The monarchy did not leave these acts unpunished, but King Richard began by confiscating to his own benefit the fruits of the pillage.

Material considerations seem here to have taken precedence over the emotional atmosphere that accompanied the preaching of the crusade elsewhere. The appearance of luminous crosses in the sky during sermons preached in Friesland by Oliver of Paderborn was well attested; they seem to have caused the founding of a religious congregation. The psychologists of today may speak of collective hallucinations; the historian can only record a sign that is indicative of the climate of emotion and exaltation that surrounded the preaching of the Fifth Crusade.

Other phenomena were recorded at this time; there was another appearance of luminous crosses during a sermon aimed at recruiting crusaders for the Albigeois, near Châteaudun in 1212. That same year miraculous manifestations accompanied the strange movement which produced the children's crusades.

Though their existence is historically well documented, the events surrounding these crusades remain obscure. Were there two distinct movements, or only one, which was unobtrusively propagated before erupting at two points far removed from each other? Contemporaries, especially the men of the mid-thirteenth century, believed that these movements had been instigated by agents, but could not agree as to their identity.

If we put aside the still unresolved problem of the link between these two movements, whose chronology is difficult to establish, we are left with a shepherd by the name of Stephen, from the villages of Cloyes in the region of Vendôme, who claimed to have received from a mysterious pilgrim a letter which he was to deliver to the king of France. A crowd of people, most of them from a similar background to his and also young, joined him and marched in procession to St Denis, where they were received by Philip Augustus. They are supposed to have submitted their message to the masters of the university of Paris, who cast doubt on its supernatural character, and the thirty thousand or so people Stephen had collected eventually dispersed. We know that these young people had made banners, and that they cheered and shouted invocations such as: 'Lord God, exalt Christianity! Lord God, give us the True Cross!' The movement was essentially lay in origin, and some groups set out independently of that led by Stephen. The reference to the True Cross, which had been lost at Hattin, allows us to class the movement as a crusade.

The 'children' who set out from Lorraine, the Low Countries and the Rhineland, and who took as their leaders a certain Nicholas of Cologne, more clearly constitute a crusade. They too marched in procession, singing Latin and German songs, behind banners whose iconography is unknown. They descended the Rhone valley, and reached Genoa and north Italy. One story, probably legendary, has the young pilgrims taken up by shipowners from Marseilles who loaded them onto seven ships; two were shipwrecked, while the others, having reached Bougie and Alexandria, delivered their passengers to the Muslims who sold them into slavery. In fact, we know that the groups of 'children' from the Rhineland split up, that many of them returned home, and that others remained in Italy.

Those who followed Nicholas, and perhaps others from various parts of France, proclaimed their intention of going to the Holy Land and obtaining from God, armed only with penitence and thanks to Our Lord's love for children and the poor, the recovery that had eluded the powerful and the rich despite the resources at their disposal. The clergy as a body showed little enthusiasm for this movement; the townspeople, for example at St Quentin, gave them a warmer welcome.

The origins of this widespread movement remain unclear. The pope had asked the bishops to organise large processions of penitents, at Whitsuntide 1212, in the context of the imminent crusade against the Almohads, after preaching campaigns related to the crusade to the East and that against the Albigensians, and it has been suggested that this may have triggered, among large numbers of the faithful disturbed by all this propaganda, a premature departure of processions of a different type. Others have conjured up a vast and quasi-spontaneous popular movement. The fact remains that, in 1212, the theme of the cross and of Jerusalem drew bands of young pilgrims onto the roads, unclear as to their immediate purpose but inspired by an idea of crusade which was not that being prepared by the pope. This movement was still reverberating in 1213, when a number of English took the cross before having been officially asked to do so.

This movement of 1212 calls to mind others which did not have Jerusalem as their goal, those processions which marched in particular through Italy singing Alleluias, preaching an end to rancour and vengeance, and submission to divine will. The 'children' of 1212 included some who resorted to that spectacular manifestation of penitence, public self-flagellation. The processions of flagellants became more numerous. In 1260 there emerged in Perugia a great movement which filled the roads of Italy with flagellants and which lasted for several years. The eastern Christians were surprised, in 1260, to see flagellants land at Acre and process through Frankish Syria. Did they, too, feel a special devotion to Jerusalem and the desire to contribute to its liberation? The place of the Holy Land in the religious thinking of the thirteenth century means we cannot exclude this possibility. To bring about the reintegration of the Holy City into Christendom by way of penances – such as flagellation – and prayer rather than by force of arms was a notion not entirely alien even to pontifical admonitions.

The movement of the Pastoureaux of 1251 was of a different type. It emerged just when the king of France, after the defeat suffered by his troops in Egypt, had recovered his liberty and, from the Holy Land, had appealed to the queen mother and to his subjects to send more troops and further financial assistance. This news probably became widely known within the kingdom of France; in any case, it was the emotion aroused by the disaster suffered in Egypt that gave rise to this new movement, though the chroniclers imply that Blanche of Castile reacted as if her son remained a captive, which seems anachronistic.

The facts that are known, even though presented in very different forms in the different sources, again present us with a charismatic leader, the Master of Hungary, who, according to some, had left a Cistercian monastery, and who was probably called James. He appeared in northern France, on the borders of Picardy, Flanders, Hainault and Brabant, and claimed to have received from the Virgin Mary a letter giving him a mission to lead the movement. Once again shepherds, the least stable element in the rural population, formed the nucleus of his troops; he galvanised them by reminding them that, on Christmas night, it had been to shepherds that the angels had announced the birth of Christ, thus justifying their choice from among the faithful. The goal he proposed was the liberation of Jerusalem and of the captives.

The Master's army, whose members seem to have taken the cross, preceded by banners bearing the image of the crucified Lamb, numbered thirty thousand by the time they reached Amiens and almost twice that number when they arrived before Paris. The Pastoureaux were armed, with swords, axes and knives. When she was in Paris, Queen Blanche had a meeting with James, whom she welcomed, thinking that this mass levy might be useful to the king's projects. Till then, apparently, the movement seemed harmless. But it became suspect during the weeks that followed, when groups marched towards Rouen, where they caused the archbishop some problems, towards Orleans, where there was a full-scale riot between the Pastoureaux and the students of the university, twenty-five of whom were killed, and lastly towards Tours. Increasingly they attacked the clergy, whom the Master reviled, blaming Dominicans, Franciscans, Cistercians, Benedictines, canons and prelates, and denouncing the Roman curia, repeating the accusations of greed which found a ready audience in the mid-thirteenth century. The queen, informed of this shift of attitude, became uneasy and put the local authorities on the alert.

At Bourges, where the inhabitants opened the gates to the Pastoureaux in spite of the *bailli*, the exhortations of the Master of Hungary turned against the Jews, whose synagogues were invaded. The burgesses and the royal officers came to their defence and the repression began. The Master of Hungary and his main leaders were killed and their followers dispersed.

Others marched on Marseilles, but were stopped on the way. Others reached Bordeaux, where Simon de Montfort asked them to disperse. Yet others went to England, to Shoreham; they, too, were turned away and Henry III forbade them entry to his kingdom.

A significant number of the Pastoureaux eventually managed to reach the Holy Land and join the royal army, accepting the usual rules of the crusade. But the movement itself had combined two contradictory aspects: the wish to bring to the king of France, in difficulty overseas, that assistance that these peasants alone could provide, and the conviction of the moral superiority of the poor and the shepherds over the clergy and the nobility, whose greed and pride had angered God and caused the crusaders' failures.

Many of them said, we are told, that the Lord had chosen the weak to confound the strong. In fact, alongside a sincere piety and an incontrovertible desire to join the king's crusade overseas, there emerged an anti-establishment movement aimed both at the ecclesiastical world and at that of the lords.

Contemporaries went much further. It was alleged that the Master of Hungary had been behind the unhappy 'children crusade'. Others saw him as an impostor, fabricating false miracles and disseminating doctrines verging on heresy. It was even said that the sultan, through his agents, had tried to sow discord in France. In reality, the motives of the Pastoureaux were probably not very different from those of the knights who had taken the cross four years earlier. They, too, felt a sincere devotion for the Holy Land; the nobles, after all, saw themselves as poor pilgrims in Christ's service. But the 'shepherds' believed that they alone were able to maintain their purity of purpose, ignoring the inevitable constraints of an expedition such as theirs.

The crusade of the Pastoureaux was not a totally isolated and spontaneous movement; it can be seen as another crusade launched and organised in the usual fashion, but introducing an element which was alien to the schema desired by the Church. The fact that it was crushed when it attacked the Jews of Bourges is not without significance. The Jews were under royal protection, and this protection, which often failed, was here enforced.

The disorderliness of the years prior to the late twelfth century could now be avoided; the crusade had achieved the maturity of an institution, and there was no longer any place for anarchic initiatives, even in a kingdom that had suffered as badly as France, whose king had been routed in Egypt.

The crusade, in the definitive form it had assumed by the time of Pope Innocent III, had proved its efficiency in that it had made it possible to assemble large numbers of warriors, and to provide them with an embryonic organisation under the control of the pontifical legates, whose role had changed over time, and also with the means to reach their theatre of operations and remain there, sometimes for a very long time. Though regularised, it had not lost its character as a redemptive work, and the response of the faithful remained remarkable; between 1215 and 1270, indeed even between 1204 and 1215, there was a complete absence of disaffection.

Nevertheless, the loss of Jerusalem and of the Holy Places, which were not recovered till 1229 and then only precariously for some fifteen years, gave a different significance to their engagement. The indulgence retained all its power to motivate; thirteenth-century Christians sought out every type of grant of indulgence; when it was necessary to bury the victims of the Ayyubid raid on Sidon, the legate Eudes of Châteauroux attached an indulgence to the performance of this charitable work. St Louis was not the last to undertake this macabre labour to earn the indulgence.

But the trend that had started in the time of Alexander III had gathered pace. The remission of sins linked to participation in the expedition was dissociated from the visit to the Holy Sepulchre. This encouraged the use of the plenary indulgence for other enterprises than for the recovery of the Holy Land. Innocent III resorted to it for his battle against Markward of Anweiler, to combat the Albigensian heretics and to halt the Almoravid offensive in Spain. His successors continued down this road.

It was not that the pilgrimage to the Holy Places had lost its appeal. On the contrary, reading the crusade songs one is made aware that it was all pervasive. But it was less the visit to the Holy Sepulchre than the idea of its liberation that mattered, and this was linked to meditation on Christ's Passion, the object of a devotion which remained very strong, and on the debt owed by the Christian to his Redeemer.

To make this visit was clearly less easy than in the previous century. It is difficult to know how many Latin pilgrims were able to go to Jerusalem in periods of hostilities, though Christians of other rites, like the Armenians mentioned by Joinville, certainly made the pilgrimage.

At times of truce, the visit was possible, although Pope Gregory VIII had stipulated that in principle it ought to be authorised by the sovereign pontiff. The combatants who had laid down their arms hastened to Jerusalem; St Louis refused to take advantage of the safe conduct offered by the sultan, so as to follow the example of Richard the Lionheart; others were less scrupulous.

There were also large numbers of pilgrims who went to the Holy Land without belonging to a crusade. The statutes of the maritime towns regulated the conditions of their transport. The agreement reached in 1233, thanks to the efforts of the constable Eudes of Montbéliard, at Acre, between Marseilles and the military orders, stipulated that the Marseillais would allow the Temple and the Hospital each to load nine ships for the two passages of Easter and August, together receiving up to fifteen hundred pilgrims; they reserved for themselves the possibility of carrying many others, whom we find mentioned in contracts.

The guides intended for the pilgrims continued to be written, such as that of Albert of Stade which dates from 1251–2, and then the fullest of them, the *Description of the Holy Land* by the Dominican Burchard of Mont Sion, written after a journey across the country when it was under Mamluk occupation in 1285. The Muslims allowed the pilgrimage to be made, not least because it was very profitable to them; a note prepared for the pope in 1217 says that the sons of al-Adil who received the income from the sanctuaries obtained 20,000 bezants a year from visitors to the Holy Sepulchre; this compares with 30,000 bezants from Mecca.

The Holy Land remained present in Christian minds. If the crusade was itself an institution which promised participants the customary spiritual privileges, the liberation of the Holy Places and their restoration to the kingdom of Christ remained a very powerful motive. One need only compare the number of those who took part in the crusades to the Holy Land with those attracted by other expeditions that earned equivalent indulgences to realise this.

9

WAR AND DIPLOMACY: THE REBUILDING
OF THE KINGDOM OF JERUSALEM

The brief crisis which followed the end of the truce agreed four years earlier, in 1211, between Aimery of Lusignan and the sultan al-Adil, was to have far-reaching consequences. Al-Adil and most of the Frankish leaders wanted to renew the truce, but the Templars pressed for it to be broken, which provoked a surge of enthusiasm in Damascus, where the women offered their hair to the prince al-Muazzam, the town's governor, for the war machines destined to attack Acre. The sultan built a powerful fortress on Mount Tabor, which seemed to the Franks to be a direct threat to their city, though this construction was part of a whole programme of fortification undertaken by the sultan.

At this point, Maria of Montferrat, heiress to the kingdom, married John of Brienne, the baron from Champagne recommended by Philip Augustus to the Frankish envoys sent to ask him for a husband for their queen. John succeeded in restoring the truces with al-Adil. But the crisis had been serious and had revealed the fragility of the peace which had survived the Fourth Crusade.

This desire for peace should not, however, be forgotten. The Franks still aspired to reoccupy their ancient kingdom, but a longing for stability was apparent, and years of truce far outnumbered years of war. Richard the Lionheart and Saladin had tried to find a lasting *modus vivendi* between Muslims and Franks in the past. In 1207, al-Adil had agreed to sacrifice some of his possessions in order to restore peace. The Fifth Crusade was to show once again the power of the westerners and, paradoxically, pave the way for the peaceful settlement which the emperor Frederick II would, if only briefly, achieve.

INNOCENT III AND THE FIFTH CRUSADE

The deviation of the Fourth Crusade, a consequence in part of the disappointing response to the appeal launched in 1198 by Innocent III, had been a setback for the project the pope had conceived at the very beginning of his reign. His desire to liberate the Holy Sepulchre had not diminished, but he had been obliged, in the meantime, to turn his attention to the Albigensian Crusade, not forgetting the conflict between Otto of Brunswick and Frederick II in which he was involved.

The events of 1211 raised once again the problem of the East. And though it was not until 1213 that he announced the promulgation of a bull of crusade, the pope had indicated his concern for the East in 1211, as is shown by the letter he sent to the queen of Georgia to seek her help in the defence of the Holy Land. Then in 1212 and in 1213 he was concerned to organise great processions designed to appease God and to remind Christians of their duty to the Holy Places. In 1212 he even considered ending the Albigensian Crusade so that he could concentrate all his efforts on the question of Jerusalem.

The ardent desire to recover Jerusalem remained the main motive for the pope's actions, but the crusade was to take place in a changed atmosphere. That of the years 1188–1204 had something of the epic about it; the atmosphere of that of 1213–21 was more apocalyptic. It is tempting to evoke the figure of Joachim of Fiore, the Calabrian hermit who had died in 1202, leaving a work of prophetic character, in which he emphasised the gravity of the blows Islam had dealt to Christendom and announced its impending collapse. Innocent III was probably not directly influenced by Joachimite ideas, but he, too, had meditated on Islam in the context of the Apocalypse; for him, as for Joachim, the religion preached by Mahomet was imminent; the number of the Beast (666) was believed to be the number of years it would reign, which put the end of its reign in the thirteenth century. The end of Islam was thus close, and the crusade would hasten it. In fact, it was not only the Christian world that was affected by movements of an eschatological nature, since there was among the Jews, at this same period, an appeal for a return to their country of origin; in 1212 they arrived in large numbers, some at Acre, some at Jerusalem, others in Egypt.

Innocent III tried to make his crusade as large as possible; he contacted the Georgians, who were then advancing into Greater Armenia at the expense of Muslim states. He tried also, though without success, to achieve a reconciliation with the Byzantines of Nicaea; it was to them that he sent his legate Pelagius, to try to revive the negotiations that had been underway before 1204, at the time of the great council which, in November 1215, proclaimed the bull *Ad liberandum*.

But, while planning to resume the crusade on an unprecedented scale, Innocent III tried, though without much hope, to find peaceful means of establishing a lasting accord between the Ayyubids and the Franks. He wrote to the patriarch of Jerusalem instructing him to ask the Christians of the Holy Land to mend their ways so as to deserve to appease God's wrath, while awaiting the fulfilment of the project for the liberation of the Holy Land that was to be finalised by the Council.

The stubborn obstinacy of the Saracens is not accustomed to allowing itself to be softened by the humble prayers of Christians. However, to show our humility . . . we have written, taking the advice of wise men and fearing God, to the sultan of Damascus and Cairo. We wish to imitate the example that God gave us when he said of himself in the Gospel: 'Learn of me that I am sweet and humble of heart',

he wrote, asking the patriarch to convey his letter to 'Saphadin', the sultan al-Adil.

So we humbly beg Your Highness to be of wiser counsel and restore to us that land, so that its occupation is not the occasion of new effusions of human blood. From this occupation you probably draw less profit, vainglory apart, than trouble. When you have returned it to us, and the captives have been freed, we will consign to oblivion all the griefs to which these battles have given rise, so that the condition of those of our citizens who live in your country is no worse than that of your citizens in ours.

Al-Adil seems not to have replied to this missive. But the idea of a peaceful return of the old kingdom of Jerusalem to the Latins was not confined to Innocent III. The pope had wanted to be informed about the situation of the Muslim princes who had been Saladin's heirs and the patriarch of Jerusalem sent him a report which must date from 1217. It said that Saphadin had eliminated Saladin's direct heirs, his nephews, with the exception of the sultan of Aleppo; in fact, one of Saladin's sons, al-Zahir, maintained his independence in northern Syria, thanks to the support of the Seljuks of Konya. The patriarch listed his sons: al-Kamil, who would succeed him in Egypt; al-Muazzam, who held Damascus; al-Ashraf, in Mesopotamia; and he named a dozen others, each of them paying his father an annual sum of 20,000 bezants, equivalent to the income from the Holy Sepulchre. He added that the Ayyubids would be willing to return the land of Jerusalem to the pope if they could be sure that the Christians would hold it in peace, and that they would even be ready to pay tribute to the pope and the patriarch to be assured of peace.

The patriarch was no doubt deluding himself, but it is useful to know that the idea of an entente with the Muslim princes was not unique to

Innocent III. The Ayyubid empire, then at its height, was not ready to surrender Saladin's conquests. Al-Adil, though lacking enthusiasm for military adventures and having experience of war against the crusaders in 1188–91 and again in 1197–8, was securely established in power, but he maintained courteous relations with the Christians of the West, which may have deceived some of them as to his true intentions.

The pope's invitation was not followed up and preparations for the crusade went ahead. Plans were drawn up in 1213. But the truces would not expire till 1217. Innocent III decided to include the project to recover the Holy Land among the matters to be discussed at the Fourth Lateran Council, which he had convened for November 1215, and which was attended by eastern prelates, the patriarch of the Maronites and representatives of the Melchite patriarch of Alexandria; it was at this council that the bull *Ad liberandum* was drawn up.

But the legates had begun to preach, in particular Robert of Courçon in France, where his initiatives provoked a hostile reaction on the part of the French clergy. On 15 July 1215 at Aachen, the young Frederick II, when he received the royal crown of Germany, took the cross, apparently unexpectedly. The troubadours echoed the appeals of the preachers and we have already noted the atmosphere of enthusiasm that surrounded the preaching of men like Oliver of Paderborn. Peace had been restored in England, making it possible to extend recruitment to that country. But it was necessary to mollify the French nobility, who asked the pope to delay their departure by one year. The date fixed by the council, 1 June 1217, was therefore honoured by only some of the crusaders.

Large contingents, nevertheless, departed on that date. Those of Friesland and the Rhineland, with the counts of Holland and Wied, set sail on 29 May with almost 300 ships; some of them delayed long enough en route to seize the castle of Alcaser do Sal. King Andrew II of Hungary had negotiated with Venice to procure ships, relinquishing possession of Zara, but his army was so big that not all of it could embark; the dukes of Austria and Merano, who had reached Split before him, left more quickly. The effects of the preaching of James of Vitry were also felt in the East, since the barons and knights of the Latin East, with Bohemond IV of Antioch-Tripoli, Hugh I of Cyprus and John of Brienne, were present at the rendezvous. The army was so large that it was impossible to ensure that it was adequately provisioned and some of the crusaders re-embarked so as not to die of hunger; others engaged in acts of pillage.

The campaign began on 3 November 1217 with an offensive in the direction of the Jordan. The sultan al-Adil, rejecting the advice of his son al-Muazzam who urged a vigorous counter-offensive, abandoned

Bethsan, where he had established himself, and withdrew to Damascus. The crusaders crossed the Jordan and panic reigned in Damascus, but the Franks contented themselves with this demonstration. At the beginning of December they marched on Tabor, but after two unsuccessful assaults they withdrew in the direction of Acre. Al-Muazzam decided, nevertheless, to dismantle the fortress, apparently concluding that it was less impregnable than had been thought. A raid led by a Hungarian detachment into the hinterland of Sidon ended in disaster. At the beginning of 1218 Andrew II, who was sick, decided to return to Hungary. Hugh I of Cyprus and Bohemond IV accompanied him as far as Tripoli, where the former died, and he returned to his kingdom after crossing Armenia, the land of the Seljuks and the empire of Nicaea.

While awaiting the second wave of the crusade, the crusaders occupied themselves in rebuilding the fortifications of Caesarea and in constructing a new castle to bar the coastal route to the south of Acre; Walter of Avesnes took charge of this operation, and the fortress, called Chastel Pèlerin, the 'Castle of the Pilgrims' (Athlith), was entrusted to the Templars.

The Frisian and German ships arrived at Acre on 26 April 1218. Other contingents were expected, in particular the crusaders from Rome and the surrounding regions, for whom Innocent III had organised ships and assigned the sum of 3,000 silver marks, but whose equipment in all cost over 20,000 marks; the crusaders were to leave in summer, most notably the contingents of Duke Eudes III of Burgundy and of Hervé of Donzy, Count of Nevers and Hugh of Lusignan, Count of La Marche, with many prelates, including the archbishop of Bordeaux; but their appointed leader, Eudes III, died almost immediately after setting out.

Some English crusaders, with the earl of Chester, set out at the same time. The arrival of the emperor Frederick II was expected, but he gave no sign of making preparations and it was only on the orders of Pope Honorius III, at the end of 1218, that he announced his intention of convening a diet with the German princes in March 1219. Nevertheless, the participation of the 'king of the Romans' (Frederick was crowned emperor only in 1220) was assumed by the crusaders.

This staggering of departures gave a specific character to the Fifth Crusade. The French and German crusaders, who had arrived in the spring of 1218, were proposing to return to the West in the autumn; Duke Leopold of Austria, who had acted as the crusaders' leader after the departure of the king of Hungary, left in April 1219, after spending two years in the East and leaving a large sum (6,000 marks) to the Teutonic knights. His departure, unlike that of the king of Hungary, was regarded as quite normal; barons rarely spent more than two years on crusade.

The case of the English is typical; the earl of Chester left when the earl of Winchester arrived, and a third contingent, with Philip of Aubigny, arrived just as the crusade was ending.

In fact, preaching had continued. Pope Honorius III continued to support the crusaders by sending them reinforcements and money. It was only in 1221 that the cardinal-bishop of Ostia, Hugolin of Segni, proceeded through Lombardy to collect contributions and encourage the towns and the great lords to provide their contingents to the army, which was to be led by the marquis of Montferrat; he was to receive the sums collected, inasmuch as they were not sent to the East where the legate Pelagius was demanding money. The crusade showed signs of becoming a long war, with new contingents arriving to relieve those who had completed their service overseas.

The initial plan, that of a massive offensive, had thus been replaced by a longer-term project, which frustrated the plans of al-Adil. The sultan, imposing his views on his son al-Muazzam, was banking on the crusaders growing weary, expecting that, after an initial offensive conducted with vigour, they would soon lose heart and abandon active operations, which would have allowed him to recover the ground he had ceded.

It has been suggested that King John of Brienne and the barons of the Holy Land, counting on a massive arrival of crusaders, planned to double their Syrian campaign with another in Egypt, so as to force the sultan to loosen his grip on Palestine. In any case, at the beginning of 1218, John of Brienne obtained an agreement to transfer operations to Egypt, on the ground that the heat and lack of water ruled out a direct march on Jerusalem during the summer season.

The campaign of 1217–18 was not without its achievements: the fortress of Tabor had ceased to pose a threat to Acre, now covered to the south by Chastel Pèlerin. The first part of Innocent III's programme, the pope having died on 16 July 1216 trying to pacify central Italy with his crusade in mind, had been achieved.

THE EGYPTIAN CAMPAIGN OF THE LEGATE PELAGIUS

On 27 May 1217 the first ships that had left Acre with the crusaders on board, under the command of count Simon of Sarrebruck, appeared at the mouth of the branch of the Nile that commanded the town of Damietta, one of the three principal fortresses of Egypt. The troops landed and occupied an island where they would be safe while awaiting the arrival of the forces of King John, the duke of Austria and the military orders, and they began to dig entrenchments. By common assent, they chose John of Brienne as their leader. Warned by carrier pigeon, al-Kamil, who ruled Egypt for his father, who was in Syria, hastily assembled an army which took up a position opposite the Franks.

The choice of Egypt as the theatre of operations had already been discussed, as we have seen, and the Fourth Crusade had intended to attack 'Babylon', that is, Cairo. But there were two possible scenarios. Of all his possessions, Egypt was the one that provided the sultan with most in the way of resources and the means to maintain his military forces; some of the crusaders, including, it seems, John of Brienne, believed that, if Egypt was attacked, the sultan would prefer to sacrifice the Holy Land, which was much less rich and was remote from the great centres of Alexandria, Cairo and Damascus, rather than risk Egypt's loss or devastation. For others, Egypt was itself a tempting goal, devoid of the mountain ranges that could shelter resistance, lacking great fortresses other than Alexandria, Cairo and Damietta, and capable of supplying an army on campaign. Its conquest would allow the restoration of a Christianity that was still very present, the return of Christian worship to venerable churches, and the cult of Biblical souvenirs and of the sites redolent with memories of the Holy Family. Already, in 1168–9, King Amalric had dreamed of the conquest of Egypt; and we should remember that south of it lay the Christian kingdom of Nubia, and further south still that of Ethiopia.

But Damietta was a formidable fortress, protected by triple ramparts, commanding the entry to the Nile by means of a great tower, the Tower of the Chain, to which were attached the chains which barred access to the river. This tower, the first obstacle the crusaders would have to overcome, was defended by a strong garrison (three hundred men) equipped with balistas with which the defenders could bombard the assailants' ships. A first assault failed on 23 June, and a second on 1 July, when the ladder loaded with soldiers were toppled into the river. Oliver of Paderborn then constructed a floating wooden tower, mounted on two great ships, from which the assailants launched footbridges which enabled them to penetrate the tower's defences; it capitulated on 25 August.

The fall of the fortress made a deep impression on the Arab world, and it was said that the death of the sultan al-Adil on 31 August was caused by the shock. But the crusaders, faced with the Nile floods, decided to wait for reinforcements.

The Romans, the French and the English joined them between the end of August and the end of October. With them came two papal legates, Robert of Courçon, who died at the beginning of winter, and Pelagius, cardinal-bishop of Albano, who soon assumed a dominant role in the crusader council; as papal representative and because of the

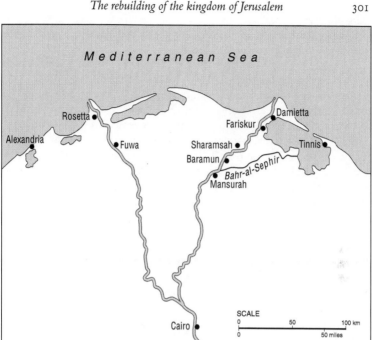

Map 15   The Nile Delta and the operations of 1218–21 and 1249–50

religious implications of the various decisions taken by the crusaders, he claimed an authority which eclipsed that of King John, whom many of the crusaders were in any case reluctant to recognise.

Al-Kamil, who had taken the title of sultan in Cairo at the same time that his brother, al-Muazzam, had taken it in Damascus, tried to block the course of the Nile upstream of the town. On 9 October 1218 he attempted a landing on the west bank, which John of Brienne was able to beat back. But then, discovering a conspiracy, al-Kamil fled, leaving his army leaderless. Panic ensued, and the sultan was only able to regroup his forces thanks to the arrival of al-Muazzam. But the crusaders had seized everything in his camp and had been able to establish themselves on the east bank. The siege of Damietta began (5 February), soon after Pelagius had ordered a general fast.

It was at this point, it seems, that the two Ayyubids decided to open negotiations with the crusaders. Al-Kamil offered, if they would evacuate Egypt, to relinquish the kingdom of Jerusalem, except for Kerak and Montreal, and to conclude a thirty years' truce. John of Brienne, the

Frankish barons and the French wanted to accept; Pelagius, supported by the Italians and the masters of the military orders, rejected these proposals, even improved by the offer of an indemnity of 30,000 bezants to compensate for the omission of Kerak and Montreal.

Despite the failure of the negotiations, the Ayyubids persisted in thinking that their adversaries would eventually accept their offers. Al-Muazzam ordered his officials in Syria to embark on the systematic dismantling of the fortresses of the old Latin kingdom, including Saphet, Banyas, Toron and, above all, Jerusalem, which provoked a wave of panic among the Muslim and Jewish populations. At the same time, he put pressure on the Jews and Christians of Egypt by extorting huge sums from them; the Copts and the Melchites were the victims of a general persecution, which provoked the exodus of many thousands of Copts to Nubia.

The siege of Damietta continued, the crusaders benefiting from the arrival of new contingents with the spring 'passage' of 1219. New engines were built to batter the walls; a general assault, attempted on 8 July, was repulsed by the defenders, who used Greek fire, and thanks to attacks by the sultan's army on the Christian rear. New assaults, on 13 and 31 July, suffered the same fate. On 29 August, in spite of the advice of the knights, the footsoldiers decided to launch an attack on the sultan's camp, which ended in disaster; John of Brienne and the knights were able to cover the army's retreat but it had suffered heavy losses through the numbers killed or taken prisoner.

The sultan, worried about the state of the besieged town, reopened negotiations. This time he promised to pay for the rebuilding of the fortifications of Jerusalem, to free those captives who could be found and to return the True Cross to the Christians. The two parties that had formed in February stuck to their positions, except that the English joined that of John of Brienne. But Pelagius, who was suspicious of the sultan's intentions, once again rejected his offers.

Finally, after the failure of an attempt on the part of the sultan to get provisions into Damietta, on 3 November 1219 it was decided to make a new effort to take the town. It fell almost without a battle, the garrison exhausted and the population depleted by famine (5 November 1219). The booty was considerable, but it seems that those who wanted to were allowed to leave the town. A few days later, the neighbouring town of Tinnis fell in its turn to the crusaders.

The occupation of Damietta divided the victors. The Italians accused the French of having defrauded them in the division of the spoils; Pelagius, who tried to reconcile them, was threatened, and there was fighting in the streets. The legate claimed the town as having been conquered by a crusade and refused to relinquish it, even in part, to John of Brienne, who claimed it as a dependency of the kingdom of Jerusalem; it was decided to put the decision in the hands of the pope.

In the end, by an agreement reached on 2 February 1220, the various quarters of the town were assigned to the different nations. The great mosque became a cathedral; in their quarter the English dedicated one church to St Edmund and another to St Thomas Becket. But the legate tried to prevent the future citizens of Damietta from settling in the quarter which had fallen to the kingdom of Jerusalem. Honorius III had confirmed his authority and he took advantage of this to behave as master of the city, especially when the departure of John of Brienne, who was anxious to press his claims to the throne of Armenia, left the field clear. He tried to forbid people from leaving, restricting the movement of ships; this allowed Muslim corsairs to burn, off Cyprus, the boat of the count of Katzenelnbogen, and many other ships fell victim to their attacks.

The capture of Damietta had an enormous impact on the Muslim world; the destruction of the walls of Jerusalem aggravated fears. Egypt now seemed defenceless and liable to fall into the hands of the crusaders. Al-Kamil appealed to all the forces of the Ayyubid empire, in particular to his brother al-Ashraf, who reigned in Diyarbakir.

The eastern Christians were equally uneasy. Thanks to Paul Pelliot we are able to attribute to them prophetic texts, copies of which were even found in Damietta. One is attributed to a 'Hannan son of Isaac', almost certainly the famous translator Hunayn ibn-Ishaq, who died in 873, who was regarded as an author of prophesies. The other is an *Apocalypse of St Peter* supposedly written by his disciple Clement. In fact, these two texts were clearly written under the impact of the events of 1219. The *Prophetie de Hannan*, which was written in Arabic, and which Pelagius had translated, foretold the ordeals suffered by the Christians, the capture of Acre, the massacre of the garrison, and the capture of Damietta by a 'tall, thin' man accompanied by a large army, which would be followed by the conquest of Cairo and Babylon, Aswan and Qus. There would then come a king of Abyssinia, who would destroy Mecca; a king from overseas would meanwhile have taken Damascus and both would meet in Jerusalem. The *Apocalypse of St Peter*, also written in Arabic, provided a history of the world up to the coming of the Anti-Christ, emphasising the fall of Damietta and the arrival of the two kings by whose hands the law of Mahomet would be destroyed.

The similarities between these texts and the ideas about the end of Islam expressed by Innocent III in his bull of 1215 are striking. They reveal, as Pelliot has shown, that the Christians of the East, whether they were 'Nestorians' or 'Jacobites', were also disposed to believe in the collapse of Islam, and that some of them wished to encourage the crusaders by disseminating prophesies which tended in this direction.

Another, very different, text, the *Relatio de Davide*, appeared the following year. It had been communicated to Bohemond IV by the spies he maintained in Muslim territory; less complete versions of it had been brought by merchants from Mesopotamia. This was the story of the conquests made at the expense of the Muslims by a 'King David', whose kingdom was located in the Indies and who had successively vanquished the sovereigns of the Kara Khitai, reigning beyond the Pamirs, of Ghazna and of Khwarizm and the Muslim dynasties of Iran, and who was on the point of subjugating the Abbasid caliphs of Baghdad. In fact, this referred to a real historical personage, the Naiman prince Küchlüg, who had conquered the land of the Kara Khitai and who had originally been Christian. But the *Relatio de Davide* was unaware that he had been defeated and killed by the Mongols of Genghis Khan and that it was the latter who had subjugated the Khwarizm and Iran.

In Damietta, the crusaders readily accepted this version of events and Pelagius made haste to communicate it to the pope, who made it known to the archbishops. The idea of the intervention of a powerful Christian king, reviving the hopes inspired by the figure of Prester John before the Second Crusade, was very encouraging. But the authors of these texts found it difficult to explain why these conquerors, deemed Christian, had attacked the kingdom of Georgia and inflicted a serious defeat on it.

For Pelagius, the Georgians were potential allies; he had asked them to support the crusade. In fact, they had expressed their regret that the unexpected attack of the Mongols had prevented them from bringing their assistance to the crusaders, which they would probably have done by attacking the Ayyubid lands ruled by al-Ashraf. The latter had had to decide between the help demanded of him by the caliph against the Mongols and that demanded by al-Kamil against the Franks. It is understandable why the historian Ibn al-Athir regarded the year 1219–20 as the most dangerous that Islam had yet experienced.

It is also understandable why, to Pelagius, more or less accurately informed about the problems of the Islamic world, the exchange of Damietta for the kingdom of Jerusalem seemed derisory; banking on the help of the Georgians and of the king of Ethiopia, he was expecting the imminent arrival of Frederick II who, according to the prophesies, would conquer Damascus.

The accounts of Oliver of Paderborn and James of Vitry reveal the influence of these texts within the legate's entourage. Al-Kamil seems to have repeated his offers to renounce all of Saladin's conquests except for the Transjordan and Arabia Petraea, but Pelagius was unimpressed.

Al-Muazzam tried to harry the Franks in Syria; he attacked Caesarea, whose fortifications had just been rebuilt; the Genoese were able to evacuate the town by sea before it fell. Chastel Pèlerin, twice besieged and defended by the Templars, successfully resisted (October 1220). Al-Kamil, meanwhile, had his troops build, at the point where the Bahr al-Saghir separates from the Damietta branch of the Nile, a great fortress, which he called 'The Victorious One' (al-Mansûra), to give Cairo the cover that Damietta could no longer provide.

A number of crusaders had returned to the West, feeling that they had done enough, but new arrivals were expected, in particular the troops of the emperor Frederick II, from his kingdoms of Germany and Italy.

Frederick got his projected crusade ratified by the Diet of Nuremberg in October 1219, four years after taking the cross. After his coronation and that of his son, Henry, in 1220, preparations had been speeded up. Cardinal Hugolin had obtained from Lombardy the support of nearly 450 knights, who were to be led by the marquis of Montferrat; the German princes had brought their contingents to Apulia and the first of them embarked in April 1221. Others followed in June. But Frederick had given orders that operations should not commence before his arrival.

Why did the legate decide to proceed with the attack as soon as the first imperial contingents arrived? It was suggested by Winkelmann that Pelagius, faithful to the pontifical conception of a crusade wholly directed by and to the benefit of the papacy, was unenthusiastic about a massive intervention by the emperor because it would deprive him of the fruits of his victory; he wanted to conquer Egypt before Frederick arrived. But James Powell has noted that the army led by Pelagius represented only part of the forces available at Damietta. Among those who supported his scheme was the duke of Bavaria, who declared that he had come to fight and that the Nile floods would soon render operations impossible. John of Brienne, who arrived with his troops on 6 July, tried in vain to argue the opposite case; the legate accused him of treason.

Was the plan to conquer Egypt, or simply, as James Powell believed, to drive the sultan's army out by expelling it from Mansurah? The approaching flood ruled out a prolonged campaign. In the event, it was as short as it was unhappy. Having set out on 17 July, the army occupied Sharamsah on 21 July. Three days later (still in spite of John of Brienne) it spread out along the Nile, flanked by an imposing flotilla, and reached Baramun.

But the three Ayyubid princes had assembled a large army. As the Nile swelled, the sultan was able to send ships by a secondary canal to cut the Franks off from Damietta, on which they depended for supplies. Land forces completed their encirclement, and retreat was impossible, especially as the flood was rising. An emissary, William of Gibelet, was sent to negotiate with al-Kamil, who, worried about the arrival of the emperor, refused to listen to those who advised him to destroy the Frankish army. King John negotiated with him and obtained fresh supplies.

The capitulation of Baramun was nearly not accepted at Damietta, where the imperial fleet had just arrived, commanded by the admiral, Henry of Malta, the chancellor of Sicily, Walter of Palear, and the chancellor of the empire; they took refuge behind the instructions of Frederick II.

The Venetians, and others from the imperial forces, wanted to attack the houses of the king, the Hospitallers and the Templars, and it was necessary to threaten to surrender Acre to the sultan to get the capitulation ratified. On 30 June 1221, this was done; the crusaders abandoned Damietta; an eight years' truce was concluded, with the stipulation, as in 1198, that it would cease to be effective if a crowned king took the cross. There was to be an exchange of prisoners, without ransom. The Muslims promised to return what they possessed of the True Cross.

The retreat of the crusaders was an immense relief to the Muslims, in proportion to the depth of their fears; the eastern Christians had to lick their wounds, and the patriarch Nicholas of Alexandria wrote to the pope to this effect.

The West had experienced a wave of enthusiasm to which the stream of contingents departing for Damietta bears witness. The disappointment was expressed in attacks on pontifical policy and demands for money; above all, the poets raged at the legate Pelagius, whose undeniable energy had greatly contributed to the victories, but whose stubbornness and inflexibility had helped to poison relations between the crusaders and the Franks of the East, before dragging the army into the unhappy episode of Baramun.

The vain wait for the imperial army had also contributed to the final defeat, and Pope Honorius III, in a letter of November 1219, reproached Frederick II for his procrastination. But the Fifth Crusade had, for the first time, made the Westerners listen to the eastern Christians. The appearance of the Mongols on their horizon had been only fleeting; it was to make itself felt more strongly in the following decades. Nor should we forget the apparently minor episode of the intervention of St Francis of Assisi, who penetrated as far as the sultan to ask him to accept the Christian faith; with him, the idea of mission made its appearance in the crusade.

FREDERICK II, KING OF JERUSALEM: ON THE MARGINS OF THE CRUSADE

The absence from the Fifth Crusade of Frederick II, whose arrival had been awaited with so much hope by the crusaders and with so much fear by the Muslims, weighed heavily on the course of events. It was probably because he was expected that active operations were abandoned during 1220, and this expectation probably encouraged the enemies of the compromise providing for the exchange of Damietta for Jerusalem, who were banking on the enormous power that would be at the crusaders' disposal once they were reinforced by the emperor's troops.

Frederick took the cross in 1215, but it was only in 1218 that he announced the meeting of a diet which would prepare the crusade for March 1219; it was held late in the year and, as we have seen, the first contingents of his army did not depart until 1221. Frederick had probably been anxious that his coronation as emperor, and that of his son Henry, should take place first. Honorius III reproached him for having let more than five years elapse in this way and Frederick agreed to depart on 24 June 1225.

The pope had also convoked a council of war, attended by John of Brienne and the masters of the military orders, to prepare the new expedition. It was then that it was decided to strengthen the emperor's resolve by marrying him (he had been a widower since the death of Constance of Aragon in 1222) to the daughter of John of Brienne by Maria of Montferrat, Isabella, heiress to the crown of Jerusalem, when she reached the age of fourteen. It was probably the pope who was behind this scheme; at any rate he made haste to grant the necessary dispensations – Isabella, through the Montferrat, being Frederick's cousin. Philip Augustus expressed reservations about this scheme.

The master of the Teutonic knights, Hermann of Salza, its principal negotiator, had promised John of Brienne that he would remain king of Jerusalem for life, and it was understood that Frederick would be crowned, according to custom, in the East. The marriage, celebrated in Tyre by proxy, was followed by the arrival of the young bride at her husband's side; he, without delay, had himself crowned at Foggia, adopted a new seal incorporating his title as king of Jerusalem, demanded that the barons who had accompanied Isabella did homage and informed John that he had no further right to the crown. Frederick may have feared that his father-in-law would form a party, as a result of the links of

the Brienne with the old Norman dynasty of Sicily. John protested but
had to leave Sicily, while Frederick sent the bishop of Melfi to receive
the homage of his new vassals and appointed the able Thomas, count of
Acerra, to govern the kingdom.

Frederick's marriage had earned him a further delay. By the treaty of
San Germano (25 July 1225), he promised to leave for the East on 15
August 1227 with a thousand knights to serve for two years, on pain of
excommunication.

The scale of the preparations was stepped up and the numbers
assembled exceeded what had been promised, though it had been
necessary to use force to obtain the contingents and financial aid of the
Lombard communes. On 15 August 1227 a large part of the army left
Brindisi. Frederick embarked on 8 September, accompanied by the
patriarch of Jerusalem, Gerold of Lausanne, but he left him to continue
alone and returned to port because he had fallen ill. The new pope,
Gregory IX, refused to believe in his sincerity and launched against him
the excommunication stipulated in the treaty of San Germano (29
September 1227). The pope probably had other reasons for quarrelling
with Frederick than the exasperation caused by his procrastination, in
particular with regard to the rights claimed by the papacy in the
kingdom of Sicily. But the conflict became increasingly bitter.

Frederick was in no hurry to reach the East. He set sail only on 28
June 1228, and then defying a formal prohibition by Gregory IX, who
had learned that he was taking with him only a hundred knights, and
who wanted him first to get the excommunication lifted.

The emperor's crusade thus began inauspiciously. He left under
sentence of excommunication, which, in principle, prevented other
Christians from having dealings with him, a prohibition that was largely
ignored by the emperor's vassals, but which greatly embarrassed the
Templars and the Hospitallers, who would only join his army on
condition that orders were not given in his name. The pope had not
appointed a legate to accompany the crusade, and the powers of legation
belonged to the patriarch of Jerusalem, who was determined to assert the
rights of his see. Above all, Frederick left wielding a dual sovereign
authority, that of the emperor and that of the king of Jerusalem. As
emperor, he could exploit the suzerainty which the kings of Cyprus and
Armenia had recognised to his father Henry VI. As king of Jerusalem, he
was in the paradoxical situation of a king who had taken the cross to
bring aid to his own kingdom.

Frederick was determined to exercise his rights both as emperor and as
king. He made this plain as soon as he arrived in Cyprus, which was then
governed in the name of the young King Henry by his uncle, John of

Ibelin, sire of Beirut. The Ibelin, a powerful lineage well established in the Holy Land and related to the royal families of Cyprus and Jerusalem, had made enemies, in particular among the families of the companions of Guy of Lusignan who had left Poitou to settle in Cyprus, the chief of whom was Aimery Barlais. They had made contact with Frederick, who intended to deprive John of Ibelin of his position, basing himself on the customs of the empire which allowed him to exercise wardship over heirs of fiefs who were minors and collect the revenues. Taking advantage of a meal to which he had invited John of Ibelin, he instructed him to surrender this government and account for his administration. John gave way on the first point. But Frederick also demanded the return of the fief of Beirut, as having belonged to the estate of the kings of Jerusalem. John refused, on the grounds that it had been given him as a fief at the time of its reconquest by the crusaders in 1197 and Frederick eventually accepted this.

He had nevertheless succeeded in imposing his authority on the kingdom of Cyprus and in enforcing imperial rights there. As he was short of money – so much so that he had to borrow 30,000 bezants from the sire of Gibelet – he could now hope that Cyprus would provide him with financial resources and the assistance of its army for his expedition. He failed, however, in his attempt to obtain the homage of Bohemond IV, prince of Antioch and count of Tripoli, who, to escape the emperor's power, feigned a fit of madness and managed to return to his lands without complying.

Frederick was to revisit Cyprus on his return from the Holy Land, in 1229; he took advantage of this to marry King Henry to a Montferrat, binding the Lusignan more closely into the imperial system, and entrusted the government of the island to five barons from the party hostile to the Ibelin, demanding from them a payment of 10,000 silver marks. To obtain this sum, the barons were obliged to put pressure on John of Ibelin's supporters. A conflict erupted, which quickly ended in a victory for John (June 1230) and the siege of Kantara, where his enemies had taken refuge and which capitulated early in 1231.

In his kingdom of Jerusalem, Frederick could count on the unconditional support of the Teutonic knights. His aim was twofold: the recovery of Jerusalem, the purpose of the crusade, and the consolidation of royal authority. As regards Jerusalem, he was successful thanks to negotiations with the sultan of Egypt to which we will return, but the restoration remained partial and the handful of other places returned to the Franks amounted to very little. Few of the barons of the kingdom recovered any of their lands; it was not they who benefited from this recovery, with the exception of Balian of Sidon, one of the emperor's cronies. Frederick, who had granted a fief of ten knights to a new arrival, the German Conrad of Hohenlohe, tried to recreate for the benefit of the Teutonic knights the great lordship that Count Joscelin had assembled before 1187 round Acre. He confirmed their purchase from one of Joscelin's daughters of her share of this lordship, and forced James of La Mandalée, son of Joscelin's other daughter, to surrender the other part, which enabled Hermann of Salza to build above Acre the powerful fortress of Montfort. Frederick granted them the royal manor of Jerusalem, and proposed also to give them Toron which the sultan had granted him; but the heiress of the former lords insisted on her rights and Frederick gave them instead the castle of Maron, while awaiting the outcome of the lawsuit. The impressive series of privileges given to the Teutonic knights at the time of Frederick's departure (April 1229) seemed highly significant.

But Frederick had taken pains to exclude the patriarch Gerold from his negotiations. This was resented all the more fiercely in that the patriarchs claimed a temporal as well as a spiritual authority; the memoir addressed in 1217–18 to the pope by the patriarch Ralph envisaged that, in case of an agreement with the sultan, the latter would be a tributary 'of the patriarch and of the Holy Roman Church', ignoring John of Brienne. Gerold vigorously denounced the treaty of Jaffa and, citing Frederick II's excommunication, wanted to place Jerusalem under an interdict, which would have prevented the crusaders from worshipping in the Holy Sepulchre. But Frederick was too quick for him; he marched to the Holy Sepulchre with the army, seized the crown from the altar and put it on, after which Hermann of Salza read a list of his grievances against the pope. The archbishop of Caesarea, instructed to announce the interdict, only arrived the next day.

Fearing an attack by the emperor, Gerold surrounded himself with troops. Frederick returned to Acre and prepared an assault on the residence of the patriarch and on that of the Templars, ordering all those who had armed against him to leave the town. But he was obliged to return as quickly as possible to his kingdom of Sicily, which had been invaded by John of Brienne. He left after giving orders for the destruction of the arms and the war machines that might be used by the patriarch. It is noteworthy that the barons of the kingdom were careful not to compromise themselves with the prelate; John of Ibelin remained in the emperor's entourage right to the end.

Although the crusade itself ended on a successful note, Frederick left behind a deeply divided country. Soon after his departure, a rival, Alice of Champagne, arrived, to claim the crown on the grounds that the death of Queen Isabella had deprived Frederick of his rights. But the barons recognised that the throne reverted to Isabella's son, Conrad, and asked the emperor, according to custom, to send him to the Holy Land within a year. Frederick was slow to reply. His representatives, Balian of Sidon and Garnier the Aleman, were torn between his desire to be obeyed and the stubborn opposition of the barons. When Frederick ordered them to deliver Toron to the Teutonic knights, in disregard of the judgement of the court that had recognised the rights of Alice of Armenia, she summoned her peers to join with her in refusing armed service, and Balian had to give way.

It was the recapture of Cyprus by John of Ibelin that struck the most serious blow to Frederick's authority, just when he had been reconciled with the pope. His response was to banish John and his principal supporters from the kingdom and seize their fiefs. Balian of Sidon was unable to enforce this command, as John had emphasised that he had in no way violated the king's rights in his kingdom of Jerusalem, and had got his peers to support him. Frederick then sent to the East an army composed of subjects from his kingdom of Sicily – called 'the Lango-bards' because they came from 'Langobardia' – under the command of his marshal, Richard Filangieri, who was to replace Balian as ruler of the kingdom. Filangieri besieged Beirut, but was unable to take it. John of Ibelin brought reinforcements from Cyprus and appealed to his suppor-ters in Acre. There, the knights and the bourgeois formed themselves within a fraternity into a self-defence league which became a commune and elected John as mayor (April 1232). Filangieri took advantage of the defeat of his enemies at Casal Imbert to carry the war to Cyprus, but he was defeated at Agridi and his troops, who had taken refuge in Kyrenia, eventually capitulated (3 April 1233).

Gregory IX had taken Frederick's side and tried in vain to find a compromise solution, on the basis of the replacement of Filangieri by someone less suspect in the eyes of the barons of the Holy Land, the grant of an amnesty to the rebels, the dissolution of the commune and the recognition of the king's authority. Frederick was reluctant to compromise, but was unable to repeat his effort of 1232.

The crusade of Frederick II had unforeseen consequences. The dispatch of Filangieri's army, which was large when compared with that of the Franks, had been intended not to contribute to the defence of the Holy Land, but to maintain Frederick's authority. The failure of this operation had resulted in the extension to the Latin East of the communal movement against which he was fighting in Italy.

But the coalition of the patriarch, the Temple and the Hospital, which had been formed in the aftermath of the emperor's excommuni-cation, did not last. Gregory IX had strongly rebuked Gerold of

Lausanne for his support of the commune of Acre, temporarily with-drawing his powers as legate. The Temple and the Hospital had been punished by Frederick who had confiscated their property in Sicily; but the Hospitallers had been reconciled to him, and he had restored their possessions. The Templars remained irredeemably hostile, and they made common cause with the barons opposed to the emperor. It was not by chance that, at the end of his life, the sire of Beirut became a brother of the Temple. And the Ibelin had rid themselves by exile of their enemies in Cyprus.

There remained, however, a third party which, without sharing the emperor's grudges, remained loyal to him; in their eyes, he was, in law, only the guardian of the true king, Conrad of Hohenstaufen. Balian of Sidon and Eudes of Montbéliard were its chief figures, and the former continued to be regarded by the barons as holding authority, Filangieri's investiture not having been properly performed. This enabled the king-dom's institutions to function regularly, that is, the Haute Cour, supreme juridical authority in feudal matters, the *parlement* which occasionally discussed common matters, and the officers, castellans or viscounts, who were responsible for everyday administration. But the deep divisions which existed made the pursuit of a common policy impossible. In a kingdom whose existence was based on an equilibrium in the middle of its powerful neighbours, this situation was fraught with danger.

Historians have been divided as to the causes of this crisis. It is clear that the way in which Frederick II, victorious in his kingdom of Sicily over the barons' aspirations for autonomy and enemy of the Italian communes which challenged his power, conceived the rights and powers of a sovereign was difficult to reconcile with the attachment of the barons of the Holy Land to their customs and privileges. The fact that he had to rely, to govern his kingdom, on someone so ill suited to compromise and maintain him so long in his position, was a consequence of his customary absence. But this, of course, was precisely because Frederick had gone as a crusader in order to assume the government of a kingdom which had come to him by hereditary right. This was the background to the crusades of the period 1228–44.

THE SIXTH CRUSADE AND THE TREATY OF JAFFA

The truces of Baramun, which, in 1221, had ended the Egyptian campaign, could not and did not appear as other than a temporary armistice; the representatives of Frederick II who had tried to prevent the surrender of Damietta to the Egyptians considered that the crusade had not ended since the emperor had not yet arrived.

In East and West alike, his imminent arrival was assumed. A few months after the evacuation of Damietta, Honorius III assembled the leaders of the Latin East to prepare the new campaign. Honorius had taken over the projects of Innocent III, and his successor, Gregory IX, who had preached the crusade in Lombardy and Tuscany when he was Cardinal Hugolin of Segni, was equally enthusiastic.

The feelings of the eastern Christians were no different. Queen Russudan of Georgia wrote to the pope, probably late in 1223, to tell him that the Georgians, prevented from responding to Pelagius' appeal by the Mongol invasion of 1221, intended to join the emperor's crusade, and asking him when it was due to depart. Iwane, constable of Georgia, had taken the cross and expected to lead forty thousand warriors. The kingdom of Georgia, then in full expansion, was in a position to intervene effectively against the Ayyubids in the Khilat region. The pope answered on 12 May 1224, rejoicing at the queen's news and extending the benefit of the plenary indulgence to the Georgian crusaders and their leader. Unfortunately, the Georgians had to face the attacks of the Khwarizmians of the sultan Jalal al-Din in 1226, and those of the Seljuks of Anatolia, and in 1228 it was Gregory IX who tried to organise a crusade to set out from Hungary, through the land of the Cumans (north of the Black Sea), to bring assistance to the Christians of Georgia.

In the West, there was no preaching campaign comparable to that which had preceded the Fifth Crusade. The crusade was preached in the territories belonging to the emperor, but not in France. In England, where the campaign had been slow to get off the ground, preaching continued. Many people left; Peter des Roches, Bishop of Winchester, took the cross in 1221; William Brewer, Bishop of Exeter, did the same, perhaps to fulfil the vow of his uncle, who had left him a treasury of 4,000 marks on deposit in Acre.

The Sixth Crusade was therefore partly an English crusade. It was on this occasion that Peter des Roches altered the constitution of the English hospital founded at Acre during the Third Crusade under the name of St Thomas Becket to make it a military order on the model of the Teutonic knights, the order of St Thomas the Martyr of Acre.

But the crusade was primarily that of Frederick II. Bishop Conrad of Hildesheim had preached it in Germany, where the landgrave of Thuringia and the duke of Limburg had taken the cross. In Lombardy, the towns at first resisted the emperor's demands, and the pope had to intervene before they would agree to send 400 men to join his army. The kingdom of Sicily provided 250 armed men. The 1,000 knights that Frederick had promised to lead had been found, even exceeded, but an epidemic caused many deaths. On the date agreed, 15 August 1227, the fleet set sail, carrying the new duke of Limburg, Henry, who was to be the leader of the crusade.

Frederick himself, as we have seen, left on 6 September but quickly returned, in all likelihood really struck down by the epidemic. Hermann of Salza had continued with twenty galleys, but it was only in May 1228 that the emperor followed, after sending a new detachment under the command of Richard Filangieri in April. Frederick had used the winter to recruit new troops, especially in Sicily, where he had ordered the levy of one knight in eight. But his own detachment was relatively small, only forty ships being needed to carry it.

As a result of these staggered arrivals, it had been impossible to embark on operations before Frederick's arrival; the agreement made at Baramun allowed for the truce to be broken only if a crowned king arrived in Syria. When a group of crusaders led a raid of pillage into Muslim territory, Richard Filangieri punished them harshly and returned their booty and prisoners to the sultan's officials. A large number of crusaders then decided to return to the West, though no doubt fewer than the 40,000 that has sometimes been suggested; the army present at Caesarea the following year numbered in all some 800 knights and 10,000 men.

The presence of the army and the financial resources at its disposal had been put to good use in a programme of fortification. The French, unable to rebuild the walls of the town as a whole, reconstructed the 'sea castle' of Sidon. The bishop of Winchester largely paid for the restoration of the ramparts of Caesarea and began work on those of Jaffa. The Germans put themselves at the disposal of the Teutonic knights to build the powerful fortress of Montfort.

As a result of his stay in Cyprus, Frederick arrived at Acre only on 7 September. It was not until November that he left. In fact, unknown to the majority of the crusaders and probably to the Franks of the Holy Land, he had probably decided even before his arrival not to risk his fate in battle.

Since 1226, in fact, the emperor had been in contact with the Ayyubid sultan, al-Kamil. The accord between al-Adil's sons had not long survived their father's death; al-Muazzam, who ruled in Damascus, feared he would be dispossessed of this town by al-Kamil and had turned to the sultan of Khwarizm, Jalal al-Din, who, driven out of his eastern territories by the Mongols, was building himself a new dominion south of the Caucasus. Al-Muazzam recognised his sovereignty and had his name proclaimed in public prayers in place of that of the sultan of Egypt. Al-Kamil, in his turn, took fright. Fearing treachery on the part of his emirs, he sent Frederick a confidential messenger, Fakhr al-Din Ibn al-Shaikh, seeking the assistance of the emperor against his brother, and offering in return to restore Saladin's conquests. Frederick responded to these overtures by sending Archbishop Berard of Palermo to Cairo, though also then on to Damascus to sound out the intentions of al-Muazzam, whose reply was a blunt refusal.

Al-Kamil pressed on with negotiations which probably stipulated generous concessions to Frederick. But in November 1227 al-Muazzam died, and al-Kamil made haste to invade the lands of his son, al-Nasir Dawud, occupying, in particular, Jerusalem. So, before Frederick had left the West, circumstances had altered radically: al-Kamil and his brother al-Ashraf, from whom Jalal al-Din had taken Khilat, made an agreement to share al-Muazzam's inheritance, and the assistance of Frederick II became superfluous.

Frederick reacted by sending Thomas of Acerra and Balian of Sidon to the sultan of Egypt to remind him of his promises. Fakhr al-Din having returned, Frederick used all his skills to try to convince him that he, Frederick, had come to the East only in response to his invitation, and that he could hardly leave without achieving some tangible result, or he would lose face.

When the sultan procrastinated, Frederick decided on a show of force and marched his troops to Jaffa, to complete the rebuilding of the fortifications. To his barons and to the crusaders, he explained this move by his desire to assure himself of a convenient base for an imminent campaign with Jerusalem as its goal. But he received disturbing news from Italy and, we are told, he had already instructed his admiral, Henry of Malta, to have his ships ready for him to return in spring. A speedy settlement was necessary; happily for him, the siege of Damascus by the two Ayyubid brothers dragged on, and al-Kamil, too, wanted to have his hands free.

So, on 11 February 1229, Frederick's representatives concluded with those of the sultan the treaty of Jaffa, which had been negotiated in the strictest secrecy and whose text was not even communicated to the patriarch. This treaty consisted of the proclamation of a truce for ten years, five months and forty days (the length corresponding in the Muslim calendar to ten years in the Julian calendar – the text that survives is a French translation of an Arab original); it applied only to the kingdom of Jerusalem, excluding the principality of Antioch, the county of Tripoli and the domains of the Hospital and the Temple at the Crac, Chastel Blanc, Tortosa and Margat, Frederick prohibiting his subjects from providing assistance to the latter in the event of conflict with the sultan. The crucial clause was the grant to the emperor of 'Jerusalem the exalted', which he would have the right, it seems, to fortify; the town had been dismantled, as we have seen, by al-Muazzam.

But al-Kamil had refused to include the mosque al-Aqsa and the Dome of the Rock, even saying that the caliph would call him an unbeliever if he abandoned places as holy for the Muslims as the Holy Sepulchre was for the Christians.

Christian pilgrims would be allowed to visit the Temple, on condition that they behaved with due devotion and discretion; Nazareth and Bethlehem were also returned to the Christians, each of them to have a corridor connecting with Frankish territory.

A Muslim judge was to reside in Jerusalem to hear the cases of his co-religionists. A few minor territorial concessions completed the treaty: full ownership of lands hitherto contested or divided (Sidon, Jaffa and Caesarea) and the grant of Toron, which must not be refortified. Lastly, prisoners of war were to be returned.

This treaty has been much discussed by historians; it is particularly instructive to compare the pages devoted to it by René Grousset in his *Histoire des croisades*, where he shares the hostility of thirteenth-century Frankish authors, with those written by the same historian in his *Figures de proue*, after a reconsideration of the personality of Frederick II. Setting aside the accusations of Islamophilia and amateurism that have been made against the emperor, he raised the question of deeper motives.

Certainly, Frederick II, in his relations with the Muslim princes, played the role of a sovereign open to Arab civilisation, taking pleasure in exchanges of correspondence, just as his Norman predecessors at Palermo had maintained at their courts poets who sang their praises in the Arab language; during his stay in the East, he adopted attitudes bordering on the provocative with regard to the Latin Church, praising the Muslims for choosing their caliphs from the family of the Prophet when Christians chose popes of obscure origins, and imposing silence on Christian priests to demonstrate his respect for Muslim worship.

But it was also Frederick who dismantled the structure of Sicilian Islam and deported the Muslims in Apulia, and who respected the Christian faith more than his enemies allowed. Were Frederick and al-Kamil two spirits ahead of their times who had realised the necessity of bringing to an end a conflict that was leading nowhere, by adopting a lasting compromise? The Holy Places of Islam under Muslim control; those of Christianity under Christian control: this was a solution to the problem of Jerusalem found at other periods. But the question remains: the conclusion of a truce, and not a peace treaty, was a retreat from the solution considered in 1213 by Innocent III. The compromise of 1229 may have been the product of the reflection of two political minds anxious to establish a lasting peace, or an expedient allowing each of them to extricate himself from a situation in which he had been placed by intrigues and mishaps.

The reception given to the treaty, on both sides, suggests a general unpreparedness to accept it. On the Muslim side, al-Nasir of Damascus tried to exploit against his uncles a withdrawal which he presented as shameful; the preachers in the entourage of al-Kamil demonstrated their hostility by uttering, at the door of his tent, off-key appeals to prayer.

In the crusading army, the Germans and most of the English were delighted at the prospect of fulfilling their vow and visiting the Holy Places, which made them deeply resentful when the archbishop of Caesarea tried to prevent them. Others expressed their discontent; one of the English preachers of the crusade, the Dominican Walter, as a sign of protest, celebrated a mass outside the walls of the Holy City.

The barons of the Holy Land were inevitably divided, especially since Balian of Ibelin had been one of the negotiators; Frederick had paid little attention to the interests of the barons dispossessed by Saladin's conquests. The most vociferous critic, however, was the patriarch Gerold, when he at last managed to get hold of a copy of the treaty. He commented on its clauses in a document which Gregory IX disseminated widely. Some historians have presented Gerold as a fanatic, immovable in his hatred of the Saracens and unable to envisage any other relations with them than in war; in fact, he criticised the emperor for having failed to use the military force at his disposal to impose a less scandalous treaty on the Muslims.

To the patriarch, the scandal was that Frederick had negotiated in his own name, without regard for the Church or the pilgrims, and that he had conducted his negotiations while deceiving them as to his intentions; in fact, he had decided on his departure well before Christmas, on the grounds that he was short of money, and excluded the patriarch, legate of the Holy See, from the negotiations. Further, dealing with al-Kamil, who had just occupied Jerusalem, he had ignored the probable claims of the sultan of Damascus, thus exposing the city to his designs.

The recovery of Jerusalem, he went on, was incomplete. The town had been granted to the emperor without its hinterland; the ecclesiastical institutions – the patriarchate, the Hospital, St Mary Latin, Mount Sion, Josaphat, the Mount of Olives and the Temple of the Lord – would not recover the property on which they depended. Only the Templars recovered several places on the road from Jerusalem to Jaffa. To leave the Temple to the Muslims was to forget what it meant to Christians (the pope spelled this out: it was the place where Christ had preached, Jerusalem's first cathedral); Christian visitors would be admitted if they believed what the Saracens believed, whereas all Muslims could enter Bethlehem without having to meet any conditions.

The exclusion of the other Christian lands from the benefits of the truce also provoked the patriarch's wrath. Gregory IX repeated these grievances, claiming that, by dealing in this way with the sultan, the emperor had deprived himself of his office. Hermann of Salza, on the other hand, emphasised the scale of what had been recovered – the road from Jerusalem to Bethlehem and to Jaffa, with the villages through which it passed, that from Acre to Nazareth, etc.

The protestations of the patriarch were not without some foundation. The question of the right to rebuild the walls of Jerusalem had been left obscure. The French text of the accord ('qu'il en face que ilh vodra de garnir ou autre chose') allowed for the possibility of fortifying the town; Arab authors claimed that this was precluded. Frederick assembled the leaders of the crusade and the great barons to discuss this refortification, but, when the town was put under an interdict, he left it before a decision had been taken. Some work was later done on the walls, but it was never completed; given the enclave constituted by the Temple and the mosque al-Aqsa, difficulties were inevitable.

Did the town become entirely Christian? We know that prior to 1187 the Jews and the Muslims were not allowed to reside there on a permanent basis. The treaty stipulates the presence of a *qadi* to adjudicate in Muslim cases. Frederick seems initially to have forbidden the Jews the right to live in Jerusalem, but, as before 1187, exception was made for the Jewish dyers, whose right to give lodgings to those of their co-religionists who came on a pilgrimage to the Holy City was expressly authorised in 1236.

The conditions under which the treaty was signed, both the fact that the emperor was excommunicate and that the patriarch was excluded from the negotiations, and the hurried nature of some of the clauses, which left many matters unclear, meant it could not provide a permanent solution. Frederick could probably have obtained more favourable conditions by giving his support to al-Kamil at the period when he had felt himself to be in real difficulties, that is, before the death of al-Muazzam. But Frederick would then have been faced with a sultan of Damascus exercising real power in Jerusalem.

Gregory IX was reconciled with Frederick II in May 1230. The treaty then became that obtained by 'our very dear son Frederick', thanks to whom 'this city has been restored except for the Temple of the Lord', which remained 'abandoned to the stain' of the infidel. The pope accepted it, whilst recognising it to be provisional and incomplete.

THE BARONS' CRUSADE

In letters written to the English on 4 September 1234, and to the French on the following 7 November, Pope Gregory IX warned them that the truce concluded with the sultan was about to come to an end, and that time was short to prepare the expedition that was indispensable to the survival of the Holy Land. He suggested that its situation remained precarious.

In fact, the Frankish occupation following the treaty of Jaffa remained very restricted. Even in Jerusalem, those who had resettled there and who quickly began to rebuild it, especially in the quarter assigned to the Teutonic knights, were exposed to sudden attacks. By the end of 1229, the Muslim villagers of the surrounding region, stirred up by their *faqi* (the preachers in the mosques), attacked the town, which had only makeshift defences. The two *baillis* of the emperor, Balian of Sidon and Garnier the Aleman, warned in time, were able to rescue the inhabitants, who had taken refuge in the Tower of David.

But this showed the necessity of rebuilding the walls. The pilgrimage route, meanwhile, was so unsafe that the pope, on 9 March 1238, instructed the Templars to restore its security by garrisoning it with armed men, because the Saracens were ambushing pilgrims between Jaffa and Caesarea. He added that, if they were unable to do this, the protection of the route would be entrusted to Count Walter of Brienne, who held Jaffa, for a period of five years, in return for a payment of 2 *tournois* by every pilgrim.

The truce concluded in 1229 did not apply to the lands situated to the north of the kingdom of Jerusalem, in particular those belonging to Tripoli, the Crac des Chevaliers and Chastel Blanc. The Hospitallers of the Crac demanded payment of tribute by the Ayyubid prince of Hamah, which he refused. A series of raids conducted by the knights between 1229 and 1233 culminated, in October 1233, in a much larger campaign in which the contingents of Bohemond V of Antioch-Tripoli, the Templars, and knights from Jerusalem, led by Peter of Avallon, and from Cyprus took part.

They were preparing another attack early in 1234 when the army of the sultan al-Kamil, marching north against the Seljuks, camped near Hamah. The sultan imposed his mediation and the prince of Hamah accepted a compromise. But the conflict seems to have resumed over the castle of Montferrat, which commanded the pass leading from the Crac to Hamah, which had been occupied (probably in 1236) by the Hospitallers, then recovered and dismantled by the Ayyubid in 1238–9.

The Templars, meanwhile, had attempted a surprise attack on Darbsak, on the borders of Aleppo, which failed (1237).

But these frontier disputes hardly endangered the Holy Land. Gregory IX thus felt able to respond to the appeals reaching him from the Latin Empire of Constantinople, where John of Brienne had assumed the imperial crown to rule in the name of the young Baldwin II of Courtenay (1230). Threatened by a coalition between the tsar of the Bulgars, John Asen, and the emperor of Nicaea, the two emperors asked for assistance, and the pope suggested to those who had already taken the cross that they go to Constantinople rather than to the Holy Land (1236). This appeal had some success; some crusaders left, some by sea with John of Béthune (1238), others by land with Humbert of Beaujeu and Thomas of Marle, to whom the king of France had provided financial assistance comparable to that which he gave to the young Baldwin II, who pawned his county of Namur to him. The tsar having changed his policies, the crusaders confined themselves to a few operations in Thrace (1239).

The majority of the crusaders, however, remained faithful to the initial aim of the crusade, and Gregory IX switched his attention back to that. This crusade assumed a specific character. It was essentially the act of the great feudatories of the kingdoms of France and England. In France, the rebellions which had marked the first years of the reign of Louis IX had led, as a form of punishment, to a commitment by many barons to go overseas; they included the duke of Brittany, Peter Mauclerc, who had promised that as soon as his son was old enough to govern, he would go to the Holy Land for five years (1234). Thibaut IV of Champagne, king of Navarre, had already taken the cross when the king, having put down his revolt (1236), insisted he spend seven years outside the kingdom of France. Ties of lineage, in particular within the families of Dreux and Blois-Champagne, led others to take the cross, including Duke Hugh IV of Burgundy, John of Braine, Count of Mâcon, Guigues, and Count of Forez and Nevers, and the counts of Bar le Duc, Grandpré and Sancerre; others, such as Amalric of Montfort and Robert of Courtenay, did the same.

The king of France encouraged them to take the cross; he bought the country of Mâcon from John of Braine, brother of Peter Mauclerc; he gave generously towards the crusaders' equipment; he agreed to accept as security castles, such as Champtoceaux, pawned to him by the duke of Brittany, in return for cash loans. And he gave 32,000 *livres* to the constable of France, Amalric of Montfort, granting him the right to wear his arms. Thus the expedition, which comprised some 1,500 knights, took on the appearance of a campaign by the royal army, under the royal banner.

In England, the crisis experienced by the kingdom during the minority of Henry III had discouraged recruitment, but the crusade appeared to some barons as an opportunity to be reconciled with their enemies, for example the king's brother, Richard of Cornwall, and Gilbert Marshal, in 1236. Simon de Montfort, Earl of Leicester, William Longsword and others took the cross. Gregory IX, however, wondered whether Richard had a more pressing duty, that of helping his brother to keep peace in his kingdom, and he asked him not to leave (1238). But the earl of Cornwall, worn down by the conflicts he had tried ceaselessly to resolve, stuck to his decision. Nevertheless, it was only on 12 November 1239, at Northampton, that the barons of the two parties swore to go to the Holy Land, ignoring the other proposals.

The French barons had preceded them. They had contacted Frederick II, who had insisted that they delay their departure till 1239 in order not to break the truces, and who, pressed by them to assume leadership of the expedition, had promised to join them or at least to send his son, Conrad; this would have been a way of reviving his plans of 1228, by giving the young prince, in theory recognised by all the barons of Jerusalem as their legitimate king, the occasion to act as king. But the resumption of his conflict with Gregory IX, who excommunicated him in March 1239, and his campaign against the Lombard towns prevented him from following up his proposal. He had offered the ports of his kingdom as a base for their departure, and facilities for revictualling. Gregory IX persuaded the barons not to accept his offers. In the end, some left from Brindisi and the others from Marseilles or the ports of Languedoc.

On receiving news that the crusade was under way, the leaders of the Holy Land – the archbishop of Nicosia, Eustorgius of Montaigu, vicar of the patriarch of Jerusalem, the archbishop of Nazareth, the bishops of Lydda and Acre, the abbot of the Temple of Our Lord, the masters of the Temple and the Hospital, Eudes of Montbéliard, in his capacity as constable, Walter of Brienne, Balian of Sidon and John of Caesarea – met at Acre on 6 October 1238 and wrote a letter to Thibaut IV, who had been elected leader of the expedition. They recommended, contrary to Frederick II, not waiting for the expiry of the truces, since these were not being observed (in the attacks on pilgrims) and urged a landing in Cyprus to procure the necessary provisions and to finalise a plan of campaign, in particular to decide whether to proceed to Egypt or to Syria.

In fact, the pope had agreed to defer the departure till the following

year. And when the crusaders arrived in the East, the truces had expired;
it was in September 1239 that Thibaut of Navarre, who had been
recognised as leader after Frederick II had refused, landed at Acre. But
the situation they found in the Near East was no longer what they had
expected. The Ayyubid empire, already divided at the time of Frederick
II's crusade, was disintegrating. It had faced in succession the offensive of
the sultan of Khwarizm, Jalal al-Din, then, after his death (1231), the
advance of the Seljuks of Anatolia towards the Jazirah.

Al-Kamil had installed his eldest son, al-Salih Ayyub, in this region, at
Hisn Kaifa; but, on his death, in September 1238, Ayyub revealed his
intention of disputing Egypt with his younger brother al-Adil II, who
had been proclaimed sultan there, and he eventually occupied Damascus
in December 1238; his uncle, Ismail, took the town from him on 30
September 1239 and was himself captured by his cousin Dawud, prince
of Kerak, who freed him the following year, allowing him to become
sultan in place of al-Adil in May.

The crusaders arrived just as Damascus separated from Egypt, and
when none of the rivals had yet thought of making contact with the
Franks. It was thus difficult to open a line of negotiation as had been
done in 1228–9. It was decided first to reconstruct the walls of Ascalon,
then to march on Damascus, which had the serious disadvantage of
alienating both the sultan of Egypt and the future sultan of Damascus,
though the two rulers seem not to have attempted to act in concert.

Before setting out for Ascalon, the Count of Brittany, Peter Mauclerc,
launched an attack on a large caravan which was carrying foodstuffs from
Egypt to Damascus and seized a considerable quantity of booty which
provided food for the army (4 November 1239). The count of Bar,
anxious to equal this success, surprised an Egyptian detachment which
was heading for Ascalon, despite the entreaties of Thibaut, who had not
been informed.

The king could only assemble the main body of his troops to support
these advance elements which comprised some 400 to 600 knights. They
had already crossed the stream which marked the frontier near Gaza and
settled down to eat in a valley surrounded by dunes. Walter of Brienne
gave the alarm, but the crusaders were already encircled; Amalric of
Montfort deployed his crossbowmen and the knights charged, falling for
the stratagem of the simulated flight. The count of Bar was killed,
Amalric and about eighty knights and many sergeants were captured; the
bodies of 33 knights and 500 footsoldiers remained on the battlefield.
The duke of Burgundy and Walter of Brienne had been able to join the
main army, which gathered up a number of fugitives but which dared
not pursue the enemy for fear of provoking a massacre of the captives (13

November). They returned to Acre, where they decided to rebuild the castle of Saphet.

The defeat encouraged the king of Transjordan, Dawud, who had already tried an attack on Jerusalem towards the end of August, to march on the town, which had hastily begun to fortify. The defenders withdrew into the Tower of David, which held out for nearly a month; they capitulated and were allowed to return to Acre under escort (mid-December 1239), but Dawud razed the citadel to the ground.

The quarrels between the Muslim princes, however, grew worse. The prince of Hamah, a supporter of Ayyub, feeling threatened by his neighbours of Damascus and Homs, was the first to ask for help from the Franks; he sent them a missionary he knew, William Champenois, who may be the famous Dominican William of Tripoli, letting it be understood that, if the Franks came to his aid, he would declare himself a Christian. Thibaut led his army to Tripoli, to learn that the prince, having got rid of his enemies, had broken off discussions.

In May 1240 Ayyub had just acceded to the throne of Egypt after the deposition of his brother, in collusion with Dawud of Kerak. This made his uncle, Ismail, master of Damascus, extremely uneasy, and he opened negotiations with the king of Navarre, promising to surrender immediately to the Christians the hinterland of Sidon, with the fortress of Beaufort, Tiberias and Saphet, and promising to return other lands – according to some the whole of the old kingdom of Jerusalem as far as the River Jordan – but these were lands held either by Dawud or Ayyub.

In return, the Franks promised not to make a peace or a truce with the sultan of Egypt without his consent, and to march on Jaffa and Ascalon to bar the route to the sultan of Egypt.

This agreement was strongly resisted by the garrison of Belfort and Ismail had to besiege it before he could return it to the Franks. The Hospitallers demonstrated some hostility (perhaps because they were attached to the policy of entente with Egypt, in line with Frederick II) and the relatives of the captives complained that they had been forgotten.

The army then returned to Ascalon; it was joined, near Jaffa, by the sultan of Damascus and his troops. It has been claimed that the allies met an Egyptian force which inflicted a defeat on them; if this was the case, it was probably on a small scale. But Thibaut was approached by emissaries of the sultan Ayyub, who proposed a truce, promising to free the captives.

This assumed that the promises made to the sultan of Damascus would not be kept. But before resolving these problems, Thibaut of Navarre and the count of Brittany took advantage of the truce to make their

pilgrimage to Jerusalem and, in mid-September 1240, they re-embarked.
The crusade had not finished; the arrival of the English crusaders was
expected, and many problems remained, which it would be for the
brother of the king of England to resolve.

Historians have been very critical of Thibaut's crusade, but this
criticism needs to be qualified; he had succeeded, without engaging in a
major battle, in adding to the land which Frederick II had earlier
recovered. The barons of 1239–40, whatever their love of dashing
military deeds, had adopted the programme outlined at the time of the
Fifth Crusade, that of a combination of a military presence and
diplomatic activity. The king of Navarre had successively deployed his
forces in response to the approaches of the prince of Hamah and the
sultan of Damascus, before finally concluding an agreement with the
sultan of Cairo. The idea of solving the question of the Holy Land by
negotiation had entered into people's thinking.

Nothing reveals this more clearly than the compilation at this period
of a memorandum entitled: 'This contains all the land held by the
sultan'. It lists the lordships comprising the kingdom of Jerusalem,
mentioning in passing who had formerly held them: Ascalon, Gaza,
Sebastia and Nablus, Grand Gerin, the Casal des Pleins and La Fève,
Hebron, the Castle of Figs, Tafila, the Crac of Moab, Montreal and the
places around it, and Le Vaux Moyse (Wadi Musa), in other words all
the land of Montreal and Oultrejourdain. It returned to Galilee with
Sephorie, Neeme, Bethsaida, Tabor, Buria, Belvoir and the Jordan valley
as far as the Dead Sea, Jericho, the whole land of Tiberias, the Cave de
Sueth, Saphet, Châteauneuf, Jacob's Ford, Banyas with all the mountains
beyond Tyre, Beaufort, Belhacem and the whole mountainous country
of the diocese of Beirut.

This list, which shows what the Franks hoped to be able to recover,
was probably drawn up to facilitate the negotiations with the sultan. It is
probable that it antedates the treaty of 1240, since Saphet, Beaufort and
Tiberias are still given as in the hands of the sultan. But the recovery of
these places became a matter of negotiation.

'OUR ROYAL TREATY' AND THE END OF A POLICY

The ships which were carrying Thibaut of Champagne and Peter
Mauclerc back to Europe may well have crossed at sea with those taking
out to the East some eight hundred knights from the kingdom of
England, with an unknown number of other combatants, under the
command of the earl of Cornwall. Richard, like the other English
crusaders, had had to overcome the reservations of Gregory IX, who

may have been reluctant to see the arrival in the Holy Land of the emperor Frederick II's brother-in-law; he had nevertheless benefited from the financial concessions of the pope, and of Henry III, who, in particular, granted him 3,000 marks raised from the Jews. Richard was to arrive in the East with a well-filled treasury which enabled him to take impoverished crusaders into his pay. He and the other English crusaders, among them Simon de Montfort and William Longsword, had left England on 10 June 1240; they had been warmly received by the king of France, who accompanied Richard as far as Lyons. Having embarked at Marseilles, they reached Acre on 8 October next.

They were to discover a complex situation in the Holy Land. The successive conclusion by Thibaut of a treaty of alliance with the sultan of Damascus and truces with the sultan of Egypt had bewildered many crusaders. Some had laid down their arms and returned to France with the king of Navarre; others regarded themselves as bound by their commitments to Ismail. The Hospitallers had returned to Acre, with some of the barons of the Holy Land; the duke of Burgundy and the count of Nevers were busy rebuilding the fortifications of Ascalon, in accord with the promises made to the sultan of Damascus, with whom the Templars remained on good terms. However, the bishop of Marseilles, Benoît of Alignan, who had made a pilgrimage to Our Lady of Sardenay (Sidnaya, near Damascus), had returned impressed by the strategic value of the castle of Saphet and insisted that they start to rebuild it, a project considered and rejected in 1239; work commenced on 11 December 1240.

Richard of Cornwall found opinions divided; the imperial party, to which he was bound by his family tie with Frederick II, inclined towards the Egyptian alliance, the anti-imperial party towards that with Damascus. He decided to join the duke of Burgundy at Ascalon and assist with its fortification.

The sultan of Damascus had kept his promises, granted facilities to the pilgrims and led out his troops to cooperate with the Franks. The sultan of Egypt had promised to liberate his prisoners but delayed doing so (it was said that he was anxious first to complete the work on the fortress of Roda on which they were employed); in practice, all his concessions were of places which were in the power either of Ismail or of Dawud. The treaty concluded with him began to look like a fool's bargain. To fortify Ascalon was to put pressure on him, and this may have decided Richard, like Hugh of Burgundy before him, to undertake this task.

In the end, Richard, finding the pride of the grand master of the Temple insufferable, swung round to support the Hospitallers; he met the duke of Burgundy to accept new overtures from the sultan Ayyub,

Map 16   The kingdom of Jerusalem reconstituted in 1241–4

who promised to persuade his ally, Dawud of Kerak, to evacuate Jerusalem. And, on 13 April 1241, the prisoners taken at Gaza and in other skirmishes were freed. Richard of Cornwall won great prestige by this liberation, as from the burial he provided for those who had died on the battlefield of Gaza. The French barons remembered it during the campaign in Poitou between the king of France and Henry III. But Richard was also able to take credit by decrying the activities of Thibaut of Navarre. Richard, brother-in-law of Frederick II, seems to have tried to negotiate an agreement between the emperor and his rebellious subjects. It was to the imperial castellan of Jerusalem that he delivered Ascalon when it was completed. He did no more to restore Frederick's authority, but the latter nevertheless wrote to him several times over the next few years to keep him up to date with events in the Holy Land.

In these letters, the emperor lost no opportunity to criticise the intrigues of the Templars and the Frankish barons, holding them responsible for every failure. He seems to have regarded Richard as having acted as his representative. In a letter of 1244, he refers to 'our royal treaty, that we have concluded in our name in agreement with the convent and the masters of the houses of St John (the Hospital) and St Mary of the Germans'. Frederick II had thus adopted as his own the policies of the earl of Cornwall, which were in line with his own entente with the sultan of Egypt, and which the great embassy he sent to Cairo in 1242–3 probably only confirmed.

But one name was missing from this treaty, that of the master of the Temple, who seems not to have been associated with the treaty concluded with Egypt. In 1242 the Templars, in disregard of this treaty, launched an attack on Nablus during which they sacked the town, obliging the sultan to send his troops against them. The Templars' contempt for imperial authority went so far as to authorise them to wage their own war against the sultan of Egypt.

The quarrel between Frederick II's representative and the party led by Balian, son of John of Ibelin, took a new turn in 1241. Richard Filangieri had secretly made contact with two of the bourgeois of Acre who introduced him into the town; but a new arrival, Philip of Montfort, who had come with the crusade and who had married the heiress to Toron, Maria of Antioch, prevented him from pressing his advantage; Balian of Ibelin tried to seize him by besieging the house of the Hospitallers, but he had already left. At this point, Frederick wrote to the barons of the kingdom that Conrad was about to attain his majority and must be recognised as king of Jerusalem.

The emperor's enemies decided that, in Conrad's absence, they would appoint as legitimate heir his nearest relative, Queen Alice, now remarried to Ralph of Soissons, and hand over to her the government of the kingdom. Without further delay, they marched on Tyre and seized the lower town. Frederick had recalled Richard Filangieri, and the castle was held by his brother, Lothair. Chance, in the form of a high wind that had seriously damaged his ship, forced Richard back into port, where he was captured by his enemies who threatened to hang him; Lothair surrendered the castle, probably on 10 July 1243, though this date is disputed.

The new *bailli* sent by the emperor, Thomas of Acerra, could only establish himself in Tripoli; Frederick ordered him to surrender Ascalon to the Hospitallers. A new legal quibble enabled the barons of the kingdom to avoid surrendering to Alice the town of Tyre, which they retained; she was allowed only the title 'lady of the kingdom', which allowed her to receive homage and appoint *baillis*. This was on the pretext of safeguarding Conrad's rights for when he came to his kingdom.

The Franks had not realised that in depriving Frederick II of his authority they would provide the sultan of Egypt with an excuse, behind which he could shelter when the pope asked him to renew the truces broken in 1244, arguing that he could negotiate only with the emperor as he was committed by the earlier agreements.

In the short run, the Franks embarked on a reconstruction. In 1241 the sire of Arsur started to restore his castles. Eudes of Montbéliard began to rebuild the citadel of Tiberias; the monks of Mount Tabor returned to their monastery. Giles, lord of Sidon and Beaufort, which he had just recovered, restored one of his vassals in the land of the Schuf. The Muslim emirs of the mountains found themselves faced by a revived Frankish power; two of the Bohtor of the Gharb were killed in 1242 in the Kesrouan, east of Beirut, and the Maan of the Schuf in 1245 attempted an attack on Sidon. The pope encouraged the donations and bequests destined for the reconstruction of the fortifications of Jerusalem and Ascalon, 'to take advantage of the discord of the sultans'.

All these efforts were to be compromised by new troubles which shook the Ayyubid empire. The sultan Ayyub, at last master of Egypt thanks to his cousin Dawud of Kerak, had taken reprisals against those who had recognised his brother al-Adil; he then quarrelled with Dawud, who was reconciled with the sultan of Damascus, Ismail. As before, Ismail sought an alliance with the Franks, and the two allies offered to restore the part of Jerusalem that the treaty of Jaffa had left to the Muslims. In order to keep his alliance with the Franks, Ayyub did the same. During the winter of 1243–4, Christian worship was resumed in the Temple.

Ayyub, however, fearing that he might be deposed by his enemies, now having been joined by the king of Homs, sought help from a quarter which had already given him assistance, the Khwarismian bands of Bereke Khan; since Jalal al-Din's death, they had served both the Ayyubids and the Seljuks, always pillaging on their own account. But the arrival of the Mongols in the region of the Caucasus and the defeat they had inflicted on the sultan of Turkey made their situation perilous (1243). They therefore jumped at the chance to go to the rescue of the sultan of Egypt. Before this threat, the three allies turned once again to the Franks, this time offering them not only all that remained unrecovered of the kingdom of Jerusalem, but part of Egypt, in return for a military assistance to which the Franks, all parties in accord, readily agreed.

The Khwarismians, however, having devastated the Beqa'a, arrived before Jerusalem. The patriarch and the masters of the Temple and the Hospital went to put the citadel, which had then been rebuilt, in a defensive state, but they stayed only briefly. The castellan and the preceptor of the Hospital were killed trying to surprise the Khwarismians in a sortie. The citadel resisted, but the defenders, seeing no help on the horizon, asked to be allowed to reach the coast under the protection of the king of Kerak. Thanks to a trick, the Khwarismians lured them to below the walls of the city and killed two thousand of them. Bandits picked off the rest on the road; scarcely 300 refugees managed to reach Jaffa. The victors killed the few priests they found in the Holy Sepulchre, among them the Greek patriarch. The Armenian community had been massacred in its convent (23 August 1244).

The Khwarismians then joined the army of Ayyub, confined near Gaza, facing that of the three Ayyubids of Syria who had joined forces with the Franks. The king of Cyprus had sent 300 knights, the prince of Antioch a similar number; there were 348 knights of the Temple, 351 of the Hospital, 440 Teutonic knights and a body of knights of the order of St Lazarus, and the lay and ecclesiastical barons of the kingdom had brought their vassals, reinforced by a large number of indigenous auxiliaries; in total, there were perhaps 2,000 knights, plus many turcopoles.

The king of Homs argued that they should stay where they were, banking on the enemy breaking up; he was ignored and an attack was launched. Some Ayyubid contingents fought valiantly, that of Homs losing 1,720 of its 2,000 Turks; others fell back.

The Franks, surrounded, were almost wiped out; of the contingents of the military orders, only three Teutonic knights, thirty-six Templars and twenty-six Hospitallers escaped; the grand master of the Temple was

captured with the count of Jaffa; the master of the Hospital was killed.
The patriarch, who managed to escape, estimated the total losses at
16,000 men; the campaign army of the Frankish kingdom had been
destroyed (17 October 1244). The battle of La Forbie, as serious on the
military plane as that of Hattin, marked the collapse of the patient
reconstruction of the Latin kingdom.

Frederick II was to blame 'the proud order of the Temple and the
arrogance of the indigenous barons brought up in delights ... who had
forced the sultan of Egypt into an unjust and ill-prepared war'. In fact it
was the rivalry between the Ayyubids which had allowed the restoration
of the Holy Land, which the agreement made in the summer of 1244
with Ismail, Dawud and their allies had completed. But the success, up
to 1241, had been linked to a prudent strategy, avoiding pitched battles.
The defeat of 1244 was the result of abandoning this strategy. The
policy, however, remained the same.

But the consequences of the defeat were slow to be felt. Philip of
Montfort, escaping capture, rushed to Ascalon and put it in a defensive
state; Walter of Brienne, led out by his captors to below his castle of Jaffa
and placed on a gibbet to encourage the defenders to capitulate, exhorted
them to stay firm; he was to die in the prisons of Egypt. The
Khwarismians were refused entry to Egypt; they ran riot over the
countryside, pillaging and ravaging everything in sight, as far as Nazareth
and Saphet, and threatened Acre. Ayyub had seized Judaea and Samaria
from his cousin Dawud; he took possession of Jerusalem then marched
on Damascus, which endured a pitiless siege and fell in October 1245,
restoring Syrio-Egyptian unity. The rupture of the alliance between the
Khwarismians and the sultan, which was followed by the destruction of
the former by the king of Homs in October 1246, delayed the beginning
of the reconquest of Frankish lands threatened by Ayyub that year.

The papacy ordered public prayers on behalf of those captured at La
Forbie; the Templars and the Hospitallers offered to redeem their
brethren, but met with an outright rejection. The pope wrote to the
sultan to seek a truce. Ayyub replied that he approved of his desire for
peace, but that he would put the matter in the hands of the emperor,
who he knew had quarrelled with Innocent IV (3 June 1245). The
proclamation of a general crusade (July 1246) was to follow from the
failure of these negotiations.

It was not until 1247 that the Egyptian army attacked the Frankish
fortresses. It laid siege to Tiberias, which fell on 17 June, then Ascalon.
The Egyptian fleet, which was participating in the siege, was driven onto
the coast by a Cypriot squadron, but the timber from the ships was used
to support a sapping trench, through which the attackers penetrated the

fortress (14 October). The hermits of Mount Carmel had to evacuate their monastery and the inhabitants of Acre itself expected a siege.

The slow reconquest, which had been embarked on after the setback of the Third Crusade and had achieved significant results, had been thrown into question. The campaign of 1244, undertaken without warning, had lacked western help. It is true that this had assumed a new form during the previous decades. Initiated during the Fifth Crusade, the negotiations with a view to the recovery of the Holy Land had at first been designed to use the pressure of a serious military threat from the West to obtain the exchange of Egyptian conquests for Jerusalem.

With Frederick II, Thibaut of Champagne and Richard of Cornwall, it was an alliance with one of the warring Muslim princes, combined with the presence of a credible armed force, that had made it possible to obtain these surrenders. The coalition of 1244 had pursued the same objective, but with ambitions which probably exceeded the power of the Franks of the East. It was now once again the turn of crusaders from the West.

IO

THE TURNING POINT OF 1250

The year 1250 may seem to be one of those pivotal dates which determine the destiny of peoples. It was the year of the defeat, captivity and liberation of St Louis, which saw the end of the type of crusade that had existed since the early days of the century. It was the year of the death of Frederick II, in the middle of the crucial stage in the battle between empire and papacy whose repercussions weighed heavily on the fate of the Latin East. And it was the year of the accession to power in Egypt of the Mamluks, who were soon to create an 'Islamic empire' based on a military dictatorship.

But the choice of one year as a symbol only serves to obscure developments taking place over the longer term. For the history of the crusades, the defeat of La Forbie in 1244 marked a staging post, by depriving the Franks of the means to use a military power that was still real to impose a solution to the problem of the Holy Land. For the West as for the East, it was between 1240 and 1245 that there emerged the Mongol threat, which brought home the fragility of the frontiers of the Christian as well as of the Muslim world. And it was not until around 1260 that the Mongols began to be seen not as a mortal danger but as a new hope of resolving that same problem of the Holy Land.

THE HOLY LAND NO LONGER IN THE FOREFRONT OF EUROPE'S PREOCCUPATIONS

In 1240, while Thibaut of Navarre was hesitating between the alliance with Damascus and the prospect of a truce with Egypt, the Mongol threat suddenly emerged to the east of Europe. The campaign led by two

Mongol leaders against the Cumans of the Ukraine and the Russian princes, in 1222, was over in a flash. The reappearance of the Mongols on the Ural and the Volga, around 1236, did not pass unnoticed by the Hungarians, and the devastation of the Russian principalities which had followed had been noted, in particular by the Dominicans who were endeavouring to evangelise the peoples of the steppe. But the flight into Hungary of the Cumans expelled by the Mongols, and their crossing of the Carpathians and invasion of Poland led the Poles, the Germans and the Hungarians to oppose them with armies that were destroyed at Chmielnik, Legnica and on the Sajo (18 March, 9 April and 11 April 1241). The victors devastated Hungary, reaching Dalmatia and the approaches to Vienna, before returning, in 1242, to their camps on the Lower Volga. On the way, one of their leaders, Qadaan, encountered the emperor Baldwin II of Constantinople, whom he defeated.

Rumours circulated, rousing fears that the invaders were intending to push even further. The historian Matthew Paris assembled a collection of letters which attest to this terror; refugees arrived even from Russia, where the Mongols had sacked Kiev, bringing reports of atrocities. The Hungarian King Bela IV had managed to escape, not without having briefly been a prisoner of the duke of Austria; he tried to obtain help. But Gregory IX and Frederick II were then at each other's throats, and each was attempting to blame the other for the disunity of Christendom in the face of the 'Tartars'. The emperor announced that he was raising an army to be commanded by his son, Conrad; the pope proclaimed a crusade against the Tartars, but confined its preaching to the provinces bordering the regions they had invaded (June 1241). Innocent IV renewed this appeal in 1243, by which time the danger had passed. The Mongols had evacuated Hungary, both because of the death of the *qaghan* Ogedei which recalled their leaders to Mongolia and, probably, because the Hungarian plain could not feed their cavalry.

Though the Mongols had left central and eastern Europe, they were present on another front, that of the Caucasus. The *noyan* Baiju, who commanded the army stationed in this region, had invaded and devastated Georgia, then Greater Armenia and, lastly, Turkey. The Seljuk sultan had summoned all his Christian and Muslim vassals, and his army included Frankish mercenaries, but was nevertheless routed at the battle of Köze-Dagh (1243). Some of the princes subject to the Seljuks made haste to join the victorious camp, among them the king of Little Armenia. But there was anxiety in the Frankish and Muslim lands of northern Syria, especially when the prince of Antioch received an ultimatum asking him to dismantle his fortresses, pay a tribute equal to the annual revenue of his lands and hand over three thousand young

girls. His neighbours of Aleppo submitted; Bohemond V did not follow
suit, but sent the patriarch of Antioch to warn the West of this new
danger; he visited the court of Frederick II (1244), then that of the pope.

The prince of Antioch's appeal succeeded where the invasion of 1241
had failed, and Innocent IV, who then convened the Council of Lyons,
included the *Remedium contra Tartaros* in its agenda. But even before the
council met, he decided to sound out the Mongols' intentions. To
Western minds, war was a means of obtaining reparation for an injury or
injustice; Innocent IV asked the Mongols what the motive was for their
attacks on the Christians, towards whom they had no reason to be
hostile, and proposed what we would call a treaty of non-aggression.
Three embassies, that of Andrew of Longjumeau and that of Ascelin of
Cremona, which left from Acre, and that of John of Plancarpin, which
left from Lyon, reached the command posts of the Mongol armies, at
Tabriz, at Sisian in the Karabagh, and on the Volga. Plancarpin pushed
on into Mongolia, where he attended the enthronement of the *qaghan*
Güyük (1245–6). But all these ambassadors returned with one message
which specified the Mongols' objectives: to make all the princes of the
world submit to the *qaghan*, he being invested with a mandate that
conferred on him world empire.

Güyük put it like this:

You have sent us these words: 'You have taken all the lands of the Magyars and
the Russians; I am amazed. Tell us what they had done wrong.' We have not
understood your words ... In the power of God, from the East to the West, all
the lands have been granted to us ... Now, you must say with a sincere heart:
'We will be your subjects: we will give you our power.' Come yourself, in
person, at the head of all the kings without exception, come to offer us service
and homage. Then, we will recognise your submission. And if you ... contra-
vene our orders, we will know you to be our enemies.

The letter which Baiju entrusted to Ascelin of Cremona gave short
shrift to the pope's admonitions regarding the massacres committed,
seemingly without valid reason, by the Mongols, retorting:

The intangible precept of God and the edict of he who contains all the land [the
qaghan] is this: 'Whoever hears this edict, let him remain on his land, his water
and his heritage, and let him lend his power to he who contains all the land.
Those who do not confirm, but act otherwise, will be destroyed and lost.'

He, too, demanded that the pope come in person to make an act of
submission.

The situation was only too clear: in the absence of a submission they
were not ready to make, the Christian West and the Latin East risked the
same destruction as that inflicted by the Mongols on the peoples they

had vanquished. They must expect an imminent offensive; the edict which Güyük sent to Baiju in the spring of 1247 instructed him to transmit the order to submit to all he could reach.

Nevertheless, the pope waited for the threat to assume a more definite form before organising a response. The envoys who returned from the Mongol countries had gathered information about the invaders' military power and their methods of war, leaving few illusions as to the resistance that the West could offer. But in the years which preceded the crusade of St Louis, the internal crises of the Mongol empire granted a respite. The assignment of the part of that empire that adjoined the Christian lands of Europe and the Caucasus to Batu, one of the grandsons of Genghis Khan, was not accompanied by a sufficient endowment of troops to permit an aggressive policy, and Batu confined himself to getting his suzerainty acknowledged by the Russian princes and the Georgians. It was not until 1253–4 that Alexander IV thought it necessary to preach a crusade in this direction.

The eastern frontier of Europe seemed an area liable to ignite in an unpredictable manner. It accordingly became a land of crusade, which was already the case with certain regions adjoining the Baltic, where the Livonian, Lithuanian and Prussian peoples resented the presence of islands of Christianity on their soil. In 1274, a Bohemian prelate was to question the utility of a crusade in the Near East when the real danger, in his eyes, came from the pagans of eastern Europe.

The arrival of the Mongols changed the situation as far as a Near Eastern crusade was concerned; the collapse of Seljuk power made it possible to speculate as to the vulnerability of Turkey if a crusade were to decide to land there. In 1248 an Armenian prince sent as ambassador to Mongolia to perform an act of submission suggested to his cousins, the count of Jaffa and the king of Cyprus, that they might find common ground with the Mongols. But it was too soon for the Franks to understand such language.

While eastern Europe was giving cause for concern, the Iberian peninsula, in contrast, offered the prospect of a significant Christian expansion. Since the victory of las Navas de Tolosa (1211), Almohad power had been broken and the Christian kings of Spain pressed ahead with the *reconquista*. The fall of Seville, which coincided with St Louis' arrival in Egypt, made a deep impression on the Muslim world. But Spain had ceased to attract crusaders from beyond the Pyrenees. At most, Henry III of England considered joining his relative, Alfonso X of Castile, on an expedition into Africa.

The main problem then preoccupying the Christian West was the battle between empire and papacy, which posed a serious threat to the crusade. It was essentially because of Italian matters that Frederick II and the popes were at odds. The emperor had settled to his advantage, soon after his return from the crusade, the differences relating to his kingdom of Sicily, and Gregory IX had admitted defeat. But in Lombardy and central Italy the Patrimony of St Peter was threatened, and the protection traditionally accorded by the pope to the league of Lombard towns had broken down. Gregory IX had eventually, in April 1239, after Frederick had made one of his sons king of Sardinia in spite of papal rights over the island, excommunicated the emperor for the second time; the imperial army had conquered the larger part of the Patrimony and prevented the pope from holding the council at which he had intended to proceed to Frederick's deposition.

It was at this point that Gregory died. His successor, Celestine IV, was only briefly on the throne. It was a cardinal regarded as favourable to the emperor, Sinibald Fieschi, who was elected as Innocent IV. The new pope had realised that the struggle between empire and papacy, especially since the emperor was determined to secure power over the whole of Italy, was inevitable. By leaving Rome and Italy to seek refuge elsewhere, he was safeguarding himself against an attack by imperial troops. As the king of France had not authorised him to establish himself in his kingdom, he settled at Lyons, on imperial territory, but close to France, where he might eventually take refuge. On 3 January 1245 he announced the meeting of a council in that town, which, this time, the emperor could not prevent, though he forbade the prelates of Germany and Italy to attend. The meeting was intended to address the dangers threatening Christendom as a result of the loss of Jerusalem, the situation of Constantinople and the Tartar invasion, and the schemes of the emperor. Frederick's relations with the infidel appeared among the complaints formulated against him. The emperor's representative claimed that his master wished in future to devote himself to the battle against the enemies of the Church, the Tartars and the Saracens, but he could not prevent the council from confirming the excommunication (17 July) and pronouncing Frederick's deposition. Louis IX intervened in vain.

Now under a ban throughout Christendom, Frederick II faced a proclamation granting the crusading indulgence to the military operations designed to implement the conciliar sentence, as had been the case in 1228 and in 1239. The election of an anti-king in Germany (first Henry Raspe, then William of Holland) opened the hostilities that were to continue even after Frederick's death, although his son Conrad IV had regained ground. Some crusaders participated, and the pope even secretly urged his legate to encourage volunteers to go to Germany rather than to the Holy Land, only to reverse this decision and forbid the transfer of the vows the Frisians had taken for the crusade in the East to the support of William of Holland.

The battle between empire and papacy had two consequences. The first was to divert towards Italy and Germany the pope's efforts to raise the men of war and the money which might otherwise have been available for the East; Frederick's propaganda, repeated by the *trouvères* and other poets, emphasised this, not that the emperor showed any sign of going to the Franks' assistance. The second was to drag the Latin East into the equation. Frederick proposed, more or less sincerely, to resign from his duties and transmit them to his son, going to end his days in the Holy Land. On his death, he left a large sum of money to be used on its behalf, as directed by Conrad (and when he died, a cross was placed on his mantle to show that he remained faithful to his vow of crusade). Alexander IV suggested that Conrad renounce the empire and Sicily to devote himself to his kingdom of Jerusalem. In 1247, Innocent IV ended the empire's rights of suzerainty over the kingdom of Cyprus, which he made responsible for the protection of the kingdom of Jerusalem.

Another matter discussed at the council of Lyons was the future of the Latin empire of Constantinople. The emperor Baldwin II had been one of those who had tried hardest to bring about a reconciliation between the pope and Frederick, who had brokered a truce between him and the Greek emperor of Nicaea. At the council, he obtained a levy on pontifical resources for the defence of his empire, as his financial situation was disastrous. When the truce had expired, John Vatatzes had seized from the Latins two of their towns in Thrace, and threatened Constantinople. But Innocent IV, ever hopeful of a reunion of the Churches, had negotiated with Vatatzes with a view to ending the Graeco-Latin schism, Vatatzes implying that he was ready to recognise pontifical supremacy. In 1254 Vatatzes even dangled the prospect of an agreement by which a council would meet to proclaim the union, Rome agreeing in return to restore Constantinople to the Byzantines and to replace the Latin patriarch by a Greek patriarch. Innocent replied that he had no proper grounds for deposing Baldwin II, but that if it should so happen that Constantinople fell into Vatatzes' hands, the pope would agree to the Greek patriarch occupying the see of that city. Alexander IV confirmed these proposals in a letter to Theodore II Lascaris in 1256. But Baldwin II had no intention of relinquishing his empire; he even asked the new emperor Michael VIII, in 1259, to restore Thessalonika, or simply Serres, which he refused. In 1261, as we know, Constantinople became his.

That Rome should put the spiritual interests of Christendom before the preservation of a Latin rule that might prove an obstacle to the union of the Churches was in line with the missionary orientation which increasingly emerged under Innocent IV. It was many years since the presence of the Franks in Constantinople had been regarded as being of value to the establishments in the Holy Land. The life-and-death struggle in which papacy and empire were engaged was a different matter; the Mongol danger, though remote, might yet re-emerge at any moment. This did not lead to a disengagement with regard to the Holy Land, but it is difficult to avoid the conclusion that a joint effort to recover lost ground in the Holy Land ranked low in the priorities of the pope, the emperor and many kings.

It was in these circumstances that St Louis came to play a major role. In the middle of the thirteenth century, the king of France became identified with the crusade.

THE CRUSADE OF ST LOUIS

The convening of the council of Lyons, three months after the defeat of La Forbie and six months after the loss of Jerusalem (3 January 1245), heralded the resumption of the crusade. A letter from the pope to Thibaut of Navarre, dated 15 January, was even more specific on this point. But the king of France had already taken the initiative; in this sense, his crusade is reminiscent of that of his ancestor, Louis VII, who had also decided to depart for the East even before Pope Eugenius III had appealed for a crusade.

The historians tell us that the king had fallen gravely ill, and was not expected to live when, regaining consciousness, he asked to take the cross, which was given him by the bishop of Paris. At the end of December 1244 it was rumoured that Louis had had a vision which had made him decide to leave for the East. It is likely that the king was still unaware of the disaster of La Forbie, news of which seems to have reached Innocent IV only towards the end of December, but that he knew of the sack of Jerusalem. Joinville says that Blanche of Castile did everything in her power to persuade her son to go back on his vow; the king returned his cross, then asked for it back, this time irrevocably.

The king's decision seems to have taken his entourage by surprise, but his interest in the crusade was not new. What survives of his accounts testifies to his generosity to crusaders, especially to those of 1239 who represented, as we have seen, a large part of the forces of his kingdom and were commanded by his constable. The obligation to serve in the Holy Land which he imposed on his rebellious barons, and, in 1237, on the citizens of Narbonne guilty of molesting inquisitors, points in the same direction. In 1239 his devotion to Christ's Passion had been shown by the purchase of the crown of thorns and, between 1242 and 1248, by the building of the Sainte-Chapelle.

Those around him, however, doubted whether his health would withstand the rigours of the expedition, and whether his kingdom would be safe in his absence, given the intentions of Henry III of England, who was demanding the restoration of the fiefs – Normandy, Anjou and Poitou – confiscated from his father and who, after his defeats at Taillebourg and Saintes, had made a five-years' truce which was due to expire in March 1248. Lastly, the state of relations between the pope and the emperor seemed not to favour the mobilisation of a crusade.

But the king persisted in his project and the pope gave his agreement; at the end of the council, which had repeated the measures taken at the Fourth Lateran Council, he appointed a legate with responsibility for preaching the crusade, the French bishop, Cardinal Eudes of Château-roux.

On 9 October 1245 Louis IX convened in Paris an assembly of barons and prelates at which many of them took the cross, including the archbishops of Reims and Bourges and the bishops of Orleans and Beauvais. The barons who had clashed with royal authority in previous years and those who had already been to the East in 1239 promised to accompany the king. The usual measures were taken: proclamation of a moratorium on the interest on debts contracted by crusaders; prohibition of all private wars for three years, until 3 June 1249; imposition of a tax payable by the towns and rural communities. The pope granted the king a twentieth of the revenues of ecclesiastical benefices, payable not only within the kingdom but also in the dioceses of Lotharingia and the Rhineland which belonged to the empire.

The recruitment of the crusaders seems not to have met with any real hostility, though it was rumoured that the king had arranged for crosses to be sewn onto the robes he distributed to his knights at Christmas, making them, in a sense, crusaders whether they liked it or not. The count of Champagne was absent, having gone to his kingdom of Navarre, which excused him from joining the crusade, but even here many people took the cross; Joinville, seneschal of Champagne, reported that thirty-five knights banneret, that is lords who dispensed high justice, from the county were killed in Egypt. A number of estimates agree in putting the number of knights participating in the crusade at 2,800, most of them from the kingdom of France.

St Louis, who wanted to associate as many European sovereigns as possible in his enterprise, informed Frederick II that he had taken the cross. The emperor congratulated him in a very friendly letter; he put at his disposal the resources and ports of his kingdom of Sicily, authorised him to purchase horses, arms and ships there and promised to grant safe-conducts to the crusaders. He also tried to exploit the king's desire to strengthen his crusade to obtain his support in his conflict with the pope.

But Ibn Wasil tells us that an envoy from Frederick, whom he called Berto, disguised as a merchant, came from the emperor to warn the sultan of the king of France's plans, and to ask him to put his country in a defensive state. It is possible that Frederick was seeking to maintain his alliance with the sultan Ayyub while manifesting his good will towards the crusader king. Some German barons joined the crusade, but not very many; Innocent IV had restricted the legate Eudes of Châteauroux's activities in those parts.

Louis IX was counting on King Haakon of Norway, who he knew had taken the cross some years before; the Norwegian fleet could be extremely useful to the French army. The chronicler Matthew Paris was given the mission, but Haakon rejected this request on various grounds, including the difficulty of making two peoples so alien to each other live together.

There remained England. Henry III, for whom the defeats of 1242 still rankled, was ill disposed towards the king of France's crusade; he refused the bishop of Beirut permission to preach in his kingdom in 1245. But in the face of the English barons' desire to join the expedition, he eventually gave way, authorising the preaching, but refusing to allow the English benefices to be taxed for the crusade; England was at that time extremely hostile to the financial aspects of papal policy. The king's brother, Richard of Cornwall, sent £1,000 to the Holy Land through the intermediary of the Hospitallers; his half-brother, William Longsword, Simon de Montfort, Earl of Leicester and the bishop of Worcester took the cross, as did another half-brother of the king, Guy of Lusignan, to whom the king gave large sums of money, in a sense making him his representative. But in 1247, Henry asked the pope to allow the English crusaders to depart a year after the French crusaders, which was agreed; the two hundred or so knights from England and their leaders (less Simon de Montfort, whom the king sent to Gascony) left in 1249.

The crusade, essentially French but with significant English participation, left in 1248, with a few contingents delayed until 1249, that is, one year after the date initially set. The delay was due to the need to assemble money, provisions and the necessary ships.

In the meantime, St Louis took a remarkably ambitious step. To put his conscience at rest before his departure, but probably also to leave his kingdom in good order, he launched a major enquiry whose purpose was to right the wrongs he, or his officials, might have done his subjects, and also to restore to victims of the arbitrary deeds of his predecessors property that might be regarded as ill-gotten. The enquiries were entrusted to members of religious orders, Dominicans and Franciscans initially, so as to place this enquiry into the procedures of government firmly within the moral perspective appropriate for a crusade. Royal fiscality (and papal fiscality in the king's service) was a heavy burden on the eve of the expedition, but St Louis wanted to exclude injustice and the profits of injustice. This decision can be seen as having a wider application; the knights and barons who left on the crusade must also have felt obliged to ask themselves similar questions. The enquiries of St Louis throw light on the moral preparations for a crusade. Joinville tells us how, having assembled his vassals before taking the cross, he said to them: 'My lords, I am going overseas and I do not know if I will return. Step forward, if I have done you any wrong. I will make reparation', and he left it to the court to judge the claims. This move of Joinville's part, at the lower level, was in response to the same preoccupations as those of the king.

The material preparation for the crusade was also meticulous and took longer than expected. The French clergy met and decided to allocate to the king not the twentieth of its revenue, as the council had stipulated, but the tenth, and for three years. This measure met with recriminations on the part of those who had not been present. The order of Cluny sheltered behind its exemption, and a long conflict ensued; the king of France instructed his *bailli* of Mâcon to seize the priory of Lourdon, and the duke of Burgundy sacked several of the abbey's dependencies (Givry, Paray, Toulon-sur-Arroux), for which he was excommunicated, which did not stop him from demanding to be paid what was due. For the pope had arranged for the revenue of these tenths to be handed over to the leaders of the contingents who had to equip and transport them. Thus Dreu of Mello was to receive a sum of 500 silver marks from Eudes of Châteauroux, drawn from the twentieth and other revenues, and his companion Landry of Fleury 50 marks; Humbert of Beaujeu was to receive 3,000 *livres tournois*.

The burden was equally heavy on the towns of the royal demesne, which were obliged to borrow in order to pay the sums demanded. Roye, in Picardy, had to find 1,200 *livres* for the crusade, which did not stop Blanche of Castile from demanding three further payments from them – 1,000 *livres* in all – to send to the king in the Holy Land. A large war treasury was amassed by such means. It enabled the king to take into his pay crusaders who had reached the end of their resources, like Joinville, and to bear the costs of the expedition and of his ransom.

The crusade of St Louis was also innovatory in the way the king established, as had been suggested by the barons of the Holy Land in 1238, what amounted to a rearguard base where grain, wine and other foodstuffs were assembled in advance to await the crusaders' arrival in Limassol. Purchases were made on the king's orders in Apulia as authorised by Frederick II. His crusade was not to be entirely dependent on the speculations of merchants.

The provisioning of ships got under way as early as 1246, with a view to a departure in 1247. The king obtained a promise of twelve large sailing ships (*nefs*) and four smaller boats from Genoa, and of twenty sailing ships from Marseilles, and had ships specially built to carry the horses. The barons procured their ships not only from Marseilles but in the West and even in Scotland. Two Genoese, Ugo Lercaro and Jacopo de Levante, were made admirals of the fleet, that is, they were made responsible for preparing and provisioning the king's ships; the king paid for the purchase of tackle, sails and munitions (crossbow bolts). Other crusaders booked their passage aboard ships. Genoa also provided the assistance of its bankers, who were to advance the sums the king needed, recovering them by means of assignments on the royal treasury. Louis IX's army was to assemble in the newly built port of Aigues-Mortes, where work was pressing ahead with a view to the impending crusade; it was in 1246 that the town received its charter, granting it a consulate.

Diplomatic preparations were also made. Henry III of England was demanding the restoration of the Angevin inheritance and refusing to renew the truces, so the king had to leave his mother, whom he made regent, with the means to resist a possible attack. Above all, he tried to make peace between Innocent IV and Frederick II. Matthew Paris, very hostile to the pope, says that the king of France was annoyed to find him inexorable. In November 1245 the pope and the king met at Cluny; their discussions failed to produce a reduction in the sentence pronounced against the emperor, but the king obtained the grant of the necessary dispensations for the marriage of his brother, Charles of Anjou, to Beatrice of Provence, the queen's sister. A second meeting, in 1247, gave Frederick the opportunity to propose to the pope, in return for his absolution, the transfer of the emperor's crowns to his son, Conrad; Frederick would spend the rest of his life in the Holy Land; but Innocent IV questioned the sincerity of this proposal.

Though the king of France was able to leave his kingdom at peace, his attempt to pacify the West on the eve of the crusade was a failure. At least he had left nothing to chance.

In his absence, he entrusted the government of the kingdom to his mother, along with wardship of his elder children; Queen Margaret was to accompany him to the East.

St Louis took the cross at St Denis on 12 June 1248, and, by way of Sens, Vézelay and Lyons, where he once again met the pope, he reached the Rhône valley, where he demolished the castle of la Roche-de-Glun, whose lord was imposing a toll on pilgrims. When he arrived at Aigues-Mortes he was surprised to find thousands of volunteers, crossbowmen and footsoldiers, who were hoping to accompany him, but whom he could not accept. The fleet set sail on 25 August 1248.

Other departures followed. Raymond VII of Toulouse had planned to leave in 1249, but died before he could do so, on 27 September of that year, leaving instructions for the repayment of the sums he had received to finance his crusade and for the dispatch of fifty knights to the East. Alphonse of Poitiers had experienced some difficulty in recruiting combatants, and it was 25 August 1249 before he left Aigues-Mortes.

The English had already left and they travelled more quickly. Henry III himself took the cross in March 1250, without, apparently, any immediate intention of leaving. The Latin East had also responded to the preaching of the crusade; the knights of Cyprus and the Holy Land were to participate, as was the prince of Achaia, with four hundred knights, who joined the royal army in Cyprus.

THE EGYPTIAN CAMPAIGN

In proceeding to Cyprus, where his ships landed on 17 September 1248, Louis IX may have been responding to the suggestions made in 1238 by the Frankish barons and prelates; or he may have had strategic concerns in mind, as the accumulation of foodstuffs on the island would seem to suggest, that is, the desire to have an operational base near to his military objectives. In any case, it was at Limassol that the crusaders gathered as they arrived, and it was a little to the north of that town, at Camen-oriaqui, that they made their camp.

Some observers said that the king wanted to proceed immediately to the attack but was persuaded of the need first to assemble his troops, including the latecomers. A long winter followed. The island's climate proved lethal for the new arrivals, and many notable crusaders died of disease, including John of Montfort (who was later venerated as a saint and whose tomb, with the Cistercians of Beaulieu near Nicosia, worked miracles), and many crusaders of lesser rank also died. Nevertheless, the army maintained its strength thanks to the arrival of new detachments from the West and even from the Latin East, in particular Morea.

Finding he was in for a long stay in Cyprus, St Louis had time to reflect on a plan of campaign. Some claimed that, in their fear of a crusade, the Egyptian authorities had poisoned the pepper destined for the West in 1247, but Matthew Paris says that this was a rumour circulated by merchants anxious to offload their stocks. In fact, the sultan Ayyub, though he had taken measures for the defence of Egypt, was preoccupied by his struggle against his cousin of Aleppo, who was disputing Homs, and he left for Syria to try to recover that town.

To conduct negotiations with the eastern princes had ceased to be exceptional and their success had resulted in the restoration of the Latin east between 1229 and 1241. There had been other such contacts. Even the 'Old Man of the Mountains' (probably the sheik of the Ismailis of northern Syria rather than the leader of the sect in its distant retreat of Alamut, in northern Iran) is reported to have sent an embassy to France and England in 1238; this has been related to the threat of a new Mongol invasion. The Seljuk sultan had also tried to make contacts with the king of France; Baldwin II of Constantinople had contemplated marrying a French princess to the sultan in order to reinforce their alliance against the empire of Nicaea. The idea of using Frankish force to the benefit of eastern dynasties had become commonplace in the East. The various masters of the orders had made contact, in one case with an Egyptian emir plotting against his sultan, in another with Aleppo at war with the same sultan. It seems that they had even considered the possibility of exploiting the weakness of the sultan of Turkey, defeated by the Mongols, by suggesting a landing on his shores.

St Louis put a stop to all such projects, which in any case were rather vague, forbidding any negotiations with the Muslims. It is possible that the condemnation of Frederick II, whose relations with the sultan had been used to accuse him of betraying Christendom to the benefit of Islam, discouraged St Louis from adopting such a course. But he may simply have been afraid of seeing the strength of the crusade dissipated in intrigues beyond his control. Or perhaps he remained attracted by the very classic conception of the Fifth Crusade: the seizure of a great Egyptian port, preferably Damietta, and a march on Cairo. His entourage appear to have taken a close interest in the flooding of the Nile, which ruled out a campaign in the Delta during the summer, to avoid a repeat of the catastrophe of 1221.

While waiting, the king put his time to good use. The legate Eudes of Châteauroux turned his attention to religious matters; he held a council to reform the Latin Church of Cyprus and made contact with the island's Greeks. The king, meanwhile, received envoys and visits: that of the empress mother of Constantinople, who asked for his aid for Baldwin II; and that of the prince of Antioch, Bohemond V, battling against the invasion of Turkoman bands set into motion by the weakening of Seljuk power. The first military operation of the crusade was the dispatch of five hundred knights to Antioch to assist the prince. The arrival of Mongol envoys raises questions; should it be regarded as a proposal for an alliance with the Mongols, or was the representative of the *qaghan* in Iran intending to guard against any temptation the king of France might feel to attack the territories under Mongol sovereignty?

The king, lastly, had some difficulties with his army and his fleet. During the winter, while the sailors were preparing the flotilla of embarkation craft that would carry his troops to the shore, the captains of the Genoese ships had gone to Acre where they had started a small war against their Pisan rivals; at the beginning of spring, the king had to wait for this conflict to be settled before he had access to his boats. Some of the barons had grown impatient and gone to the Holy Land, against the orders of the king, who wanted to keep his army together.

At the beginning of May, everything was ready. The knights of the duke of Burgundy, who had spent the winter in Morea, and those of the prince of Achaia, had arrived in Cyprus, as had the contingents of the barons of the Holy Land and the military orders. The English had also arrived. The army comprised at least 2,500 to 2,800 knights, 5,000 crossbowmen and about 15,000 other combatants, not to speak of the *vivandières*, the washerwoman and others who accompanied them.

The army sailed towards Damietta, where it intended to land on the beach close to the town. Joinville has left us a famous description of this landing: of the knights carried to the shore aboard small boats and taking to the water themselves when the boats could go no further, while they had to hold the king back; of the units rapidly regrouping under the fire of enemy archers; of the knights sticking their lances into the ground to repel the Egyptian cavalry, composed of troops of high quality; of the panic that seized the Egyptians who, not content with abandoning the town to the enemy, evacuated it in great haste, followed by the entire population, forgetting even to cut the bridge. On 6 June 1249, a fortress that had held out for more than a year in 1219–20 had been taken after a single engagement.

The king could hardly have expected such rapid success. Everything suggests that he was assuming it would take some time to achieve the fall of Damietta and that, at best, the campaign would be resumed at the end of the summer, after the Nile floods had subsided. In fact, the river would begin to flood the Delta at the end of June. Was it this that caused a certain hesitation? It was rumoured, and reported by Matthew Paris, that the sultan, immediately after the fall of Damietta, offered the king, in return for its restoration, the whole country of Jerusalem and the liberation of the Christian slaves; the chronicler added that the purpose of the crusade ought to be confined to the recovery of the Holy Land, but this was a theme dear to the heart of Matthew Paris, for whom the sin responsible for the failure of the crusade was the desire to substitute for this legitimate objective a conquest of Egypt for which there was no justification. Muslim historians tell of an exchange of letters between the sultan and the king of France that took the form of an exchange of challenges, the king reminding the sultan of the victories won in Spain and threatening him with a similar fate, even if he submitted and embraced the Christian faith (words it is difficult to imagine coming from St Louis). There are other references to Ayyub's offer to become a Christian. In fact, there is no evidence of the opening of negotiations on this basis. On the contrary, the sultan Ayyub, then in the final stages of the illness that would kill him, demonstrated great energy, cruelly punishing those responsible for the precipitate evacuation of Damietta and putting Cairo into a defensive state.

The king of France, like the crusaders of 1220, organised his conquest. He restored the cathedral founded in Damietta in 1220, which he endowed with a chapter and temporalities; one of the clergy in his entourage, Giles of Saumur, became its archbishop (his tomb and cross are preserved in the church of Nantilly near Saumur). Everything points to a permanent settlement, and probably the conquest of Egypt, which, it has been said, Louis had in mind as a kingdom for his brother, Robert of Artois. Robert was denounced after the event as having been the evil genius of the campaign, but it is possible that, after his death at Mansurah, he was made a scapegoat by those looking for someone to blame. For Joinville, blame lay with the sins committed by the crusaders: the evil behaviour of too many of them, their greed and excessive luxury. And the king, always anxious for the victualling of the army, had, contrary to custom, set aside from the division of spoils the foodstuffs found in Damietta, which had deeply shocked the chronicler.

Robert of Artois seems to have played a decisive role during the council at which the next stage of the campaign was decided, rejecting the plan to complete the capture of Damietta with that of Alexandria, which would have the advantage of depriving the sultan of his other great port, and of providing the march on Cairo with an easier route than that of the Delta (the experience of Napoleon Bonaparte's march by this route, lacking watering places, casts doubt on this thesis). For Robert, it was crucial to crush with all speed the snake's head, that is, to take Cairo. The arrival of the count of Poitou was still awaited (24 October); a dispute between Robert of Artois and William Longsword had led to the English temporarily withdrawing to Acre, from which they returned two months later to rejoin the army for the march. At this point, a storm erupted, in which many ships – 140 according to Joinville – were lost.

On 20 November, the army set out on the route south. It was accompanied by a flotilla which sailed up the Nile and assured it of provisions. On 24 November the sultan Ayyub died; the news was suppressed to give his heir, Turanshah, time to arrive from the Jazirah. The leader of the army, Fakhr al-Din (who had earlier negotiated with Frederick II), managed to resist the advance of the Franks, who were marching on the fortress of Mansurah, but who had first to face a formidable obstacle, the crossing of the arm of the Nile which led to Lake Menzalah, the Bahr al-Saghir.

St Louis had with him a body of workmen, led by his engineer, Joscelin of Cournaut, who started to construct a dike across the river. But the Egyptian engineers began digging at the other side, to maintain the width of the channel, while the formidable Greek fire rained down on the wooden castles built by the crusaders on boats. Joinville has described the terror felt by the knights when it was their turn to guard these constructions, which risked bursting into flames, or when the flaming projectiles exploded.

Finally, a local inhabitant told the Franks of a ford, downstream of the confrontation. The king gave orders for it to be crossed in good order (the crossing was dangerous and many knights were drowned) and for the army to regroup on the other bank. But the advance guard, without waiting, launched into an attack on the Egyptian camp which it surprised and took; Fakhr al-Din was killed before he could put on his armour, and his troops took flight. Robert of Artois wanted to follow up this first success; while the king's 'battles' crossed, one by one, by the ford, he set out in pursuit of the fleeing army, which took refuge behind the walls of Mansurah. The Franks followed. The grand master of the Templars, Brother Giles, warned the count of Artois of the danger he ran; denounced as a coward, he followed him; ten knights sent by the king to stop him failed in their aim.

In the streets of the fortress, the battle assumed a different character; the Mamluks of the Egyptian army regrouped under the command of the emir Baybars al-Bundukdari; the Franks' horses were exhausted, and the advance guard was almost entirely massacred. The count of Artois was among the dead; it was a Hospitaller, Henry of Ronnay, who escaped, who had to tell the king. William Longsword and the English had been swallowed up in the defeat.

By this rash act, the success achieved by the royal army almost turned into a disaster. A whole section of the army, in particular its cross-bowmen, remained on the left bank of the Bahr al-Saghir. The knights had to regroup in difficult terrain, crossed by irrigation channels, and it was only in the evening of a day marked by heavy losses that the duke of Burgundy was able to lead his crossbowmen, by means of a bridge thrown across the river, in time to gather up the exhausted cavalry (8 February 1250).

A rapid retreat to Damietta would probably have saved the army. But the battle of Mansurah ended in success, because the Egyptians were finally obliged to beat a retreat. If he abandoned the march on Cairo, the king could hope to exploit the threat still constituted by this Frankish army at the mouth of the Delta to negotiate advantageous terms with the sultan. According to Joinville, the negotiations, conducted in particular by Philip of Montfort, who was both a vassal of the king and a great baron of the Holy Land, were far advanced; the king's council and that of the sultan had set a date for a treaty; the crusaders would restore Damietta to the sultan and he would restore the Holy Land to them. The king had even stipulated that his war-machines and provisions of 'salt-meat' could remain at Damietta until he could collect them and that the sick could remain there till they recovered. But one Egyptian demand, that the king surrender himself as a hostage until Damietta had been restored, caused the project to fail; one of the 'goodly knights' who formed a sort of royal general staff, Geoffrey of Sergines, argued strongly against it.

The army's health, meanwhile, was deteriorating. The river link with Damietta, unknown to the king, had been intercepted, the Egyptians having introduced galleys into the Nile which were seizing the boats sailing upriver. As a result, the army was reduced to living on salt meats, and began to suffer from scurvy. Food was running short. Joinville blamed the 'army sickness' on the Nile fish – the *barbotes* – which they ate for want of anything better and which had fed off the corpses thrown into the river. The army, at any rate, suffered badly; Charles of Anjou said that of the thirty-six 'battles' the king had led south, only six remained in fighting condition at the end of the expedition; a 'battle' or *eschelle* usually consisted of between fifty and a hundred knights. The ships accompanying the army were laden with the sick.

In these conditions, there was little point in persisting. On 5 April the king began the retreat to Damietta. The Egyptians, who had decided, after a new defeat on 11 February, to leave the crusaders alone, quickly discovered that they had left; it seems that Joscelin of Cournaut had failed to cut the cords of the pontoon bridge built on 8 February. The Egyptians fell on the stragglers, among whom was St Louis, laid low by another attack of dysentery, but who refused to board a ship. He had to be left in a house with a woman (a Parisian) who nursed him and a few companions, while Walter of Châtillon tried to prevent anyone entering. The larger part of the army arrived at Fariskur, a day's march from Damietta. Philip of Montfort succeeded in finding the emir with whom he had negotiated and offered to surrender Damietta to the sultan provided he would allow the rest of the army to regain the town. At this point, according to Frankish sources, a sergeant by the name of Marcel shouted that the king had ordered them to lay down their arms, and the combatants obeyed (6 April 1249). The victors could thus exploit the fact that there had been no formal capitulation.

They took advantage of this to indulge in a systematic massacre of the sick, the Egyptian galleys having seized the ships that were carrying them; Joinville owed his life to the fact that he was recognised as a cousin of Frederick II. Many crusaders were invited to choose between apostacy and death, among them many great barons. Louis IX, however, after his capture at Munyat Abu Abdallah, was handed over to an emir, Fakhr al-Din, and treated with respect. Very quickly, those who had taken him, and who were embarrassed by the large number of their captives, entered into discussions. The emir Husam al-Din, to whom the king was entrusted, was struck by the simplicity and intelligence of the prisoner. The crusaders insisted that it was not in their power to surrender fortresses in the Holy Land, because they belonged, by law, either to Frederick II and his vassals or to the Temple or the Hospital. Accordingly, the negotiations were confined to the fixing of a ransom.

St Louis insisted on negotiating in everyone's name to avoid individual bargains. A global sum was agreed for the ransom of the king and his companions, but Louis refused to be included, offering Damietta as the price of the redemption of his person, as he was not someone who could be bought for money; this led the sultan, not to be outdone in magnanimity, to reduce the sum of the general ransom. Eventually, the sum of 400,000 *livres tournois* (800,000 gold bezants) was agreed, and the king insisted that the payment should be made accurately and in full. To procure the cash needed for the first instalment, it was necessary to appeal to the Templars, who initially took refuge behind the inviolable nature of the deposits they had received, but who quickly gave way in the face of a symbolic act of violence: Joinville seized an axe and, making as if to break open a chest, made this axe the 'king's key'.

In fact, the agreement was overtaken by an unforeseen event, the murder of the sultan Turanshah by his father's Mamluks, in collusion with his widow. She married the Mamluk Aibek, who took over the government in the name of a young Ayyubid prince. The new rulers nevertheless ratified the conventions; on 6 May, a month after his capture, St Louis was freed with his principal barons.

The surrender of Damietta had not been without problems. Queen Margaret, who was about to give birth to a son, John Tristan, had to exercise all her authority to prevent the Italians from abandoning the town immediately Louis was captured, then from refusing to surrender it when he was freed. The clauses relating to the sick and to the foodstuffs and war machines were violated as soon as the town passed into the hands of the Mamluks, who massacred the former and burnt the latter. But, when payment of the first instalment of the ransom was made, the hostages left as security, among them Alphonse of Poitiers, were freed. The fleet carrying the king and his companions could then set sail for Acre.

The Egyptian campaign of 1249–50 ended in failure. For contemporaries, it was a massive disappointment, because it had been embarked on in the most favourable of circumstances, and prudently led by men who were above reproach. Its failure marked a decisive stage in the history of the crusades.

ST LOUIS IN SYRIA

If the crusade of 1250 was a turning point, it was because the king of France, obliged to abandon his scheme to occupy Egypt, chose to give a different significance to his stay in the East.

In leaving Damietta, St Louis was probably not too concerned about leaving the Latin East exposed to new blows at the hands of the Egyptians. The death of the sultan Ayyub, then that of his successor, led to new splits in the Arab and Turkish worlds, and the conflict between Aleppo and Cairo which had broken out in 1248 might indicate to those with knowledge of the East that the direct heirs of Saladin, long reduced to a tiny principality of Aleppo, were again in a position to rival the descendants of al-Adil, for so long predominant. The Frankish barons, while St Louis and the majority of them were in Egypt, had rediscovered their fighting spirit, as is shown by the attack made in December 1249 by the sire of Arsur, at the head of the knights of Acre, on Bethsan, which he pillaged, at the same time seizing some 600 cattle from a Turkoman tribe. It was clear that the departure of the king of France would leave them once again to face Muslim dynasties, and in a much less strong position than in 1241, but the gloomy atmosphere of the years 1246–7 had lifted.

In fact, as he himself wrote to his subjects, Louis IX was preparing to return to France, as several of his barons had already done. Joinville has described, not perhaps without embellishing his own role, the two councils held by the king on 26 June and 3 July. At the first, only a few voices were raised in favour of prolonging the king's stay in the Holy

Land; they were in such a minority that Joinville contemplated entering the service of the prince of Antioch. A song (*Nul ne pourrait de mauvaise raison bonne chanson ne faire ni chanter*) supported them, describing 'the land of Outre-mer ... in the balance' and evoking the prisoners who remained in Mamluk hands.

But just before the second council, it was learned that the ships sent to Egypt to bring back the captives the sultan had promised to free had returned without them. Since the Muslims had failed to keep their promises on this point, St Louis felt it was morally impossible for him to return to France leaving his men in the prisons of Egypt. He gave their liberty to his barons and his brothers, and decided to remain in the Holy Land to consolidate its defences, until he had procured the liberation of the captives. In this way he would escape the reproaches levelled at Thibaut of Champagne for not having obtained the immediate release of the prisoners taken at Gaza.

This would be expensive. Admittedly, in spite of paying his ransom (or rather the first instalment), which was roughly equivalent to one year's income from his kingdom, his treasury was not empty. But the recruits he needed to attract to rebuild his army demanded a high price. Joinville, accused by the king's counsellors of being too greedy, defended himself by presenting a budget showing what it would cost to maintain his men for one year, on top of their wages. According to him, it was on this basis that the new fighting men were recruited. But the king also wrote to his mother and to the regency council to ask for volunteers to join him and for more money.

It seems unlikely that there were many new recruits. It is possible that the movement of the Pastoureaux was in part a response to the king's appeal, but Henry III of England and many English knights had taken the cross before news of the king of France's misfortunes had arrived (March 1250), and it was only in 1252 that Henry announced for 1256 a departure which never materialised. A few barons, like Elnard of Seninghem, arrived in dribs and drabs; Alphonse of Poitiers was still intending to return. The passengers on the Marseilles ship the *St Victor* had to get the Messina authorities to make the ship's masters with whom they had negotiated a passage to Damietta carry them instead to Acre. The royal army received reinforcements, but not in large numbers.

Blanche of Castile was able to provide additional money by obtaining an extension of the levy of the tenths and new aids on the towns. Many consignments were dispatched; one of them was lost en route, the barrels full of pennies sinking along with the ship that was carrying them. The king of France could still resort to loans from the Italian bankers and military orders, whom he reimbursed by assignments on his treasury.

In his letter of August 1250, the king referred to the disputes emerging between the sultans; the usurpation of Aibek, even completed by marriage to a young Ayyubid wife, had provoked the hostility of all those Mamluks recruited by Ayyub's predecessors, bound by ties of loyalty to the family of Saladin and al-Adil. In July 1250 the sultan of Aleppo, al-Nasir, marched on and occupied Damascus, then sent messengers to St Louis to seek his assistance with a view to the occupation of Egypt, in return for the surrender of Jerusalem. It was a tempting offer, and the king sent the Dominican Yves the Breton to Damascus for discussions with the sultan's officials, serving as interpreter to his official ambassadors. But they could only give one response: if the emirs of Egypt did not keep the promises they had made to him, 'he would willingly assist him to avenge his cousin the sultan of Babylon whom they had killed'.

In fact St Louis' hands were tied; the Mamluks still held a number of prisoners and there was a danger they might suffer reprisals. The king therefore preferred to exploit the Egypt–Damascus conflict to obtain the implementation of the agreement made with the Egyptians who had so far almost entirely ignored it. In two successive missions, John of Valenciennes, sent by the king, succeeded first in bringing back all the knights still held captive (about two hundred), then the children who had been taken prisoner – an attempt had been made to convert them to Islam – along with the heads of the Christians exposed on the walls of Cairo since the defeat of Gaza and the body of Walter of Brienne. He also managed to get the remaining 200,000 *livres* of the ransom waived.

At the beginning of 1251 the Mamluks, threatened by a new offensive from Damascus, offered to make an alliance with the king of France to repel it, promising to restore the kingdom of Jerusalem. A meeting was arranged for this purpose, but the Damascenes set up a camp at Gaza to intercept the contacts between the Franks and the Egyptians. And the Egyptians, though making the king a gift of an elephant (whose picture survives in a manuscript of Matthew Paris), failed several times to turn up for these meetings; the surrender of Jerusalem, Bethlehem and the lands this side of the Jordan remained no more than a promise, while the king of France prolonged his stay in Jaffa, waiting for his allies to arrive (May 1253–April 1254).

The troops of the sultan of Damascus, on whom the Mamluks had inflicted a serious defeat when they had tried to penetrate Egypt, remained on guard in Gaza, observing the king's army without embarking on operations against it. Nor was St Louis anxious to provoke them. It was against his advice that the master of the order of St Lazarus led a raid of pillage in the region of Ramla which turned out badly for his knights. The sultan al-Nasir even offered the king of France a safe-conduct to enable him to make his devotions at the Holy Sepulchre; the king, basing himself on the example of Richard the Lionheart, did not take up the offer. The two parties avoided confrontation, al-Nasir perhaps hoping for a change of mind on St Louis' part. But the king remained faithful to the truce concluded with the Egyptians, and when he learned that the master of the Temple had entered into negotiations with the Damascenes to settle a frontier dispute by sharing the revenues of the contested territory, he insisted that the agreement should be broken and that the Templars apologise.

The caliph of Baghdad tried to achieve a reconciliation between al-Nasir and the Egyptians. His envoy was successful and the sultan of Damascus and Aleppo agreed to restore Palestine to his opponents, who still showed no sign of carrying out the promises made to the king of France. Louis was now faced with an Ayyubid army which no longer needed to tread carefully. He found himself in a situation that had become familiar to the Franks of the Holy Land, exposed the length of their frontier to Muslim attacks and without the possibility of exploiting the hostility between Egypt and Damascus which had dominated their policies for the previous twenty years.

During the year that the king of France was still to spend in the Holy Land (April 1253–April 1254), he devoted himself to improving the defences of the Frankish lands, assuming the role of protector of the kingdom of Jerusalem and even of the Frankish states as a whole; he received the young Bohemond VI, the new prince of Antioch and count of Tripoli, whom he dubbed a knight, and whom he managed to reconcile with his mother, persuading her to allow him to govern part of his lands. The Ismailis of Masyaf even approached him to try to intimidate him by extracting protection money against an 'assassination' and by attempting to obtain through his intermediary release from the tribute they paid to the Temple and the Hospital. The king frustrated their manoeuvre by giving their envoys an audience in the presence of the masters of the two orders, and the status quo was maintained. It seems that he was regarded as exercising a sort of sovereignty over the Latin states as a whole.

During the year he spent at Jaffa, St Louis was not idle. Like many crusaders before him, he set to work on rebuilding dismantled fortifications. Jaffa had only a citadel surrounded by a ruined enceinte, which he restored. He did the same at Caesarea, where recent excavations have revealed the bastioned ditches and the base of the enceinte flanked by the towers of what was one of the most perfect of thirteenth-century castles. He also strengthened the defences of Acre. At Sidon his engineers worked on the 'land castle' which sheltered the town's population. And when the king announced his intention of returning to the West, the legate Eudes of Châteauroux confided to Joinville his desire to use what remained of the treasury which he had on deposit to fortify the suburb of Acre.

But when the Damascenes regained their freedom of action, the army that al-Nasir had stationed at Gaza returned north. Joinville has described the progress of the Muslims in front of the Frankish army and the skirmishes between some of its men and the archers of the king of France. St Louis then in his turn began to lead his men north, after the army of Aleppo and Damascus, which attacked Acre in passing, devastating villages and trying to extort a tribute from the citizens to spare others. At Sidon, the Damascene army was able to surprise the knights who were guarding the workers engaged on the construction of the enceinte. The crusader army arrived too late and the Muslims massacred the Christians who had not been quick enough to take refuge in the sea castle. St Louis himself helped to bury the victims. He had to be dissuaded from taking part in an operation attempted by several companies of knights against Banyas. The Franks eventually succeeded in occupying the town, but an attack on the fortress of Subeibe almost ended in disaster. The company commanded by Oliver of Termes managed to rescue the others who fell back on Sidon; the king stayed on in the town until the walls had been completed.

The news from France, the death of Blanche of Castile, the troubles in Gascony and the affairs of Flanders and Hainault were giving increasing cause for concern, and the king's return became essential. Louis held a council and explained his dilemma; his duty to his kingdom required him to return, but he found it hard to leave the Holy Land exposed to the attacks of Muslim princes with whom no truce had been concluded. The Franks of the East themselves acknowledged that the effort put into restoring the system of fortifications that protected their possessions was an essential element in the security of their lands. A truce was therefore made with Damascus, for a period of more than ten years. The king could embark, on 24 April 1254, for a voyage which was not without its difficult moments, and which ended on 10 July when he reached Hyères, though it was only on 12 July that he could be persuaded to go ashore rather than to proceed to Aigues-Mortes where he would have been in his kingdom.

Louis IX did not regard himself as released from his obligations to the Holy Land. A body of a hundred knights paid by the royal treasury and commanded by one of the best warriors of his kingdom, Geoffrey of Sergines, remained stationed at Acre, at the disposal of the authorities of the kingdom, to participate in its defence against the Muslims. This was a new situation, since these knights had in practice the status of crusaders not integrated into the structures of the Latin kingdom.

Geoffrey of Sergines himself eventually became seneschal of the kingdom and, briefly, *bailli*, invested with power by Queen Plaisance (1 May 1259). But he remained essentially the permanent representative of the king of France in the Holy Land and the captain of his warriors, as did his successors after him. Rutebeuf, in his *Complainte de Monseigneur Geoffroy de Sergines*, portrayed him as the ideal crusader.

Conrad IV died while St Louis was on his journey home (May 1254). The king of France had been careful not to encroach on the prerogatives of the titular king of Jerusalem, though nor had he responded to Frederick II's requests that he deliver the fortresses to the officials he appointed; Frederick had made a show of intervening to procure St Louis' liberation from captivity, but not gone beyond declaring his intentions.

It was necessary to resolve the difficult situation of the kingdom, which remained at war with the 'emirs of Egypt'. The barons of Acre, led by the *bailli* John of Ibelin-Arsur, and the masters of the orders negotiated with the Mamluks and obtained a truce for ten years, ten months and ten days, but Jaffa was excluded from the truce, probably to leave the Mamluks the possibility of protecting themselves against new attacks from Damascus, which the Franks might support. At Christmas 1255 Geoffrey of Sergines and the other Frankish leaders marched on Jaffa. A raid allowed them to seize a large quantity of booty; the Muslims responded with another raid, more profitable in both captives and cattle. A more serious engagement, in April 1256, cost the emir of Jerusalem his life. Finally, in October, the truces were renewed, this time including Jaffa; the situation that St Louis had found in 1248, on his arrival in the East, had been stabilised, at the cost of what had become a permanent commitment on the part of the king of France.

Seen from Frankish Syria, the balance sheet of the Capetian crusade was positive: the places that had been faltering in the face of the reconquest undertaken by the sultan of Egypt had been strengthened, their walls consolidated, and the morale of their defenders raised. Muslim Egypt and Syria remained separate; it could hardly be expected that negotiations would produce gains comparable to those of the years 1229–41, but they made it possible to maintain the status quo.

Seen from the West, the balance sheet appeared negative. An excellent army and a king whose moral worth was generally recognised, enjoying exceptional financial support, had set out for the East amidst high hopes, and the early successes had exceeded expectations. The failure had been all the harder to bear. There was a response to the new appeals of the king of France, but not on the scale of that of 1244–8.

It cannot be said that the notion of the crusade had suffered. But it is clear that in the years after 1250 the sense of urgency as regards the recovery of the Holy Land seemed to have subsided, since other problems seemed equally serious.

While St Louis was preparing to leave Egypt for Syria, a new sovereign solemnly took the cross and announced his departure for the Holy Land, Henry III of England. Those close to him did the same, in March 1250. The failure of the French army was not as yet known, and the motives behind Henry's decision remain unclear; he had made no effort to join the king of France, against whom he had been asserting claims since the beginning of his reign. But the king's resolution was not in doubt; he began to accumulate a war chest during the course of 1250 and made economies at Christmas that year; but he also asked the pope to allow him to postpone his departure.

In 1252, the situation was clarified; Henry announced his departure for August 1256; he appealed to the military orders to provide ships and lodgings for his advance party; in March 1253 he enquired how many crusaders would come from Ireland and began to negotiate with Marseilles for the transport of his army. A propaganda campaign was launched; the English had not forgotten the crusading exploits of Richard the Lionheart.

At this point, Henry was diverted by events in Gascony; the intrigues of Simon de Montfort made it necessary for him to go in person to the duchy, taking the crusaders with him, and to spend there a large part of the money he had accumulated, including the tenths demanded of the churches. The king still intended to leave for the East. But in 1254 he was showing interest in the pope's schemes for the kingdom of Sicily and, at the end of the year, he promised the king of Castile to get his crusading vow commuted so that he could accompany him on his proposed expedition to Africa. This was a project he discussed again in 1256, and even in 1262; he remained *crucesignatus* and his commitment was to the Holy Land, but if he could he would get the pope to change its destination so that he could join the African expedition, which never materialised. The pope pressed him, in 1255, to leave for the East, but the king still hesitated.

On 9 April 1255 Henry III made an agreement with the new pope,

Alexander IV, accepting the offer of the throne of Sicily for his second son, Edmund, which obliged him to lead his knights to Sicily and pay the costs incurred by the papacy in the Sicilian affair, a total of 135,541 marks. This was a large sum, which led the king of England to negotiate with the king of France, renouncing the rights he claimed to the Plantagenet inheritance, confiscated by Philip Augustus, in exchange for a substantial indemnity which would be used to pay knights 'employed in God's service'. This led on to the treaty of Paris which lifted the threat to the kingdom of France constituted by the claims of the English king, leaving Louis IX's hands free to assist the Holy Land.

The history of Henry III's abortive crusade is significant. Though he had taken the cross in all sincerity to go to the Holy Land, Henry was seduced by other prospects in other spheres of action. While Haakon of Norway managed to get his vow of crusade to the East commuted so that he could instead fight the Estonians, the king of England preferred the conquest of the Sicilian crown which had been offered to him by the pope.

The Sicilian affair became one of the major preoccupations of the papacy. Until the death of Frederick II, though Innocent IV's attempts to undermine the kingdom of Sicily had not borne fruit, the pope had supported the Lombard communes against the emperor, and succeeded in making William of Holland a 'king of the Romans' recognised in north-eastern Germany. On Frederick's death, it was one of his illegitimate sons, Manfred, who acted as regent, while the pope tried to exploit this situation to take possession of Sicily; finally, Conrad IV arrived from Germany and his half-brother surrendered the kingdom to him; Innocent IV found himself in a false position. He had declared that the Hohenstaufen had forfeited their rights to reign in Germany and Italy, and stripped them of the crown of Sicily. He was nevertheless reduced to negotiating with Conrad, who refused to renounce his rights to the crown of the king of the Romans and behaved as both king of Sicily and king of Jerusalem. The pope had been liberal with grants of crusading indulgences to anyone who assisted William of Holland or the Italian towns, but he had been met with only moderate enthusiasm, though the German crusaders had helped William to take Aachen in 1248. The crusade preached in Germany against Conrad was hardly more successful. It was primarily on the financial plane that these appeals had yielded results, since they had made it possible to tax the ecclesiastical benefices. To offer the crown of Sicily to a foreign prince was a different matter; neither Richard of Cornwall nor Charles of Anjou had succumbed to the temptation.

The death of Conrad IV changed the situation (May 1254). Manfred had let Innocent IV take possession of the kingdom (it was at Naples that the pope died, in December) and negotiated with Alexander IV for a compromise. But in the end, he remained sole master of the kingdom, of which he proclaimed himself king in 1258, ignoring the rights of his nephew Conradin. Alexander IV appealed for a crusade against him, and against his supporters in northern Italy, in particular Ezzelino da Romano. He declared that Manfred had no right to reign and offered the throne to Edmund of England, then, when Henry III, preoccupied with the revolt of his barons and financial problems, had to abandon this project (July 1263), his successor, Urban IV, appealed to Charles of Anjou.

All these negotiations, attempts and local wars were punctuated by appeals to a crusade; in 1263 volunteers were invited to expel the supporters of the Hohenstaufen from Sardinia, with the promise of the indulgences granted to crusaders. But it was the expedition of Charles of Anjou which was really organised in the manner of a crusade to the Holy Land, with preaching in central Italy and an appeal for volunteers elsewhere. The poet Rutebeuf, who had already written a *Complainte de Monseigneur Geoffroy de Sergines* and a *Complainte de Constantinople*, composed a *Chanson de Pouille* which invited the knights to come and fight against Manfred in the same words he had used to invite them to leave for the East. The privileges granted to the crusaders by Urban IV were identical to those granted for the crusade overseas.

Such a crusade still had a place in papal policy; once the Sicilian affair had been settled, and with Germany disputed between two rival kings of the Romans, Richard of Cornwall and Alfonso of Castile, the West could devote itself to the defence of the Holy Land. In this sense, the victory of Charles of Anjou at Benevento in 1266, even though it was not until 1268 that the last Hohenstaufen, Conradin, was defeated and executed, removed one of the obstacles which had inhibited the resumption of the crusade. But precious time had been wasted.

The quarrel between papacy and empire and the Sicilian affair were not the only occasions on which the crusading indulgence was offered to others than to those who left for Acre. The Latin empire of Constantinople had tried in vain to obtain papal and western aid to resist the relentless advance of the Byzantines. Malcolm Barber has noted that the more the principality of Morea, under the Villehardouin, proved attractive to western knights, the greater their indifference to the Latin empire, while its constant appeals for financial aid were an irritant to public opinion. But the fall of the imperial city, after a bold attack by a small Byzantine detachment (25 July 1261), provoked deep emotion. The emperor Baldwin II rallied the leaders of the Latin states of

Romania, then Manfred, to his cause, and arrived at Viterbo where the new pope, Urban IV, had already received an ambassador from Michael Palaeologus seeking recognition of the *fait accompli* by promising to work for the union of the Churches; he had been sent packing. Manfred offered to restore Baldwin to his throne in return for recognition of his right to the throne of Sicily; the pope dismissed this proposal too, and issued a bull in which he ordered the preaching, first of all in France, of a crusade for the recovery of the Latin empire. He excommunicated the Genoese, allies of the Byzantines, and he ordered that the sums raised for the assistance of the Holy Land should, for three years, be assigned to the proposed expedition (1262). Rutebeuf wrote a *complainte* to encourage the future crusaders.

But by 1263 circumstances had changed and the urgency of the help needed in the Holy Land put the projected crusade in abeyance. Baldwin II attempted to find allies from among the French nobility, offering great lordships, which had first to be conquered, to the count of Champagne and the duke of Burgundy, before concluding a matrimonial alliance with Charles of Anjou, who gave his daughter in marriage to Baldwin's son Philip, and marrying his son to the daughter of the prince of Morea. But Venice, which was associated in Baldwin II's manoeuvres, and which had inflicted a crushing naval defeat on the Genoese in 1263, was approached in 1265 by the Byzantine emperor with the offer of a peace treaty. The anti-Byzantine crusade remained a dead letter, and Michael VIII resumed his relations with Rome in 1267.

Though the Mongol threat had failed to materialise since the retreat of the army that had advanced as far as the Adriatic in 1241, the eastern frontier of Europe had continued to offer crusading opportunities. Here, the conversion to Christianity of the Scandinavian peoples, achieved in the eleventh century, and that of the Poles, the Bohemians and the Hungarians had preceded the first attempts at the evangelisation of the Finnish and Baltic peoples and of those of the Steppe. These were under way by the beginning of the thirteenth century, though already, in the last decades of the twelfth century, Danes and Swedes had embarked on conquests accompanied by the destruction of idols and by conversions, in Finland, Estonia and Livonia, which have sometimes been compared with crusades. It was with the preaching of the Cistercians in Prussia and Livonia that clashes occurred that led the papacy to intervene. In 1206 Innocent III gave the Cistercians of Lekno the right to preach in Prussia; a bishop of Livonia appeared in 1200. These 'new plantations of the faith' were exposed to return offensives by the pagans, and by 1199 Innocent III felt it necessary to preach a crusade for the defence of the Christians of Livonia. Other crusades sporadically followed for similar reasons, particularly in Prussia, and King Waldemar I of Denmark had to intervene in Prussia and Pomerelia in 1210.

A characteristic feature was the organisation of 'Christian knight-hoods', military orders in the service of the local Churches; the first seems to have been that of the Sword Brothers, created by the archbishop of Livonia for the protection of his Church; in 1228 the Polish Duke Conrad of Mazovia founded at Dobrin another 'Christian knighthood' in imitation of it, to defend the new Christianity of Plock from Prussian attacks. There were also appeals to foreign orders; the knights of Calatrava appeared in Pomerelia, but most important were the Teutonic Knights, established in 1226 by the Polish duke of Chelm 'to fight against the Prussians and other Saracens', who, in 1223, had captured some missionaries.

The Teutonic Knights were also established in Transylvania, in 1211, in the face of the Cumans of the Ukrainian plain, and their estates had been enlarged in 1222 by the king of Hungary 'for the defence of the kingdom against the Cumans'. But their claim to depend only on the Holy See, in other words to escape royal authority, led King Andrew II to eject them. The country of the Cumans, in any case, passed under Hungarian protection after a defeat inflicted on the Cumans by the Mongols, and the protection of the Knights was no longer needed. In 1228, however, the pope was still contemplating a crusade to protect the Cuman converts against those who had remained pagan.

During the years 1240–60, the danger took new forms. The Cumans and other nomads, the Alans (Jasc in Hungarian), had sought refuge from the Mongols in Hungary, and though they had been made welcome by the king, they were responsible for a revival of paganism which eventually became a source of anxiety for the papacy. But problems were erupting all along the frontier of the Baltic peoples. The Sword Brothers had been beaten by Alexander Nevsky in 1242; the Teutonic Knights were asking for a crusade to defend them from the pagans in Prussia, Livonia and Courland (1256). Between the Vistula and the Pripet were the Jatwings who were causing anxiety both to the Russians and to the Poles. Alexander IV instructed the Franciscan Bartholomew of Bohemia to preach a crusade against them in Poland (1255); the collusion of the duke of Cujavia and those of the Lettigallians who had adopted Christianity also caused problems with the Teutonic Knights (1257).

But Alexander IV may have harboured larger ambitions; Oskar Halecki has suggested that we should see in both the creation of the bishopric of Lukow for the Jatwings, thus recognised as an independent people, and the grant of royal crowns to the grand-duke of Halicz,

Daniel, and the Lithuanian prince Mindaugas (1255), a project for a federation of the peoples of eastern Europe directed against the Mongols. The pope wanted to complete the formation of this league of princes who sided with the Church of Rome by organising a crusade against the Tartars, which proved impossible. When the Mongols advanced, and their pressure was felt by 1257, the league collapsed, the princes in question making their submission, as Alexander Nevsky himself had done.

How many of the faithful likely to be moved by appeals to a crusade responded to this tangle of initiatives sanctioned by, or even emanating from, the papacy? We know that certain princes, who might have taken the cross to go to the Holy Land, such as the king of Bohemia, Ottokar II, in fact set out for Prussia; it was in his honour that the Teutonic Knights named their new fortress Königsberg. As we have seen, there were volunteers even to go to Sicily or to support William of Holland in his battle against the Hohenstaufen. At a time when the fate of the Holy Land seemed stable and when other appeals were being made, those who wanted to earn the crusade indulgence did not lack opportunities.

THE JURIDICAL THEORY OF THE CRUSADE AND THE EMERGENCE OF THE MISSIONARY PERSPECTIVE

During Louis IX's crusade in Egypt and in the aftermath of its defeat, voices were raised in criticism of the project attributed to him, not without reason, of conquering Egypt, and of having wished to destroy the power of the sultan – 'to crush the snake's head' in the words of Robert of Artois – and convert that country to the Christian faith, when, as Matthew Paris said, the purpose of the crusade ought only to be the reconquest of Jerusalem.

This was a debate that had been started by the great thirteenth-century canonists who, commenting on the 'five books of the Decretals', that is, the collection of texts on which canon law was based, had discussed, under the heading of the vow (*de voto*), the implications of the vow of crusade. This led them to establish a distinction between the vow by which a crusader promised to fight and that of the pilgrim, made for a purely spiritual end. Already well established by Sinibaldo Fieschi (the future Innocent IV) in the 1230s, this distinction was very clear in the work of Henry of Suse, cardinal of Ostia, who was writing after 1260. Hostiensis, however, tried to show that there was no difference in nature between the crusade overseas (*crux transmarina*) and the crusade which fought the enemies of the Church on European soil (*crux cismarina*), while Innocent IV pondered the legality of a crusade directed against schismatics or against Christians who rebelled against the teaching of the Church; in his eyes the heretics, who disobeyed the Church knowingly, alone merited repression by means of a crusade.

The position of the cardinal of Ostia was, in fact, more radical than that of the future Innocent IV. Hostiensis regarded as lawful a crusade launched against the infidel which resulted in deprivation of lands, because the coming of Christ had transferred to Christians the rights and the powers which had previously belonged to non-Christians. Sinibaldo Fieschi, on the other hand, believed that the infidel enjoyed the rights of every human being; the crusade, he said, was only legitimate to the extent that it aimed to restore to the Christians lands to which they had valid rights but of which they had been deprived without justification. This applied in particular to the Holy Land, which had belonged to the Roman empire, and which had been sanctified by the life and passion of Christ.

Had this historical line of argument been continued it would doubtless have ended by casting doubt on the legitimacy of the right of the Muslim princes to occupy other territories which had belonged to the Christian emperors up to the seventh and eighth centuries. But those who accepted the arguments of Innocent IV, who were in a majority in the thirteenth century, were persuaded to recognise this occupation as legitimate to the extent that the princes did not oppress the Christians or oppose the free preaching of the faith of Christ.

Further, a deeper knowledge of Muslim beliefs made it possible to go beyond the ideas of the people of the twelfth century, for whom Mahomet was no more than a disciple of the heresiarchs of the first centuries, and to discover the biblical basis of the doctrines laid out in the Koran. A letter from pope Alexander IV to the sultan of Konya is highly significant in this regard. The pope wrote to the sultan, replying to letters from him, that he understood that he had received a whole part of the Bible, the Pentateuch included, and that he was well disposed with regard to a preaching which might even persuade him to embrace the Christian faith; Matthew Paris even accepts that the sultan had been baptised in secret. Dialogue with the Muslims appeared, then, to be a possibility.

This new conception of the situation of the infidel with regard to Christianity led to the adoption of another new attitude. It was not a matter of replacing the crusade by mission, as many historians have too simplistically stated, but of making a place for mission alongside the crusade. We may recall the occasion when St Francis of Assisi proposed to the sultan al-Adil that he prove the verity of the Christian faith by subjecting himself to ordeal by fire. We should also note the many conversions to Christianity which took place in the twelfth century, in particular on the part of captive Muslims. James of Vitry, at the time of the Fifth Crusade, preached to Muslims, that is, to those in the Frankish lands. Such preaching continued, not without encountering a degree of obstruction on the part of the Frankish owners of Muslim slaves who feared they might escape their servile condition by embracing the Christian faith. Gregory IX, in 1237 and in 1238, had to remind the lords of the kingdom of Jerusalem of their duty to allow their infidel slaves to attend, at least once a month, the sermons intended for them, and to receive baptism, without prejudice to the freedom they would acquire by the fact of their conversion. The legate Eudes of Châteauroux returned to this point in 1252, threatening to excommunicate those who obstructed the baptism of their slaves.

But the evangelisation acquired another dimension between 1230 and 1250, as a result of the intervention of members of religious orders who were no longer tied to a convent and to the obligation to serve a sanctuary, and who were consequently able to penetrate non-Christian lands to spread the Gospel there and to urge the Christians separated from Rome to unity in the faith. The Franciscans were the first to arrive, with Francis of Assisi. In 1238 Pope Gregory IX gave one of them the task of taking the sacraments to the Christian captives of the sultan of Aleppo, whom he authorised, in default, to resort to Jacobite priests. The Dominicans followed, and it is known that St Dominic, when he founded his order, had in mind the preaching of the faith to the pagans of eastern Europe; they were therefore ideally suited to go out among the infidel and the schismatics.

Under Gregory IX, the duty of mission in the East assumed another form. In 1235 the pope recommended the Dominican William of Montferrat to the lords, merchants and other Christians when he sent him to the countries which did not obey the Church of Rome. Letters were addressed by the same pope to the leaders of the eastern Churches to invite them to the union of the Churches, and the prior of the Dominican convent of Jerusalem, Philip, reported that he had sent his brethren to the eastern prelates, and even to the *catholicos* of the Nestorians, who lived in Baghdad (1237). The easterners discovered with interest these exemplary and educated religious; the king of Armenia asked for the foundation of a convent of friars preacher, but, in the absence of brethren, had to be content with founding the convent of Tiflis (1240).

The mission to Christians separated from Rome assumed even greater importance under Innocent IV. The council of Lyons (1245) was for this pope an opportunity to promulgate an encyclical in which he asked the patriarchs, *catholicos* and archbishops to send their profession of faith and a declaration of support for the unity of the Church. He received many favourable responses, though the controversial issues were avoided.

These conversations took a particular turn in the case of the Greek Churches. The papal envoys, Dominic of Aragon, Laurence of Portugal and John of Parma, acting as spokesmen of Innocent IV, agreed to very major concessions to the Greek Church, to the detriment of the predominant position claimed by the Latin prelates of the East. Rome accepted that Greek patriarchs and Greek archbishops should enjoy the same dignity and authority as their Latin peers, by recognising the primacy of the pope, but without in future depending on the Latin primates who had hitherto claimed to exercise a superior authority. The Greek patriarch of Antioch, David, was recognised by the pope; the Greek archbishop of Cyprus was confirmed by Eudes of Châteauroux despite the protests of the Latin archbishop of Nicosia; a lawsuit followed which was settled only by a compromise under Alexander IV, in 1260. And the Greek patriarch of Constantinople was to be restored to his patriarchal see, with the title of ecumenical patriarch, without having to renounce his liturgical particularisms, on condition that he accepted Roman primacy.

In fact, in the middle of the century, in relations with the Christians of the East, the desire to achieve the union of the Churches was regarded as more important than the rights that the Latin prelates of the East regarded as established. The idea of mission took precedence over other considerations. But the union of Churches was not its only objective; the conversion of the infidel to the faith of Christ emerged as an imperative at the same time. In 1233 Gregory IX sent the principal Muslim sovereigns letters urging them to embrace Christianity, which were conveyed by religious who were instructed to explain to them the points of the faith. These religious kept in contact; it was one of them, William Champenois of Tripoli, who in 1239 served as intermediary for the prince of Hamah when he wanted to get the crusaders to intervene in his favour. In 1245, as well as the letters they carried to the eastern prelates, Innocent IV's representatives sent letters to the Muslim princes to invite them into the faith. The prince of Kerak replied very courteously to his, expressing his regrets that he had been unable to prevent the Khwarismians from sacking Jerusalem, but without replying to the pope's appeal; the prince of Homs said he regretted that the religious had not known enough Arabic for it to have been possible for him to organise a debate. Only the Seljuk sultan of Turkey agreed to enter into a religious discussion, though without following up the pope's invitation.

These friendly exchanges did not, however, result in the freedom to preach the Christian faith in Muslim lands, and the hopes based on the persuasiveness of the missionary initiatives with regard to the Muslim princes were dashed. The attempt, however, is indicative of a state of mind shared by Gregory IX, Innocent IV and Alexander IV, that is, by the popes of the mid-thirteenth century: a confidence that the brethren trained by the mendicant orders could establish a religious dialogue capable of converting the Muslim princes themselves to the Christian faith, without having recourse to armed force.

The appearance of the Mongols on the horizon was to arouse other hopes. Gregory IX had no alternative but to proclaim a crusade to oppose these invaders with a resistance which it was never, in fact, necessary to organise. Discovering that the Mongols professed no known religion, Innocent IV conceived the idea of offering them, along with a treaty of non-aggression, a conversion to the Christian faith. This invitation was very badly received by the *noyan* Baiju, whose entourage made Ascelin of Cremona understand that it might be insulting to propose to the victorious Mongols that they exchange their religion and identity for those of the Christians, a word which, to them, represented the people they had conquered. The *qaghan* Güyük replied simply to the pope: 'We have not understood your demand.' And this was the reply that John of Plancarpin reported to the sovereign pontiff. The third mission, that of Andrew of Longjumeau, turned out differently; the Dominican had met in Tabriz a monk from the Far East, Simeon Rabban-ata, who had been made responsible for the protection of Christians. He had discovered that there existed among the Mongol people a Christian element which enjoyed a certain influence.

This information was confirmed when there arrived in Cyprus, during Louis IX's stay, and when Andrew of Longjumeau was also present, a letter from the constable of Armenia, Sempad, to his Frankish cousins, in which he told them of his journey to Samarkand, which he left for the Mongol court, describing this Christian world, in general of the Nestorian rite, in the oases and steppes of central Asia.

The message sent to the king of France by the representative of the khan in the Iranian lands, Eljigidei, was itself conveyed by two Christians, Mark and David, one of whom had already been encountered by Andrew of Longjumeau in Simeon's entourage. The message, at least in its translation, probably the work of other Christians, consisted of expressions of good will towards the king and for his victory over the infidel. Louis IX concluded from this that the Mongol sovereign was well disposed towards Christianity, and sent Andrew of Longjumeau back to the Mongol court with presents including a tent-chapel of precious cloth decorated with religious scenes. Andrew returned in 1253 with a disappointing reply; the regent Oghul-Qaimish was asking him once again to make an act of submission, without replying to the invitations to baptism made to her by the king and the pontifical legate.

So, when a Franciscan already familiar with the East, the Fleming William of Rubruck, told the king of his desire to go out and settle in Mongol territory in order to preach the Gospel there, because he had heard, probably from Armenian sources, that the Mongol prince Sartaq, son of the khan Batu who ruled the lands between the Volga basin and Turkestan, had received baptism, St Louis was cautious. He provided William with letters of recommendation for Sartaq, whom he congratulated on having accepted the Christian faith, expressing his desire for friendly relations, but carefully avoided anything that might be seen as an overture of a political nature. He and the queen also gave the Franciscan jewels, books and money. Passing through Constantinople, William obtained other letters of recommendation from the emperor Baldwin II as well as information from the knight Baldwin of Hainault, who was returning from a mission he had made to Mongolia on behalf of the Latin emperor.

William's expedition did not turn out as expected. The letters he carried to Sartaq had been translated into Arabic and Syriac, but, before being handed over, were translated once again. Perhaps because the translators, who were Armenians, wanted the king of France to co-operate with the Mongols against their Muslim enemies, the letters took the form of a proposal for an alliance. Sartaq, who William was hoping would authorise him to preach the Gospel in the lands he ruled, was reluctant to take it upon himself to reply to a proposal of this kind; he sent William to the court of his father, Batu, who, in his turn, sent the Franciscan to the court of the *qaghan* Möngke.

William of Rubruck was thus to have an extraordinary experience; conducted with great speed by means of the Mongol post as far as Karakorum, in central Mongolia, he crossed the whole of central Asia, discovering the people, the customs and the country. He had personal contacts with the *qaghan* and met westerners who had been deported, such as the Parisian goldsmith William Boucher and a Pasquette of Metz from Lorraine, and adventurers, Russians who had come to make an act of submission and Christians of various rites, including one of the wives of the sovereign. He took part in a theological debate, he brought spiritual assistance to the Christians of Karakorum and learned that German miners had been established in Dzungaria. He discovered a mission field. But the letters from the king to which he owed his adventure had got lost. He left, regarded as an ambassador from the king, with a new invitation to the king to recognise Mongol sovereignty.

He was followed by the king of Armenia, Hethoum, who was hoping to provoke that Mongol intervention to the benefit of Christianity in the Near East that Rubruck had done everything to avoid (1254–6). The westerners had not yet anticipated such a possibility; for them, the discovery of the immense Mongol territories, the possibilities they offered for the task of evangelisation, the presence of 'Christian captives of the Tartars' and of groups of Christians belonging to eastern rites but often deeply ignorant, all opened up new horizons. Already, while Rubruck was returning from Karakorum, passing this time by the shores of the Caspian Sea and Armenia, he had met a group of Dominicans who were on their way to preach the faith among the Mongols; and in 1258 Pope Alexander IV accorded the privileges granted to the missionaries to the Franciscans who, it seemed, were proposing to settle in the countries adjoining the Black Sea, under the rule of the 'Tartars'.

We cannot discuss the development of these missions more fully here, but we should note that, in parallel, the Roman Church refined its missionary doctrine in the lands of its eastern frontier that were still pagan, by seeking to create national Christianities, to the detriment of the ambitions of the Teutonic Knights. This was the case, for example, when the Jatwings invaded the borders of Poland. Alexander IV had given the Franciscan Bartholomew of Bohemia responsibility for preaching the crusade against them in Poland (1255). But in 1256 he learned that some of them had become Christians and had put themselves under the protection of the duke of Cujavia; when he proposed to create a bishopric for them, this was opposed by the Teutonic Knights, who wanted to place this people under their rule, which earned them a papal excommunication (1257). The missionary doctrine defined between 1240 and 1260 was aimed at freeing the new Christianities from the political ambitions of the Latins who based their rights on the crusade, seeing this as an opportunity to impose obedience on the peoples in their area who were not subject to the Roman Church.

The years that separated the fall of Jerusalem from the second Mongol attack on Europe, seen from the viewpoint of the history of the crusades, are dominated by the preparation, events and consequences of Louis IX's expedition to Egypt. The hopes it had raised and the spectacular nature of its early successes only deepened the disillusionment which followed. But by prolonging his stay overseas, and by leaving a detachment of his own men guarding the Holy Land, the king of France prevented the failure of the Egyptian campaign from leading to further discouragements. The duty to preserve the Frankish positions in the Holy Land, point of departure for its recovery, remained etched into the consciousness of the West, in spite of the reservations articulated by Rutebeuf through the voice of his *Décroisé*.

That the loss of Jerusalem led to only a single major departure, that of the king of France – to the extent that the crusade can be seen as his personal affair – shows that other problems seemed as urgent as the recovery of the Holy City, all the more so in that the palace revolution which had cost the life of the sultan Turanshah had not yet resulted in the establishment of a 'Mamluk imperialism' capable of causing concern to Christendom; the 'emirs of Egypt', as they were called in the entourage of St Louis, who had broken with Ayyubid legitimacy, appeared rather as an anarchic element, likely to weaken the power of the Saracens.

Did the proliferation of appeals to the crusade for what the canonist Hostiensis called the *crux cismarina* make people forget the *crux trans-marina*, which, he noted, was less attractive to the simple faithful? The settlement of the conflict with the Hohenstaufen on the one hand and the building of the defences of the northern confines of eastern Europe on the other diverted attention from the problems of the Holy Land. But it was probably because these were less pressing that the West left the crusade temporarily in abeyance. The Franks of the East themselves did not, at this period, seek the help of their co-religionists; the questions which were then preoccupying them were nothing to do with the crusade.

IN THE HOLY LAND: A NEW FRANKISH
SOCIETY

Whereas the crusades of the twelfth century had of necessity to be integrated into the framework created by the presence of the Latin states of the East, those of the thirteenth century were rather superimposed on it. Nothing reveals this more clearly than the stipulation which appeared in the truces made between the Franks and their Muslim neighbours at the end of Henry VI's crusade, and also in the treaties of the sultan Qalawûn and the Frankish lords after 1275: the arrival of a Western sovereign would automatically end the truce, without responsibility for the rupture being imputed to the Franks of the East.

The Frankish establishments were unable to exert the same influence on political decisions as in the previous century. They had changed in size and structure and all had been affected to some degree by the crisis of 1187. The new economic conditions contributed to these changes by giving growing importance to commercial interests; changes to the juridical system on which these states were based also played a part. But the main cause of these changes was the Muslim conquest of 1187 and its consequences in both the demographic and territorial spheres.

THE CONSEQUENCES OF SALADIN'S CONQUEST AND THE RECONSTRUCTION

Saladin's attempt in 1187–8 to eliminate the Frankish presence in Syria had not been wholly successful for three main reasons: the strengthening of the defences of the great coastal fortresses following the arrival of the first reinforcements from the West; his own difficulties in keeping his troops in the field over long periods; and western reactions. The resulting situation varied according to region: in the kingdom of Jerusalem, only Tyre with its immediate environs remained Frankish; Acre and a few dependencies were to be recovered. In the county of Tripoli, on the other hand, the occupation of Gibelet, Botrun and a few places of secondary importance had not seriously eroded the county; the Hospitallers and the Templars had retained their principal castles. The principality of Antioch had lost Latakia and Jabala, only briefly reoccupied before 1260, and the castles in the interior covering the route from Aleppo to Latakia, such as Saone, had been permanently lost; the principality was reduced to the region round Antioch, with St Simeon as its only port. Saladin had even at one stage occupied the fortresses to the north of Antioch.

With the exception of certain parts of the county of Tripoli, the Franks had lost most of their rural estates, that is, the lands cultivated by indigenous tenants which provided their Frankish lords with most of their income. They had also lost all the small towns with Frankish populations, which are listed, probably incompletely, in the *Assises de Jérusalem*, which gives about thirty names, cited as meeting places of a *cour de bourgeois*. A large number of castles had been dismantled. The towns themselves had been emptied of their Frankish inhabitants, though Saladin had often offered them the possibility of reaching the coast rather than being reduced to slavery, which had been the fate of many from the villages and small towns.

All the same, if Saladin had hoped to compel all these Franks to return to the West, which many of them had never seen, he miscalculated. Frankish nobles and bourgeois took refuge in the towns that remained in their power, at the risk of overcrowding. As we know from the example of Acre, they hoped to recover their houses and property as soon as a crusade made this possible. In the meantime, a whole uprooted population was crammed into the towns still held by the Latins.

Richard I's conquest of Cyprus offered them an outlet, especially when the island came into the hands of the first two Lusignan. As we have seen, Guy has been credited with having appealed to the ruined nobles, the widows, the orphans who had lost their inheritance and the bourgeois deprived of their lands to find compensation in Cyprus. The Armenian baron Leo, who in 1197 succeeded in getting his lordship of Cilicia elevated into a kingdom, also attracted Frankish nobles, in particular those from the principality of Antioch who had clashed or would clash with prince Bohemond III or his son Bohemond IV. Many barons and knights from Antioch went to settle in Armenia, where Leo offered them fiefs and titles, which produced some conflicts of loyalty. The family of Ibelin profited from its dominant position in Cyprus to exercise exceptional influence in the kingdom of Jerusalem. In contrast, the brothers of Tiberias, the stepsons of Raymond III of Tripoli, having lost their fine lordship, served many sovereigns in succession – king of Jerusalem, prince of Antioch, emperor of Constantinople and king of Armenia – without ever acquiring an endowment comparable to the one they had lost.

Only a few great vassals rebuilt, thanks to the reconquests, those lordships grouped round a great fortress and secondary castles which had existed in the twelfth century, as did the sires of Beirut, Sidon and Toron, the counts of Jaffa, and the sires of Arsur and Caiphas. Eudes of Montbéliard was briefly able, between 1241 and 1247, to recreate a lordship of Tiberias. But many were content with a few villages from which they received the usual payments, and rents on royal revenues, organised into money fiefs. The Tripolitanian vassals seem better endowed than those of Jerusalem.

This did not prevent some of the barons from living in a surprising degree of luxury. We owe to Wilbrand of Oldenburg, who visited Beirut in 1211, a dazzling description of the palace recently rebuilt by John of Ibelin, with its fountains cooling the air, its mosaics and its paintings executed by Greek, Syrian and Muslim decorators who were masters of trompe-l'oeil. Wilbrand was amazed to discover houses in Antioch which were unimpressive from the outside but had luxuriously decorated interiors. The richness of clothing had already impressed visitors in the twelfth century and the patriarch Heraclius had been criticised for his use of perfume and for the luxurious fabrics of his robes. The rich bourgeois were unlikely to be less richly clothed.

With the disappearance of the bourgeoisie who could be described as rural, who had inhabited the fortified places of the interior, there now existed an essentially urban bourgeoisie, engaged primarily in commercial activities. As we have seen, at the time of the crisis of 1187 the moralists denounced this bourgeoisie for having exploited the pilgrims and the crusaders to profit from their presence. The description left by James of Vitry, bishop of Acre at the time of the Fifth Crusade, of the Latins of the East who were his diocesans, reveals such resentments. These *poulains*, he said, were effeminate; they wore loose-fitting clothing more suitable for women, used perfume and had lost their warlike qualities; they made truces and peace treaties with the Saracens and engaged in civil wars in which they were not afraid to involve the latter, while they appealed to the 'pilgrims' to come to their aid, although refusing to break the truces; one detects here an echo of the war between Bohemond IV and Leo of Armenia, and Aimery's refusal to break the truces. They locked up their women like the Muslims and the

Syrians, forbidding them even to go to church. And they mocked the 'sons of Hernaud', the Westerners gullible enough to come to their assistance, accusing them of not understanding the East.

This diatribe may be largely unjust, but it shows that the customs of the Latin East could come as a shock to those arriving from the West with the intention of sanctifying themselves there. Acting, no doubt, on information provided by St Louis or his legate, Innocent IV fulminated in 1248 against the people of Acre, including the religious, who rented their houses to courtesans; many popes reproached the Frankish lords for opposing the baptism of their slaves, motivated by greed, since baptism led to enfranchisement, though ties of patronage were maintained. There was truth in the accusation that some of the crusaders led a life of pleasure in Acre. They gambled, and for high stakes; this was how Julian of Sidon lost his fortune, and the banished Englishman arrested in Vienna as a Mongol spy had also ruined himself gambling.

But we should not forget that nobles and bourgeois had to bear their share of the burdens of the war. James of Vitry himself collected many commitments to the Egyptian crusade. The heavy losses suffered at La Forbie in 1244 hit knights, sergeants and turcopoles. Succeeding the bloodbath of 1187, this catastrophe inevitably had demographic consequences. The remarriage of widows was one of the problems it posed for sovereigns.

For this and other reasons, there were large numbers of immigrants, from many different countries. New arrivals, thanks to marriage, took their place among the nobility of the Latin East; among the lords of Caiphas, we find a García Álvarez and a John of Valenciennes; the English Hamo l'Estrange became lord of Beirut, and the lists of knights that appear in royal and seigneurial acts contain many new names. The same is true of the bourgeoisie, reinforced by men who arrived from the West, not all, perhaps, for wholly honourable reasons, since they included many who had been banished and were seeking refuge and pardon for their offences. The growth of commercial and artisanal activity attracted many foreigners.

The development of confraternities was linked to this immigration. The *Assises de Jérusalem* assigned them a role, specifying that, to start proceedings against the perpetrator of a crime, the initiative might be taken by the victim's relations or, if they had none, by members of their fraternity, which therefore served to bind together people without roots or local family. The fraternity of St Andrew of Acre, which dated back to before 1187, constituted a form of association that enabled the adversaries of Frederick II to band together. In 1219 a fraternity of the Holy Spirit was founded by Italian goldsmiths, which brought together the Italians of Acre, except for those of the merchant towns who had their own institutions. It gave them the opportunity to practice a devotion to which they were particularly attached; it provided them with assistance thanks to a treasury stocked by their subscriptions and by donations; and it helped them to equip themselves for war and pay their ransom. It was not unique; the Spanish had a fraternity dedicated to St James, and they associated it in the prayers of the Hospitallers; the English founded a fraternity of St Edward, which Edward I in 1278 made responsible for guarding the tower he built in Acre. The 'Syrians' seem to have been grouped into a fraternity of 'St George and Bethlehem'. We get a picture of a society articulated into groups which bound together those of common origin, which is hardly surprising in an East where the various 'nations' were anxious to maintain their identity and internal links. These groups also constituted military forces; that of the Holy Spirit had its arsenal, and when its members fought it was under the fraternity's banner. These associations divided the Christian community into a collection of juxtaposed parts capable of opposing each other.

At the same time, within these Frankish towns Christians of different confessions moved closer to each other in a way already celebrated by Fulcher of Chartres. Acts in French were drawn up before the *cour des bourgeois* of Acre by persons with indisputably 'Syrian' names who were therefore very close to their 'Frankish' homologues. A great merchant, Saliba, 'bourgeois of Acre', whose brother was called Bedr and whose nephew was called Sarkis, described himself as a brother of the Hospital, and in his will of 1264 made bequests to the Dominicans, the Franciscans, the Carmelites, the Repentant Sisters, the hospitals of St Antony and the Holy Spirit, St Lazarus and the churches of St Agnes and St Magdalen. He may have remained firmly rooted in his community of origin, but his devotions and contacts placed him also in Frankish circles. Juridical texts distinguished the Christians of 'the law of Rome' from those who belonged to other rites, but the latter, who also enjoyed urban franchises, seem to have had many contacts with the former.

The rural population is known to us thanks to what are often very full texts, such as that drawn up by the *bailli* of Venice, Marsilio Zorzi, at the time of the recovery of a third of the dependencies of the lordship of Tyre in 1244. It lists the tenants of the rural estates by name; the majority of them were of servile status (they are called *homeliges*), and some of their names indicate Muslims. They were obliged to hand over to their lords a third or a quarter of their crop, a hen and a dozen eggs at Christmas, a payment for the use of the woods and, at the beginning of Lent, a cheese; special rents were paid for vineyards and olive groves; the sugar cane plantations were often directly exploited to the lord's benefit. There were also free peasants, who paid lower rents. These agricultural lands, which surrounded the coastal towns, were usually very fertile and well watered, which contributed to the prosperity of these towns.

The towns were dependent on an industry which we know primarily from its cloth production; weavers produced silks and woollens. Joinville, making a pilgrimage to Our Lady of Tortosa, was instructed by St Louis to buy, in Tripoli, pieces of cameline, a rough cloth which the king intended to give to the Franciscans. These fabrics were dyed, providing work for dyers. There were also many goldsmiths, and the glass and pottery industries employed many artisans. Other industries were based on agricultural products, in particular sugar, important in Tripoli, Gibelet, Tyre and Acre. Oil was used for the manufacture of soap.

We must conclude that the Latin colonies had recovered from the disaster of 1187, which had affected them to varying degrees, and from the vicissitudes of the crusades of the thirteenth century, which had been marked by raids of pillage and occasional devastations; the loss of lands previously recovered, as between 1244 and 1247, failed to sap their vitality; they attracted immigrants of different origins; the human losses were compensated for by the arrival of newcomers.

But this immigration and rebuilding were essentially to the benefit of the towns. In the twelfth century, Latin society had been distributed between small towns endowed with franchises, some 'new towns' with Frankish populations, and the castles and towns of the coast and the interior; though Jerusalem was reoccupied between 1229 and 1244, it never recovered its pre-1187 population; the Latin society of the thirteenth century was primarily based on an urban structure, the rural parts of the Frankish states constituting, except in certain regions such as the county of Tripoli, a sort of outlying suburban zone around towns and the few castles which had been reestablished in the reconquered territories of the Lebanon and Galilee. Figures for the Frankish population are difficult to estimate; we know that the towns grew in size and were surrounded by suburbs which were taken into the ramparts, like the Montmusard quarter at Acre, home of a substantial number of immigrants; Matthew Paris says it was here that most of the English congregated.

These towns were also home to Italian, Catalan and Provençal colonies, not forgetting the nationals of the countries under Muslim rule, all attracted by their commercial activity. Antioch was a case apart, as, in the thirteenth century, it experienced a falling off in its activity and influence; political circumstances – the remoteness of the prince, who mostly lived in his Tripolitanian lands, tension in the face of Armenian expansion, the community of interests between Latins and Greeks in a town where the Greek patriarch was often resident and where both communities lived – gave a unique character to its urban structure. But Antioch was increasingly isolated from the rest of the Frankish states. The rebuilding was primarily effective between the regions of Tripoli and Jaffa, which was where the principal centres of maritime commerce were located, whose influence in the political and economic life of the Latin East was increasing.

THE ATAVARS OF THE FRANKISH LORDSHIPS

The three Frankish states which had survived Saladin's conquest were reduced to two by the extinction of the Saint-Gilles dynasty in Tripoli; Count Raymond III had named as his heir (reserving the rights of the counts of Toulouse) his godson Raymond, elder son of Bohemond III. But Bohemond got these arrangements amended, so that it was his second son, Bohemond IV, who succeeded Raymond III and received the homage of his vassals.

A quarrel then erupted between the Armenian baron of the Mountain, Leo, and Bohemond III, over the castle of Baghras, which Saladin had dismantled and which Leo had restored and returned to the Templars. Leo laid an ambush for the prince of Antioch (October 1193) and demanded that he grant him the city. Bohemond agreed; but one of the Armenians introduced into the town offended Frankish feelings by announcing that the dedication of the church of St Hilary was to be changed to St Sergius. A riot broke out; the patriarch put himself at the head of the Latin and Greek bourgeois, who formed a commune, and Leo had to abandon his occupation of the town; but he was able to obtain his release from the ties of vassalage which bound him to the prince, and the marriage of his niece to Raymond heralded the future union of Antioch and Armenia. Leo got his royal title recognised by the pope and the emperor; an agreement was concluded between the Roman and Armenian Churches, and the new kingdom, with an aristocracy both Frankish and Armenian, took its place among the Latin states (1199).

But Raymond died in 1197, leaving a very young son, known as Raymond Roupen. The commune of Antioch, fearing an Armenian protectorate, tried to deliver the town to Bohemond IV; Leo intervened and restored Bohemond III, who died in 1201. There followed a long conflict, in which the Muslim princes became involved, al-Zahir of Aleppo supporting Bohemond, al-Adil Raymond Roupe. King Aimery, the patriarchs and the pontifical legates tried to broker an agreement, but in vain. Leo expelled Bohemond IV from Antioch, but was driven out in his turn. The patriarch Peter I, having taken Raymond Roupen's side, was deposed by Bohemond, who replaced him with a Greek patriarch (1206); Peter was thrown into prison, where he died (1208). Bohemond appealed to the sultan of Turkey to invade Armenia. The conflict was complicated by the fact that Leo had taken Baghras from the Templars, and that the papacy treated the Armenian king warily, while at the same time trying to do justice to the order. Finally, in 1216, Leo managed to recover Antioch, and Raymond Roupen was consecrated by the new patriarch, Peter II. But his success was short lived; Bohemond IV recovered Antioch in 1218, was reconciled with Leo, who gave his daughter Isabella in marriage to his son, Philip, and permanently united Antioch and Tripoli; he was careful, nevertheless, to maintain the individuality of each of the territories.

The union of Antioch and Armenia was thus definitively ruled out, especially when Philip was arrested, imprisoned and probably poisoned by the head of a great Armenian family, Constantine, who married Isabella to his own son, who was consecrated in 1226 with the name of Hethoum I. The links between Armenia and the Frankish states nevertheless survived.

Successive kings of Jerusalem, Henry of Champagne, Aimery of Lusignan or John of Brienne, had tried to intervene in Antioch's war of succession, but their authority was no longer what it had been in the days of the Baldwins and Fulks of the past. The quarrel was settled without reference to them.

The crown of Jerusalem, which had gone to Conrad of Montferrat on his marriage to Queen Isabella, passed after his death to Isabella's two next husbands, Henry of Champagne and Aimery of Lusignan; but it was Isabella's daughter by Conrad, Maria of Montferrat, who remained heiress to the kingdom. Henry, in view of the precariousness of his title, refused to take the crown and called himself only *seigneur du royaume de Jérusalem*. Aimery, who had received, in 1197, the royal title granted by the emperor for Cyprus, was less scrupulous. He managed to get Henry of Champagne to cancel the debt which Richard of England had contracted with Guy of Lusignan and transferred to his nephew Henry; the two kingdoms of Cyprus and Jerusalem were independent of each other and Aimery was careful to preserve their separate administrations.

We have seen how, after Aimery's death in 1206, Maria of Montferrat married John of Brienne, who soon lost his wife and married his daughter to Frederick II, who had by her a son, Conrad, titular king of Jerusalem as a result of his mother's premature death; Conrad himself transmitted his rights to his son Conradin. As we have seen, Frederick was deprived of the exercise of his rights, those of Conrad and Conradin being scrupulously respected, though only to become effective when they arrived in the East to take possession of their kingdom, which meant that from 1243 power was exercised by a 'lord of the kingdom', the nearest heir to the throne after the legitimate king. In succession, Queen Alice of Cyprus, daughter of Henry of Champagne, her son Hugh I, his widow, Plaisance, and her grandson, Hugh II were recognised as lady and lords of the kingdom and received the homage of their vassals. The kings of Cyprus were represented by a *bailli*, usually chosen from among the liege men of the kingdom and appointed in the presence of the Haute Cour, in fact with its agreement; Plaisance tried to give this office to her husband, Bohemond V of Antioch, but one faction refused to accept this.

In these circumstances, the power of the monarchy was inevitably weakened. Henry of Champagne and Aimery of Lusignan had both been energetic sovereigns who had been obeyed; the former had ruled one of the great fiefs of the kingdom of France; the latter had long experience of the East and had given the kingdom of Cyprus its institutional structures, avoiding constituting either great feudal lordships or vast ecclesiastical estates. The compilation of a *Livre au Roi*, one of the oldest customary texts in French, was made under his direction; it included the rules established by King Baldwin II to authorise the king to seize the fiefs of his vassals if they failed in their duties, rules which later authors were careful not to retain, and it defined the duties of the great officials of the kingdom. Not content with equipping the monarchy with this code, Aimery managed to limit the application of one of the provisions of the *Assise sur la ligece* of King Amalric, which authorised vassals to band together to deprive their lord of their service if he refused to put their cause before his court; when Ralph of Tiberias was suspected of having led an attack against him, and was banished from the kingdom, the king maintained his sentence despite an attempt to call on the *Assise sur la ligece*. He was unable, however, to prevent one of the principal heiresses to a fief, Beatrice of Courtenay, from marrying the count of Hennenberg, in spite of his right to authorise the marriage of heiresses.

After him, however, the barons managed to use this right of coalition, for example against Frederick II; as a result, it was the Haute Cour, that is, the feudal court of the kingdom, which controlled the exercise of royal authority. This did not prevent conflicts between men and between lineages; the *bailli* of the kingdom had great difficulty in getting their decisions obeyed, being themselves subject to the decision of the liege men at the time of their appointment.

There emerged a school of jurists trained in customary law, which managed to prevent the penetration of Roman law into jurisprudence, whereas this law had been used as a means to strengthen monarchical power in the kingdoms of the West. The refusal in 1254 to put into writing the decisions of the Haute Cour, which were to be confined to the 'record of the court' in the oral tradition, attests to the strength of this rejection. The great jurists, John of Ibelin, Count of Jaffa, Philip of Novara, who wrote for the kingdom of Cyprus, and their followers, codified this customary law in books which remain the great collections of the law applied in feudal matters in the Latin East. There existed, however, a rival school expert in Roman law, which included other jurists such as, probably, James Vidal and Stephen of Sauvegny, and written law penetrated the collection of the *Assises de la cour des bourgeois* drawn up around 1240. Nevertheless, the development of this juridical culture, with its attachment to the values specific to the feudal world, was one of the unique features of the Latin kingdom and the ability to manipulate the juridical concepts favourable to them helped the vassals to maintain their privileges vis-à-vis the king.

The decision of 1243 that made it possible to disseise Conrad IV without depriving him of his rights was one of the great achievements of these jurists. At the same period, they managed to remove the town of Tyre from the royal demesne to give it to the lord of Toron on the pretext of preserving it for the legitimate heir to the throne, and to get Alice of Champagne to accept this deposition. Even the appointment of the sovereign was within the competence of the Haute Cour, which scrutinised the rights of the claimants and decided which one should receive homage.

This was the case after the death of Henry I, when it was necessary to appoint the *bailli* of the kingdom; the court chose between two cousins of the young Hugh II, Hugh of Antioch and Hugh of Brienne, noting in favour of the former that his mother had been invested as *bailli* before him (1263). In 1268, Hugh II having died almost immediately, the death of Conradin obliged the Haute Cour to replace the 'lords of the kingdom' with an effective king. They discussed the respective rights of Hugh of Antioch and his aunt Maria of Antioch, who was a spinster granddaughter of Aimery of Lusignan and Isabella of Jerusalem, whereas Hugh was only his great grandson; they decided in his favour, nevertheless, which did not stop Maria from protesting against the decision at his coronation (1269).

Although Hugh III had achieved a reconciliation with Philip of Montfort by recognising his possession of Tyre, he encountered so many obstacles to the exercise of his power that he left Acre in 1276 after 'many quarrels he had with the religious orders, the [Italian] communes and the confraternities that he could neither rule nor command as he wished'. The true masters of the kingdom were the great seigneurial lineages, closely linked to each other by matrimonial alliances, but divided by problems of succession. The different branches of the Ibelin family, which possessed Jaffa, Arsur and Beirut, the sires of Sidon and Caesarea and the Montforts were in effect independent in their lordships, and even made private treaties with the Muslims. Interventions by the military orders, also practically independent – in 1276 the Temple refused to seek royal assent for the purchase of a *casal* – and by the Italian colonies helped to render the sovereign ineffectual.

The situation of the other state of Frankish Syria, which compromised the principality of Antioch and the county of Tripoli, was very different, though it, too, experienced institutional problems. The princes – Bohemond III till 1201, Bohemond IV (1201–33), Bohemond V, who in 1238 married a niece of Innocent III, Bohemond VI (1251–75) and Bohemond VII, who died in 1287 – were all strong personalities; Bohemond IV, who succeeded in replacing Raymond Roupen as prince of Antioch, was regarded as one of the foremost jurists of the Latin East. They managed to keep out of the struggle between the Ibelin and Frederick II, without breaking with the emperor. Their principality of Antioch was in practice administered under their authority by the commune founded in 1197; the barons of the county of Tripoli, originally from the Languedoc, seem not to have objected to the accession of the Poitevin dynasty.

The most immediate cause of conflict was the determination of the princes to insist on their right to marry the heiresses of fiefs. Bohemond IV's half-brother could thus marry the daughter of the Pisan Plebain, lord of Botrun. But Raymond, sire of Nephin, disregarded the count's rights by marrying the daughter of the lord of Gibelcar, and he won the support of the brothers of Tiberias and of Aimery of Lusignan and Leo of Armenia; there followed a war which ended in victory for Bohemond, now master of Nephin and Gibelcar (1204–5). A new conflict broke out for a similar reason between Guy of Gibelet and Bohemond VII, in 1278–9. The marriage of Bohemond V with Lucia of Segni brought to the county many 'Roman' knights, who packed the comital entourage, and also ecclesiastics who occupied the prebends of the chapter of Tripoli; it was this that, in the context of the conflicts that marked the 'war of St Sabas', provoked a war between the prince and his principal barons, led by Bertrand of Gibelet. The latter's death in a peasant ambush paved the way for a solution to the conflict. We learn in this way that the prince's vassals complained that they were unable to obtain justice in his court, which was dominated by the new arrivals, and that it was necessary to constitute a mixed commission of thirteen members to settle the differences between them and the prince. The most determined of the opposition withdrew to Acre (1258).

A new quarrel broke out after 1275 because Bohemond VII's mother, Sibylla of Armenia, had entrusted the government to the bishop of Tortosa, Bartholomew Mansel, who broke an agreement for the marriage of Guy of Gibelet's brother to the daughter of Hugh Saraman, whom he wanted to marry to his own nephew; Guy had the marriage celebrated and obtained the assistance of the master of the Temple. The conflict thus opposed the powerful family of Gibelet, allied to the Templars, to the knights of the party opposed to the 'Romans', led by the bishop of Tortosa. The massacre of some knights and canons of the 'Roman' party, the occupation of the house of the Temple and other exactions led the pope to intervene, and Tripoli was put under an interdict; Guy of Gibelet's supporters besieged Nephin and defeated the prince, several of whose vassals were killed (1278). Peace was restored but then violated by a surprise attack on Tripoli by Guy of Gibelet who was finally forced to surrender to the prince, who threw him into a dungeon where he starved to death (1283). But his party benefited from the death of Bohemond VII (1287), who was succeeded by his sister, married in Sicily to Narjot of Toucy, to form themselves into a commune and demand that the princess promise to respect it, referring to the 'evils, outrages and [acts of] force' inflicted on them by Bohemond V and Bohemond VI. Rifts emerged between them and Lucia of Toucy was finally able to enter Tripoli, shortly before the fall of the town.

These often implacable wars, the inherited hatreds, the overthrowing of alliances and the interventions of the Italian 'communes' and the military orders gave a character to these faction fights, these quarrels between barons, and between them and the sovereigns, which recall the judgement of James of Vitry. The strong feudal structure which had characterised the Latin East in the twelfth century had been replaced by a microcosm in which the barons, the confraternities and the other components of the ruling class fought for apparently futile reasons.

The kingdom of Cyprus also suffered from these rivalries. Behind the conflict which erupted in the time of Frederick II was the hostility between the descendants of the knights established on the island by the Lusignan and the Ibelin, the latter destined to rule by their kinship with the second wife of Aimery of Lusignan, the former finding themselves excluded from the favours of the *bailli*; personal abuse and acts of violence had preceded the confrontation between the regents appointed by Frederick and the sire of Beirut and his supporters. The regents had either left the island for Sicily (Philip Chinard, who had defended Kyrenia for Filangieri, was made governor of Corfu) or taken refuge in the county of Tripoli. It was only the policy of King Henry I, who encouraged marriages between the hostile lineages, that allowed peace to be restored in his kingdom.

The picture presented by the *Assises de Jérusalem* of a coherent juridical system, functioning without conflicts, must therefore be qualified. The feudal institutions of the thirteenth century suffered the consequences of the instability following the crisis of 1187 and the other ordeals experienced by the two kingdoms, the principality and the county.

TRADE IN THE LATIN EAST

At the end of the twelfth and the beginning of the thirteenth centuries, in the aftermath of Saladin's conquests, trade routes changed throughout the East. Constantinople probably retained its position, though the Venetians had taken advantage of the fall of the Byzantine empire to penetrate the Black Sea, previously forbidden to western ships; it was still some time, however, before the ports of the Crimea began to give access to the Asian interior. But the establishment of the two sultanates, that of the Ayyubids and that of the Seljuks, created a peaceful climate from which the western merchants profited, and they were soon setting out on the roads of the interior. The sultan of Aleppo granted facilities to the Venetians to enter that town by using the port of Latakia and passing under the castle of Saone. Simon of St Quentin describes a Turkey frequented by merchants from the West; two of them had leased the alum mines of Kutahya. The Seljuks opened a route leading from Sinope to Adalia. This made it possible to deal directly with the markets of the Near East without the need to stop in the ports of Frankish Syria. The opening up of Mongol Asia, around 1260, made Ayas, in Armenia, one of the ports of the Asian interior.

Nevertheless, Frankish Syria, except perhaps for Antioch, seems not to have suffered from this competition, any more than from the busy trade of the Egyptian ports, Damietta and Alexandria, to which the sultans continued to attract merchants by offering privileges and exemptions. Acre, Tyre, Beirut and Tripoli were all well sited for trade with the West, and we need only read, thanks to Pegolotti's *Pratica della mercatura*, which uses a thirteenth-century text, the list of equivalences of the measures of Christian Acre with those of other towns to appreciate the far-flung contacts of this great mercantile town: it was useful to be able to convert the weights and measures of Acre not only into those of Alexandria, Aleppo, Latakia, Tripoli, Damascus, Antioch, Ayas, Sivas and Constantinople, but also those of Thessalonika, Clarence and Thebes, for Romania, and Venice, Florence, Pisa, Nîmes, the fairs of Champagne, Marseilles and Messina, the two last ports providing wine, whilst Sicily, that is, the coast of Apulia, provided grain. So many places were in direct or indirect contact with the port of Acre that the Franks had to improve it, though they were unable to make it a totally safe harbour.

Our best source of information for the trade of Acre is a document which is sometimes regarded as a customs tariff and which was inserted into the *Livre des Assises de la cour des bourgeois*. In fact, it is a list of the 'dues of the *funda*', that is to say of the taxes levied on the market to the benefit of the king; it therefore does not differentiate between merchandise imported by land or by sea and that exported, and it includes local produce. It tells us, nevertheless, what goods were being traded in the town around 1245. Contracts of charter enable us to complete the list.

One could procure in Acre oriental products, some from India or the East Indies, such as pepper and spices of every sort; incense from Arabia; medicinal drugs, perfumes, silks and raw silk, ivory, morocco leather, fabrics such as buckrams and muslins; from Muslim countries came ceramics, wine and even salt fish from Egypt, and products demanded by western industries such as alum, and various dyestuffs, such as indigo, and woollens, cottons and cotton fabrics. Local production was represented by shoes, pottery, vegetables, fruits, olives and oil; sugar came either from the local industry or from external markets.

The West made a large contribution to the victualling of the towns with cargoes of wheat, wine, dried fruits, especially almonds, and salt pork. Woollens and canvas were in great demand, the former coming from Douai, Ypres, Châlons, Provins and Louviers, the latter from Champagne, Lille, Bâsle and Arras. Hemp, copper and other metals, iron and saddles also came from the West. These products were for the most part destined to be exported to Muslim countries; Egypt was a favoured market, and the ships which put in at Acre often quickly left for Alexandria; the merchants might sell their bales on arrival, use the money to make new purchases which they then offered to buyers in Egypt so as to procure new goods to carry back to the West; they could re-export to Egypt anything they had been unable to sell in Acre.

The activities of these merchants, which provided a livelihood for a whole population of intermediaries, brokers (called 'sensars') and interpreters, were controlled by royal agents. On arrival, they stored their merchandise in their *fondouk*, administered by an officer called by the Marseillais a *fondiguier*. The *fondouk* consisted of a number of houses, rooms and shops, completed by facilities which had originally been *banalités* belonging to the king but which each merchant community endeavoured to appropriate, that is, bath, oven, etc. The king provided public weights and measures, and these, too, were often appropriated; at Acre, Pegolotti refers to the hogsheads of the *funda* (those of the king), and of the Pisan, Venetian, Templar and Hospitaller quarters, each of them collecting a payment for the use of these measures.

We find a very similar picture when we look at other towns, for example Tyre and Tripoli, which were probably scarcely less busy than Acre, though it was Acre that most impressed contemporary observers. The income from the 'lordship' seemed exceptionally high to the author of the 'route planner' attached to the chronicle of Matthew Paris, which notes that the city was worth 50,000 *livres* a year to its lord, a sum corresponding to roughly a tenth of the budgetary receipts of the king of France. We must also allow for all the tax exemptions and reductions granted both to the Frankish bourgeois of the town and to the natives of the privileged maritime cities, the 'communes'. The Syrians were prohibited from settling 'downstream' of the *funda* to prevent them avoiding taxes through proximity to the Italian quarters.

Putting aside this population of artisans and local traders, peasants from the vicinity bringing their produce, and officials of the lords and the churches selling their surplus on the market (where we hear of planks, beams, equipment destined for building sites, firewood and poultry being offered for sale), the merchant world is revealed as very varied. The westerners are known to us primarily through the privileges they tried to obtain. Hans Meyer has shown how Marseilles, whose traders established themselves in the twelfth century with those of Languedoc – from St Gilles or Montpellier – succeeded in acquiring a whole series of privileges thanks to the discovery by a consul from Marseilles of documents he had bought around 1250; these documents actually came from the workshop of a forger and, thanks to them, the Marseillais could claim a privileged status.

Conrad IV, without having taken possession of his kingdom of Jerusalem, granted franchises to the merchants of Messina; the pope granted others to those of Ancona, and the list of privileged towns grew, revealing that their natives frequented the market of Acre. We hear of Florentines who visited even the Muslim towns of Syria; the merchants of less important cities must also have participated in this commercial life. For all of them, Syria was reached by a sea voyage. Merchant navigation grew rapidly as a result, and there were also technical advances; the first certain mention of the compass concerns a ship which was in Tripoli around 1240. Contracts, for example those made in front of the notaries of Venice, reveal the agreements signed by those who joined together in a *colleganza*, like the two merchants who, in 1211, contributed 418 and 836 *livres* respectively to go to Tyre and trade there, sharing the profit on return. Others entrusted to a fellow citizen, in the form of a *commenda*, sums which the latter engaged to turn to good account, buying a load of goods to trade in the markets of the East, selling, buying and reselling as the opportunity arose. One bought alum in Egypt to sell on in Tyre, another received an order for cinnamon, cotton thread and sendal which he bought in that town to carry back to Europe.

These Western merchants were far from being the only ones to frequent the Frankish towns of the coast. There were others who scarcely appear in our texts, but the chroniclers record occasional roundups of horses, camels and other beasts at the expense of the nomadic herdsmen, who must normally have supplied these animals to the markets of the Frankish towns. The provision of new mounts for the Frankish cavalry had been a major problem from the beginning; it is referred to, for example, by Fulcher of Chartres. Great war horses, raised in the studs of the West, and in particular in Spain, were imported by sea, but, as well as Arab horses, unsuited to bearing the weight of armed knights, we hear of the 'turkomans' which were more robust, and which had probably been brought from Syria or Turkey.

Ibn Jubayr, referring to the years before 1187, mentions two rich Damascus merchants who had their factors all along the coast of the Frankish states, and whose caravans crossed the frontiers without hindrance. Under the Ayyubids, this situation had been widespread; Muslim – or Christian – merchants, in particular from Damascus, were common in Acre, Tyre and Tripoli; the 'dues of the *funda*' mentions the products which came from or were destined for Muslim countries, paying a tax of roughly ten per cent. In 1290 Italian pilgrims massacred both Muslim peasants who were bringing their produce to market and some merchants under the protection of the sultan. In 1268, among the victims of acts of pillage committed by the Genoese, we find an 'Esbolez' of Damascus and a 'Bogaleb' (Abu Ghalib), also from Damascus, who said they were men of the lord of Tyre, a Suleiman, again from Damascus, who lived in Acre, and merchants of Acre of whom at least one was a Muslim.

A particularly interesting community is that of the 'Mosserins', who formed a confraternity enfeoffed to the order of the Temple, which took an active part in the conflicts arising between the different national groups in Acre between 1256 and 1290. This group was not purely confessional, like others; it seems to have been composed of merchants or other Christians originally from Mosul, probably mostly of the Nestorian rite, but whom the *assises* distinguished from the local

Nestorians. The presence of merchants from Mesopotamia trading in precious stones, spices and luxury fabrics is attested in 1221, when they passed on to the Franks the first rumours of the Mongol invasion. They are referred to in several other texts, and were reputed to be very wealthy. With the establishment of Mongol domination, they readily took the route which, by Tabriz and Sivas, arrived at Ayas, from which they reached Acre by sea; previously, they must have crossed Muslim territory to reach Antioch or Tripoli. It seems likely that their presence considerably antedates the 'Mongol peace' which opened up the roads of Asia Minor.

If we accept that these 'Mosserins' are from Mosul, we must see them as easterners, belonging to various Christian denominations, who engaged in trade in precious goods over very long distances, and who had frequented the trade routes before the merchants from the West also began to risk the routes which led into central Asia; it was in 1271 that the Polo brothers, setting out from Acre, passed through Ayas to travel as far as China, after a first voyage which had taken them from Soldaia, in the Crimea, across the basin of the Volga and Turkestan as far as distant Cathay. The establishment of the Mosserins in the city of Acre, where they enjoyed a recognised status and where they were able to form a confraternity, is reminiscent of that of the privileged Italians. We must imagine caravans of asses and camels heading for the Frankish cities, as well as the ships sailing along the coast to connect them with the ports of Egypt, Armenia and Turkey, alongside the merchant fleets from the kingdom of Sicily and the shores of Italy, Provence, Languedoc and Catalonia.

The fleets not only transported merchandise (and, eventually, the slaves that sometimes appear in contracts). The transport of pilgrims remained a lucrative activity, which the king recognised by claiming to levy to his own benefit a third of the price of the passage. Statutes and contracts had to limit the space taken up by the merchants' bundles to prevent them encroaching on that of the passengers. These pilgrims took their food with them; they spent in the East the sums necessary for their upkeep, thus contributing to its economic activity.

Crusaders and pilgrims might have need of money, in which context we should remember the Templars and Hospitallers who organised transfers of money between East and West. Nor should we forget the Italian bankers, particularly from Siena and Piacenza, who also made such transfers, nor the local capitalists. It was to an Ibrahim, a money changer of Acre, that, around 1280, Pope Adrian V entrusted a deposit of more than 6,000 *livres tournois*. The Jews also lent money, sometimes large sums, in particular to the Frankish barons.

There was also a traffic in precious metals and coin, which was the subject of agreements making provision for their transport to the East. Money changers kept their 'tables' in the *fondouks* or, in Tyre, in the rue du Change; they converted western money into the local currency; they are mentioned in contracts specifying the sums that must be repaid on leaving the Latin East. This consisted of gold bezants 'in the coin of the king of Jerusalem', subdivided into the carat or the 'carouble' (one twenty-fourth). The royal mint also struck silver 'dragans', or dirhams. Western pennies were also in circulation, and are found in large numbers in hoards.

The *sarrasinois* bezants of Acre and the *tripolaz* bezants of Tripoli continued to duplicate Fatimid types, to cater for long-distance international trade. The legate Eudes of Châteauroux was offended by the fact that coins struck by Christian princes bore the year of the Hegirah and Muslim inscriptions. Innocent IV then ordered an end to such abuses, and in future the bezants bore the image of the Cross and Christian inscriptions (1253). The kingdom of Cyprus, however, remained faithful to a coinage of the Byzantine system, the white bezant.

We know that in 1259–60 the Franks manipulated the coinage, considerably reducing the fineness of the silver dirham, which provoked a crisis in the neighbouring Muslim countries, where the devalued money drove out good money. This manipulation may have been a consequence of the political crisis which was then affecting the Frankish states ('the war of St Sabas'), but the episode reveals the sensitivity of the Muslim world to the economic difficulties of its Frankish neighbours and, consequently, the imbrication of their economies. The Latin east was fully integrated into a whole which, with the Muslim states, was soon to extend to the Mongol possessions.

THE 'COMMUNES' AND THE WAR OF ST SABAS

The defeat suffered by the Franks at Hattin profoundly altered relations between them and the maritime cities of Italy which, thanks to their participation in the conquest of Jerusalem and the coast, had been able to obtain commercial privileges and territorial concessions. These they had retained more or less; their nationals who had received the lands as a fief of the commune had become the vassals of the count or the king, as in the case of the Embriaco of Gibelet in Tripoli and the Contarini of Tyre in Jerusalem. The presence of their merchants was a source of wealth much appreciated by the sovereigns of the Latin states, but they succumbed to the temptation to reclaim revenues covered by the diplomas granted to the different towns. Admittedly, these diplomas were not always above suspicion, and historians have questioned the interpolations they have detected in them.

But when Saladin's armies attacked the towns of the coast, the support of the Italians was once again appreciated. At Tyre, Raymond III and the baronial survivors of Hattin granted concessions to the Pisans and the Genoese to persuade them to share in the town's defence; Conrad of Montferrat confirmed and extended them; Guy of Lusignan accepted them, if only to deprive his rival of Pisan support. It was only Henry of Champagne, after the Pisans had intrigued with Guy of Lusignan and because of their acts of piracy, who attempted to reduce their privileges and limit their presence to an agreed number to avoid the risk of a raid. They were unreliable allies, in whom one could not be confident, quick to attack defenceless ships and ready to sell themselves to the highest bidder.

Henry of Champagne and John of Brienne tried to recover lost ground, but the 'communes' were in a position to apply pressure. The Genoese, to obtain compensation for damages, withdrew from Acre and transferred their *échelle* to Beirut, where John of Ibelin was only too pleased to welcome them. This sort of embargo, which deprived the lords of fiscal resources, was extremely effective. And the dependence of these same lords on Italian moneylenders also disposed them to treat them leniently.

The three great communes enjoyed more or less analogous positions. They had won the right to extend their jurisdiction to their natives, including those who claimed their protection, especially those Syrians who in Cyprus were called 'white Genoese'. The royal court alone remained in principle competent to deal with crimes of blood, feudal matters and affairs concerning tenures *en bourgeoisie*, but it was the consuls of the Venetians, the Genoese and the Pisans who exercised within their concession the office of viscount, and who claimed the right to judge their compatriots even in criminal matters. Courts sat in the 'lodge' of each commune, and the notaries of each drew up documents. On taking office, the consul swore an oath of fealty to the king, but he also promised to be faithful to the commune. It was he who collected in its name the revenues from the hire of rooms and shops, and from the *banalités* due for the use of collective facilities. Even the church which each commune built in its quarter (its *rue* or 'street') claimed to depend directly on the bishopric of the city of origin and not on the local bishop.

This was probably one of the reasons for the severity of James of Vitry with regard to these colonies, whose role in the defence of the Holy Land he acknowledged, but whose greed and excessive liking for independence he denounced. They had participated in the crusades, especially that which, in 1219–20, had occupied Damietta, where they were hoping to secure similar establishments and which they evacuated only reluctantly. But they also participated in civil wars, transferring to the East quarrels originating in the West; the Pisans were deprived of their privileges by Filangieri as a punishment for their encroachments, but had all their rights restored by Frederick II to reward them for their support for the imperial cause. John of Ibelin managed to secure Genoese aid during his war against Filangieri, which helped him to move to Cyprus, where he granted the Genoese their first privileges.

It was Venice that did best out of this quarrel between Guelphs and Ghibellines. The *bailli* Marsilio Zorzi, having failed to get Filangieri to restore the rights of Venice of which he had deprived them in Tyre, played an active part in the plot to replace imperial rule by that of Alice of Champagne; he provided her with a galley and thirty knights, which contributed to the capture of Tyre; but it was only thanks to the support of the master of the Temple that he managed to get the promises honoured.

It is thanks to these events that we have a very full account by this same *bailli* of the rights, possessions and revenues of Venice in Tyre, which, perhaps for the first time since 1124, corresponded to the concession the barons of the kingdom had granted to the city of the doges, and which applied to a third of the town and its lordship: many villages, sugar-cane plantations, lands, vineyards, gardens, mills and a sugar factory outside the town; a large *fondouk* and other smaller ones, churches, baths and ovens; the right to have their own measures, to levy taxes on transactions; the right to administer justice; exemptions from dues imposed for the king's benefit, though he managed to retain some of them, which the *bailli* regarded as an injustice. All this constituted a coherent quarter in the town, a large estate outside it, all sorts of facilities for the Italian merchants and a quasi-extraterritorial status which was expressed in the oath of fealty to the doge sworn by all the natives of the lordship of Venice. Venice, which had been promised similar concessions in Ascalon, also had a trading post at Beirut, another at Acre and establishments in Tripoli and Antioch.

The rights of Genoa and Pisa were perhaps slightly less extensive than those enjoyed by the Venetians in Tyre, but the two towns ran her close. In their footsteps, other maritime cities, including Marseilles and Ancona, had tried to go beyond the franchises and exemptions they had acquired to secure consular jurisdiction, a *fondouk* and rural property. This privileged situation left them free to trade with the Muslim countries, especially Egypt, on the sole condition that they did not supply them with strategic material, in particular wood, iron and arms, a condition which seems often to have been ignored. Indeed, the Genoese made a speciality of transporting to Egypt slaves from the Black Sea countries, which was one of the routes for Mamluk recruitment.

The natives of the communes transferred to the East the enmities which divided them in Europe. Genoa and Venice remained on good terms for a long time, but the quarrel between the Genoese and the Pisans dated back to the twelfth century, the latter disputing hegemony in the Tyrrhenian Sea with the former. In the conflict between Frederick II and the papacy, Pisa sided with the imperial party, in contrast to the other two great communes. Innocent IV wished to punish this stance and, in 1247, he deprived the church of the Pisans in Acre of its parish status; in 1248 Pisan ships were forbidden to enter Acre under the imperial flag. Pisans and Genoese then resorted, in the streets of the town, to a war during which they used machines such as perriers and mangonels, and which, after almost a month of fighting, only ended thanks to the mediation of the sire of Arsur, the commune of Acre, the Templars and the Hospitallers (1249).

Other scuffles occasionally broke out; in 1257 Marseilles and Montpellier fought over the latter's claim to have their own consul. But it was a quarrel arising in Acre itself that involved the Venetians and the Genoese in a battle which was to assume major proportions.

Between the Genoese and the Venetian quarters stood a group of buildings and a church belonging to the monastery of St Sabas. Both Genoese and Venetians coveted these buildings and, we are told, both obtained a letter from the pope giving them satisfaction. The Venetians committed their letter to the patriarch, the Genoese to the prior of the Hospital. This was in 1256. It is not clear what exactly led to open war; in any case, the Genoese, this time allied with the Pisans, invaded the Venetian quarter, where the Venetians were soon in difficulties. But the metropolitans intervened; Pisa and Venice were reconciled and the Pisans of Acre joined the Venetians (1257). The Genoese retaliated by concluding a treaty with John of Arsur, representing the 'lordship' of Acre, and seized the tower of the Pisans; like all Italian towns, Acre bristled with towers. At Tyre, Philip of Montfort, lord of Toron, who held the town in the name of the lord of the kingdom, took the opportunity to seize the Venetian quarter and its dependencies; so, among the barons of the kingdom, there were some supporters of Genoa, and others, like John of Ibelin, sire of Arsur, who sided with Venice.

Driven out of Tyre, the Venetians took their revenge in Acre. A fleet commanded by Lorenzo Tiepolo took control of the port, destroying the Genoese ships; Venetians and Pisans reoccupied the parts of their

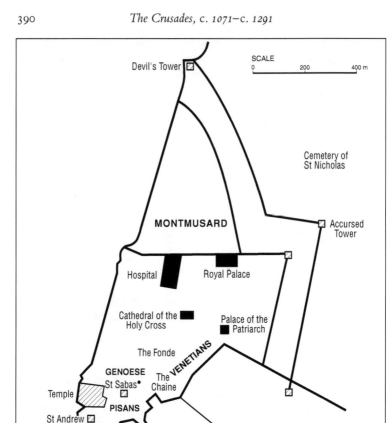

Map 17   Acre in the thirteenth century

quarters that had been conquered by their enemies, including St Sabas. The local barons, this time including John of Arsur, supported their action.

The divisions worsened. In February 1258 Queen Plaisance of Cyprus came to Acre with her brother, Bohemond VI, and her son, the infant Hugh II, and asked the barons to recognise Bohemond as *bailli* of the kingdom in her capacity as its lady. But the Genoese suspected Bohemond of being favourable to the Venetians; it was, in fact, the master of the Temple and the count of Jaffa who had asked him to come in the hope that he might be able to end the conflict. At this point, the

Genoese, the Hospitallers and the brethren of St James of the Spanish had the clever idea of denying Plaisance her status as lady of the kingdom and affirming that they recognised no authority except that of Conradin himself. Bohemond then came down against them; but when he ordered one of his barons, Bertrand of Gibelet, to charge the Genoese, he made common cause with them, because the sires of Gibelet, descending from the Embriaco, were of Genoese origin. The conflict spread to the county of Tripoli, where the rising of the Tripolitanian barons against the count of his 'Roman' entourage was led by Bertrand. Philip of Montfort, meanwhile, supplied food and reinforcements to the Genoese who were blockaded in Acre, and this was probably what started the war between him and the sire of Sidon. The Maronite archers of the sire of Gibelet lent their assistance to the Genoese, who also enjoyed the support of the Syrian confraternity of St George. Machines of war hoisted onto all the towers of the town bombarded each other, and it was said that Acre looked like a town destroyed by a siege.

The papacy had tried to impose its mediation on 6 July 1258, but the legate sent by Alexander IV arrived only the following year. And the disaster suffered by the Genoese fleet of Rosso della Turca in Syrian waters, on 24 July 1259, forced the Genoese to capitulate, evacuating their quarter, relinquishing their jurisdictional privileges and passing between lines of their enemies standing with drawn swords. They were still permitted access to the port of Acre on condition they struck their flag, which shows that it was less the securing of commercial monopolies that was at issue than the desire to demonstrate a political supremacy. Genoa retained, in any case, a strong position in Frankish Syria, since Philip of Montfort, having deprived the Venetians of their rights in Tyre, granted these rights in full to the Genoese.

The war between the communes continued. In August 1259 the Genoese fleet of Benedetto Zaccaria suffered a serious defeat before Tyre; in 1261, after the fleet of Simon Grillo had captured a Venetian convoy and taken it to Genoa, the Venetians launched a raid in Tyre; it failed only because Philip of Montfort armed the local peasantry and appealed to his supporters in Acre. The Genoese, meanwhile, had negotiated with Michael Palaeologus (the treaty of Nymphaeum), and his capture of Constantinople assured them of commercial advantages over their rivals, but drew them into other military operations. The conflict that had arisen over possession of the church of St Sabas had by now assumed major proportions, and dragged on. In 1267 Luccheto Grimaldi, with a Genoese squadron, attacked Acre and seized merchant ships as far away as Gorigos. It was only in 1270 that St Louis was able to reconcile the two towns.

This reconciliation was slow to take effect. The agreement of 1270 allowed the Genoese to return to Acre, but without recovering possession of what they had lost to the Venetians and the Pisans; it was only in 1288, after their defeat at Meloria, that the Pisans restored their part of the Genoese quarter. At Tyre, it took the intervention of the master of the Temple, William of Beaujeu, to persuade John of Montfort to reinstate the Venetians in their possessions, in 1277.

At the same time, the new prince, Bohemond VII, had arranged for the return of Bertrand of Gibelet's son, Bartholomew, who had in 1259 been exiled to Acre, and who witnessed an act of Bohemond in favour of the Venetians. The old quarrel seemed to be forgotten. But when a new conflict arose between Bohemond and Guy of Gibelet, the master of the Temple became involved, this time on the side of the descendant of the Embriaco, whom John of Montfort tried to assist. And when the knights of Tripoli formed a commune to curb princely authority, Bartholomew of Gibelet put himself at their head, with the support of the Genoese, who asked for the restoration of their quarter and privileges, which the princes had not respected.

The political life of the Frankish cities was thus dominated by the quarrels of the Italian communes, into which, as a result of alliances, the other maritime towns were drawn, those of Provence and Languedoc on the side of the Venetians and the Pisans, those of Ancona and Catalonia on that of the Genoese. For the Frankish lords, the presence of the merchant colonies had been a guarantee of the growth of the economic activity of their towns, and, as a result, of their resources. They were now faced with veritable powers which conducted on the territory of Frankish Syria wars for far greater stakes. Genoa aspired to acquire a hegemony in the seas of the eastern Mediterranean and came into conflict with the ambitions and interests of Venice, allied with Pisa, its perennial rival. The Frankish barons could do little more than give their support to the warring cities, and the situation was only aggravated by the rivalries of the military orders and the intrigues of their supporters.

The communes enjoyed other advantages, thanks to the privileged situation they had also been able to acquire in the Byzantine empire and in the Muslim states. The Genoese may, in 1263, have approached the sultan Baybars to get him to intervene against their enemies in Acre. And Genoa was hand in glove with the Byzantines against the Venetians.

The war of St Sabas left a trail of devastation. What is known of the state of Acre speaks volumes: Pisans and Venetians used the stone from the buildings of the Genoese quarter to construct a fortified enclosure round their own streets, surrendering a few enclaves such as the church of St Demetrius to round off their domain. The buildings of the

Venetian quarter in Tyre were also in ruins. And as we have seen, it was at precisely this point that the effects of a weakening of the money struck by the Franks were felt.

Finally, this war and its repercussions attest to the deep divisions within the Frankish world. James of Vitry had already, in his *Historia orientalis*, noted that 'the men of the famous cities of Genoa, Pisa and Venice ... living in the East ... would be formidable for the Saracens if they renounced jealousy and their insatiable lust for profit, not having between them wars and discords without end'. These discords eventually spread to the Frankish world as a whole.

After the quarrel between the Guelfs and the Ghibellines had been transposed to the Latin East in the form of the war between the supporters and the enemies of Frederick II, other conflicts then revealed the fragility of the structures of a kingdom and a principality largely reduced to a string of towns.

THE LATIN CHURCH IN THIRTEENTH-CENTURY FRANKISH SOCIETY

The defeat of 1197 struck a serious blow to the ecclesiastical structures of the Frankish states. Saladin had wished to eliminate the presence of the Latin clergy from the Holy Land; it was only after the Third Crusade that he allowed a few Latin clergy to serve the Holy Sepulchre. The episcopal hierarchy was swept away; the patriarch and the canons of the Holy Sepulchre had to leave Jerusalem, the archbishops and bishops, with their chapters, their episcopal cities.

The consequence had been the retreat of all these ecclesiastics, if they had escaped captivity, to the towns of the coast, that is, to Tyre and Tripoli. At the beginning of the reconquest they had also found asylum in Acre and in the other reoccupied towns, but as refugees. But many churches had owned property and rents in the coastal towns, or in the West, before 1187; they were not all without resources, and the survival of its temporalities enabled a community or a prelate to survive.

At first, there was some confusion; bishops expelled from their see and canons driven out of their cathedral settled, for want of an alternative, in towns which already had their ecclesiastical structures. As late as 1220, James of Vitry compared his town of Acre to a 'monster', where resided the patriarch and the bishops of Lydda, Nazareth and Tiberias among others, not to speak of the regular communities. It was not until the patriarchate of Haymar ('Haymar the Monk'), between 1197 and 1202, that this hierarchy was reorganised: three archbishoprics and seven bishoprics, those which had the means to support themselves, were preserved, and their episcopal series survived, thanks either to the election of the prelate by his chapter, even if this was now skeletal, or by the metropolitan himself filling the vacant post. In fact, like the barons deprived of their lordships, the bishops and archbishops were waiting for the time when they would recover their sees. This sometimes happened. In 1217 a bishop was appointed to the see of Sidon; the town had not yet been reoccupied, and the prelate lived for many years in Sarepta, which was in his diocese, before returning to Sidon. Tiberias, too, received a new bishop, if only briefly, in 1241. Some of these prelates never recovered their see; some found other employment in the West. At the end of the century, there were systematic creations of titular sees, as in the case of Hebron, restored in 1251 though no Latin prelate was reinstated in this town.

The situation was slightly different in the patriarchate of Antioch, where there had survived since the middle of the twelfth century an archbishopric of Apamea whose archiepiscopal town was in Muslim hands, but whose incumbent retained suffragens, such as the bishop of Valania. In 1233 he obtained the right to celebrate divine office in Latakia, where he had a chapel though the town was under Muslim administration. Tarsus and Mamistra also retained an archbishop and a cathedral, thanks to an agreement made with the kingdom of Armenia. In contrast, in the county of Tripoli the hierarchy survived almost intact, its dioceses hardly eroded.

The patriarch of Jerusalem had found asylum in Acre, though it was in the cathedral of Tyre that, when Jerusalem was inaccessible, the king was consecrated. It was not till the pontificate of Urban IV, however, who had himself been a patriarch of Jerusalem, that the episcopal see of Acre was incorporated into the patriarchate. The importance of the patriarch's role had not diminished, especially since he was now permanent legate of the pope in the Holy Land; though the patriarch Gerold was at one time deprived of the legation as a result of his difficulties with Frederick II, he had been reinstated. But the patriarch increasingly appeared as the representative of pontifical authority in the Holy Land, invested with a wide range of responsibilities and missions, rather than as leader of the local hierarchy.

The patriarch of Antioch had experienced serious problems with the princes Bohemond III and Bohemond IV, the latter having even caused the death of the patriarch Peter I, during his battle with Raymond Roupen. His see had sometimes been transferred to a Greek patriarch, under Bohemond IV and, later, during the Mongol protectorate. Still enjoying great authority in the first half of the century, he was then increasingly frequently an absentee.

The papacy began to intervene with greater frequency in ecclesiastical matters; the episcopal and archiepiscopal sees, and even the patriarchates, were filled by ecclesiastics close to the Roman curia, even from papal families, as in the case of Opizo dei Fieschi at Antioch, or Paul dei Conti at Tripoli. In this, the Church of the Holy Land was in a very similar situation to that of the Churches of the West, but the influence of the lay sovereigns seems to have been less; prelates from outside were, accordingly, all the more numerous. What characterised this Church, both secular and regular, was now its urban character. The Latin parish network had not been particularly dense, but there were now no villages with Frankish populations to be served. In the towns, in contrast, churches proliferated. A list of the indulgences that could be earned by visiting those of Acre, in the last decades of the thirteenth century, recommended no fewer than forty. The majority were the churches of religious communities, but some must have been parish churches, in particular those of the privileged Italian quarters: St Mark's of Venice, St Peter of the Pisans, and St Laurence, probably the church of the Genoese. This list is very much what would be found in a western town, with dedications like St Agnes, St Bridget and St Leonard, not previously customary in the Eastern churches.

Like every large town in Latin Christendom, Acre had convents belonging to the new religious orders: Franciscans, Dominicans, Brothers of the Sack and Magdalenes; the mendicant orders had appeared very early, with the visit by St Francis to the crusade in 1219, and they had prospered. The Franciscans, in particular, had convents in most towns, and by 1230 had organised a province of the Holy Land.

The eremitical movement of the twelfth century had lost impetus, in part because the new orders had attracted the vocations which would have turned, in the previous century, to the hermitages. It had nevertheless given birth to an original form of religious life: what a pilgrim guide described as 'the Latin hermits that are called the brethren of Carmel' had settled near Mount Carmel, close, that is, to Caiphas, perhaps around St Brocard, a pious hermit who had fought in the Third Crusade. They enjoyed some success until the wanderings of the Khwarismians and Egyptian raids obliged them to take refuge in the town; there they turned into a new mendicant order, destined to a great future, which spread throughout the West. At Antioch, pious women had come together in an original community, that of the Carpitanes, which probably shared some features with the Carmelites, going by their adoption of a robe made up of pieces of different colours, which they only abandoned for that of the Benedictines after moving to Cyprus, where they adopted a new dedication, Our Lady of Tortosa, consigning that of 'the Cross of Antioch' to oblivion. At Acre, as well as the Cistercian nuns of St Magdalen, there was a house of Clares.

One of the old hermitages survived, that of St Mary of Jubin, in the Black Mountain near Antioch; the patriarch Peter II, once a monk of Locedio, persuaded it to adopt the Cistercian rule, to the displeasure of his successor, Albert of Rizzato, who would have preferred it to remain subject to patriarchal authority. But the popularity of the Cistercian order continued; Beaulieu was founded in Cyprus; the bishop of Gibelet persuaded the abbot of La Ferté to send monks to found St Sergius of Gibelet.

But these monastic foundations outside, if not remote from, towns remained rare. Rather, there was a retreat of monasteries into the towns, and a retreat to the coastal towns of the communities that served the sanctuaries of the interior. Many establishments probably disappeared without trace, among them the Cistercian convents of Salvatio and St John of the Woods. But the regular canons and the monks established near the Holy Places withdrew to Tyre or Acre, to survive on what remained of their ancient endowments. These largely consisted of estates in the West, and some of them soon transferred their base overseas. The monks of Josaphat settled in Palermo, those of St Mary Latin in Agira in Sicily; those which left houses situated in the principality of Antioch or the county of Tripoli, during the course of the thirteenth century, took refuge either in Cyprus, like St Paul of Antioch, which merged with the abbey of the Cross (Stavrovouni), or further afield after an initial period in the island, like Jubin, which moved to Genoa. Others preferred to remain in the Holy Land, in the hope of recovering their original sites, even if it meant retaining only a priory in the Holy Land. In the 'pardons of Acre', we find St Samuel of Mountjoie, St Lazarus of Bethany, the Holy Sepulchre, Our Lady of Josaphat, St Mary Latin, Bethlehem, St Anne, St George (of Lydda); the Temple of Our Lord also had its dependencies on the coast. The reoccupation of Jerusalem, Bethlehem and Nazareth, between 1229 and 1244, was accompanied by a partial resettlement; Frederick II had made no attempt to recover the *casals* constituting the endowment of these establishments, which were therefore in very reduced circumstances. Thus Josaphat was content, in 1241, to reestablish a prior in Jerusalem, the larger part of the community not accompanying him.

This stubborn persistence of the monasteries and convents attached to the great sanctuaries, in the hope of a return to conditions favourable to the revival of their earlier vocation, is worthy of attention. The flow of pilgrims continued; they submitted to the demands of the Muslims, masters of the sanctuaries, who had no wish to deprive themselves of the revenues they provided. But unable to find in Jerusalem or Nazareth the communities which supported their devotion, they went to Acre or to Tyre to ask for their prayers or to form ties of brotherhood. The large number of indulgences granted to Acre – there was even one for the town gate – suggests that they may have been at least in part intended to make the port a substitute for Jerusalem, at a time when access to the Holy City was impossible.

For ships continued to bring their annual cargoes of pilgrims. There was no shortage of sites to venerate in Frankish territory. Joinville described how he went on a pilgrimage to Our Lady of Tortosa, where a miraculous icon (later taken to Cyprus) was venerated and which was the oldest church dedicated to the Virgin. Nazareth remained in Frankish hands for a long time and continued to be served by their canons.

Elsewhere, pilgrims found the sanctuaries in the hands of the Greeks, who had usually managed to get the sultans, in the first instance Saladin, to recognise their right to serve the Holy Places, if not to occupy the Latin churches, which had often been destroyed or transformed into mosques; some had been allowed to fall into ruins, like that of the Table of Christ where Ricoldo of Monte Croce celebrated mass during a pilgrimage. But Saladin had authorised two Latin priests and two deacons to officiate in the Holy Sepulchre, and also in Nazareth and Bethlehem; so, in different circumstances, the coexistence of the previous century continued. The Latin canons resumed their place between 1229 and 1244, but lost it later.

Eastern pilgrims, too, visited the sanctuaries of the Holy Land, even if they found fewer establishments than, for example, John Phocas when he had made his pilgrimage. The monasteries of the Greek rite were still in existence, and there is no evidence that they were less respected by the Latins; the Armenians were still at St James and the Georgians still at the monastery of the Cross. Burchard of Mont-Sion, in 1280, met the Greek patriarch of Jerusalem, who assured him of his good will with regard to union with Rome. Relations with the eastern clergy were even favoured by the missionary orientation of the mendicant orders; while the Dominicans were in Jerusalem between 1229 and 1244, the Jacobite patriarch Ignatius travelled to the Holy City, visited them, made his profession of faith and even donned the habit of their order. A Jacobite *maphrian* who had retired to Tripoli was accompanied to his last home by processions of Frankish clergy. The convent of Dominicans in Jerusalem was the starting point for the mission to the East. In Antioch, the intrusion of a Greek patriarch in the time of Manuel Comnenus, then under Bohemond VI, who had used him against the Latin patriarch, had been a source of conflict, but the presence of the patriarch David caused no greater problem than the Latin patriarch's annoyance at the equality of treatment that Rome seemed to wish to show the two prelates; this was the case also in Cyprus, where the Greek archbishop was maintained in his see by Innocent IV and Alexander IV.

One of the peculiar features of the history of the Latin Church in the thirteenth century is the development of works of assistance. The hospital of St John of Jerusalem lost its great establishment in the Holy City; it was transferred to Acre, where an indulgence of forty days was granted to those who made the tour of the 'palace of the sick' for every occasion on which they performed this devotion. It had not forgotten its hospital vocation and continued to receive pilgrims. But there had grown up alongside it other communities which also devoted themselves to the care of the sick and wounded. During the siege of Acre, two hospitals had been founded, one for the Germans, the other for the English; St Mary of the Germans and St Thomas of the English settled in the town after its capture and continued to operate there, the Hospital having been unable to insist on its right to a monopoly of the exercise of hospitality. A hospital of the Holy Spirit, attached to the congregation of that name, appeared and, on 29 August 1254, a hospital of St Martin was founded for the Bretons. The reception of pilgrims played a major role in the activities of these hospitals, too, further evidence of the importance of the former to the kingdom in the thirteenth century. Despite the fall of Jerusalem and the relative brevity of its reoccupation, the kingdom of Outremer continued to be the kingdom of pilgrimage, and the Church continued to serve it. When a pope, soon after the fall of Tripoli, wanted to forbid visits to the Holy Sepulchre so as to deprive the sultan of his income from this source, the patriarch intervened to get the decision rescinded, against the interests of what survived of the kingdom.

In the case of the Teutonic knights, as in that of St Thomas of Acre, hospitallers were converted to a complementary vocation, that of war. The first religious of St Thomas devoted themselves to the care of the poor, the burial of the dead and the redemption of captives, though this last task increasingly devolved on the Trinitarians, who also had an establishment in Acre earning indulgences. But in 1227–8, the bishop of Winchester, Peter des Roches, anxious to find a remedy for the poverty and lax life of these regular canons, assigned them a new house and gave them the duty of fighting the infidel in the manner of the Teutonic knights. Enriched with pontifical privileges, and expanding its endowment primarily in England, this little order shows that the association of the military and hospital functions had come to seem natural to the people of the Holy Land. But St Thomas was less lucky than the

Teutonic knights, for whom the transformation was more rapid and who, even before they were favoured by Frederick II, had been summoned to Hungary by King Andrew II. The order of St Lazarus (St Lazarus of the Knights was another of the churches to which a visit earned indulgences) also continued throughout the thirteenth century to perform its dual mission of care for the lepers and the provision of a place for those who wished to remain combatants and for those who, from piety, wished to be associated with them.

The diversity of the religious life of the Holy Land meant that the clergy were omnipresent. The rich endowments granted to the religious establishments of the preceding century had been much reduced. Defensive necessities had persuaded the pope to authorise the conversion into a fortress of the convent of Mount Tabor, already, in fact, destroyed by the Muslims; but the income of the churches remained very substantial given the diminution of the landed base of the kingdom, the principality and the county.

But the resources of these Frankish establishments were to a large extent dependent on the fraternal charity of the Christians of the West. The registers of the pontifical chancellery are full of encouragements granted by the popes to ensure that the communities of the Holy Land, and the kingdom itself, would receive financial support: people left money to fortresses in their wills; preachers urged their audience to give alms for the Holy Land; a Burgundian noblewoman left money 'to redeem the captives of the land of Outremer'; a knight destined his horse and his weapons for those who defended it. It is impossible to keep track of the donations and foundations which, through the intermediary of their priories situated in Europe, were made to the benefit of the churches of Outremer.

The Church thus played an important role in providing for the Holy Land, through religious establishments and by the collections made at the instigation of the papacy, subsidies and assistance of every type. But the sums deriving from legacies, the restitutions made by usurers, the tenths and other contributions from ecclesiastical benefices, passed increasingly though the intermediary of the patriarch. He, at the time of the Fifth Crusade, regarded himself as having rights in the government of the Holy Land; we have seen an example of this in the anger of Gerold of Lausanne at not having been consulted by Frederick II about the treaty of Jaffa. In future, the patriarch appeared as a lessor of funds that came from the West and were assigned to the Holy Land by the popes; his role, which was also that of permanent legate of the Holy See, was accordingly enhanced. But the characteristics of the religious life of the Latin East give an original touch to the picture of Frankish society.

This religious life was intense; it gave birth to foundations which take their place in the great pious movements of the time. The Carmelites and the Carpitanes had original features; churches proliferated in the towns; the religious mendicants and the hospitaller orders enrich this picture.

The desire to maintain the existence of the communities and episcopal sees in spite of the Muslim occupation was in itself very significant. It shows that Frankish society aimed to preserve ecclesiastical structure which it expected to revive as soon as the 'recovery of the Holy Land' was achieved. The exodus to the West was delayed as long as possible. The Church of the Holy Land lived in hope of this reoccupation of lost territories.

THE MILITARY ORDERS: A PERMANENT WESTERN PRESENCE

After the defeat of Hattin, the grand preceptor of the Temple, Thierry, sent news of the disaster to the West. Sixty knights of his order had been left on the battlefield of Cresson in May; 230 had perished at Hattin, most of them beheaded on Saladin's orders. There remained some Templars in fighting condition, but they had retreated into their castles; that of Saphet was particularly defensible. The situation of the Hospitallers was similar. The two orders had been almost wiped out.

But when Richard the Lionheart led his crusading army through Palestine, he found contingents of both orders. When Gerard of Ridfort was killed, the king of England provided one of his vassals, Robert of Sablé, to succeed him as master of the Temple. And it was to the Templars that he granted the island of Cyprus, to which the order dispatched a detachment of knights, sergeants and turcopoles, also paying the king a large sum of money. Like the Hospital, the Temple had made up its losses in a remarkably short time.

This is one of the main reasons for the position occupied by the military orders in Syria after Hattin. Kings, princes, barons and prelates had difficulty in replenishing their army or their treasury, but the masters of the Temple and the Hospital, and soon of the Teutonic knights who modelled themselves on the two earlier orders, could seemingly draw on inexhaustible reserves.

But the Templars and the Hospitallers had suffered badly. They had been driven out of their houses in Jerusalem, whose size had been a source of amazement to travellers; the stables of the Temple were said to have room for two thousand horses. The Temple had lost its great castles of Gaza and Saphet, the Hospital those of Bethgibelin and Belvoir, not to speak of the smaller fortresses that covered the route from Jaffa to

Jerusalem. The Temple had also lost its fortresses situated on the frontier of the principality of Antioch and of Cilicia, Darbsak and Baghras; Leo of Armenia recovered them, but it was 1216 before he agreed to return them to the Templars, despite the entreaties of the pope. On the other hand, Leo showed great favour to the Hospitallers, granting them many fortresses (Til, Silifke) and estates around them; he later granted Amudain to the Teutonic knights. The Temple, however, had received substantial donations in Cyprus. And the conquest of Saladin had left almost intact the two vast estates possessed by the two orders on the border of the principality and the county of Tripoli: for the Temple, Tortosa and Chastel Blanc, for the Hospital, that created by the counts of Tripoli between 1142 and 1180, the length of the frontier covering the county from the direction of the Orontes valley, with large fortresses of which the most important was the Crac des Chevaliers. A little further north, the lord of Margat had, in 1186, in return for a large rent, granted his castle to the Hospitallers and Saladin had been unable to take it. Bohemond III even wanted to add the castle of Maraclea, destroyed by the Muslims, on condition they restored it, but the Ismailis, already kept at a distance by the Hospitallers, to whom they paid tribute, feared a new addition to their power and obliged Bohemond, on threat of assassination, to revoke his grant (1199). But the two orders remained in possession of large and profitable lordships.

It was they who were called on to guard many of the fortresses the crusaders had rebuilt. This was the case, for example, with Chastel Pèlerin in 1217, which was handed to the Templars; they recovered Saphet when Benoît of Alignan had the castle rebuilt. But the treaty of Jaffa had been very disappointing for the Templars, who had recovered only a small castle at the point where the road from Jaffa to Jerusalem plunged into the mountains; the pope was to complain that the order neglected its primary vocation which was to protect the pilgrims following this route. In contrast, Frederick's crusade had been very profitable for the Teutonic knights, who had obtained a manor in Jerusalem and managed to acquire a very large estate north of Acre, the old lordship of Count Joscelin.

Between 1234 and 1238, the Hospitallers had attempted to make a reality of their rights over Montferrand, Rafaniyah and the adjoining territory, by making war on the Muslim prince of Hamah, but the operations had scarcely gone beyond the level of skirmishes and reciprocal razzias; the order was not really capable of recovering land from the Muslims. But an incident occurring during the course of St Louis' crusade reveals that the Templars had negotiated with the sultan of Damascus a division of the revenues from certain frontier territories.

In fact, while the orders did not neglect the revenues they drew from the exploitation of their eastern estates, their resources came mainly from elsewhere. In the East, they possessed *casals* whose inhabitants paid rent, plantations worked by slaves, fortresses, rents, houses and fortified manors in the towns; in the West, they had a network of commanderies, that is, rural estates.

The commanderies of the Temple and the Hospital largely consisted of the villages and property given to the two orders by lords or knights when they joined their ranks, or in other circumstances by pious donors. They also included a far from negligible number of hospitals, such as the 'maisons-Dieu' intended for the accommodation of travellers on the roads, which has led to the suggestion that the two orders tried to establish their houses along the roads which led to the Holy Land; in fact, it was often in an attempt to ensure the regularity of the life of those who served these houses that they were incorporated into recognised orders.

Their number was considerable; each of the two orders had many hundreds, scattered throughout the West and even in Spain, where the crusaders had made little impact but where pilgrimage was hardly unknown. Each took the form of a small community, comparable to a priory but without the same liturgical functions; it was in principle expected to provide hospitality to poor travellers; the Templars were criticised for having neglected this obligation. Its principal role was to extract the profits from a rural estate, not only to support the commandery but to provide the order with financial resources, each one being required to send an annual contribution to the treasury of the order, which were known as the 'responsions'.

These houses also played a role in recruitment to the order, receiving the recruits who wished to join the ranks of the knights. The conditions for joining varied; alongside the professed knights, who took monastic vows, there were knights who joined for a fixed period, whose position was very close to that of the *soudoyers*. But the commanderies kept locally a body of men which has been regarded as excessive in the light of the needs of the Holy Land; when disaster struck, as, for example, at La Forbie, the master of the order could call on these reserves to fill the gaps made in his troops.

A reservoir of both men and money, each of these orders had to organise their conveyance to the East. The Temple and the Hospital each had a fleet. In 1216 they both had to negotiate with Marseilles concerning their right to build ships and carry pilgrims and merchants; in 1233 this right was restricted to the transport of 1,500 pilgrims and the use of two ships annually. But the orders owned other large sailing ships and galleys; the famous adventurer Roger Flor commanded one of the Templars' ships, the *Falcon*.

The conveyance of money led the Templars, in particular, to perfect a system that has been called a banking system. In fact, the Temple served primarily as a deposit bank; the Capetians, from Philip Augustus to Philip the Fair, entrusted their revenues to the treasury of the Temple, kept in the tower of the Templars in Paris. Crusaders entrusted their cash and jewels to the Templars, who made sure that their chests were opened only by the depositors. We have already recalled Joinville's story of how, to obtain the money needed to pay the first instalment of St Louis' ransom, he appealed to the commander of the Temple, whose ship was anchored off Damietta; when the Templar refused to open the chests, Joinville seized an axe, which allowed the master to appear to be giving in to force. But it was common practice for the Templars to make credit transfers from one place to another, advancing in the East sums they recovered in the West, or vice versa, thanks to the movement of funds which they had to make on their own account.

The orders had access to the financial resources that were often lacking to the barons. As we have seen, in 1187 it had been necessary to resort to the deposits made with them by Henry II of England to rebuild the kingdom's defences. In the thirteenth century they catered for the needs of the Frankish lords, accepting securities or sales, sometimes on a considerable scale. In 1254 the sire of Sidon, Julian, had to sell his fief of Casal Robert to the Hospital; in 1256–7 he ceded the lordships of the Schuf, Gezin and the fort of the Cave de Tyron to the Teutonic knights, in return for 23,510 bezants; in 1261 he sold the land of Sidon and Beaufort itself to the Templars. The sire of Arsur mortgaged his land to the Hospitallers in 1261.

This had the result of placing an increasing share of the burden of the defence of the Frankish states on the orders. Thanks to their ample means, they were in a position to build fortresses employing the most advanced techniques, as in the case of the Crac des Chevaliers and Margat. In 1240, however, the Temple hesitated about rebuilding Saphet, and Benoît of Alignan had to encourage the knights and appeal to the crusaders to cooperate. In 1255 the Hospital paid 1,500 bezants for the ruins of the monastery of Mount Tabor, whose monks had withdrawn to Acre, in order to build there over the next ten years a castle which would have a garrison of forty knights; the order embarked on the fortifications almost immediately.

In addition to this network of fortresses, garrisoned by several hundred knights, sergeants and turcopoles, there were other men, normally stationed in the manor houses owned by the orders in the great towns of the kingdom or the county; that of Tripoli was besieged during the battle between Bohemond VI and the Temple; that of the Hospitallers at Acre, which still stands today, was blockaded in 1242 by the enemies of Filangieri. It was they who had to assure the defence of the towers, barbicans and sections of the enceinte of Acre which had been granted to the Hospitallers, the Teutonic knights and the knights of St Lazarus and of St Thomas. And when the army of the kingdom was assembled under the royal standard, each order sent its own contingent under its own banner; these contingents might comprise as many as 300 or 400 knights without it being necessary to denude the fortresses of their garrisons.

The maintenance of these forces entailed other costs, such as equipment, war machines, victualling and the provision of fresh horses, which the Templars brought from Spain. The commanders of the Vault of the Temple in Acre had been urged to look after the corn stored there, and one of them was dismissed for having let it overheat. If we add the cost of purchasing many rural estates, often probably in response to appeals from owners in difficulties, one realises that the orders had to incur considerable expenses.

Their establishments, as a result of their combined religious and military nature, led them into close contact with the Frankish, and also the Syrian, populations; Syrians from Latakia 'commended' themselves to the Hospitallers of Margat. In commending themselves to the prayers of the knights, the barons and the fraternities joined the confraternity of either the Temple or the Hospital; there survives a deed of 1254 by which the priors of the fraternity of St James of Acre undertook to take an oath of fealty to the master of the Hospital, all their brethren being at the same time received into the confraternity of the order. As a result, the order came to be surrounded by a whole clientele which, during the war of St Sabas, lined up behind the knights.

Within the Latin states, the orders constituted political powers which, on the ecclesiastical plane, enjoyed exemption from the normal jurisdiction of the bishops, even of the patriarch, though the legation received by the patriarch from the Holy See slightly reduced their independence in his case. At the level of lay rulers, they were protected by the excommunication which the papacy was ready to pronounce against kings or princes who molested them, and the Temple exploited this against the king of Armenia. But, given the dwindling forces and resources of the princes, they represented a power which counterbalanced them.

In 1210 the Temple leaned on the barons of the kingdom of Jerusalem to resume hostilities against the sultan; we have already seen how, in the war of succession in Antioch, it took the side of Bohemond IV; how in

1228–9 it was almost openly at war with Frederick II; and how in the period 1240–1, it argued for an alliance with Damascus rather than with Egypt, in contrast to the Hospitallers and the Teutonic knights. Its stance in the war of St Sabas and in the conflict between Bohemond VI and the sire of Gibelet shows the masters of the order behaving independently of the sovereigns of the various states. The Hospital did the same; it, too, pursued its own policies, though with perhaps more restraint than the Temple; with the Teutonic knights, it accepted Frederick's authority when the Templars supported the rebel barons.

The orders were occasionally, however, forces for reconciliation. Gregory IX at one point considered entrusting the defence of Tyre to the Teutonic knights to get round the obstacle of the barons' hostility to Filangieri, and, in 1259, it was the master of the Temple who mediated between Bohemond VI and his rebellious barons.

But one of the darker sides of the military orders was their rivalry. Despite frequent agreements and reconciliations (at one point, both masters belonged to the family of Montaigu), this led them to take opposing positions. At other times, they demonstrated their amity; during the Egyptian campaign and during that of Louis IX in Syria, they were usually of the same mind when advising the king. They then demonstrated considerable understanding of the East and of the tactics of the combatants and often represented the voice of caution.

The last master of the Temple in Syria, William of Beaujeu, had to calm the warlike ardour of the young brethren newly arrived from the West; contrary to a received image, the Templars were not a band of knights avid for mighty deeds and bold acts, but a group of experienced fighting men, as ready to negotiate as to fight; indeed, they were reproached for this at the time of their trial. The Muslims recognised that they kept their word; this may have been what prevented the Temple, in 1241, from abandoning the alliance with Damascus. It should be added that, bound to obey their rule, the knights were subject to a discipline which was evident during their operations.

Their establishments outside the Holy Land may give the military orders the appearance of organisations of an international character, whose interests were likely to be much influenced by the imperatives of their endowment in Europe. This might be the case, for example, when Frederick II seized their property in the kingdom of Sicily. In fact, everything was subordinated to their vocation in the Holy Land. The Spanish kings, especially in Aragon, entrusted them with estates and castles on the border with the Muslims; the Templars showed little enthusiasm for fighting against the latter and, in the end, orders specific to Spain were preferred to them. The Teutonic knights, despite their establishment in Prussia and Livonia and their increasingly deep involvement in the Christian expansion in the face of the Balts and Estonians, kept Montfort (Starkenberg) as their headquarters until its fall in 1268 obliged the grand master to transfer the convent's base to Marienburg. The Templars and Hospitallers also remained primarily attached to the Holy Land and disinclined to lend their support in other theatres of operations.

Contemporaries were often critical of the orders; as early as 1274 it was suggested that they be merged into one body to end their rivalry. Their wealth, which was exaggerated (in 1244, the Temple was said to have 9,000 manors, the Hospitallers 19,000), led the dean of Lincoln to propose, at the same date, making them wholly responsible for the defence of the Holy Land; it was believed that too many knights lived on their estates in the West instead of going out to the East.

But if these criticisms were sometimes well founded, it remains the case that the Temple, the Hospital, the Teutonic order and their imitators played a crucial role in the preservation of the Latin East; they assured the permanence of a flow of foodstuffs, money and relief troops, without which the Latin establishments would have been constantly at the mercy of the always uncertain support of the West. It was this permanence which made the cooperation of the orders in the crusading enterprise so valuable. And this recruitment was sustained; the ideal of the Christian knight, which St Bernard had associated with that of the first Templars, survived and attracted to the orders a constant stream of new recruits of whom, many, at some time or another, went to the Holy Land.

As it had been reconstituted or maintained after the catastrophe that had ended the first epoch of the kingdom of Jerusalem but less profoundly affected the two northern states, Frankish society demonstrated an undeniable will to survive, though it had to adapt to new conditions. The few towns which remained in Frankish hands or were gradually recovered became active commercial centres, whereas the countryside lost its Frankish population. The weakness of the monarchy allowed the barons and liege men to put it into tutelage, even abeyance, thanks to their refusal to allow the last of the Hohenstaufen to exercise power.

Forces that were new, or which had assumed new forms, were able to assert themselves: the privileged Italian 'communes', the fraternities, the community of liege men which managed to form itself – temporarily in the case of Acre – into a sworn commune.

As a result, this society, living in principle in the expectation of the rebirth of a Frankish Syria which only a crusade could bring about, seemed to adapt to this existence, though territorially restricted, and though deprived of what had been its raison d'être, the possession of the Holy Places. At the time of the war of St Sabas, which dragged on long after the original conflict, one has the impression of a society not of crusaders but of communities jealous of their autonomy, whose horizons were restricted to their own city. Even the county of Tripoli, which had long resisted this tendency, was eventually riven by conflicts between national groups.

But though the Latin churches, too, were confined in their activities to the towns, they could not forget that they were maintaining the tradition of a Latin presence in the great sanctuaries, and that they were awaiting its revival. And the military orders, despite their rivalries and oppositions and the severe restriction of their immediate perspectives, represented an element which maintained on a permanent basis the vocation of the crusaders. They could only contribute, however crucially, to the survival of the Frankish Syria which might, at any moment, serve as the base for a new crusade, but they acted as conduits for the influx of men and resources which made this survival possible.

For the recuperation so longed-for to come about, a crusade remained indispensable. It was to experience an unexpected revival in its darkest hour.

12

THE CRUSADE AND THE MONGOLS

Since the catastrophe of 1244, the Latin East had been conscious of the precariousness of its situation. An act of 1248 stipulated that, if there were to be a Muslim conquest, the rents specified in contracts would still be paid if Acre and Tyre remained in Christian hands, but would lapse if these two towns were lost. St Louis' crusade had put new heart into the Franks, but their situation remained difficult.

Within six months of the king of France's departure, however, the outlook had been transformed; the creation of an empire extending over a large part of Asia and as far as the borders of Europe had quite unforeseen consequences. The appearance of a powerful ally in the East raised once again the question of the reoccupation of the Holy Land, and the prospect of a crusade appeared in a new light.

In the twelfth century, certainly, there had been talk of a possible intervention by Christian princes from the Far East, of whose existence people were dimly aware; the victory of the Khitan of the Kara Khitai over the Seljuks of northern Iran had been seen as a sign of Prester John's desire to assist the Christians of the Near East. And in the circles of the legate Pelagius, Bohemond IV and John of Brienne, the campaign conducted by the Mongols in Iran had also been attributed to a Christian king 'in whom the people', said James of Vitry, 'had recognised Prester John'. But these were interpretations originating with the Christians of Iraq, and illusions were soon shattered. The appearance of the 'Tartars' on the European and Asiatic scene, between 1240 and 1245, had taken a very different form.

Between 1260 and 1274, however, these daydreams were to materialise. The transition from the prospect of a formidable invasion to that of an actual alliance happened so rapidly that not everyone was quick to grasp its significance.

In February 1253 the *qaghan* Möngke, who was to receive Rubruck a few months later, summoned to the source of the Onon, east of Lake Baikal, the *quriltai*, the assembly of the Mongol princes. There he proclaimed the resumption of the great enterprise to subject peoples to the empire founded by Genghis Khan, defining three directions: China, which he would conquer with his brother Qubilai; Europe, which would be subjected by his uncle Batu; and the Near East, which was to be the sphere of operations of his other brother Hülegü, who took the title of il-khan. In fact, this project was slow to get off the ground; the movements of these princes were accompanied by a veritable migration of people and flocks. It was early in 1254 before Hülegü was on the Amu-Darya.

Meanwhile, Möngke had received the visit of Hethoum, king of Armenia, who had come to swear allegiance, and who had described to him the situation of his kingdom and the neighbouring lands, emphasising the potential importance for the Mongols of the Christian factor. The *qaghan*, as we know from Rubruck, was not ill disposed towards Christians; it is even possible that he agreed to be baptised by an Armenian bishop, though he seems to have been more attracted by Buddhism. It is far from certain, however, that the king of Armenia succeeded in making him favourable to the Latins of the Holy Land, if we are to believe the historian Rashid al-Din, who says that Möngke ordered Hülegü to subject Syria and the Muslim countries as far as the furthest limits of Egypt, and to drive out the sons of France and England.

In fact, the first consequences of the implementation of Möngka's programme were felt on the eastern frontier of Europe. Batu died in 1256; his son Sartaq (to whom Rubruck had taken a letter from St Louis) and Sartaq's son both soon died, and it was the khan Berke who, in 1257, took command of the Golden Horde. Berke was a Muslim; it is possible that his mother was a daughter of the sultan of Khwarism, conquered by Genghis Khan. He was more interested in the Asian part of his possessions and was to clash with Hülegü over the Caucasus, which had probably been assigned to Batu's sphere of influence. But he began to carry out the programme laid down in 1253; his messengers invited the sovereigns of eastern Europe to submit. In 1257 he exacted obedience from Daniel of Halicz; in 1259 he entered Poland and burned Sandomir and Cracow. The Lithuanians who, under Mindaugas, had responded to the approaches of Alexander IV, changed sides and, in 1260, inflicted on the Sword Brothers the defeat of Durben. The king of Hungary, Bela IV, who had made an act of submission to Batu, was invited to join the Mongol army, but managed to evade this demand. All Alexander IV's efforts to build a dike to contain the advances of the 'Tartars' had been in vain.

In the Near East, the prospects were no better. The Hülegü's army had first destroyed the principality founded by the Ismailis south of the Caspian Sea, seizing Alamut and the Old Man of the Mountains himself, who was put to death. It then entered Kurdistan, subduing the local princes, before marching on Baghdad, where the caliph had been unable to maintain the prudent policy of his predecessors, and where the rivalries between Shi'is and Sunnis had become increasingly bitter. The capture and sack of the town, early in 1258, the extinction of the Abbasid dynasty and the execution of the caliph caused consternation throughout the Muslim world. The eastern Christians, spared by the conquerors, who had shown particular respect for the *catholicos*, saw this as a punishment inflicted on a city which, for them, symbolised oppression. Hülegü had then gone to Azerbaijan and upper Mesopotamia, subjecting or eliminating the local princes. In January 1260 he arrived before Aleppo, which fell after a siege lasting only a few weeks; its sultan had taken refuge in Damascus, which fell in its turn on 1 March. Al-Nasir, the last of the Ayyubids of Syria, eventually surrendered to the victors.

The Franks had followed these events with unease; in 1256 the patriarch had warned the pope of the danger that threatened the Holy Land, and the pope had given instructions for bequests intended for the fortifications of Jerusalem and Ascalon to be assigned to preparing the defences of the Holy Land against the Tartars. The letters of the following years show that the danger was felt to be coming closer. But, under the influence of his father-in-law, the king of Armenia, the prince of Antioch had opted for submission to Hülegü, and sent troops to assist him in the siege of Aleppo; he himself had occupied Baalbek and, having entered Damascus with the Mongols, had had the satisfaction of seeing mass celebrated in the great mosque, the former cathedral of St John. The biography of a Chinese general tells how he had sent a demand for submission to a Frankish 'sultan' whose name, transcribed O - fu - wu - tu, could be that of Huguet, king of Cyprus; his answer, full of hyperbole but without specific commitments, could be taken as an agreement.

The attitude of the prince of Antioch caused a scandal; the patriarch of Jerusalem excommunicated him and Alexander IV put his case, with that of Daniel of Russia and Hethoum of Armenia, on the agenda of the council he was about to convene; it was deplored that 'Christian Antioch' should have submitted 'without even brandishing its shield and its lance', and the author of the romance *Claris et Laris*, in 1261–2, regarded the town as lost to the Christians. In fact, Bohemond had obtained important advantages from Hülegü. He had been obliged to accept the restoration of a Greek patriarch, Euthymius, to the patriarchate of Antioch (the Latin patriarch, Opizo, was then in Europe) and the presence of a Mongol resident, but the il-khan had agreed to the restoration of everything taken from his principality by the Saracens: Darkush and Kafardubbin in the plain of the Orontes, Latakia and Jabala, which the Templars and Hospitallers helped him to reoccupy. This was in line with a policy of restoring princes whose rights the Mongol regarded as legitimate; another was the Ayyubid al-Ashraf, who recovered his principality of Homs.

The reaction of the Franks of Acre may have been less clear cut than is admitted by most historians. Admittedly, a letter from the barons and prelates of the Holy Land to Charles of Anjou, dated 22 April 1260, presents the Mongol invasions as a calamity and bemoans the falls of the Ayyubid rulers, but another letter raises the possibility of taking advantage of the vacuum created to make conquests in Syria. In fact, a Frankish baron, Julian of Sidon, reckoned the time was ripe for a raid in the valley of the Litani. There, he met a Mongol detachment, which he defeated, killing its leader, who turned out to have been the nephew of Kitbuqa, a Nestorian Christian, the leader of the army that Hülegü had left in Syria. Kitbuqa retaliated with a raid on Sidon, sacking the lower town. And when the Mamluks of Egypt decided to take on the Mongols, they opened negotiations with the barons of Acre which, but for the caution of the master of the Teutonic knights, might have led to a formal alliance; in any case, they authorised the Mamluks to cross their territory in return for a promise to be able to buy cheaply the horses seized from the Mongols, and so contributed to the Egyptian victory of Ayn Jalut, in Galilee, on 3 September 1260.

But at the same time, when they had received the invitation to submit which had been conveyed to them on Hülegü's behalf at the beginning of February, these same barons and prelates had replied by sending several ambassadors to the il-khan, including an English Dominican, David of Ashby, who had friendly discussions with Hülegü. In fact, the attitude of the Franks of Acre was ambivalent.

That of the pope, in contrast, was very clear. Alexander IV had at first been preoccupied with the threat emerging in eastern Europe and, in 1259, he preached the crusade in that region, though he was unable to give effective aid to the king of Hungary. On 25 May 1260, warned of

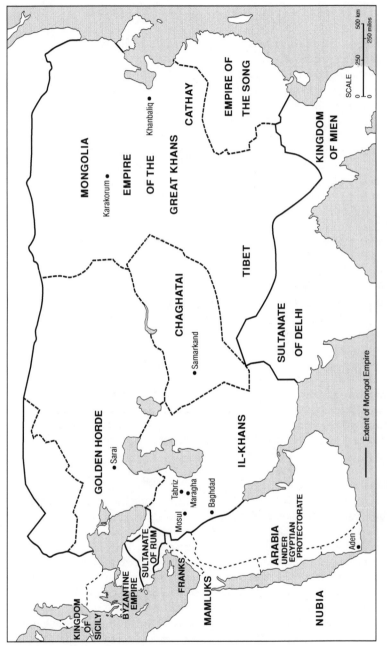

Map 18   The Mongol Empire after 1260 – Hülegü's offensive (1260)

the situation in Syria, he sent the bull *Audiat orbis* to the bishop of
Marseilles, Benoît of Alignan, giving him the task of organising a crusade
to defend the Holy Land against the Tartar threat; Benoît left for the
East, where he rediscovered the castle of Saphet which he had built
twenty years before. On 27 November the pope's plans became clearer.
He addressed all the princes and prelates of Christendom and announced
the meeting of a council for July 1261, to be preceded by provincial and
national councils. Councils were duly held in Mantes and Bordeaux to
prepare for that held in Paris, in parallel with those held in Lambeth,
Mainz and Ravenna. The kings of France and England then summoned
their barons to assemblies, that in Paris for 10 April 1261. Public penances
were ordered; gambling and tournaments were forbidden; it was decided
to renounce luxurious clothing and banquets, much to the annoyance of
trouvères such as Rutebeuf, who feared losing their livelihood. The
council was preceded by meetings in the Curia; the affairs of the Holy
Land and the 'remedy against the Tartars', as at Lyons in 1245, were on
the agenda.

All seemed set, then, for a general crusade, when Alexander IV died
(25 May 1261). His successor was none other than the patriarch of
Jerusalem, James Pantaleon of Courpalay, who took the name Urban IV
and who, well informed about the situation in the East, put first things
first. Though he announced the preaching of a crusade, he asked that it
be preceded by a financial contribution, believing that what the Latin
East needed most was money. But the French clergy, asked to provide a
voluntary aid, refused at a meeting in August 1262, pointing out that the
Holy Land was covered by the truce concluded with the Saracens.
Urban IV then decided to institute a tax of a hundredth on ecclesiastical
resources throughout Christendom, for a period of five years, but he was
again met with reluctance on the part of the French clergy, and he was
obliged to entrust the collection to Giles of Saumur, archbishop of Tyre,
and John of Valenciennes, both arrived from the Holy Land. The
purpose was clearly spelt out: 'To assist the Holy Land at a time when it
is in great danger on account of the Tartars.' In Germany, Albert the
Great was made responsible for this collection, which did not begin till
the end of 1263.

By then, the situation had changed. In March 1263 Urban IV was still
speaking of 'this cruel and damnable people, the Tartars, who crush
those they have reduced to slavery under intolerable burdens'. On 13
June, he added to the Tartar peril that of the Saracens, and soon it was
they alone who were mentioned. He had already, on 26 May 1263,
suspended the sentence of excommunication pronounced against

Bohemond VI after receiving his explanation of his alliance with the Mongols.

Nevertheless, the Mongols remained formidable adversaries, who were threatening the eastern borders of Europe. It is possible that the great Mongol embassy which went to Paris in 1262 was that of the khan Berke, carrying an ultimatum to St Louis. In November 1265 Pope Clement IV thought it necessary to preach a crusade against the Tartars in Hungary, Poland, Brandenburg, Bohemia, Austria and Carinthia. In fact, the khan of the Golden Horde had relatively few troops at his disposal, and we know that his attention was primarily focused on the frontier of the Caucasus. Nevertheless, he kept up his pressure on the Christian countries.

In Frankish Syria, meanwhile, events had taken another direction. There was no longer any thought of conducting a crusade against the Mongols; the talk was now of a crusade in collaboration with them.

THE EMPIRE OF ISLAM FACE TO FACE WITH THE FRANKS

The Franks had not been mistaken in signalling, when Damascus fell to the Mongols, that Syria was for the taking. But it was not the westerners who were to profit from the disappearance of the Ayyubid sultanates of Syria, which had been united by al-Nasir Yusuf, sultan of Aleppo.

Mamluk Egypt was among Hülegü's objectives. But soon after the fall of Damascus, he learned of the death of his brother, Möngke, and of the problems caused by his succession, disputed between Qubilai and Ariq-Buqa. He left for Iran. If we are to believe the letter he wrote to St Louis and some evidence in eastern writings, he had another reason for withdrawing most of his troops from this theatre of operations, that is, the exhaustion of the Mongol horses, deprived of their usual pastures, oppressed by the heat and, being unshod, suffering on ground that was harder than that of the steppe. In any case, the il-khan withdrew his troops, leaving the *noyan* Kitbuqa with a relatively small occupying force.

In Egypt, the Mamluks' rule had experienced problems thanks to Ayyubid claims and battles between the different clans of the Mamluk caste. The emir Baybars, who had been one of the authors of the victory at Mansurah, had at one point entered the service of al-Nasir. Aibek, who had taken power in 1250, was murdered by his former comrades, one of whom, Qutuz, replaced him.

Qutuz was presented with demands for submission from the Mongols, who, what is more, despised these slaves who had acceded to power by murdering their sultan, many of whom came from lands they had subjected (Khwarismians or Qipchaqs from the Kazakh and Ukrainian steppe), and who seemed to them fugitives who had escaped their rule and were destined for punishment. Qutuz answered by putting their envoys to death, an unpardonable insult in the eyes of the 'Tartars'. He reinstated the emirs expelled by his predecessor, then assembled a large army, swollen by those who had fled from Syria during Hülegü's offensive, and set about recovering territory lost by the Muslims. Scattering in passage the thousand men left at Gaza by the Mongols, and having negotiated a passage along the coast with the Franks (who had received his emirs in Acre), he met and routed Kitbuqa's troops at Ayn Jalut. The Mongol leader was captured and killed after he had demonstrated his disdain for his adversaries. One of his lieutenants, the *noyan* Ilqa, gathered the remnants of the Mongol army and led them north, where the Armenian Hethoum received and re-equipped them. The Egyptians had entered Damascus, where they took reprisals against all those who had colluded in any way with the Mongols, in particular the Christians, the Jews and the Shi'ites. They pushed on to Aleppo, whose Mongol garrison had withdrawn. But Qutuz did not enjoy his victory for long; he was murdered by his comrades in arms and Baybars, chief instigator of his murder, became sultan in his turn, though the governor of Damascus refused to recognise him as such. Baybars led his army back to Egypt and refused to keep the promises made to the Franks of Acre.

Hülegü sent a new army which briefly reoccupied Aleppo, but which was defeated by the princes of Hamah and Homs, clients of the sultan. There was confused fighting in the region of the Euphrates, which the Mamluks learned to render impenetrable to the Mongol horsemen by systematically burning the spring pastures. Hethoum and Bohemond VI asked for assistance from Hülegü, who could only attack the frontier town of al-Bira (1264–5). But the sultan had already turned his attentions in another direction.

It was Baybars who was responsible for the transformation of the Mamluk state, which in the time of Aibek and Qutuz had been largely formed in the mould of the Ayyubid sultanate, into a solid political formation, based on a military dictatorship. The last Ayyubid sultan, al-Nasir, had died, executed on Hülegü's orders; the sultan of Cairo now reigned over Damascus and Aleppo, though the Damascenes and their governors on more than one occasion proved unruly. Ayyubid feudalism and its Kurdish elements had been replaced by a more centralised system, where the *iqta* of the Mamluk emirs formed endowments without territorial consistency. All recruited from non-Muslim slaves, usually Turks (and including the occasional westerner), the Mamluks were trained in arms and instructed in Islam, then enfranchised, while retaining a bond of loyalty towards their master; they were united by a camaraderie which did not preclude rivalries, and they alone acceded to high military and government office. But the army also included groups of different origins.

Baybars had welcomed an Abbasid prince who had escaped from Baghdad and recognised him as caliph; he then got rid of him in favour of a successor who was accepted by the Mamluks as sovereign of their state, and as leader of the hierarchy of judges and clerics. This made it possible for them to present this state as 'the empire of Islam', on the pattern of the old Abbasid caliphate, and in spite of the claims of other princes, such as the king of Tunis. Together with the fervour common among recent converts, this gave their empire a stronger religious coloration than that of their predecessors, and enabled them to demand obedience from all the princelings of the region, especially after the gradual eclipse of the Seljuks of Asia Minor, in which Baybars cooperated.

The adversary that the Franks now faced had undeniable qualities as a statesman, but also a lack of scruple and a brutality that made him formidable even to his allies, more than one of whom he dispatched by the dagger or by poison. To this was added an anti-Christian fanaticism intensified by his hatred of the Mongols.

In 1261 the emir of Jerusalem harried the pilgrims who were arriving in the Holy City that year in large numbers, imprisoning them, to be released in return for a ransom, and encouraging attacks on them on the roads. The count of Jaffa and the sire of Beirut opened negotiations, proposing an exchange of prisoners and asking for the return of the small town of Zarin (Petit Gerin), which they had been promised by Aibek. Baybars refused (1262), but in 1263 reopened negotiations. In the meantime, he had led his troops to Antioch and laid siege to the town, which was saved by a Mongol show of force. His chief demand was for an exchange of prisoners, on terms which were more favourable to the Muslim captives. But he was also demanding the evacuation of Saphet and Beaufort, on the grounds that the treaty of 1240 which had recognised their possession by the Franks had been invalidated when they had allied with the sultan of Damascus against Egypt. The count of Jaffa and the Hospitallers of Arsur agreed to the exchange, but the Templars and the other Hospitallers refused, anxious, it was said, not to lose the cheap labour provided by their captives. Baybars denounced the greed of the two orders and, ignoring the truces, attacked Nazareth, Mount Tabor, the Table of Christ and Bethlehem, whose sanctuaries he pillaged. But an attack on Acre failed, on 14 April 1263. The sultan then returned to Jerusalem and embarked on the construction of a caravan-serai as a signal that the Muslim reoccupation of the Holy City was permanent.

This brutal rupture of the truces, and of a whole equilibrium reached over more than thirty years, aroused deep unease among the Franks, who lost no time in warning Urban IV. 'Those who believed they had escaped the formidable threat of the Tartars were confounded by the fury of the Babylonians', wrote the pope on 20 August 1263. The Latins of the East appealed for aid. Urban IV authorised the use of the hundredth, originally intended for the defence against the Mongols, to stave off these new dangers; he urged the completion of the fortifications of Jaffa.

Left to fend for themselves, and taking advantage of the fact that the sultan was once again occupied in northern Syria, the Franks risked an attack on Lyon, led by the Templars and Hospitallers, a raid of reprisal against Ascalon and another against Bethsan, which could hardly bring any lasting relief from Mamluk pressure. In the West, the papal legates summoned people to the crusade, though Urban IV was more concerned with Sicily. In 1265 Baybars returned to the attack. From 27 February to 5 March he besieged Caesarea and reduced in turn the lower town and the citadel, recently fortified by St Louis. On 15 March he destroyed Caiphas, which the Franks had evacuated, but he was checked at Chastel Pèlerin. From 21 March to 29 April he besieged Arsur, which capitulated, and, breaking his word, clapped in irons the Hospitallers who had been promised their freedom.

The appeals for aid had not been in vain, but the response was very limited; Oliver of Termes brought reinforcements to Geoffrey of Sergines at the end of 1264, and the regent of Cyprus his contingents in March 1265. More significant was the arrival, in October 1265, of the elder son of the duke of Burgundy, Count Eudes of Nevers, with fifty or sixty knights, which amounted to a little crusade, raised at the cost of the duke and count and maintained thanks to the income from the hundredth. It was too small a force to drive back the armies of the sultan, but it prevented him from taking Acre.

Eudes of Nevers was not to leave, dying at Acre in 1266. Erard of Valery, who had accompanied him, agreed to prolong his stay and keep with him the majority of the companions of the count of Nevers, still at the expense of the pope, who sent the money collected from the hundredth to the king of France. At the latter's request, the payments were made through Italian bankers who delivered the amount to the patriarch or to the masters of the orders and were reimbursed in Paris from the royal treasury.

The presence of this little crusade – an expedition of this type came to
be called a *passagium particulare* – had not prevented Baybars from
carrying on with his conquests. In 1266 he attacked Saphet, which was
defended by a strong garrison of Templars and which put up a stout
defence; he suffered, as a result, heavy losses. But he was able to exploit
the discord between the knights and the Syrian sergeants, one of whom,
Leo, gave the knights to understand that the sultan would grant them
free exit. On the grounds that he had sworn no oath, Baybars had them
led some distance away and gave orders for all but one of them to be
killed. The Templars all refused to deny their faith, encouraged by some
Franciscans. The people of Acre asked for permission to bury the bodies;
Baybars launched an attack on their territory, massacring the Christian
peasantry, to show that he could provide them with fresh martyrs. He
then took Toron without difficulty, which he destroyed. But he ordered
the repair of the damage suffered at Saphet, to make it a citadel provided
with a strong garrison commanded by an emir who made himself master
of all the land around Acre, where he raised taxes. On 28 October he
intercepted a Frankish detachment which was on the way to raid the
region of Tiberias.

Baybars had pushed his advantage in the direction of Tripoli, seizing
three of the fortresses, Arcas, Halba and Coliat, which covered the
approaches to the town. He forced the Hospitallers to renounce the
tribute they were paid by the Ismailis and came close to obtaining the
cession of the half of Jabala which the Templars were ready to abandon.
A contingent that had marched on Antioch made an about-turn, its
leaders, it was claimed, having let themselves be bought by the prince.
But a catastrophe decisive for the future of the principality intervened in
the form of the devastating offensive conducted by the prince of Hamah,
al-Mansur, in the kingdom of Armenia; the Armenian army was defeated
and one of Hethoum's sons was killed, the other captured. The
Armenian king then devoted all his efforts to procuring the latter's
liberation; this achieved, he became a monk (1270). Antioch could no
longer count on Armenian help.

The year 1267 passed without too many losses. Nevertheless, the sire
of Tyre was obliged to accept a truce, involving payment of a tribute for
the eighty-nine villages left to him, and he renounced Toron and
Châteauneuf. The sire of Beirut, too, had to submit to the sultan's
demands, which included the liberation of Muslim prisoners.

But in 1268 the sultan began by obtaining, in March, the capitulation
of Jaffa, which put up no resistance because the count believed he was
covered by a truce. On 15 April Beaufort fell, and the sultan's army
marched north, demanding in passing a new tribute from Beirut. Baybars

tried to seize Tripoli, which resisted; he had to be content with ravaging the surrounding countryside, even felling the fruit trees, and massacring the peasants. Then, marching on Antioch, he defeated the troops of the constable, Simon Mansel, who was captured and invited to enjoin Antioch to capitulate. The defenders refused, but could hold out only for three days, and the enemy entered the town by force on 18 May 1268; the citadel held out for two more days. The victors indulged in an orgy of killing and destruction. Baybars lovingly described these scenes in a letter to Bohemond VI:

If you had seen your knights trampled under the horses' hooves, your houses stormed and ransacked by the looters, your wealth weighed by the quintal, your women sold in lots of four at a time, and bought for a dinar from your own treasury! If you had seen your churches thrown down with the crosses, the pages of the false gospels scattered, the tombs of the prophets toppled! If you had seen your Muslim enemy trample the place of the mass, the monks, the priests and the deacons with their throats cut on the altars, the patriarchs struck by an unexpected misery, the royal princes reduced to slavery! If you had seen fires spreading through your palaces, your dead burning in the fire of this world before burning in the next, your palaces rendered unrecognisable, the churches of St Paul and St Peter prostrated and destroyed!

Its inhabitants massacred, reduced to slavery or dispersed, its monuments and houses destroyed, Antioch was never to recover from this catastrophe. The sultan also seized St Simeon with the ships in the port, and the towns in the Orontes valley recovered in 1260, and the Templars abandoned all their territory to the north of Antioch, in particular Baghras. All that remained of the principality were the towns reconquered after the Mongol invasion, Latakia and Jabala, and, until 1275, the castle of Cursat, which was spared thanks to the good relations existing between the castellan and the Muslims. The sultan had taken advantage of his march past Tripoli to launch an expedition into the valley of the Qadisha, to seize the fortified caves held by the Maronite leaders, beheading their defenders.

It remained to take the powerful fortresses held by the military orders. Baybars attacked the Crac des Chevaliers, which held out for a long time (21 February–7 April 1271) and whose defenders were conducted to the coast. The neighbouring castle of Gibelcar, which had served as a base for raids of pillage far to the east of the Orontes valley (Baybars punished the Christian inhabitants of Qara whom he regarded as accomplices of the Franks), fell on 12 May.

The Templars of Tortosa and the Hospitallers of Margat obtained a truce, but at the price of renouncing the tributes paid them by their Muslim neighbours and abandoning Chastel Blanc. After this Baybars returned south and laid siege to the great fortress of the Teutonic knights, Montfort, near Acre. It held out till the end of June 1271, but eventually capitulated; Baybars immediately embarked on its destruction, though he had the Crac des Chevaliers restored, for it to become the residence of the emir responsible for controlling the region around Tripoli.

Baybars was anxious to demonstrate that, in his eyes, these conquests were irrevocable, and that there was no question, as had happened under the Ayyubids, of any of them being abandoned to the Franks thanks to some shift in policy. The conquest had been systematic, eliminating the Frankish fortresses of the interior. Works of fortification were begun, and the sultan put his mark on them; the 'lions of Baybars' were found everywhere such work was undertaken.

The West had not observed this collapse without some attempt to react, though it was caught up in Charles of Anjou's campaign in Sicily and Baldwin II of Constantinople was launching an operation to reconquer his capital. Giles of Saumur preached the crusade till his dying breath, and Simon of Brie succeeded him. Eudes of Châteauroux has left us a crusade sermon. The Dominican Odo persuaded the margraves of Brandenburg and Misnia and the duke of Bohemia to take the cross, and Clement IV wanted to give command of the expedition to the first of these, but he died on 4 April 1266. On 28 May the pope rekindled the zeal of the crusaders of Germany, Saxony, Bohemia and Navarre – the counts of Juliers, Cleves and Luxembourg had taken the cross – and he proposed a departure for the month of March 1267. But the project was cut short, probably because of the announcement that the king of France had taken the cross, which led to the proposed *passagium particulare* being abandoned in favour of a *passagium generale* on a grand scale.

THE MONGOL PROJECT

As we have seen, in 1249, having received an ambassador from the Mongol leader, Eljigidei, St Louis had replied by sending costly gifts and a message which left open the possibility of further discussions. The reply received from the regent Oghul-Qaimish had been hardly encouraging, but the *qaghan* Möngke, receiving Rubruck, still regarded it as too friendly and denounced the regent's weakness, demanding from the king a submission in conformity with the requirements of the 'mandate from Heaven' devolved on the Mongols. The idea of Franco-Mongol military cooperation, circulating, it seems, in some Christian circles in the entourage of the khans, remained alien to the Mongols. Hethoum and Bohemond VI had enjoyed Mongol support, but by becoming the subjects of the *qaghan*. And the westerners could conceive of the Mongols only as implacable enemies.

It is easy to understand, therefore, the surprise of Louis IX, and of Pope Urban IV, whom he at once informed, when they learned of the letter of the il-khan Hülegü written at Maragha on 10 April 1262 and dated the Year of the Dog, according to the Mongol calendar. The letter had been brought to the king of France by a Hungarian by the name of John. Its wording bore signs of the intermediary of a western scribe, probably the il-khan's Latin notary, Rychaldus. It still conformed to the protocol of the Mongol chancery, recalling first the Heavenly mandate of which the *qaghan* was the recipient and the universal obligation of submission to him. In support of this demand, Hülegü recalled how the order of Eternal Heaven had been transmitted to Genghis Khan by the shaman Kököchu – the Teb-Tengri – and how it had been confirmed by the victories won by the Mongols empire over an impressive number of potentates, which he listed. But, if he was implying that the king of France ought also to take account of this, he was careful to differentiate his letter from the ultimatums which had preceded it. He recalled the embassy of Andrew of Longjumeau and the splendour of the gift sent by the king, which, he said, the Mongol court had accepted as a sign of friendship. And he explained how it had long been believed that the pope was the leader of the Christian people before it had been realised where true power lay among the French.

It was after these preliminaries that the il-khan, who styled himself 'destroyer of the power of the Muslims and friend of Christianity', turned to the events of 1256–60. He described his campaign against the Assassins, the caliph and the sultan of Aleppo and Damascus, which, he said, had been provisionally halted by a retreat caused by heat and famine. But he announced his intention of destroying the power of the Mamluks, which was why he was seeking the cooperation of the king of France, whom he begged to equip ships to join in a common campaign. He added that it was his intention to return the Holy City of Jerusalem and the Holy Land to the pope and that in token of his good will he had already given orders to seek out and liberate those Christians who had come to the East with the crusades and had been reduced to slavery by the Muslims; John of Hungary had drawn his attention to their lot.

This letter maintained the principle of universal submission to the Mongol empire, and to request the cooperation of the Franks in operations led by the Mongols was also in line with earlier policies. But this time, unlike earlier invitations to 'bring their forces to he who contains the whole earth', the king of France was not asked to accept the customary marks of submission to which Bohemond VI, for example, had had to conform. What Hülegü was offering was an alliance. And, contrary to what has long been written by the best authorities, this offer was not in response to appeals from the Franks.

St Louis seems to have been uncertain how to reply to such an unexpected message. He sent John and his letter to Pope Urban IV, who, in the brief *Exultavit cor nostrum*, sent his congratulations to Hülegü on his expressions of goodwill towards the Christian faith (which John claimed he was ready to embrace), while asking the patriarch of Jerusalem to make new contacts.

The origin of this first official contact between il-khans and western sovereigns with a view to joint action must be sought in the events of 1260. As we have seen, in response to the demand for submission sent by Hülegü, the papal legate, then Thomas Agni of Lentino, and the barons and prelates of the kingdom of Jerusalem had sent him their own messengers, who had also spoken in the name of the king of Cyprus.

The result of these negotiations is known to us through the report of it made by the notary Rychaldus at the council of Lyons. The envoys found Hülegü in Iran; he received them warmly and affirmed his friendly intentions towards Christians; his wife, Doquz-khatun, was a Christian, and some eastern Christians went so far as to see them as a new Constantine and a new Helen. He had no objections to extending to the Latin clergy the privileges granted to ecclesiastics by Genghis Khan: exemption from taxes and public dues, in return for their prayers for the *qaghan*. He prohibited molestation of the Frankish establishments and promised to restore Jerusalem to the Franks. Whether the liberation of the captives was in response to the approaches of David of Ashby or John the Hungarian is unclear.

The promise to restore Jerusalem was in line with the concession obtained by Bohemond VI: the Mongols agreed to recognise the Franks as legitimate owners of the lands of which they had been deprived by Saladin and, if the sultan was defeated, they would allow them to take possession. From the perspective of the crusade, this opened up new and encouraging possibilities.

But the initial reaction of the pope was on a different plane, and the papacy stayed true to its position; its prime concern was not so much the participation of the Mongols in the reconquest of the Holy Land as their conversion to the Christian faith. In 1266 Clement IV was to specify that, not being Christians, the Mongols could not enjoy the crusade indulgence, even though they were the crusaders' allies against the Saracens. And in all the conversations between the popes and the il-khans, this difference of approach remained; the il-khans spoke of military cooperation, the popes of adhering to the Christian faith.

Hülegü seemed very close to Christianity, but his successors, Abaga and Arghun, inclined rather towards Buddhism, and they encouraged its diffusion throughout their empire. Arghun was to reply to a letter from the pope: 'If one recognises the God of Heaven and conducts oneself well, does one need baptism?'

The embassy of John the Hungarian, who probably returned to Maragha late in 1262, was followed by another, but this was intercepted on its arrival in the kingdom of Sicily by Manfred, who prevented the envoys from reaching the pope. It is not impossible that the Latin-speaking notary from the Mongol chancery was part of this embassy; in 1266–7 new envoys brought Clement IV a letter written in the Mongol language, which no one at the Curia could read. But the envoys repeated the message of their master, Abaga, who had succeeded Hülegü, and the pope was able to arrange for them to be present when the king of France took the cross (April 1267). In 1268 Abaga sent a new letter to the pope, which followed another missive sent to the king of Aragon, in which he announced his intention of joining the army of this king or of sending his brother Aghai to join it when it landed in Cilicia. Further, he announced to the westerners that his father-in-law, Michael Palaeologus, would also lend his support to their expedition, in particular by supplying it with provisions.

In fact, Abaga, in 1265, had married an illegitimate daughter of Michael VIII, Maria, and he had found Michael ready to join the war against the Mamluks; the Byzantine emperor was seeking to get his reoccupation of Constantinople accepted by cooperating with the Franks elsewhere. But the il-khan did not have his hands free; the khan of the Golden Horde, Berke, had declared war on him as a result of Hülegü's annexation of the Caucasian lands claimed by Batu's successors. In 1262 Hülegü had led an offensive in a northerly direction, and been driven back. In 1266 Abaga had repulsed the prince Nogai, who had invaded his states, and Berke was preparing to renew this attack when he died later that year. The conflict was to be widened as a result of the division of the Mongol princes between obedience to Qubilai, who had proclaimed himself *qaghan* in China, and that to his brother Ariq-Buqa, who had been recognised in Mongolia and who had the support of Baraq, the khan who ruled in Transoxiana. In 1269–70 Abaga had to resist an attack by the latter, whom he defeated in July 1270. The battle against the Mamluks was only one strand in his policy.

The sultan Baybars aimed to exploit the dissensions between the Mongols. In 1262 he concluded a treaty with Michael VIII to obtain free passage for his merchants in the Straits; at the end of 1263 he sent his messengers to Berke to ask him, in the name of Muslim solidarity, to

attack the allies of the Christians. And in 1264 he got Michael
Palaeologus excommunicated by the patriarch of Alexandria for having
broken their treaty of 1262 and thus having violated his oath. The
coalition between Franks, Mongols and Byzantines was matched by a
coalition between the Golden Horde and the Mamluks; in 1265 Berke
got Nogai to attack the Bulgarian frontier of the Byzantine empire.

It was therefore impossible for the new il-khan to repeat the massive
descent into Syria of 1260. But the Mongol alliance could mean the
intervention of a large army and other forms of assistance which could be
helpful to a crusade. It is hardly surprising that, for nearly forty years, the
Westerners remained hopeful of achieving this combination of their
efforts and those of the sovereigns of Persia, and that this should appear
so dangerous to the sultans.

THE EIGHTH CRUSADE

For many people, the Eighth Crusade is the second 'crusade of St Louis',
decided on by the king at an inopportune moment, against the tide of
public opinion, and doomed, consequently, to failure. It had every
appearance, on the contrary, of a common enterprise, the response of a
large part of Christendom to the disasters suffered by the Holy Land, and
backed up by the prospect of a Mongol alliance which was in no way a
chimera born of western illusions.

The role of St Louis was decisive, however, in that, by undertaking to
leave for the East, the king of France transformed the project conceived
by Urban IV and Clement IV, which was under way, into an enterprise
on a much larger scale. The expedition prepared by a few princes from
the empire, from the Elbe valley and the Low Countries, was turned
into a crusade in which many sovereigns would take part. The former
would have been a *passagium particulare*, bringing a little assistance to a
hard-pressed Latin East; the latter, had it received Mongol and Byzantine
support, might have resulted in the reoccupation of the Holy Land.

In August 1266, Clement IV announced to the barons of the Holy
Land the departure, in the next spring 'passage' (April 1267), of the
bishop of Liège and the counts of Cleves, Juliers and Luxembourg, who
would be accompanied by two thousand crossbowmen provided by the
kings of France and England; he had written to Michael VIII, to Abaga
and to the king of Armenia to ask for their assistance, and he was busy
assembling galleys. Alphonse of Poitiers intended to join the expedition;
the pope agreed to grant him the revenues from the tenths.

But, in September 1266, the king of France secretly informed the
pope of his intention of taking the cross. This was awkward for Clement

IV, who was obliged to abandon his own project to devote his efforts to the preparation of a 'general passage'. He rallied round, however, and, on 25 March 1267, during the feast he gave for the Annunciation, Louis IX announced his decision to his barons and, before them, made his vow on the relics of the Passion. His three sons did the same, followed by many barons. We know that Joinville refused to join them, making himself the spokesman of those who took the cross only reluctantly, so as not to lose the king's favour. But enthusiasm was greater than the seneschal of Champagne suggests, and, at the feast given for the knighting of Philip the Bold on 5 June, more people took the cross.

The resolve of the crusaders was stiffened by many sermons: by Simon of Brie, by another cardinal, Ralph Grosparmi, appointed legate to the crusade, and by Humbert of Romans, master of the Friars Preacher, who wrote a manual for the use of those preaching the crusade. Songs were also written for their benefit, among them Rutebeuf's *La Voie de Tunes* and his *Disputaison du Croisé et du Décroisé*, which takes the form of a debate in which the arguments in favour of the crusade prevailed over those of the knight unable to see why it was necessary.

The financing of the crusade called for economies in the ordinary expenses of the king, and also of Alphonse of Poitiers, who resorted to all sorts of expedients (sale of enfranchisements, proceedings against usurers and the felling of woods) and the usual aid from the king's subjects. The levy of a tenth, when it was proposed, met with the opposition of the French clergy, but they were obliged to yield. The king made contracts with the lords who, with their men, enlisted in his own 'household'.

The kingdom of England had barely emerged from civil war; it was on 4 August 1265 that the Lord Edward, the future Edward I, defeated and killed Simon de Montfort at the battle of Evesham. But Edward, too, intended to leave for the crusade; his father, Henry III, prevaricated, because he was still bound by a vow he had never fulfilled, but he eventually gave in and, in June 1268, authorised his son to take the cross. Edward did not intend to lead his crusade independently; in August 1269 he reached an agreement with St Louis to participate in a joint expedition.

The departure had initially been planned for 1269. Louis IX and Edward decided to postpone it for a year, which made it impossible for them to combine their operations with those of the king of Aragon, James I. He, though under sentence of excommunication because of his marital situation, had taken the cross at the end of 1266. He assembled a fine army of eight hundred knights and several thousand *almogavares* (mercenaries) and footsoldiers. He had made contact with the Mongols, to whom he had sent Jaime Alarich of Perpignan, who returned towards the end of 1267 with Abaga's proposals, which were for a landing in the kingdom of Armenia, where the Mongol troops and those of the king of Aragon could join forces. Michael Palaeologus was to supply them with provisions, which he duly did.

James I set sail on 4 September 1269, but his fleet, which consisted of some thirty ships, ran into a storm in which many of them were lost. The king, who was sick, was put down at Aigues-Mortes, from which he returned to his kingdom. Nearly half his army did the same; 2 of his sons reached Acre, with 18 sailing ships carrying 442 knights. Most of them left after spending a month waiting for the king to arrive and fewer than two hundred of them remained with the two princes. They participated in the defence of Acre, but were unable to prevent the Mamluks from successfully ambushing Geoffrey of Sergines' successor as head of the French detachment, Robert of Cresèques, who was killed; but they were able to restrain the Franks who were preparing to confront forces superior to theirs. They left without waiting for the other crusade.

Nothing had come of Abaga's proposed plan of campaign. The il-khan had intended to join the crusaders and he had issued his challenge to Baybars early in 1269. But the unexpected attack made by Baraq on Merv and Nishapur had obliged him to turn his attention to this new enemy.

St Louis was counting on the aid of his brother the king of Sicily, Charles of Anjou, whom he had supported in the conquest of his kingdom and who had made a large hole in the available military manpower of the king of France's states. Charles procured all the necessary facilities – provisions, ships and war machines – but delayed taking the cross, which he did only in March 1270. In fact, though he, too, had made contact with the Mongols, Charles of Anjou was playing a complex game. He had defeated Conradin's attempt to reconquer Sicily only in 1268; in his kingdom he found the tradition of peaceful relations with Egypt. In 1267 he had made an agreement with Baldwin II of Constantinople with a view to Baldwin's recovery of the throne of the Latin emperors, completed by a marriage between his daughter and Baldwin's son, and another agreement with William of Villehardouin, whose heiress was to marry one of Charles' sons; the alliance with Michael Palaeologus which had preceded the crusade was at odds with this policy. King Charles joined the crusade but with reluctance.

A campaign in the East, involving the transport of large numbers of combatants with their weapons and horses, required the support of the naval powers. St Louis put pressure on the republics of Genoa and Venice to end the conflict which had been going on since 1256; they eventually came to an agreement in 1270. But the king, remembering that in 1249 he had been at the mercy of his carriers, intended this time to have absolute control over his ships, and a French admiral, Florent of Varennes, was given command of the fleet.

To assemble this fleet, the king of France turned to the various maritime cities. Venice offered him three large three-decker sailing ships and twelve smaller ones, but demanded that the king grant privileges to its nationals, and was anxious not to compromise the favourable situation enjoyed by its trade with Alexandria. Marseilles offered to hire out its ships, but it was Genoa which offered the king of France the best conditions, both to hire and to build ships. In October 1268 the king's envoys negotiated with the podesta and with various shipowners for the construction of several large sailing ships, the king agreeing to provide tall trees from his forests for the masts, the lateen yards and the beams which would serve as rudders. Others hired their ships to the king, undertaking to equip them for the transport of the horses (as many as fifty could be accommodated in the larger ships). The king stipulated that these ships should be ready at Aigues-Mortes by 10 May 1270, that he could take them wherever he wished and that they should remain at his disposal if the fleet put in somewhere and even over the winter. These conditions left him free to employ his ships as he wished, whereas Venice had imposed much stricter rules. For the crusaders, such freedom of action was new. Genoa joined in the crusade by providing a large contingent of footsoldiers and crossbowmen. Other barons, in particular Alphonse of Poitiers, made arrangements elsewhere.

The Eighth Crusade took the form of a coalition in which the king of France was the dominant partner, at least on the western side. Baybars, who was kept informed of these preparations by his spies, was worried; he scaled down his activities against the Frankish towns during 1269 and devoted himself to putting the defences of his lands in order by works of fortification and also by destroying castles where the crusaders might find a base. Damietta, already twice occupied by them, was a danger for Egypt when it was in enemy hands; the sultan gave orders for its walls to be thrown down, and for Ascalon also to be razed.

Meanwhile, the crusade had lost its prime mover. Clement IV died on 29 November 1268, and his death was followed by the longest vacancy in the history of the papacy. Divided into two groups, one hostile to Charles of Anjou, the other favourably disposed towards him, it was 1271 before the cardinals appointed a successor. Clement IV had been very aware of the defensive needs of the Latin positions in Syria; it was only after some hesitation that he had agreed to the transformation of the crusade planned for 1267 into an expedition which did not leave for another three years, giving Baybars time to deal some severe blows to the Frankish possessions. It is possible that, had he lived, Clement might have intervened during the course of the crusade, which was to take a wholly unexpected direction.

THE CRUSADE OF ST LOUIS AND EDWARD OF ENGLAND

The expedition which set out in 1270 has remained for historians the 'Tunis crusade'; it was already known by this name in the thirteenth century, when Rutebeuf gave the title *La Voie de Tunes* to the song he had composed in 1267 to summon people to the crusade, calling on the knights to follow the example of the king and also of Alphonse of Poitiers, 'who governs a whole people' (he had added the county of Toulouse and its dependencies to his Poitevin apanage). To begin with, nothing suggested that Tunis was its destination, and the Genoese had underwritten letters of exchange payable in Syria. It was only after putting in at Cagliari, in Sardinia, that the king revealed the direction in which the fleet was heading; in 1269 he had been intending to land at Syracuse and he had told Charles of Anjou that he expected to be there on 24 June 1270.

There had been a change of plan between the end of 1269 and the summer of 1270. This change has puzzled historians, who have wondered how a landing in Tunis was expected to bring assistance to the Holy Land, then in dire need.

Tunis was ruled by the Hafsids, who had freed themselves in 1228 from Almohad domination, and who were on friendly terms with the Christian kingdoms; they paid a tribute to the king of Sicily in return for their merchants having access to Sicilian grain supplies. The replacement of Manfred by Charles of Anjou had caused some difficulties, which seemed on the way to being solved, even though Hohenstaufen supporters had been made welcome in Tunis. The hypothesis that Charles was using his brother's army to solve his problems is difficult to sustain.

Others have suggested that the sultan Abu Abdallah Muhammad, who had claimed the title of caliph after the fall of Baghdad (he called himself, in imitation of the Abbasids, al-Mustansir bi-llah), was thought likely to lend his assistance to the sultan of Egypt against a Christian offensive, and that St Louis was intending to cut Egypt off from the aid it might expect from the Maghreb. But relations between Baybars and the Hafsid were not particularly close.

Muslim historians have pointed to a sum of 300,000 dinars which was owed to Provençal and Italian merchants by a rich Tunisian trader whose property Abu Abdallah had confiscated. But it is difficult to see how this could explain the diversion of the crusade to Tunis; even Charles of Anjou's influence over his brother the king of France was not so strong as to have drawn him into serving Provençal and Italian interests in this way. In any case, Charles asked Louis not to attack Tunis so as not to hamper the negotiations that were under way.

It seems to me that two events must be taken into consideration: the arrival of a Tunisian ambassador in Paris in October 1269, and the crossing of the Amu-Darya by the khan of Transoxiana, invading the Khorassan, during the same year.

The reason for the presence of the Tunisian ambassadors remains unclear. It has been suggested that it was in connection with the settlement of commercial problems, though these were of little concern to the kingdom of France, or with a request for mediation between Abu Abdallah and Charles of Anjou. What is certain is that the sultan's envoys were at St Denis on 9 October 1269, for the baptism of a celebrated Jew. The king then told them that he would be ready to spend the rest of his life in prison if the sultan and his people would receive baptism. Perhaps the scheme to persuade the Tunisian sovereign to embrace the Christian faith had been conceived during this embassy. It has been suggested that the religious (perhaps Dominicans) who are likely to have accompanied the envoys may have emphasised the good will of the sultan to suggest that the appearance of a Christian army before Tunis would remove all the obstacles to a public acceptance of the Christian faith. We should note that the Dominicans had a convent in Tunis by 1250, that the emir, now sultan, had a guard composed of Christian knights, and that St Raymond of Pennafort expected his conversion to Christianity. It is obviously extremely unlikely that a sultan who posed as successor to the caliphs had any intention of abandoning Islam; it remains possible that such illusions might have been fostered by his discussions with the missionaries.

We must also consider the messages that St Louis had received from Abaga. The latter had fixed a rendezvous with the Franks to embark with them on a campaign against Egypt. The king of France had probably warned him that he would be in a position to embark on operations in 1270; had Abaga changed his own plan of campaign? We do not know. But, when his cousin and enemy Baraq attacked his frontier and invaded his territory, early in 1269, it became impossible for him to keep his commitments to the Franks. It seems to me likely that he then asked them to postpone their campaign till 1271, to give him time to repel the invader, and it was, indeed, in 1270 that he seized Bokhara and inflicted a decisive defeat on Baraq.

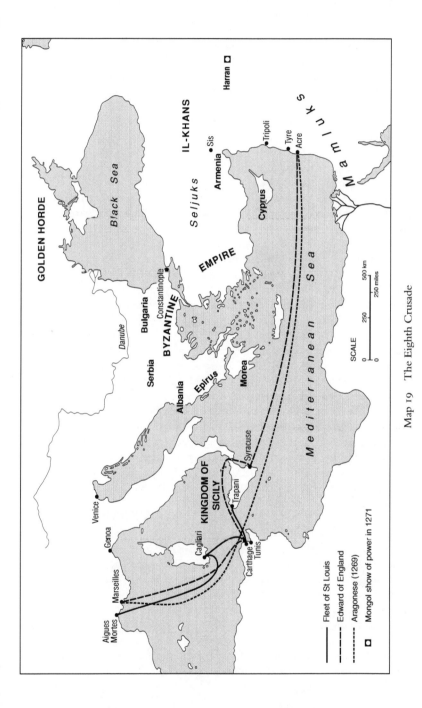

Map 19   The Eighth Crusade

In which case, the king of France may have kept to the departure date assigned to the various contingents, without warning them of the change to his plans, and altered the direction of the campaign by transferring to Cagliari the rendezvous originally fixed for Syracuse. The diversion to Tunis may have appeared as a way of facilitating a campaign with Egypt as its objective, either by adopting the land route to reach that country, or by reducing the sultan of Tunis to the status of vassal or ally, and taking advantage of his kingdom's resources to strengthen the crusade. This campaign, early in 1271, after overwintering as anticipated in the contracts of charter (probably with reference to the overwintering of 1248–9 in Cyprus), would have enjoyed Mongol support.

Other theories can no doubt be devised to explain the adoption of a plan of campaign that is, on the face of it, so surprising. The loss of the registers of the French chancery which might have contained evidence of diplomatic correspondence and that of the accounts means we are unable to confirm them.

The king had put the affairs of his kingdom in order, and appointed two 'guardians', the sire of Nesle and the abbot of St Denis. He left Paris on 15 March and reached Aigues-Mortes, where he was joined by Thibaut of Champagne. There, they suffered a first disappointment; not all the ships were ready, which meant a loss of nearly two months, during which a major row erupted between the Catalans and Provençals and the French. Other crusaders departed from other ports; when the king left Aigues-Mortes on 2 July, it was understood that all the ships would gather at Cagliari, where they arrived up to 15 July. It was then that the king announced the destination of the expedition, which provoked some murmurs of protest. The legate had to calm the scruples of those who asked whether such a diversion was compatible with a vow to go to the Holy Land.

The sultan was not caught unawares, information having apparently reached even him. He had repaired the enceinte of Tunis, accumulated reserves of grain and recruited warriors from Morocco, and he had asked for assistance from Baybars, who prepared an expeditionary force and dug wells along the route it would take. But the crusaders were allowed to disembark on the tongue of land which closed the port (18 July), a position it was soon necessary to abandon in the absence of watering places, in order to march towards Carthage, which was stormed. The king accommodated the sick inside this little town, he himself and his army camping under canvas on the plain.

With the sultan showing no sign of the expected conversion, and his troops harassing the crusader positions, St Louis imposed a very strict discipline. He wanted to wait for the arrival of Charles of Anjou before mounting an attack on Tunis. The wait was painful, and it was necessary to surround the camp with an entrenchment. Disease spread through the army. The king's second son, John Tristan, born at Damietta, died, followed by the legate Ralph Grosparmi. The king himself fell ill and was confined to his bed for three weeks before dying, on 25 August 1270.

The envoys of the Byzantine emperor, of Abaga and of the king of Armenia arrived at the camp too late to discuss with the king the next stage of the crusade. The number of deaths was large; the Muslim attacks continued. But Charles of Anjou had assumed command of operations. While some were still expecting to attack Tunis, he opened negotiations and, on 30 October, reached an agreement. He was unable to get the sultan to allow the Christian faith to be freely preached in Tunis, but he obtained a doubling of the tribute paid to the kings of Sicily, the expulsion from Tunis of the banished refugees, and an indemnity of 210,000 ounces of gold; Edward of England, who arrived on 10 November, was not allowed a share in this indemnity. All that remained was to re-embark. Most of the crusaders proposed to continue their journey to Syria, with Alphonse of Poitiers, while the new king, Philip III, returned to France. Charles of Anjou, who had been able to exploit the situation in which he had found the army, proposed to take many barons into his pay in order to fight Michael Palaeologus in Greece.

On 14 November the fleet arrived at Trapani; during the night of 15–16 November a storm broke out which, according to Baybars' spies, caused the loss of forty ships and almost a thousand persons. The French crusade had lost the means to continue its journey. The king, Alphonse of Poitiers and Thibaut of Champagne set off for France, which not all of them were to reach: the count of Poitiers died at Savona on 21 August 1271 when on his way to Genoa in search of ships; at about the same time, Richard of Cornwall's son, Henry of Almain, who was on his way to join his cousin, Edward of England, was murdered at Viterbo by the son of Simon de Montfort.

It is difficult to estimate the size of the crusade. Many historians think it was considerably smaller than that of 1248–9, as a result of the supposed lack of enthusiasm among the knights for this expedition. Muslim historians have suggested very high figures: 7,000 knights and 30,000 footsoldiers, according to Maqrizi. Ferdinand Lot reduced this figure to 10,000 men. The true figure probably lies somewhere between these two estimates.

One of the crusaders, Edward of England, decided to continue the crusade. His ships seem to have escaped the disaster, but his contingent was much smaller, and could be carried in only thirteen ships. With his brother Edmund, having spent the winter in Sicily, he landed at Acre on 9 May 1271. Some elements of St Louis' army had not taken the detour to Tunis; the Frisians and the count of Luxembourg had gone straight to Acre, though they had been too few to play a significant role in the resistance to Baybars. When the English prince arrived, Baybars was mounting a campaign against the Crac des Chevaliers; he then moved to Montfort and, despite being so close, Edward was unable to prevent the castle from falling.

On landing at Acre, Edward had at once sent his messengers to Abaga. He received a reply only in 1272, when he had left the Holy Land. The il-khan apologised for not having kept the agreed rendezvous, which seems to confirm that the crusaders of 1270 had devised their plan of campaign in the light of Mongol promises, and that these envisaged joint operations in 1271. In default of his own arrival and that of his army, Abaga ordered the commander of his forces stationed in Turkey, the '*noyan* of the *noyans*', Samaghar, to descend into Syria to assist the crusaders. In fact, Samaghar and the troops of the Seljuk sultan, led by that sultan's *perwaneh* (first minister), confronted Baybars' army near Harran, and were beaten. But this allowed Edward to launch from Acre operations with limited objectives, one against St George, in the mountains of Acre, the other against Caco, a castle which controlled the road to Tiberias, which they did not risk besieging (November 1271). In spite of Baybars' absence, the English crusaders and their Frankish allies did not dare to launch a large-scale campaign.

Edward's crusade had been useful, nevertheless. The prince had built a tower to reinforce the enceinte of Acre; one of his companions, Hamo l'Estrange, married the heiress to Beirut. Above all, it was probably the reinforcements he had brought the people of Acre that decided Baybars to conclude a truce with them (he was effectively renewing the truce he had made on 27 May 1268, and broken in 1269) to last for ten years and ten months, which allowed the Christians free access to Nazareth. But it had also been necessary for Charles of Anjou to intervene with the sultan of Egypt (22 May 1272).

Edward had also offered his good offices to settle the differences between King Hugh III and his barons, and he left behind, like Louis IX, a detachment of knights, commanded by Otto of Grandson. But though his undeniable military qualities had been demonstrated by his victory at Evesham, Edward's stay in the Holy Land had done little to improve the Franks' situation. The great crusade conceived by St Louis and approved by Clement IV had ended by fragmenting into a series of operations none of which had any tangible effect on the fate of the Latin East. The death of St Louis and the disaster suffered by his fleet off Trapani had contributed largely to the failure of this grand design. But the absence of the Mongols, due to unforeseen circumstances, had been equally important. The *passagium generale*, supported by eastern alliances, had failed to materialise.

THE CRUSADE OF POPE GREGORY X

While Edward – who became king before he reached home – was in Acre, the Sacred College appointed a successor to Clement IV; this was one of those who had been close to him, Tedaldo Visconti, a native of Piacenza, who had preached the crusade and who had gone directly to Acre at the end of 1270. There he had received the visit of two Venetians who had arrived from China with a message from the *qaghan* Qubilai for the pope; the Mongol sovereign asked to be sent some learned religious, able to perform miracles, and some oil from the lamp of the Holy Sepulchre. The Polo brothers and their nephew Marco set off back without having been able to accomplish the first part of their mission; they were at Ayas when they were recalled by the new pope, who appointed two Dominicans, William of Tripoli and Nicholas of Vicenza, to accompany them.

The cardinals, still very divided, had agreed on Tedaldo because of his devotion to the Holy Land. On the basis of a vision, the new pope believed he was appointed to liberate the Holy Land and restore the Greeks to union. The sermon he preached to the Christians of the Latin East before he left Acre amounted to a programme.

The whole of Gregory X's pontificate (1271–6) was to be dominated by the crusade. He sent a succession of knightly contingents for the defence of the Holy Land: with the patriarch Thomas in 1272, with Oliver of Termes in 1273, and with William of Roussillon in 1275; these contingents were provided by the king of France, Philip III, who continued the policies of St Louis. The king had proposed sending an army to the East, without waiting to organise a more important crusade. Gregory, to whom this proposal had been taken by John of Acre, son of John of Brienne, rejected it and asked the king to send experienced men of war to the Holy Land to study the conditions for the enterprise he had in mind.

On 31 March and 1 April 1272, Gregory X announced a council, which was to be held at Lyons in two years' time. In the bull *Salvator noster* he defined the programme for his council, which was to remedy the ills of the Church: the Greek schism, the situation of the Holy Land and the evil conduct of Christians. He called for preparatory reports to be drawn up. On 11 May 1273 he renewed his appeal, emphasising the 'scandals of the Church'. He was aiming to bring together a whole dossier, one of whose chief purposes would be the preparation of the crusade.

One of the matters raised was the proliferation of the religious orders; the council decided to merge several mendicant orders, for example the Brethren of the Sack were incorporated into the Franciscan order. The military orders, too, presented an 'excessive diversity'. We know that the possibility of merging the Temple, the Hospital and probably other orders was discussed. But the discussion came to nothing, Gregory X having invited the new master of the Temple, William of Beaujeu, to attend the council.

The memoirs drawn up on this occasion were analysed in depth in 1940 by Palmer Throop, a historian with a particular interest in detecting in them themes which had appeared during the course of the thirteenth century in the songs and other accounts which expressed objections to the crusade or to the way it had been used.

The Franciscan to whom we owe the *Collectio de scandalis Ecclesiae* (perhaps Gilbert of Tournai) attributed responsibility for the failure of the crusades to the sins of Christendom, which was hardly new. But he analysed more particularly the abuses found in the preaching and organising of the crusades. He made himself the spokesman of the clergy, who denounced the collection of the tenths and other taxes, including the aids demanded by the lords, as a means of providing the nobles, by pressurising their subjects and extorting money from the clergy, with sums which were used for their own benefit. The poor were being taxed to support the rich.

He also criticised the redemption of vows; preachers exhorted their hearers to commit themselves to costly and perilous expeditions, after which they suggested that they convert a vow made in all sincerity into a cash payment; some crusaders were even pressurised into redeeming their vows. Others made their vow knowing in advance the cost of redeeming it. It thus became a form of taxation.

He also denounced the princes who persisted in their rivalries and conflicts when the crusade presupposed peace. The practice of forcing criminals to take the cross as a substitute for the punishment they deserved was also criticised; the register of the archbishopric of York for 1274–6 reveals that, out of three hundred redemptions of vows, only eleven were made by persons who had not taken the cross under compulsion. This made it possible to evade the sentences pronounced by the courts. The Franciscan complained that many crusaders saw the act of taking the cross as a means of acquiring impunity. He concluded that there were serious faults in the system. The role of the Church, as far as the crusade was concerned, was primarily to pray without ceasing and thus obtain the aid of the Lord. The participation of occasional combatants, each of whom spent only a limited time overseas, might, he said, profitably be replaced by the imposition of a general contribution which would make it possible to support paid soldiers who would be stationed in the Holy Land on a permanent basis.

Humbert of Romans, author of another memoir, reviewed the objections to the use of force by the Church. Leader of a missionary order, he defined two complementary attitudes: the Church ought to 'plant the faith' through preaching, but defend the faithful by resorting to force. He still decided in favour of the legitimacy of the crusade, but in making it a permanent duty.

William of Tripoli had drawn up for Tedaldo Visconti, before he became pope, a *De statu Saracenorum* in which he drew the lessons of his long experience as a missionary. His sympathy for the Muslims is evident; he emphasises their virtues, notes the similarities between their faith and the Christian faith, and recommends persuasion as the means to convert them rather than coercion. To preach the word of God to the infidel needed missionaries, and he himself had been responsible for enough conversions to vouch for the efficacy of preaching. On the basis, lastly, of the prophecies which foretold the end of Islam, he argued that the crusade might be unnecessary. His position as regards the rejection of force as a means of conversion was shared by many of his contemporaries, notably his colleague, Thomas Aquinas, who died on his way to the council.

A report requested from a Franciscan, Fidenzio of Padua, which was not put into writing until 1291, expressed doubts as to the effectiveness of preaching, the Saracens being too hardened in their error, and even as to the possibility of preaching; he asserted that the Muslims were a danger to the faith of the Christians and recalled that they had put missionaries to death. For him, the crusade was a means to the removal of these obstacles.

Voices were raised – in particular by the count of Foix, during the council – to condemn the use of the crusade against Christians. There was even a troubadour, Folquet of Lunel, who questioned the sincerity of Gregory X's enthusiasm for the crusade, suspecting him of planning to use it to further papal interests in Europe.

Bishop Bruno of Olmütz, who was probably expressing the views of King Ottokar of Bohemia, claimed that European problems should take precedence over problems in the East. For him, peace should first be restored by ending the Great Interregnum, by appointing an emperor; the gravest danger came from the East, where the pagans were omnipresent thanks to the welcome the Cumans had received in Hungary, the hostility of the Lithuanians and the Tartar threat. A crusade ought therefore to be directed against all of them and, once they had been dealt with, it could turn against the Saracens.

The divergences of view that emerge in these memoirs, in which we find echoes of the debate which was at the heart of the *Disputaison du Croisé et du Decroisé*, written some years earlier, reveal that the crusade had been the subject of much reflection, and that Gregory X had prepared for the council with great care.

It opened on 7 May 1274, but the pope had been in Lyons since November 1273, along with St Bonaventure, who seems to have been one of his most influential advisers. He had already taken steps to resolve the crisis created in Germany by the disappearance of the Hohenstaufen; the death of Richard of Cornwall (2 April 1272) and the lack of support for his rival, Alfonso X of Castile, had led him to press the archbishop of Mainz to convene the diet which, on 24 October 1273, gave the crown of king of the Romans to Rudolph of Hapsburg, on whom Gregory X was counting for the crusade.

After the first session, the pope and the cardinals embarked on a series of meetings, in particular with James I, king of Aragon, who, in his autobiography, inflated his own role. He had advised the pope to send to the Latin East a first contingent of 500 knights and 2,000 footsoldiers to hold the fortresses, while waiting for the crusade proper, in which he would lead 1,000 knights. The master of the Temple and Erard of Valery, who represented Philip III, were lukewarm towards the crusade, and believed that supporting between 250 and 300 knights would meet the needs of the Holy Land. It seems that, for them, the aim was to preserve the Frankish towns, while the recovery of the Holy Land could wait. But our source of information, that is, the memoirs of James I, may not be entirely reliable.

In any case, Gregory X pushed ahead with his project. During the second session, on 18 May 1274, he promulgated the *Constitutiones pro zelo fidei* which repeated and elaborated the conciliar constitutions of 1215 and 1245, emphasising the arrangements to be made in naval matters. The crusade was thus proclaimed, its departure fixed for 1278. The pope ordered the princes to cease their quarrels; he prohibited tournaments and jousts, which provoked some resentment among the nobility and could not be rigidly enforced. Chief among the measures intended to assure the financing of the crusade was the collection of a tenth on clerical incomes for a period of six years, throughout the whole of Christendom.

On 1 August Gregory X sent his instructions to Simon of Brie, appointed legate in the kingdom of France and the dioceses of Lyons, Liège, Cambrai, Toul, Metz and Verdun. The revenues from the tenth, which was to be collected by agents chosen by the legate, but not by the clergy of the king of France, to avoid regrettable confusions, were to be supplemented by the sums coming from redemptions of vows, confiscations of ill-gotten gains and certain fines; all was to be delivered to King Philip III, charged in a letter of 31 July with keeping the funds for the crusade; this asked him to assure the costs of maintaining the contingent commanded by Oliver of Termes.

In England, the archbishops of York and Canterbury were made responsible for preaching the crusade and for collecting the tenth, and also a hundredth on ecclesiastical revenues. The archbishops of Ireland, Scotland, Navarre, Aragon, Portugal, Sicily, Sardinia, Italy, Dalmatia, Hungary, Poland, Slavonia, Achaia, Norway, Sweden and Germany received similar letters (12 September 1274). Tenths were collected in Iceland, and the diocese of Gardar, in Greenland, paid in seal and ox skins, walrus teeth and whalebone, whose conversion into currency in circulation in Europe caused some problems, which were resolved in 1282.

Gregory X was counting on the participation of Philip III of France, whose crusading vow remained unfulfilled since he had returned from Tunis without having gone to the Holy Land. The king, the queen and their entourage solemnly took the cross on 28 June 1275. Charles of Anjou also promised to depart, or at least to send his son in his place. James I of Aragon could be regarded as favourably disposed, but had made no firm commitment. The king of Sweden had taken the cross; he left 400 marks in his will, in 1285, for the fulfilment of his vow.

The pope was relying heavily on the new king of the Romans, who had announced his intention of taking the cross at the time of his coronation. But Rudolph had to deal with the claims of Alfonso of Castile and of Ottokar of Bohemia; the pope arbitrated in the case of the former and persuaded the king of Castile to withdraw, which he did only in September 1275. Ottokar agreed to take the cross, deferring till his return from the crusade his final decision as to whether to recognise Rudolph, which was tantamount to challenging his possession of the crown. Rudolph, his wife and his barons finally took the cross in October 1275.

Gregory X's efforts to impose peace had mixed success. Philip III did not abandon his operations against the count of Foix or the king of Castile; the conflict between the king of Bohemia and Rudolph was settled only in 1278 by the latter's victory at Marchfeld. James of Aragon, meanwhile, had died.

Gregory X was not proposing to confine the enterprise to the Christian countries of the West. He revived the schemes from prior to 1270 which had aimed to involve Mongols, Armenians and Byzantines. As regards the latter, he refused to support the ambitions of Charles of Anjou, who during the pontifical vacancy had continued to prepare a campaign against the Byzantine empire. Michael VIII remained faithful to his policy of rapprochement with the papacy and alliance with his son-in-law, the Mongol il-khan, though he seems to have tried to avoid open conflict with the new khan of the Golden Horde, Möngke-Temur, and with the sultan of Egypt.

The discussions between Greeks and Latins revolved round the resolution of the dogmatic controversies. The Greek patriarch of Constantinople, John Bekkos, made an important contribution because he had stated that the Latin formulation of the procession of the Holy Spirit, principal stumbling block in Graeco-Latin negotiations, was compatible with the doctrine of certain Greek Fathers. As a result, there could be a proclamation of unity of the faith and recognition of Roman primacy by the *basileus* without it being regarded simply as a manoeuvre on the part of the Byzantines (6 June 1274).

The Mongols sent an embassy consisting of thirteen persons, including David of Ashby and the notary Rychaldus, who wrote an account of Franco-Mongol relations for the fathers of the council. What he did not say was that Abaga, in 1272, as a result of his conflict with the khan Baraq, had attempted a rapprochement with Baybars, who had received his overtures coldly. The il-khan had then returned to the policy he had pursued from 1265 to 1271. Having arrived on 4 July, the ambassadors were fêted, and the solemn baptism of their leader, in the presence of the members of the council, on 16 July, made a great impression. But, wrote a chronicler, 'the Tartars came not because of the faith but to conclude an alliance with the Christians'.

The concrete proposals they brought are known to us only through a letter from Edward I, whom they had visited after the council (28 January 1275). We know that they passed through Lyons on their return, on 13 March, and that they carried a letter for Abaga, to which he replied, in 1276, by sending the two Vassali brothers. While the correspondence with the pope dwelt primarily on the invitation to the faith formulated by Gregory X, the letter from the king of England emphasised that the il-khan had promised to campaign alongside the crusaders.

But one of the most interesting pieces of evidence concerning the Mongol presence at the council is the little treatise written by David of Ashby, *Les Faits des Tartares*, which has unfortunately been lost; we have, however, the table of contents and one chapter, which tells us that the Dominican, who, according to Rychaldus, had been present at many battles and sieges in the il-khan's army, had had the intention of informing the pope about the methods of fighting, the tactics and the customs of this army, with which westerners would have to cooperate on the battlefield.

Gregory X died in 1276 and his two immediate successors held office only briefly, but they continued the policy of cooperation between Latins, Byzantines and Mongols in the proposed crusade.

The resumption of the crusade during the years 1260–74 was entirely dominated by the presence of the Mongols at the gates of Syria. The terror which preceded their approach had brought crusaders to the East, in the wake of Benoît of Alignan. The collapse of the Ayyubid sultanate and other Muslim dominions in Syria fostered illusions among the Franks of the East, who imagined that the Tartars would not occupy the country they had invaded and that it would be free for a Frankish reoccupation; this had already begun around Antioch, but in other circumstances.

It is by no means certain that an agreement between the Franks of Acre, Tyre and Sidon and the invaders would have been enough to achieve this reoccupation. Hülegü had left too few troops to Kitbuqa for him to have withstood the Mamluk army, even with Frankish reinforcements. But, by sticking to a neutrality which was very favourable to the Egyptians, the barons of the Holy Land facilitated their victory, hence the entrenchment of a regime which saw itself as the champion of Islam against the pagans (the Mongols) and the infidel who made, or might make, common cause with them. The letters that Baybars wrote to Bohemond VI emphasise that there was no point in his expecting help from Abaga, and the truces he granted to the Franks required them to break with the Mongols. It is likely that in conducting his campaigns against Frankish Syria (and Armenia), the redoubtable sultan was seeking to deprive the il-khans of the bases that the Frankish possessions might provide for their allies from the east.

The efforts of Hülegü and his successor to obtain a Frankish alliance clearly took the pope and the king of France by surprise. But the sustained attacks by Baybars, and the successive fall of all the great fortresses, though restored and equipped, at great expense, with all the refinements of a masterly technique, converted the westerners to this alliance, which the Mongols were also able to persuade the Byzantines to join.

But the prospect of a coalition which expressly stipulated the recovery of the Holy Land by the Latins changed the nature of the crusade made necessary by the Mamluk attacks. The *passagium particulare* led by Eudes of Burgundy to the rescue of Acre was followed by a great enterprise of a very different type, because the Mongol army had become the crucial element in the proposed campaign. The attacks of the other descendants of Genghis Khan on the il-khan's frontiers prevented this plan from being implemented, and it is not impossible that they therefore diverted the crusaders from an assault on Egypt, to encourage them to wait until they could join forces with the Mongol cavalry.

The crusade of Gregory X, which revived and expanded the projects of St Louis and his allies, was based on similar assumptions. The success of an enterprise to recover the Holy Land was now assumed to depend on the Mongol alliance.

13

THE END OF THE FRANKISH HOLY LAND

From the death of Gregory X until 1291 – and even after that, since the last Franks abandoned their fortresses in 1302 or 1303 – the Holy Land that remained in the hands of the crusaders' heirs was only a shadow of its former self, dependent on the good will of the Mamluks, which could not be relied on. A transformation of the political scene in the Mediterranean as a whole gave this survival a new character, when Frankish Syria was attached to the Angevin empire. But the internal divisions became more acrimonious. King of Cyprus, prince of Antioch-Tripoli and masters of the orders all pursued their own ends. The West was preoccupied with other dramas, the chief of which was the Sicilian question, which had for decades hung over the destiny of the Frankish states. The return to earlier attitudes, at the time of Pope Nicholas IV, came too late for a crusade of any size to be launched.

But the idea which had emerged in the previous period had not been forgotten; no one felt, in 1291, that the crusades were over. Nor was it the end of the Latin East. This was destined to survive in various forms: kingdom of Cyprus, principality of Morea and adjoining lands, Venetian and Genoese islands, Hospitaller colony on Rhodes. And new types of crusade made their appearance in the first half of the fourteenth century.

THE TIME OF UNEQUAL TREATIES

Since the twelfth century, Franks and Muslims had become used to a coexistence regulated by agreements reached after their conflicts, in the form of truces: commercial truces, allowing the passage of merchants and caravans; local truces, assuring the security of the surrounding area; and truces between great lordships. Some were accompanied by the payment of sums presented as tribute, or as being in return for rights of passage. Yet others stipulated the division of crops in lands claimed by two sovereignties. The Franks had often benefited from such agreements at a time when they had been dominant. They were based on respect for provisions guaranteed by a sworn oath. One of the concerns of those who wanted to resume hostilities was to give themselves the appearance of being in the right, by imputing to the enemy responsibility for breaking the truces, by a violation of their conditions.

Baybars, too, emphasised his respect for his word. When he claimed Saphet and Beaufort, it was on the basis of the treaty of 1241; at Saphet, so as to be able to execute the Templars of the garrison, he made a pretence of having taken an oath, whilst in fact avoiding doing so. When he appeared before Acre and Jaffa in 1263, it was on the pretext of renewing the truces which had not yet expired, but accompanying the renewal with new and apparently justifiable demands, such as the liberation of prisoners. In reality, the disproportionate size of the respective forces gave him the means to impose these demands. At the end of each of his campaigns against the Franks, each preceded by a rupture of the truces, the sultan agreed to negotiate with his adversaries and, in general, to grant them a truce valid for ten years.

In 1262 the count of Jaffa and the Hospitallers of Arsur had accepted his conditions, and the truces concluded in 1256 had been renewed. This did not prevent both towns from being captured, in 1268 and 1265 respectively, without the sultan bothering to offer a justification for violating the truces.

In May 1267 the sire of Beirut obtained a truce; around the same date, Philip of Montfort, who had just lost Toron, made a similar treaty which protected the town itself and ninety-nine neighbouring *casals* against attack. In 1268 the sultan granted a truce to the Templars of Sidon; on 27 May he granted one to Acre. This did not prevent him, in 1269, from breaking the treaties made with Acre and Tyre, on the pretext, in particular, that four Muslims had withdrawn to Acre to receive baptism there.

After his campaign against the Crac des Chevaliers, Baybars agreed to grant a truce to the Templars of Tortosa, then to Bohemond VI of Tripoli (1271). On 22 May 1272 it was the turn of Acre and, also in 1272, of the lady of Beirut. In 1270 King Hethoum of Armenia, too, had obtained a truce.

These agreements were renewed by his successor, Qalawûn, despite his determination to press his advantage at the expense of the Franks.

The truce with Tortosa was renewed in 1282, that with Acre in 1283, that with Tyre in 1285.

On the expiry of the truce concluded in 1272, the ambassadors of Acre (two Templars, two Hospitallers and two of the king's knights), representing the masters of the Temple and the Hospital, the lieutenant of the master of the Teutonic knights and the seneschal Eudes Poilechien, *bailli* of the kingdom, asked for its renewal. Qalawûn agreed, and the two parties swore to the treaty, according to a formula carefully worked out so that it was surrounded by every guarantee, in the Christian as well as in the Muslim faith.

Both sides promised to respect their respective territories. The sultan ostentatiously listed all his possessions from Egypt to Tadmor (Palmyra) and from the Hejaz to Birecik and the borders of Cilicia. He was careful to give a complete list of all the 'blessed' (or 'happy') conquests made at the expense of the Franks, and it is difficult not to conclude that he wanted to drive home their humiliation.

On the Frankish side, the treaty listed what was under the authority of the Angevin *bailli* and the military orders (Tyre and Beirut were excluded, as covered by other truces): the city of Acre, its gardens, mills and vines, Caiphas and the 'marine' (the coast between the two towns), and two monasteries on Carmel, where the sultan possessed one village and the Franks thirteen others. In the case of Chastel Pèlerin (Athlith), the fortress, city, gardens, vineyards and cultivable land belonged to the Franks, with sixteen villages. The rest of the territory of this town was 'half and half', except for eight villages belonging wholly to the sultan. The Hospitallers retained possession of their property in the land of Caesarea; Iskenderun (Scandelion) and Maron, with their territory, were 'half and half'. At Sidon, the fortress, the city and fifteen villages belonged to the Franks, the rest, in the mountains, to the sultan.

The situation was similar in Tyre and in Beirut; in the former, where the lordship contained some hundred villages (the treaty lists eighty-five), five belonged to the Muslims, ten to the lord of the town, who retained it with its immediate surrounds, and the rest were held jointly.

The conditions of this 'half and half' division were defined during the course of a lawsuit concerning a dependency of the *casal* of Batiole, one of those left to the Franks. The revenues from the land were collected jointly by the officials of the lord and of the sultan and assembled in a convenient place where they were divided into two. Justice was dispensed by the officials of the two parties, acting in concert, the Christians being judged by those of the lord, the Muslims by those of the sultan; the blood price, in the case of murder, was shared between the two powers. This system, the *casals de parçon*, was probably that in force in the districts where the revenues were shared that are so often mentioned in the agreements between Franks and Muslims.

But the sultan specified that there should be no fortification of the towns covered by these agreements, while himself retaining complete freedom of action. Agreement was reached concerning the safeguards to be enjoyed by ships, and the right of the galleys of the sultan and of the countries allied to the kingdom of Acre to be repaired in the ports of the coast. If a crusade was proposed, the *bailli* and masters of the orders promised to warn the sultan two months in advance. In the case of a Mongol attack, whichever of the two parties knew of it would warn the other at once; in which case, it was stipulated that, if the sultan's troops were driven back towards the coast, the Franks would have the right to prepare their defences and provide, by negotiation, for the safety of their territory and their subjects. Provision was even made for the arrival of refugees from countries subject to the sultan, assuring them of their liberty and the protection of their property. Lastly, the Franks promised not to give aid to pirates, and so did the sultan. The treaty with Acre was completed by stipulations concerning Nazareth, where Christian pilgrims could use the church and four adjoining houses and were promised safe passage, but they were forbidden to repair the church.

These truces were concluded for a period of ten years, ten months, ten days and ten hours. They afforded the towns of the coast a precarious existence, at the mercy of an offensive from the interior, which was ruled by the Mamluk emirs.

In the county of Tripoli, Latakia, Margat, Tortosa, Tripoli and Gibelet were in a similar situation. Baybars had negotiated with the Templars of Tortosa and the Hospitallers of Margat without reference to Bohemond VI; it is possible that the sultan had also concluded a truce with Gibelet, just as he had regarded the lords of Tyre and Beirut as independent of the lordship of Acre. At any rate, he had been able to exploit the internal differences of the Franks, and the lady of Beirut, threatened with being remarried by Hugh III without her consent, put herself under his protection. The treaties made between 1267 and 1272 are striking evidence of the disintegration of the Frankish states.

The Muslim lordships which had covered these states were also affected by the retreat of the Franks. The Bohtor emirs of the Gharb, at the time of the Mongol offensive of 1260, had, like other Muslim princes, made contact with the invaders and made acts of submission; they had then tried to recover the sultan's favour, but one of them, Zain al-Din, was accused of having acted as a spy for Bohemond VI and was thrown into prison. Later, in 1280, he treated with Humphrey of Montfort, lord of Beirut, who gave him a landed fief in return for a promise to respect the borders of their lordships and not to allow Muslim captives to flee from Frankish lands. The Bohtor remained close to the Franks; similarly, certain Christian *moqaddam* from the Lebanese mountains could continue to rely on the Frankish lords to maintain their independence. But this was becoming precarious, as the Mamluk raid of 1268 in upper Lebanon had shown.

The Ismailis had been freed by Baybars from the obligation to pay an annual tribute to the Hospitallers and Templars, but were then obliged to pay it to the sultan himself. In 1272–3 Baybars made himself master of some of their fortresses.

The sultan turned his attentions further north, beyond the Amanus which had marked his frontier. In 1275 he conducted a raid into the kingdom of Armenia, plundering Sis and Ayas. Two years later, he attacked the Seljuks of Antioch, who had been made vassals by the Mongols. The Mongol army stationed in the region went to meet him and was crushed near Albistan; there seems to have been some falling off in the Turks' loyalty to their Mongol masters. Abaga arrived by forced marches to drive back the Mamluks, but they preferred not to wait for him.

Despite the failure of this attempt, Mamluk domination was assured in Syria. The Frankish territories could survive only with the sultan's consent. The death of Baybars in that same year (1277) gave them a respite.

THE HOLY LAND BECOMES PART OF THE ANGEVIN EMPIRE

When Baybars finally abandoned his attempts to seize Acre, it was in the context of a new policy, that of Charles of Anjou; the king of Sicily had acted as mediator between the people of Acre and the sultan in the lead-up to the truce of 1272. But this policy was driven by other ambitions than merely the desire to defend the Holy Land against the Mamluk offensive.

Since 1247, when Innocent IV, breaking the feudal tie which bound the Cypriot monarchy to the empire, had entrusted the protection of the Holy Land to the king of Cyprus, the Lusignan had been recognised by almost all the Franks of the kingdom of Jerusalem as 'lords of the kingdom'. But almost the only right this title conferred was that to appoint the *bailli* who governed in their name; and when Alice of Champagne died (1246), her son, King Henry I, who was chosen by the Haute Cour (even though his aunt Melisende, widow of Bohemond IV, had been a closer relative of Queen Isabella), endeavoured to achieve a reconciliation with the powerful family of Ibelin; he enfeoffed the county of Jaffa to John of Ibelin, Casal Imbert to Balian of Ibelin, sire of Beirut, and the constableship to John of Ibelin, sire of Arsur; the latter and Balian alternated as *bailli*, except for the short period when it was held by John Foignon; and after Henry's death, his mother Plaisance, sister of Bohemond VI, kept them in office. In 1254 she herself married Balian of Ibelin, but separated from him in 1255. As we have seen, during the war of St Sabas she tried to rule more directly, or at least through the intermediary of her brother Bohemond. In 1258 she decided to appoint as *bailli* Geoffrey of Sergines; for the first time since the days of Frederick II, this office was held by a baron from the West.

When Plaisance died (1261), no one wanted the regency; it was only in 1263 that her sister Isabella, married to Henry of Antioch ('Henri du Prince'), was recognised as lady of the kingdom, though not for long as she died the following year. But this recognition paved the way for her son, Hugh of Antioch, to be made regent in Cyprus; he was recognised after a debate before the Haute Cour, in spite of the claims of his cousin Hugh of Brienne.

In 1268, Conradin died; it was now possible to recognise the authority of a monarch, no longer that of a 'lord of the kingdom'. Hugh of Antioch, already crowned king of Cyprus on the death of Hugh II (1267), was preferred despite the claims of his aunt, Maria of Antioch, daughter of Melisende of Lusignan, and was crowned king of Jerusalem at Tyre in September 1269.

Hugh III was determined to make his title a reality. He began by settling a pressing question, that of Tyre, which had been entrusted to Philip of Montfort by Henry I in 1246. Since then, Philip, grandson of the leader of the Albigensian crusade, belonging to the Ibelin family through the marriage of his father Guy, sire of Castres and La Ferté-Alais, to Helvis of Ibelin, and by his own marriage to Maria of Antioch, daughter of Raymond Roupen, lord of Toron, had acted entirely independently. He had sided with Genoa during the war of St Sabas; the truce he made in 1268 with Baybars took no account of royal authority. The reappearance of a resident king deprived him of any title to retain Tyre, which ought to revert to the royal demesne. Hugh III confirmed possession of the town to Philip himself and his son, John, who married the king's sister, Margaret of Antioch-Lusignan, and Philip was destined to become the chief support of the rule of Hugh III. It was probably for this reason that Baybars had him assassinated, on 17 August 1270. Two accomplices of the Old Man of the Mountain came to Tyre to seek baptism, and one of them had the lord of Tyre as godfather; when Philip was handing him a penny for the collection, during the mass, he stabbed him, and was only just arrested before he could kill John of Montfort.

Hugh III tried to heal the wounds left by the war of St Sabas by preparing for the return of the Venetians to Tyre and of the Genoese to Acre. He had already intervened in 1265 and 1266 to lead Cypriot troops to the assistance of Acre, and he did the same in 1268 and 1269. In 1271 he was in Acre yet again. In an attempt to take advantage of the absence of the king and his knights, Baybars, in May–June of that year, launched an attack on Cyprus, equipping seventeen galleys bearing Frankish banners and carrying a small army. But eleven of these ships ran onto the coast and the men they were carrying (between 1,800 and 3,000) were captured.

It was not, however, the risks to the island as a result of these absences that provoked the discontent of the Cypriot nobility, a discontent which Edward I had managed briefly to allay in 1272, but which erupted again in 1273. The dispute concerned the king's demand for military service in Syria, for an unlimited period, from his vassals in Cyprus. The *Assises* certainly provided for such service, but within the kingdom. Cyprus and Jerusalem were united only by a personal tie; the liege men of Cyprus, through John of Ibelin, argued that they were not obliged to serve in the other kingdom; there seem to have been similar difficulties when Baldwin II had taken over the principality of Antioch. To the arguments put forward by Hugh III, based on their participation in the campaign against Filangieri and operations against the Muslims, their spokesman replied that the Cypriots had then been acting either as crusaders or of their own free will; he even claimed that the knights of Cyprus had been serving the house of Ibelin more 'than *monseigneur* the king or his ancestors'. In the end, it was agreed that the king had the right to ask for four months' service overseas. In 1279, when Hugh III led them to Syria, his knights left after their four months had expired. Hugh III could not count on the wholehearted support of the knights of Cyprus.

Other difficulties arose. The lady of Beirut, widow of Hamo l'Estrange, had been commended by her husband to Baybars. Hugh III insisted on his right to give her a new husband and occupied the lordship, taking Isabella of Beirut to Cyprus; the sultan demanded that she be allowed a free choice. The king's conflict with the Templars, who refused to seek his permission to acquire the village of La Fauconnerie, and 'many other quarrels with the Italian communes and the confraternities', and finally the refusal of the Tripolitanians to recognise him as regent during the minority of his cousin Bohemond VII, eventually made Hugh decide to abandon his rule.

He withdrew to Tyre; the people of Acre begged him to return, but the master of the Temple and the Venetians refused to join them. Hugh confined himself to appointing a *bailli*, Balian of Ibelin-Arsur, and left for Cyprus, informing the pope and the kings of the West that he had found it impossible to govern.

There was another reason for his withdrawal, namely the imminent arrival of a representative of the king of Sicily. Ever since he had taken possession of Manfred's kingdom in 1266, Charles of Anjou had harboured vast schemes embracing the whole of the eastern Mediterranean basin. He had revived the ambitions of the Norman kings regarding the eastern shore of the Adriatic, getting himself proclaimed king of Albania by the Albanian chieftains, thanks to rights acquired by Manfred in this region through his marriage to the daughter of the Despot of Epirus. His agreements with Baldwin II and William of Villehardouin had led him to contemplate the restoration of the Latin empire of Constantinople, to the benefit of his son-in-law, Philip of Courtenay, and the recovery of the places conquered by the Byzantines at the expense of the principality of Achaia, which would fall to his second son. This had put him at odds with his brother, Louis IX, and with Pope Gregory X, both committed to the Byzantine alliance from the perspective of the crusade.

The Sicilian heritage had not brought Charles any rights to the Frankish kingdoms of the Holy Land, but he remembered that Frederick II, Conrad IV and Conradin had been kings of Jerusalem, and coveted this prestigious crown. He had received in Sicily Hugh III's defeated rival for the throne of Cyprus, Hugh of Brienne; he had shown his interest in the Holy Land by intervening with Baybars in 1269 and in 1271, to ask him to grant a truce to Acre. The fall of the Hohenstaufen had not interrupted the tradition of good relations between Egypt and the kingdom of Sicily.

It is not known at what point Charles of Anjou made contact with Maria of Antioch, the granddaughter of Isabella of Jerusalem who had contested the rights of Hugh III – himself only Isabella's great-grandson – when he had claimed the throne; Maria had even instructed a notary to protest at the coronation against what she regarded as a usurpation. In 1272 Hugh had responded by asserting that only the Haute Cour of the kingdom was competent to decide in this matter. In 1276, however, Maria revived her claims, probably having been told of Hugh's quasi-withdrawal by the master of the Temple. Since 1275, Charles of Anjou seems to have encouraged the ambitions with regard to Cyprus of his vassal, Hugh of Brienne; it is likely that he was planning to exploit Maria's claims to further his designs on the crown of Jerusalem. In fact, without waiting for the ruling of the court of Rome, on 15 January

1277, in the presence of the majority of the cardinals, Maria of Antioch ceded her rights to the throne of Jerusalem to Charles of Anjou, in return for a life annuity.

Three or four months later, a little squadron carried Roger of San Severino, Count of Marsico, with a few knights, to Acre, where he announced himself as *bailli* appointed by Charles of Anjou in his capacity as king of Jerusalem. Balian of Arsur refused to surrender the royal castle, but Roger had been welcomed by the Templars, who let him into the town, and Balian had to withdraw (7 June 1277). The leader of the French garrison, William of Roussillon, had refused to support the sire of Arsur, and it was Eudes Poilechien, hitherto justiciar of the land of Otranto, who succeeded him as captain of the king of France's troops, before, in 1278, marrying Balian's widow. A series of Sicilians took possession of the great offices of the kingdom, while the bishop of Troia, Hugh of Tours, was transferred to the see of Bethlehem (5 March 1279). The Venetians had been the first to recognise the new power.

But it was recognised only in Acre. Tyre continued to hold out for Hugh III, who landed there at the head of seven hundred knights, probably early in 1279, and set out to rally the inhabitants of Acre, by a lavish expenditure of money. But the barons, who had had to agree to do homage to Charles of Anjou, would not budge, and the master of the Temple adopted a resolutely pro-Angevin stance. At this point, four months having elapsed, his knights returned to Cyprus, and Hugh could only follow them.

He made a further attempt in 1283, landing at Beirut with 250 knights. But the Mamluks laid an ambush for him; Eudes Poilechien was a stout defender of the Angevin cause, and Hugh could get no further than Tyre, where he died on 24 March 1284. The sires of Tyre and Beirut had remained his vassals, but these two lordships, the last survivors of the great baronies of the kingdom of Jerusalem, could not compensate for the possession of Acre by the supporters of Charles of Anjou.

Charles' main support came from the order of the Temple. On the death of Thomas Berard, William of Beaujeu, the commander of the order in Apulia, had been elected master, on 3 May 1273. He had arrived in the Holy Land only in September 1275, and soon revealed himself as a devoted supporter of Charles of Anjou. Himself from a great baronial family, that of the sires of Beaujeu, son of a lord of Montpensier and brother of a constable of France, he no doubt felt able to treat on equal terms with the Lusignan and the princes of Antioch. In dispensing with royal consent to purchase La Fauconnerie from Thomas of St Bertin, and in refusing to join the people of Acre in their support of Hugh III, he had demonstrated his approval, in advance, of the Angevin takeover of the town. In July 1277, it was in his tent that the peace between the Venetians and the lord of Tyre was concluded. In 1279 he opposed the attempt to restore Hugh III. The king of Cyprus in future treated him as an avowed enemy; he seized the order's property and manors on the island. The papacy intervened in vain; the king of Cyprus stuck to his guns.

William of Beaujeu also intervened in the county of Tripoli where Hugh III had been refused the regency for Prince Bohemond VII. When Guy of Gibelet defied princely authority by marrying his brother to a rich heiress, the master of the Temple received him, at Acre, into the brotherhood of the order and reconciled him with the bishop of Tripoli, Paul dei Conti, himself an enemy of the prince; he provided him with thirty knights to defend his castle of Gibelet.

This alliance led Bohemond VII to attack the houses of the bishop and the Temple in Tripoli. The use of Muslim soldiers against the order caused a scandal, as did the removal of the bells from the Templars' church; in the riot directed against the supporters of Bishop Paul several 'Roman' knights and canons lost their lives. Roger of San Severino was forced to intervene to impose his mediation and a truce to last one year (1278). But the war was resumed; Bohemond destroyed the Templars' manor at Montcocu, above Tripoli; William responded by destroying that of the prince at Botrun, besieged Nephin and won two victories over the prince's small army. He attempted a sea assault on Tripoli, to which Bohemond replied with an attack on Sidon. Finally, Guy of Gibelet, with the support of the Templars, tried on three occasions to surprise Tripoli; but his accomplices, who were meant to open the gates, were unable to get their signals through to him – his men failed to see a rocket that they launched, and mistook the rising of a star for a signal; a commander of the Temple on whom they had counted withdrew, and Guy had to surrender to Bohemond who had him killed (1283).

The war between the prince and the Temple, like that conducted against the order by Hugh III in Cyprus, shows that William of Beaujeu was behaving as if he was a sovereign. This was to be remembered at the time of the Templars' trial, but it was primarily his contacts with the Muslims that were criticised. In fact he had contacts in the sultan's entourage, and therefore access to valuable information; he was even able to negotiate agreements with the infidel. This fitted very well with the policy of Charles of Anjou, which was based, like that of Frederick II before him, on the maintenance of good relations between the king of Sicily, now king of Jerusalem, and the sultan of Egypt. But it was at odds with Gregory X's projects for western Christendom, acting in concert with the Byzantines and the Mongols; if it allowed for the recovery of the Holy Land, it was only after other, and very ambitious, objectives had been achieved.

When his envoys returned from the council of Lyons, the il-khan Abaga could hope that the crusade desired by his father and by him would soon materialise, and that the peace restored on the borders between his states and those of his cousins of the Chaghatai and the Golden Horde would enable him to combine his forces with those of the crusader princes. This is probably what the Vassali brothers, two Georgians, were sent in 1276 to tell the West. But Gregory X had been careful to inform him that it would be for his legates, who would accompany the crusade, to work out with him a plan of campaign.

Abaga did not neglect the religious questions so dear to the pope. He asked him to send some religious who would explain the Christian faith both to him and to his uncle, Qubilai. In April 1278 Pope Nicholas III appointed the Franciscan Gerard of Prato and four of his brethren, who left for the East, returning the following year, without having gone as far as China. But the safe-conduct they were granted in November 1279, which was addressed to the governor of Asia Minor, Samaghar, did not specify the content of the message they were carrying. On the other hand, the Armenian Hayton tells how, after Baybars' expedition into Anatolia (1277), King Leo III of Armenia was asked by Abaga to invite the pope and the Christian kings to send their troops for the reoccupation of the Holy Land, in the expectation of an imminent Mongol offensive in Syria.

The circumstances were favourable. Baybars had died in 1277, possibly poisoned by the cup of *qumuz* he was offering to an Ayyubid prince he wanted to get rid of. His eldest son succeeded him, to be overthrown in August 1279 by the leader of the army in Syria, the emir Qalawûn, who took the title of sultan later that year. Qalawûn announced his intention of pursuing the battle against the Franks, but the governor of Damascus, Sonqor al-Ashkar, one of Baybars' favourites, rebelled in April 1280 and proclaimed himself sultan. Qalawûn defeated him and forced him to take refuge in the castle of Sahyun (Saone to the Franks). Sonqor then appealed to the Mongols.

Abaga quickly responded to this appeal, and his army occupied Baghras and Darbsak, then seized Aleppo, many of whose inhabitants were massacred. After this, the great Mongol army withdrew in anticipation of an imminent campaign. On the Frankish side, letters sent to Edward I tell us that the king of Cyprus, Hugh III, and Prince

Bohemond VI had combined their army, but that it was unable to intervene, as the Mamluks had already taken up a position between them and the Mongols. An envoy from the il-khan came to Acre, before October 1280, to ask for the assistance of the Franks and for the provision of supplies. But the patriarch's vicar pointed to the famine then reigning and also to the fact that the king of Sicily – and of Jerusalem – was busy with other wars; the lordship of Acre remained on the margins of these events.

The Hospitallers of Margat saw this as a chance to carry out a raid as far as the walls of the Crac, in October 1280; in February 1281 they inflicted a defeat on troops led by the Mamluk emir of the Crac.

But Qalawûn acted rapidly and vigorously; he was reconciled with Sonqor; he negotiated with the Temple and the Hospital and concluded a truce with them (3 May 1281) which was extended to Prince Bohemond on 16 July. A conspiracy was planned against him; it was the Franks of Acre who warned him of it and enabled him to thwart it. Frankish assistance to the Mongols was negligible.

So, when the il-khan's brother Möngke-Temur led a large army (fifty thousand Mongols and thirty thousand other combatants) into Syria, the 'Syrian knights' it contained were only those from the kingdom of Cyprus. They took part in the battle of Homs (30 October 1281) during which the Mongol right flank, with the Armenians of Leo III, the Georgians and other Christians, routed the enemy left flank, which it pursued as far as Homs. But the centre, including Möngke-Temur, was soundly beaten; the Mongol prince was wounded and withdrew, leaving his right flank in a perilous state. Leo III had great difficulty in getting it as far as Cilicia. Qalawûn, however, was wary of pursuing the defeated army, and it was at this point that he renewed the truces with the Franks.

The importance of the non-participation of the Franks in the campaign of 1281 should probably not be exaggerated. The modest contingents they could have assembled would hardly have changed the course of the campaign. For their intervention to have made a difference, a larger army was needed, but the short delay allowed to his allies by the il-khan between the two campaigns had left little time for it to be assembled.

The following year, Abaga died (1 April 1282). His brother Teguder, who succeeded him, reversed his policy. He embraced Islam and took the title of sultan and the name of Ahmed. He invited his Mongol subjects to become Muslims, and sent proposals for an alliance to Qalawûn, which were favourably received. It took a revolt, that of Abaga's son, Arghun, supported by the *qaghan* Qubilai, to end his reign

(10 August 1284). Arghun returned to the pro-Christian policies of his father, though himself a Buddhist. The kings of Armenia and Georgia urged him to resume contact with the West.

The letter he wrote in May 1285 is in a remarkably barbaric Latin, probably attributable to one of the Franks who served in the Mongol guard and who occasionally reached positions of responsibility, rather than to the notary Rychaldus, about whom no more is heard after his visit to Lyons. Its argument ran as follows: 'The land of the Saracens lies between your land and ours. We can therefore squeeze it between us. To this end, send an army into Egypt and let us know, so that we can attack from our side.' This was to revive in a simplistic way the tactics under consideration since 1262; we do not know whether the bearer of this message, who is unknown to us, had more detailed proposals to submit to the recipients of the letter.

We are much better informed about the next embassy, which left the il-khan's encampment in the early months of 1287. Arghun, in the hope of getting a better reception among the Franks of the West, had the idea of sending them one of the highest prelates of the Chaldean Church, the 'visitor for the East', Barsauma, better known by his surname of Rabban Sauma. Barsauma was a Christian of Turkish origin, from the region of Beijing, who had set out with his disciple, Markos, to make a pilgrimage to Jerusalem. But the two monks had been delayed at the Mongol court, and Markos had been raised to the office of *catholicos*, the Nestorians believing that, as a compatriot of the il-khans, he would receive a sympathetic hearing; Barsauma, too, had received one of the highest offices in his Church.

Bearing a message whose contents are unknown to us, he set sail on the Black Sea and arrived in Constantinople, where he was warmly received by the Byzantine emperor, Andronicus II; from there he travelled to Naples, witnessing in passing a naval battle between the Aragonese and the Angevins, on 23 June 1287. He was disappointed, on reaching Rome, to find the pontifical see vacant; the consideration he was shown by the cardinals was no substitute for the negotiations he had hoped to have with the pope. By way of Genoa, where he had discussions with the rulers of the republic, he went to Paris, which he admired and where Philip III took him to the Sainte-Chapelle to venerate the relics of the Passion (10 September). At the end of October, he was in Bordeaux, where he met Edward I of England. On his return to Rome, he attended the coronation of Nicholas IV (20 February 1288), who received his message and gave him communion with his own hand, sending the *catholicos* the insignia of his office. Barsauma was back at the Mongol court in the summer of 1288.

The story of his journey, which he wrote and of which a summary survives, shows that he was disappointed at how little attention the West paid to the il-khan's proposals. It was at Genoa that, during a conclave which seemed to him interminable, he said to a cardinal: 'What shall I say to the Mongols on my return? Those who have hearts harder than stone wish to seize Jerusalem, and those to whom it belongs are not interested.' At a later stage, his discussions with the two kings and, above all, with the new pope struck a more positive note. They promised to join the next campaign directed by the il-khan against Egypt.

Arghun could therefore expect there to be a joint plan of campaign. In April 1288 he sent a Genoese from his entourage, Buscarello of Ghisolfi, to convey his proposals to the pope and to Philip the Fair. Arghun was planning to set out in January 1291 so as to be in the plain of Damascus on 20 February, where he fixed a rendezvous with the Christian armies; they were to march with him on Jerusalem to free that city, which would be restored to the Christians. But he warned them against missing this rendezvous. Buscarello also carried a memoir specifying the aid the Mongol would provide for his allies; they would find on landing the fodder necessary for 30,000 horses. Buscarello returned to the West in 1290, probably with new proposals (perhaps a change of dates?). He was accompanied by a noble Mongol, Zagan, who was baptised.

Among the projected joint enterprises was a maritime operation in the Indian Ocean to be made by a small Genoese squadron. Carpenters and sailors went to Baghdad to construct two galleys, which Arghun intended to launch on the trade route for the spices and precious foodstuffs that came from India and more distant countries to the ports of the Red Sea, Aydhab and Qusair, so as to assure the blockade of Egypt. These ships were to carry crossbowmen, who arrived by land. But the enterprise failed, as a result, we are told, of infighting among the Genoese, split between Guelfs and Ghibellines.

On 7 March 1291, Arghun died, and his two successors, Geikhatu and Baidu, did not follow up his schemes. One of Arghun's sons, Ghazan, rebelled in 1295 and, with the aid of the emir Nawruz, took possession of the throne. With him, and under the influence of Nawruz, Mongol Persia became officially part of Islam; the Oirat Mongols, who refused to accept this, had no alternative but to take refuge in Egypt. The Christians and the Buddhists were persecuted, but the Mamluks rejected Nawruz's approaches. When Ghazan got rid of him (March 1297), he revived his projects against Egypt, and the rebellion of the Mamluk governor of Damascus, Saif al-Din Qipchaq, provided him with the opportunity for a new Syrian campaign; Franco-Mongol cooperation thus survived both the loss of Acre by the Franks and the conversion of the Mongols of Persia to Islam. It was to remain one of the givens of crusading politics until the peace treaty with the Mamluks, which was concluded only in 1322 by the khan Abu Said.

The Franks may be criticised for having done too little to promote this policy. The battles for influence taking place at the Mongol court, the wars between the different khanates and the uncertainties of succession also played a role. But we need to emphasise the role of the Frankish adventurers who had entered Mongol service and who made themselves the zealous agents of the agreement between their Mongol masters and the West.

Pope Nicholas IV was to recognise their role by sending them a letter, in which he gives their names; among them is a Tommaso Ugi of Siena, *ilduci* in the il-khan's guard, who also carried a message to the West. The pope thanked them for the assistance they gave to the religious who went to preach the faith to the Mongols by conveying pontifical letters to the sovereigns. But these men, who were appreciated as men of war, even when, like Marco Polo, they also engaged in trade, were particularly well placed to inform the Mongols of the military possibilities offered by the West. Rashid al-Din drew his information about the political situation of the Frankish countries from that 'paladin', the Pisan Ciolo Bofeti di Anastasio, otherwise known as Isol the Pisan. He, in Syria, acted as a liaison officer, invested with wide powers by the Mongol sovereign.

The need for such men stands out in the comments of the Armenian Hayton, a keen proponent of the Mongol alliance, but conscious of the difficulties that would inevitably arise in the collaboration of men as alien to each other as the Franks and the Mongols. His concern was to limit the opportunities for friction between these allies.

The Franco-Mongol alliance never had to confront these difficulties. It foundered in the face of the vastness of the distances, and the impossibility of predicting events that made joint operations not feasible or of seizing chances offered. It is a story of lost opportunities.

CHARLES OF ANJOU'S PROJECTS AND THE CRUSADE

The purchase by Charles of Anjou of the rights to the crown of Jerusalem raises the question of the king of Sicily's interest in the crusade and the recovery of the Holy Land. His participation in the expedition of 1248–50 and the veneration of the memory of his brothers, Robert, killed at Mansurah, and Louis IX and Alphonse of Poitiers, both dead in the service of the Eighth Crusade, articulated in his deposition at the canonisation process of St Louis, make it impossible to doubt that his interest was real. But what had he in mind when he secured possession of the throne of Jerusalem?

That the youngest son of Louis VIII was ambitious is not in doubt. Count of Anjou by right of apanage he had, through his marriage to Beatrice of Provence, on the eve of the Seventh Crusade, inherited that county. On his return from the crusade, he revealed his desire to be sole master of the county of Provence, in spite of the claims of his sisters-in-law, who included Margaret of Provence, wife of St Louis, and that of his mother-in-law to retain the county of Forcalquier; he had subdued Marseilles, and exacted obedience from the feudal nobility of Provence.

At the same time, he got Countess Margaret of Flanders, in dispute with the sons of her first marriage, to grant him the counties of Hainault and Namur, which had brought him into conflict with William of Holland, then king of the Romans. It had needed an intervention by Louis IX before he agreed to give way.

The conquest of the kingdom of Sicily had seen him active in the service of the Church, represented by Pope Clement IV; he had given evidence of military skills, but also of a keen political sense. Despite his promises, he had retained the title of senator of Rome and vicar of Tuscany, which allowed him to maintain an army in central Italy. Having defeated Manfred, he had kept his widow, Helen, daughter of the Despot of Epirus, a prisoner, and claimed her dowry; in 1269, as a result, he was able to take possession of the Albanian port of Valona.

Here, Charles of Anjou was entering territory which had once been part of the Byzantine empire and which had since been in the orbit of the despotate of Epirus. This was in line with the ambitions long harboured by the Norman kings of Sicily since Robert Guiscard, to secure control of both shores of the Adriatic. But Charles went further, agreeing to champion the two Latin sovereigns dispossessed by Michael Palaeologus: Baldwin II, driven out of Constantinople, and William of Villehardouin who, after his defeat at Pelagonia (1259), had been forced to abandon certain territories to the *basileus*. The treaties made at Viterbo associated him with Baldwin's schemes of reconquest and assured the succession to the principality of Morea to his son, Philip of Taranto, married to Isabella of Villehardouin.

The count of Anjou was therefore posing, if not as pretender to the empire of Constantinople, as has often been claimed (it was to revert to Philip of Courtenay, husband of one of his daughters), at least as protector of the emperor Baldwin and his auxiliary in his attempts at reconquest, and as suzerain of Morea. The expedition he was planning in 1270, for which he equipped a fleet, was probably intended to allow him to accept the homage of his feudatories in Morea (which his lieutenants were to receive in his name), and perhaps to recapture places occupied by the Byzantines. The occupation of Valona could provide him with a base for operations against the latter. The duke of Burgundy and the king of Navarre, Thibaut V, had promised to support Baldwin II's efforts to reconquer the imperial throne, and the duke had gone to Sicily.

At this point, the Eighth Crusade intervened. The participation of Michael VIII and the discussions between the Greek emperor and the papacy made it difficult to open hostilities against him, and St Louis had obliged his brother to abandon his project for the time being. Receiving Michael's envoys shortly before his death, he had promised to try 'to make peace between the emperor and his brother'. Once the king was dead, Charles tried to retain some of the barons in his service for his Greek enterprise, which he was determined to revive. In 1271 he got himself recognised as king of Albania; Durazzo, Berat, Janina and Butrinto were in this new kingdom. At this point Gregory X became pope; freer with regard to the Angevin than Clement IV, a former servant of the Capetian monarchy, he opposed an attack by Charles on Michael VIII, who recovered Berat in 1274; the creation of the kingdom of Albania had not, in his eyes, abolished imperial rights over these lands. In 1277 the Byzantines also seized Kalavryta, at the expense of the Franks of Morea.

John XXI, who succeeded Gregory X, remained faithful to the projected crusade, hence hostile to an anti-Byzantine enterprise. His successor, Nicholas III, an Orsini, was primarily concerned to limit Charles' Italian ambitions by obliging him to abandon Rome and Tuscany. But these popes had shown no hostility towards Charles' schemes for the Holy Land, probably seeing them as a desire to participate in the defence of the Frankish possessions and contribute to the great enterprise of the crusade; it was in the presence of the cardinals, during a vacancy in the apostolic see, that Maria of Antioch transmitted her rights to Charles, and John XXI confirmed this transfer.

Should we conclude that the king of Sicily had persuaded these pontiffs that his aim was to combine all the forces of the Frankish East with those of his Italian kingdom to make a more effective contribution to the recovery of the Holy Land? By accepting the grant of the crown of Jerusalem to Charles, John XXI was following the example of Honorius III when he had assured that same crown to Frederick II.

But Charles of Anjou confined himself in 1277 to taking possession of Acre. On the death of his son, Philip, then that of William of Villehardouin, the following year, he secured the inheritance of Isabella, William's daughter and Philip's widow, whom he kept at his court while he occupied the principality of Morea. In 1279 he sent Hugh of

Sully to Albania to attempt, in the event unsuccessfully, to recover
Berat from the Byzantines. His immediate objective was not, then, the
Holy Land but the Balkan peninsula. Charles could take advantage of a
change of attitude on the part of the papacy by procuring the election
of the Simon of Brie who had been legate in France for Clement IV
and Gregory X and who, as Martin IV, was a devoted supporter of the
king of Sicily.

The obstacle to Charles' anti-Byzantine projects had been Michael
VIII's support for the union of the Churches. Whatever the political
motives that had entered into his decision, Michael had pursued it
wholeheartedly, and had endeavoured to overcome the opposition of
the Byzantine clergy and people; he had dealt ruthlessly with the anti-
unionists. But these difficulties prevented him from keeping all the
promises he had made to Rome, which had given rise to some
discontent at the pontifical court. Martin IV used this as grounds for
excommunicating the Byzantine emperor and encouraging the projects
of Charles of Anjou, granting those who supported him the benefit of
the crusade indulgence.

In fact, hostilities had already commenced in Epirus, Morea and the
Aegean Sea. Charles was preparing a fleet and an army which were to
leave Sicily on 1 April 1283, though their precise destination is
unknown. What is known is that, on 31 March 1282, there was an
insurrection in Palermo which quickly spread to the other towns of
Sicily, accompanied by the massacre of the knights and other soldiers of
Charles of Anjou – whether or not prepared by the agents of Michael
VIII and, more likely, those of King Peter of Aragon, basing himself on
rights he held from his Hohenstaufen ancestors. Charles' projects were
thrown into disarray. He recalled his troops to defend the island and the
continental provinces of his kingdom of Sicily. The death of Michael
VIII was also the signal for a persecution of the Greek clergy who had
supported union. Martin IV promulgated a crusading bull in favour of
the defence of Sicily against the Aragonese, and assigned the resources
that Gregory X had intended for the great enterprise in the East to
another project, the 'Aragon crusade' directed against King Peter.

This expedition, embarked on after Charles of Anjou's death (January
1285), was a failure. Charles' son became a prisoner of the Aragonese;
when he recovered his freedom, he quickly surrendered his rights in
Morea to Isabella of Villehardouin, who transmitted them to her new
husband, Florent of Hainault. As far as the kingdom of Jerusalem was
concerned, nothing had changed; but Hugh III of Cyprus, after the
recall of Roger of San Severino (14 October 1282), thought the moment
had come to re-establish his authority in Acre. The leader of the French

contingent, Eudes Poilechien, a nephew of Pope Martin IV, who was serving as *bailli* in the name of King Charles, with the support of William of Beaujeu, defeated this attempt (August 1283).

Angevin authority was maintained for two more years. But the young king Henry II of Cyprus, who acceded to the throne on 20 May 1285, negotiated with the master of the Temple, resorting to the mediation of the master of the Hospital, and an agreement was made between them. When Henry, with his knights, landed at Acre on 24 June 1286, he was received by the whole population and led in procession to the cathedral. Eudes Poilechien retreated into the royal castle, where Henry blockaded him, and he capitulated when his food ran out, on 29 June. The king of Cyprus agreed to submit to the arbitration of the king of France, and declared that he did not regard the French garrison as hostile, though it had supported the Angevins. The Angevin episode was over.

Was the great projected crusade at last to materialise? Nicholas IV revived it, and the il-khan Arghun was still counting on the cooperation of the western kings in a common enterprise. But the kingdoms of France and Aragon had just clashed fiercely, Sicily was disputed between Charles II and the Aragonese, and the king of England was fighting the Welsh. The Mongol ambassador who came to seek western aid saw for himself a sea battle off Naples.

All the labours of Gregory X were wasted. Charles of Anjou's attempt to build a new Latin empire in the eastern Mediterranean had come to nothing. Meanwhile, the sultan Qalawûn remained committed to the programme he had outlined in a letter to Sonqor al-Ashkar, at the beginning of his reign, to press on with the battle against the Franks.

THE FALL OF THE LAST FRANKISH POSSESSIONS AND THE CRUSADE OF NICHOLAS IV

The presence of Abaga at the head of the Mongol empire of Persia and the relations between the Sicilian and Egyptian courts had probably played a part in dissuading the sultan Qalawûn from attacking the Frankish territories. But the death of Abaga in 1285 left his hands freer, and the power of Charles of Anjou was hardly felt outside Acre. This may explain why the sultan chose first to attack in the north.

He had a pretext for disregarding the truce concluded with the Hospitallers of Margat. They were, it was said, exercising a reign of terror over their Muslim neighbours and had attacked the castle of Coliat. Qalawûn assembled an army, spreading rumours of an expedition against Hromgla, seat of the Armenian *catholicos*. From Egypt, his ships brought a quantity of arms, in particular tubes for launching Greek fire, and war machines. On 17 April 1285 they gathered before Margat, which put up a vigorous defence. The sultan's miners were able to cause one tower to collapse, but without the breach allowing an assault. But the Hospitallers, fearing that other parts of the ramparts had been undermined, agreed to surrender the fortress in return for free exit; their leaders paid a ransom of 2,000 dinars for the right to take with them twenty-five horses and mules. On 25 May Qalawûn took possession of Margat, where he placed a strong garrison (150 Mamluks and 1,000 footsoldiers) and an emir who was made governor of the whole region of Antioch. Jabala was already in the sultan's hands.

Qalawûn then marched on the castle of Maraclea, which its lord, Bartholomew, had refortified after its earlier destruction, exploiting its situation on a peninsula which rendered it almost impregnable. The sultan put pressure on Bohemond VII of Tripoli, threatening to break the truces which protected his county, and the prince obliged his vassal to surrender his castle, which was dismantled 'stone by stone'.

Latakia was still in Christian hands, and the people of Aleppo complained of having to pass through their territory to gain access to the port. In March 1287 an earthquake destroyed part of the ramparts. The sultan took advantage of this and claimed that the town was not covered by the truce made with Bohemond, since he had been negotiating as count of Tripoli (on which Baybars had insisted) and that Latakia belonged to the principality. He entered the town; the population retreated into the citadel, which capitulated on 30 April 1287.

Bohemond VII died on 19 October 1287. His sister Lucia was then in the kingdom of Sicily with her husband, Narjot of Toucy. The barons appealed to the prince's mother, Sibylla of Armenia, to take over the government. But Sibylla wanted to recall the bishop of Tortosa, Bartholomew Mansel, who was hated by the knights of the party of Guy of Gibelet, whom Bohemond had killed in 1283. They rebelled and proclaimed a commune, choosing for mayor another Gibelet, Bartholomew, and informed the Princess Lucia, when she arrived in the East in 1288 and succeeded in taking possession of her castle of Nephin thanks to the assistance of the Hospitallers, that they were determined 'to maintain each one his right and reason'.

In fact, the rebellion in Tripoli was part of wider developments. War had resumed between Pisa and Genoa, and Venice had joined in on the side of the Pisans (1287); the Genoese attempted an attack on Acre, blockading the port and destroying the enemy shipping. Their fleet, under Benedetto Zaccaria, was being used to pursue a policy designed to assure Genoese hegemony in the seas of the Levant, and the sultan accorded them benevolent neutrality. The citizens of Tripoli put themselves under Zaccaria's protection, whilst Bartholomew of Gibelet made contact with Qalawûn.

The three military orders, this time unanimous, tried to impose their mediation. Zaccaria made known his demands: that the Genoese quarter of Tripoli be enlarged and that the republic should nominate a podesta. The princess Lucia agreed, and the Genoese admiral ceased to oppose her taking possession of Tripoli. But two envoys from an Italian town (who may have been Genoese from the party of Bartholomew of Gibelet, or Pisans, or Venetians) went to Qalawûn to denounce the danger posed to Alexandria by the transformation of Tripoli into a Genoese naval base.

The sultan embarked on military preparations. The master of the Temple learned from an emir with whom he had close ties that they were directed against Tripoli, but his warnings were ignored; some expected an attack on Nephin, that is, on the Princess Lucia, which they would not have opposed. Unity came only when the Egyptian army hurtled down from the Crac des Chevaliers, and Princess Lucia was recalled; the king of Cyprus sent his brother Amalric to Tripoli, where he found the marshals of the two orders and the leader of the French contingent, John of Grailly.

The siege of Tripoli, which began on 25 March, was pressed energetically, thanks to the use of great catapults. On 27 April the Mamluks stormed the town, which was overrun and the population massacred. Many of the defenders managed to take refuge aboard the ships in the harbour; those who crammed onto the little island of St Thomas, a short distance from the shore, were slaughtered, on 29 April, by Mamluks who had crossed the channel on their horses; the women and children were reduced to slavery, and 1,200 captives were sent to Alexandria to work in the arsenal being built there. Tripoli was razed to the ground; Qalawûn ordered it to be rebuilt on a new site. The fall of Tripoli was followed by that of the small towns of the coast, Nephin and Botrun. The sire of Gibelet, Peter, managed to retain his lordship in return for payment of a tribute.

Was the disaster suffered at Tripoli about to engulf Acre? King Henry hastened to put the town in a defensive state. Qalawûn threatened to open hostilities, accusing the king of having broken the truces made in 1283 by sending his brother, ships and horses to the defence of Tripoli; Henry claimed that this type of help was not forbidden by a truce which applied exclusively to the territory of Acre and its dependencies. The sultan accepted his reasons and even agreed to renew the truce for a period of ten years and ten months. Henry was able to return to Cyprus, leaving his brother Amalric as *bailli* in Acre.

At the same time, he sent an appeal for help to the pope, and John of Grailly was asked to inform Nicholas IV of the situation in which the last Frankish towns now found themselves.

The pope, as we know from his discussions with Barsauma, was concerned for the Holy Land and inclined to revive Gregory X's project, which had never, in fact, been officially abandoned; in 1280 the king of Castile asked Edward I to help him to assemble ships; as we have seen, the king of Sweden bequeathed a sum for the crusade in 1285; in 1288 Edward asked the pope to grant a delay, postponing his departure till 1293. The new il-khan, Abaga, was also anxious to get the projected crusade under way, and it was for this reason that Buscarello of Ghisolfi had come to Europe; the missionary Ricoldo of Monte Croce, however, then in Mesopotamia, observed the satisfaction of the Muslims at the news of the capture of Tripoli.

Nicholas IV attended to the most urgent matters first. He sent 4,000 *livres tournois* to the patriarch of Jerusalem, Nicholas of Hanapes, then a squadron of thirteen galleys 'for the protection and defence of the city of Acre and the other lands and places held by the Christians in Outremer'; they were to spend a year at Acre, available 'according to the needs of the Holy Land and of the Christian people who live there'. On 10 February 1290 he proclaimed a crusade with as its objective 'the total liberation of the Holy Land and which, while waiting, would support the places at present held by Christians'. The crusade was preached all over, including in the Holy Land. The patriarch received the power to absolve from their faults, if they took the cross, those who had used force against the clergy, or who had supported the rebellious Sicilians or who had visited the Holy Sepulchre despite the pontifical prohibition. He forbade all commerce with the lands of the sultan, pilgrimage being regarded, in the same way as trade, as a means of contributing to his finances. In principle, the departure of the expedition was fixed for 24 June 1293.

Nicholas IV went further; he was reconciled with James II of Aragon in July 1290, and James promised to provide a contingent of a thousand *almogavares* and two thousand crossbowmen in 1291, and the same number the year after, with twenty galleys. Edward I sent Otto of Grandson to reinforce the garrison of Acre.

But as these preparations were proceeding, others were playing a different game. James II and his brother the king of Sicily negotiated with the sultan, on 25 April 1290, promising not to assist a crusade, and authorising the export of strategic material to Egypt, in return for freedom for their subjects to make the pilgrimage to Jerusalem; they renewed this treaty in 1292–3. Genoa was reconciled with Qalawûn, who extended Genoese privileges in compensation for the loss of their quarter in Tripoli. Even the patriarch of Jerusalem appealed for the lifting of the embargo on trade with Egypt, so as not to ruin the economy of the Frankish towns, to which the pope agreed on 21 October 1290.

The *passagium particulare* had begun to get under way. At Easter 1290 a Venetian fleet set out with Italian crusaders, under the command of Hugh of Sully; it carried 3,540 footsoldiers who were stationed at Acre. In August, some of them attacked Muslim peasants on their way to the market, together with some Muslim merchants. The latter took refuge in their *fondouk*, and the knights of the Temple and the Hospital came to their aid; but some twenty merchants and thirty villagers were killed, some of them, it was said, eastern Christians whom the Venetians assumed to be Muslims on account of their beards.

The sultan, if we are to believe the king of Aragon's informants, had begun to prepare in the spring. This incident provided him with an opportunity to demand the surrender of the guilty, as responsible for a violation of the truces. William of Beaujeu advised accepting, and surrendering criminals instead of crusaders. The other members of the council rejected the idea of surrendering crusaders to the Muslims and confined themselves to offering excuses, which the sultan refused to accept. The truces were broken.

The death of Qalawûn, soon after, gave hope of a resumption of negotiations. In fact, his son, al-Ashraf Khalil, was very quickly able to frustrate a conspiracy and secure himself in power. He began to assemble a very large army, circulating rumours of an expedition to Africa. William of Beaujeu's usual informers warned him of the real purpose of these preparations; once again the master of the Temple was met with disbelief. On 1 May 1291, arriving from both Egypt and Syria, an army allegedly of 70,000 horsemen and 150,000 footsoldiers – figures we have no way of verifying – assembled beneath the walls of Acre.

These walls had recently been reinforced, the countess of Blois having financed the construction of a new tower in 1287. The garrison was large, but only some 15,000 fighting men could be assembled. However, the Franks held the seas and their small boats harassed the besiegers.

But the sultan had assembled very considerable means. The two great mangonels, the *Victorious* and the *Furious*, each had to be dragged by a hundred wagons, and there were large numbers of *qarabugha*, the medium-sized catapults. Miners attacked the weak points of the ramparts in groups of a thousand men. Their sapping utilised both the outlets of the drains and the butchers' ditch. On 4 May King Henry II, two hundred knights and five hundred footsoldiers arrived from Cyprus.

Henry managed to open negotiations with al-Ashraf, who offered to allow the evacuation of Acre, leaving the sultan the land and the stones of the town which he was determined to acquire, but sparing the lives and property of the inhabitants, out of regard for the king's youth. The king's envoys replied that by accepting these proposals, Henry would bring dishonour on himself. The talks were broken off.

In vain the viscount of the town of Acre tried to set fire to the *Victorious* by means of a sortie led by William of Beaujeu. On 8 May the miners reached the foot of the wall of the enceinte. On 15 May the New Tower collapsed, and preparations began for the evacuation of the women and children, but a heavy sea made this impossible. On 16 May another assault was repulsed, but, two days later, the Mamluks gained a foothold on the curtain wall. William of Beaujeu and the master of the Hospital tried to drive them back; William was killed, John of Villiers and John of Grailly were badly wounded and the defenders of the 'Accursed Tower' abandoned their posts.

The battle continued in the streets, while the gates fell one after the other. The marshal of the Hospital was killed defending the area round the port to allow the evacuations. The fortified houses held out a little longer, in particular those of the Teutonic knights and the Hospitallers. The sultan promised to spare the lives of the defenders and had them massacred nevertheless. The keep of the Temple, a powerful fortress with five towers, still held out, under the command of the marshal, Peter of Sevrey, who was hoping to allow those who had taken refuge there to embark. The sultan finally promised to allow the refugees to leave, and a troop of Mamluks entered the castle. But they began to profane the chapel and assault the women; Peter of Sevrey fell on them, and the siege resumed. A second agreement was violated; it was only on 28 May that the castle fell; undermined, it collapsed onto the assailants and the remaining Templars. They had been on the point of cutting their horses' hocks so that the enemy would be unable to take them.

Some of the defenders had been able to leave, with Henry II and Otto of Grandson, and many of the wounded. The Mamluks massacred the Dominicans in their convent, and the Franciscans and the Clares; they rounded up the women and children and sold them into slavery. The patriarch Nicholas was drowned during the evacuation, when his small boat, overloaded, sank. News of this massacre and the sack of the town reached Ricoldo of Monte Croce in Baghdad, where he was able to buy some books from the Dominican convent.

The last fortresses fell almost without resistance; the castellan of Tyre evacuated the town and withdrew on the very day of the fall of Acre (19 May). Sidon resisted till 14 July, but, with no prospect of assistance, the

commander of the Temple evacuated the fortress. Beirut was taken by
treachery (21 May). Caiphas succumbed on 30 July and the monks of
Carmel were martyred in their convent. Tortosa was evacuated on 3
August, Chastel Pèlerin on 14 August.

The prodigious feats of courage displayed during the siege of Acre cast
an aura of heroism over the collapse of Frankish Syria in the face of the
massive forces of the Mamluk empire.

The Christians of the Lebanese mountains suffered the consequences
of this collapse, as their neighbours, the Muslim emirs, fell on their lands.
They suffered a serious defeat at the hands of the *muqaddam* of the
Maronite villages (1292). The sultans preferred to tolerate these autonomous powers, given the insubordination of the Druse or even Sunni
leaders, against whom they were obliged to conduct a punitive expedition. The Syrian citizens of the coastal towns probably suffered the same
fate as the Franks; like them, many reached Cyprus, which remained
Frankish, and which escaped the landing being contemplated by
al-Ashraf when he was killed by his emirs.

AFTER THE FALL OF ACRE

The fall of Acre was a terrible shock for western Christendom. So short
had been the siege – forty-four days – of such a strongly fortified town that
people looked for someone to blame. King Henry II, the papacy, the
military orders, the discord among the Franks and the treachery of the
inhabitants were all implicated by someone. The event itself marked the
end of a nation which had managed to survive for almost two centuries.

The fate of the Franks of the East has fascinated many people. Eastern
traditions connect them, amongst others, with Bedouin tribes and with
the mountain dwellers of the Lebanon. In fact, they were dispersed.
Many left by sea and found asylum, whether in the West, in Armenia, or
in Cyprus. The influx of refugees to this island was so great, it was said,
that the Cypriots pretended not to recognise the new arrivals so as not to
have to accept responsibility for them, and the king had to spend
massively to assist them. The creation of the new town of Famagusta
made it possible to receive large numbers of Franks and Syrians.

Many others became slaves; travellers came across them in Egypt;
some Templars had become fishermen in the service of the sultan in the
Red Sea; building sites swarmed with captive Franks. One pilgrim says
that they were not ill-treated, but that they suffered from the absence of
religious solace and their inability to observe Sunday as a day of rest.
Some went over to eastern rites; many, sooner or later, adopted Islam.
There are no further references to islands of Frankish population.

The Mamluks systematically destroyed the coastal towns and the castles that might have served as bases for another crusade; Acre, Sidon, Chastel Pèlerin and Tripoli were all dismantled, even totally destroyed. A Gothic doorway from the Holy Cross in Acre was taken to Cairo to adorn the mosque of al-Nasir, in 1303. But the libraries and works of art disappeared almost completely.

Frankish Syria was a thing of the past, and the Syrian Christians suffered great human and mental losses, finding themselves back in the condition of *dhimmi*, but the victors seem not to have persecuted them systematically; it was primarily in the towns occupied by the Mongols that they suffered reprisals. Contact with the West was lost until the missionaries tried to restore it. Some sympathies survived, however, which could sometimes be exploited.

Though Frankish Syria could no longer be a focus for the westerners' concern, the Holy Land continued to haunt their thoughts. The crusade remained, more than ever, on the agenda. It was with the fall of Acre that the age of crusading projects began.

Nicholas IV, when he heard of the fall of Acre, reimposed the embargo on trade with the lands of the sultan which he had just revoked (23 August 1291). Learning from experience, he invited the Temple and the Hospital, both of which had suffered badly during the siege, to consider combining into one order. But more urgent was the need to strengthen the defences of the kingdoms of Armenia and Cyprus, and he took immediate action. A squadron given responsibility for assuring this defence and for enforcing the embargo was rapidly equipped, and entrusted to Manual Zaccaria. This little naval force of some twenty galleys, reinforced by the fifteen galleys of the king of Cyprus, attacked Candeloro (Alaya) and Alexandria in 1293, but it could not survive the renewal of hostilities between Genoa and Venice. The Cypriot ships continued to patrol the sea to prevent smuggling, with little effect since the Italian communes had managed to get themselves exempted from the embargo. This was maintained, nevertheless, with penalties which were still enforced by Benedict VIII, because it was hoped it would significantly reduce the sultan's income from customs duties and from pilgrimage, and would cause a cessation of the import of war materials – the timber which was necessary both for the Nile dykes and for naval construction, iron, lances and swords. In fact, the 'Alexandrians', that is, the merchants who traded in Egypt and Syria, were able to obtain either export licences or absolution for infringements committed.

The preparation of a crusade remained a part of pontifical plans. A Dominican, Peter of Pennis, describing the Holy Places, was to write: 'That the Saracens occupy the Holy Land should be an incentive to prayer and penitence for the faithful.' And the Genoese, Galvano of Levanti, compiling before 1295 a *Livre de la conduite des chrétiens pour effectuer le passage contre les Sarrasins* for the benefit of the king of France, listed the reasons for recovering the 'kingdom of Christ'. In 1298 Boniface VIII commended King Sempad of Armenia to the kings of France and England, explaining that 'the kingdom of Armenia is close to the Holy Land, and that if the army of the Christian faithful goes there as expected, it is through Armenia that we may best hope to recover it'. A new opportunity to achieve this recovery was about to emerge.

On 21 October 1299 a Christian by the name of Cariedin came on behalf of the Mongol khan to propose to the king of Cyprus and the masters of the three orders that they join in a campaign which Ghazan was planning to conduct against Damascus and Egypt. Once again, the sultan's governor in Syria had rebelled and appealed to the Mongols. But, thanks to the quarrels between Templars and Hospitallers, nothing was ready when a new messenger arrived on 30 November. And, on 24 December, it was in the absence of the Franks that the Mongols and their Georgian and Armenian allies won the victory of Homs and pursued the enemy as far as Gaza. The king of Cyprus, however, had assembled an army of 400 knights and turcopoles, with 60 archers and crossbowmen, which landed at Botrun, set about fortifying Nephin and appealed to the Christians of the mountains to embark on the siege of the new town of Tripoli; without success. In July 1300 the admiral Baldwin of Picquigny, with Ghazan's representative, Ciolo Bofeti, on board, entered the Rosetta branch of the Nile, and made a landing during which several captive Christians, taken at Acre, were freed; after which he sailed up the Syrian coast, landing at Acre, Tortosa and, lastly, Maraclea. The isle of Ruad was occupied by a strong detachment which was to await the arrival of the Mongol army, announced for the end of the year.

It was February 1301 before the Mongols arrived; Ghazan had fallen ill and his general, Qutlugh Shah, led only forty thousand cavalry to Antioch. He could carry out only limited operations, leaving some twenty thousand men in the Jordan valley to cover Damascus, where a Mongol governor was installed.

Ciolo Bofeti called himself 'vicar of Syria and of the Holy Land for the emperor of the Tartars'. His mission was perhaps primarily to secure the cooperation of Franks and Mongols, and to implement the promise the latter had made to their allies, the return to them of the recovered Holy Land. Ghazan had written to the western kings and, in May 1300, James II of Aragon informed him that he was sending galleys, sailing ships and combatants, asking to be assigned one fifth of the Holy Land; King

Charles II of Anjou appointed a vicar for the kingdom of Jerusalem, Melior of Ravendel, presumably in expectation of this recovery. Ghazan had renewed his promise to the king of Armenia; at the end of 1301, he asked the pope to send troops, clergy and labourers to make the Holy Land once again a Frankish state. But meanwhile, the governor of Damascus had changed sides, and the Mongol army of occupation had been obliged to withdraw. It was 1302 before Ghazan could return, and his army was beaten at Marj al-Suffar on 21 April 1303. The little garrison of Templars (120 knights, 500 Syrian archers) who had been given Ruad had to capitulate in 1303. The last lord of Gibelet, who seems to have supported the sultan's adversaries, evacuated his town after setting fire to it.

Ghazan's campaign showed that the Mongols had not forgotten their promises, and they continued to be taken into account in crusading projects.

THE AGE OF PROJECTS

After the crisis in the Church caused by the conflict between Boniface VIII and Philip the Fair, and with the latter too occupied by events in Gascony and Flanders to give all his attention to those in the East, the election of Bertrand of Got to the pontifical throne put the crusade back on the agenda. The new pope, Clement V, had a sincere desire to implement the project planned by Gregory X.

But the preparation of the crusade was now a matter of negotiations between sovereigns, probably while waiting for a council that Clement V convened only in 1311. Like his predecessors, the pope began by seeking advice. It was during his stay at Poitiers in 1307 that he received a number of memoirs of varying importance.

That of the master of the Temple, James of Molay, began by discussing the value of a *passagium particulare* preceding a *passagium generale*; this could only take the form of the dispatch of an army to Armenia, if it was to be the starting point for the large expedition. James of Molay reckoned that, faced with the 12,000 to 15,000 horsemen and 40,000 to 50,000 archers that could be mobilised by the sultan, a large force would have to be assembled, and that Armenia and the Armenians could not provide adequate reinforcement. He himself would opt for a massive expedition, involving all the kings of the West, with a sufficient number of ships to ensure the rapid transport of the whole army – at least 12,000 to 15,000 knights, 2,000 mounted crossbowmen and 5,000 footsoldiers. They should land in Cyprus (which ought at once to be reinforced by the dispatch of a dozen galleys) in order to decide where the army was to be deployed. The master of the Hospital contributed a full description of the enemy and of his army, and of the itinerary which would take the crusaders from the Syrian–Palestinian coast to Egypt (*La Devise des chemins de Babylone*), without prejudging the plan of campaign to be adopted, but letting it be understood that its objective could only be the heart of the Mamluk empire. The king of Sicily, Charles II of Anjou, probably supported this plan; on 20 July 1307, he promised to provide the projected expedition with twenty galleys and a contingent of 300 knights, presumably with a 'general passage' in mind.

The Armenian prince, Hayton, who had arrived from Cyprus as Envoy of the regent Amalric of Lusignan, drew up, in August 1307, while in Poitiers, a very long treatise, which has been given the title of the *Flos historiarum Terre Orientalis* to emphasise the importance of the Mongol factor; the new khan Oljeitü was also favourable to the Christians (in May 1305 he had written to the kings of France and England and to the pope, and he sent help to the Armenians in 1304–5). Hayton suggested sending an army of 1,000 knights, 3,000 footsoldiers and 10 galleys either to Cyprus or to Armenia, to reinforce the blockade of Egypt and to reach an agreement with the Tartars. They would attack Aleppo, the Latins Tripoli. This would be followed by the general passage, which could travel via Barbary (the question of Tunis here reappears), or via Constantinople, or by sea (with a pause in Cyprus). A landing in Armenia would make it possible to provide the knights with fresh mounts, and they could then join those who had landed at Tripoli. Then, while the khan was conquering Egypt, the Franks would reoccupy the Holy Land.

Other memoirs followed, including one by the king of Cyprus, Henry II, before, in 1321, the more original treatise, emphasising the maritime aspects of the proposed expedition, of the Venetian Marino Sanudo (the *Secreta fidelium crusis*). Meanwhile, the order of the Temple had been destroyed. James of Molay had been received by the pope at Poitiers; he had discussed the proposals to combine the two orders of the Temple and the Hospital, submitting in advance to the pope's decision, but explaining why this union seemed to him inopportune. His arrest and that of all his brethren of France, on 13 October 1307, was totally unexpected.

The reasons for the king of France's actions need not detain us here. But they were relevant to the future of the crusade, and it was William of Nogaret, in a memoir dated 1310, who explained that 'the abomination of the Templars' was 'an obvious obstacle' to the mobilisation of the crusade. The expedition should take place as soon as possible, the kings agreeing each to provide their contingent; the loss of Syria, which had deprived the Christians of their base of departure, made things more difficult; the Tartars, the Greeks and the Italian maritime towns would have to be involved. And once the conquest had been achieved, it would be necessary to base there for at least twenty or thirty years warriors who would be frequently relieved. The revenues of the Temple and a tax on the Hospitallers and other orders should be used to provide for the cost of this occupying force.

Peter Dubois, another counsellor of the king of France, developed this idea. For him, the union of the Temple and the Hospital was beside the point; what was needed was a new military order, under the control of the Capetian monarchy. And instead of restoring the old kingdom of Jerusalem, the map of the Holy Land should be redrawn. Its defence against the infidel would devolve on the new knights.

Here there emerges an idea which would be remembered by the orders of knighthood founded by the princes of the fourteenth century. It had already been considered during the preparations for the council of 1274, but it had been in particular the subject of a memoir addressed, soon after the fall of Acre, to Pope Nicholas IV by Charles of Anjou (the *Conseil du roi Charles*). This elaborated a plan of crusade involving the dispatch of a 'small general passage', which would establish a base of operations either in Tripoli or in Cyprus to prepare the way for the 'great passage'. The conquests it made should not be restored to the princes dispossessed by the Mamluks, which is noteworthy given that Charles was titular king of Jerusalem. They should be put under the protection of a new military order, to which would be assigned the property of the Temple, the Hospital and the other analogous orders, but also that of the other 'religions' of different types, such as the Trinitarians and the Grandmontines. This order should also enjoy a regular income, secured by a tax on the property of the clergy. It would keep a permanent force overseas of two thousand knights and two hundred sergeants, and its leader should be a prince, if possible a king's son. The crusade would thus be perpetuated, in the form of a commitment by the whole of Christendom, by means of an order which would provide permanent support to the Holy Land, but getting rid of those which already existed.

But Clement V remained faithful to a more traditional approach. Forced by the king of France to act against the Templars, he tried to give them the means to defend their order and retain control of its property. The Hospitallers, who, like the Teutonic knights, had taken refuge in Cyprus after the fall of Acre, were entrusted in 1308 with the preparation of a *passagium particulare* designed to defend Cyprus and Armenia, and also to strengthen the embargo; 1,000 knights and 4,000 footsoldiers were to be deployed for five years; it was this venture which resulted in the occupation of Rhodes. It was very much in line with what had been recommended by Hayton.

The *passagium generale* was to follow in 1310. The pope, both because of the crisis caused in Cyprus by Amalric's usurpation and because of his own problems, left it to the council he convened at Vienne, which lasted from 30 October 1311 to 6 May 1312. It decided on the crusade and on the levy of a tenth for six years. The order of the Temple was suppressed without being condemned, and its property transferred to the Hospital.

New memoirs were drawn up for this council. Two Dominican missionaries, Raymond Etienne and William Adam, wrote, respectively, the *Avis directif pour le passage outre-mer* and *De modo Saracenos extirpandi*. The former, dedicated to the king of France, proposed a crusade which would have a choice between four routes – the sea route, Barbary, Italy or Germany – and recommended the last of these, which would require obtaining in passing the submission of the Serbs and the Greeks, and taking advantage of this to restore union to the separated Christians. Adam emphasised the necessity of enforcing the blockade of Egypt, but with the addition of a squadron dispatched to the Indian Ocean, and he also recommended obtaining the help of the empire of Constantinople, if necessary by force.

The increasingly impracticable nature of these projects contrasts with the modesty of the action taken. Clement V's crusade seemed likely to materialise when Philip the Fair took the cross (1313), but Enguerrand of Marigny persuaded him not to leave. Philip V considered entrusting an army and a squadron to Louis of Clermont (1318–19); Charles IV, in the aftermath of a destructive raid by the Mamluks on Ayas (1322), prepared an expedition the first element of which was to be entrusted to Amalric of Narbonne. Philip VI took the cross again in 1331.

In fact, other types of contacts were beginning to be made. Before 1295, the kings of Aragon had continued to promise the sultan assistance in the event of a crusade; later, reconciled with the pope, they had exchanged ambassadors with the Mamluks, encouraging the trade of Barcelona with Egypt and obtaining for their subject the right to visit the Holy Sepulchre. They had also intervened in favour of the indigenous Christians persecuted in Egypt. The king of Cyprus had been authorised by the pope to send 'ambassadors and informers' to that country, and commercial relations had begun to be regularised by 1326. John XXII and Charles IV themselves tried to negotiate an agreement with the sultan, from 1328 to 1330, on the basis of the symbolic grant of the Holy Places. The sultan al-Nasir refused, but agreed to the request of the Angevin king of Sicily to establish a Franciscan convent in Jerusalem.

The recovery of the Holy Land was not forgotten. It continued to foster hopes and fancies; the king of France, John the Good, considered a *passagium generale* under his own leadership in 1363, and the king of Cyprus, Peter I, led a *passagium particulare* to Alexandria in 1365, in expectation of this. But by 1334 a new conception of the crusade was emerging. It was at this period that the decline of Mongol domination in Asia Minor and the disappearance of the Seljuks of Konya was leading to the creation of Turkish sovereignties, those of the *uc-begi* or Turkoman emirs of the frontier, who engaged in piracy and made increasingly deep incursions into Byzantine territory and into the islands possessed by the Latins in the Aegean Sea. The most famous were the Ottomans, whose activities threatened the Byzantine empire and, soon, the Christian kingdoms of the Balkans; in fact, the year 1334 saw the first of the 'holy leagues' combining the maritime powers and the Byzantines against the Turks. They were granted crusading privileges.

In this way, the crusade became once again what it had been in the time of Urban II, a form of defence of the Christian world of East and West against a wave of Muslim invasions, once more by the Turks. The Holy Land was not forgotten; it continued to be visited by pilgrims who evoked with nostalgia memories of the age of the crusaders and hoped for its return; it was the objective proposed for their expeditions by the princes who went to fight against the Turks. But circumstances had changed, and the West was no longer able to combine its efforts for that 'recovery of the Holy Land' which had demanded so many sacrifices.

CONCLUSION

Two centuries of crusades inspired the authors of *chansons de geste*, those verse narrations in which the story of real events is embellished with legendary additions; there was no shortage of dramatic or heroic episodes that lent themselves to epic developments. Even during the First Crusade there were probably *trouvères* to celebrate the exploits of the valiant knights, and one suspects their influence in certain passages in a more scholarly historiography, the work of clerks or knights, which also emerged during or soon after the expedition. The *Chanson d'Antioche* of Richard the Pilgrim was the first of these verse texts; Ambroise's *Estoire de la Guerre sainte* performed a similar role for the Third Crusade. Revised, enriched with imaginary and fantastic episodes, but always exalting the chivalric values which had inspired the Christian and the Muslim heroes alike, these works are the precursors of the chivalric romances of the 'second cycle of the crusade', in which we find Kerbogha become Corbaran, Tughtekin likened to Hugh of Tiberias, Saladin and Baldwin of Bourcq, prototype of the Baudouin de Sebourc of the song. And Godfrey of Bouillon became one of the 'valiant knights' whose exploits figure in the tapestries that were hung in palaces and in Tasso's masterpiece, *Jerusalem delivered*; they fired the imagination of the men of the Renaissance, and inspired the artists who produced the innumerable paintings devoted to the loves of Rinaldo and Armida; in this way, the memory of the crusades was kept alive.

Historians then saw the crusades primarily as an epic exalting heroism and the faith, combined in a great adventure which continued in an age when the Turk was still being fought on the borders of central Europe and in the Mediterranean; Voltaire himself wrote: 'I confess that I would not be unhappy to see [a crusade] against the Ottoman empire ... I would observe with pleasure lovely Greece ... delivered from her servitude.' The eighteenth century, however, brought a quite different vision of the crusade, coloured by the Age of Enlightenment's contempt for those which preceded it. In the *Encyclopédie* of Diderot and d'Alembert, the judgement is unequivocal: it was 'a time of the deepest darkness and of the greatest folly ... to drag a significant part of the world into an unhappy little country in order to cut the inhabitants' throats and seize a rocky peak which was worth not one drop of blood'. And Voltaire goes further, speaking of 'that epidemic fury which lasted for two hundred years and which was always marked by every cruelty, every perfidy, every debauchery, and every folly of which human nature is capable'.

This interpretation remained that of doctrinaire historians. It provoked a reaction, that of the romantics, susceptible to the dimension of exotic adventure, as we see from so many historical paintings; but also that of a whole school of historians, for the most part Catholics, to whom we owe the revival of a scientific study which began in the seventeenth century with the collection of narrative sources forever associated with the name of Bongars. That of Joseph Michaud inaugurated a long series, continued by Rey, Mas-Latrie and above all Paul Riant, indefatigable editor of texts, disciple of Tobler and Röhricht. For men like these, the history of the crusades was not that of an aberration or of a sterile adventure.

The scientific aspect of research on the crusades has made great progress. Scholarly work continues, in the footsteps of those late nineteenth-century historians to whom we owe our access to a documentation which is reliable and which requires knowledge of non-European societies.

Nevertheless, those who have produced works of synthesis have come to very different conclusions. To pass judgement on the crusades involves a whole spectrum of conceptions of a philosophic, religious and political nature. It would be a fine historiographical exercise to compare all these points of view. To confine ourselves to those who have written during the past half-century, René Grousset, historian of civilisations, located the crusades in what he saw as a millenarian conflict opposing a European civilisation, daughter of Greek thought, Roman order and Christianity with a Germanic contribution, to other cultures which developed in a vast East. For him, the crusades took over a Byzantine effort that was running out of steam. And they resulted in the establishment on Asian soil of men, forms of thought and political structures from the West, constituting a sort of first form of European colonisation.

This view has been criticised, sometimes sharply, by those whom Michel Balard has called 'the heralds of the third world', in the period of decolonisation. What had appeared as a positive result of the crusades was now retrospectively denounced. Time has passed, qualifying such judgements and bringing the realisation that it was fruitless to try to compare the European expansion which was a product of the crusades to the 'colonialism' for which Europeans have been criticised, and which was once their pride.

The crusades put westerners in contact with an East, sometimes Christian, sometimes Muslim, before revealing a whole as yet unknown Asia. This discovery could have been the occasion for a reciprocal awakening to differences and similarities; sometimes it was. But the current trend is rather to emphasise how this encounter would, on the contrary, cause ruptures. The crusades have sometimes been blamed for what was not their fault. Thus, good historians have tried to minimise the significance of the Graeco-Latin schism of 1054 by locating in 1204 the moment of the true break between the Greek and Latin Churches, and the starting point for a hatred for the Latin name which was, in fact, already present among the people of Constantinople in 1182. The alleged incomprehension of the Byzantines with regard to the crusade did not prevent the emperors from using it to save their empire, or the Latins from dying in large numbers, from 1095 until 1453, to defend the imperial town from the Turkish threat.

The crusade has also been said to have deepened the gulf between Christians and Muslims; for some, it was what drove Islam to intolerance. But the crusade was not a 'war on Islam' but a battle against Muslim powers for a clearly defined objective to which Christendom believed it had more right than they, the Holy Land. And Christian warriors had confronted the Saracens on many other fronts long before 1095. It was hardly necessary to resort to propaganda in order to arouse in them hostility towards the Muslims, even going as far as distorting Islamic thought.

It can be convenient to hold the crusade responsible for conflicts which probably had many other causes. It has been blamed for the retreat of eastern Christianities, either because the Franks oppressed those Christianities they regarded as heterodox or, on the contrary, because they showed them a favour which compromised them in Muslim eyes. It is clear that the latter often caused local Christians to suffer for the failures experienced by the Latins; but it was primarily after Mongol campaigns and as a result of the conversion of the victors to Islam that there were persecutions and forced conversions. The humiliating situation of the *dhimmi* in Muslim territory and the erosion of the Christian populations date from well before the crusades.

It is hardly necessary to add that it is better not to start from contemporary situations to go back to the age of the crusades. The propaganda that had been produced for seven centuries helped to change relationships between communities, even to introduce perspectives totally alien to those of the Middle Ages. The evocation of the 'crusaders' in some sections of the press during the recent crisis in the Lebanon shows the extent to which anachronism can go. And modern forms of interconfessional dialogue have helped to give a questionable image of that of the Middle Ages.

The crusades also had repercussions for western Christianity. Here too, there has been gross oversimplification; the grant of the indulgence by Urban II has been seen as the origin of the traffic in indulgences denounced by Luther, when in fact the grant of indulgences for the restoration of churches started well before 1095.

The identification of the crusade with a 'holy war' is still debated, despite the arguments deployed by the canonists. Many historians, among them Paul Rousset, have revealed their repugnance for a war whose purpose was to impose the Christian faith on the infidel by force. In his *The Church in Council* (1960), E. J. Watkins wrote that the crusade 'was more truly defeat, a spiritual defeat of Christianity by Islam'. He implies that Christendom adopted the notion of jihad, even though some Muslims have raised objections to the simple assimilation of jihad and holy war.

The combatants did not need to have been inspired by fanaticism for the war to have assumed appalling forms. A town taken by storm was liable to experience massacre, pillage and every sort of violence; one thinks of the seizure of Jerusalem, or of Caesarea and Bilbeis, or of the sack of Constantinople, but also of the seizure of Edessa by Nur al-Din, and of Antioch, Tripoli and Acre by the Mamluks; the beheading of the Templars and Hospitallers coldbloodedly ordered by Saladin preceded that of the prisoners taken at Acre by Richard I, and the men who were captured at the Field of Blood were also systematically massacred. Blood has flowed and men have rushed to pillage in many other wars and in our own day.

One of the aims of the Church in summoning men to the crusade was the Christianisation of the lifestyle of the knights, urging them to see themselves as dedicated to protecting the weak; by a different route, the crusades helped to change western society in a way that benefited the political powers. Kings who had to struggle to obtain the obedience of their great vassals, who regarded themselves as masters in their own domains, led them to the East in their wake. The camaraderie of the camps, even shared captivity, bound together men who saw themselves as rivals, if not enemies. Many great families, in France, England and the empire, revealed over several generations a true crusading vocation, to which they sacrificed other objectives. The lord who alienated a part of his land in order to leave for the Holy Land was often abandoning a family policy of territorial aggrandisement. The collections of money made for the crusades paved the way for tax systems; the protection of crusaders' property legitimised the intervention of sovereigns. And the papacy spared no effort to reconcile adversaries with a view to their participation in an expedition or to the creation of the peaceful climate it regarded as a precondition for its success. Probably without preconceived plan, the crusades encouraged the trend towards a new political order.

Was the crusade, in the end, a failure? At the end of the three volumes of his *History of the Crusades*, Sir Steven Runciman concluded that it was, and expressed his views unequivocally: 'a vast fiasco', a series of efforts that were 'particularly capricious and inept', 'a tragic and destructive episode'. He ended with this strongly worded sentence: 'The Holy War itself was nothing more than a long act of intolerance in the name of God, which is the sin against the Holy Ghost.'

One may question the notion of intolerance; the crusaders revealed, in their contact with the East, an unexpected capacity to exercise tolerance with regard to the populations they had subjected, whether they were suspected of heresy or were frankly infidels. But to what extent can one talk of 'fiasco'? Admittedly, the Franks eventually had to evacuate everything they had occupied in Asia. But the last of them left in 1302, whereas the first had set foot in Asia in 1096. Their achievement – two centuries of presence in the East, by men who were only sporadically supported by state power, who were dependent, for the transport of their troops, materials and provisions, on methods which seem to us rudimentary, who did not enjoy a real military superiority, and who were operating some 2,000 kilometres from their nearest bases – confounds the modern observer. All the more so since, while the First Crusade faced a divided Islam, those that followed had to confront a Sunni revival supported by Turkish power, and founders of empire of the quality of Nur al-Din, Saladin and Baybars. And their efforts were frustrated by summonses to other theatres of operations, by the quarrels of western princes and by the reservations of the Byzantines.

Let us move on from overall judgements, which, though emanating from the most highly qualified sources, are so divergent. What I myself want to know is what was felt by the crusaders themselves, those who experienced events, their pleasures and pains, and who gave their life for the crusade.

The crusade, as we know, was an appeal directed at the knightly world by a pope from that world who addressed it in its own language. This was a language which had been developed for more than a century, with a view to introducing into this warrior society an ideal of life which found its highest expression in the monasteries, but without obliging them to renounce their vocation, that of protectors of the weak and defenders of an order willed by God. These knightly values, though they fell below what was required of the first Templars, found in the crusade a way of being employed in the service of God, the Church and Christians. Should we, with Jean Flori, believe that this valorisation of the knightly function was one of the essential objectives of Urban II's appeal, and that it was only partly achieved? In any case, as Adolf Waas has shown, there was a convergence between the ideology of the crusade and that of chivalry.

Sure of having been called by God to his service and of being led by him, trusting in him, convinced that eternal reward awaited him at the end of the day, the knight on crusade was like a vassal summoned to fight for his lord. He brought with him not only his professional qualities – those of the warrior skilled in managing his horse and his weapons, better trained in the discipline of battle in serried ranks than has often been claimed – but an absolute confidence in the goal he had been set. This did not, of course, preclude discouragement, acts of indiscipline or the questioning of leaders.

These men had to show bravery, in extremely difficult circumstances, since they were fighting far from home against enemies of whom they knew little and who were usually more numerous. They experienced fear; panic sometimes seized whole troops. But the Muslims and the easterners, even if they despised the westerners for their apparent ignorance, testified to their respect for this bravery. Nor was it confined to the knights; the footsoldiers needed courage to stand firm beneath hails of projectiles and blasts of Greek fire, in the face of a charge, maintaining their ranks to cover or to receive the mounted warriors, with the certainty, in case of defeat, they would not be spared like those who could pay a ransom; their lot would be slavery or death.

For all that, the Franks suffered defeats in battle, even disasters. As was natural, each time people looked for scapegoats, and alleged treachery; for Hattin, some accused Raymond III of having sold himself to Saladin, others blamed Gerard of Ridfort. The rash behaviour of the 'sergeants' when they launched into pillaging the enemy camp or when they could no longer bear prolonged inactivity was deplored. St Bernard accused the barons of having mismanaged the Second Crusade; King Conrad III spoke of complicity between the Franks of the East and the Muslims. These were knee-jerk reactions. The clergy managed to persuade the laity of their own explanation of the defeats. *Peccatis nostris exigentibus*; it was because of the sins of the crusaders, but also of all Christians, that God had refused the promised victory. They must redeem their faults through penitence, before resuming the interrupted task.

The task was hard. There were moments of exaltation – the intoxication of a victorious charge, the flight of the enemy, pillaging a camp, the joy of victory. There were small pleasures shared between comrades, and the thought of the glory to be won. But setting out was called by one songwriter the *dure départie*. It was preceded by financial worries which might entail the sacrifice of family property, and the prospect of difficult days for those left behind. There was the pain of separation; Joinville could not look back when setting out from his fine castle, where he had left his children. Goodbyes were painful; no one could be sure of seeing parents, wife or fiancée again, and the men of the Middle Ages felt the pain of leaving their loved ones just like those of today.

Those who went by land faced a long journey, and the risk of ambush and famine; those who went by sea had to cram into overcrowded ships, dreading storms, experiencing the torments of seasickness, at danger from shipwreck. The perils of battle were real – 'for the Saracens are *félons*'; the Turks also were fierce warriors; how many lost comrades were mourned, despite the conviction that God had opened for them the gates of Heaven? And the inevitable epidemic decimated the army, whether on the march, on campaign or laying siege. Lastly, as we know, the climate of the Near East is deadly for men who have not yet adopted the habits of food, lodgings and clothing appropriate to those countries.

Other ordeals awaited the crusaders; booty often provided satisfaction for the victors, but not every campaign had its victory. Everybody was short of money; the rising price of foodstuffs caused hardship; they cost a small fortune to buy. Here, organisation steadily improved, as the financial costs came to be shared by others than the combatants. Aids and tenths provided a more regular system of finance, but meant the imposition of a taxation system which was soon unpopular; the whole of the population that remained in the West was taxed, and it was not long before the collectors and the beneficiaries of these taxes were accused of profiting from them without the crusade gaining the benefit.

Gradually, the whole of society was drawn into the preparation for a crusade, whether it was a 'general passage' organised by the papacy or the simple armed pilgrimages of the twelfth century. Preachers abandoned their favourite themes to summon their audience to take the cross; the clergy collected the money. For the seigneurial world, it amounted to a general mobilisation; the suzerain led his vassals, who led their rear-vassals, assuming they agreed to volunteer. But it was difficult for a knight to refuse to follow his lord who left for the Holy Land; it was rather the latter who had to tailor the size of his contingent to his resources.

The effort was considerable, and it was sustained, more or less continuously, for two centuries. The demographic explosion, the craving for expression of men eager to establish themselves, love of adventure, the economic impact were all contributory factors, but the religious factor was crucial.

It was not a matter of anti-Muslim fanaticism, or the desire to end a schism. It consisted essentially of a visceral attachment to the Holy Land. The canonist Hostienis said – and regretted – that the *crux transmarina* attracted many more crusaders than the *crux cismarina*, and this even when the hope of visiting the Holy Sepulchre had faded. The attraction of the plenary indulgence, which was attached to other expeditions equally recommended by the papacy, was therefore no longer the main motive for going on a crusade.

To understand this attachment, we must return to the *In Praise of the New Knighthood*. St Bernard never tried to go to the Holy Land and he dissuaded his monks from doing so. But he regarded the crusade as eminently desirable for knights. For him, the 'redemption of Jerusalem' was the fulfilment of the promise made to the Jewish people in favour of the New Israel; it made it possible to erase from the Holy Places the stain of the infidel and it brought to the Christian people riches that St Bernard called 'delights of the world, celestial treasure, heritage of the faithful peoples'. He listed them: Bethlehem, Nazareth, the Mount of Olives, the valley of Josaphat, the Jordan, Calvary, the Sepulchre, Bethphage and Bethany, all places which had their mystical evocation. Bernard invited the knights of the Temple to drive out of the Holy City 'those who endeavour to steal the inestimable riches that Jerusalem reserves for the Christian people, who wish to soil the Holy Places and appropriate the sanctuary of God'.

This image of 'treasures' was taken up by others. It expressed a reality felt with varying degrees of intensity by those who took the road for the East. It seems not to have been part of Urban II's appeals, and the Byzantines, concerned though they were to save the places consecrated by the presence of Christ, had come to terms with the fact that they were under the sovereignty of the caliph. But, during the First Crusade, the simple pilgrims and the lesser knights, who had forced the decision to leave northern Syria on the barons, felt deeply drawn to the Holy Places.

The Holy Places, and the entire Holy Land, also redolent with Biblical and Gospel memories, had at first been the goal of the pilgrimage. After

Hattin, another perspective was gradually substituted for it: the Holy Land, which belonged to God, and thus to Christendom, could not be left in the hands of the infidel; its recovery was a duty owed to the Lord, just as a vassal had a duty to reconquer the heritage of which his lord had been deprived.

In the end, the purpose of the crusade was to assure Christians possession of those treasures described by St Bernard. For nearly a century, in spite of the distances and difficulties of every sort, at the cost of a constant influx of men ready to fight for it, this possession was maintained. For another century, westerners and the Franks of the East tried desperately to recover it, by organising great enterprises, and at a heavy cost in men and material goods; they succeeded for a few years. They faced an expanding power; their sovereigns were seduced by other objectives, and the very scale of the strategic projects made them less frequent. The loss of the coastal towns which had been all they retained deprived them of the bases from which they had hoped to resume the fight, and so made it less urgent to send the small-scale expeditions designed to secure those bases; but the 'general passage' so often projected was never abandoned.

The Holy Land was not forgotten by the Christians of the West, even after the age of the crusades. We need only recall the persistence of pilgrimages, the visits during which the founders of an order like Ignatius Loyola and Charles of Foucauld stiffened their resolve, or the journeys of Lamartine and Chateaubriand.

It was the crusade which anchored this idea in the imagination of the western world. The concept of the Holy Land was not created by theoreticians and preachers; it emerged, on the basis of the objectives set by Urban II, from the very fact of crusading. It was the crusaders themselves who made the crusades what they were: enterprises on an amazing scale, entailing sacrifices and ordeals, but also source of a spiritual enrichment that is difficult to measure; they remain one of the major episodes in European history.

CHRONOLOGY

1071: Byzantine defeat of Manzikert; capture of Jerusalem by Atsiz.

1074: Gregory VII's project for an expedition to the East.

1077: Recapture of Jerusalem by Atsiz.

1095 March: Council of Piacenza; Council of Clermont.

1096 spring: Departure of the first crusaders and anti-Jewish riots; August: Departure of the barons; October: First crusader defeats.

1097 19 June: Capture of Nicaea; July: Battle of Dorylaeum; December–3 June 1098: Siege of Antioch.

1098 February: Baldwin at Edessa; 28 June: Victory over Kerbogha at Battle of Antioch; August: Recapture of Jerusalem by the Egyptians.

1099 15 July: Capture of Jerusalem; 12 August: Victory of Ascalon.

1100 July: Death of Godfrey of Bouillon; August: Capture of Bohemond. Tancred regent of Antioch.

1101 April–May: Genoese Crusade. Capture of Arsur and Caesarea; 7 September: Victory of Ramla; August–September: Disaster of the Crusade of 1101.

1102: Capture of Tortosa by Raymond of Saint-Gilles; May: Defeat of Baldwin I at Ramla and victory of Jaffa.

1103: Capture of Acre. Liberation of Bohemond; siege of Tripoli begins.

1104: Defeat of Harran. Capture of Baldwin of Bourcq.

1107: Bohemond lands at Avlona.

1108 September: Treaty of Devol; Liberation of Baldwin of Bourcq and war against Tancred.

1109 12 July: Capture of Tripoli.

1110–13: Expeditions of the atabeg Mawdud.

1113–15: Occupation of Kaysun, Raban and Armenian lordships by Baldwin of Edessa.

1115: Defeat of the atabeg Bursuqi at Tell Danith.

1118: Foundation of order of the Temple; March–April: Baldwin I's capture of Farama and death; 28 June: Defeat and death of Roger of Antioch at the Field of Blood. Regency of Baldwin II.

1119 14 August: Victory of Baldwin at Tell Danith.

1123: Capture of Baldwin II.

1123–4: Venetian Crusade.

1124 7 July: Capture of Tyre.

1128: Zengi occupies Aleppo.

1129: Marriage of Fulk of Anjou and expedition against Damascus.

1131 21 August: Death of Baldwin II.

1132: Revolt of Hugh of Le Puiset.

1136: Raymond of Poitiers prince of Antioch.

1137: Attack on Antioch by John Comnenus. Siege of Shaizar. Defeat and death of Pons of Tripoli. Fulk besieged in Montferrand.

1139: First pilgrimage of Thierry of Flanders.

1142: John Comnenus at Antioch.

1142 (or 1144): The Crac des Chevaliers granted to the Hospitallers.

1144 26 December: Fall of Edessa.

1145 14 December: Proclamation of the Second Crusade.

1146 31 March: St Bernard at Vézelay; 25 December: St Bernard at Speyer.

1147 24 October: Capture of Lisbon by the crusaders; November–December: Defeat of the German armies in Anatolia.

1148 March: Louis VII at Antioch; 23–28 July: Siege of Damascus.

1149 29 July: Defeat and death of Raymond of Poitiers at Fons Murez.

1150 May: Capture of Jocelyn II; August: Grant of county of Edessa to the Byzantines.

1153: Reynald of Châtillon prince of Antioch; 19 August: Capture of Ascalon.

1154: Occupation of Damascus by Nur al-Din.

1157: War against Nur al-Din and demonstration against Shaizar. Third expedition of Thierry of Flanders.

1159: Manuel Comnenus enters Antioch.

1160: Capture of Reynald of Châtillon.

1163: First Egyptian campaign. Nur al-Din defeated at the Biqa; 11 August: Victory of Nur al-Din at Harenc.

1164: Second expedition to Egypt.

1167: Third Egyptian campaign. Defeat of Babain and siege of Alexandria.

1168: Attempted conquest of Egypt by Balbain. Capture of Bilbeis, burning of Fustat and evacuation of Egypt.

1169 October–December: Franco-Byzantine attempt on Damietta.

1170–2: Campaigns of Nur al-Din and Saladin in Oultrejourdain.

1174: Saladin master of Damascus. Death of Amalric.

1176: Defeat of Manuel Comnenus at Myriokephalon.

1177: Crusade of Philip of Flanders. Siege of Harenc; 25–26 November: Victory of Baldwin IV at Montgisard.

1180: Defeat of Baldwin IV at Banyas and at Jacob's Ford. Marriage of Sibylla of Jerusalem and Guy of Lusignan.

1183: Expeditions of Reynald of Châtillon in Arabia and the Red Sea. Saladin master of Aleppo. Siege of Kerak.

1184: Rebellion of Guy of Lusignan.

1186 September: Accession of Guy of Lusignan and rebellion of Raymond III. Seizure of the Damascus caravan by Reynald.

1187 4 July: Disaster of Hattin, followed by the conquest of Acre, Jaffa, Ḥaifa, Caesarea, Toron and Sidon, then Beirut and Ascalon; 20 September–2 October: Siege and capitulation of Jerusalem; August–December: Proclamation of the Third Crusade.

1188 2 January: Saladin lifts siege of Tyre; March: Arrival of the Sicilian fleet. Failure of Saladin before Tripoli. Conquest of part of principality of Antioch.

1189 May: Departure of Frederick Barbarossa; August–12 July 1191: Siege of Acre.

1190 10 June: Death of Frederick II in Cilicia; July: Arrival of Henry of Champagne at Acre. Philip Augustus and Richard I at Vézelay.

1191 20 April: Philip arrives at Acre; 6 May: Landing of Richard on Cyprus; 8 June: Richard arrives at Acre; 7 September: Victory of Arsur.

1192 December–January: Crusader army stationed at Betenoble. Retreat to Ascalon; 28 April: Assassination of Conrad of Montferrat. Henry of Champagne lord of the kingdom; June–July: Crusader army again at Betenoble; July–August: Richard's victory at Jaffa; 2 September: Franco-Muslim truces.

1193 4 March: Death of Saladin and beginning of rivalries between his heirs.

1194: Ambush of Baghras and Armenians lose hold on Antioch.

1197: Crusade of Henry VI. Recapture of Jaffa by al-Adil and death of Henry of Champagne; October: Recapture of Beirut. Siege of Toron.

1198: Promulgation of the Fourth Crusade.

1200: Unification of Ayyubid empire by al-Adil.

1201: Death of Bohemond III and beginning of disputed succession to Antioch; April: Treaty between Venice and the crusaders (1201–13).

1202 October–November: Siege of Zara.

1203: Landing in Constantinople. Restoration of Isaac II.

1204 12 April: Capture of Constantinople; September: Truces with Amalric; reoccupation of Sidon and Jaffa.

1210–11: Resumption of hostilities in the Holy Land.

1213: The Children's Crusade. Announcement of the Fifth Crusade.

1215 November: Fourth Lateran Council.

1217 August: Departure of the duke of Austria and the king of Hungary; November–December: Siege of Mount Tabor.

1218 28 May: Landing of John of Brienne in Egypt; 24 August: Capture of the Tower of the Chain.

1219 5 November: Capture of Damietta.

1221 30 August: Capitulation of the crusader army at Baramun and evacuation of Damietta.

1225: Marriage of Frederick II and Isabella of Jerusalem.

1227 October: Landing of German and English troops at Acre. Rebuilding of Sidon and Caesarea.

1228 7 September: Arrival of Frederick II at Acre.

1229 18 February: Treaty of Jaffa and restoration of Jerusalem to Frederick II.

1230–3: War between Filangieri and the Guelph party. The commune of Acre.

1238: Gregory X's crusade to assist Constantinople.

1239 August: Departure of the crusaders for the Holy Land; 13 November: Defeat of crusaders at Gaza.

1240 11 October: Arrival of Richard of Cornwall.

1241 23 April: Treaty between Richard and the sultan of Egypt.

1243 July: Tyre seized from supporters of Frederick II.

1244 23 August: Loss of Jerusalem; 17 October: Disaster of La Forbie; December: St Louis makes vow of crusade.

1245 June–July: Council of Lyons.

1248 25 August: Departure from Aigues-Mortes; September–May 1249: St Louis in Cyprus. Andrew of Longjumeau sent to the Mongols.

1249 5 June: Landing of the crusaders of Damietta.

1250 8 February: Crossing of Bahr al-Saghir. Battle of Mansurah; 6 April: Capture of Louis IX and disaster of Fariskur; 2 May: Murder of the sultan Turanshah and seizure of power by the Mamluks; 6 May: Surrender of Damietta.

1252: Alliance between Louis IX and the Mamluks.

1254 24 April: St Louis leaves Acre. Truce with the Muslims.

1256–8: War of St Sabas; revolt of the barons of Tripoli against Bohemond VI; February (1258): Capture of Baghdad by the Mongols.

1260: Mongol campaign in Syria. Capture of Aleppo and Damascus; September: Mongol defeat at Ayn Jalut. Accession of the sultan Baybars.

1263: Attack on Acre by Baybars.

1264: Hülegü offers alliance to St Louis.

1265: Capture of Caesarea, Caiphas and Arsur. Crusade of Count Eudes of Nevers.

1266: Capture of Saphet and Toron.

1268: Capture of Jaffa and Beaufort. Attack on Tripoli. Capture of Antioch and fall of Baghras. Promulgation of the Eighth Crusade.

1269: Aragonese crusade.

1270: St Louis' crusade; Tunis campaign and death of the king.

1271: Fall of Crac des Chevaliers, Chastel Blanc and Gibelcar, then Montfort. Edward I's crusade in the Holy Land.

1272 22 May: Truce with the Mamluks.

1274 May–July: Second Council of Lyons. Promulgation of crusade, in liaison with the Mongols.

1277 January: Maria of Antioch cedes her rights to the throne to Charles of Anjou; June: Seizure of power in Acre in the name of Charles of Anjou.

1275–82: War between Guy of Gibelet, the Temple and Bohemond VII.

1281: Mongol campaign in Syria; their defeat at Homs.

1285: Conquest of Margat and retreat from Maraclea.

1286: Restoration of the dynastic union between Cyprus and Jerusalem.

1287–8: Rabban Sauma's embassy to Rome, Bordeaux and Paris; preparations for a joint campaign with the Mongols.

1287: Loss of Latakia.

1288: Rebellion of Tripoli against the princess Lucia.

1289 26 April: Fall of Tripoli.

1290: Promulgation of a crusade.

1291 28 May: Fall of Acre, followed by the evacuation of the other towns.

1299: The Mongols enter Damascus.

1300: Frankish landings at Rosetta and Tortosa.

1303: Loss of the Isle of Ruad. Evacuation of Gibelet.

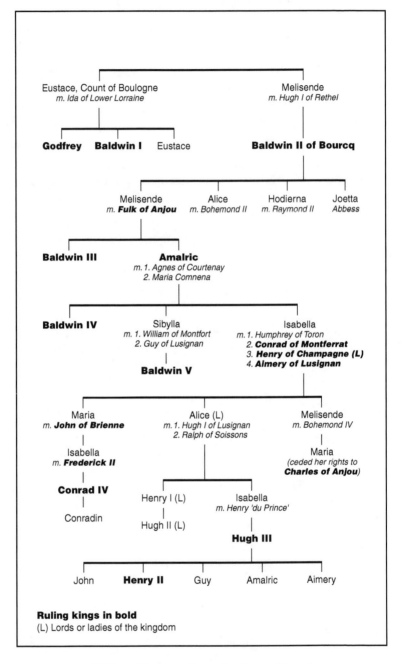

Table 1   The succession to the throne of Jerusalem

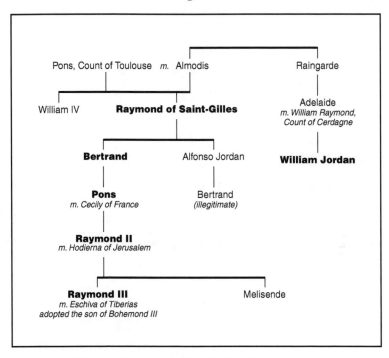

Table 2   The counts of Tripoli of the Toulouse dynasty

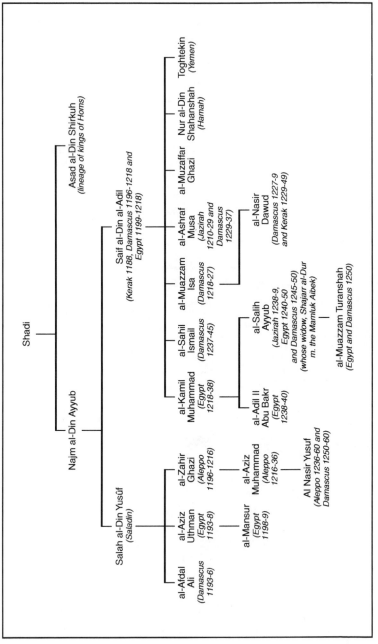

Table 3 Simplified Ayyubid dynasty

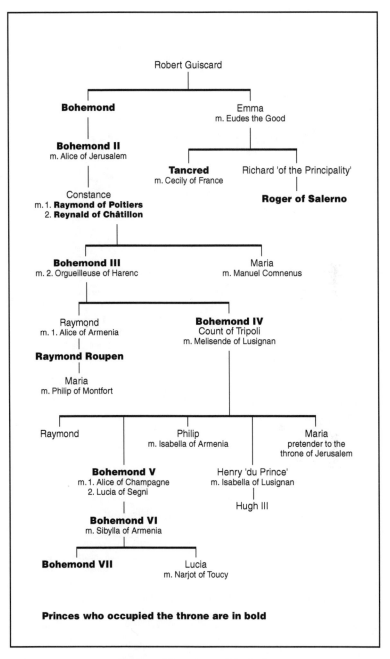

Table 4   The princes of Antioch

SOURCES AND BIBLIOGRAPHY

The sources for the history of the crusades are numerous and extremely varied. In addition to the different narrative forms, which range from the chronicle to the letter and the *chanson de geste*, there are not only juridical documents and accounts but archaeological remains and even the monuments still in place. These sources are, for the most part, 'western'. The East generally lacked the same reasons for interest in expeditions from the West, but their historians noted, sometimes in great detail, events which affected the life of their countries and communities. It is essential, therefore, to use eastern narrative sources both to write the history of the crusaders' expeditions and to understand the conditions in which they took place.

This necessity was realised at an early stage, and explains why, in the programme of the great *Recueil des historiens des croisades* undertaken by the Académie des inscriptions et belles lettres, such prominence was given to the historical texts of Arab, Syriac, Greek and Armenian origin. This vast collection comprises the following series: *Historiens occidentaux*, *Historiens orientaux*, *Historiens grecs* and *Documents arméniens*, and publication continued until 1906. It was then broken off and has been replaced by a new collection of *Documents relatifs à la histoire des croisades*, less dominated by the narrative texts. The old editions of the *Recueil* are sometimes unsatisfactory, and it is necessary to consult editions which conform more closely to modern rules of source criticism; for example, in the case of the great work of William of Tyre, that which appeared in the *Corpus christianorum, Continuatio medievalis*. Other texts have not appeared in the collection; these include the *Itinerarium peregrinorum* and the chronicle of Ernoul, among others.

The same is true of the eastern sources, some of which have been translated into western languages accessible to researchers, whilst the editions in eastern languages are not always easy of access. Also, the *Historiens orientaux* often give only extracts, since the principal aim of these works was not necessarily related to the crusades. A remarkable effort has been made to assemble the most significant extracts from the Arab historians in F. Gabrieli's *Storici arabi della crociate* (Milan, 1957) (trs. into French as *Chroniques arabes des croisades*), though it makes no claims to be comprehensive. Extracts from the interesting remarks of Ibn al-Furat have been edited and translated into English by U. and M. C. Lyons, with annotations by J. S. C. Riley-Smith, with the title *Ayyubids, Mamlukes and Crusaders* (Cambridge, 1971). There are now, happily, some complete translations appearing, such as that of the Armenian chronicle attributed to the constable Sempad, by G. Dédeyan, and that of the anonymous Syriac chronicle kept up to 1234, the work of the late Father J.-M. Fiey.

The historical output of the age of the crusades includes a large number of eyewitness accounts, some by ecclesiastics, others by laymen, who participated in the expeditions and related their memories, not without revealing their attachment to a particular leader or contingent, but providing us with their impressions, even blunted by literary conventions. The Anonymous of the First Crusade, Villehardouin, Robert of Clary and Joinville were combatants; Fulcher of Chartres, Raymond of Aguilers, Odo of Deuil and Oliver of Paderborn were clerics in close contact with the leaders of one or other of the crusades. These accounts, written as events dictated, are particularly vivid. But when a universal chronicle reported the events that occurred during the course of a crusade, it was often on the basis of the evidence of letters or accounts, which are also direct sources. The rules of source criticism still need to be applied; the historical works written in the Latin East, and even the invaluable *History* of William of Tyre, often show signs of the prejudices of their authors.

Itineraries and accounts of pilgrimages have been conveniently assembled by Father S. de Sandoli in the four volumes of his *Itinera Hierosolymitana crucesignatorum* (Jerusalem, 1978–84). The letters relating to the First Crusade were assembled and criticised by H. Hagenmeyer in 1901, but the later epistolary material remains very scattered.

In the case of archival documents, we remain reliant on R. Röhricht's remarkable *Regesta regni Hierosolymitani*, completed by an *Additamentum* of 1904. This inventory cannot, of course, take account of later discoveries, and an important work of criticism is at present under way under the direction of H. E. Mayer. We should also note the publication by R. Hiestand of the *Papsturkunden für Kirchen im Heiligen Lande* (Göttingen, 1985) and that of the documents from the Cairo Geniza by S. Goitein.

For the juridical sources, A. Beugnot's edition of the *Assises de Jérusalem* in the *Recueil des historiens des croisades* has been useful but must today be regarded as out of date; new editions of these texts are in preparation.

I should complete this brief survey by noting the existence of collections which are not scholarly in aim but are intended to make available to a wider public texts which are informative about the crusades, notably:

J. Brundage, *The Crusades. A Documentary Survey* (Milwaukee, 1962).

J. Richard, *L'Esprit de la Croisade* (Paris, 1969).

L. and J. S. C. Riley-Smith, *The Crusades. Idea and Reality, 1105–1274* (London, 1981).

The historical literature relative to the crusades is considerable and increasing, and shows no sign of drying up. The references given below are not intended to provide justification for the facts I have recorded or the interpretations I have put forward, but only to indicate works in which the reader may pursue certain themes.

I have drawn on a large number of articles that have appeared in journals, conference proceedings, miscellanies and collective works, and it would be impossible to list them all here. I should note, however, a remarkable bibliographical guide: author of a *Bibliographie zur geschichte der Kreuzzüge*, which appeared in 1960, H. E. Mayer, in collaboration with J. McLellan, has given us, in the sixth and final volume of the *History of the Crusades*, published under the direction of K. M. Setton, a *Select Bibliography of the Crusades* (1989). After a methodical description of the sources for the history of the crusades and of the Latin East, this work provides a full list of the books and articles devoted to it, completed by a list of topics tackled. This list alone fills nearly a hundred pages of small print; which is to say, it satisfies the most demanding.

Over the past few years, a large number of very innovative works have appeared. Because these works are so scattered, the Society for the Study of the Crusades and the Latin East, founded in 1980, publishes an annual *Bulletin* listing the recent publications of its members, thus making it possible to keep up to date with the progress of research. It should be added that the *Collected Studies* published by Variorum, today at Aldershot, has devoted a large amount of space to collections of articles on the crusades.

Synthesis

For the history of the crusades as a whole, there are a number of major syntheses. Without forgetting the oldest of them, I should first quote: R. Grousset, *Histoire des Croisades et du Royaume Franc de Jérusalem*, 3 vols. (Paris, 1934–6), which provides a very full reconstruction, well footnoted, of the progress of events, and remains in general very accurate.

Other syntheses have started from different positions than that of Grousset, though without challenging his account of events:

Runciman, S., *A History of the Crusades*, 3 vols. (Cambridge, 1951–4).

Cognasso, F., *Storia delle Crociate* (Florence, 1967).

Rousset, P., *Histoire des Croisades* (Paris, 1957).

Other authors have offered explanations of the phenomenon of the crusades, standing back from the events themselves, notably:

Alphandéry, P. and Dupront, A., *La Chrétienté et l'Idée de Croisade*, 2nd edn (Paris, 1955).

Waas, A., *Geschichte der Kreuzzüge*, 2 vols. (Freiburg im Breisgau, 1956).

Starting from a project of John L. La Monte, the great collective enterprise directed by Setton, K. M., *A History of the Crusades*, 2nd edn, 6 vols. (Madison, 1969–89), is the starting point for all new research.

Also useful are:

Balard, M., *Les Croisades* (Paris, 1988).

Cahen, C., *Orient et Occident au temps des croisades* (Paris, 1983).

Mayer, H. E., *The Crusades*, 2nd edn, trs. John Gillingham (Oxford, 1988).

Morrisson, C., *Les Croisades*, 4th edn (Paris, 1984).

Pernoud, R., *Les Hommes de la croisade* (Paris, 1982).

Platelle, H., *Les Croisades* (Paris, 1994).

Riley-Smith, J. S. C., *The Crusades: A Short History* (London and New Haven, Conn., 1987).

Riley-Smith's *The Atlas of the Crusades* (London and New York, 1991) goes beyond our period and deals with crusades other than in the Near East.

On the causes of the crusades:

Anderson, G. M., 'An economic interpretation of the medieval crusades', *Economic History Review*, 21 (1992).

Bartlett, R., *The Making of Europe: Conquest, Colonisation and Cultural Change, 950–1350* (London, 1993).

Cahen, C., 'En quoi le conquête turque appelait-elle la croisade?', *Bulletin de la faculté des lettres de Strasbourg*, 29 (1950–1).

Fedalto, G., *Perché le Crociate: Saggio Interpretativo* (Bologna, 1980).

On the origins of the crusades:

Becker, A., *Papst Urban II. 1088–1099*, 2 vols. (Munich, 1964–88).

Cowdrey, H. E. J., *Popes, Monks and Crusaders* (London, 1984) (a collection of articles).

Delaruelle, E., *L'Idée de Croisade au Moyen Age*, ed. A. Vauchez (Turin, 1980).

Erdmann, C., *The Origin of the Idea of the Crusade*, trs. M. W. Baldwin and W. Goffart (Princeton, 1977).

Rousset, P., *Les Origines et le Caractère de la Première Croisade* (Neuchâtel, 1945).

Studies of particular crusades

Each expedition has been the subject of specific studies, to which must be added the chapters entrusted to specialists in the *History of the Crusades*, many of which are authoritative:

First Crusade:

Bull, M., *Knightly Piety and the Lay Response to the First Crusade. The Limousin and Gascony* (Oxford, 1993).

Flori, J., *1095–1099, La Première Croisade. L'Occident contre l'Islam. Aux Origines des Idéologies Occidentales* (Brussels, 1992).

Heers, J., *Libérer Jérusalem. La Première Croisade* (Paris, 1995).

Krey, A. C., 'Urban's crusade, success or failure?', *American Historical Review*, 59 (1948).

Riley-Smith, J. S. C., *The First Crusade and the Idea of Crusading* (London, 1986).

There are many works devoted to the protagonists:

Aubé, P., *Godefroy de Bouillon* (Paris, 1985).

Eidelberg, S., *The Jews and the Crusaders. The Hebrew Chronicles of the First and the Second Crusades* (Madison, 1977).

Hill, J. H. and Hill, L. L., *Raymond IV Count of Toulouse* (1962).

Porges, W., 'The clergy, the poor and the non-combattants in the First Crusade', *Speculum*, 21 (1946).

Richard, J., 'La papauté et la direction de la Première Croisade', *Journal des savants* (1960).

Second Crusade:

Caspar, E., 'Die Kreuzzugsbullen Eugens III', *Neues Archiv*, 45 (1924).

Constable, G., 'The Second Crusade as seen by contemporaries', *Traditio*, 9 (1953).

Gervers, M., ed., *The Second Crusade and the Cistercians* (New York, 1992).

Grabois, A., 'The crusade of King Louis VII. A reconsideration', in ed. P. W. Edbury, *Crusade and Settlement* (Cardiff, 1985).

Hoch, M., *Jerusalem, Damaskus und der Zweite Kreuzzug* (Frankfurt, 1993).

Philipps, J., *Defenders of the Holy Land. Relations between the Latin East and the West, 1119–1187* (Oxford, 1996).

Third Crusade:

Baldwin, M. W., *Raymond III of Tripoli and the Fall of Jerusalem* (Princeton, 1936).

Hamilton, B., 'The Elephant of Christ, Raynald of Châtillon', *Studies in Church History*, 15 (1978).

Kedar, B. Z., 'The battle of Hattin revisited', in ed. B. Z. Kedar, *The Horns of Hattin* (Jerusalem and London, 1992).

Möhring, H., *Saladin und der dritte Kreuzzug* (Wiesbaden, 1981).

Naumann, C., *Der Kreuzzug Kaiser Heinrichs VI* (Frankfurt, 1994).

Nicholson, R. L., *Joscelyn III and the Fall of the Crusader States* (Leiden, 1973).

Fourth Crusade:

The literature concerning the Fourth Crusade is particularly abundant and judgements remain contradictory. I give below only a few of these works:

Carile, A., *Per Una Storia dell'Impero Latino di Constantinopoli. 1204–1261* (Bologna, 1978).

Frolow, A., *Recherches sur la Déviation de la 4e Croisade vers Constantinople* (Paris, 1955).

Godfrey, J., *1204. The Unholy Crusade* (Oxford, 1980).

Longnon, J., *Les Compagnons de Villehardouin. Recherches sur les Croisés de la Quatrième Croisade* (Geneva, 1974).

Maleczek, W., *Petrus Capuanus* (Vienna, 1988).

Queller, D. E., *The Fourth Crusade: the Conquest of Constantinople. 1201–1204* (Philadelphia, 1977).

A recent work on the Children's Crusade is:
Dickson, G., 'La genèse de la croisade des enfants (1212)', *Bibliothèque de l'Ecole des chartes,* 153 (1995).

Fifth Crusade:
Powell, J. M., *Anatomy of a Crusade. 1213–1221* (Philadelphia, 1986).
For Frederick II's expedition to the East, see the recent edition of the principal source with an important discussion:
Novara, Filippo di, *Guerra di Federico II in Oriente,* ed. Silvio Melani (Naples, 1994).

The Crusades of St Louis:
Jordan, W. C., *Saint Louis and the Challenge of the Crusade* (Princeton, 1979).
Lefevre, R., *La Crociata di Tunisi del 1270 nei documenti del distrutto archivio angioino di Napoli* (Rome, 1977).
Lloyd, S., 'The Lord Edward's crusade', in *War and Government in the Middle Ages. Essays in Honour of J. O. Prestwich* (Woodbridge, 1984).
Richard, J., *Saint Louis. Crusader King of France,* ed. S. Loyd and trs. J. Birrell (Cambridge, 1992).
    'La Croisade de 1270, premier "passage général"?', *Comptes rendus de l'Académie des inscriptions* (1989).

For the last years of the Frankish Holy Land and the crusade projects:
Herde, P., *Karl I von Anjou* (Stuttgart, 1979).
Holt, P. M., 'Qalawûn's treaty with Acre in 1283', *English Historical Review,* 91 (1976).
Housley, N. J., *The Later Crusades from Lyons to Alcazar. 1274–1580* (Oxford, 1992).
Laurent, V., 'La croisade et la question d'Orient sous le pontificat de Grégoire X', *Revue historique du Sud-Est européen,* 22 (1945).
Schein, S., *Fideles Crucis. The Papacy, the West and the Recovery of the Holy Land. 1274–1314* (Oxford, 1991).
Throop, P. A., *Criticism of the Crusade: a Study of Public Opinion and Crusade Propaganda* (Amsterdam, 1940).

The Latin States of the East

These have been the subject of much historical research. Each has one or more full histories:

Amouroux-Mourad, M., *Le Comté d'Edesse. 1098–1150* (Paris, 1988).
Cahen, C., *La Syrie du Nord à l'Epoque des Croisades et la Principauté Franque d'Antioche* (Paris, 1940).
Prawer, J., *Histoire du Royaume Latin de Jérusalem,* 2nd edn, 2 vols. (Paris, 1975).
Richard, J., *The Latin Kingdom of Jerusalem,* trs. J. Shirley, 2 vols. (Amsterdam, New York and Oxford, 1979).
    Le Comté de Tripoli sous la Dynastie Toulousaine. 1102–1187 (Paris, 1946).

'Les comtes de Tripoli de la dynastie antiochénienne et leur vassaux', in ed. P. W. Edbury, *Crusade and Settlement* (Cardiff, 1985).

The internal history of the kingdom of Jerusalem and its institutions is a large field. I note, in particular, Hans Mayer's *Mélanges sur l'histoire du royaume de Jérusalem* (Paris, 1984) and the collections of his articles published by Variorum; also the works of J. Prawer, J. S. C. Riley-Smith, S. Tibble and D. Jacoby.

The religious history of the Latin East:

Cipollini, G., *Cristianità-Islam. Cattività e Liberazione in Nome di Dio. Il Tempo di Innocenzo III dopo il 1187* (Rome, 1992).

Fedalto, G., *La Chiesa Latina in Oriente*, 3 vols. (Verona, 1973–7).

Hamilton, B., *The Latin Church in the Crusader States. The Secular Church* (London, 1980).

Jotischky, A., *The Perfection of Solitude. Hermits and Monks in the Crusader States* (Philadelphia, 1995).

Mayer, H. E., *Bistümer, Klöster und Stifte im Königreich Jerusalem* (Stuttgart, 1977).

Richard, J., *La Papauté et les Missions d'Orient au Moyen Age* (Rome, 1977).

The military orders:

Barber, M., *The New Knighthood. A History of the Order of the Temple* (Cambridge, 1992).

Demurger, A., *Vie et Mort de l'Ordre du Temple* (Paris, 1985).

Favreau, M.-L., *Studien zur Frühgeschichte des Deutschen Ordens* (Stuttgart, 1974).

Forey, A., *Military Orders and Crusades* (Aldershot, 1994).

Riley-Smith, J. S. C., *The Knights of St John in Jerusalem and Cyprus, c. 1050–1310* (London, 1967).

For regional participation in the crusades:

Favreau-Lilie, M.-L., *Die Italiener im Heiligen Lande (1098–1197)* (Amsterdam, 1988).

Riant, P., *Expéditions et Pèlerinages des Scandinaves en Terre Sainte au Temps des Croisades* (Paris, 1869).

Tyerman, C., *England and the Crusades. 1095–1588* (Chicago, 1988).

Military History

This area, once associated with Delbrück and Boutaric, is now an English speciality:

France, J., *Victory in the East. A Military History of the First Crusade* (Cambridge, 1994).

Marshall, C., *Warfare and the Latin East. 1192–1291* (Cambridge, 1992).

Smail, R. C., *Crusading Warfare. 1097–1193*, 5th edn (Cambridge, 1987).

Deschamps, P. *Les Châteaux des Croisés en Terre Sainte*, 3 vols. (Paris, 1934–73).

Economic History

The two classic works remain:

Heyd, W., *Histoire du Commerce du Levant au Moyen Age*, trs. F. Raynaud, 2 vols. (Leipzig, 1885–6, repr. 1967).

Schaube, A., *Handelsgeschichte der romanischen Völker des Mittelmeergebeits bis zum Ende der Kreuzzüge* (Munich, 1906).

More recently:

Ashtor, E., *A Social and Economic History of the Near East in the Middle Ages* (London, 1976).

Pryor, J. H., *Commerce, Shipping and Naval Warfare in the Medieval Mediterranean* (London, 1987).

Also the many articles of Claude Cahen reprinted in *Turcobyzantina et Orient Latinus* (London, 1974).

On the financing of the crusades:

Cazel, F. A., 'The tax of 1185 in aid of the Holy Land', *Speculum*, 30 (1955); (see also his chapter in the *History of the Crusades*, vol. 6).

Constable, G., 'The financing of the crusades', *Outremer. Studies in the History of the Crusading Kingdom of Jerusalem Presented to J. Prawer*, ed. B. Kedar *et al.* (Jerusalem, 1982).

Gottlob, A., *Die päpstlichen Kreuzzugsteuern des 13. Jahrhundert* (Heilgenstadt, 1892).

Purcell, M., *Papal Crusading Policy. 1244–1291* (Leiden, 1975). This book is also extremely useful on the subject of the conception and organisation of thirteenth-century crusades.

Conception of the crusades

For spiritual and juridical aspects and relations with pilgrimage:

Brundage, J., *Medieval Canon Law and the Crusade* (Madison, Wisconsin, and London, 1969).

   The crusades, Holy War and Canon Law (London, 1991).

Cardini, F., *Studi sulla storia e sull'idea di crociata* (Rome, 1993).

Gotlob, A., *Kreuzzugablass und Almosenablass* (Stuttgart, 1906).

Paulus, N., *Geschichte des Ablasses im Mittelalter*, 2 vols. (Paderborn, 1922–3).

Richard, J., *L'Esprit de la Croisade* (Paris, 1969).

Riley-Smith, J. S. C., *What were the Crusades?* (2nd edn, London, 1992).

Rousset, P., *Histoire d'une Idéologie: la Croisade* (Lausanne, 1983).

Sigal, P.-A., *Les Marcheurs de Dieu. Pèlerinages et Pèlerins au Moyen Age* (Paris, 1974).

Villey, M., *La Croisade; Essai sur la Formation d'une Théorie Juridique* (Paris, 1942).

Wilkinson, J., *Jerusalem Pilgrims before the Crusades* (Warminster, 1977).

   Jerusalem Pilgrimages. 1099–1185 (Warminster, 1989).

Willemart, P., *Les Croisades. Mythe et Réalité de la Guerre Sainte* (Verviers, 1972).

Preaching and the crusade

Cramer, V., 'Kreuzpredigt und Kreuzzugsgedanke von Bernhard von Clairvaux bis Humbert von Romans', *Das Heilige Land in Vergangenheit und Gegenwart* (Cologne, 1939).

Leclercq, J., 'L'Encyclique de saint Bernard en faveur de la croisade', *Revue Bénédictine*, 81–2 (1971–2).

Lecoy de La Marche, A., 'La prédication de la croisade au XIIIe siècle', *Revue des Questions Historiques*, 48 (1890).

Maier, C., *Preaching the Crusade. Mendicants, Friars and the Cross* (Cambridge, 1994).

The question of the crusades and 'public opinion' is discussed in many of the works cited above and is also the subject of a monograph:

Siberry, E., *Criticism of Crusading. 1095–1274* (Oxford, 1985).

Works on the literature produced by the crusades are too many to deal with here.

The East

On Constantinople:

Bréhier, L., *Le Monde Byzantin*, 3 vols. (Paris, 1947–50).

Chalandon, F., *Les Comnènes: Etude sur l'Empire Byzantin aux XIe et XIIe Siècles*, 2 vols. (Paris, 1900–12).

On relations with the Franks:

Buisson, L., *Eroberrecht, Vassalität und Byzantinische Staatsrecht auf den Ersten Kreuzzug* (Hamburg, 1985).

Geanakoplos, D. J., *Emperor Michael Paleologus and the West* (Cambridge, Mass., 1959).

Lamma, P., *Comneni e Staufer: Ricerche sui Raporti fra Bisanzio e l'Occidente nel Secolo 12*, 2 vols. (Rome, 1955–7).

Lilie, R. J., *Byzantium and the Crusader States. 1096–1204*, trs J. C. Morris and J. E. Ridings (Oxford, 1993).

On relations with Constantinople seen from the West:

Daly, W. M., 'Christian fraternity: the crusaders and the security of Constantinople, 1097–1204: the precarious survival of an ideal', *Medieval Studies*, 22 (1960).

Kindlimann, S., *Die Eroberung von Constantinopel als Politische Forderung des Westerns im Hochmittelalter* (Zurich, 1969).

Setton, K. M., *The Papacy and the Levant (1204–1571)*, 4 vols. (Philadelphia, 1976–84).

On the Eastern Christians:

Atiya, A. S., *A History of Eastern Christianity* (London and Notre-Dame, 1968).

Fiey, J.-M., *Chrétiens Syriaques entre Croisés et Mongols* (Rome, 1974).

On the Maronite Church:
Salibi, K. S., 'The Maronites of Lebanon under Frankish and Mamluk Rule', *Arabica*, 4 (1957).

The literature on the Armenians is abundant and impressive. Among others:
Mutafian, C., *La Cilicie au Carrefour des Empires*, 2 vols. (Paris, 1988).

On the attitude of these Christians to the crusaders:
Lüders, A., *Die Kreuzzüge in Urteil Syrischen und Armenischen Quellen* (Berlin, 1964).

History of the Muslim States:
Among many works:
Elisseef, N., *L'Orient musulman au Moyen Age. 622–1260* (Paris, 1977).
Tate, G., *L'Orient des Croisades* (Paris, 1991).
On the different states:
Cahen, C., *Pre-Ottoman Turkey* (London, 1968).
Eddé, A.-M., 'Ridwan, prince d'Alep de 1095 à 1113', *Mélanges D. Sourdel, Revue des Etudes Islamiques*, 54 (1986).
Elisseef, N., *Nur al-Din, un Grand Prince Musulman de Syrie au Temps des Croisades*, 3 vols. (Damascus, 1967).
Gottschalk, H., *Al-Malîk al-Kâmil von Egypten und sein Zeit* (Wiesbaden, 1958).
Irwin, R., *The Middle East in the Middle Ages: the Early Mamluk Sultanate. 1250–1382* (London, 1986).
Lewis, B., *Les Assassins* (Paris, 1982).
Lyons, M. and Jackson, D., *Saladin: the Politics of the Holy War* (Cambridge, 1982).
Mouton, J.-M., *Damas et sa Principauté sous les Seljoukides et les Bourides* (Cairo, 1994).
Thorau, P., *Sultan Baibars I von Aegypten* (Wiesbaden, 1981).

For the Muslim view of the crusades:
Maalouf, A., *Les Croisades vues par les Arabes* (Paris, 1985).

For relations between Franks and Muslims:
Kedar, B. Z., *Crusade and Mission. European Approaches to the Muslims* (Princeton, 1984).
'The Subjected Muslims of the Frankish Levant', in Powell, J., *Muslims under Latin Rule, 1100–1300* (Princeton, 1990), pp. 135–74.
Köhler, M. A., *Allianzen und Verträge zwischen Frankischen und Islamischen Herrschern in Vorderen Orient* (Berlin and New York, 1991).
Schwinges, R. C., *Kreuzzugsideologie und Toleranz. Studien zu Wilhelm von Tyrus* (Stuttgart, 1977).
Sivan, E., *L'Islam et la Croisade: Idéologie et propagande dans les Réactions Musulmanes aux Croisades* (Paris, 1968).

The Mongols

The classic work remains:
Grousset, R., *L'Empire des Steppes* (Paris, 1939).
See also:
Morgan, D., *The Mongols* (Oxford, 1986).
Spuler, B., *Die Mongolen in Iran* (3rd edn, Berlin, 1968).

For their wars with Egypt:
Amitai-Reiss, R., *Mongols and Mamluks. The Mamluk–Ilkhanid War. 1260–1281* (Cambridge, 1991).

For relations with westerners:
Schmieder, F., *Europa und die Fremden. Die Mongolen im Urteil des Abendlandes vom 13. bis 15. Jhdt* (Sigmaringen, 1994).

INDEX OF PERSONS

Cambridge Medieval Textbooks

Already published

9169023

Made in the USA
Lexington, KY
01 March 2011